PROBATE RECORDS

OF

ESSEX COUNTY
MASSACHUSETTS

VOLUME III
1675–1681

Essex Institute

HERITAGE BOOKS
2025

HERITAGE BOOKS

AN IMPRINT OF HERITAGE BOOKS, INC.

Books, CDs, and more—Worldwide

For our listing of thousands of titles see our website
at
www.HeritageBooks.com

A Facsimile Reprint
Published 2025 by
HERITAGE BOOKS, INC.
Publishing Division
5810 Ruatan Street
Berwyn Heights, MD 20740

Salem, Mass.
Published by the Essex Institute
1920

International Standard Book Number
Paperbound: 978-0-7884-3310-8

LIST OF ESTATES

THE PROBATE RECORDS OF ESSEX COUNTY, MASSACHUSETTS.

Estate of Jonathan Gage of Bradford.*

Inventory of the estate of Jonathan Gage taken Mar. 22, 1674-5: weareing apparel linen & woollen, 3li. 15s.; bed & beding, 3li., books, 6li., chests, & boxes, 8s., 3li. 14s.; iron, bras, pewter, earthen and wooden ware, 3li. 8d.; sword and belt, 12s., utensills for husbandry, 2li. 1s. 6d., 2li. 13s. 6d.; cattle & swine, 15li. 6s.; bridle, sadle & pillion, 13s., provisions, 17s., 1li. 10s.; 8 acres of broken up land and a orchard, 29li.; houseing, 3li. 10s., Rough land 52 acres. 52li., 55li. 10s.; total, 114li. 9s. 2d. Debts due from the estate, 47li. and 20s. per year to old goodwif Gage during her life.

Attested in Ipswich court Mar. 30, 1675 by Hester Gage, relict of Jonathan. *Essex County Quarterly Court Records, vol. 5, page 270.*

Whereas Mr. Francis Wainwright had power granted to him to administer upon the estate of Jonathan Gage at Ipswich court, in Mar. 1675, and had paid part of the debts, as per account brought in, the remaining part being mostly in land, is willing the widow should make the best of the estate, and resigned his administratorship Mar. 28, 1676. Court granted administration to Hester Gage, the widow. *Ipswich Quarterly Court Records, vol. 5, page 279.*

Estate of Thomas Browning of Salem.†

Whereas there were several lands that were given and bequeathed by Thomas Browning, deceased, by will to Joseph Williames and Isaac Meachum, his sons-in-law, which lands were undivided, said Joseph and Isaack agreed as follows: that Joseph Williams was to have the ten acre lot in the south field between Nathaniell Pickman's and John Pickering's lands, one acre of salt marsh lying by Marblehead

*See *ante*, vol. 2, page 425.
†See *ante*, vol. 2, page 228.

bridge, one acre of bastard marsh lying in the south field between some marsh of Richard Prince and Paule Mansfield's
marsh, and one quarter of an acre of marsh lying by the
Deacon's marsh by the mill pond, with the fence belonging to
the said ten acre lot lying at the field gate; and for the house
and ground in the town, Joseph is to have for his part one-
half of the land with the house that was said Thomas Browning's, being the south end of the land next to the water, he
paying the said Isaack or his heirs at the decease of Mary
Browning their mother-in-law, 12li.; Isaack was to have for
his part the five acres called Mousers with the fence that belongs thereto, also three-quarters of an acre of salt marsh
that lies between some marsh of Joshua Buffum and some
marsh of Richard Prince and the one half of the ground in
the town, being that half that lies from the water to the north,
said Joseph paying to said Isaack, 12li. at their mother's decease, in consideration of the housing that stands upon the
said Joseph's part, as aforesaid. Witness: Hilliard Veren, sr.
and John Batcheler.

Sworn, 17:2:1675, before Wm. Hathorne, assistant. Recorded in the records at Salem, book 9, fol. 109, by Hilliard
Veren, recorder.

Essex County Quarterly Court Files, vol. 23, leaf 44.

ESTATE OF JOHN COLLINS, SR., OF GLOUCESTER.*

"I John Collins Sen. of Gloucester in the County of Essex
in New England being by Gods providence visited with much
Sickeness & weakenesse & not knowing how neare the time
of my departure out of this world may be at hand doe therefore make knowne this my last will & Testament in manner & forme following first I committ & commend my
Soule into the hands of God the ffather of Spirits & my
Body to the Grave to be decently buried by my Surviving
Freinds. And for my Goods first I Give & bequeath unto
my eldest Sonne John all my wearing Apparell also I doe
give and bequeath unto my Sonne John my great Gun or
fowling peice and all the rest of my Ammunition both Sword
& bandeleirs Also I doe give unto him and to his Heires
all my Land in the ffishermans ffeild So commonly called.
As also all my Meadow or marsh Ground in Annasquam So
common [ly called] lying neare to the Cutt and adjoyning
to the Land of mr Stevens & Steve [en Glover: *copy*] Also
I doe give and bequeath unto my Sonne John all that parcell

*Copy, Ipswich Deeds, vol. 4, pp. 1, 2.

of [land that: *copy*] his Dwelling house now Standeth upon
being about an Acre more or [less.] I give and bequeath unto
my Daughter Anna James halfe an Acre of [land at the:
copy] upper End of my planting Lott or the Land where
now my Corne g[roeth the same: *copy*] to injoy to her &
‖her‖ heires for Ever. Item I give & bequeath unto my [son
James: *copy*] Collins & to his Heires two Acres of my planting Lott where my Corn [now groweth: *copy*] next & adjoyning to his Sister Annas Land abovesayd over whar [the sayd:
copy] planting Lott and on that Side of his Sister's Land
abovesayd towards [the harbour on: *copy*] the Southeast provided alwayes that if my Sonne James doe sell the sayd [land:
copy] his Brother John Collins abovesayd shall have the first
refusall thereof also I doe give & bequeath unto my Sonne
James & his Heires five Acres of Land upon the Easterne
point So commonly called adjoyning to the Land of Steve[n]
Glover on the East & running up to the Great pond at the
East End of it. Also I give him two Acres of Marsh lying
next to Osmand Dutches Island in little good Harbour Also
I doe give ‖him‖ my Muskett Sword & Bandeliers. Item I
give & bequeath unto my Daughter Mary three Acres of
Land be it more or lesse lying & being Situate on the Easterne side of her Brother James his Land abovesayd and at
the sayd Easterne poynt the Same to injoy to her & her
Heires for Ever. Also [I] doe give unto my Daughter Mary
the Swampe with all the wast Land that lyeth betweene the
Lotts & the Sayd Swampe to her & her Heires for Ever
the Sayd Swampe being Situate & adjoyning to the Marsh
of Robert Elwell and at the Easterne poynt abovesayd Also I
doe give unto her two Islands of Marsh lying in Starke
naught Harbour pond so commonly called & all the rest of
[my marsh *lying in*: *copy*] Starke Naught Harbour lying on
the South East Side of the River the [same to: *copy*] injoy to
her & her Heires for Ever. Item I give & bequeath unto
my daughter Anna & her Heires three Acres of Land (upon
the Easterne poynt) be it more or lesse the Sayd Land lying
on the west End of the Long Beach a[nd] [adj]oynin [to]
the Land of Steven Glover on the North East.

  "Also I doe give unto her & her Heires halfe my Marsh lying on the Northwest Side of Starke Naught Harbor River
and adjoyning to the Meadow of Isaac Elwell on the Northwest. Also I give unto my Daughter ‖Anna‖ one cow also I
doe give her two pewter platt. Also I——Tin [jordan: *copy*]
And after her Mother's Decease I doe give her my [great

chest: *copy*] & my second great pott of Iron. Item I give
& bequeath unto my Gr [and] Daughter Mary Scampe the
full & just Summe of three pounds Sterling to be payd
unto [her] by the Executor at my decease if shee be of age.
Item I give & bequeath unto my deare and Loving wife
Joan Collins & to my Sonne John Collins all my Housing
& Land Orchyards & Gardens and all my Land &
Meadow yet ungiven the Same to injoy & improve joyntly
together after my Decease during the time that shee Contin-
ueth my widdow But if my wife doe marry agayne my will
& meaning is that then shee shall only injoy the thirds of
this land last mentioned & one cow during her naturall
Life & after her decease the sayd Land last mentioned shall
all be returned unto my Sonne John & his Heires for Ever
as his & their proper Right. Also I doe give & bequeath
unto my sayd wife & my Sonne John abovesayd all the
Rest of my Household Goodes and Cattell not disposed of as
long as my wife doth live my widdow my Sayd wife and
Sonne to injoy & improve them together But if Shee doe
marry agayne then the Sayd Goodes and Cattell last mentioned my will & meaning is that my Sonne John & his
Heires shall have and Injoy them for Ever. And to the end
that this my Last will and Testament may be duely &
truly performed I doe by these p^rsents constitute appoynt &
ordayne my Sonne John Collins to be Sole Executor and doe
by these presents also further give & bequeath unto my
Daughter Anna Collins the full Summe of foure pounds
Sterling besides that which I have given her abovesayd and
doe appoynt my Sonne John Collins to pay it unto her after
the decease of my Selfe & my. wife if my Sayd Daughter
Surviveth us both but if my Daughter Anna doe dye before
my Selfe & my wife then my will and meaning is that my
Sayd Sonne John shall keepe the Sayd foure pounds & injoy it to his owne proper use & behoofe. And further my
will & meaning is that if my Sonne James Collins abovesayd should not returne agayne from Sea or this voyage that
he is now upon or that he should otherwise dye before hee is
marryed that then also my Sonne John Collins abovesayd
Shall have & injoy the sayd portion—ents of Lands (that I
have given him in this my last will & Testament) to his
owne proper use & behoofe as also his Heires after him for
Ever & it is to be remembered & understood and hereby
it is declared that all the sayd Lands Expressed in this my last
will & Testament which I have given & bequeathed unto

any and all my Sayd children are in the Towne of Glocester aforsayd Any thing [heerin: *copy*] [c]ontayned to the Contrary in any wise Notwithstanding In wittnesse w[hereof] or unto this my last will and Testament I have hereunto Set my hand & Seale the five & twentieth day of this Instant August Anno Dom. one thousand Six hundred & Seaventy foure."

John (his † mark) Collins Senr.

(SEAL)

Witness: William (his ‡ mark) Vinson, Senr., Thomas Millett, junior.

Proved in Ipswich court Apr. 21, 1675 by the witnesses.

Inventory taken Mar. 31, 1675, by William Vinson, Sr., Thomas Millet and Thomas Riggs: the house and Lands, 80li.; 2 oxen, 3 cowes, one steare, 20li. 10s.; one mare, 1li. 10s.; Cart and wheales, tumberall, yokes, Chaines, Cart rope, Shovels, forkes, plow share and Coulter, 3li. 15s.; swine, one hide, o; Iron, bras and peuter, 2li.; wearing Clothes, 9li.; beds, beding and bedsteads with what belongs to them, 9li.; axes, betell, wedges and other toules, 15s.; Chists, Chairs, table and Spining wheals, 1li.; bridle and Sadell, 6s. 8d.; debts, 4li.; mony, 4li. 8s.; one fouling peace, one muskett, two swords and other amunishon, 3li. 10s.; total, 139li. 14s. 8d.

Attested in Ipswich court Apr. 21, 1675 by John Collins, executor of his father's estate.

John Collins executor of the will of his father, John Collins, having died without fulfilling the will, James Davis, sr. and Mary his wife, and Anna James, daughters of John Collins, sr. late of Gloster being legatees in said will petition the court Oct. 5, 1697, that the executor, Ezekiel Collins son of the deceased, who has the estate in his hands, may be cited to appear in order to take administration on said will or to renounce the same, that what is necessary may be done according to justice.

Essex County Probate Files, Docket 6,074.

ESTATE OF SAMUEL MOODY OF NEWBURY.*

"Newbury March 22, 1674-5. The last Will & Testament of Samuel Moodey I Samuel Moodey of Newbury being weak in Body, but in perfect Memory doe make & ordain this to bee my last Will & Testam^t. hereby re-

*Copy, Ipswich Deeds, vol. 4, pp. 3, 4.

vokeing all form[r] Wills whatsoever. I give unto my Eldest
Sonn W[m]. Moodey my now Dwelling House with all y[e] other
Houseing thereabout, together with y[e] Orchards & Areable
Land & Pasture adjoyning thereunto about fifty Acres bee
it more or lesse, & five Acres of Pasture land lying in Benj.
Rolfe's Pasture, & ten Acres of ffresh Meadow lying below
Benj. Rolfe's Land, & a Tenn Acre Lott of Salt Marsh lying in y[e] Marishes below y[e] Old Towne, with two Acres and
Halfe of Salt Marsh purchased of W[m]. Stevens, & an Addition of Marsh granted mee by Exchange. All w[ch] lies joyning
together as it is bounded. Also I give him my Priviledge of
Comonage or ffreehold, & all this to come. into his Hands
when hee shalbee of y[e] Age of Twenty one yeares. Also I
make him mine Heire & further give him my Negro Boy
when he shall bee at y[e] Age afores[d]., Obligeing my said Heire
to pay to each of his Sisters five pounds within one year after
theyr marriage, & if they marry before hee is of Age, then
to pay y[m] y[e] s[d] Sume within one year after his coming to Age.
I give & bequeath unto my second Sonn John Moodey
all y[t] pcell of Land before John Knight's House, both Areable, Pasture & Meadow, being fiveteen Acres more or lesse
as it is now fenced, & y[e] Island of Marsh over y[e] Great
River which is between W[m]. Ilsly and mee, y[e] s[d] W[m]. Ilsly
being to divide & I to chuse, y[e] s[d] Marsh containing about
ten Acres. Also I give him my pcell of Marsh about Sixe
Acres at y[e] Lower end of Rich[d]. Dole's Pasture. I give unto
my 3[d] Sonn Sam: Moodey All my Meadow in Lob's Pound,
being about nine Acres more or lesse, & my pcell of Upland
by Elisha Ilslye's about tenn Acres more or lesse, & my
pcell of Pasture Land lying next Hen. Short's Pasture, w[ch]
I bought of Ric. Dole, being about Sixe Acres more or lesse.
"I give unto my 4th Sonn Cutting Moodey my twenty five
Acres of Land now in possession of John Davis wth my House
& Barn thereupon, & my Sixe Acres of Meadow in y[e]
Birchen Meadowes with five Acres of Salt Marsh w[ch] is part
of y[e] 20 Acres of Marsh y[t] was Grandfather Cutting's & y[e]
Priviledge of Comonage or ffrehold thereunto belonging. And
my Will also is y[t] each of these three Sons forementioned
shall have y[e] Estate afores[d] come into y[r] hands at y[e] Age of
twenty one years. And if my son William dye without Issue.
then I appoint my Son Samuel to be my heire & to have all
I have given to William & [Samuells portion: *copy*] shalbe
Equally divided between John & Cutting Moodey, & if
either John or Cutting dye without Issue, then theyr Estate

to bee equally divided between yᵉ two youngʳ Brothers, &
three younger Sisters.

"I give unto my Eldest Daughter Sarah Moodey Sixty
pounds & to my three youngʳ Daughtʳˢ Mary, Hanna &
Lydia fivety pounds a peice to bee paid by my Executrix in
Household Goods, Corn & Cattle an equall share of each,
to bee pᵈ each of yᵐ at theyr Marriage if they marry before
twenty years of Age, or however when they are at yᵗ Age,
whither married or not. And if any of yᵉ Daughters dye
before yᵉ time comes for theyr receiving theyr Portion, the
surviveing Daughters shall have yᵉ Portion of yᵉ Deceased
equally divided betwixt them. I appoint my Dearly beloved
Wife Mary Moodey to bee yᵉ sole Executrix of yˢ my Last
Will & Testamᵗ & give her yᵉ thirds of my Houseing &
Land dureing her Naturall life, & the use & Improvemᵗ
of my whole Estate in yᵉ Minority of my children, to bee ordered by Advice of the Overseers in yᵉ best Mannʳ for yᵉ
bringing up of my Children till they come to Age. And
further dureing her Widdowhood shee shall have yᵉ
use of my dwelling house with yᵉ Household Stuffe,
and halfe yᵉ fruit of yᵉ Orchards. If she marries she shall
have fivety pounds in yᵉ like specie yᵗ my Daughters
portions are payable in. And if yᵉ stock will not hold out to
pay yᵉ Daughter's Portions, then my son William shall make
up yᵉ rest, & shall have such Time allowed him as my overseers shall judge meet, & yᵉ overplus of yᵉ stock (if any
bee) when my wives sᵈ 50li. and Daughters portions are paid
shalbe divided equally among my 4 daughters. And further
if my Executrix shalbe straitened to pay my Daughters Portions, shee shall have two years time after theyr Marriage to
pay it in. Finally for yᵉ better performance of yˢ my Will according to yᵉ true intent & meaning thereof I request &
appoint my mᶜʰ respected Uncle Nicho. Noyes, & my beloved Brothers Joshua & Caleb Moodey together wᵗʰ Benjamin Rolfe to bee my Overseers. ffurther giving full Power
to my Executrix with yᵉ Advice of my sᵈ Overseers to make
Sale of my Land at Wells for yᵉ payment of my Debts. In
Testimony to all & singular yᵉ pʳmises I set to my Hand
& seale this 22. (1)ᵐᵒ 1674-5. It is to bee understood &
I doe further will that what Cattle and goods were Given to
my Daughters Sarah or Mary by either of theyr Grandfathers
or Grandmothers, & is now among my Estate is to be theyrs
besides & distinct from what I have here bequeathed them."

                              Samuell Moody. (SEAL)
  Witness: Nicholas Noyes, Jno. Dole, Caleb Moody.

Proved in Ipswich court Apr. 21, 1675 by Nicholas Noyes
and Caleb Moody.

Inventory taken 14:2:1675, by George (his —— mark)
Little and Benjamin Rolfe: the dwelling house, Barn and
other houseing thereabout together with 50 Acres of plow land
& Pasture about ye House & ye orchard, ye land at 6li. per
acre, 650li.; Sixe Acres of land by ye other bought of Rich.
Dole, 36li.; Eleven Acres of upland near adjoyning, 44li.;
Nine Acres of Meadow in Lob's Pound, 45li.; Five Acres
Pasture below Ben. Rolfes, 20li.; Ten Acres below that, 50li.;
Five Acres of salt Marsh joyning to James Brown, 35li.;
Fiveteen Acres Meadow & upland by John Knight, 75li.;
Thirty two Acres of salt marsh in several pcells, 192li.;
Thirty Acres of land at New Town wth House, Barn, orchard
& 6 Acres Meadow in ye Birchen meadow, 150li.; a parcell
of land at Wells, 40li.; 5 acres of land at N. Town, 5li.;
11 horses, mares and foales, 26li.; 100 sheep, 50li.; 10 cowes,
40li.; 4 oxen, 24li.; 3 steeres, 9li.; 7 2 yr. olds, 14li.; 3
yrlings, 4li.; 4 young calves, 2li.; Swine, 12li.; 1-4 Bark
Flower, 37li.; 2-3 of an Hay boat, 5li.; Gun, sword and
amunition, 2li.; wearing clothes, 14li.; Bedding, an High &
low bed wth appurtenances, Table, Joyn stooles, chaires, cupboards, chests in ye Parlor, 22li.; Table Cloth & Napkins,
3li. 10s.; Cushions, 1li. 10s. 6d.; sheets & pillow beeres,
6li.; Curtain cloth, 4li. 10s.; yarn & cloth, 8li. 2s.; Iron
Utensils in ye Kitchin, 5li.; Brasse, 5li. 15s. 6d.; Pewter, 3li.
3s. 6d.; Trayes, earthen ware & other vessells in ye
Kitchen, 3li.; 4 feather beds with all theyr Appurtenances
above in ye chamber, 36li.; chest, 10s.; Bed, Sacks, Tubbs etc.
in another chamber, 5li. 10s.; Caske in ye Cellar, 2li. 10s.; a
dram Cupp & whittle, 1li. 8s.; corn, 10li. 11s.; Hemp &
Flaxe, 36s. 8d.; sheeps wooll, 40s.; Bacon, Pork and Beefe,
3li.; sadles & Bridles, 30s.; cupboard, 2 Tables & a Bedstead, 4li.; 2 Cushions, 6s.; 5 pr. sheets, 8li.; 6 pillowbeers,
20s.; 5 napkins, 10s. 6d.; Featherbed & Furniture, 12li.;
carts, wheeles, Ploughes, chaines, yoakes with all other Tackling for Oxen & Horses, Axes and other Tooles, 12li.; a
Negro Boy, 25li.; Books, 1li. 10s.; so much silver due to ye
estate, 13li.; so much more in other pay, 19li.; more due in
Corn, 3li.; so much in Cattle recd. from Sarah Moodey wch
is in ye stock, 21li.; so much in Cattle belonging to Mary
Moodey added also to stock, 11li.; total, 1838li. 3s. 8d. Some
desperate debts about 16li. The estate is Dr. to ye 2 children
last mentioned, 32li.; debts to severall, 45li.; total, 77li.;
what is due to severall Physitians not yet known.

Attested June 24, 1675 by Mary Moodey, executrix of the estate of her late husband, Samuell Moody.
Essex County Probate Files, Docket 18,621.

ESTATE OF JOHN JONES.

John Joanes's will was proved Apr. 21, 1675 and inventory delivered. *Ipswich Quarterly Court Records, vol. 5, page* 264.

ESTATE OF JOHN BLACK, SR.

John Black dying intestate and there being an inventory of his estate brought in to court amounting to 11li. 10s., administration was granted July 20, 1675, to John, his son, who was ordered to pay out of the estate to his three sisters, Eliza Kemboll, Pearcis Follett and Lydia Davis, 50s. each. *Salem Quarterly Court Records vol. 5, leaf* 86.

Copy of the inventory of the estate of John Blacke, sr., who died 16 : 1 : 1675 taken 12 : 2 : 1675, by Thomas Lawthropp and John Hill, and copy made by Samuell Hardie: his wearing Clothes, 2li.; linnen sheets & shirts, 1li. 5s.; small Linnen, 5s.; bed, bolster & Pillow, 2li. 15s.; bedstead, Chest & Chaire, 1li.; one Cow, 4li.; a Small Gunne, 5s.; total, 11li. 10s. "There was another Cowe: that was Sold p the now Deceased person in the time of his life for two pounds in money: the charge of the funeral & other maters amounted to more & therefore we thought not meet: to put that into the Inventory." *Essex County Quarterly Court Files, vol.* 23, *leaf* 104.

ESTATE OF ELIAS WHITTEE OF SALEM.

Administration on the estate of Elias Whittee, intestate, granted July 20, 1675, to Henry Skerry, marshal, and there being an imperfect inventory presented, he was ordered to perfect it, pay the debts, and make return to the next court. *Salem Quarterly Court Records, vol. 5, leaf* 86.

Inventory of the estate of Elias Whity, who was servant to Robt. Stone, and was drowned at Winter Island from a boat carrying fish ashore, Edw. Mould and John King being chosen by said Stone to appraise his goods: one hatt, 7s. 6d.; one Caster hat, 8s.; 4 yds. Broad Cloth at 5s. 6d. p yd., 1li. 2s.; 12 yds. narrow Cotton at 1s. 8d. p yd., 18s.; 4 pr. shoes, 13s.; 1 Coate & A pr. of Britches, 1li. 1s.; 1 Coate & pr. of

Britches, 14s.; 2 waistcoats, 9s.; 3 old pr. Drawers, 3s.; a prsell of old Cloaths, 8s.; 2 shirts & 4 neckcloth, 1 pr. Gloves, 9s.; 1 gunn, 1 Chest & a rayser, 11s.; 1 Line & Hooks, 4s.; one horse & a sadle, 2li.; mony Robt. Stone owes him, 1li. 7s. 5d.; total, 11li. 9s. 11d.; Charges for his Burien, 3li. 4s.; washing & Lodging Last winter and diet for five months, 4li.; for last summer, 1li.; mony Lent him p Wm. Russell, 1li. 10s.; total, 9li. 14s. *Essex County Quarterly Court Files, vol. 23, leaf 105.*

ESTATE OF THOMAS WHITE.*

Ruth White, administratrix of the estate of Thomas White, deceased, made oath July 20, 1675, that all the debts were paid, and was discharged. *Salem Quarterly Court Records, vol. 5, leaf 88.*

Account of payments made by Ruth Whitt, administratrix: to Capt. George Corwinn, 7li. 10s. 10d.; to Capten Lothoerup, 4li. 15s. 4d.; Jonathan Wade, 9li. 8s. 11 1-2d.; Mr. John Rucke, 2li. 16s. 6d.; Mrs. Elizabeth Newman, 4li. 7s. 4d.; Mr. John Gidny, sr., 4li. 1s. 2d.; Wiliam Story, 3li. 6s. 8d.; Decon Goodhew, 2li. 13s. 4d.; Ezekell Woodward, 7li. 12s. 8d.; Insigne Gold, 3li. 6s. 8d.; Richard Hutten, 8li.; Zebulon Hill, 2li.; John Denice, 15s. 8d.; Daniell Kilham, 11s. 4d.; Thomas Ives, 4s. 10d.; Goodman Goldsmith, 1li.; Thomas Fisk, 1li.; Andrew Petter, 14s. 8d.; Insigne Corning, 4s. 8d.; four swine lost out of ye estatt, 2li.; one load of hay from Chebako, 1li.; An horss Lost out of ye estat prised at 4li.; for driving swine to decon goodhus, 4s.; to Robertt perce of Ipswich, 1li. 14s.; taken by marshal Scery, 10s.; Thomas Rix, 4s. 8d.; taken by Jno. West, 19li.; total, 73li. 16s. 7 1-2d. *Essex County Quarterly Court Files, vol. 23, leaf 114.*

ESTATE OF THOMAS COLDAM OF LYNN.

"March 14th 1674-1675 This is the Last will, & testament of Thomas Couldum of Lynn the Countye of Essex, aged about eightye six yeares, being weake of bodye, but of perfect memorye, & understanding Imp^r: I Comitt my bodye to the earth, & my spirrit to him that gave it It: I bequeath to my wife Joannah Couldum, all my planting ground in the Township of Linn afforesd Containing in estimation about twenty foure acres (viz) twelue acres of it, in estimation being my house Lott bee it more, or Lesse: & the rest of it,

*See *ante*, vol. 2, page 306.

with mowing ground ajoyning to it, being Called by the name
of Turkye ffeild the whole Containing in estimation foareteen
acres, & an halfe, bee it more, or Lesse & is bounded with the
Lands of Richard Moore & Joseph Mansfeild: And alsoe the
use of all my houseing, and alsoe all my medow ground (viz)
five acres of salt marsh ground Lyeing in Rumnye marsh, betwixt Edward Bakers marsh, & the marsh of Richard Haven
Alsoe two acres of salt marsh in Rumnye marsh Lyeing betwixt the marsh of Mr Whiteing, & the marsh of Andrew
Mansfeild & two acres of salt marsh Lyeing in the Marsh
beefore the Towne Lyeing by the Marsh of Moses Chadwell
(viz) dureing her naturall life, not Crossing a Couenant, or
agreement made betwixt my selfe, & my grandchild Samuell
Simonds, touching my Considering, or a Loweing him, for
his manageing my affaires.

"I give vnto my wife Joannah the one half of all my Liveing stocke both in Neat cattle, horse kind, sheep, swine &c.: &
halfe the increase of them, & halfe the produce of the whole
Liueing accordinge to the affore hinted Covenant, or agreem^t
with the Afore sd Samuell Simonds, as her owne proper:
right & interest. It: I give unto my wife Joannah, all my
moueable estate both within dores, & without dores, to bee at
her free dispose. It: I give vnto my sonn Clement Couldum
his heires & assignes for ever one halfe, of all my Lands
houseing, & medow as his owne proper right, & interest forever, with all Comon Liberty and previlidges belonging thereunto with halfe the orchard

"I giue vnto my sonn Clement Couldum (after my owne,
& my wifes deseace my bed that I Lye uppon, with all the
Appurtenances belonging there vnto, my great chist alsoe
with my Cubberd, Iron pott, & Iron kettle,) notwithstand my
guift of my moveables vnto my wife which is expressed as
to her in generall Tearmes as abouesd. It. I hereby Confirme vnto my Grandchild Sam^{ll} Simonds to him his heires,
& assignes forever as his owne proper right & interest, And
that vppon Consideration of his Agreem^t with us to manage
& Carrye on all o^r buisinesses according to the sd agreem^t
That hee the sd Sam^{ll} Simonds shall have & enjoye to him,
his heires, & assignes for ever one halfe of all my houseing
Lands medowes & marsh ground & halfe the orchard as aboue
exp^{r}st, wth all Comons, Libertyes & p^{r}vilidges (viz) after my
owne & wife's desease. It: I make choyce of my Loueing wife
& my Loueing Brother & Freind Mr Henrye Rhodes Joynt
executo^{rs}. Last I desire my Loueing Friend Andrew Mans-

feild & John Newhall seni^{or} to bee overseers of this my will:
In wittnesse whereof I have sett my hand, & seale the daye &
yeare afore written."

Thomas (his ‡ mark) Couldum. (SEAL)

Witness: Samuell Rodes, Joseph Rhodes.

Proved in Salem court 21:5:1675 by Andrew Mansfeild
and Joseph Roads.

Inventory of the estate of Thomas Couldum of Lynn, who
died Apr. 8, 1675, taken by Francis Burrill and Nathaniell
Handforth: wearing apparrill, Lyning, woolen, stockins,
shoos, hats, 5li. 7s.; Bedding, 6li. 18s.; Bedding, 1li. 6s.;
Bedding given to Clemond Coldum according to will, 5li.
10s.; Lyning, 6li. 8s.; Brasse & puter, 1li.; 2 Iron pots, 1
Iron Ketle, a ringer, wedges, hake, hookes, tooles, 4li. 8s.; 2
Cheere Tables, Couberd, formes & Chest, 1li. 15s.; Armes &
Amunition, 1li. 15s.; 16 sheepe & 7 Lambs, 9li.; English &
Indian Corne, 4li. 2s. 6d.; flax, Hemp, wool & yarne, 1li.
16s.; Boards & shingles, 1li. 8s.; Uncut cloath, 1li. 4s.;
monyes, 8li. 6s.; Lumber, wheeles & Barrills, 3li.; Porke,
1li.; Neate Catle, 36li. 5s.; Horse kinde, 5li. 10s.; Swine,
12s.; Houseing, 27li. 10s.; Upland & medow ground, 175li.;
carts, plow, Grindlestones & Haye, 3li. 14s.; A sadle & pillion,
1li. 5s.; total, 313li. 19s. 6d.

Attested 21:5:1675 by Joana Coldum, relict and executrix.

Essex County Quarterly Court Files, vol. 23, leaves
116, 117.

ESTATE OF HENRY LEA OF MANCHESTER.

"The Last will & testement of Henery Lea of Manchester
Henery Lea being weak & sick of body but of pfit memory
doe ordaine this his last will & testement Imprymes I giue
& bequeth to my well beloveed wife Marey Lea my wholle estate personalle & reall, my depts being payed ye estate is lift
to her w^t is remayning except som small Legeacyes y^t I giue
to my chillderen to my son John Lea I giue twenty shillens
to my other too sonns Samuell & Thomas Lea I giue ten
shillens apeace to each of them & to my too daughters Hanah
& Sarah Lea too each of them I giue & bequeth ten shillings
a peace and for ye p^rformenc hereof I haue made & doe
apoynt my wife meary Lea afore saide execuetor & my well
beloued friends Thomas Jones & willam Benet as ouer sears
to assist her in any busnes as she shall desire of them con-

sirning the said estate whereunto I here set my hand for ye confirming of ye same."

Henry (his ‡ mark) Lea.

Witness: Samuell Freind, Aron (his † mark) Bennet. Manchester the 12 of feberary 1674.

Proved in Salem court 21 : 5 : 1675 by William Bennet and Samuell Freind.

Inventory of the estate of Henery Lea, taken Mar. 29, 1675, by John West and Willam Bennet: hows & land with priveledges there unto belonging, 100li.; Cattell & Swine, 24li.; Bedding wth other howshold Goods, 20li.; total, 144li. Debts to be paid, 28li.

Attested 21 : 5 : 1675 by Mary, relict and executrix.

Essex County Quarterly Court Files, vol. 23, leaves 118, 119.

Estate of Mrs. Margaret Sanden of Marblehead.

"The last will & Testament of Margarett Sanden of Marblehead: made this twentieth day of August Ann Dom 1667: I Margeret Sanden, widow & late wife of Arther Sanden, late deceased, being Ancient & weake of body & my dayes seeming to draw neere their end, but through the Lords mercy of pfect memory do make this my last will & testament as followeth Imp^{r}s I giue unto Samuell & Ephraim Sandin the children of John Sanden, my son, late deceased: twenty shillings each of them to be paid in 6 months after my decease It I giue vnto the children of nicholas meret by mary my daughter, being in number eight sons & daughter, now surviving all the rest of my estat when all debts & other charges are paid to be equally devided among those that survive of them to the age the sonns at 21 years & daughters at 18 years or maryed: It I doe appoynt my son nicholas merrett & mary his wife my daughter to be sole executors of this my last will & testament, and in witnes heare of I haue set to my hand & seale the day & yeare first above written."

Margeret (her ‡ mark) Sanden. (SEAL)

Witness: Mary (her ‡ mark) Veren, Henry West, Hillyard Veren, sen.

Proved in Salem court 23 : 5 : 1675 by Hilliard Veren, sr. and Henry West.

Inventory of the estate of Margreet Sanding, deceased, taken by Cristover Lattemore, William Browne and Nathenell Walton: one Feather Bed, 2li.; 1 Bolster and 2 Pil-

lowes, 15s.; 2 old Blanketts & 1 old Rugg, 10s.; 1 old Cattaile & old Bedding, 12s.; 1 old Couerled, 12s.; 1 old Chair,
2s.; 1 old bedstead and 1 old Bedd matt, 10s.; 1 pare Cur-
tans and old. Vallins, 12s.; 1 Looking Glace, 1s. 6d.; 1 old
Warming Pann, 4s.; 2 Pare Pillowbeers, 6s.; 3 old pillowbeers fitt for nothing but tinder; 6 sheetes, 1li. 16s.; 5 old
sheetes, 15s.; 1 Table Cloth, 1 Bolster Cloth, 10s.; a small
parsell of table Lining fitt for tinder; 1 old Chest made of
pine, 5s.; 1 old wainscott Chest, 7s.; 1 frame Table, 12s.; 5
Joynt stooles, 1li. 7s. 6d.; 1 Brass Kettle, 1li. 5s.; 1 Iron
pott, 15s.; 1 old Iron pott and pott Hooks, 8s.; 2 old Iron
Skilletts, 5s.; 1 pessell & morter, 5s.; 1 pare of old Scales,
2s.; 1-2 a dussan of puter Dishes, 16s.; 2 old puter platters &
2 old plaits, 4s.; 2 old puter Candle sticks, 3s.; 2 old Candlesticks, 2s.; 1 quart, 1 wine quart, 1 wine pinte, 1-2 pinte, 1
nogin, 6s.; a parcell of old puter, 9s.; 1 Trambell, 3s.; 1 old
friing pann, 1 old pare of Tongs & an old Shouell, 3s.; total,
17li. 3s.

Attested in Salem court 23 : 5 : 1675.

Essex County Quarterly Court Files, vol. 23, leaves 112, 113.

ESTATE OF SAMUEL COGSWELL.

Administration upon the estate of Samuell Cogswell was
granted, Aug. 26, 1675, to John Coggswell, his brother, who
was ordered to bring in an inventory to the next Ipswich
court. *Ipswich Quarterly Court Records, vol. 5, page 271.*

Inventory of the estate of my Brother Samuell Cogswell :
a Sae Cape, 1s.; a payer of old stockins, 6d.; a payer old
Sleves, 1s. 6d.; a peyer old Bridges, 1s.; payer old draers, 2s.;
one old wascoote, 3s.; payer old Bridges, 1s. 3d.; one old
Coote, 1s. 6d.; one old Coote, 6s.; one old kerseye Coote, 2s.
9d.; two old haets, 4s.; one payer Sarch Bridges, 9s.; one
Sarch wascoote 9s.; one sae gouwne, 15s.; one karseye Coote,
1li. 7s.; one old Coote, 7s.; one Cheast, 5s.; total, 4li. 17s.
6d.

Some things praysed by Thomas Varny and William Goodhuw: a payer old shoes and Incorn, 16d.; a little pello, 2s.;
pestolls and Cootlach, 1li. 5s.; in the hand of Samuell Pyppin
not payeable in ayght yeares, 7li. 19s.; total, 14li. 5s. Due by
bill from Gabriel grub, 25li. 17s.; Bill from Rob. Crosse, 28
li. 10s.; Bill from Stefen Crosse, 5li. 9s.; total, 74li. 1s. His
Debts: furnerall Debts, Silver, 4li.; fish at the Ils of Sholles,
—; Samuell *French, all* silver, 2li.; deakon goodhuw, 1li.

10s.; goodman howard, 15s.; goodman Crosse, 8s. 6d.; goodman Varny, 9s.; quartermaster Perkins, 8s. 9d.; Mr. Baker, 4s. 11d.; goodman Woodward, 5s.; Tanner Clark, 4s. 6d.; Mr. Lord for Admynestration and Coppy, 2s. 6d.; duw to Mr. Andrews for Rent, 20li. 18s. 2d.; money Borrowed of Mr. Tho. Androws, 5s.; total, 31li. 11s. 4d. Attested in Ipswich court Sept. 28, 1675 by John Cogswell.

An addition to the inventory given in by John Cogswell to be annexed: 1 ades, 4s.; 2 weges, 3s.; on mortising actes, 1s. 6d.; 2 betell ringes, 2s.; on short draft chain, 5s.; as aperes by lease, 5s. pur yer; of the rent recovered, 1li. 15s.; total, 2li. 10s. 6d. Entered 1685.

Essex County Probate Files, Docket 5,861.

The addition to the inventory given in to the Ipswich court Mar. 30, 1686 by John Cogswell. *Ipswich Deeds, vol. 4, page 223.*

Estate of Thomas Manning of Ipswich.

Administration on the estate of Thomas Maning, who was slain in the war, granted Sept. 28, 1675, to his brother Daniell Maning, and an inventory was left in court. *Ipswich Quarterly Court Records, vol. 5, page 272.*

Inventory* of the estate of Thomas Maning late of Ipswich, taken Sept. 30, 1675 by John Appleton and John Whipple: waring clothes Linen and woolin with one hatt, 3li. 3s.; two Ruges, one blankit, 1li. 4s.; fether beed with one bolster, 5li. 10s.; two old sheets, 6s.; bookes, 1li. 10s.; a box with 6 glases, 3s.; payer of gloves, 2s. [6d. *copy*]; two boxes, 5s.; two chests, one cubburd, 1li. 3s.; pewter, 10s.; brasse, 1li. 7s.; thre smal iron potes with pothooks, 17s.; two chayer, one foorme, 7s.; two barels, two tubes, 4s.; two powdering tubes, one paile, 5s.; one bedsted, 5s.; one Keeler, a meall troofe, 4s. 6d.; Carpender tooles, 4li. 3s.; a xcut sawe and one axe, 1li. 17s.; a twibill, 8s.; firepane, tongs, tramell, griggon, a sive, 8s.; fethers, 2s., a sithe with snath, [7s. *copy*]; two fowling peces, 4li.; horse saddle, [3li. *copy*]; sevrall small things, [5s. *copy*]; 65 acres of Land at Topsfeild, [30li. *copy*]; abought nine acers of march in welles, 36li.; 150 accers of Land in welles as apers by severall deeds, 10li.——; total, 107li. [14s. *copy*].

*Copy, Ipswich Deeds, vol. 4, page 15.

Attested in Ipswich court Sept. 28, 1675 by Daniell Maning.   *Essex County Probate Files, Docket* 17,573.

ESTATE OF RICHARD KIMBALL, SR. OF IPSWICH.

"The Last Will & Testament of Richard Kimbell S^r of Ipswich in Essex in New England who, Allthough weake in body
yet of perfect Memmory Doe dispose of my Lands & Estate
in maner & forme as ffolloweth— Ips. To my Loveinge wife,
My will is, that shee shall dwell in my House, and haue the
Improuement of my ground & medow belonging thertoo, with
the use & increase of my whole stock of Cattell, one whole
yeare affter my discease, and then at that yeares end, the
fforty pound due to her According to Contract at marriage to
bee paid her, and that houshould stuff shee brought with
her. And to haue Libertie to Live in the parlor end of the
house, the rome wee now, Lodg in; & Libertie for her Nec-
esarie use, of som part of the seller, allsoe the Libertie of one
Cow, in the pasture the Executors to provide winter meate
for the same. And to haue a Quarter part of the fruit of the
orchard ‖and firewood,‖ as Long as shee Lives ther, and iff
shee desire to Remoue to her owne house, then to be sett in itt,
with what shee haue, by my Executors And to be alow,d forty
shilings yearly as Long as she Lives, And to my Eldest son
Henery, my will is, To give him, three score & Ten pounds, To
bee paide Twenty pound, a year & half after my Discease, and
the Remaining parts, in the Two following years, after that.
To my son Richard I give fforty pound To my son John I
give Twenty pounds To my son Thomas I give Twenty five
pounds to bee paid two years and a half after my discease, and
to his children, I give seven pound to be devided Equaly
among them, & paid as they come of age, or at day of marriage, provided if any die Before then, that share to be distributed Equaly amongst the rest. And to my son Bengamin,
Besids the Two Oxon allredy Received I give the sume of
Twenty five pounds, Ten pound To be paid a year & halfe
after my discease, the rest in the two years ffolowing. Allsoe
to his children I give six pound Equally to be devided and
paide as they come of age, or at day of mariage, in case any
die before, that part to be Equally devided to the rest.
"And to my son Caleb, I give that peece of Land known by
the name of Tings Lot, and all my Land at wattels-Neck, with
my marsh at the hundreds, knowne by the name of Wiats

marsh, and all my working Tooles except Two Axes, all to be delivered present after my discease. Allsoe I give fourtene pound to his seven children Equally to be devided, To be paid as they Come of Age, or at day of mariage, and if any die before, that part, to be Equaly devided amongst the rest. To my son in Law, John Severnes, I give Ten pound, To be paid Two year and a halfe affter my discease, And to my Daughter Elizabeth I give Thirty pound Ten pound to be paid a year & half affter my discease and the other Two parts the Two following years after that. To my Daughter Mary, I give Ten pounds five pound to be paid a yeare & halfe After my discease the other five pound the yere after that. To my Daughter, Sarah, I give fforty pound, five pound to be paid the year and half after my discease and the rest, five pound a year Till itt be all paid. Allso to her children, I give Seven pound Ten shilings, To be paid To them as they Come of Age, or at day of mariage, iff any die before, that part to be Equally devided to the rest: And to my daughter Sarah, abouesd, I allsoe give the bed I Lie, on, with the ffurniture, after one years use, off itt by my wife To my wives Children, viz, Thomas, jeramiah, & Mary, To Thomas, and mary I giue fforty shilings apeece to, be paid a year & halfe affter my Discease, & to Jeramiah I give fffifteene pound, to be paid at the age off one & Twenty I give alsoe Eight pound to the Two Eldest Daughters of Gilles Senrs [Gyles Cowes: *copy* :* that hee had by his first wife,] to be paid and Equaly devided to them at the age of sixteene, if Either of them die before, Then the whole, to be given to that that Remaines I allsoe give fouer pound to my Cozen Haniell Bossworth And doe Ordaine & Appoynt my Two Sonns ab,sd Richard, And John Kimbell, to bee my Lawfull & sole Executors, And my Cozen haniell Bossworth aboue,sd to be my overseeer that this my Last Will & Testement bee duely and Truely Performed: And thus I Conclude w,ᵗh setting Too my hand and seale, This fift of March 1674/5."

Richard (his ⌐ mark) Kimbell Sᵉʳ.
(SEAL)

Witness: Moses Pengry, Senʳ., Aaron Pengry, Sᵉʳ.

Proved in Ipswich court Sept. 28, 1675 by Decon Pengry and Aaron Pengry.

Inventory* of the estate of Richard Kemball, Sener, deceased June 22, 1675, taken July 12, 1675 by John Brewer, Sr.; and Simon Stace: The dwelling house & barne with the

*Copy, Ipswich Deeds, vol. 4, page 12.

orchyard, homestead & pasture fenced in containing
twenty five akers, 200li.; fourteene akers of land lying in
the comon field betweene Edward chapmans and mark Quil-
ters land, 70li.; one six aker lot caled tings lot, 30li.; ten
akers of land lying by yt caled Bradstrets farme, 25li.; fourteene akers of land lying in yt caled Wattells neck, 40li.;
Twenty akers of hundred marsh cald Wiats marsh, 50li.;
Twenty akers of marsh caled the point, 120li.; Sheepe &
lambs, 9li.; too old oxen, 11li. 10s.; foure oxen, 20li.; Six
cowes & one bull, 23li. 10s.; too heifers too yere & vantage
old, 4li. 10s.; four yerelings & vantage, 6li.; Three calves,
1li. 16s.; two horses, one mare, one yereling colt, 6li. 15s.;
Eight akers of upland by ye marsh cald ye point, 22li.; Six
hoggs & five shoats, 6li. 10s.; His wearing apparell, 10li. 9s.;
one Duzen of Napkins, 1li. 4s.; four pillow cases, 10s.; three
table cloaths, 15s.; Three towells, 3s.; Seven sheets, 2li. 2s.;
one paire of Blanketts, 12s.; two cushins, 2s.; The bed in ye
parler, one bolster, too pillows, one blew Rugg, one Blankett
with ye curtains & valants & matt, 6li.; another bed & Rugg,
one blanket & too pillows, 4li. 10s.; Three Blanketts & too
Ruggs, 3li. 10s.; one Blankett, 8s.; bookes, 12s.; money, 17s.;
one Bedstead, too chests, too Boxes, one cubbard, 3li.; Three
Brasse Kettells & one scillit, 4li.; one Brasse pot, 1li.; one
warmeing pan & three Brasse pans, 18s.; one iron Kettle, one
slice, a paire of tramells, a spit, 1li.; fire shovell, pot hooks,
tongs, 8s.; pewter & a lanthorne, 1li. 4s.; one frying pan,
mustard Quarnes, one iron foot, 9s. 6d.; two chaynes & a span
shackell, 12s.; Three yoaks, too plowes & tacklings, 1li. 6s.;
cart ropes, 8s. In the celler & leanto in tubs, buter & meat &
other things, 3li. 3s.; cubbard, meale trough, litle table, three
chaires, 14s.; one great chaire, pailes & trayes, 5s.; too Bedsteads with Bed cords, 1li. 4s.; one saddle & Bridle, [5s.
copy]; one musquet & one barrill of a gun, 1li. 5s.; too siths
& tacklings to them, 5s.; one fann, [9s. copy]; sheeps wooll,
1li. 10s.; Indian Corne, 18s.; three sacks & too wheelles, 13s.;
one cheese press, grindstone & winch, 12s.; one pair of New
wheeles, 1li. 10s.; for feloes & spoaks, 6li.; four pair of Beetle
Rings, 7s.; five axes & one adds, 1li. 2s.; Three Beers, 12s.;
Three sawes, 1li.; too shaves & seven augors, 17s.; one square,
too chizzells, one gouge, 4s. 6d.; one sledge, one fro, one pair
of gromes, 8s.; paire of compasses, one file & spiling chizell,
2s.; one Dung forke, spade, four wedges, 1li.; cart & wheeles,
1li. 18s.; one Tumbrell & slidd, 1li. 2s.; Timber in ye woods,
1li.; due by Booke, 15li. 11s.; total, 737li. 3s. 6d. Owing in

debts in small parcels. 36li.; to Tho. Dow, 8li. 10s.; Aaron
Pengry, 1li. 10s.; more, 1li. 12s.; total, 47li. 12s.
Attested in Ipswich court Sept. 28, 1675 by John Kimbell.
Essex County Probate Files, Docket 15,723.

ESTATE OF HUGH ATKINSON.

Hugh Atkinson, sometime of Kendall in England, dying
intestate at sea, court Sept. 28, 1675, granted administration
of his estate to Mr. Joseph Hills of Newbury, who was ordered to bring in an inventory to the next Ipswich court.
Ipswich Quarterly Court Records, vol. 5, page 272.

ESTATE OF SAMUEL STEVENS OF NEWBURY.

Administration on the estate of Samuell Steevens of Newbury, who was slain in the war, granted Sept. 28, 1675, to
Wm. Titcombe, and an inventory was presented, which was
dered to bring in an inventory to the next Ipswich court.
Ipswich Quarterly Court Records, vol. 5, page 272.

Administration upon the estate of Samuell Steevens, who
was slain in the wars, was granted 22 : 10 : 1675, to Rebecka,
relict of deceased, who brought in an inventory. She was to
have the estate for her own use, but was to pay to Sara, the
daughter of deceased, 10li. at eighteen years of age or marriage with the mother's consent.

Inventory of the estate of Samuell Stevens, taken Nov. 30,
1675, by Henry West and Nathaniel Putnam: one tenn acker
lott in the northfeild, 25li.; one tabel & Joyn stooll, 16s.; tow
Bedsteds, 1li. 10s.; one feather Bed & Curtaines, 2 pillows &
bolster, 1 Rugg & 2 blankets, one coverlid, 1 paire of sheets,
6li. 10s.; Tow pare sheets, table linin, 6 pillow bers, 2li. 17s.;
vutter, tinn, smothing iron, earthen war, wood ware, 1li. 10s.;
wareing aparell, 7li.; Carsei and sargge, 1li. 12s.; Warming
pann, Brasse, 1li. 12s.; iron ware with potts, hakes, firepann,
tongues, 1li. 12s.; Boxes and Cheests and Chares, 1li. 13s.; 1
hameker and Bookes, 1li. 3s.; Barrels, tubes with other lumber, 12s.; spade, spitt, hamer, 2 pare sheers, press iron, 16s.;
one Cow, 3li.; his Wages, 2li.; one axe, one Reapper, 13s.;
one Creadell, 1li.; one pillion, 2 glasse bottles, 12s. 6d.; 3
yards of linn. Cloth with staffe, 12s.; total, 62li. 2s. Estate
Dr. about 14li.
Essex County Quarterly Court Files, vol. 24, leaf 77.

Wm. Titcomb having formerly been appointed administrator of the estate of Samuell Stevens and an inventory now being brought in amounting to 38li. 6s. 4d. clear estate, said Titcomb was allowed 10li. and court Mar. 28, 1676, ordered the rest of the estate to John Steevens, his brother.

Ipswich Quarterly Court Records, vol. 5, page 278.

ESTATE OF THOMAS MILLET OF (GLOUCESTER?).

Administration on the estate of Thomas Millet, intestate, granted Sept. 28, 1675, to Mary Millet, the relict.

Ipswich Quarterly Court Records, vol. 5, page 274.

ESTATE OF JOHN GODFRY.

Administration upon the estate of John Godfry granted Sept. 28, 1675, to Benjamin Tompson. *Ipswich*

Ipswich Quarterly Court Records, vol. 5, page 272.

Peter (his P mark) Godfary, aged about forty years, deposed, Sept. 12, 1675, that John Godferry being at deponent's house about a month before he died, "I Asked the said Godfary when hee would Com and order mattrs conserning his bills or bonds hee tould mee vary speedelly: said I to him you may dy and leave youar things to you know not hoo : to which John Godfary Answered as for Jams Jakman hee shall have his bond or bill upe of the wheat and Indian corn for I have Resaued full sattisfaction from him the said Jakman and am greatly Ingeaged to him therfor no person shall molest or trubll him the said Jakman or his wief or childarn after him." Mary (her ‡ mark) Godfary, aged about thirty-nine years, deposed the same. Sworn, Sept. 9, 1675, before Samuell Symonds, Dept. Gov., and copy made by Robert Lord, cleric.

Essex County Quarterly Court Files, vol. 24, leaf 87.

ESTATE OF JOHN FRINK OF IPSWICH.

"In the Name of God Amen. I John ffrink of Ipswich in America by the prouidence of God being called to make a voyage into Europe, not knowing how it may please God to deale with mee before I returne, Doe dispose of that small estate God hath lent mee as followeth, first as touching my loueing wife with whom I Coupled myself in the feare of god liueing with her in the blessed estate of honorable wedlock, by whom also by the blesing of god I haue now twoe sonnes viz. John, & George, & albeit I doubt not but y^t God after my

departure acording to his pmise wilbe unto her a husband,
yea & a father, a patron & defender & will not suffer her to
lack if she trust feare & serue him dilligently, calling upon
his holy name, yet, forasmuch as God hath blessed mee with
sum worldly substance, I therefore giue unto her & bequeath
for terme of her naturall life if she remaine, so long unmar-
ried, the use & benifit of all my whole estate, where ever it bee
eyther in old England or New, be it lands monyes or other
goods, rents or dues, debts or demands that are or may be due
or belonging unto mee at or after my decease. what other land
or estate I leaue beside what falls to my heire by heritage or
intaile. I bequeath to my wife one third p^t of the same & to
my sone George one third p^t. & to my sone John one third pt.
my debts being all paid by my executrix Mary my wife whom
I make my sole executrix of this my last will & testament, &
Decon Goodhew of Ipswich my Supvisor to Counsell my wife
& puide for her & my Children while I am wanting & my
will is that hee shall pay himself out of my estate what is due
to him, for what he doth lay out or expend in my Absence
for my wife & Children: In witness wherof I haue hereunto
set my name & Seale December^r 26. in the yere of grace 1674."

John ffrinke (SEAL)

Witness: Thomas Sparke, Mary (her ‡ mark) Wilson.

Proved Sept. 29, 1675 by Deacon Wm. Goodhue and Mary
Willson before Samuell Symonds, dep. Gov. and Maj. Gen.
Denison.

Essex County Probate Files, Docket 10,231.

ESTATE OF ABEL OSEPH.

At Boston, 6 : 9 : 1675, administration upon the estate of
Abell Oseph, ship carpenter, who was slain in the wars with
Capt. Lothrop, was granted to Mr. Edmon Batter, on behalf
of and for the use of Jon. Oseph, his brother, living in Bostone with widow Johnson, and Hilliard Veren, clerk of the
court, was to present this to the court at Salem for confirmation, which was done.

Salem Quarterly Court Records, vol. 5, leaf 91.

Administration confirmed 21:10:1675, by Samuel Symonds, Dept. Gov., and Daniel Denison.

Essex County Quarterly Court Files, vol. 24, leaf 50.

Mr. Edmund Batter, administrator of the estate of Abell
Oseer, was ordered 28 : 4 : 1676 to pay the remainder of the estate after the bills were paid to the brother of the deceased,

John Oseef (also, Osuf), who acknowledged satisfaction.
Salem Quarterly Court Records, vol. 5, leaf 96.

Inventory of the estate of Abell Osier, who was slain in the
fight with the Indians, taken by Simon Horne and William
Ropes: serdge suet & fustian drawers, 2li.; shirt & other linen,
7s.; 2 p gloves, 2s., & old stocking, 12d., 3s.; 1 Bible, 2s.;
knife & Inckhorne, 6d.; 20 bisket, 16d.; Chest, 4s.; carpenters Tools, 4s.; total, 3li. 1s. 10d. To worke done for the new
meeting house for Mr. Nicolet, 5li. 1s. 6d. Debts, to Mr. Phill.
Cromwell, 4li. 6s. 6d.; Rats pd. to Constable Marsten, 1li. 3s.;
Symon Horne, 1li. 10s.; to Jno. Norman, 2s.; total, 6li. 1s.
6d.

Attested 28 : 4 : 1676 by Mr. Edmond Batter, the administrator.

Essex County Quarterly Court Files, vol. 25, leaf 56.

ESTATE OF JOHN LITTLEHALE.

Administration upon the estate of John Littlehale, who was
slain in the war, was granted, on Nov. 25, 1675, to Edmond
Bridges and Mary his wife, late wife of Richard Littlehale
and mother of said John, who were ordered to bring in an inventory to the next Ipswich court.

Ipswich Quarterly Court Records, vol. 5, page 275.

Inventory of the estate of John Littleale being slaine with
Capt. Laithrop: in cloathes, 4li.; one hatt, 10s.; shirtes and
sleeves and neckcloathes, 1li. 10s.; one payre of Breeches,
10s.; peuter & tin ware, 13s.; one musket, 12s.; a loome and
gares to it, 5li. 10s.; his wages for his service, 1li. 17s. 8d.; a
debt we find in a paper, 2li. 9s.; one sheepe, 8s.; Three sheep
lett unto Tho. Kimbell for three yers to the half, 13s.; total,
18li. 18s. 4d.

Delivered in Ipswich court Mar. 28, 1676 by Edmond
Bridges and his wife.

Essex County Probate Files, Docket 16,888.

ESTATE OF JOHN TREBIE.

Administration on the estate of John Trebe, was granted
30 : 9 : 1675 to Mary Trebe, the widow. She brought in an inventory and the two daughters, Elizabeth and Sara, were ordered to have 4li. each at age or marriage, and the house and
land to stand bound for the payment.

Salem Quarterly Court Records, vol. 5, leaf 90.

Inventory of the estate of John Trebie, deceased, taken
Nov. 24, 1675, by John Peach, sr. and James Dennes: house
and ground, 40li.; 4 Swine, 1li. 10s.; calfe, 12s.; fether bed,
one Bolster, 2 pillowes, 3li.; pare of Blankets, 16s.; one Rugg,
10s.; 2 Curtains, 6s.; Cabbin Bed and Blankets, 15s.; 2
Chears, 5s.; spining wheel, 3s. 6d.; 3 Barrills, 4s.; a Coate,
wastcoat, Breeches & Drawers, 1li. 5s.; a sea Coate &
Breeches, 7s.; 4 pare sheets & an odd one, 4li. 14s.; 5 pare pillow beres, 2li. 5s.; 6 Napkins & a Table Cloth, 18s.; 3 old
Shurts & 3 old pare Drawers, 1li.; a Chest, 3s. 6d.; a Leverre
Coubert, 1li. 15s.; Trundle Bedstead, 6s.; Table and 2 Joynt
stooles, 12s.; 4 Cheares, 6s.; Chest & 2 Boxes, 10s.; 2 Coubert
Cushings, 5s.; Little small table, 3s.; new Caster hatt, 13s.;
2 Coats, a pare Breeches & wastcoate, 2li. 10s.; pare shoose,
3s. 6d.; 5 pare stockins, 10s., 2 pare Gloves, 3s. 6d.; a Casse
and 5 Botles, 2s. 6d.; Cradle, 5s.; pare small Iron Doggs, 6s.;
a Cruck, fire shovell & Tongs, 6s.; spitt & Gridiron, 4s. 6d.;
pare Bellows, 1s.; 2 Iron pots & pott hooks, 15s.; Iron kettle,
8s.; 2 Brace Kettels & a Brace skellit, 1li. 10s.; percell
yerthen ware, 8s.; 6 peuter Dishes & a sauser, 1li.; 2 pewter
pots, a Bowl & a puter Botle, 6s.; 8 peuter porringers and a
little skillet, 10s.; 6 spoones & a Latten Dripen pann, 2s. 6d.;
an hour Glase & Looking Glace, 2s. 6d.; Smoothing Iron, 1s.
6d.; 4 Tubs & a Bucket, 4s.; one Gun, 1li.; sword, Belt &
Bandilears, 12s.; total, 74li. 11s. 6d.

The debts: to Mr. Ambrose Galle, 2li. 18s.; John Furbush,
16s.; Thomas Pitman, sr., 6s.; Mr. Moses Maverick, 5s. 9d.;
Samuell Clark, 1s. 6d.; Edward Humphreys, 1s. 6d.; Robert
Rowles, 17s.; Thomas Dixcy, 14s.; Mr. Ed. Batter, 1li. 2s.
7d.; Mr. John Gidney, 1li. 7s. 5d.; Edw. Holman, 10s.; Mr.
Christopher Lattemore, 15s. 10d.; James Dennis, 2s.; Mr.
Wm. Browne, sr., 25li. 17s. 4d.; total, 35li. 14s. 11d.

Attested in court 30:9:1675 by Mary, relict of the deceased and administratrix.

Essex County Quarterly Court Files, vol. 24, leaf 46.

ESTATE OF GEORGE COLE.

"I Jeorg Cooll being very aprehencsiue of my present deso-
lution doe committ my body to the earth and my soull to god
that gaue it i now being in my right mind and of sound understanding and judgment doe thus dispose of that Estatt
that god hath giuen me i giue to Mary Davis home i used to
call mother: forty shillings. item: i giue to my master John
Dauis all my timber: it: i giue the rest of my estatt to my

sister mary tuck and my other sister Elezibeth Cooll to be
equally deuided between them: i doe allsoe will and intreat
my Loueing freind danell Johnson and my Master John Dauis
to tak Care to se my just debpts that i owe be paid out of my
estatt as alsoe to gather in thos debpts that are dew to me and
to tak what Caare thay Cane that my will may be performed
for which i doe alsoe will and desire that thay haue resonable
sattisfaction for thar Care and paines herin out of my estatt
this Eaight of nouember one thoussand six hundred seuenty
fiue as wittnes my hand."

                    Georg (his *G* mark) Coolle.
Witness : Thomas Ferman, Samuell Foster.
Acknowledged Nov. 12, 1675, before Samuell Appleton,
Com. in Chief.
Proved 30 : 9 : 1675 and Daniell Johnson and John Davis
were appointed administrators.

Inventory of the estate of Georg Coall, taken by Samuell
Hartt and Eleazer Linse: 3 saues, 8s.; 2 goynters & fore-
plaine, 6s.; 3 smothing plains & a draing knife, 3s. 6d.; 2 plans
& 2 revolving plains, 10s.; 4 round plains, 5s.; 3 rabet plains,
4s.; 3 holou plains, 3s. 6d.; 9 Cresing plains, 10s. 6d.; 6 torn-
ing tools, 9s.; 3 plaine irons & 3 bits, 1s. 6d.; 1 brase stok, 2
squares & gorges, 1s. 6d.; 1 brod ax & 1 fro, 2s.; holfast, 1s.
6d.; hamer, 1s. 6d.; 6 gouges, 2s.; 9 Chisels, 5s.; 2 ogers & 1
draing knife, 3s.; 1 bench hooks, 2 yoyet irons, 1s.; a glue-
pot, 1s. 6d.; 1 bible, 3s.; 5 yards & a halfe of cloth, 1li. 13s.;
clothing, 2li. 5s.; for what work he has done in his shop, 1li.
10s.; 1 cow, 3li.; 1 horse, 2li. 15s.; 2 calfe, 10s.;
total, 15li. 16s.
Attested 30 : 9 : 1675 by John Davis.
Essex County Quarterly Court Files vol. 24, *leaves* 73, 74.
More in money, 1li. 16s., brought to be entered 23 : 11m :
1681.
          Essex County Probate Records, vol. 301, *page* 71.

ESTATE OF PETER BARRON OF MARBLEHEAD.

"Be it knowne vnto all men by these p^rsents y^t I Peter
Barroon off Marblehead New England ffisherman being now
prest and Commanded away to Goe a Gainst the Indians not
knowing where it may please ye Lord to spare my Life to Come
a Gain : Therefore I haue a Desire and Doe by these p^rsence
ffreely Giue unto my Master Elias Hendly all whateuer I
haue either money Goods o^r any other thing or things to his
own proper use and Behoofe to doe and use at his own will
and pleasure and further Doe Impower ye sd Elias hendly to

be my true and Lawful Attourney for me and in my name to Requir Recouer and Receiue all Debts. Dues Demands in money, o^r moneys Goods or other things whatsoever that is of property and of due belonging to me from any person or persons what ever: and upon any ye Refusers of payment thereof it shall & may be lawful for my sd Atourney to sue them Rest Implead Condemn Imprisson & upon payment of any such money o^r Goods for my Atourney to Giue aquitance o^r Discharges for ye same & in all to be as Good as if I were personally p^{r}sent at ye Doeing ye same in witness Thereof I haue set my hand this 28th: August 1675."

Petter (his O mark) Barroone.

Witness: Edw. Humphreys, John Merrett.

Proved 15 : 10 : 1675 by the witnesses.

Essex County Quarterly Court Files, vol. 24, leaf 78.

Inventory of the estate of Peter Barron, taken Nov. 26, 1675, by Nathanel Walton and James Dennes: one wascotte, pare of breshes & Jakett of stufe, 2li.; a pare of ould stufe briches & 2 pare of wolling drayers, 7s. 6d.; ould carsy cotte & breshes & one wascot of penestone, 16s.; one hatte & cape, 4s.; 2 fishing Linnes, 4s.; one pare of stockins & gloves, 3s.; two long neckcloth & hancershers, 9s. 6d.; one winter shirt & drayer, 14s.; 2 cors shirts & one ould pare Drayers, 10s.; one green ruge & one blankett, 1li. 8s.; one cheast, 5s.; mony sellver, 3li. 7s.; total, 10li. 8s. Debts due: to vini vinson, 17s.; to Mr. William Browne, sr., 1li. 16s.; to Cristopher Lattemore, 1li. 12s.; to John Furbush, 15s.; total, 5li.

Essex County Quarterly Court Files, vol. 25, leaf 92.

Elyas Henly was appointed 27 : 4 : 1676 administrator of the estate of Peter Baroone, who was slain in the war against the Indians, and was ordered to fulfill the mind and will of deceased as expressed in that writing given in and proved as his act and deed.

Salem Quarterly Court Records, vol. 5, leaf 94.

ESTATE OF CAPT. THOMAS LOTHROP OF BEVERLY.

Capt. Thomas Lothrop being slain in the war against the Indians and dying intestate, or not having left a formal will, Bethiah, his wife, was appointed 21 :10 :1675, administratrix of his estate and she brought in an inventory. There being some evidence of what the said Thomas Lothrop expressed concerning his mind and will in his lifetime, the administratrix was ordered to fulfill it accordingly.

Salem Quarterly Court Records, vol. 5, leaf 91.

Inventory of the estate of Capt. Tho. Lathrop of Beverlye, who died in the wars betwixt the English and the heathen, taken Nov. 11, 1675, by Paul Thorndike and John Hill: his wearing Apparrill, yt of it which was most Considerable hee had along with him into the service, & that which remained at whom, 4li. 17s. 6d.; 1 fether Bed, 1 Boulster, 2 pillows, 5li. 10s.; 1 flock Bed & pillow, 1li. 10s.; 1 Rug, 1 Covering, 1 sett of Curtins & vallans, 1 Bedstead & matt, 6li. 15s.; 2 fether Beds, 3 Boulsters, 8li.; 1 Rug, 1 Covering, 2 pillows, 2li.; 1 Cabbin Bedstead, 1 Curtin, 1 Curtin rod, 1 Trucle bedstead, 18s.; 1 Flock bed, 1 Boulster, 1 Truckle bedstead, 1 Covering, 1 Blankit, 1li. 10s.; 1 fether bed, 1 Boulster, 5 pillows, 1 Rug, 1 Blanket, 9li. 5s.; 1 Bedstead, 1 set of Curtains, Curtin rods & mat, 3li. 4s.; 9 pare of sheets, 1 single sheet, 4 pillow beers, 9li. 13s.; Table Lyning, with some other Lining, 1li. 14s. 6d.; Puter, 2 silver Cups, 1 silver spoone, 4li.; Monyes, 1li. 10s.; Brass, 6li. 8s.; 2 Carts, 1 pare of wheels, 1 plow, 1 pare of fetters with appurtenances, 4li.; 2 oxes, 1 Ads. 1 pare of Andirons, some tools & Lumber, 1li. 15s. 6d.; iron potts & ketles, pot hookes, fire shovell & tounges, hakes, Trevit, 1 iron morter & pestle & Tinn ware, 4li. 3s.; Trunkes, chests, Tables, cheers, stooles & formes, 1li. 10s.; 1 Lookeing glass, Barrills & Lumber, 17s. 6d.; 1 Brass ketle, 2 Fryeing panns, 7s.; Bookes, 2li. 8s. 6d.; 40 Bushels of Barlie, 12 Bushell of Rye, 10li. 8s.; 7 Bushels of Oates, 50 Bushels of Indian Corne, 8li. 6s.; 6 swine, 7li.; sheepe, 3li. 10s.; neat Catle, 27li. 10s.; the house Lott in estimation, being ten acres with the houses & orchard uppon it, 130li.; 23 acres in estimation Lyeing in the plaine, joyning or neare adjoining to the house Lott, 103li. 10s.; 20 Acres of Land Lyeing at an hill called snake hill, 30li.; 6 acres of medow Lyeing by Samll. Cornish his farme, 27li.; 1 acre & halfe of salt marsh neare Richard Leeches on Royall syde, 10li. 10s.; Haye, 7li. 10s.; 1 pare of scales & 1 Handvise, 4s. 6d.; A farme which was Major Hathornes land & medow, 98 acres, 98li.; A Farme which was Capt. Davinports land & medow, 74 acres, 79li.; Fifteene acres of Land Lying by Crumwells medow, 15li.; sixtye acres of Land, 60li.; In Horse kinde, 20li.; In cash Received uppon the account of my housbands wages, 9li. 13s.; total, 734li. 4s. Debts due to the estate, 4li. 14s. Debts due from the estate, 50li. 3s. 3d.

Petition of Ezekiel Cheever, schoolmaster, to the court: "Whereas Capt. Thomas Lowthrop, who lately lost his life in yᵉ service & cause of God & his countrey, being his wives' own,

dear, naturall brother, dying intestate, & without issue, he
humbly conceives himself on ye behalf of his wife to be y^e
true, naturall, proper heir of his estate left, & therefore his
duty to make his humble address to this Honoured Court,
that he may declare & legally plead ye same. To which end
‖ he came ‖ & attended ye court neer a weeks space, But y^e
Court by publick ocasions of ye Countrey being necessarily
adjourned, he was forced to return home, & resolved (God
willing) to attend ye Court, ye time appointed. But by y^e
providence of God, ye season being extraordinarily stormy, &
himself under bodily infirmity, he could not possibly come
without apparent hazard of life, limb or health. Yet had
cautiously left order, & instructions for his son to appear for
him in such an exigence which accordingly he did, though not
in season, being by the same providence also hindered. So
that the Honoured Court (no heir appearing) granted Administration to his sister Lowthrop, according to what then
appeared. But seing ye estate was not then setled, nor ye case
fully issued, many things alledged being dark & dubious &
nothing proved, & he hath much to say, to invaledate y^t very
writing given in, & ye seeming force of it. He humbly requests this Honoured Court, that being a party so neerly concerned, and interested, he may have ye liberty of making &
pleading his claime, & title according to law. And for y^e
better securing of what shall be judged to be his right, he may
be joyned together with his sister Lathrop in administration
of ye said estate."

Bethiah Lowthropp's statement: "My deare husband
neuer spake word to me concerning the giuing of any of his
Land Lying in the woods to his sister Cheeuers her children.
But only that Lying in the woods about Snake hill. But seriously considering my deare husbands expressions I doe conclude he gaue the plaine & the pasture by it together with the
Land at Snake hill to his sister cheeuer. for thus my dear
husband was pleased to expresse himselfe to me as we Rode
together to wenham the last spring in the week before the
court of election. Speaking to mee concerning the disposeall
of his land as he had formerly done, he said the house Lot I
giue to the towne for the use of the ministrey not to any particular person. But to the town for the use of the ministry
hoping it will be an acceptable seruice to god. And as we
were Riding ouer part of his Land belonging to Snake hill he
said this Land here I intend for my sisters children except
god take my Brother cheeuer away before my sister, then it

shall be for her use as long as she liueth, & afterward for her children, whereupon I doe conclude he gave the other land mentioned which lyeth but a little way from it to his sister, else that at Snaak hill would not be so usefull for my sister if god should be pleased to take my Brother away before her, & so I haue faithfully declared what I apprehend was my husbands will & pleasure concerning this matter which he said he did intend to put in writting. But the prouidence of god was pleased to preuent it in calling him forth upon public seruice."

Bethiah Lowthropp's statement: "Whereas it is expressed By my Honoured Brother Mr Ezekiel Cheeuer that my deare husband did not willingly take Sarah gott into his house but was perswaded & preuailed with by others to doe it, Humbly Requesting leaue, I shall humbly present the Honoured Court with the whole truth concerning this matter. When the childs mother was dead my husband beeing with mee at my cousins buriall & seeing our friends in so sad a condition the poore babe hauing lost its mother & the woman that nursed it being fallen sick, I then did say to some of my friends that if my husband would give me leaue I could be uery willing to take my cousins little one and nurse it for him a while till he could better dispose of it. whereupon the childes father did mooue it to my husband. my deare husband considering my weaknesse & the incumbrance I had in the family was pleased to Returne this Answer. hee did not see how it was possible for his wife to undergoe such a burthen. the next day their came a friend to our house a woman which gaue suck & she understanding how the poore babe was left beeing Intreated was willing to take it to nurse and forthwith it was brought to her. But it had not bin with her 3 weekes before it pleased the Lord to visit that nurse with sicknesse also and the nurses mother came to me desiring I would take the childe from her daughter, and then my deare husband obseruing the prouidence of god was freely willing to Receiue her into his house. But she was then Receiued only as a nurse child & so she Remained aboue a quarter of a yeare before her father did tender her to my husband to accept of her for his Adopted Child."

Left. William Dixie deposed that coming to Capt. Lawthrope's in the time of his last sickness, Mrs. Lawthrope and Mrs. Got went out of the room, and Capt. Lawthrope said to him, "I am glad you are come for I would have you to take notice: that I give unto my wife all my estate so long as she

liveth: and after her decease I giue unto the Ministry of
Beverly: my tenn acre lott at home and my house upon the
same." Upon asking him if he had acquainted his wife with
it, he said he had and that she approved of it. Also he said
he gave the ground in the woods to his sister Chevises children: Sworn in court.

"My wife affirms that her brother hath oft spoke in her
hearing dissatisfiedly concerning Noah Fisk being brought to
his house, when his mother was very weak, & not able to look
after him being very weak also, y^t he never knew upon w^t
termes he kept him, & wondred what they did intend to do,
she saith Lieut. Dixey told her, my brother told him when he
had brought him up fit to go to apprentice, he had done, he
should do no more." [Testimony of Ezekiel Cheever?]

Reasons for the claim of the wife of Ezekiel Cheever: 1. "It
does not appear, that my brother ever set himself seriously,
as the thing requires, to make his last will. But all that is
said, is, that he expressed such and such purposes at such
times, but purposes and actions are different things. 2. No
man but in case of absolute necessity, when he is surprized by
sudden weaknes and inability, will make such a nuncupative
will, and then he will do it in the surest and strongest way
that may be, by postive and peremptory declaring it his last
will, and confirming it by sufficient witnesses that are legall.
But in this case no such thing is found. 3. The persons testi-
fying in this case are persons concerned and interested, and
not so competent witnesses in law in any case, much lesse in
such a weighty one, as a last will and testament. Beside they
agree not in their testimony, but in some things directly con-
tradict each other, which does demonstrate that either they
mistook my brother, and he never expressed such purposes
and desires, or that his purposes and desires altered. 4. It
seems to be an act of prudent and deliberate choice in my
brother not to make a will For (1) He was oft importuned to
it by my sister, but did it not. (2) He had warning of death
by a long and dangerous sicknes last winter, in which, after
some degree of recovery, he had severall relapses. (3) After
that by the mercy of god he was recovered to perfect health,
he had time sufficient for such a work, if he had judged it
expedient. 5. I conceive that the true reason of his not
making a will was, he could not do for his own sister, and her
children, what he thought was most just and right, and they
might be likely to need after the decease of his brother
Cheever; but he should displease his wife, and her relations,

who would be expecting more, though he had done in his lifetime so much for them : and nothing for his sister and her
children. And he well knew the equity and justice of the law
which makes provision for the widow and the next of kin, but
nothing for strangers, as also the faithfullnes of the magistrates in doing things according to law. 6. The matter which
they testify is so unjust and unreasonable, that none that
knew my brothers goodnes and love will beleive, that my
brother would be so unnaturall to preferr strangers before his
owne naturall sister and her children, whom he so dearly
loved, as many that knew them both can abundantly testify.
7. My Brother, when he brought his sister from England
with him from all her friends and relations very loth to part
with her, used this as a great argument with her Mother to
perswade her. Viz : That he had no children of his own, nor
was likely to have any : and otherwise he must give what he
had to strangers. And her mother told this to friends in her
hearing, that that was a great motive that induced her to be
willing to part with her ; and commited her to the love, and
care of her brother as a Father, with great confidence and assurance of his tendernes toward her. 8. His sister by coming
over, lost the value of twenty-five pound, beside what her
mother would have given her at her decease. 9. My brother
having one of their relations with him already. viz. Noah
Fisk whom he brought up from a little one was unwilling to
take Sarah Gott : but was importuned, and prevailed with to
take her, not upon loose terms, as he did the other, but as his
own : so that her father might not have power to take her away
from him, when she might grow up to be serviceable, as is oft
done in such cases. As for her calling them father and
mother, it is no more but what is ordinarily done to nurses or
servants, and what another, whom he had brought up before,
was used to do, who went away from them, when she might
have been serviceable to them. My sister brought no estate
with her, as I ever heard of, hath no charge, her husband by
her own confession gave her none of ye land to dispose of as
her own."
Essex County Quarterly Court Files, vol. 24, leaves 50-55.

Court 27 : 4 : 1676, gave judgment upon the settlement of
the estate of Capt. Thomas Lothrop, of which Bethiah, the
widow, was administratrix, being moved by the petition of
Mr. Ezekiell Cheevers, as follows : that all the estate remain
in the widow's hands during her life ; after her decease, the
farm called Maj. Hathorn's to be Sara Gott's ; the housing,

ten acre lot and appurtenanc, after the widow's decease, to be
for the use of the ministry in Beverly forever; that the debts
and legacies were to be paid, and the lands and meadows expressed in the inventory, being understood to be the lands in
the woods, after the decease of the widow, were to be given to
Ellenor, wife of Mr. Eze. Cheevers and her heirs; the rest of
the estate to be sold for the benefit and disposal of the said
Bethia.

Upon further consideration, court found that Capt. Lothrop intended the legacies of 40li. bequeathed to Noah Fisk
and the four youngest children of Joshua Rea should be paid
out of the land in the woods towards said Rea's farm, which is
part of that land assigned by the court to Mr. Cheevers. It
was therefore ordered, with the consent of Mr. Grafton and
his wife, the relict of the said Capt. Lathrop, that Mr.
Cheevers should have present possession of all the lands formerly allotted to him by this court, excepting only the land in
Beverly belonging to and now used with the house there, said
Cheevers paying the legacies of 40li.; also that what disbursements should be laid out upon the house and land in Beverly
by Mr. Grafton, should be repaid by the said town to whom
the house and land were given, after the death of Mrs. Grafton. This judgment was to be submitted to the General
Court for approbation.

Salem Quarterly Court Records, vol. 5, leaf 95.

The act of the County Court at Salem, June 27, 1676,
being presented to this Court, determining the settlement of
the estate of the late Capt. Lathrop, this court Oct. 15, 1679
confirms and allows the same.

For a final settlement of the estate of Capt. Lauthrrop, this
court June 11, 1680, having heard the several pleas, determine
that the widow, now wife of Joseph Grafton, have the moveable estate and to pay the said Lawthrops debts and twenty
pounds to the children of Joshua Rey; also to have the use
of the houses and lands during her life; at her death to revert
to the wife of Mr. Ezekiell Cheevers and her issue, the heirs
of the said Capt. Lawthrop. The costs for the hearing was
five pounds which Mr. Ezekiell Cheevers paid.

The court Oct. 13, 1680 ordered that no alienation should
be made of the reversion of the said Lawthrops lands and
houses during the life of his widow; but if there should appear need for her relief she may make application to the
Court of that county, who are impowered to order the sale of

any part thereof as to them may appear necessary.

Mass. Bay Colony Records, vol. 5, pp. 252, 298.

Agreement made between Ezekiel Cheever of Boston, gentleman, in behalf of Ellin his wife (sister of Capt. Lathrop late of Beverly) and the children he hath had by her, as the proper heirs of the said Capt. Thomas Lathrop on the one part and Joseph Grafton of Salem, mariner, in right of Bethiah his wife relict and administratrix of the estate of sd. Capt. Thomas Lathrop, on the other part, relating unto the estate left by Capt. Lathrop as of right belonging unto the said Ellin, and her children and for a final settlement of the same; that Ezekiel Cheever shall pay unto Joseph Grafton 60li. in consideration whereof Joseph Grafton and his wife Bethiah relinquish all their right in said estate of housing and lands left by Thomas Lathrop, and they shall enjoy the estate clear from all debts owing from said estate and bequests pretended to be made by him. Signed and sealed, Nov. 30, 1680.

The true meaning of the above is not that Mr. Grafton and his wife shall make good in law, the just title of any part of the aforesaid lands against any that may lay claim thereto, but only to give in any legal evidence they can to the justices of any controversy about them.

Witness: John Higginson, sr., Hilliard Veren.

Acknowledged April 4, 1681, by Joseph Grafton and Bethiah his wife.

Essex County Quarterly Court Files, vol. 34, *leaf* 91.

ESTATE OF RICHARD PRINCE, SR., OF SALEM.

"The Last will and Testament of Richard Prince, senior, of Salem, aged 61 yeares or thereabouts. Imprimis, I giue and bequeath vnto my sonne Joseph Prince, the one halfe of the Ten acre lott, bought of William Lord, Senior, I say the one halfe of that part of the lott, that lyeth South ward, & so from the highway westward to the end. Also I giue vnto him halfe an Acre of marsh ground more or lesse, lying at the further side of the south field of Salem, Joyneing on the one side to an Acre of marsh of goody Lemmans that was, & butting on m^r George Gardners upland. Item, I giue vnto my sonn Samuel Prince, the other part of the ten Acre lott which I bought of goodman Lord, lying Northward, & running from the highway to the end westward. Also I giue vnto him that halfe acre of marsh ground, more or lesse, lying neere the bars that goeth out of ye South field.

"Also I giue vnto my sonne Samuel my now dwelling house, with my warehouse & barne, & all the houseing theireto apertayning, with the ground whereon the said dwelling house standeth, from the ffront or street Eleuen pole downeward towards ye North, & adioying to his brother Richards grounds on ye East, & his broth^r Jonathans on ye North, Item, I giue & bequeath vnto my sonne Richard Prince, a fiue Acre lott, lying in the South field of the Towne, neere Joseph Hardye, fiue Acre lott, lying in the same field

"Also I giue vnto him, out of that lott that my dwelling house standeth on, two pole & an halfe in bredth front to the streete, namely of the ground betweene my dwelling house & the land of Mr William Browne, junior, & adioyneing next to ye land of ye said William Browne on the East, & Contayning in Length Eleuen pole downward into ye orchard. Item, I giue vnto my sonne, Jonathan Prince, the other part of the Ten Acre lott, that I bought of goodman Lord, lying from the highway Eastward the whole bredth. Also I giue vnto him halfe an Acre of marsh grounds, more or lesse, knowne by the name of Wallers halfe acre. Moreouer I giue into him the remainer of that ground on which my dwelling house standeth, that is the North part of my orchard Contayning the whole bredth of it, adjoyneing to the End of his brother Samuell & Richards ground, & so to the land. Item, I giue & bequeath vnto my daughter Mary Daniel Twenty pounds, to be paid after my decease & after the decease of my wife Item I giue vnto my two Grandchildren, Steven & Mary Daniel, Five pounds apiece, to be paid, after my Decease in money.

"Lastly, I leaue & ordaine my sonn Joseph Prince to be the sole Executore of this my last will & Testament Haueing in his hands all the remainer of my Estates to beare ye Charge of maintayning my wife after my decease whom I giue and Committ to his Care to be maintained the whole tyme of her naturall life, And after her death, those Legacyes being paid to my daughter & her Children, with my debts and funerall Charges, what remaines of my Estate upon true Inventory taken, my will is that it be divided into four equall parts, & my four sonns to haue each of them his share of it And I intreat my loueing friends—Bartholmew & Mr Joseph Grafton, sen^r to be ouerseers of this my last will & Testament, which I haue made & ordained being sicke & weake in body, but of perfect understanding & memory blessed be God

and haue hereunto Sett my hand & seale, this 21th of the
seuenth month. 1675."

Richard Prince (SEAL)

Witness: Stephen Daniell, Edw. Norrice.

Proved 21:10:1675 by the witnesses.

Inventory of the estate of Mr. Richard Prince, sr., of Salem,
taken Oct. 21, 1675, by Joseph Grafton and Francis Skerry:
bed, boulster, pillow, Coverlet & blankets, with bedsted &
Curtaines, as it stands, 7li.; bed, boulster, Covering, blanket,
4li.; bed, boulster, 3 blankets, rug, bedsted, 4li.; bed, boulster,
pillow, rug, blanket, bedstead, 7li. 10s.; 10 pair of sheets, 6li.;
30 yards of Cotton & Lining Cloth, 3li.; 3 yards of Cotton
& Lining Cloth, 12s.; 2 pair of pillowbeares, 12s.; 4 bordclothes, 1li. 4s.; 2 Corse bordclothes, & six napkins, 8s.; 2
Trunkes, 12s.; 1 Chist, 1li. 5s.; 4 Joynt stoles, 8s. 4d.;
Chaires, 12s.; 1 table, 14s.; 2 tables, 1li.; 2 old Chists, 2 old
boxes, 3s.; 2 whells, 6s.; 1pr. Cards, 2s.; 3yd. Cearsie, 1li.
15s.; 2 grosse butons, 8s.; a psell silke, 16s.; 16 bushels
Indian Corne, 2li. 8s.; 2 old brasse, 1li.; 1 old bras pot, a
skillet & Chafeing dish, 12s.; 2 Iron pots & a skillet, 13s.; 1
bell metell morter & pestill, 8s.; 1 small bras scelles & waits,
8s.; 1 frying pan, 1s.; warming pan, 6s.; 12 platers, 3li. 7s.;
2 basons, one Culender & 2 pots, 24s.; 6 peces of old puter,
14s.; 2 small puter pots & a Chamber pot, 8s.; 6 porengers,
7s.; fouer puter Candell stickes, 8s.; 4 sasers, 2s.; 1 Lanthorn,
2 dripin pans & 2 Candellstickes, 9s.; Earthen weare, 8s.; 3
old tables & an old Cobart, 1li.; 7 Chaires, 12s.; Iron ware,
18s.; small bag Cotton, 4li. 17s.; 7 Lod hay, 7li.; 1 horse &
an old mare, 3li.; 2 Cowes, 7li.; 1 hog, 2li.; 4 paier sheares,
2 Irons, 10s.; one smothing Iron & heats, 2s.; 1 pr. bellows,
1s.; books, 1li. 10s.; 1 gun & sword, 1li.; 4 spones & 2 old
small Cupes, 2li.; Monie, 90li.; 15 Akors of upland & An
Acre of Salt marsh, 76li.; the house & ground belonging,
130li.; the Cloths, 5li. 10s.; total, 386li. 18s.

Attested 21:10m : 1675, by Joseph Prince, executor.

Debts owing Richard Prince: Capt. Georg Corwin,
5li.; Mr. Graves, 2li. 2s. 6d.; Nath. Beadell, 2li. 8s. 4d.; James
Powland, 19s. 6d.; Capt. Price, 3li. 6s.; Mathew Standly, 1li.;
John Gardner, 1li. 10s.; Thomas Gardner, 1li. 10s.; Daniell
King, 1li. 4s. 9d.; John Grafton, 3li.; John Watters, 12s.;
Francis Scurrie, 1li.; Tho. Ives. 1li.; Samuell Willyams, 1li.;
Capt. Moore, 2li. 7s.; Jacob Barnie, 19s.; Samuell Pittman,
1li. 10s.; John Brown, 1li. 17s.; Mark Bacheler, 10s.; Mr.

Bartholmu, 5li.; Robart Hodg, 18s.; Abraham Bartholmu, 11s.; Sam. Gachell, 16s.

Richard Prince debtor: to Willyam Brown, senr., 5li. 1s. 5d.; Phillip Cromell, 4li. 15s. 6d.; Willyam Brown, 2li.; Manasah Merston, 5s.; John Holmes, 1li.; total, 13li. 1s. 11d. *Essex County Quarterly Court Files, vol. 24, leaves* 56-58.

GUARDIANSHIP OF JOHN CREASY.

John Creasy chose Joseph Bacheler as his guardian, and it was allowed 21 : 10 : 1675.

Salem Quarterly Court Records, vol. 5, leaf 91.

ESTATE OF WILLIAM DEW.

Administration on the estate of William Dew, who was slain in the wars against the Indians, was granted 21: 10: 1675, to Edward Bishop, jr., and he was to bring in an inventory to the next Salem court.

Salem Quarterly Court Records, vol. 5, leaf 91.

Edward Bishop, having been appointed at the last Salem court administrator of the estate of Will. Dewe, made oath to the inventory which he brought in to court 27:4:1676.

Salem Quarterly Court Records, vol. 5, leaf 97.

Inventory of the estate of Will. Dewes, taken by Edward Bishop: Recd in Marchandabel Fish, 4 li. 17. 3d.; for ye contrey Servis under Capt. Page of Boston, 2li.; for ye countery Servis under Capt. Thomas Lawthrope, 1li. 10s. 6d.; by his Cloaths and Chist, 2li.; 3 sheepe, 1li. 1s.; 3 gall. Traine oyle at 2s. pr. Gall., 6s.; mony of Ephraim Fellowes, 6s.; mony of Marke Haskoll, 2s.; total, 12li. 2s. 9d.

Attested in Salem court 30:4:1676 by Edward Bishop.
Essex County Quarterly Court Files, vol. 25, leaf 74.

ESTATE OF SAMUEL CRUMPTON.

Administration on the estate of Samuell Crompton, who was slain in the wars against the Indians, was granted 21: 10: 1675, to Jane, his wife, who brought in an inventory. She was to have the estate for her own use, "there being noe relations of her husbands known of in this country."

Salem Quarterly Court Records, vol. 5, leaf 92.

Inventory of the estate of Samuell Crumpton, taken 29: 9:1675, by Hilliard Veren, sr. and Henry West: a parcell of small trunks unfinished, 3li.; 3 leather chaires, 1li. 4s.; 8 sadles, 20s. p., 2 side sadles, 3li.; 1 dozen skins, 3s.; pcell of nayles, 2li. 10s.; pcell of soft sope, 16s.; 100 of skins, 5li. 8s.; 6 bridles, 5s. p. & 3 at 3s. p., 1li. 19s.; pcell of Inkle, 5s.; 1 gross of civills, 12s.; 6 p^r of sterrop Irons, 8s.; pcell of girtnes, 3s.; a gross of plates, 1li. 10s.; 1-2 gross of buckles, 4s. 6d.; 1,000 bullen nailes, 8s.; 5 p^r raines of bridles, 7s.; 2 chests, 7s. 6d.; a brass Kettle, 1li. 7s.; 5 yd^s cource cloth, 12s. 6d.; 10 drest skins, 1li. 5s.; cloath cloak old, 25s.; yards home made stuff, 1li. 4s.; a caster, 12s.; 3 shirts, 12s.; 2 p^r stockens, 3s.; 1 p^r shooes, 4s.; a bed & furniture, 5li.; pewter, 20s.; 6 chaires, 36s.; fire pan, tongs, frying pan, 7s. 6d.; scillet, som earth dishes & bottles & som lumber, 5s.; a little table & 2 Joyn stooles, 10s.; woolen wheele, 4s.; by 2 sadles & a bridle prest into ye service, 2li. 6s.; for his wages while upon the service, ——; the estate is credit by severall men, 13li. 11s. 6d. Estate is Dr. to severall men, 5li.

Attested 21 : 10m : 1675 by Jane, relict and administratrix. *Essex County Quarterly Court Files, vol. 24, leaf 62.*

ESTATE OF STEPHEN WAIMAN.

Administration on the estate of Steephen Waiman, intestate, granted 21 : 10 : 1675, to George Bonfeild and Rebeca, his wife, and they were to bring in an inventory to the next Salem court.   *Salem Quarterly Court Records, vol. 5, leaf 92.*

ESTATE OF GEORGE ROPES OF SALEM.

Administration on the estate of George Roapes, who was slain in the wars against the Indians, was granted 21 : 10 : 1675, to Wm. Roapes, brother of the deceased, who made oath to the inventory brought in, and after all debts were paid, the remainder was to go to Mary Roapes, the mother, during her life. The estate was not enough to pay the debts by about 12li.   *Salem Quarterly Court Records, vol. 5, leaf 92.*

Accounts due from the estate to Jno. Price, John Pickering, William Andrew, Wm. Browne, sr., Thomas Rix, Thomas Ives, John Guppy, Jacob Pudeator, Phillip Cromwell and William Reeves.

Inventory taken by Edw. Norice and Benjamin Gerrish: bed & blankett, 3li. 10s.; rugge, 2li.; 2 hatts, 1li. 8s.; Curtaines & Vallians, 10s.; Bible, 7s.; Cloake, 2li. 10s.; horse, 2li. 10s.; shirt, 10s.; 3 pillowbeeres & 2 napkins, a little towell,

12s.; 6 platters, 1li. 5s.; 2 Chayres, 6s.; 1 matt, 2s.; 2 Chests, 13s.; saddle, 4s.; 3 boxes, 7s.; white Coate, 4s.; bedstaves, 2s.; 6 yds. course canvas, 6s.; another Chest, 4s.; an axe, an adz & 2 sawes, 10s.; other tooles, 15s. 3d.; pr. new shoos, 7s. 6d.; total, 20li. 2s. 9d. George Roapes Dr. to Thomas Rix, 9s. 4d.; to Capt. Geo. Corwin, 1li. 14s. 6d.; Jacob Pudeater, 1li.; Mr. Phill. Cromwell, 5li. 18s. 4d.; John Guppy, 3li. 1s. 6d.; Mr. Browne, sr., 11s. 6d.; Mr. Ruck, 2li. 5s. 7d.; Mr. Price, 5li.; Wm. Reeves, 3li. 5s. 8d.; Tho. Ives, 7li. 15s. 10d.; John Pickering, 1li. 16s. The creditors were to be paid at the rate of 11s. per li.

Essex County Quarterly Court Files, vol. 24, leaves 69, 70.

Estate of Peter Wolfe of Beverly.

"In the name of God Amen: I Peter Woolfe: of Beverly yeoman: being though sick in body: yet of sound & perfect mind & Memory praised be God for it: Doe make and ordain this my present last will & testament in Maner & form following (Viz) first & principally: I comend my soull into the hands of Almighty God: hoping through the merite death & pasion of my Saviour Jesus Christ: to have free pardon & forgiveness of all my sins & to Inherit everlasting life: and my body I comit to the earth to be decently buried: at the Discristion of my executor herafter named and as touching the discretion of all such temporall estate as it hath pleased: God to bestow upon me: I give & dispose the rest as followeth first I will that my debts & funerall Charges shall be paid & Discharged: Item I give unto my two Granchildren Mary & Sarah Solace to be divided between them A yearling heifer: in my son Blacks hands Item. I Give unto Martha: my Loving wife: the sume of twelve pounds wch is Due from Nicholas Grove; of which sume there is now paid fourty shillings and the residue is to be paid in w^t my said wife shall need; only four pounds of it in Money if she require it: All the rest and residue of my personall Estate Goods & Chatells whatsoever, I doe give & bequeath unto my Loving Sonn John Black full & sole executor of this my last will and testament. And I desire that my body may be buried and I doe herby revoke disanull & make void all former wills & testaments by me hertofore made in witness wherof: I the said Peter Wolfe to this my last will & testament, being Contained in one side of this halfe sheet of paper: set my hand & seall this twentieth day of November in the year of our lord God one thousand six hundred & seventy five."

Peter (his ╱ mark) Woolfe. (SEAL)

Witness: Samuell Hardie, Humphrey (his H W mark)
Woodbery, Senior.
Proved 21:10:1675 by the witnesses.

Inventory of the estate of Peter Woolfe of Beaverley, who
deceased 6:10:1675, taken Sept. 13, 1675, by Humphrey
(his H W mark) Woodbry and John Hill: waring aparill, 1li.
10s.; 3 paire & one shete, 9s.; 3 Sherts, 1li. 10s.; one bed, pel-
ows & covering, 3li. 16s.; one Iron pot & pothooks, 9s.;
one friing pan & lumber, 3s.; one warming pan, 4s.; one
paire of belles, 1s. 6d.; one chest & to boxis, 10s.; one cuberd,
5s.; one churne & to tubes, 5s.; five badgs, 7s.; one skillet &
other small things, 4s.; one paill, 1s. 6d.; 3 Iron wedges, 2s.
6d.; 1 tube & to barills, 4s. 6d.; 3 trays & to pots, 2s. 8d.; to
stools & on chayer, 2s.; to swine, 2li. 8s.; neat Catell, 11li.;
3 lode & half of hay, 3li. 10s.; one lode of strawe, 7s.; 16 bushells of barly, 3li. 4s. 8d.; Indian corne, 1li. 15s.; one bushill
& halfe of ry, 6s.; one bedsted, 5s.; one paire tramels & nary-
ing bars, 1li. 10s.; hows & orcherd together with 8 ackers of
land, 68li.; Due from Nich. Legrove, 10li.; total, 112li. 11s.
10d. Debts due from the estate, 4li. 12s.
Attested in Salem court 21:10:1675.
Essex County Quarterly Court Files, vol. 24, leaves 71, 72.

The will and inventory of Peeter Woolfe were proved and allowed 21:10:1675. John Black, the executor, agreed to maintain the widow of deceased during her life, if said Black sur-
vived so long, and it is to be understood that the 10li. given to
the widow by will, was to be used by her for her maintenance,
but she was not otherwise to dispose of it.
Salem Quarterly Court Records, vol. 5, leaf 92.

ESTATE OF CALEB KIMBALL.

Administration upon the estate of Caleb Kemball, who was
slain in the war, was granted 21:10:1675, to Henry and
Richard Kemball, the latter making oath to the inventory
which was allowed.
Salem Quarterly Court Records, vol. 5, leaf 92.

Inventory of the estate of Caleb Kemball, slain with Captain Laythrop in the country service, taken 25:9:1675, by
Charls Gott and Walter Fayerfield: one hous and twenty-four
akers of land, 34li. 5s.; one hors, 3li.; one mare, 2li. 10s.; 15
bushells and 1-4 of inden corn, 2li. 5s. 9d.; tools, 17s. 6d.;
one muskett, 1li. 5s.; by 7 wekes wadges dew from the coun-

try, 2li. 2s.; one chest and boox and on par of shoes, 10s.;
tining ware and other small things & bible, 10s. 6d.; wearing
clothes, 3li. Debts due from the estate: to the hayers or administrators of Henery Kemball his father, 25li.; to Deakon
Goodhew, 4li. 3s.; Walter Fayerfeld, 2li.; Ezekell Woodward,
2li. 3s.; Master Batter, 1li. 5s.; Thomas Ives, 1li. 2s.; Peeter
Chevers, 2s. 6d.; Mr. Phillip Cromwell, 6s.; Mistres Newman,
5s; Goodman Hayward the hatter at Ipswich, 13s. 6d.; to
John Baker of Ipswich, 4s. 6d.; John Safford, 5s. 6d.; Cornitt
Whipple, 9s.; John Sparks, 1s.; his unkle Richard Kembal's
estate, 4s. 6d.; to Leweie Elford, 2s.; that his father Henery
Kemball had in money, 17s.; delivered to Elizabeth Norten
by Caleb's order a chist and box and tin ware, 8s.; four bushels and half of Indien corne that henery Kemball his father
had of Caleb Kemball's corn, 15s. 9d.; debts that are dew and
out of my hand of Caleb Kembal's estate, 38li. 7s. 3d.; the
17s. in money and 15s. 9d. in corne is dew from the estate of
his father henery kemball and a paile the window kemball
hath, 1li. 13s. 9d.

Administration on the above estate granted to Hen. and
Richard Kimboll and said Richard attested 30 : 9 : 1675, to
the truth of this inventory.

The said Henry being deceased sole administration is
granted to Richard and he was ordered to pay to the twelve
children of the deceased Henry Kimboll 18s. at age.

Essex County Quarterly Court Files, vol. 25, leaves 81, 82.

Estate of Philip Nowell.

Philip Nowell dying at sea, intestate, Mr. Habbackuck
Turner was appointed 21 : 10 : 1675, administrator of his estate, who made oath to the inventory of the estate left aboard
the ship, and was ordered to bring in the perfected inventory
to the next Salem court.

Salem Quarterly Court Records, vol. 5, leaf 91.

Inventory of the estate of Phillip Nowell, taken by Habb.
Turner: two blankits, 7s. 6d.; 1 wastcoate, 5s. 9d.; a coate
and wastcoate, 8s.; a payre of shoos, 5s. 6d.; a bed sack and
two shurts, 12s.; a wastcoate and drawers, 15s.; a coate and
britches, 1li. 18s.; a coate and wastcots, 19s. 6d.; wastcoat
and briches, 17s.; a coat and Chest, 16s. 6d.; 5 1-2 mo. wages
at 30s. p mo., 8li. 5s.; 5 1-2 yds. of corse carsey, 16s. 6d.;
2 hhs. of brandy, 20li.; 1 quarter cask of brandy, 5li.; a small
burding peace, 10li. 10s.; total, 41li. 16s. 3d.

Inventory of the estate of Phillip Nowell, not brought in
by Mr. Turner, taken by Richard Croade, John Beckett
and John Pallet (also Pollard) brought in by Wm. Dicer,
money in william Dicer's hands, 5li.; in my hands, for fish
received of Good. Buckly, 1li.; due from John Archer, 1li.;
due by Richard Flinder, 10s., due by Richard Maber & from
Jon. Cliford, 10s., 1li.; due for 10 pr. of stockins sold to Hen.
Rich. at 2s. 6d., 1li.; due from John Pollard for 2 1-4 yds.
carsy, 5s. 7 1-2d.; due from John Pollard for 2 pr. woemen's
stockins, 3s.; due by Mr. Habbacuck Turner, bookes, bedding & Cloathes, wch as I am Informed were sold at ye mast
as ye manner of the sea in such cases is, 7li.; 3 very large
Hogsds. of brandy wch ye sd. mr. Habbacuck Turner must
give accompt of,——; in the custody of Mrs. Mary English, 1
wt. Jackett new, 1 new wascoat, 1 black castor Hatt almost
new, ——; in my custody, 10 pr. womens' stockens at 18d.,
15s.; 1 pr. of drawers, 3s.; 1 paceboard Hatt case, 1s.; 2 1-2
yrds. red carsey at 2s. 6d. per, 5s. 7d.; 1 pr. old worsted stockins, 1s. 6d.; 2 neck cloaths, 2s. 6d. A chest left in my hand, as
followeth, 2 pr. old silver buttens, 1s. 6d.; in money, 4li.
10s. 7 1-2d.; 1 pr. of falce sleeves & a remnant of fustin, 3s.;
1 loose broad cloath coat, 1li.; an old pr. of drawers, 2s.; 1 pr.
of camlett breeches, 12s.; 1 holland shirt, 5s.; 5 yds. wt.
flanning at 18d. p yd., 7s. 6d.; 1 pr. wt. Jerzey stockens. 2s.; 1
new red rugg, 1li. 10s.; 1 new ivory comb, 1s. 3d. A very smale
pr. of stilliards which he left in my house, & sd. they should
be for the use of the house, 2s.; what is due to him from Mr.
Turner for his wages ye Tyme he sayled with him, ——; a
smale pcell of pipes not valued. Debts owing by Phillip
Nowell, to me William Dicer, 8s. 6d.; to Mr. Jonathan Corwin
for Buttens, 1s. 6d.; to the constable of Salem for rates, to
charges for drawing the Inventory & appraisers, ——.

Said Nowell was drowned Nov. 15, 1675, upon the coast
of New England, from a vessel commanded by Mr. Habbacuck
Turner, bound for Salem from France, and William Dicer,
as attorney to said Nowell, petitioned for administration to
be granted to him "that I may with a good conscience make
an honest discharge vnto whomsoeuer of his relations most
propperly claymeing the due of right thereto."

Pay for Phillip Nowells Rates: Indian to Mr. Cleford, 1li.
5s.; Indian Rate, 8s.; Ministers Rate, 5s.; towne Rate for the
yeare 1674, 4s. 6d.; more payd William Diser by Maj.
Harthornes order for charges on the estate and 8s. 6d. Phillip
oade Diser, 1li. 12s.; to Mr. Verin for writing the inventory

and severall things, 4s. 6d.; my atending on the Cort 8 dayes, 12s.; costoms of his brandy, 1li.; for frait, 1li.; to Constable Cleford for his tyme spent on serving warrents and other things, 5s.; the work for inventory &c., 2s.; total, 6li. 15s.
Essex County Quarterly Court Files, vol. 24, leaves 47-49.

ESTATE OF JOHN BATCHELER OF SALEM.

"I John Batchelor aged 63 being in pfect memory do make this my last Will and Testament in the year of o^r Lord 1673 and the 25 year of the Reigne of o^r Soveraigne Lord Charlse the Second King of England &c Inp^r I Bequeath my Soul to the Lord Jesus my Redeemer and my Body to my ffriends by them decently to be intered and what estate the Lord hath given mee I dispose off as followeth I give unto my loving Wife Elizabeth my dwelling House during her natural life & then to be my Son John Batchelors allso I give her all my movable estate wheresoever it is, (shee paying fifteen pounds in legacyes as here after is willed) & 6 pound p anu. so long as shee remains unmaried and the keeping of two Cowes, & fire-wood for her necessary use to be paid for at the charge of my Two Sonns as it is here after expressed also I appoynt her to be my Executrix. It. I give my Son John Batchelor ‖ my house I dwell in, after my wives decease ‖ & twenty Acres of Land which I bought of John Scuder (except six Acres more or less as it is now bounded, which I give to John Cressy as is here after expressed) and takes it begining at Abram Warrens well, so downe to the brooke to the Common the brook being the boune between his Land & his Brother Josephs, and allso a piece of Land that lyes at the uper end of the sd twenty Acres without the fence, with the hither end of my salt marsh up to a place commonly called the Rocks where they cart downe wood. I Give my Son Joseph Batchelor all my land in the field together with the orchard & Barne & the salt marsh lying beyond the sd Rocks commonly called Ducks Cove & halfe an Acree of marsh y^t I bought of Joseph Roots & halfe an Acre of Jeoffry Massy. my Will is that my two Sonnes aforesd shall pay their mother the yearly rent of six pound p. anum during her widowood & keep two Cows & prouide fire-wood for her necessary use and the charges there of to be equally borne by each, and the sd 6 pound to be yearly paid in such specia as she shall desire. Also I give my Daughter Hanah Corning ten pound to be paide by my loving wife be-fore her decease. It. I give my Grandchild John Cressy six Acres of Land lying within my sonne Johns Land as a foresd along Royals neck & five pound to be paid by my loving wife before her decease. Allso I intreat m^r Henry Bartholmew & Deacon Prince to see this will truly pformed. In witness whereof I have hereunto set my hand & seal the year above written may the 17."

John Bacheler Senr (SEAL)

Witness: John Swinnerton, Bethiah Archer.

Proved in Salem court 22 : 10 : 1675 by the witnesses. John and Joseph Bachelor, sons of deceased, were appointed administrators.

Inventory of the estate of John Bachelor of Salem, who died Nov. 13, 1675, taken Dec. 4, 1675, by John Raiment and Andrew Eliott: 45 acres of upland, 90li.; two Acres of Salt marsh, 10li.; one dwellinge house and one Barne, 30li.; all his wareinge Clothes, 8li.; all his beddinge, 16li.; whome made Cloth, Lining and woollen, 30 yds., 4li.; 20 pound of wooll and yarne, 1li. 10s.; Three Bibles, 8s.; other houshold stuff, brass and Iron, 2li. 10s.; one Copper quart with other Earthen ware, 5s.; 2 pewter platters and other smale things, 10s.; one Chest and fiue trays with other wooden ware, 15s.; Irons for husbandry for wheels & ploughs, 2li.; pease and Indian Corne, 11li.; fouer bushell of barley, 16s.; one quarter of beafe, 16s. 8d.; one yoke of Oxen, 10li.; two steers, 7li. 10s.; five Cows and one heifer, 18li.; one yearling and two Calves, 2li. 10s.; one horse, 2li.; eleaven swine, 7s.; seaventeen sheep, 4li. 5s.; one Lininge wheel, 5s.; total, 230li. 8d. To be paid out in debts, 12li., in legacies, 15li.

Attested in Salem court 22 : 10 : 1675 by John and Joseph Bachelor.

Essex County Quarterly Court Files, vol. 24, leaves 75, 76.

ESTATE OF MARK BATCHELDER OF (WENHAM?).

Administration upon the estate of Marke Bachelar was granted on Jan. 16, 1675, to John Bacheler, his brother, who was ordered to bring in an inventory to the next Ipswich court.   *Ipswich Quarterly Court Records, vol. 5, page 275.*

Inventory of the estate of Marke Bacheler taken 25 : 10 : 1675, by Thos. Fiske, Will. Fiske and John Batcheler: the homestead with a small pcill of medow, 100li.; Catle, 10li.; Barly in the strawe, 16 Bu., 3li. 4s.; flax, 4s.; foder, 1li.; pease, 6 Bu., 1li. 4s.; oats, 13 Bu., 1li. 6s.; Indian Corne, 6 Bu., 1li. 1s.; fethers, 31li., 1li. 11s.; wooding lumber, 1li. 4s. 8d.; Iron & Brass, 1li. 6s. 6d.; pewter, 12s.; sword & belt, 8s.;

Book, 4s.; Clothes, 13s.; Butter & Cheese, 8s.; Swine alive, 1li. 15s.; porke, 2li. 14s. 9d.; Boards, 1li. 16s.; Iron pot & skelct, 9s.; total, 131li. 11d.

Attested in Ipswich court Mar. 28, 1676 by John Bachelour brother of Marke Bacheler.

Deed on back of inventory: "John Portter Seno^r of ye towne of Salem in the Countie of Esex yeoman And Wiliam Dodge of ye towne of Beauerly yeoman Thee Execetters of Samuell Portter Late deceased: wee Thee Aforsaid Execetters doe in ye Behalffe of John Portter Juno^r thee proper Heire vnto thee ffarme of thee Aforsaid Samuell or Any other that doth or shall lay claime unto ye farme in thee Right of Samuell Portere doe make ouer settell and confirm unto marke Batcheler A small parsell of Land bee it more or lesse with the Bounds as ffolloweth North upon ye land of marke Batcheler which hee Bought of m^r Fisk east upon the lannd of John Fesk at ye corner of his felld where there is A stake and an heape of stons for thee bounds and from thence bounded by thee farme easterly, thee South bounds is A stake and an heape of stons that is made at ye west side of A Reed oak bee-twen thee upland And thee swampe and the weest bounds is the land of marke Batcheler that was giuen vnto his father by thee towne of Salem: and one thee east ther is A small ash that is Asi—bounds By Agrement: This parsell of land to bee thee Aforsaid marke Batchelers His heirs Execeters Asigns peacably to Inioy with out Any denyall or lawfull disturbance from Any thee Aforsaid propryetters or ther heirs Excettors or Asigns or Any by them — Marke Batcheler hath possession Accordinge unto Law befor thee signing heroff: where vnto wee haue sett our hands And seal. This land is thee Aforsaid marke Batcheler by way of exchang for A parsell of land neare thee great pond with the bounds thereof as it is specified in his deed."

John (his $\mathcal{F}$ mark) Porter, Willim Dodg, Sen. (SEAL).

Witness: James Moulton, John Carpenter.

Essex County Probate Files, Docket 2,100.

ESTATE OF ALLEN PERLEY OF IPSWICH.

"In the name of God Amen I Allen Perley of Ipswich in the county of Essex in New England being by the good blessing of God in good health & enioying my vnderstanding and memory yet sencible of my mortall and changable condition heere And desireous to sett my house in order doe therfore make my last will and testament first I committ my soule

into the hands of Jesus Christ my blessed Saviour & redeemer
my body to be decently buryed in what place the Lord shall
alott for me to depart this life in assured hope of a joyfull
resurection at the last day And for my outward estate that
God hath gracously given me I thus dispose, my three elder
sonns viz. John Perlye Thomas Perley and Samuell Perlye
Taking there liberty at the age of one & twenty to leave me
&c yet I have given unto them, three parts of the Land beyond Bachelours brooke (each of them a part wᶜʰ they are
possest of and doe enioy) exsepting the great meddow which
I doe reserue, And ‖all‖ that part of Land which was Na-
thaniells my sonn who is departed this ‖life wᶜʰ‖ I doe give
& bequeath unto my two daughters Sarah and Martha Perley.

"And my house and ‖the res of my‖ land & the great meddow I giue & bequeath unto my sonn Timothy when he shall
attaine to the age of twenty three years, provyded still my beloved wife Susanna shall haue one roome to ‖her‖ owne use
dureing her naturall life, Item I give vnto my beloved wife all
my cattle & moveable goods and one third part of the land
bequeathed to my sonn Timothy dureing her naturall life, for
her comfortable maintenance and after ‖her‖ decease my will
‖is‖ the house & land be vnto my sonn Timothy and the cattle
& moveable goods be equally devided among all my children
then liveing and my will and mynd is that if my sayd wife
shall marrye that then the Land and roome in the house be
vnto my sonn Timothy & he to paye vnto his mother seaven
pounds a yeare dureing her life And I doe make my beloved
wife sole executrix of this my last will my will further is
that my sonn Timothy at the age of 23 yeares shall haue the
use ‖of‖ pt of the stock to the value of thirty pounds dureing
the life of my wife & then to be returned to be devided as is
above expressed In wittnes wherof I have heerunto sett my
hand seale the 23 of June Anno Dom. 1670."

Allan Perly (SEAL)

Witness: Robert Lord, Mary Lord.

"The 16ᵗʰ day of Novembar 1671 I Allen Perley as an ex-
planation of that clause in my will within mentioned con-
cerneing my wife haveing given vnto her my cattle & moveables
dureing her naturall life besyds the thirds of land & a roome
in the house and in case of hir mariage to leave the roome in
the house and Land & to have seaven pounds a yeare payd her
by my Sonn Timothy but nothing spoken about the cattell &
moveable goods my will is that shee returne also the cattel &
moveables to be dvyded among my children as is expressed in

the sayd will wittnes my hand the day & yeare above written."
Allen Perley.

Witness: Robert Lord, Mary Lord.
Proved Feb. 3, 1675 by Robert Lord, Sr. and Mary Lord before Mr. Samuel Symond, Dept. Gov., and Maj. Gen. Denison. *Essex County Quarterly Court Files, vol.* 24, *leaf* 121.

Inventory of estate of Allen Perley, deceased the 28th of December last past, taken Jan. 19, 1675, by John Kimball and Nehemiah Abbot: the house, barn and orchard with the homstead, grate madow and madowe about home with som littelle upland belonging to the madow, 201li.; The half part of that land as was Nathaniell Perleys, 20li.; The madow that was Nathaniell Perleys, 16li.; two oxen, 10li.; 3 Cows, 10li. 10s.; 2 Cows, 5li.; a haifer, 1li. 15s.; a calf, 1li.; a horse mare and colt, 5li.; 20 sheep, 8li.; 9 swine, 4li.; his wareing cloeths, 4li.; 3 beds with what doe belong to them, 7li.; 2 payer of sheets, 1li. 10s.; a table cloth, 8 napkins, 1li. 2s.; 4 pelow ceases, 10s.; Traye, 3s.; peauter, 1li.; 20 pound of butter, 10s.; cheese, 5s.; 20 pounds of cotten wolle, 16s.; 20 pound of sheeps wole, 1li.; 12 pounds of wolen yarn, 1li. 10s.; linien yarn, 1li. 10s.; 3 guns, 2li. 10s.; 5 bushells of wheat, 1li. 10s.; 4 bushells of Rye, 16s.; 18 bushells of indian corn, 3li.; beefe, 1li. 10s.; 2 Iron pots and a morter, 1li.; brass, 15s.; pans, dishes and spoons and som small things, 10s.; payle, half bushell, half peack, 4s.; a churn, a bariell, a meat tub and som old tubs and a bariell, 10s.; 2 tramiells, frying pane, pothooks and a gredgiron, fyer pan and tongs, 15s.; 3 axces and a how, 10s.; an old Cart, tombrell, whells, plow, yoak and Irians belonging to them, 1li. 10s.; an oger, a chisell, 2 payer of fork tins, 4s.; a Rope, 2s.; a payer of bellows, 2s.; chayers and chusens, 3s.; a table, cotten whele and forme, 5s.; a smothing Irion, 2s.; Seeves 2s.; a bible and a psalm book, 6s.; sacks, 2s.; haye and flax, 3li. 5s.; a cheast, 4s. 6d.; cards, 4s.; 5 bushells of barley, 1li.; a stear, 3li. 10s.; total, 320li. 2s. 6d. The debts: Mr. Windrit, 6li. 3s.; the counstable, 2li. 14s.; deaken goodhue, 18s.; Captain Curwin, 10s.; Mr. Cobbit, 11s.; thomas perley, 3li. 12s.; Joh freanch, 6s.; deakon Knolton, 4s. 6d.; James How, Sr., 3s. 6d.; total, 15li. 2s.

Attested in Ipswich court Feb. 3, 1675 by Susanna Perly, the widow of Allen Perley and executrix of his estate, before Mr. Samuell Symonds, Dep. Gov., and Maj Gen. Denison.
Essex County Probate Files, Docket 21,445.

ESTATE OF MRS. MARGARET KIMBALL OF IPSWICH.

Administration upon the estate of Margaret Kimball of Ipswich, late wife of Richard Kimball, was granted on Mar. 4, 1675-6, to Daniell Dow and Thomas Dow, sons of said Margaret, who were ordered to bring in an inventory to the next Ipswich court.

Ipswich Quarterly Court Records, vol. 5, page 275.

Inventory of the estate of Margreat Kimball, widow, deceased in Ipswich Mar. 1, 1675-76, taken by Walter Ropeer and John Caldwell, Sr.; due from the exceketers of her husband Rich. Kimball by contract at mariage, 40li.; Twenty five bushels of Indian Corne, 4li. 7s. 6d.; one bedstead, bed and furniture, 7li.; pewter dishes, cups potengers, 3li.; Tine ware, 6s.; one Table, Two Chests, 1li. 4s.; one grate Trenches glase, 4s.; Two Iron pots, one Iron skellet & gridiron, 1li. 7s. 1d.; one morter & pestell, one small skellet, scumer, 8s. 6d.; Two glase botels & erthen ware, 6s.; one bible and other bookes, 15s.; her wering aparell linen & woolen, hud & scarfe, 11li.; sheetes and Napkins, Table cloth, towels, 3li. 13s.; Two pillowes, hat case, two pere of shooes and Two hats, 1li. 13s.; one box, thre Cushiones, pilion, pillion cloth, spectacles, one Tub & one locke, 1li. 2s. 6d.; Cotton wooll, two pare of Cards, basket, combe parsell bellows, one peare candlestick, Trunckes, one linnen wheele, 2li. 3s.; meate & Two cheeses, 1li. 2s.; fouretene Bushels of wheat & one pek, 4li. 5s. 6d.; Barley 18 bushels, 3li. 12s.; foure bushels of Ry & Six of pease, 2li.; Three shoats, two calfes, three lambs, 1li. 11s.; Combe, Sithes, one bag, 3s. 6d.; hay, 4li.; Debts due to the estate, 6li. 10s. 5d.; debts due from the estate, 3li. 3s. 2d.; total clear estate, 98li. 10s. 9d.

Attested in Ipswich court Mar. 28, 1676 by Daniell and Thomas Dow, the administrators.

Inventory of the goods of Margret Kimball of Ipswich that are at Hampton, taken Mar. 21, 1675-6, by John Moulton and James Hobes: an ould Brass kittell, 1li.; two tramills & a speet, 10s.; 3 chayrs & a stooll, 6s.; an earthin pot & pan, 6d.; 1 Iron pot & pot hooke, 5s.; a paire of chese tongs, 4d.; bed teeking an ould one, 8s.; one ould spinin whell, 1s.; total, 2li. 10s. 10d.

More to be added prized Mar. 27, 1676, by Joseph Dow and Hannah Philbrick: frying pan, tray, stoole, 3s. 6d.; a pr. of cops, a Ringle and staple, 5s.

Attested in Ipswich court Mar. 28, 1676 by Daniell Dow and Thomas Dow, the administrators.

Essex County Probate Files, Docket 15,671.

Administration having been formerly granted to Daniell and Thomas Dow of the estate of Margaret Kimball, their mother, and an inventory being brought into court amounting to about 100li., and there being four children left, court Mar. 28, 1676, ordered to Daniel Dow of Hampton, 20li. The remainder of the estate was to be equally divided among the other three, Thomas, Jeremiah and Mary Dow.

Ipswich Quarterly Court Records, vol. 5, *page* 277.

ESTATE OF ROBERT ANDREWS.

"The will and testomony of robort Andrus I doe Commit my Soul and body to the keping of the gra lord of oste and if it be his good wile to Cal me out of this world that i retorne not a gaine to my frindes and estate that god hath given me i doe wile and beques to each of my brothers and sisters twenti shilens a pese and fiue pound to marey towne and the rest of my estat when my detes ar payed to be *be* equelly deuided ‖betwen‖ my mother ‖and‖ broth^rs John and Joseph Andrus and dow make my brother Samuel Symonds my exsekter to louk after the true performens of this my las wile and dow giue him that which ensin goule ad danel blaike doth owe to me ad this is my tru wile ad testamoni as witnes my hand this 6 day of desember in the year of our lord 1675."

Robard Andru[s].

Witness: Samuel Symonds, Josue Bisson.

Proved in Ispwich court Mar. 28, 1676 by the witnesses.

Inventory of the estate of Robard Androus, taken by Abraham Reddington and John Gould who were chosen by Samuel Symons: 2 oxen, 10li.; 1 Coue, 4li.; 3 piges, 1li.; 1 parcell of flaxe, 1li. 12s.; 1 mare, 2li.; 1 new bariell, 3s. 6d.; 1 old bariell, 2s.; 1 parcill of befe and suate, 2li.; 1 parcill of porke, 1li. 15s.; 1 parcill of clothes, 4li. 4s.; nailes, 6s.; 1 chest, 16s.; 1 saddell and stuirup and sturips Lethers, 1li. 1s. 4d.; 1 bridall, rains and bits, 4s.; 4 axes, 1 howe, 2 okers, 1li.; 2 boshiall of wheat, 12s.; 2 boshiall of rie, 9s.; 22 boshiall of Indon Corne, 3li. 17s.; 5 boshiall of Lime, 5s.; 1 siseth and takiling to et, 4s. 6d.; 1 pike, 4s.; ye halfe part of a whipswa, 4s.; 2 weges, 3s.; 1 gr. 2lb. bar Iron, 6s. 6d.; 1 share and Coulter, 6s.; 1 slead, 3s.; 1 brake, 1s.; 1 mine Carte, oo.; total, 36li. 18s. 10d.

The remainder of the inventory taken by Abraham Redington, Samuel (his O mark) burtt: a lese of medowe, 3li.
1s. 6d.; tene akers of earabel land and medo, 25li.; the house,
28li.; a hundred and fiftie akers of land, 150li.; a sarg sute,
1li. 8s.; a bybel, 5s.; a short, 3s.; sadel Cloth, 2s.; 1q and 26
pound of bar Eiren, 11s. 6d.; total, 208li. 11s. The deptes
ar that do as yet apear, 22li. 5s. 6d.

Attested in Ipswich court Mar. 28, 1676 by Samuell
Symonds, executor.

Essex County Probate Files, Docket 710.

ESTATE OF THOMAS NEWMAN, SR.

"The Last will & testem: of Thomas Newman sr Jan^r: 8th:
1675 In the name of god almighty amen: &c. I Thomas Newman Beinge Weake in Body though in perfect strenth of memory &c Comit my spirit to god that gaue it & my Body to bee
desently Buried—Doe beequeath & giue to my sonns, Thomas
Newman & John Newman. all the houses & Lands thay Now
stand possest wth all. and also doe giue unto Each of them:
two Cowes & tenn sheepe, (weathers & Eaws one with the
other, wth rams) p ps and I do giue to my sonn Thomas one
mare of a Blacke Brown Cullour of 7 years old, & my mare of
a flexen meaine & Taile of 4 years old to my sonn John: &
also I giue my two red oxen to my sonn Thomas: and I do
giue my Dwelling house with all my Lands unto my sonn
Benjamin Newman together with all my household stuffe &
goods with all the rest of my Cattle, Carts plows, &c. wch
sonn Benjamin I make my Executor, out of wch estate
abouesd giuen to him I order that my sd sonn Benjamin, shall
Let my wel beloued wife Sarah Newman, In Joy all the East
End of my now dwellinge house, with such a part of the seller
as she shall Judg necessery for her own use, & also Let her
haue & in Joy so much of the household stuffe, as shee shall
Judg necessery for her use, & Let her haue two Cowes & six
sheepe, & maintaine the same both winter & sumer & finde
her with Conuenient firewood as much as shee shall neede, all
wch I do order & will my sonn Benjamin to find & p^ruide
together with Eight pounds p yeare, Either in wheat barly or
Indian Corne: or to his mothers Content all wch shall bee
duringe her Naturall Life and further I do order my sonn,
Benjamin: to deliuer unto my sonns Thomas Newman &
John Newman: one acker of Land (in John Mannings)
Neck: per. ps: afer my welbeloued wifes decease: together
with that Lot at plum Island I bought of symon Tuttle, to bee

Equally deuided betwixt them: and also wʳ as it hath pleased god by his prouidence to call my sonn Benjamin: into the warrs. in case hee should not returne, but yᵗ god should take him away to him selfe: then it is my will, that what so Euer I ‖haue‖ given to my sonn Benjamin, that it shall bee Equally deuided between my sonn Thomas: & my sonn John thay to performe to my wife what so Euer I haue appoynted my sonn Benjamin to doe."

Thomas (his † mark) Newman, sr.
Witness: ffrancis Wainwright, John Wainwright.
Proved in Ipswich court Mar. 28, 1676 by the witnesses.

Inventory taken Feb. 9, 1675 by Francis Wainwright and John Whipple: in moneys, 7li.; Wearing apparel, 8li.; 2 beds in ye parler wth one rugg, 3 blanchets & bedsted, curttaines and Valins, 9li.; chests & table Chaire & Cuchings & forme, 2li. 4s.; 7 pr. of sheets, 3li. 2s.; 5 pillowbears, table cloath, 1li. 15s.; 1 fine wicker bascet, 5s.; Cobbirons, 10s.; pewter & tin wares, 2li. 7s.; one warming pan, 10s.; pessel & morter, 9s.; basting ladle, 1s. 6d.; one grater & lanthorn, 3s. 6d.; one larg Kettle, other brase, 3li. 15s.; potts & Kittle of Iorne, 3li.; Iorn skillet & spit, 10s., 3 guns, 4li.; 2 swords & belts, 5li. 10s.; bellows, salt box, tonges, 6s. 6d.; slice, 4s.; 4 chairs, 6s.; frying pan, 4s.; wheele, 5s.; one small chest, 5s.; another wheele, 3s. 6d.; cards, 6s.; 3 beere barrels, 7s.; Cheese, 3li.; butter, 15s.; chest & appls, 8s.; 3 trays, 4s.; one hogshed, 12d.; churn, 5s., beef, pork & tubbs, 4li. 5s.; Earthen ware & wooden dishes, 10s.; 2 sives, 3s., 2 Kellors, 2 tubbs, 18s.; 3 payls, 5s.; scayls, 12d.; bed & steed & furniture, 6li.; 300li. wool, 9li. cotton wool, 5li. 9s.; hempe, 10s.; fethers, 20s.; more heemp & flex, 15s.; more beding, 3li.; Indian Corne, 10li.; pease 20 bushells, 4li.; barly 15 bushels, 2 hogdhds, 4s., 3li. 4s.; 2 shovels, 7s. 4d.; 1 pr. Fetters, 5s.; sadle & bridle, 1li.; 3 siths & forks, 1li.; hoos & sickles, 9s.; Utensall for Husbendry, 6li. 11s.; Cannows, 2li.; wheat & ry, 15s.; woolin, 4li.; dwelling house & barns & land adjoininge, 200li.; land in manings neck, 36li.; marsh behind ye hill, 50li.; marsh at plum Iland, 24li.; 4 oxen & 2 steers, 30li.; 8 Cowes, 30li.; young Cattell, 8li.; 4 maires, 6li.; 3 young horses, 5li.; 40 sheep, 16li.; 4 swine & foules, 2 li. 10s.; Hay, 10li.; tramels, 4s. 2d.; debts due to ye estate, 11li.; total, 538li. 19s.

Attested in Ipswich court Mar. 28, 1676 by Benjamin Newman, executor of his father's will.

Essex County Probate Files, Docket 19,434.

ESTATE OF SAMUEL SIMONS OF LYNN.

Administration upon the estate of Samuell Simons, intestate, was granted Mar. 28, 1676, to Clement Coldom, who brought in an inventory amounting to about 16li.
Ipswich Quarterly Court Records, vol. 5, page 278.

Inventory of the estate of Samuell Simons, grandchild of Tho. Couldum of Lynn, who died in the beginning of August 1675, taken Dec. 6, 1675 by John Burrill, Thomas Browne and Joannah (her —— mark) Couldum: 1 Hatt, 1 Coate & 1 Carsye Coate, 1li. 10s. 6d.; Breeches & jackit, 12s.; shooes & Lumber, 6s. 6d.; 1 Pistle, 1 chest, 7s. 6d.; neate Catle, 3li. 16s. 6d.; sheep, 1li. 2s.; Horse Flesh, 3li.; 1 gun Lock, 8s.; Indion Corne 27 bush., 4li. 1s.; Barlye 5 bushell, 1li.; wheat 1 halfe Bushell, 2s. 6d.; total, 16li. 6s. 6d.

Attested in Ipswich court Mar. 28, 1676 by Clement Coldam.   *Essex County Probate Files, Docket 27,133.*

ESTATE OF MRS. MARGARET ROGERS.

Administration upon the estate of Mrs. Margret Rogers, intestate, was granted Mar. 28, 1676, to Mr. John Rogers, her eldest son, who was ordered to bring in an inventory to the next Ipswich court.
Ipswich Quarterly Court Records, vol. 5, page 278.

ESTATE OF JOHN AYRES OF BROOKFIELD.

Administration upon the estate of John Ayres of Qaboag, intestate, was granted Mar. 28, 1676, to Susana Ayres, the widow. There being an inventory brought in amounting to 195li., and there being seven sons and a daughter, court ordered 95li. to be divided among the children, the eldest son John, with what he already had to be made up a double portion, and the remainder to be equally divided, the widow to have the rest of the estate.
Ipswich Quarterly Court Records, vol. 5, page 278.

Inventory of the estate of John Ayres of Brookfield taken Sept. 13, 1675, by John Brewer, sr. and Simon Stace: six oxen, 33li.; ten cowes, 30li.; two steers two yere old, 5li. 10s.; two heifers the same age, 5li. 10s.; one heifer more & too yerelings & one bull, 8li. 10s.

Inventory taken Mar. 27, 1676 by John Brewer, sr. and Simon Stace: one Kettle & too scillets, 1li. 10s.; pewter plat-

ters & pots & other small things, 4li. 14s.; foure coverlids &
one Rug, 7li.; Three paire of curtaines & vallants, 4li. 10s.;
six good blancketts & foure old ones, 6li.; six feather beds,
nine bolsters & nine pillows, 28li.; some woolen & linen cloath,
1li. 8s.; one old bed teeking & bolster, 15s.; two
paire of sheets, five paire more of worne sheets, 4li.
15s.; twelve pillowbeers, 1li. 16s.; one hollen sheete,
three bord cloaths, 2li. 5s.; twelve napkins & three
towells, 1li. 3s.; two Guns and three cutlashs, 5li. 1s.; one
sith, four sack & one bag, 11s. 6d.; a mantle, a sive botom,
three spoones, 17s.; Bibles & other Bookes, 1li. 16s.; wearing
cloathes, 7li. 12s.; in money, 34li. 10s.; total, 195li. 13s. 6d.

Attested in Ipswich court Mar. 28, 1676 by Susana Ayres,
the administratrix.

Statement of Susanna Ayres that she had seven sons and
one daughter and that her eldest son hath had of her husband
too oxen, one cow, a fatt hogg, one sow & piggs, one pewter
dish, a fether bed & bolster, one Rug & blancket & a paire of
sheetes.

Essex County Probate Files, Docket 1,089.

ESTATE OF THOMAS SMALL OF SALEM.

Upon request of Ruth Small, whose husband deceased intestate, court Mar. 28, 1676, appointed her administratrix of
his estate, and ordered her to bring in an inventory to the
next Salem court.

Ipswich Quarterly Court Records, vol. 5, page 279.

Inventory of the estate of Thomas Small, who deceased
Jan. 26, 1675, taken by John Putnam and Richard (his
R mark) Leach: housing and land, 250li.; two oxen, 10li.; 13
cows, 48li. 15s.; 5 Cataill of 2 year old, 12li. 10s.; 5 of a year
old, 6li. 5s.; 25 sheep, 12li. 10s.; 3 mares & a horse & a Coult,
5li.; sadel, Bridle, Pistolls & houlsters, Belt, Rapyer, 3li. 10s.;
a Gune, 1li. 10s.; his wearing Cloaths, 13li. 2s.; feather bead,
Boulsters & Pillows & Beadsteed, Curtins & valians & a Ruge
& a Blanket, a pair of shets, 10li.; 3 sheets & other Linen, 1li.
6s.; mony, 10s.; 10 lb. of Coten woolle, 10s.; 17 lb. of woollen
yearn, 1li. 15s.; Cheese & Boxes, 15s.; Chairs, 10s.; a Litell
Table, 5s.; a trundle Bead & Beading, 2li. 10s.; Bead & Beading & Beadsteed, 3li.; 32 lb. of Sheeps woole, 1li. 12s.; a pair
of stillyards, 1li.; Cart Rope & Pilion, 18s.; for a fanne, 4s.;
old Barills, 13s.; 17 Bushills of Barill, 3li. 8s.; 2 bushells of
Rye, 8s.; 15 bushells of pease, 3li.; 80 bushells of Indian

Corn, 12li.; sacks, 12s.; chains, 1li. 6s.; shars & Coulters, 1li.; axes, 16s.; hous, 10s.; Betell & wedges & old Iron, 1li.; swin, 4li.; Keards & whells, 10s.; siths & Tackeling, 6s.; 2 Iron potes, 1li.; a friing pan & warming pan, 3s.; Barills & other wooden warr, 1li.; wooden with other things, 2li.; meat, 2li. 10s.; Cart & whells, 1li.; 8 Bushells of Barlly, 1li. 12s.; Hemp & flax, 15s.; Glase, 4s.; total, 427li. Debtor to several persons, 135li. 7s. 4d.; debts due from severall persons, 58li. 10s. 5d.

Allowed in Salem court 30:4:1676.

Essex County Quarterly Court Files, vol. 25, leaf 62.

Ruth, the relict of Tho. Smale, was appointed administratrix of his estate and made oath to the inventory, 30:4: 1676. She was bound with Edward Groves.

Salem Quarterly Court Records, vol. 5, leaf 96.

Petition, dated Salem, Mar. 25, 1676, of Ruth (her ♅ mark) Small, John (his † mark) Small, Edward Grove, John Putnam and John Buxton, that the estate of Thomas Small should be divided as follows, said Ruth having taken advice of her father Small, her uncle Grove, her brother John Buxton and Mr. John Putnam: that the court make her administratrix; that she have liberty to bring up her four children herself, to continue with her until they come of age unless she see cause to dispose of them otherwise for their better education; that her son William as soon as he comes of age may have the one-half of the farm that is undisposed of, with the meadow belonging, having his part on the east side of the farm adjoining Nathaniell Putnam's, not meddling with the housing or any part of the improved land; that as soon as her daughters Lidia, Hanna and Ann come of age, they were to have 40li. each; that her father John Small, her uncle Edward Grove, her brother John Buxton and Mr. John Putnam be overseers.

Allowed in Salem court, 30:9:1676, the 40li. disposed of to the child deceased to be equally divided between the mother and three children.

Essex County Quarterly Court Files, vol. 24, leaf 120.

Estate of Freegrace Norton.

Administration upon the estate of Freegrace Norton, who was slain in the war, was granted Mar. 28, 1676, to Mr. Francis Wainwright, and there being not a sufficient amount to satisfy the debts, court ordered that the debts be paid according to proportion. If any were not satisfied with their proportion, they were given liberty to take their course, if they could find any other estate not inventoried.

Ipswich Quarterly Court Records, vol. 5, page 279.

Thomas Borman, sr., Walter Roper, Abraham Tilton and Elihu Wardal, chosen to appraise the work done by Freegras Norton for Docter Dane, found it to be worth 24li. 12s. 6d. Approved by the court, Mar. 30, 1676. Robert Lord, cleric.

Inventory of the estate of Freegrace Norton, taken Mar. 28, 1676: 1 orchard of three quarters of an acre, 15li.; 1 bedsted curtains & valins, 3li. 10s.; 1 Cubbord & Cubbord Cloath, 3li. 4s.; 1 table & one forme & one Carpit, 1li.; 6 chairs & 3 Cushins, 14s.; one Chest with Locke & key, 5s.; 2 pr. sheets, 2li.; 2 table Cloaths & 6 napkins, 10s.; one Bible & one sermon booke, 7s.; one silver dram cupp & 1 pr. shooe buckles, 7s.; 1 settle & 1 small table & 1 Inkhorne, 10s. 6d.; 1 brass skillet, 1 Kettle, 1 warminge pann, 1li. 10s.; 3 pewter Dishes & 3 porringers, 14s.; one Pewter pot & 3 Cupps, 5s.; one Tin kettle & 4 Tin pans, one tunnel & 1 sass pan, 7s. 6d.; 1 pr. tonges, fire shovell & Grid Iron, 10s.; one fryinge pann, 1 pr. Bellows, 5s. 6d.; one spitt, one Jacke & waite, 1li. 5s.; 3 pailes & 1 pigen, 5s.; 2 boules, 3 dishes, 6 trenchers, 3s.; Earthen ware, 2s.; spoons, 12d.; 4 barrels, & 2 halfe barrels & 1 meshinge tubb, 1li.; 3 Keelers & one trucklebed sted & 2 Chests, 6s.; one broadax & one Narrow ax, 7s.; working tooles & 1 pr. beetle rings, 19s.; 1 Candlesticke, 2 hookes & staples, 2s. 6d.; one seate in the meeting house, 1li.; total, 36li. 10s. What Charge Freegrace Norton was in repaireinge the house, by 1,000 foote pine Boards, 3li.; Laying 2 floors, findinge all nailes & sleeprs., 15s.; 2 doors, 2 pr. hooks & hinges, one Locke, pettel, &c., 15s.; stoninge a seller, 5s.; 2 pr. staires, 8s.; 1,000 brickes, 20s.; for whiteing ye roome, 9s.; Glass, 14s.; Ensigne Tho. Burnum Walter Roper, Abra. Tilton & Elihu Wardell being Chosen p Docter Deane & Goody Norton to apprise the worke Freegrace Norton did for ye sd Deane & thay finde it worth 24li. 12s. 6d.; Goodman Bridges is dr. to the estate, 6s.; total, £68. 2s. 6d.

Essex County Quarterly Court Files, vol. 25, leaves 122, 123.

Francis Wainwright renounced his administratorship of the estate of Freegrace Norton granted in March last.

John Wainwright was appointed Sept. 26, 1676, administrator of the estate of Freegrace Norton. He was to allow the widow her thirds of the land and to pay no debt except to his

satisfaction due and legally proved; also to pay as far as the
estate could be sold for.

Ipswich Quarterly Court Records, vol. 5, page 283.

ESTATE OF JOHN WITT, SR., OF LYNN.

"This is the Last will, & testament of John witt senio^r of
Lynn in the Countye of Essex written the tweluth daye of
September, Ano: Domni 1675: whoe being sicke, & weake of
bodye, but of good memorye, & understanding. Imp: I bequeath my bodye to the earth, & my spirrit to the Lord that
gaue it It: I giue to my daughter Ann Barnitt, five shillings
shee haueing receiued her portion alredye. It: I giue to my
Daughter Elizabeth five shillings shee also haueing receiued
her portion alreddye. It: I give to my daughter Sarah six
pounds to bee paid to her with in two years after my deseace.
It: I give vnto my daughter Marye twentye pounds to bee
paide vnto her with in three yeares after my deseace but in
case shee shall marrye, sooner, then it, to bee pd: at her
marryage It: I give vnto my daughter Martha, twentye
pounds to bee paid, vnto herr ‖in‖ foure yeares after
my deseace, but if shee shall marrye Sooner, then it to bee
paid her, at her marryage. It: I give vnto my son John witt,
my now dwelling house & house Lott with all my houseing
vppon it to him his heires & assignes for ever, with all
Comons, Libertyes, & p^{r}vilidges what soe ever be Longing
there vnto (viz) to take possession of at his now Mothers
marryage if shee shall marrye againe, but if shee shall not
marrye againe but remaine a widdow then my Son John not
to haue it in his possion untill his said mothers death, & then
to possesse it. It: I give to my Son Thomas witt, all my
Land by the meeting house which I bought of m^r: King with
all Comons Libertyes & p^{r}vilidges what soe be Longing there
vnto, to him, his heires, & assignes for ever & alsoe ten acres
of my marsh ground this being to bee vnderstood that I
hereby doe give vnto my affore sd son John witt all the rest
of my marsh ground & doe referr vnto the overseers of this
my will the Layeing out for my Son Tho: witt: ‖y^t sd‖ ten
acres of my marsh indifferentlye they haueing an eye to the
goodnesse & badnesse of my marsh the convenience, & incon-
veniencye soe y^t neither of my sonns maye be wronged & hee
the said Thomas to haue possession of his whole guift both of
vpland, & marsh ground at the death of his now mother

"It: I give unto my wife Sarah the vse, of all my affore
said houses Lands & marsh ground with all there appurten-

ances & privilidges as aboue said to improue for her best advantage dureing all the tyme shee shall remaine my widdow
It: I giue vnto my affore sd wife all my Catles & Liveing
stocke of all sorts to gether with debts due to mee, & also
all my moveable estate both within dores, & without to bee
at her dispose for ‖her‖ owne Comfortable Livelyhood dureing the tyme shee shall remaine my widdow & if shee shall
dye my widdow then shee is to dispose of what parte of my
moveable estate maye bee then Left to all, my children in
generall, or ‖to‖ which of them shee pleases but if shee shall
marrye with any man Then my will is, & I doe here by impower my Son John witt to enter possession vppon two
thirds of all my houseing Lands & marsh ground, as abouesd
to bee disposed of as abouesd, I herebye giueing to my wife
one third part of all my houses Land, & marsh ground as
aboue sd dureing her naturall life.   Alsoe my will is y^t if my
wife Sarah shall marrye againe, that before shee doe marrye,
shee doe devide all my moueable estate as aboue sd which then
maye be Left, amongst all my children in generall ‖as shee
pleases‖ & doe hereby impower my son John, with the overseers of this my will, to see it be don: It: I bequeath to my
grandchild Hester witt one ewe Lamb.   It: my will is that in
Case any of my children shall dye before the tyme the shall
receiue their respectiue Legacyes as aboue said then their
Legacyes to bee paid to their brethren or brother abouesd if
Liveing.   It: My will is that where as their are severall
Legacyes to be paid as abousd, & alsoe: ten pounds to be paid
by mee to my Grandchild Hester witt, as it being soe willed
by her father Jonathan witt: that soe much of it as shall bee
due to bee paide dureing ye tyme my estate in generall shall
bee in my wifes hands as abouesd, shee shall paye it out of the
moveable estate but soe much of it as maye not bee due to bee
paide whilest the tyme of the deseate, or marryage of my wife
Sarah with some other man as aforesd My two sons John: &
Tho: witt shall paye it after this proportion to my son: John
Thirtye five pounds & my Son Thomas ffifteen pounds & that
vppon this consideracon y^t I haue giuen y^m all my houseing
Lands & marsh ground, as aboue sd this being to bee understood, that how far short that which my Sons: John, &
Thomas maye paye of it shall be of fiftye pounds the shall
make it up fiftye pounds to be paid to her to dispose of It:
I make my wife Sarah my Lawfull: Executrix Last I doe
desyre & apoynt my Loueing ffriends John Burrell Nathaniell Kertland senio^r, & Mathew farington to be overseers

of this my will In: witt: whereof I haue put my hand this
being to bee vnderstood to bee the meaning of that fiftye in
the interline next before where I make my wife my executrix
that iff my sons shall paye noe pt of y^e. 10^{li}: nor of the
Legacyes abouesd then John: shall paye to the assigns or
assignie of his mother 35^{li} & Tho: 15^{li}: but if the shall paye
any part of it by soe much the shall deduct & the tyme of the
payment is at their mothers death."

John (his □ mark) witt Senio^r.

Witness: Andrew Mansfeild, Joseph mainsfeild, Deborah
(her ✔ mark) Mansfeild.

Proved in Ipswich court Mar. 28, 1676 by Andrew and
Joseph Mansfield.

Inventory of the estate of John Witt, Sr. of Lynn, deceased Dec. 2, 1675, taken Dec. 14, 1675 by John Fuller and
Andrew Mansfeild: weareing Apparill, Lyning & woollen,
2li. 15s.; Bed Coverings, 2li. 2s.; five pare of sheets, 5li. 10s.;
fether Bed, 1 boulster, 3 pillowes, 6li.; fether bed with other
Bedding, 8li. 1s.; more Bedding, 1li. 4s.; Bedstead, 1li. 10s.;
Table, Carpitt, Table Lining, 4li. 2s.; Lining Cloth, 4li. 1s.;
woolen Cloth, 3li. 17s. 6d.; Flax, woole, 3li. 12s.; Puter &
Tinn ware, 3li. 11s. 2d.; Iron & Brass potts & ketles, pestile
& morter & posnets, 2li. 1s. 6d.; Fryeing pan, 2 Hakes, 1
Grid Iron, 1 spit, 1pr. tonngs, 2li. 4s.; 1 spade, 3 axes, 1
Hamer, 1 Hooe, 1 Mattake, 1 Hetchell & haye Hooke, 1li. 3s.
6d.; wedges, beetle rings, Hoops & boxes for cart whells, 1li.
1s. 6d.; Armes & Ammunition, 1li. 10s.; chest, Boxes, cheres
& Fann, 1li. 16s.; Bookes, 1li.; English & Indion Corne, 14li.
5s.; Neate catle & sheep, 57li. 12s.; swine Flesh, 11li. 2s.; To-
baccoe, 2li.; Carts, plows, chains, yoks & Apurtenances, 4li.
12s.; Butter, cheese & Beefe, 3li. 10s.; spining wheels, woole
cards, smoothing iron, 12s. 6d.; Syder, chees press, cheese
fatts, 3li. 6s. 6d.; Pailes, Doe tub & some Lumber, 18s.; 1
Horse, 2li.; A Loome for to weave in, sleas & Harniss &c.,
5li.; grindle stone, syths & sickles, 1li. 1s.; new Iron, 2
Bottles, a baskitt, pannill & sadle, 1li.; monyes, 1li. 4s.; The
house lott, 6 acres in estimation wth ye houseing & orchard
vppon it, 160li.; 5 acres by the meeting house with the orchard uppon it, 32li.; marsh ground, 115li.; total, 472li. 7s.
Due to the estate in monyes, 5li. Debts due from the estate,
2li. 6s.

Attested in Ipswich court Mar. 28, 1676 by Sarah Witt,
widow and executrix.

Essex County Probate Files, Docket 30,221.

ESTATE OF DANIEL ROLFE.

Administration on the estate of Daniell Roff, intestate, granted by the Ipswich court Mar. 28, 1676, to his brother Ezra Roff, and there being an inventory brought in of 38li., the court ordered the estate to be left in his hands.

Inventory of the estate of Daniell Rooffe, slain in the "wars at the Narogaynseths": one Cloke, 2li. 12s.; one Koote made of Sarch, 1li. 10s.; one Clooth Koote, 18s.; a payer of drawers, 6s.; a doblet & bridges, 1li.; one old Cloth Clooke, 1li.; a payer draers and waskot, 1s.; 2 payer old Bridges, 1s.; thre hats, 6s. 6d.; one shert and drawers, 8s.; 2 bands, a Neck Clooth and one payer of sleefes, 12s.; one belt and ponts, 4s.; small Tools, 12s. 3d.; Coopers tools, 3li. 7s.; one ax, 2s. 6d.; one gone stik boer, 1s. 6d. Debts due by a bill of Schoer Wilson, 3li. 9s. 5d.; Jo. Chack for a gun, 8s.; my father Rooffe, 13li. 6s. 8d.; Jas. Smith, 8s.; Jos. Lee, 5s.; Mr. Lord, Clerk, 10s.; Jon. Kindrik, 3s.; total, 18li. 10s. 1d. More by 2 goons and 4 barrels of goons, 3li. 1s.; goodman Wood of Rowly, 2li. 10s.; Jaemes Myrick of Newbery, 1li. 10s.; 3000 of Barrel Staves and heading, 4li. 10s.; a bill of Joseph Wilson of Andifor, 3li. 10s.; debts due from the estate, 4li. 4s. 6d.; total clear estate, 42li. 8s. 4d.

Attested in Ipswich court Mar. 28, 1676 by Ezra Roffe, administrator.

Essex County Probate Files, Docket 24,105.

ESTATE OF DANIEL SOMERBY OF NEWBURY.

"I Daniell Sumerby beeing Caled to goe forth to war by gods prouidens: this is my will that my sister Elizabeths Clarkes eldest soon shall bee my Ayre of all my Lands exep[t] that twoe acors of medow liing with goodman hals below the ox Comon: that I doe alot to henry hale: and the heire of my Land shall pay to my sister Saras 2 Children Thomas and Judah fiue pound a pees and to the rest of my sisters Elizabeths Childred forty shillins apees: and the rest of my estate after my Lawfull debts are payd I doe: giue to my brothers and sisters Equally to be deuided: and I doe a point my father Coffin: and my brother Nathanell Clarke: to see this Last will and testament of mine performed: this was written the 26 of october in the 1675 yere of our Lord:"

Daniell Sumerby.

(SEAL)

Witness: Mary Coffin, John (his ✕ mark) Wolinford.
Proved in Ipswich court Mar. 28, 1676 by the witnesses.
Essex County Probate Files, Docket 25,842.

ESTATE OF THOMAS SMITH OF NEWBURY.

Administration upon the estate of Thomas Smith of Newbury, who was slain in the war, was granted Mar. 28, 1676,
to James and John Smith, his brothers, and court ordered
that it be equally divided between them.
Ipswich Quarterly Court Records, vol. 5, page 277.

Inventory of the estate of Thomas Smith of Newbury who
was slayne when Capt. Lathrop was slayne, taken Mar. 22,
1675-76 by Robert Long and Anthony Somerby: foure acres
of plowland, 3 acres of pasture, 4 acres salt marsh & 3 acres
of swamp or slow land, 55li.; A yoke of oxen & a 4 yeare old
heifer, 16li. 10s.; His weareing apparrell, 5li.; A Chest,
Crosscut saw, broad Axe, 2 Augurs, maul, 2 Addes, Rule & a
Raypier, 2li. 8s.; snapsack & a bible & 2 paper bookes, 8s. 6d.;
debts due to him about 1li.; total, 80li. 6s. 6d. The debts he
owes, 10li.

The deceased was out in the Country service about 7 weeks,
he was at first Corporall & after Sergent under the said Capt.
Lathrop & had all his Armes & Amunition well fixt which is
all lost except the Rapier.

Received in Ipswich court Mar. 28, 1676.
Essex County Probate Files, Docket 25,780.

ESTATE OF SAMUEL STEVENS.

Inventory of the estate of Samuell Stevens who was slayne
when Capt. Lathrop was slayne taken Sept. 27, 1675 by Anthony Somerby and Augustin Steadman: his crop of corne of
all sorts, 5li.; a yoake of oxen, a cow & a calfe, 14li. 15s.; horse
and a 3 yer old mare & 2 yerling colt, 8li. 10s.; 5 or six sheep,
1li. 15s.; Apparrell, skins, tooles & lumber, 2li. 10s.; his book
debts about 16li.; sadlers ware, 1li.; four load of Hay, 2li.;
total, 51li. 10s. His debts about 20li.

Addition to the inventory above; A sute of clothes, 1li.
10s.; a remnant of broadcloth, 1li. 10s.; his wages, 1li. 17s.
8d.; a new trooping sadle, 1li. 10s.; sadlers ware sold to Anthony Somerby, 2li.; more for sadlers ware, 5li.; a new sadle
& bridle & gunne pressed away for the Countryes service.
New debts that did not appeare till of late: to Mr. Wayn-

wright, 2li. 7s. 4d.; Rates, 2li. 4s.; deduction of debts, 2li.;
due to Benaia Titcomb, 1li. 6s.; total, 7li. 17s. 4d.
Attested in Ipswich court Mar. 28, 1676 by Wm. Titcomb.

Essex County Probate Files, Docket 26,419.

ESTATE OF SIMON THOMPSON OF IPSWICH.

"In y⁰ name of God Amen. I Simond Tomson of Ipswich,
weake in body, but of perfect understanding and memory,
after ye bequeathing my soule into ye hands of my mercifull
Redeemer, and my body unto decent buryall, doe in case of
death thus dispose of my estate, wᶜʰ God hath graciously given
mee: Inprimis, I give unto Rachel my beloved wife, my dwelling house and land, wᶜʰ was part of Hayfeilds farme, and now
in yᵉ use and tenure of Thomas Atwood, wᵗʰ two cowes, two
bullockes, six sheep during yᵉ terme of her naturall life, provided she remaynes a widow; but in case she marryes agayn I
give her in lieu thereof six pound yearly out of yᵉ same during yᵉ sayd terme of her naturall life: Item I give unto her all
ye houshold stuffe wᶜʰ she brought wᵗʰ her at her marryage, to
her and her heyres for ẻver: Item I give to her during ye
terme of her naturall life my best coverlet, wᵗʰ ye new bed-
teek, my new trunke, my new box, one Iron pot, one por-
renger, one pewter dish, a spoon, chafing dish, warming pan,
brasse fire pan and tongs one of ye green say cushions, but
after her decease I give them all to my Grandchild Mary
wood. Item I give unto her four pound a year so long as she
liveth, due by bill from my son in Law Abraham Fits. Item
I give unto my Grandchild Simond wood my house wherein I
now dwell wᵗʰ all ye priviledges, and appurtenances thereunto
belonging, wᵗʰ all yᵉ land, pasture, arable, and meadow, not
after disposed of, he allowing liberty to his brothers Samuell
and William to keep three cowes apeice in ye cow pasture,
himselfe keeping foure. I give ye sayd pʳmises to him and
to ye heyres of his body lawfully begotten for ever; and for
want of such heyres, I give all ye sayd premises to his brothers
Thomas ‖and tomson‖ wood in like manner, provided alwayes
yᵗ he pay unto his Sister Joannah, and to his cousin Sarah
Fits, thirty pounds ‖a peice‖ when they come to yᵉ age of
twenty one yeares. Item I give the dwelling house and ye
land belonging to it at Hayfeilds Farme, after my wives decease to my Grand Children Thomas wood, and Thomson
wood, equally to be divided betwixt them, provided they pay
thirty pound betwixt them to their Sister Sarah, when she
comes at age, and after they come unto ye possession of ye

sayd house and land. Item I give unto my Grand child Sam-
uell wood ‖the house his father lives in‖ wth all ye priviledges,
lands & appurtenances thereunto belonging after ye death of
his father and his mother, according as is mentioned in a deed
concerning ye same, but my will is yt ye sayd be nulled after
this my will comes to take place, provided alwayes yt ye five
Acres I bought of Thomas Lee, be not included in this devise.

"Item I give unto my Grand child william wood the house
and land I bought of Goodman More wth ye Marsh at Plumbe
Island belonging thereunto, the five acres I bought of Thomas
Lee, after ye decease of his father, and mother. Item I give
unto my Grandchild Mary wood one acre of land towards M^r
Hubbards Corner, being part of ye house Lot, I bought of M^r
Jonathan wade, or George Hadly, as also I give unto her, six
acres of land bought of Deacon Goodhue adjoyning to Goodman Hunts land, and next ye High way. Item my will is y^t
my Grand children Abram Fits, and Sarah Fits shall enjoy
my halfe of ye house and land possessed by their father, after
his decease : But ye six acres I bought of Richard Nicholls, at
ye east end of heart-breake hill, I give unto my Grand child
Abraham Fits. Item my will is yt my daughter wood shall
enjoy the house where she now dwells wth all ye land belonging thereunto, according to ye true intent of a deed concerning ye same, wch sayd deed I leave in ye hand of a friend to
keep for yt end. Item my will is yt in case any of my Grand
children should dye before they come to age, or leave no issue
behinde them lawfully begotten. that then the land or legacyes
bequeathed unto them, be equally divided amongst ye rest of
their brothers and sisters. Lastly my will is yt my debts be
all payd wth convenient speed, after my funerall charges, and
to that end I constitute and appoynt my son-in-law Isayah
wood the sole Executo^r of this my last Will and Testament,
hereby disanulling all former Wills, In witnes whereof I have
hereunto set my hand and seale this 25th of June in ye yeare
1675. Further My will is, yt in case my daughter wood be
left a widow, yt her Sonne Simond shall pay unto her fourty
shillings a yeare during ye time of her widowhood and yt ‖her
sons‖ Thomas wood, and Thomson wood shall pay her in ye
like manner twenty shillings by ye yeare each of them, while
she remayns a widow; likewise I desire my loving friends M^r
W^m. Hubbard, Mr John Rogers, and Deacon W^m. Goodhue, to
be ye overseers of this my last Will; Item I give ye new teek

mentioned above to my wife for ever, not wth standing w^t ever
is above expressed."

Simon (his M mark) Tomson.
(SEAL)

Witness: William Hubbard, Jno. Rogers.
Proved in Ipswich court Mar. 28, 1676 by the witnesses.

Inventory taken Nov. 20, 1675: money, 2li.; his wearing
Aparell, 14li.; 7 pr. of Sheets, 5li.; 8 pilowbeares, 1li. 8s.; 4
pilowbears, 12s.; pilowbeares, napkins &c., 3li. 7s.; 1 bagg with
hops in it, 9s.; Cushons and small things, 8s.; new linnen,
13s.; 2 tabls in the parlor, 5 chayres, 1 forme, 15s.; 1 trunk, 1
Chest, 15s.; 1 bedsted, bedding &c., 3li. 5s.; small linen, 13s.;
peuter and tinn, 2li. 2s.; brasse and Iron stilyards &c in
kitchin, 5li. 4s.; 1 bagg with meale, 1li. 4s.; in the Chamber,
Indian corne, 5li.; 1 fether bed, 1 blankit, 3li. 10s.; 1 pike
and Costlet, 1li.; sawes and severall tools, 3li. 5s.; 1 musket,
1 sword, bandeliers, &c., 1li. 15s.; 1 bed with beding in the
chamber, 3li. 10s.; 86 1-2li. wooll put out to hallves, 4li. 6s.
6d. Things willed to goode Tomson for life: 1 Coverlitt, 1li.
10s.; 1 trunke, 15s.; 1 box, 4s.; 1 Iron pott, 9s.; 1 poringer,
2s. 6d.; 1 peuter dish, 3s. 6d.; 1 spoone, 6d.; 1 Chafing dish,
2s.; fire shovell, tongs, 10s.; 1 Cushon, 4s.; 110li. of Cheese,
1li. 3s.; onions, 1s.; 2 sives, 2s.; 2M. nayls, 20s.; 1 box of buttons, &c. 10s.; yarne, 2s.; 1 Table, 4s.; 3 boxes, 6s.; 1 blanket,
8s.; 1 Curtane, 2s.; Some small things in the dary house,
12s.; severall things in the seller, 4li.; things in ye leaneto,
12s.; severall small things in a box, 18s.; his dweling house
and homsted being 9 acres and a halfe, 137li.; mores howse
and land with marsh and comg, 60li.; 34 acres at the pasture,
170li.; 10 Acres of marsh at laboring vane, 50li.; 4 acres 1-2
marsh at Plum Iland, 9li.; 6 acres bought of Thomas Lee,
36li.; 60 Acres and apurtnases at hafilds farme, 260li.;
swine, 4li.; timber, 12s.; crow, 5s.; 4 oxen, 20li.; 4 stears,
16li.; 7 cows, 24li. 10s.; 2 yerelings, 3li.; 2 calvs, 1li. 10s.; 2
horses, 3li. 10s.; 43 shepe, 14li.; plows, carts, chayns &c., 3li.
3s.; Inglish Corne in the barne, 24li.; 16 load of hay, 8li.; debts
due Abram fitts, 8li.; Atwod, 1li. 8s., due from Nathaniell
[R]ust, 2s. 8d.; total, 926li. 12s. 8d. Debts due from the estate: to Deacon Goodhue, 29li. 12s.; Mr. Francis Wainewright, 12li. 6s.; widdow Redings, 4li.; Mr. John Rogers,
4li.; Sam. Hunt, 6s.; Tho. Newman, 11s.; John gaines, 8s.;
John Dane, 12s.; John Sparkes, 3li. 5s. 10d.; Deacon Knolton, 18s.; Robert Perce, 13s. 7d.; Rates due to Mr. Willson,
2li. 18s. 8d.; more due to Mr. Willson, 2li. 12s.; 6d.; to Seth

Story and Daniell Ringe, 12li.; Edward Bridges, 7s. 4d.; Obadiah Bridges, 8s.; John Burnam, Junior, 8s.; Ensigne frensh, 12s.; Thomas Burnam, Junior, 7s.; Reonall Foster, Junior, 2li. 9s.; for minester rats, 1li.; total, 81li. 15s. 1d.

Attested in Ipswich court Mar. 28, 1676 by Isaiah Wood to be a true inventory of the estate of his father in law Symon Tompson.

William Hubbard one of the witnesses to the will of Symon Thompson attested in Ipswich court Mar. 28, 1676, that the said Thompson did expressly order when his will was drawn up that he did give thirty pounds per piece to Johannah Wood and Sarah Fitts to be paid by Symon Wood, and that upon the best of his remembrance it was so read to the said Thompson before he signed it, though the words (a peece) were occasionally omitted in the writing of the said will.

John Rogers the other witness attested that he believed it was the said Thompsons meaning, according as it was expressed in a former will signed by himself the year before and which was now shown before the Court, that Johannah and Sarah should have thirty pounds apiece for their legacies.

Essex County Probate Files, Docket 27,525.

ESTATE OF JAMES BROWNE.

Inventory of the estate of James Browne, taken Apr. 7, 1676 by Joseph Grafton and Wm. Browne, jr.: in parlour chamber, 1 bedd, bolster, pillow, rugg coverled, curtaines & vallens with the bedsteed, 7li.; 13 chaires, 5li., chest of drawers, 20s., trunk, chest & smale desk & smale table, 20s., 7li.; 11 pr. worne holland sheets, 7li. 10s., 3 damask & 18 diaper naptkins, 15s., 8li. 5s.; 43 naptkins of canvis & holland, 1li. 10s.; 7 pr. pillowbeers, 4 table cloathes, 2 cubbord cloathes, 2li.; severall remnants of lining & wollan cloath with som haberdashery, 16li.; a pcell of wearing cloathes, 6li., spice, 10s., an old watch & a pr. buttens, 10s., 7li.; 4 peeces of goold & 15li. 12s. 6d. in English money, 19li. 12s. 6d.; a pcell of plate, 35li., a goold ring & other small things, 40s., 37li.; New England money, 31s. 6d., a pcell of brass things, 55s., 4li. 6s. 6d.; a pcell of pewter, 3li., earth ware & glasses, 10s., a pcell of old bookes, 10s., 4li.; a hatt & 2 basketts, 10s., a cubbord cloath, 3s., 13s. In the hall chamber: 1 bedd, bolster, pillow, blankett, coverled, curtains, vallens, bedsted, 6li.; bed, ruge, cradle ruge, two trundle bedsteeds, 1li.; a chest, cubbord & cloath with other small things, 2li.; 6 greene chaires & six leather, 3li., a round table, 10s., 3li. 10s.; 2 looking glasses &

1 pr. Andirons, a wicker chaire & curtains, 1li. In a smale
clossett severall small things, 1li. In the poarch chamber:
child bed linen & blanketts, 2li. 10s.; a table, desk, smalle
trunk, spice box, 2 stooles & old bookes, 2li. 5s.; a sadle, 3
bridles & other furniture, 30s., 3 pr. pistolls, 2 pr. holsters, 3li.
10s., 5li.; 3 belts & a rapier & other small things, 2li. 5s. In
the Kitchen chamber: 3 beds & furniture, 10li., chest of drawers & other things, 1li., small things in ye closett, 10s., 11li.
10s.; pcell of old linen, 30s., a smale table, 5s., 1li. 15s. In the
Garrett: smale things com to 3li.; 14 B. Indian & a hhd. malt,
3li. 10s., a wheele & other old things, 10s., 4li.; 2pr. old bootes
& other small things, 30s., meale, 5s., 1li. 15s. In the Hall: a
table & a still, 1li. 10s. In the parlor: a press, a table & a glass
case, 5li. In the Kitchen severall pcells of pewter, brass, tin
& Iron ware & a copper, 8li. 10s. In the barne severall things,
55s., a bed, blankett & 4 pillowes, 20s., 3li. 15s.; 2 cowes, 1
heifer 2 year old, 8li., 2 piggs & 3 hens, 20s., a smale negroe
girle, 8li., 17li.; 3 mares & 2 young horses runing in the
woods, 8li.; 2 horses & a muskett prest into ye warrs agst the
Indians, 6li.; a pcell of land by the planters marsh, 20li., 2
small garden plott, 12li., 32li.; a dwelling house together
with out houseing & ye ground joyning to it, 200 li., total,
444li. 12s. Then there is som land in the nargansett contry
together with a small plot at the burying place at Salem.
Then there is in debts due by book from severall men, 31li.
18s. 5d.; the remainder of a bill due from John Browne, jr.,
18li. 4s. 5d. Due from Abra. Kick in holland as by his accot.
appeers, 880 Guilders. The estate is Dr. to Samll. Shrimpton
as by his acct. given in due to him, 217li. 12s. 8 1-2d.; Abra.
Bartholmew, 8li. 15s. 3d.; severall other small debts, 4li.;
total, 230li. 7s. 11 1-2d.

Attested Apr. 26, 1676 by Mrs. Hanna Browne, relict of
Mr. James Browne, and administratrix of his estate, before
Samuell Symonds, Dept. Gov. and Edward Ting, Esq., Assist.
Essex County Probate Records, vol. 301, page 93.

ESTATE OF GEORGE GIDDINGS OF IPSWICH.

Administration upon the estate of George Gettings (also,
Geddings) was granted 27:4:1676, to Jane, the relict, who
was ordered to bring in an inventory to the next Salem court.
Salem Quarterly Court Records, vol. 5, leaf 94.

Inventory of the estate of George Giddings, late of Ipswich,
taken June 19, 1676 by John Whipple, sr., Henry Benet and

Nathaniell Wells: his waring Clothes, wollin & Linon, 7li.;
money & platte, 4li. 10s.; housing with Comonidg, 60li.; in
the parlor, a beed sted with a fether beed & what belongs to
it, 11li.; cubbord with drawers, 2li. 10s.; table, two chayers 4
cushins, 1li. 18s.; boxe, one baskit, truncke, 12s.; 6 yds. of
Cloth, 1li. 10s.; more of the same, 7s. 6d.; pewter, 4li.; a table
cloth & 6 napkins, 1li.; two payer of pillowbeers, two towels,
tablecloth, 1li. 6s.; one payer of sheetes, 1li.; fower payer of
sheets, small table cloth, 1li. 10s.; 3 payer of pillow beers with
other linen, 1li. 10s. 6d.; beedsted with a fetherbeed & three
blankits, 7li. 10s.; an old table, one old chest, 5s.; trundle
beed with what belongs to it, 2li. 15s.; sheeps wooll, 140lb.,
7li.; flax, yerne & flaxe with som tooe, 1li.; old tubes, 2s. 6d.;
10 bush. of Indian Corne, 2 bush of malt, 2li. 3s.; 3 sackes,
one bush. of wheat, 12s. 6d.; one sadle and bridle & pilion, 1li.
4s.; tubes & Keelers, 1li.; pailes, trayes, other wood dishis,
1li. 1s.; old Cubbard, 10s.; smalle table & 4 Chayers, 10s.; a
Copper, one cetle, 2li. 5s.; two Iron potes, 1li. 7s.; two
tramels, two payer of pott hooks, 11s.; an Iron barr, payer of
Andjrons, 16s.; slice, paire of tonges, 4s.; morter & two scillits,
10s.; tin ware, 10s.; one worming pann, one payer of belis,
7s. 6d.; one smothing Iron, with heaters, 3s.; Chespres, 8s.;
gridiron, 11s.; two spining wheels with cardes, 11s.; Ches
moats & sives & spits, 13s. 6d.; powdering tub, two barrels,
7s. 6d.; a Cherne, a runlit, 7s.; bookes, 2li.; seed plow, 9s.;
two Chaines, two yoacks with Irone, 19s.; Cart & wheeles
with spanshakle, 2li.; beetle with ringes, 5 wedgis, one axe,
14s.; 9 Cows & 3 hayfers, 36li.; thre two yer old hayfers, 4
oxen, 27li.; one yearling, 6 Calves, 3li. 10s.; 60 sheep, 40
Lames, 27li.; one hors, 3 maares, one year old coult & two
foales, 8li.; 6 swine, 4li.; poark, backen & cheese, butter, 3li.
10s.; 152 accers of Land, 760li.; 6 accers of march at Plom
iland, 12li.; total, 1021li. 12s. 6d. Debts owing from the estate, 24li.

Attested 27:4:1676 by Jane, relict and administratrix.
Essex County Quarterly Court Files, vol. 25, leaf 49.

For the settlement of the estate of George Gittins, deceased,
by agreement of the widow, administratrix and the five sons,
it was ordered Sept. 26, 1676, that all the estate be delivered
into the hands of the five sons, Thomas, John, James, Samuell
and Joseph Gittins, to be divided, Thomas to have a double
portion. They were to give security to pay the widow during
her life 25li. per annum and her living in the house, with the
use of the household stuff, and to pay to their three sisters,

Rebecka, Abigaill and Mary, 50li. each, deducting so much as any of them have formerly had as their portion from their father.

Ipswich Quarterly Court Records, vol. 5, page 283.

Agreement of Thomas, John, James and Samuel Giddinge sons of George Giddinge, deceased, that Thomas the eldest son shall have a double portion of the estate of his father together with the land that was formerly given him by his father where he now lives; and they also agree not to sell any of their land from one another and to bear proportionably their part in fencings.

Allowed by the Ipswich court Sept. 26, 1676.

Essex County Probate Files, Docket 10,829.

ESTATE OF THOMAS KIMBALL.

Administration on the estate of Tho. Kemboll, who was slain by the Indians, was granted 27 : 4 : 1676, to Mary, the relict, and she was ordered to bring in an inventory to the next Ipswich court.

Salem Quarterly Court Records, vol. 5, leaf 94.

Inventory of the estate of Thom. Kimball, taken May 18, 1676, by Shu. Walker and Samuell Gage : wearing apparill, all ye Indians left, 2li. 10s.; Tabel lining, 1 sheete, 3 pillowberes, 1li. 15s.; vallence and Curtaine and 4 Cushins, 10s.; 2 Rugs, 2 blankets, and a parcill of old beading, 3li. 5s.; peautar, 3li. 3s.; 1 Iron pot, 1 warming pan, 2 tubs, 2 barills, 1li. 10s.; saddle and pillion and a parcill of sheeps wool, 1li. 5s.; Tools for his traid and utensils for husbandry, 5li.; six oxen, five Cowes, two heifers of 3 yere old, 3 steres of 2 yere old, 2 yerlings, 5 Calves, 66li. 15s.; a horse and a mare and a Coult, 6li.; 12 swine, 7li.; 7 shepe, 2li.; housing and about 422 acres land and medow, 450li.; glass, 1li. 10s.; Corne and provisions, 3li; 5 yards of Cloath, 1li.; total, 556li. 3s. Wearing cloaths of Goody kimbals, 3li. 16s.; cloaths of Joanna Kimball, 2li. 10s. Debts due to the estate : Gilbort Wilford's estate, 1li.; Daniell Boreman, 1li.; John Wicom, 1li.; Joseph Bond, 1li. 2s.; Ensigne Chandler, 1li. 10s.; by John Kimbal, 12li.; total, 17li. 12s. Debts due from the estate : Mr. Wainwright, 9li. 18s. 6d.; Capt. Gerish, 9li. 19s. 1d.; Sergent Wait, 6li. 18s.; John Pickard, 1li. 10s.; Stephen Webster, 1li. 10s.; Will. Barker, 2li. 16s.; Decon Jewit, 18s.; David Haseltine, 1li. 1s.; Hunt of Ipswich, 1li. 2s.; Decon Goodhue, 1li.; Mr. Cobbit, 10s.; Shu. Walker, 12s.; Joseph Hardy, 1li. 10s.; Nath.

Gage, 15s.; Samull Haseltine, 2li. 2s.; Francis Jordon, 2s. 6d.; Josiah Gage, 18s., John Stickne, 3li.; Mr. Buship, at present not known; Anthony Somersby, 1li. 5s.; Phillip Fouler, 6s.; total, 50li. 8s. 1d.

Attested in Ipswich court Sept. 26, 1676 by Mary relict of Thomas Kimball.

Essex County Quarterly Court Files, vol. 25, leaf 124.

An inventory brought in, amounting to 520li. clear estate was ordered Sept. 26, 1676, to the eight children and widow as follows: to Richard the eldest son, 80li., and to the rest of the children, 40li. each, and the remainder of the estate to the widow, the land to stand bound for the payment of the children's portions.

Ipswich Quarterly Court Records, vol. 5, page 284.

Estate of Thomas Alexander of Salem.

Administration upon the estate of Tho. Allexander, who was slain in the war, was granted 27 : 4 : 1676, to Samuell Eb-borne, sr., who brought in an inventory which was allowed.

Salem Quarterly Court Records, vol. 5, leaf 94.

Account of what Thomas Alexander left in Salem when he was pressed away with Captain Lathopp upon the country's service, appraised June 30, 1676, by John Loomes and William Traske and allowed 30 : 4 : 1676, in court: six bushell of corne, 18s.; due from John Mecarter, 10s.; a young horse, 1li. 10s.; another very good horse prest upon the countrey service, 3li.; eight yards of irish cloth, 12s.; a coat, 7s.; 3 shirts & 2 pair of drayrs, 7s.; 3 coats, 5s.; one capp, 1s. 6d.; due to him for his time in the country service, 1li. 16s.; 3 old horse shoes, 1s.; total, 9li. 7s. 6d.

Allowed 30 : 4 : 1676.

Essex County Quarterly Court Files, vol. 25, leaf 93.

Estate of Joseph King.

Administration on the estate of Joseph King, who was slain in the wars against the Indians, granted 27 : 4 : 1676, to Mr. John Ruck, who brought in an inventory which was allowed.

Salem Quarterly Court Records, vol. 5, leaf 96.

Inventory of the estate of Joseph King, who was slain with Capt. Lawtrup in the wars against the Indians, taken 13 : 4 : 1676 by Hilliard Veren, sr., and John Rucke, sr., one ould

Cloath Coate, 10s.; 2 pair of shoues, 9s.; 3 pair of woren drawrs, 7s.; a large wascote & Briches Worne, 16s.; Coate & Briches of stuf, 2li.; 2 Colard & 1 white neckcloth, A hankecher, 1 pr. glovs, a card buttens & 2 yds. Inkle & a feue tobaco pipes, 5s.; hatt, 5s.; 3 pair ould stockens, 4s.; 10li. Tobacco, 4s. 4d.; 1 pair pocketts, 6d.; 6 shirts, 15s.; 2 pair wore Cloth Briches, 12s.; 2 wascoats, 10s.; 4 Rubstons, 12d.; 1 pair ould drawes, 12s.; cash, 22s.; 2 chests, 8s.; 3 ould seithes, 4s. 6d.; due from the widow Spooner for work, 2li. 10s.; what is due from the Cuntry the time he was out upon the sarvis wth Captin Lawtrup 6 weeks 3 dayes, 1li. 18s. 6d.; total, 11li. 2s. 8d. The Estat is Dr. for his diet had of the widow Spooner for 40 weekes, 8li.

Allowed 30 : 4 : 1676, upon oath of Mr. John Ruck, the administrator.

Essex County Quarterly Court Files, vol. 25, leaf 54.

ESTATE OF WILLIAM PITMAN.

Administration upon the estate of William Pickman was granted 27 : 4 : 1676, to Elizabeth Pickman, the relict, and she was ordered to pay to her son William, 40s. at the age of twenty-one years.

Inventory of the estate of William Pettmand, taken June 2, 1676 by Robt. Glanfiell and John Sanders: one old fether Bead & Boulster & one Pelo & to old Blankets, 1li. 5s.; three pr. of sheets, 3li.; five Pello drawers & fower napkins, 15s.; small parcell of Linnin, 5s.; sutt of aparall of his, 2li.; two sharts & three neck cloths, 10s.; parcell of old Sea Clothes, 1li.; Chest & Box, 10s.; 1-2 Doz. of Chairs, 7s. 6d.; small tabell, 5s.; parsell of Earthen ware, 7s.; 1-2 Doz of bottls, 2s.; an old musket & Rope, 15s.; sea Chest & three hamars & to Chizels, 10s.; old peuter platters, six poringers and Little bason, one Drincking Cup 1-2 doz Spuns, 15s.; tinnin poringrs, one bras Candel sticke, 1s. 6d.; cash, 5s.; one Iron pott & skellet & gred Iron, 8s.; mony, 1li. 10s.; small prcell of Land, being twelve pol or rod, 6li. 6s. Debtr to John Cromwell, 2li. 4s. 3d.

Attested 27 : 4 : 1676 by Elizabeth Pickman, the relict of William Pickman.

Essex County Quarterly Court Files, vol. 25, leaf 58.

ESTATE OF SAMUEL PICKWORTH.

Administration upon the estate of Samuell Pickworth, who was slain in the wars against the Indians, was granted 27 : 4 :

1676, to Sara his wife, who made oath to the inventory brought in. She was ordered to pay to Samuell Pickworth, son of the deceased, 10li., and to the other children, Sara and Hana, 5li. each, at age or marriage, the house and ground to be security. *Salem Quarterly Court Records, vol. 5, leaf 96.*

Inventory of the estate of Samuell Pickworth who was slain in ye warr, taken 15 : 4m : 1676, by Hilliard Veren, sr. and Bartholmew Gedney : the house & ground adjoyning, 55li., 1 fetherbed, bolster & all appurtenances, 5li. 10s.; 60li. 10s.; trundlebed stead & appurtenances, 30s., side cubbord, 18s., warming pan, 5s., 2li. 13s.; searge & som lining for lininge a sute of cloathes, 28s., wearing cloathes, 30s., 2li. 18s.; swine, 8s., table, 10s., a smale pine table, 30d., 1li. 6d.; 3 old pine chests, 10s., 6 old flagg chaires, 6s., a box Iron, 12d., bellowes, 12d., 18s.; 2 Iron potts & Kettle, 2 skilletts & old frying pan, 1li. 5s.; 2 hatts, 10s., pewter, 12s., earth ware, 2s., 3 pr. of sheets, 20s., linen left at home, 12s., 2li. 16s.; 3 pr. old stockins, 5s., torne garments & lumber, 5s., 10s.; a looking glass, 3s., a peece of cloath before the window, 2s., 5s.; 1 old pr. cards, barrells, tubbs & some lumber, 5s.; carpenters tooles, 15s., severall yeares time in a youth, 40s., 2li. 15s.; debts oweing to the estate by Joseph Miles about 3li.; by Richard Roberts about 3li., some smale debts about 20s., 4li.; total, 83li. 15s. 6d. The estate is Dr. about 10li.

Attested in Salem court 30 : 4m : 1676 by Sarah the relict of Samuell Pickworth, and she was ordered to pay to Samuell Pickworth 10li., and to Sarah, Hanah and Mary, 5li. each, being all the children of the deceased, at age or marriage. *Essex County Probate Records, vol. 301, page 85.*

ESTATE OF JOSEPH SMALL OF SALEM.

Administration upon the estate of Joseph Smale, intestate, was granted 27 : 4 : 1676, to Lidea, the widow, and she made oath to the inventory. The court ordered the estate to remain in the hands of the said Lidia and to pay 20li. to Elizabeth, the child, at age or marriage, and the land was to stand as security.

Inventory of the estate of Joseph Small of Sallam deceased May 30, 1676 taken by Joseph Huchinson and Jonathan Walcott : four akars & a halfe of medowy or broshy land, 7li.; sixteen akars of vakante land, 16li.; four akars of Improved land, 11li.; a hous, 32li. 10s.; two narow axes & a broad axe, 13s.; a barkinge Iron, drawinge knife, hamer, 5s.; plow Iorns & 2

Barills, 10s.; Bedsted mate & bed Rope, 1li.; Lookinge glace, trays & brod how, 9s.; sith & takline, 2 chairs & shovell, 8s.; three hundred of bords, 15s.; hors, 6 swine & three piges, 6li.; fouer Coues & a yearline, 16li. 11s.; firepan, tonges, friing pan, tramill, 16s.; a pot, citell, feters, 1li. 10s.; fether bed, boulsters & pillows, 5li.; Ruge, blankit, & three pare of shets, 4li. 10s.; four shurts, three pare of drawers, 2li.; six boshills of Indion corn, 18s.; Bakon, 30li.; wool & hopes, 4,000 shingle nails, 18s. 6d.; bridl & sadle, 13s. 6d.; Indion corne upon the ground, 1li. 5s.; peas, barly & oats upon the ground, 2li. 10s.; pair of shoos, neckclos & three par of stokins, 15s.; four shillings in money, a belt, 8s. 6d.; a hat & waringc Clothse, 2li. 12s.; two Chests, a ber barill, pouder & bolits & basket, 19s. 6d.; a Bible, 4s.; total, 118li. 16s. Debts due, 50li. 4s. 7d. Debts due to her, 2li.

Allowed in Salem court 30 : 4 : 1676.

Essex County Quarterly Court Files, vol. 25, leaf 61.

ESTATE OF JEFFREY THISSELL OF (BEVERLY?).

"In the name of God ᵗAmen. The last will and Testament of Jeffery Thissell of Abbetsbury in yᵉ County of Dorsett in old England but at pʳsent in New England being in perfect health and Memory but being bound to sea Not Knowing how God may Deale by him and take him out of this world and haueing an Estate hath Giuen and Disposed as ffolloweth Impms I Bequeath my soul to God that Gaue it and my body to the earth to be Buried in Good christian like manner 2ly. I make Richard Reith and Mathew Clark both of Marblehead New England to be my sole Excecutors to see those things truly and Rightly performed as shall be pessified & Mentioned. 3ly. I Giue vnto my Eldest son Richard Thissell twentie shillings siluer which George Darlin of Salem is Indebted to mee and one halfe Barrill of oyl of Geo. Tuck and tenn shillings in old England Money which I leaue in one of the Excecutors hand Richard Reith as alsoe all my Fishing Craft that is in my Chest at Clem English house in Salem, 4ly. I Giue vnto my Daughter Jone Thissell in Abbetsbury in yᵉ County Dorsett England a Bond that is in yᵉ hand John Hedgcock in Abbetsbury of 30ˡˡ pound princeple with the use of it for fiue years at this Date : as alsoe I Giue vnto her all that is Due vnto me from Mʳ Henry Feavor as alsoe all my whole propriaty that I haue in England either in Goods or any other thing what Ever 5ˡʸ I Giue to my Grand Child Jeffery my son Richards Son Twentie pounds New England mony siluer that lieth in

Richard Reits hand as alsoe I Giue to him all that is Coming
to me of the voyage along with John Darlin of Salem which
Ezekiell watters hath yᵉ Doeinge of as alsoe I Giue to my said
Grand Child Jeffery all my whole venture that I now Carey
with me. This voiag as allsoe what wages may be due to mee
as alsoe fifteen Acres of land that lieth at Bass Riuer more or
Less 6ˡʸ I Giue vnto my son Richards Daughter mary tenn
pounds in siluer of New England mony which lieth in yᵉ
hands of Richard Reith I also Giue vnto my Grand Child
Jeffery my Chest and Bedd that is at Clem English in Salem
I Doe Further order what is Coming from yᵉ voiag of Ezekiell
Watters shall be paid to Richard Thessell Towards yᵉ Land
for the use of the boy this to be paid at yᵉ prouing the will and
that it may be put into my Excecutors hands and that yᵉ
twentie pounds and yᵉ tenn pounds that I Giue vnto yᵉ Children shall be Kept in yᵉ Executors hand tell they Come to age
and if either of the Children dieth to Goe to that as Remaines
aliue and Land and all to Goe from Generation to Generation.
Lastly I Giue Unto Richard Reith and Mathew Clark my
Excecutors Twentie Shillings a peice that is in hand and
twentie shillings a peice more out of the voyage now in hand
which I Goe. In witness hereunto I haue Sett my hand and
Seale this 29ᵗʰ: of October in yᵉ year of our Lord 1675."
                    Jeffery (his ⚒ mark) Thissell. (SEAL)
    Witness: Samuell Morgan: Edw. Humphreys.
    Proved in Salem court 27: 4: 1676 by the witnesses.

    Inventory of the estate of Jeffery Thissell, taken by Sam-
uell Morgan and Edw. Humphrey: For the Land in yᵉ Bounds
of Beaverly, 30li.; money Left in Richard Reith hand, 30li.;
wages which is in ye hands of Richard Reith, 7li. 17s.; money
in Ezekell waters hand, 9li. 2s.; money in Henery Haymans
hand, 3li. & six pence in old England money and six Shillings
in New England, 3li. 6s. 6d.; Cloase Chest & a sea Bedd, 3li.
13s. 6d.; total, 83li. 19s. As for the Land abovesd and the
Cloase Chest and Bead was prised by vs at money silver of
New England and it is to be vnderstood that all yᵉ Rest is
silver. Debts, in silver, 17li. 10s.
    Attested 27: 4: 1676 by Richard Reith and Mathew Cleark,
the executors.

    Robert White, aged twenty-nine years, testified on June 27,
1676 that Jeffery Thistell being aboard the "waymouth
marshent" sailing from Saltatudes bound for New England
was taken sick on the way and on his death-bed called for

Hendry Heman, whom with deponent he asked to go to his chest and take out 3li. in English money and 6s. in New England money. Said Heman brought it and Thistle told him to carry it home and give it to his daughter, which he did. Sworn in court 19 : 5m : 1676.

Essex County Quarterly Court Files, vol. 25, leaves 67-69.

Whereas there was entered in the inventory of Jeffery Thistle, deceased, 3li. 6d. in old England money and New England coin, which money was left in the hands of Henry Hayman and there being testimony given in that the said money was ordered before the death of said Thistle to be delivered to his daughter in England, and Hayman promising to do so, it was ordered July 18, 1676, that the said sum be discounted as so much paid upon the said inventory.

Salem Quarterly Court Records, vol. 5, leaf 98.

ESTATE OF EDWARD IRESON OF LYNN.

"This is the last will and testament of edward Ierson. I doe giue to my sone Sammuel forty ackkers of land which is my farme lying next to John hokes grond on one side and this land which I doe giue him is to goe to the next yares after his decease allsoe I doe giue to my sone bengamen my hose and land Joyning to It and 4 akkers of meddoe lying up in the conterry and 2 akkers of mash lying in Romely mash and this hee is not to haue tell after his motheres decease but if the sayed bengamen dost liue with his mother and improues this grond and lickwise the stock of cattell doth prouide for them then is hee to haue halfe the corne and half the cattell, allsoe I doe giue to my dafter elissybeth twenty pond to bee payd out of the stock, allsoe after my deceace I doe giue to my dafter Ruth one yow and one lame, allsoe It is my mind my wif shall haue all the moueables at her dissposing, and this hee did in parfet memory datted in the yeare 1674 october the 26."

[No signature]

Witness : Henery Sillsbey, Henry Collins.

Proved 27 : 4 : 1676, and Alce, the relict of the deceased, ordered to fulfill the mind of the deceased according to the above written. She also made oath to an inventory which she brought in.

Inventory of the estate of Edward Ierson of Lyn, taken 20 : 11 : 1675, by Thomas Laughton, Henry Collins and Henry Sillsbey : one dwellinge house & barne and orchard and five acres of upland adjoininge to the house and tow Acres of salt mach, 70li.; tow oxen, 8li.; foure cowes, 12li.; Tow steers, 4li. 10s.; tow Heifers, 3li.; tow caulfes, 2li.; tenn sheepe, 4li.; five swine, 3li. 10s.; one Horse & one mare & colt, 5li.; Fourty Acrse of up Land in the countrey, 10li.; Foure acres of Fresh meadow in the countrey, 8li.; One Bedstead and Beding and curtaines & vallance belonging to it, 9li.; Eight paire of sheets, 5li.; Tow table cloathes and fourteen Napkins, 1li. 10s.; five pillowbears, 10s.; Tenn yeards of course cloath, 15s.; Fifteen yeards of new cloath, 1li. 18s.; Five yeards of new cloath, 1li.; wearing cloathes, 3li. 12s.; a paire shoos & stockings and tow old shirts & a old coat, 14s.; one Bedstead and bedinge & curtaines & valance belonging to it, 6li. 10s.; one Bedstead and Bedinge, 4li.; Three score Bushill of Indian corn, 10li. 10s.; tow Bushill & halfe of rye & one Bushill & halfe wheat & a bushill pease, 1li. 1s. 6d.; Barley, 3li.; oats, 2li. 4s.; sheeps woole, 1li.; flax, 1li. 10s.; Hay, 10li.; chairs and cushens, 1li.; table & forme & tow old cubbards, 1li.; Iron pots and scillets and other Iron tooles & axes & wedges & tonges, 3li.; pewter dishes and Pewter pots & poringe dishes & other pewter & cups, 3li.; musket & sword & powder & Bulletts, 1li. 10s.; Earthen dishes & pots, 6s.; spininge wheels & woole cards & a hatt, 9s.; pork, butter & cheese, 2li. 10s.; chests, boxes, chirnes, tubs, pailes, a chees presse & woden trayes, 1li. 16s.; a briddle and saddell & a cart saddle, 1li. 6s.; a Bible & other bookes & yearne & lookinge glasses & tow old stoles, 16s.; one cart & wheeles and a chaine & plough & cart rope, 2li. 6s.; In old sackes & winnow sheets & a fork & old tools, 14s.; debts owing to him, 2li. 13s.; debts to be paid, 6li. 12s.

Allowed 27 : 4 : 1676.

Essex County Quarterly Court Files, vol. 25, leaves 71, 72.

ESTATE OF RICHARD KEMBALL OF WENHAM.

Samuell and Tho. Kemboll, sons of Richard Kemboll, deceased, were appointed 27 : 4 : 1676, administrators of their father's estate, and made oath to the inventory brought in.

Salem Quarterly Court Records, vol. 5, leaf 97.

Inventory of the estate of Richard Kemball, taken June 17, 1676 by Walter Fayerfeld and Thomas Patch: the dwelling hous and 132 Akers of Land and 17 Akers of meddow belonging, 370li.; 40 Akers of upland at Lords hill with meddo, 92li.; at Lords hill 21 Akers of upland and one of meddow, 40li.; 20 Akers of upland lieing by Mr. Newmans, 28li.; 6 Akers of Land caled poulands and 12 of medow, 71li.; 200

Akers of Land in Rowly village, 164li. 10s.; corne in the hous
and corne in the grass, 13li. 15s.; cattell, shep, horses and
swine, 79li. 1s.; beads and beding and a parcell of yerne, 8li.
15s.; Arms and ammunition, 5li. 5s. 6d.; peuter and brass
and Ioron potts, 7li. 5s. 6d.; chests and bookes and bedsteds
and a cord, 2li. 18s.; earthen ware and other Implements in
the hous, 2li. 12s. 6d.; fether bead and other beding and a bedsted, 4li. 16s.; a weavers loom and tacleng, 2li. 5s.; a percill
of yern and tubbs and other Lumber, 4li. 1s.; husbantre
Implements, 7li. 9s.; dew from his fathers exsecitors, 35li.
10s.; cattell and houshould goods which his wife brought to
him, 19li. 16s.; his wearing clothes, 6li. 7s.; dew from daniell
gott by a bill that he gave to Richard kemball of 23 pounds
ther being but 4li. 5d. paid, 18li. 15s.; dew from daniell gott
for Rent thre pownds per yer during the naturall life of mary
the wife of the Late Richard kemball of wenham more severall
small debts dew to this estate, 3li. 9s.; dew from the contry
for wages and other debts, 2li. 16s.; total, 980li. 16s. 6d. Debts
due from Richard Kemball's estate: to Mr. William Browne,
sr., 21li. 4s. 8d.; Doctor Avery of Dedham, 31li.; Doctor Endi-
cote of Salem, 6li. 4s.; Rebecah Bondfield of Marblehead, 1li.
10s.; Deaken Goodhew of Ipswich, 16li. 10s. 9d.; Mr. William
Browne, jr., 4li. 3s.; Mr. Georg Corwin, 3li. 16s. 6d.; Mr. Edmond Batter, 1li. 14s. 7d.; Thomas Ives, 18s.; Andrew Wod-
bery, 5s.; Mr. Joseph Gieresh, 1li. 19s. 3d.; Captin Nathaniell
Saltingston, 3li.; Captin John Corwin, 6s.; Timothy Lindall
of Salem, 8s.; Thomas Kirks, Salem, 6s. 8d.; David Perkens,
8s.; John Safferd, 8s. 6d.; Mr. Francis Wainwrit, 11s.; Andrew Ellet, 1li. 10s.; John Lovet, cooper, 7s.; Walter Fayerfeld, 12s.; Thomas Patch, 5s.; Hayward, the hatter of Ipswich, 8s.; other debts, 1li. 4s.; debts, 18li. 5s. 8d.; by the warr
rate and Elizabeth Brooks, 7li.; total, 123li. 5s. 7d.

Essex County Quarterly Court Files, vol. 25, leaf 83.

In copy of the inventory there are the following additional
debts: to goodman bigsbe of Rowley Village, 1li. 8s.; Mr.
Verin of Salem, 5s.; making total debts, 125li. 18s. 7d.

Samuell and Thomas Kemball sons of Richard Kemball of
Wenham and administrators of his estate, with Mary Kemball their mother in law having left it to this court to proportion the estate between them it is ordered as follows: there
being 800li. estate the widow shall have what she brought
with her which is the 19li. 16s. and the 18li. 15s. mentioned
in the inventory, and also the 3li. per year mentioned in the
said inventory and also she shall be allowed 3li. per year dur-

ing her life paid out of the estate by the children of her husband, and while she remaineth a widow and dwelleth with them they are to keep her a cow, 4 sheep & one swine winter and summer, with the room in the house which she lives in, this to be in full for her thirds out of the estate of her husband; the 800li. is to be divided equally between the eight children of the deceased Richard, only to John the eldest son a double portion, and the other six children are to allow out of their proportion to their brothers Samuell and Thomas for their cost about their part of the estate; also the administrators are to be allowed out of the estate for all their trouble in paying the debts, the land to stand bound for the performance of the same.

ΙAllowed in Ipswich court, Sept. 26, 1676.

Essex County Probate Files, Docket 15,724.

ESTATE OF HENRY KEMBALL.

Elizabeth, relict of Henry Kembeel, was appointed 30 : 4 : 1676, administratrix of her husband's estate, and she brought in an inventory to which she made oath.

Inventory of the estate of Henery Kemball, taken 16 : 4 : 1676, by Thos. Fiske and Richard (his R. H. mark) Huttn: house and twelve akrs of Land which was the widow's before shee maried with him, 40li.; Neate catle, 25li. 10s.; one old horse, 1li. 5s.; sheep, 2li. 10s.; swine, 5li. 12s.; Graine upon the land, 4li.; 6 Bushels of Corne, 1li. 1s.; Beding & Bedsteads, 7li. 10s.; wearing Clothes, 4li. 18s.; Iron & Brass, 5li. 14s.; workeing Tools, 3li. 2s.; sword & Belt, 10s.; Ammunition, 3s.; Lumber, 3li. 15s. 6d.; books, 5s.; yarne, 2li.; Hemp & flax, 8s.; sheep's wooll, 15s.; hoops & Boxes & other Utensils, 1li.; Debt due from his son Caleb late deceased upon the account of howse & Land, 25li.; to ye Remnant of a Legicie given him by his father yet in the execetrs hand, 40li.; debt due from Thomas Fiske, 3s.; timber, 1li. 15s.; a Grindstone, 10s.; warming pan & old pewter, 6s.; two Bags, 3s.; total, 177li. 11s. Debts: to Mr. William Browne, 3li. 1s. 1 1-2d.; county Treasurer, 2li. 5s.; Mr. Georg Corwine, 16li. 9s. 7 1-2d.; Mr. Georg Corwine, a payer of wheels with hoops & Boxes, 2li. 12s.; to be paid to him according to a note under his hand for ye widow White, 1li. 1s.; Richard Dodg, 1li. 10s.; the Remainder of Legacies to Humphery Gilbert's childrin, 6li. 11s.; two oxen & two Cowes mentioned in humphery Gilbirth's will, 20li. 5s.; two akers of Land belonging to Humph-

ery Gilbert's farm which William Rayner Recd. of Thomas
Fiske & gave bond that the Heires should Give a deed of it
wn. he Come of Age, 5li.; to Jno. Carpenter, 14s.; Daniell
Killim, 1li. 6s.; Goodman Rix, 7s.; Daniell Killim sr., 7s.;
Osmond Traske, 3s.; Goodman Stackhouse, 14s.; William
Rayner's children according to an order of Ipswich Court, 1li.
15s.; to ye Constable of Ipswich for ye war rates & others, 3li.
14s. 2d.; to Thos. Ives, 1li. 7s. 5d.; Richard Gooldsmith, late
deceased, 1li. 10s.; Deacon Goodhue, 1li. 5s.; Mr. Wainewrite,
2li. 10s.; Mr. Wade, 1li.; Samuell Fiske, 12s.; Mr. Browne,
3li. 8s. 11d.; total, 76li. 8s. 3d.

Allowed 30 : 4 : 1676.

Essex County Quarterly Court Files, vol. 25, leaf 80.

Agreement made between Richard and John Kemball sons
of Henery Kemball, for themselves and all the rest of their
father's children, and Elizabeth Kemball the relict of Henry
Kemball, that the said Elizabeth, relict and administratrix
shall give up and resign all her right she hath in her husband's estate to her sons in law, Richard and John Kemball
and they acquit her of all debts that may be due from the said
estate, also that she shall have all the estate she brought to
their father; whereupon the said Elizabeth discharged the said
Richard and John from paying any debts of her former husband Rayner or of herself before she married her late husband
Kemball.

Dated Sept. 26, 1676.

Witness: Walter Fayerfeld, John Gilbertt.

Allowed by the Ipswich court Sept. 26, 1676.

Inventory of the estate of Henery Kemball taken May 17,
1676, by Richard Hutten and Walter Fayerfeld: one cow, one
ster, 3 sheep, 10li.; Iron poote, one Iron kettell & skelet, 2li.;
thre old sithes, one fryeing pann, 9s.; a sword and belt and
warming pan, 9s. 6d.; pewter dishes, pots and cups, 1li. 6d.;
tools in the shop and Iron Implements in the hous, 2li. 18s.;
grinding ston and a morter, 10s.; tubs and wooden ware and
lumber, 19s. 3d.; powder and shott, 3s.; one peck and nails
and lumber, 3s. 10d.; one old bed and beding all old, 2li. 5s.;
his wearing clothes lenning & woolen, 4li. 18s.; tenn bushels
of corne, one of Ry, 1li. 16s.; dew from the exsecitors of his
fathers estat to this estate, 40li.; dew from Caleb Kembals
estat, 25li.; a parcell of timber, 1li.; sum flax and other small
things, 5s.; total, 93li. 17s. 1d.

The court Sept. 26, 1676 granted administration to Rich-

ard and John Kimball of the estate of their father Henry
Kimball according to agreement dated Sept. 26, 1676, and
they to pay the debts.

Debts due from the estat of Henery Kemball: to Mr. Wil-
liam Browne, sr., 4li.; the country treasurer, 2li. 5s.; Mr.
George Corwin a pr. of whels & irons, 2li. 12s.; Richard Dodg,
1li. 10s.; John Carpenter, 14s.; Daniell Killam, jr., 1li. 6s.;
Daniell Killam, sr., 7s., Osmand Trask, 3s., 10s.; goodman
Rix, 7s.; goodman Stackhous about 5s.; the warr and other
Rates, 3li. 14s. 2d.; Thomas Ives, 1li. 7s. 5d.; Richard Gold-
smith, desesed, 1li. 10s.; Deakon Goodhue, 1li. 10s.; Mr.
Wainwrit, 50s., Mr. Wade, 28s., 3li. 18s.; Samuell Fisk, 12s.;
Richard Kemball, 2li. 4s.; other small debts, 1li. 15s.; Mr.
Pain, tresurer, 14s.; Mr. Newman, 2s., to Woodward and
other debts, 17s. 8d.; total, 31li. 11s. 3d.

At the court held at Ipswich Sept. 26, 1676, Richard and
John Kemball sons of Henry Kimball, deceased, administer-
ing upon their father's estate according to agreement between
them and their mother in law, engage to pay all debts out of
their father's estate which they have taken into their hands,
and also to pay to their mother in law Elizabeth Kimball 15li.
for the bringing up of their younger sister Deborah out of
which the mother is to pay her 15li. when she is of age; also
they are to pay to their ten brothers and sisters fifty shillings
a piece when they come to age and the rest of the estate to be
theirs, Richard the eldest son to have a double portion.
Essex County Probate Files, Docket 15,592.

ESTATE OF HENRY COLBURN.

Administration upon the estate of Hen. Coleborne was
granted 30 : 4 : 1676, to Sara Coleborne, the relict, who brought
in an inventory and to administer so far as the estate goes
only.
Salem Quarterly Court Records, vol. 5, leaf 95.

Inventory of the estate of Henry Colburne, taken June 26,
1676, by Richard Croade and Henry West: a bed, being an old
bed & but half feathers, a coverled & blanket well worne, 1 pr.
of sheetes, 4 old pillowes, an old sett of Curtains & vallents &
ye bedsteed very little worth, 3li. 10s.; a Trundle bed being a
straw bed with ye old Rugg & Blankett & ye other Small matter belonging to it, 15s.; 5 old pillowbeers, 5s.; 2 paire of
sheetes well worne, 1li.; one Table cloth above half worne out,
2s.; one chest, 8s.; an old Trunke, 3s.; an old warming pan,

an old kettle & an old skillett, 12s.; Iron pott & pott hangers,
fire shovell & a broken paire of Tongs, a grid Iron, an old pr.
bellowes & Fryeing pan, 13s.; old beare vessell, 3 Tubbs & a
Little salt beefe, 6s.; 3 qrt. earthen Juggs, 2 old Candlesticks,
2 old pewter potts, a Little old pewter & old Jarr, 5s.; 4 Small
pewter platters, 10s.; 2 earthen platters, 2s.; an old Cubbard,
2 Joyne stooles & an old Table, 5s., an old cradle, 2 old Sea
chests, & 4 or 5 old chaires, 4s.; 2 old Sives & a little old
Woodden ware, 3s.; an old hatchet & 2 henns, 2s.; debts owing
from Henry Frend, 10s., Richard Richards, 4s.; Wm. Shaw,
2s.; Nathaniel Felton, 1s. 6d.; total, 10li. 2s. 6d. "What my
husband carried with him to Virginea but it being I am sure
ye most of his estate I cannot giue acct. of Neither can I giue
an Exact acct. of what my husbands debts are."
Allowed 30 : 4 : 1676 upon oath of the widow Sara.
Essex County Quarterly Court Files, vol. 25, leaf 52.

ESTATE OF RICHARD SIBLEY.

Administration upon the estate of Richard Sibly, intestate,
was granted 30 : 4 : 1676, to Hanna, the relict, who made oath
to the inventory brought in. She was to pay to the seven children, Samuell, the eldest, 6li., and Hana, Sara, Damaris,
John, Mary and Elizabeth, 3li. each, at age or marriage, the
house and ground to be security.

Inventory of the estate of Richard Sibley: dwelling house
and barn with the Ground belonging to it, 60li.; two feather
beds wth Cloths belonging to them, 8li.; Bedsteds, 18s.; one
hat & wearing Apparell, 3li. 2s. 6d.; pewter, 14s; earthen
ware, 5s.; Brass, skellets, worming pan & spoons, 14s.;
Glasses, 2s.; two old seives, a frying pan & Smothing Iron,
6s.; two Iron pots, 14s.; one Iron Ketle, 14s.; two Ruggs,
15s.; a pr. of Andiarns, 8s.; fire shovell, tongs, hakes, pot
hooks & Gridiron, 1li. 3s., spitt, 2s.; 3 saws, 8s.; pr. of Bellows & a pail, 2s.; five old Axes, 11s.; two drawing knives &
two round Shaves and a hollowing tool, 10s.; two old ladders
& Meal vessells, 5s. 6d.; two adsess, 7s.; two Smal frows, 2s.;
two bigger frows, 3s.; one Auger, 2s.; & three hammers, 4s.;
paire of Chezells & Goudge, 4s.; a hollowing tool & pincers,
4s.; three old hoes, 3s.; 6 old chaires, 6s.; looking Glass, 2s.;
one Winscot chest, 15s.; another chest & box, 12s.; an old
Trunke, 3s.; two spining wheels & a p of cards, 10s.; smal
table, 4s.; an old smal bed & Covering & pillows, 20s.; five
sheets, 24s.; parcel of house lining, 16s.; 6 pound of yearn at

2s. p pound, 12s.; 5 pound of cotton woll, 3s. 9d.; 9 pound of flax, 6s. 9d.; 3 pound of woolen yearn, 6s., and a brish, 6d.; 2 Bed Curtains, 10s.; one Cow & a heifer, 5li. 10s.; total, 94li. 1s.

Allowed 30:4:1676 upon oath of the widow.

Essex County Quarterly Court Files, vol. 25, leaf 55.

ESTATE OF JOHN SILSBY.

Administration upon the estate of John Silsby, intestate, was granted 30:4:1676 to Bethia, the relict, and she was ordered to pay to her son John, 20li. at age, the house to be given for security.

Inventory of the estate of John Silsby, taken June 26, 1676 by Hilliard Veren, sr., and Edmond Feveryeare: dwelling house with ground belonging, 50li.; fether bed, rug, curtains, bedsted, 5li.; 2 pr. sheetes, 20s.; 1 doz, napkins & 6 towells, 1li. 15s.; 3 shirts, 12s.; 3 pc. old linen drawers, 5s.; 3 pr. pillow beers, 5s.; a carpett, 15s.; 4 pr. old & 1 pr. new stockens, 10s.; 2 pr. old cards, 3s.; wearing apparrell, 50s.; a hatt, 4s.; 5 old neckcloath, 2s. 6d.; 3 chests, 20s.; marrenrs instruments & callender, 14s.; 6 flag chaires, 6s., a cradle, 5s., a stoole table, 30d., 13s. 6d.; 1 pr. tonges, fire pan, hake, 5s.; Iron pott, 5s.; Skillett, 3s.; pewter, 6s.; earthware, 2s.; spoones, trenchers & lumber, 3s.; glasses & an old case, 2s.; Corne, 24s.; a box Iron, 2s.; a gun & sword, 20s.; 3 baskett, 2s.; a bible & 2 old bookes, 5s.; the estate is creditt, 18s.; a Cow, 50s.; 5 sheepe & 2 lambs, 45s.; a mare, 20s.; more on sea bede & Covering, 10s.; total, 74li. 16s. The estate is Dr. 21li.

Allowed 30:4:1676 upon oath of Bethiah, the widow.

Essex County Quarterly Court Files, vol. 25, leaf 57.

ESTATE OF JOHN KITCHEN OF SALEM.

"The last will & Testament of John Kitchen the twentith day of December in ye year one thousand six hundred Seventy fiue, being in parfect Memory & understanding I doe bequeth My dwelling house & land belonging to it and about an Acre of Salt Marsh by Castill hill unto my wife dureing her life time & to my Son Robert after her decease Secondly I doe giue & bequeth My Orchard and Ground behind it vnto My son Robert Kitchen: prouided y^t ye one halfe of ye produce of both be for my wifes use & to her dispossall dureing her life Thirdly as for ye rest of My estate i giue to my wife to be for her use dureing her life time & after her decease to be dispossed of to ye rest of my children fouerthly i doe by this My will Make my wife & My Son Robert kitchen exseccetrice and exseccetor."

John Kitchin

Witness: Sam^ll: Shattocke, Abraham Cole.

Proved in Salem court 30:4:1676 by Samuell Shattock who affirmed and Abraham Cole who made oath.

Inventory of the estate of John Kitchin taken May 30, 1676 by Edward Flint and Richard Croade: A dwelling house & a Small Barne with the Land upon wch the said howse & barne stands being by Estimation about a qrtr. of an acre, 160li.; Orchard & another ps. of Land adjoyning to it being in whole about Two acres of Land, 60li.; about an acre of Salt marsh lyeing in the Sowth field neer Castle hill, 7li.; one Cow, 3li.; a mare, 3li. In the parlor his Lodgeing roome the goods there, a Feather bed & Furniture, 11li.; Trundle bed being likewise a Feather & Furniture, 4li.; cubbard, Table & Joyne stooles, 2li.; Small Table & 2 Carpetts, 1li. 5s.; Chest, box & a little Forme, 15s.; pr. of cast dog Irons, 10s.; Case of Bottles, 4s.; 7 chaires, 15s.; glass Bottles & small cups & a small pcs of silver plate, cushen & cubbard cloth on the Cubbards head, 1li. 5s.; his wearing Apparrell, 20li.; 3 bibles & some other bookes, 1li. In the parlor Chamber, Feather bed & furniture, 18li.; Trundle bedsteed, 6s.; 3 blanketts, Rugg & Coverled, 2li. 10s.; Cubbard with the Furniture in it, 3li.; Table & 6 Joyne stooles, 2li. 5s.; 6 Chaires, 12s.; 3 Cushens stuffd, 9s.; chest & a small Trunke, 12s.; a wiccar baskett & looking glass, 6s. In the porch chamber, Feather bed, bedsteed & furniture, 8li. In ye garret, 5 bush. of wheate, 4 bush. of corne, 1li. 17s.; Tubbs, a wheel & some other Lumber, 6s.; a hammocke, 8s., in the kitchin, In pewter & brass, 10li. 6s.; a pestell & morter, 4s.; a still, 8s.; pewter, 4s.; Letten ware, 15s.; earthen Ware, 15s.; 3 doz. Trenchars, 3s.; a Jack, Andirons, Fire Shovels, Tongs, 2 spitts & a pr. of Stilliards, 2 smoothing Irons, hakes, Fenders & chafing dish with some other small Iron Things, 3li. 11s.; 3 Iron potts & a Kettle, 1li.; 2 Iron wedges, 2s.; 2 Little Tubbs & 4 Chaires, 8s.; A meale Trough, 2s.; Bowls & Trayes, 3s. In the shop, 4 bush. malt, 16s.; 1 1-2 bush. wheate, 7s. 6d.; Tubbs & barrels in the cellar, 15s.; In Lynnen as Table cloths, napkins towels sheets & pillowbeers, 15li.; money, 40li.; debts due, 6li.; saddle & bridle & 2 pillions & pillion cloth, 2li.; 3 payles whereof Two with Iron hoopes & bayles, 4s. 6d.; a

Lynning wheel, 3s.; 2 Chests, 4 Jarrs & a handsaw, 7s.; A spade & a pr. billowes, 5s.; total, 398li. 4s.

Allowed 30 : 4 : 1676 upon oath of Robt. Kitchin.

Essex County Quarterly Court Files, vol. 25, leaves 59, 60.

ESTATE OF JONATHAN WILDES.

Administration upon the estate of Jonathan Wiles, intestate, granted 30 : 4 : 1676 to John Wiles who made oath to the inventory.

Salem Quarterly Court Records, vol. 5, leaf 96.

Inventory of the estate of Johnnathan Wills, taken June 28, 1676 by John How and William Aver [ill] : a mar and ould sadell, 2li.; a small Gun, 15s.; thre saws, 18s.; a beres, 5s.; Broad ax, 5s.; square, 2s. 6d.; mortis auger, 2s.; ould Iorans, 1s. 6d.; an ould ax, 2s.; an inch auger and a payer of Chisells, 3s. 6d. There is a parsell of Land about 15 akers which was to be Johnnathan's after his fathers decase : this to be consederd whither to be in the Inventory or no.

Allowed in Salem court 30 : 4 : 1676.

Essex County Quarterly Court Files, vol. 25, leaf 63.

ESTATE OF WILLIAM PITCHER.

"estate I dispose —— Inpr. I will that all my due debts which I owe to any manner of person be truly satisfyed by my executours hereafter specifyed I give and bequeath of that estate I have to my elder Brother John Pitcher living in England att Kenton in Devonshire, forty pounds to be paid to him by my Executours, or to his order here in New England, and in case of my Brothers decease to be paid to my Brothers eldest sonne living, and the remainder of the estate I give and bequeath to my loving Freind Andrew Tucker : in whose house I now ly sicke : Item by these present I doe appoint, ordaine & constitute my loving Freinds Andrew Tucker and Rich Rith to be my Executours of this my will and Testament, leaving it to the care & ingenuity of my Executours to take care of satisfying my debts, and taking care of my ffunerall; In witness of which premises I have here unto sett to my hand and seale this twenty fift day of November, in the year of our Lord, one thousand six hundred and seventy five."

William (his W mark) Pitcher. (SEAL)

Witness : John (his ‡ P. mark) Pederick, William (his ⊙ mark) Venning.

Proved in court 30 : 4 : 1676 by the witnesses, who made oath 14 : 1 : 1675-6 before Wm. Hathorne, assistant.

Inventory of the estate of Wm. Pitcher, taken May 22, 1676
by Robert (his R mark) Hooper and Edw. Humphrey: For a
Green Rugg, pillow & fethers, 9s.; a silver Lace wastcoat and
another wastcoat with Gollon, 1li.; one Coat, 2 pare Breeches
and one pare Red Drawers, 18s.; Coate and Breeches, 1li. 2s.;
two Remnants of stuff, 13s. 8d.; a Remnant of Ticken, 18s.;
percell of Lining, 10s.; a hatt & some other Small things,
8s.; an old pare Boots and a Chest, 8s.; Little Trunk, 2s. 6d.;
2 pare stockings, 2s. 6d.; total, 6li. 11s. 8d. Debts owing to
him, 77li.

Attested 30 : 4 : 1676 by Andrew Tucker, the executor.

Charges of Andrew Tucker on account of Wm. Pitcher: the
first Month of his sickness Diat, tendance and Licquor and
watchers & other Necesasaryes, 6li.; 2 month for Diat tendance and Licquor & watchers & other Necessaryes, 8li.; 3
month Hee Growing worse and worse for Diate, Tendance &
for watchers p 2 every night & for Brandy for y⁰ watchers,
firewood and Light, 12li.; 4 Month For Diat Tendance & for
2 Watchers every Night & for Brandy for the watchers Firewood and Light, 12li.; 5 month to Diat and tendance p one
whole month after the will was made & for 2 watchers Every
Night To Brandy p his watchers victualls and Fire wood,
13li.; To Doct. Daniell Wells, 6li. 17s.; to Doct. Richd. Knott,
2li. 1s.; To 2 Journeys to Charlstown & pd to Doct. Check-
ing, 1li. 10s.; 1 Journey to Boston to Doct. Snelling & wt. I
had of him, 16s.; To a Journey to Lin to Goody Edmonds &
by his owne Order & for horse & man to fetch her & Cary her
home, 18s.; paid to ye Constable of marblehead for Countrey
and towne Rate, 8s. 6d.; To his Funerall, 6li.; for my own
Labour and my wife Goeing Early & Late to Marblehead,
Salem, Boston & to and again & Use of my horse, 6li.; paid
to Richard Reith, 17s.; to Edward Humphreys, 4s.; to Robt.
Hooper, 2s.; total, 77li. 1s. 6d.

Essex County Quarterly Court Files, vol. 25, leaves 64-66.

ESTATE OF MATTHEW LEGROE.

Administration upon the estate of Mathew Legroe, who was
slain in the wars against the Indians, was granted July 18,
1676, to Nathaniell Brickett, who brought in an inventory,
and was bound.

Salem Quarterly Court Records, vol. 5, leaf 97.

Moses Litell, aged about nineteen years, and Joseph Poore,
aged about twenty-two years, testified that Mathew Legro

was a servant to Elisha Ilslie when he was pressed for the war, that he was a covenant servant and was bound to serve as an apprentice from about the beginning of May, 1675, for two years and six months to learn his trade. Sworn, June 22, 1676, before Daniel Denison.

Owing to Mathew Logrow: by Mr. Short, 10s.; by Jno. Celly, 5s.; by Peter Tapon, 6s.; by Dan. Lunt, 4li. 4s.; by his wages for his being a souldier, 14li.; mony in his Chest, 1li.; clothing in his chest, 2li.; total, 22li. 5s. Account of what he owed to Mr. Adkinson, 3li.; Capt. White, 12s. 3d.; Mr. Thomas Woodbridge, 4s.; George Major, 19s.; widdow Moody, 17s.; total, 5li. 12s. 3d. Nathaniell Bricket declared that what was due to Mathew Lougrow he had given to him.

Attested in Salem court 18 : 5m : 1676 by Nathaniell Bricket.

William Fannen, aged about thirty years, deposed that immediately before Mathu Groe went away toward Hadly as a soldier, he was witness to a will made in favor of Nathaniell Bricket of Newbery, but he did not have time to finish it and told deponent that he gave his estate to said Bricket in consideration of his kindness and charges during his sickness. John Mitchell, aged about twenty-five years, testified to the same. Sworn, June 26, 1676, before Daniel Denison.

Richard Dole testified that he was also a witness to the same and that Grow asked him at deponent's house just as the soldiers were marching away. Sworn in court, June 26, 1676.

Essex County Quarterly Court Files, vol. 25, leaves 84, 85.

ESTATE OF MRS. ELEANOR ROBINSON OF SALEM.*

Whereas an account was brought into court of the estate of Ellenor Robinson, deceased, by Mr. Henry Bartholmew, administrator, there being 25s. left of the estate, the court July 18, 1676, allowed said administrator 15s. for his pains and the other 10s. was to be paid to Mr. Edmund Batter toward his debt.

Salem Quarterly Court Records, vol. 5, leaf 97.

Edmond Batter's account of the estate of Elinor Robinson, deceased, dated 21 : 5 : 1675 : Creditor to mony Received of Goody Mascall, 1li. 16s.; to mony Recd. of my wife, 3li. 19s.; for hire of 2 Cowes, 1li. 8s.; to 2 Cowes that being killed come to 4li. 5s.; total, 11li. 8s. Debter: to Capt. Joseph Gardner,

*See *ante*, vol. 2, page 246.

expense of her buriall, 7s. 8d.; paid for her, 15s. 4d.; total, 1li.
3s. Edmund Batter's receipt for 9li. in silver, dated Aug. 6,
1675, from Mr. Henry Bartholmy for a debt due from Elinor
Robinson.

Essex County Quarterly Court Files, vol. 25, leaf 85.

ESTATE OF JOHN WHITRIDGE OF SALEM.

Administration upon the estate of John Whitterig, who was
slain in the wars against the Indians, was granted July 18,
1676, to John Baxter, who was to bring in an inventory to the
next court.

Salem Quarterly Court Records, vol. 5, leaf 98.

GUARDIANSHIP OF BETHIA LONGHORNE.

Bethia Longhorne chose her uncle Thomas Longhorne as
her guardian, Sept. 26, 1676.

Ipswich Quarterly Court Records, vol. 5, page 282.

ESTATE OF THOMAS MILLETT, SR., OF GLOUCESTER.

Administration upon the estate of Thomas Millett, intestate, was granted Sept. 26, 1676, to Mary Millett, relict of
said Thomas.

Ipswich Quarterly Court Records, vol. 5, page 282.

Inventory of the estate of Tho. Millitt, Sr. which he left in
his wife's possession taken Gloster 23 : 7m : 1676 by William
Vinson, James Stevens and William Sargent: his hows & land,
marsh & upland liiing to the hows, 50li.; 12 Akers of upland
upon the Iland, 12li.; 8 akers of marsh at the Iland, 2li.; 4
Akers of marsh at the Cove, 12li.; on Cow, 3li.; 10 sheepe,
3li.; in waring Clothing, 3li. 6s.; lining, 1li. 10s.; beding, 3li.
10s.; bookes, 17s.; a dept due in a litell tyme, 4li.; lomber in
the hows, 1li. 15s.; a small remnant of Eresh Cloth, 4s.;
shepes woole, 1li.; total, 128li. 1s.

Attested in Ipswich court Sept. 26, 1676 by Mary Millet,
administratrix of the estate of her husband Thomas Millet.

The agreement between Thomas Millet, Nathaniel Millet,
Thomas Riggs, Isaac Elwell and Sarah formerly the wife of
John Millet late deceased, concerning the dividing of the es-
tate of Thomas Millet, Sr., their father, who died intestate,
into five equal parts: to Thomas Millet the eldest son of said
Thomas Millet, Sr., Nathaniel Millet, Thomas Riggs, and
Isaac Elwell 12li. each; to the four children of John Millet
and Sarah his wife, 12li., Sarah to have the use of it until the

children come to age and then to be paid to them, she also shall have 12li. for her own use this to be for the tending of their mother Mary Millet late deceased, and for what their mother had of her both in sickness and in health, also upon the said account to have the use and profits of the house and land about it, wherein she now dwelleth; the remainder of the estate shall be for the payment of the debts of Thomas Millet, Sr. and Mary his wife.

Signed Sept. 26, 1682.

It was agreed before the assignment hereof that the parties above mentioned engage to pay their equal share of what debts may be due more than the remainder of the estate.

Signed Sept. 27, 1682 by Thomas Millet, Nathanell (his ⌐mark) Millet, Thomas Riggs.

Presented and allowed in Ipswich court Sept. 26, 1682 and administration granted to Thomas.

Essex County Probate Files, Docket 18,484.

ESTATE OF RICHARD JACOB OF IPSWICH.

"In the name of god Amen I Richard Jacob of Ipswich in new England being weak in body but of perfit understanding & memory: doe Comit my body to desent buriall & my Soul: to the lord Jesus Christ my most mersyfull Sauier & Redemer in hope of Reserection to euerlasting liff doe thus dispos of my estat that god hath gratiusly giuen me: it I giue to my brother Thomas Jacob thirty pownds to be paid seuen years after my desseas I Giue to my brother John Jacob sixty pownds to be pd as foloweth fiueten pownds two years after my desseas fiueten pownds more fower years after my desseas: fiuetene pownds six years after my desseas fiuetene pownds eight years after my disseas: I giue to my brother Joseph Jacob: sixty pownds to be pd as foloweth thirty pownds within one year after my desseas: the other thirty pownds to be pd fiue years After my disseas: I giue to my Sister martha Jacob fiuety fiue powndes: forty fiue of it to be pd in my housall goods I Giue to my Sister Judeth Jacob forty fiue pownds: thirty fiue pownds of it in houshold goods: all the rest of my estat housing lands Catll and good and debts from whomsoeuer due my debts ‖and legesys‖ and funerall Charges being pd: I giue to my brother Nathanell Jacob whom I make Sole executor of this my last will & testament: I doe desir my two unkle Appltons to be ouerseers of this my

will In Confemation whereof I haue set two my hand and
Seale this 8th June 1676."

Richard Jacob (SEAL).

Witness: Samuell Appleton, John Whipple.
Proved in Ipswich court Sept. 26, 1676 by Capt. Jo.
Whipple.

Inventory taken June 26, 1676 by John Appleton and John
Whipple: his waring Clothes linon & wooline, shos, boots,
hats, 12li.; a Fowling peece, 25s.; pistills, holsters, 25s. a
watch bill, 5s.; pewter, 17s. 6d.; glassis, 1s.; whit ware, 3s.;
thre juges, 3s.; candlstiks, 1s.; 8 spones, 3s. 6d.; 2 dus. trenchers, 2s.; 2 Chayers, 6s.; two joined stooles, one foorm, 5s.: 4
cushins, 4s., a clever, 2s.; a payer of sheers, 1s.; hammer &
pincons, 2s.; books, 12s.; a payer of tonges, 4s.; beedsted &
fetherbeed with Curtins & valans & what belongs, 12li.; 50
bush. of indian Corn, 8li. 15s.; 4 bush. of ryy, 18s.; 6 bush. of
oats, 15s.; a Costlit, 20s.; beedsted & a flok beed with what
belongs to it, 3li. 10s.; sheeps wooll 16lb., 16s.; 8 pown of
yarne, 1li.; a beed Coard, 2s.; cotten yarn & cotten wooll, 1li.
6s.; a small table & a baskit, 4s.; *Coatue* box, 5s.; two firkins
of butter, 3li.; two barrells of poark, 7li.; poarke & baaken,
2li. 5s.; old chees 100 wait, 2li.; 12li. of candle, 6s.; soape,
20s.; barrels & tubes, 20s.; beame & scales & waites, 1li.; friing
pann, 2s.; 3 sives, 6s.; 22 cheeses, 50s.; chees pres & churne,
15s.; in brase, 4li.; paiels, tubes, Keelers with other wood
ware, 1li. 10s.; beetle & wedgis, 10s.; one axe, 3s.; wimbls,
chisels, 5s.; thre sawes, sadle & hamer, 17s.; tomberell, wheels,
plow Irones. 3li.; yoakes, chaine & spanshakell, 17s.; Grind-
ston & Sythes, 10s.; corn on the ground, 20li.; Earthen weare,
beese, 15s.; 150 accerse of Land with housing & comonidg,
750li.; a bill from the Cuntry, 13li. 5s. 10d.; 9 cowes, 31li.
10s.; two oxen, 11li.; two bules, 5li.; 4 steers, 16li.; two 2
year olds, 40s.; 12 year olds, 15li.; 10 Calvs, 5li.; one hors,
4li.; sheep, 3li. 10s.; swine, 20li.; due from Richd. Huttin,
40s.; from good. Abbit, 4li.; malt, 4li.; in goods aprised by
itself for the two sisters, 61li. 12s. 5d.; total, 1067li. 2s. 3d.
Debts due from the estat, 26li.

Attested in Ipswich court Sept. 26, 1676 by Nathaniell
Jacob, executor of the estate of his brother Richard Jacob.

Essex County Probate Files, Docket 14,726.

ESTATE OF SAMUEL GAGE OF HAVERHILL.

"I Samuell Gage being by the grace of god in som Competent mesure of vnderstanding and daile waiting for my

Change doe make this as my Last will and testament: and doe herby appoint my beloued wife faith Gage my Executrix of this my will first my soule I Comitt and all what I am and haue Into ye hands of god my most gracious and Loueing father in and thorough Christ Jesus my body I Leaue to the descrecion of my friends to be desently buried for my temporall Estate I do bestow as foloweth first all my debts to be paied and then I giue and bequeath to my beloved wife faith gage: which is my sole Executrix: all my moueabls ‖ad Cattel ad debts due to me‖ and my house and house Lot that I bought of my brother Josiah gage which is about sixtene accres to hir and hir heires for Euer she y^t is my beloued wife and Executrix paing oll my Debts out of this part of my Estat which I haue here giuen to hir: and then all the rest of my Land both in Bradford and Hauerill doe I giue franke and free to my dere daughter Elizabeth Gage only my beloued wife to haue the Improument of it till my daughter Come of age: but in Case my daughter should be remoued by death before she be of age then my will is that all the Land that I haue here giuen to hir shall goe to my brothers Daniell gage Nathaniell gage Josiah gage to be Equaly diuided betwene them three In Case thay be then Liuing or in Case not to ye heire Lawfuly begotten of the body of ye deseased brother or to so many of them *of them* as shall be then Liuing farther I doe giue to the towne of bradford: the beter to Enabel them to promot the Intrest of Christ: forty shilings which my Executrix is to parforme In witnes that this is my Last will and testament I have set to my hand and seale this 19th July 1676."

Sa[m]uell (his G mark) gage
(SEAL)

Witness: Shubaell walker, David Haseltine.

Proved in Ipswich court 26 : 7 : 1676 by the witnesses.

Inventory taken Aug. 18, 1676 by Shu. Walker and Daniell Wicom: wearing apparill Linnin and woolen, 11li. 12s.; artillery, 1li. 10s.; bead and beading, 14li.; bookes, 10s.; peuter, brass and Iron ware, 4li. 10s.; chest, boxes and Tubs, 1li. 10s.; utencils for husbandry, 1li. 10s.; saddell and pillion, 1li.; swine, 4li. 15s.; Neate Cattell, 20li.; horses, 6li.; 5 accres of English Corne in ye barne, 10li.; 5 accres Indian Corne upon ye ground, 7li. 10s.; a house and 16 accres land about it, 60li.; about foure score accres Land in bradford, 80li.; about forty accres land at haverhill, 20li.; saks, sheeps woole and a wheele, 16s.; total, 245li. 3s. Debts due to the estate, 5li. Debts due from the estate to Mr. Wainwright, 6li. 12s. 1 1-2d.; to Mr.

lion of Rowly, 1li.; to Doct. Benitt of Rowly, 1li. 5s. 6d.; to
Josiah gag of Bradford, 32li.; total, 40li. 17s. 7 1-2d.
Attested in Ipswich court Sept. 26, 1676 by Faith Gage,
executrix of the estate of her husband Samuell Gage.
Essex County Probate Files, Docket 10,504.

ESTATE OF NATHANIEL PIPER OF IPSWICH.

"In the Name of God Amen. I Nathaniell Pyper of Ipswich in America, being weake in body, but of good and pfect
memory blessed be God, doe dispose of that estate God hath
lent mee as followeth. Inprimis I giue vnto Sarah my loueing wife, my howse & house lott barne & orchyard, & all my
lands at Hogg Iland with all my marsh both there, & else
where in Ipswich, & all my stock of Cattle & sheepe with all
my howsehold goods & debts during hir widdowhood, & vntill
my Children Come to the age of one & twenty yeares, or be
marryed. And then my will is that my Daughter Sarah shall
haue five pounds payd hir by hir moother so soone as she can
conueniently. Also I give vnto my Sonne Nathaniell Tenn
pownds, at the age of one & Twenty yeares, or at his day of
marryage. Also I give vnto all my other Children, Josyah,
John, Thomas, Mary, Margaret, Samuell, & Jonnathan, five
pownds a peece, as they come to age or marry away. Also my
will is that none of these legasies shalbe payd soe as to hinder
my wife hir Comfortable subsistance while she liues. And also
my will is that if any of my Children shall depart this life
before they Come to age, that then their portion shallbe
equally diuided amongst the rest of my Children that shall
suruiue. Also my will is, that if my wife should marry againe,
that she shall haue one halfe of my howse, & halfe of the home
lott duringe hir naturall life, and the vse of halfe my househould goods. And after hir decease my will is that my sonne
Nathaniell shall haue all my howse & home lott, & all my land
at Hogg Iland with the marsh there & else where, all these
beinge prised & equally deuided amongst all my Children then
liueinge euery one of them alike, onely my sonne Nathaniell
to haue a double portion out of the same. I doe make Sarah
my loueing wife my sole Executrix of this my last will & Testament. Dated the Seauenth day of March in the yeare of
grace Sixteene hundred seauenty and five 1675/76 In
witnes whereof I haue herevnto set my hand & Seale."

Nathaniell Piper. (SEAL)

Witness: Francis Wainwright, James Chute, Senr.
Proved in Ipswich court Sept. 26, 1676 by the witnesses.

Inventory* of the estate of Nathaniell Piper late of Ipswich, deceased Apr. 7, 1676, taken by James Chute and Nathanell Rust: the dwelling house, barn & homestead, 120li.; land at Hogg Iland, 50li.; 3 acres & 1-2 marsh, 9li.; 2 oxen, 9li.; 3 Cows, 9li.; 13 sheepe & lambs, 4li. 10s.; 1 Calf, 10s.; 3 swine, 40s.; 1 mare & old horse, 2li. In the Parlor: 1 fetherbed & furniture, 6li. 10s.; trundle bed, Coverlet & bolster, 2li. 10s.; Cupbord & a Chest, 2li.; small Chest, 3s., a long table, 1li. 13s.; 3 Chaires, 6s.; Andirons, 7s.; Earthin ware, 4s.; 2 small silver Cups, 15s.; Cradle & things in it, [14s. *Copy*]; things in the Cubbord, [10s. *Copy*]; box & a tub in ye Closet, [1s. *Copy*] 6d.; Cushen & other things, 4s.; gun & a Cutles, 2li.; an old Sithe, 12d.; his waring Clothes, 5li.; A small spoone, 4s.; wearing Lining, 3li.; 18 pr. gloves, 9s. In the hall: pewter, 2li. 10s.; brass, 3li.; pots, trames & pot hooks, 1li.; warming pan, morter & a spitt, 13s.; Alcumy spoones, 3s.; 2 tables, 12s.; 5 Chairs, 6s.; tubs & wooden ware, 30s.; earthen ware, 7s.; 2 frying pans, 5s.; byble & bookes, 10s.; 3 wheeles, 10s.; 3 pr. Cards, 10s.; 3 howes & an Axe, 10s.; 42li. woollen yarne, 4li.; 10li. linnen yarn, 1li.; 5li. Cotton yarne, 10s.; 8li. Cotton wooll, 8s.; 4 sives, 2 brushes, a basket, 6s. In ye hall Chamber: 15li. sheeps wool, 15s.; trundle bed & other things, 2li. 10s.; flax, 6s.; oynyons, 4s.; Corn & Chese, 5s.; 3 bushell of Pease, 12s. In ye Parlor Chamber: fetherbed & beding, 5li.; Chest, 4s.; Apples, 10s.; hay & Corn in ye barne, 4li.; a box Iron & brand Iron, 5s.; 5 baggs, 5s. Debts in ye booke, due about 20li. Debts owing, 45li.

Attested in Ipswich court Sept. 26, 1676 by Sarah Pyper executrix of the estate of her husband Nath. Pyper.

Debts due to the estate of Nathaniell Piper this Sept. 26, 1676, which belong to Iles of Shoals & Piscattaqua, 13li. 6s.

Essex County Probate Files, Docket 22,022.

ESTATE OF WILLIAM TITCOMB, SR., OF NEWBURY.

"The last will and testimen of william Titcomb Sen˚ of newbery in the County of Essex in new ingland: which is as foloweth: ferst in gods Apoynted time I resien my soule into the hands of god that giaue it and my body to the dust vntell the day of the resurecksion of the Just: with asuered hop att that day to reseue itt acording to the gracious promis of *of* the god of grace and truth in Christ Jesus: and for my Temperall goods which the lord haue giuen mee I despose of them as foloweth: I giue to my to Eldest daughters Sara and

*Copy, Ipswich Deeds, vol. 4, page 52.

mary twenty shillings a peice as a pleg of my loue who haue reseud thayr porsions in my leif time: I giue to my daughter Elizabeth bartlut tene pound who haue likewise reseud part of her porsion in my life time: I giue to my sonns benaia william: thomas: and John: together with my other fowr daughters rebeca: tersa ledy and anne: twenty pounds a peice: and thes porsions to bee paid to them within one year after my deseas to as many of them as shall be of age that is to say my sonns to be of twenty one years and my daughter att Eightine years and if any of them bee vnder the years aboue Exprest att my deseas thay shall not reseue thair porsions vntell thay Come to that age: and if it shall ples god that any of them shall dey before my selfe or after my deseas before thay Come to the age aboue exprest then my will is that thayr porsions shall be equally deuided to all them whether sonns or daughters to whom I haue giuen twenty pounds a peice and to my daughter Elizabeth to whom I haue giuen ten pound I giue to my louing and dear wife/the therds of all my lands for her ves and benifet with the therd of my howsing dewring her naturall leife and then to retorn vnt my hair: lastly I doe make and hearby apoynt my sonn peniell tictcomb to be my hair to inioy all my land and housing and all my Estat beseids whom I doe here by apoynt my holle and solle executor to reseue all my estat in lands goods and depts whom I doe order and apoynt by this my will to pay all my depts that I doth owe and all the legasies that I haue giuen acording to the true entent of this my will: and that this is my last will and testimen hauing my perfecht memory and vnderstanding witnes my hand. I ad to what is aboue writen before my sining hear of that in Case my hair shuld deseas without Children all my land and howsing shuld be poseased and inioyed by my sonne benaya otherwise benomine or by the next Elldest survising att the death of my sonne peniall whom I haue apoynted my hair by this my will as witnes my hand in presenc of richard bartlut sen[r] and thomas bartlut eaighteinth day of sebtember one thouson six hundred seuenty and six."

William Titcomb

Witness: Richard bartlet, Thomus Bartlet.
Proved in Ipswich court Sept. 26, 1676 by the witnesses.

Inventory of the estate of William Titcomb late of Newbury, deceased Sept. 24, 1676, taken Sept. 26, 1676 by Anthony Somerby, John Bartlett, Sr., Samuell Plumer, Sr. and Richard Bartlet, Sr.: his house, Barne & thirty two acres & halfe of upland and two freeholds, 200li.; 30 acres of salt

marsh meadow, 150li.; three plumb Iland Lotts, 50li.; five
acres in Birchen meadows, 20li.; foure oxen, 22li.; five cows,
20li.; one yerling heifer & a calfe, 2li.; thirty sheep, 12li.; 12
swyne great & small, 7li.; corne in the barne of barly Rye
pease & wheat, 16li.; Indian Corne on the ground, 8li.; Hay,
9li.; his wearing apparrell, 10li.; one featherbed, 2 flock beds
& furniture, 15li.; Brasse & pewter & Iron pots & kettles &
warming pan, 6li.; old Indian corne, 2li. 10s.; 2 chests, 1li.
10s.; two ploughs, 2 chaines & a paire of wheels, 2li.; carpenters Tooles, Hooes & sithes, 2li. 10s.; pott hangers, 2 cottrells,
pr. of Andirons, Tongs & fire shovell, 1li. 10s.; buckets,
trayes, keilers, Tubs, hogsheds & other lumber, 2li.; beetle
Rings, felling Axe, 4 wedges, &c., 12s; Debts due to the deceased, 270li.; total, 829li. 12s.

Attested in Ipswich court Sept. 26, 1676 by Peniall Titcombe executor of the estate of his father Wm. Titcombe.

Essex County Probate Files, Docket 27,743.

ESTATE OF JOHN DAVIS OF NEWBURY.

"The will of the deceased was a Noncupatiue will He desired that his debts might be paid and that his son John
might haue four pounds, which he borrowed of him, and that
the rest of his estate may be left in his wiues hands so long
as she liues she paying twelue pence a peice to her other foure
sons & also to his daughter & his wife to dispose of what is
left to his children at her death."

[no signature]
Witness: Tho. Brown, Anthony Somerby.

Inventory of the estate of John Davis, deceased Nov. 12,
1675, taken Nov. 16, 1675 by Anthony Somerby and Samuell
(his ♒ mark) Poore: a mare, 3li.; two cowes, 7li. 10s.; a
cow and a 3 yerling heifer, 6li. 10s.; three 2 yerlings one of
them a steere, 6li.; one yerling calfe, 1li.; Eleven sheep, 4li.;
of corne in the barne, Rye, barly, oats & Indian, 12li.; Hay,
6li.; five small swyne, 1li. 10s.; cart & wheels, sled, 2 chaynes,
plow & irons, 3 yoakes, 2 hooes, 3 prongs, harrow & *sider
trough,* 4li.; a cannoe, 1li.; his wearing apparrell, 13li.; three
beds, six blanckets, 2 coverletts, 6li.; two Iron potts & pott
hookes, tramel, spit, pr. of Andirons, tongs, box of Irrons,
gridiron, 2li. 15s.; musket, 2 swords & belts, 2pd. of powder,
2li. 15s., 2 pr. of bullet mouls, worme scowrer, 42 bullets, 2li.
15s.; In provisions, 4li.; two *chests,* a powdering tub, 2 barells, 2 boxes, meale tub & trough, buking tub, three chayres &
other lumber, keeler, 4 trayes, 1li. 10s.; two bucketts, 4 seives,

wooden morter, three wheeles, cart rope & pr. of cards, 1li.
2s.; an hower glasse & a bible, 11s.; 3 small hamers, pinssers,
2 seithes, 2 axes, 3 booreers, shave, crosscut saw, froo, beetle,
4 wedges, mortessing axe, peck measure, 2 meale baggs, a
hayre bag, 4 sickles & 4 hooks, 2li. 15s.; a quart pot of pewter & a pint pot & a pewter candlesticke & pewter dish, 12s.;
3 ladders, a double breaker, 2 Churnes, 2 doore locks, a frying
pan, 1li. 4s.; An Iron bar, trowel & lumber, 8s.; sheeps wooll,
1li.; total, 80li. 2s.   The debts of the deceased: to Capt. Gerrish about 4li. 16s.; Mr. Thos. Woodbridg about 3li. 15s.;
Capt. White about 2li. 10s.; Richard Kent about, 1li. 4s.;
widdow Moody, 2li. 10s.; total, 14li. 15s.

Attested in Ipswich court Sept. 26, 1676 by Elnor Davis
widow, and administratrix of her husband's estate.

Essex County Probate Files, Docket 7,280.

ESTATE OF CAPT. SAMUEL BROCKLEBANK OF ROWLEY.

Inventory of the estate of Capt. Samuell Brocklebank
taken by Maxemillian Jewett, Ezekil Northend and Nehemiah Jewett: House & homestead with killne, Barne & Lott
9 Acers, 80li.; The Farme towards Bradford, 150li.; 11 Acers
of upland at Towne End towards Mill, 22li.; 4 Acers of Cow-
bridg marsh, 8li.; 2 Acers of marsh at Oyster poynt, 8li.; 2
Acers of marsh at stackyard, 10li.; Salt marsh at Mr. Nelsons
Isleand, 10li.; Hog Isleand Gate marsh, 10li.; Highway
marsh, 5li.; 1 Acer 1-4 at Batchelor meadow, 2li.; 4 Acers of
upland in the Marsh farme, 8li.; 5 Acers of upland at Long
hill, 5li.; total, 318li.   2 Oxen, 10li.; 4 stears, 14li.; 1 Bull
4 yr. old, 3li. 10s.; 1 Bull 2 yr. old, 2li.; 5 Cowes, 15li.; 3 two
yr. olds, 6li.; 2 yearlings, 2li.; 2 Horses, 6li.; 2 mares, 4li.; a
two year old Colt, 1li.; 2 yearling Colts, 1li. 10s.; 12 sheep &
2 Lambs, 4li.; 8 Hogs, 4li.; Bookes, 1li.; Mony & Apparrell,
5li.; sheets, pillowbears & Napkins, 3li.; Beds, beding & bedsteads, 15li.; Hemp, wool & flax, 2li.; Brass warming pan,
kettls, skilletts, brass potts, 2 frying pans, 3li. 11s.; peuter,
1li. 12s.; 2 Iron potts, morter & pestle, 1li. 3s.; Andirons, Tramills, Lamps, pott hooks, fire pan & tongs, trevet,
1li. 5s.; Barrills, Tubs, traies, Basketts & other Lumber, 1li.;
Table, chaires, cushins, chest & boxes, 15s.; Cart, plows &
Irons, cheins, Axes, yoaks & other utensels for Husbandry,
5li.; screen, Haircloth & measures, 1li. 5s.; Bricks, 5li.; corne
& baggs, 1li. 10s.; two Guns, 1li. 10s.; 8 Acers of Land at
Bradford, 2li.; total, 442li. 11s.

Debts due to Mrcht. Wainwright, 3li.; to Henry Rylay, 4li.

10s.; the Colledg, 2li.; Thomas Leaver, 10s.; Leonard Herriman, 14s.; Jno. Pearson, Sr., 10s.; James Barker, Sr., 1li.
14s.; Mr. Wade, Gd. Pearce, Gd. Russ, Gd. Howard, 1li. 7s.;
Mr. Anthonie Stoddar, 2li. 3s. 6d.; Goodman Woodin, 1li.
5s.; total, 17li. 13s. 6d. Estate Cr. to Ralph Hall, 13li. 16s.;
Joseph Williams, 5li. 5s.; what is due for Country service,
4li. 3s.; total, 23li. 4s.

Attested in Ipswich court 26:7:1676 by Hanah Brockle-
banke administratrix of the estate of her husband.

The court 26:7:1676, ordered the distribution of the estate as follows: to Samuel Brocklebank, 80li., and lands to
the rest of the children, viz. Joseph, Hannah, Elizabeth,
Mary, Sarah and Jane, to each 40li. as they come to age or
marriage, Joseph to have his portion in lands. The rest of the
estate to the widow and all the lands are bound for the payment of the said portions.

The agreement dated Oct. 9, 1701, of the children
of Capt. Samuel Brocklebank and Hanah his wife
late of Rowley, deceased, concerning the division of the estate they left: to Samuel Brocklebank the eldest son, the farm
in Rowley about five miles from the meeting house, which he
now dwelleth upon; to John Stickney, one halfe of the twenty
two acres by Kilburns and half the eight acres by the little
pond towards Bradford, eleven acres of upland joining upon
the west end ox pasture and four acres of land in the comon
feilds; to William Dole, one half the twenty two acres by Kilburns, one half the eight acres by the little pond towards
Bradford and four acres of the Cowbridge marsh; to John
Tod, two acres of marsh at hog Island, two acres of marsh at
Oyster Point and a commonage; to Nathaniel Coffin, one
third of the marsh at Nelson Island and four ninths of the
lot of land south of Long hill; to Abiell Somerby, two thirds
of the marsh at Nelson Island and five ninths of the lot of
land south of Long hill; to Joseph Brocklebank the youngest
son, the house and land on the same side of the way as the
house, twenty eight acres in the west end ox pasture for the
40li. allowed him for his portion, and the house lot on the
other side of the way against the how and the marsh called
Stack yard marsh about two acres, allways provided that he
live to want it for his maintenance or if he leave a child, but
if he die before he want it for maintenance, or if he leave no
child, then the house lots and Stack yard marsh is to return
to the five sisters or to their children, Joseph is also to have
one freehold.

Signed by Joseph (his X mark) Brocklebank, Samuell
Brocklebank, Sarah Coffin, Jane (her X mark) Sumerby,
John Sticknee, William Dole, John Todd, Nathaniel Coffin,
Abiel Somerby.
Witness: Samuell Platts, John Higginson, 3d.
Acknowledged Oct. 13, 1701 by the subscribers before the
Hon. Jonathan Corwin, Esq. and Oct. 13, 1702 the agreement
was allowed.

Essex County Probate Files, Docket 3,388.

ESTATE OF GILBERT WILFORD OF HAVERHILL.

The relations of Gilbert Wilford of Haverhill not appearing to take administration of his estate, no executor being appointed by any will of said Willford's, upon motion of Capt.
John Whipple of Ipswich, he was appointed Nov. 14, 1676,
administrator and was ordered to bring in an inventory to
the next Norfolk court.

Salisbury Quarterly Court Records, vol. 2, leaf 66.

Inventory of the estate of Gilberd Wilford taken July 28,
1676 by Henry Palmer and Robert Ford: a dwelling house
unfinished, 10li.; five acres of broken up land neare ye house,
15li.; 30 acres of wilderness land neare ye house, 30li.; two
cowes, 6li.; a two yeare old steire, 2li.; a three yeare old
heiffer, 3li.; a horse, 4li.; an Iron pot & a little brass pott,
10s.; two axes, 5s.; a yoke & cheyne, 10s.; an Iron tramell &
skillett, 6s.; two spining wheels & cards, 10s.; tubbs, kivers &
barrills, 12s.; Indian corne upon ye ground, 1li. 10s.; two
ploughs & plough irons, 1li.; two sickles, 2s.; bedding &
bookes & wareing clothes, 2li.; an old frying pan, 1s. 6d.;
total, 75li. 6s. 6d.

Debts as appears to be due from ye estate as per a note of
particulars: Mr. Wainewright, 5li. 3s.; Capt. Saltonstall,
17s.; Mr. Walker, 4li. 1s.; Josiah Gage, 1li. 16s.; Nathll.
Clarke of Nuberie, 1li. 12s.; Ensigne Chandler, 3li. 8s. 2d.;
Robert Eyers, 12s.; Henry Palmer, 7s.; Richd. Swan, 1li. 5s.;
Jno. Light, 2li. 4s. 1d.; Jno. Simons, 10s. 8d.; Decon
Goodhu, 14s. 6d.; Joseph Plumer, 1li. 4s.; Good. Haseltine,
rates, 1li. 2s.; Jno. Haseltine, 4s. 6d.; James Kinsbery, 12s.;
Cornet Whipple, 42li. 12s. 7d.; for charges of going to the
court, 6s.; for entring administracon & copi of it, 1s. 6d.; for
recording ye inventory, 2s.; total, 68li. 15s. The widow had
for necessarie maintenance for herselfe & children before ye
administrator entered, 6li.; ye 3d part of ye land wch ye

widow challengeth wch ye administrator is not charged with.
Attested in Salisbury court Apr. 10, 1677 by Capt. John
Whipple.

Copy, Norfolk Deeds, vol. 3, part 2, page 29.

Upon motion of Capt John Whipple of Ipswich, administrator of the estate of Gilbert Willford, court Oct.
9, 1677, or-
dered him to make publication according to law at the several places mentioned of the death of said Wilford, and that
his estate is looked upon as being insolvent, so that the creditors might be satisfied. Capt. Jno. Appleton, Deacon Wm.
Goodhue and Sergt. Tho. Waite of Ipswich were appointed a
committee to hear the claims of the creditors at said Whipple's house in Ipswich and settle them.

Hampton Quarterly Court Records, vol. 2, leaf 55.

According to the appointment of the court held at Hampton Oct. 9, 1677, John Appleton, William Goodhue and
Thomas Waite met together Sept. 21, 1678, about the estate of
Gilbert Wilford and find many bills brought in, some they do
approve of and others that have no proof. The following
judged legally due: Capt. John Whipple, 42li. 12s. 7d.;
Francis Wainwright, 4li. 11s. 2d.; Constable of Bradford for
10 rates, 1li. 18s. 2d.; Ensigne Chandler of Andevor, 3li. 16s.
2d.; Deacon Wm. Goodhue, 14s. 11d.; Mr. Jonathan Wade,
18s.; total, 54li. 11s. Other bills not proved legally: Shuball
Walker, 4li. 1s.; Jno. Light, 2li. 4s. 1d.; Jno. Simonds, 10s.;
Richard Swan, 1li.; James Kingsbury, 12s.; Josiah Gage, 1li.
16s.; Nathaniel Clarke, 1li. 12s.; Joseph Plumer, 18s. 6d.;
Robt. Eyres, 12s.; Henery Palmer, 6s. 6d.; Capt. Dudlay
Bradstreet, 1li. 10s.; Mr. Habaccock Glover, 8li.; Capt.
Nathl. Salstonstall, 17s.

The court having considered the return of the committee
and finding according to the inventory of the estate, ye widow's thirds being by it declared to be deducted, that the estate falls short of the sum that the debts amount unto, it was
ordered Oct. 8, 1678, that the administrator pay the debts
allowed of by the committee, Capt. John Appleton, Deacon
Wm. Goodhew and Serg. Thomas Waite, deducting 2s. upon
the pound and according to that proportion upon all the debts
allowed of.

Essex County Probate Files, Docket 29,865.

ESTATE OF THOMAS DOW OF HAVERHILL.

"June 16 1676 the last will and testament of thomas dow
being of perfect memory doe here mak my last will as fol-

loweth first my desire is that all my debts may be satisfyed which I haue made knowne to my unkell biniamin kimbole whom I doe desire and constitut to be my overseer first I giue my eldest sone to Joan haseltine the wif of John haseltine till he be 21 yeares of age but if she dyes before he coms to ye age of 21 yeares then her sone John haseltine shall haue the remainder of his time now for the satisfying of my debts I leaue my whole estate to my unkell beniamine kimbole and when my debts ar satisfyed then what remaines of my estate to remaine to my wif during her natural life but if she marry then she to haue what two men shall judg yearly payd hur by my sonn whom I make my heire of all the land that shal remaine but my wife shal haue *noth[ing]* to doe with any of my land these two men to be chosen one by my wife the other by my sone or Joan haseltin or John haseltin her son & I doe likwise enjoine my sone to giue unto my daughter when he comes to posese this land so much as shalbe judged by two men chosen by them or if my wife be with child now when I dy to haue the like only my will is that my sone shal haue a double portion if my children all dy without marying then what land remains to remaine one half to my wife if liueing the other halfe to my brother steuen dow and my sister mary. and martha ore theire children."

Thomas (his' I mark) dowe (SEAL)

Witness: henry palmer, William White.

Presented in Salisbury court Nov. 14, 1676, and an order made upon it, no executor appearing administration was granted to Henry Kemball of Haverhill.

Inventory taken July 4, 1676 by Daniel Hendrick and Robert Ford: ye House and orchad and Improved and ye unimproved land, it being about Eighty Ecers, 120li.; one Hors, 5li.; one steer, 3li.; tow Colts, 2li.; tow Swine, one Swine more, 1li. 6s.; tow Calves, 16s.; one Saw and to Axes, 14s.; one ax mor, 3s.; one wedge, a paire of bittle Rings and one froo, 7s.; a pike, 5s.; one tub, one barrell, 3s.; tow pots and a little Cettle, 12s.; a bedsteed, 5s.; sled and a yoke and Hookes, 8s. 6d.; one old Saddle, 5s.; a peece of meadow, 3li.; spining wheel, a paire of Cards and in wooden trad, 6s.; beden, 1li.; a paire of shoes, 3s.; Due from Daniell brodley to ye estate of ye Deceased, 2li. 3s.; Due from gilbord wilford to ye estate, 1li. 10s.; total, 148li. 6s. 6d.

Attested in Salisbury court Nov. 14, 1676 by Henry Kemball as administrator.

The account of the debts of Thomas Dow: to Leuft. Brown of Haverhill, 4li. 15s.; Mr. John Knight of New-' bury, 8li.; Capt. Saltonstall, 11s. 6d.; Samuel Stickne and the weddow gage, 11li.; Capt. Geresh of Newbery, 3li. 6s.; Capt. Dudle Brodstreet, 1li. 10s.; his beuriell the hole charge, 18s. 6d.; John Perle, 1li. 10s.; Thomas Estman, 5li.; Nath. gage, 5s.; Beniemin Kimball, 5li.; Samuell Lad, 6s.; Robert Ford, 7s.; Steven Webster as constable, 16s.; Robert Clemments for ratts, 17s. 6d.; Robert Clements for debts, 10s.; Edward brommag, 2s. 6d.

Presented in Salisbury court Apr. 9, 1678 by Henry Kimbal to be added to the inventory of Thomas Dow.

Henry Palmer, Ensign Pecker and Tho. Whittier were appointed a committee to meet at sd. Palmer's house to proceed according as is ordered in ye case of Capt. Jno. Whipeles, Hampton court Oct. 1677.

Essex County Probate Files, Docket 8,236.

Henry Kemball of Haverhill was appointed administrator of the estate of Tho. Dow. deceased, and was ordered Nov. 14, 1676 to proceed according to the mind of deceased as by a paper presented as a will, dated June 16, 1676, and witnessed by Henry Palmer and William White, except that the widow should have her thirds according to law or what her husband allowed if the estate were sufficient.

Salisbury Quarterly Court Records, vol. 2, leaf 67.

Upon motion of Henry Kimball, administrator of the estate of Tho. Dow, court July 15, 1678, ordered him to make publication according to law at Boston. Bradford, Haverhill and Amesbury of the death of said Dow and that his estate is insolvent, in order that the creditors may present their debts before Henry Palmer, Ensign Pecker and Tho. Whittier at said Palmer's house, who were appointed to hear the claims.

Salisbury Quarterly Court Records, vol. 2, leaf 89.

Petition of Henry Kimble administrator to the estate of Thomas Dow of Haverhill, deceased, to the court at Boston May 11, 1681, for power to sell so much of the land as will pay the debts of the deceased.

The court May 18, 1681 granted the petition of the administrator and he to take the advice of L^t. Browne and Wm. White of Haverhill and make return of his acts to any County Court in Essex for their approbation. Edward Rawson, Sec.

Mass. Archives, vol. 16, papers 210-211.

ESTATE OF THOMAS CARTER OF SALISBURY.

"October y⁰ 30ᵗʰ 1676 In yᵉ name of God Amen I Tho:
Carter of yᵉ town of Salisbury in yᵉ County of norfolk, Mas-
sechusets Collony in New england being weake of body butt
of pfect memorie doe make this my last will & Testamᵗ as followeth, revoking all former wills by mee made: either by
word or wrighting Imprimis I doe giue & bequeath my Soule
vnto allmighty God my maker: in hope of mercy & pardon
of my Sinns through the infinite merritts & Satisfaccon of
Jesus Christ my Savioʳ & blessed redeemer: & my body to yᵉ
earth from whence it was taken to bee decently buried as to
my Executrix Heare after named shalbe thought meet: And
as for my worldly goods wᶜʰ yᵉ Lord in mercy hath lent vnto
mee: my will is yᵗ my honest debts being first payd & my funerall expences discharged: yᵗ yᵉ remaynder of my estate be
disposd of as followeth first I giue vnto my beloued wyfe yᵉ
vse & impumt of all my lands meddow marsh & upland: &
howsing duering her naturall life: pvided alwayes: yᵗ if shee
marry againe: then one halfe of all my sd lands marsh &
meadow: shalbe delivered vnto my two sonns forthwith shee:
to choose wᶜʰ halfe she thinks good to haue: Itt. I giue to my
sone Jn° Carter all my howsing & yᵉ one full half part of all
my upland: i: e: yᵗ halfe lyng next to yᵉ land of Joseph Norton & will: Brown: to rang fro yᵉ Pawwaus river up to yᵉ
high way also I do giue vnto my sd Son Jn°: yᵉ one full &
compleat half part of my great division ‖of land‖ aboue yᵉ
mill: as also all yᵗ part of my marsh att brushie Iland. wᶜʰ
lieth on yᵗ side of yᵉ dead Creek next to goodman Busels
marsh lot up to a Spring by yⁿ side of yⁿ beach as also my
adicon of yᵉ first higle dee pigledee: lot of Salt marsh liing
next: Jn° Cloughˢ: as also: my two acre lott of marsh liing
at a place cald yⁿ rocks as also all my lott of marsh in yᵉ bare-
berry meadow ‖wᵗʰ yᵉ adicon‖ liing between yᵉ lotts of Tho:
Mudget & Jn°. Clough: as also: yᵗ lott of marsh neare fox
Island wᶜʰ I exchangd wᵗʰ Oneze: Page: for my lott att mʳ
Halls farme: as also three cow comonages wᵗʰ all after divisions belonging thervnto Itt: I do giue & bequeath vnto my
Sone Samᵘ: Carter: yᵉ other half part of my upland: next:
mʳ Bradburies land: as also yᵉ one full halfe part of my great
division of land aboue yᵉ mill. As also my Six acre lott of
cow comon marsh:: & three Cowes comonages: & yᵉ remaynder of my marsh lot at yᵉ beach vpon yᵉ northermost side of yᵉ
dead creek next to brushie Iland/
"It: I do giue & bequeath vnto my daughter Mary fiue

povnd: wch my will is shalbe payd vnto her by my Son Jn°
out of w^t estate I haue giuen vnto him: when my sd Son:
shall come to y^e ‖ful‖ possession of his estate bequeathed vnto
him: to bee made: in good pay att comon price It I do giue
& bequeath vnto my daughter Martha: fiue povnd to be payd
by my Executrix w^{th}in twelue months after my decease in some
good pay att: comon price: It: I do giue & bequeath vnto my
daughter Elizabeth fiue povnd, to be payd vnto her by my
Executrix wth in twelue months after my decease in good pay
at comon price. Itt: I giue & bequeath vnto my daughter
Abigail fiue povnd to be payd vnto her by my Executrix w^{th}
in thelue months after my decease to be payd in good pay att
comon price It: I giue & bequeath vnto my daughter Sarah
ten pound: fiue povnd of it: to bee payd vnto her by my Sone
Sam^{ll}. when he shall come vnto ye full possession of his estate
bequeathed vnto him in good pay att comon price: & ye other
fiue povnd to bee payd vnto her by my Executrix wth in:
twelue months after my decease Itt: I do appoint my welbeloved wife Mary Carter sole Executrix vnto this my last will
& Testam^t & In wittness: vnto this my last will & Testam^t: I
haue here vnto sett my hand & Seale ye day & yeare first aboue
written :"
                Tho: (his T mark) Carter (SEAL)
    Witness: Tho: Bradbury, William Buswel.
    Proved in Salisbury court 14:9m:1676 by the witnesses.

    Inventory taken 13:9m:1676 by Samll. Felloes, Sr. and
Ephraim Winsley: his aparell, 3li.; thre beds and furniture
thereto belonging, 15li.; two iron potts, a warming pan and
two pewter platters, 1li. 10s.; other houshold stuff, 3li. 10s.;
Indian Corne, 4li. 10s.; English corne, 3li. 10s.; Cart, plow,
cheines and other iron tooles, 3li. 5s.; thre oxen, 14li.; 4
Cows, 12li.; 3 yearlings, 5li.; 3 calves, 1li. 10s.; mare, bridle,
and sadle, 2li. 5s.; 12 shepe, 4li.; 8 swine, 5li.; houseing and
ye land adjoining therreto and comonage, 110li.; 16 acres
meadow, 50li.; a peice of outland aboue ye mill, 5li.; in armes,
1li. 6s.; 20li. of sheeps wooll, 14s.; total, 245li.
    Attested in Salisbury court 14:9m:1676 by Mary Carter.
        Essex County Probate Files, Docket 4,796.

ESTATE OF RICHARD GOODALE OF SALISBURY.

    "In ye name of god Amen I Richard Goodale of ye Towne
of Salisbury seny^r in ye County of norfolke Masachusets in
New england being in good health and of pfect memory

praises be giuen to god for ye same knowing ye vncertainty of
this life and being willing to settle things in order conserning
such things as ye lord hath in mercy lent me I make this my
last will and Testam^t vz Im^t I doe hereby frustrat and make
void all wills formerly per me made Im^t I doe giue and bequeath my body to ye earth from whence it was taken and my
soule to god who gaue it assuredly beleiueing ye pardon and
remishon of my sins in and Through ye blod of my lord and
Saviour Jesus Cht Im^t my debts being first payd : I doe hereby
make my beloued wife Mary my sole execut^r of all my estate
as houses lands and w^t ever other estate I leaue for the time
of her life and after her dcease I doe giue and bequeath vnto
my son Nehemiah all my house and lands y^t I am now
possest in ye Towne of Salsbury with all rites and p^rveledges
thervnto belonging and also w^t stock is remaining execepting
my   division   of vpland   being   my   share   and   ppor-
tion of ye devision of the fiue hundred acres being layd out for
twenty acres be it more or less as it is layd out and bounded
being in two pcels a loott of march being a Cow Comon loott
wch two divisions of vpland and march I doe giue and bequeath vnto my son Richard and also y^t halfe of Comon right
wch was my ffather Richard Goodales all laying and being in
y^c Towneship of Salsbury Also I doe giue and bequeath vnto
my son Richard all my land y^t I am now possest of att kanect-
ticutt ‖laying and being in y^c township of midletowne‖ with
all ye rights and p^rveledges therevnto belonging and also all
my working tooles att my decease to be his and the best bed,
and furniture therevnto belonging att ye decease of my wife
Also I doe giue and bequeath vnto son Nehemiah all my share
of my kech cald vnity being thre eights also my son Nehemiah
is to pay vnto my thre daughters twenty pounds apeice when
he is possest of ye abouesd estate after ye decease of my wife
wch I haue given him in ye first yeare to pay vnto my daughter Mary ye wife of John Ewell twenty pounds in corne or
Cattle att mony price in ye second yeare after ye decease of
my wife to pay to my daughter Elizabeth ye wife of Jeremia
Tower twenty pounds in corne or cattle att mony price and in
ye third yeare after my wifes decease to pay to my daughter
Martha ye wife of John Gill twenty pounds in corne or cattle
att mony price and for the rest of ye moueables to be parted
equally alike among all my children
  "Memorandm Im^t my will and meaning is y^t if any of my
thre daughters dye then the legacie giuen them is to be payd
vnto their heirs and if any of them dye without heirs then

their legacie is to be payd to ye children of ‖my‖ other daughters this third day of ffebruary in ye yeare of our lord one Thousand six hundred and seaventy and thre wittness my hand and Seale."

Richard Gooddall (SEAL)

Witness: Ephraim Winsley, Mary (her M mark) Winsley, Mary (her No mark) Greley.

Proved in Salisbury court 14:9m:1676 by Ephraim Winsly and Mary his wife.

Inventory taken Sept. 28, 1676 by Ro. Pike and Hen. Browne: a house & barne with ye Land about it being betweene 2 or 3 ackers orchard, 40li.; a pastur containing 3 ackers mor or less lying between ye Land of Henry Browne & John Ilsly in ye Towne, 50li.; a 3 acker Lott planting Lying by henry wheellers pastur, 10li.; his Lott of upland yt was of ye five hundred ackers about 10 acker, 12li.; Thirty ackers of upland above ye mill, 7li. 10s.; a medow Lot at ye beach barrs being accounted 3 ackers, 18li.; 3 ackers higgly pigly Lot at salt marsh, 10li.; a salt marsh Lott at Mundays Pound higly Pigly, 6li.; at ye beach eight score Rod of salt marsh or meddow, 2li.; a six acker Lott of meddow in ye cow comman, 18li.; a bed & Furnettur standing in ye new Roome, 9li.; a bed & Furnetur belonging to it standing above in ye chamber, 6li.; a draw cubberd, 2li.; six pewter platters, 2 plats, 3 porengers, a bole, a cadle cup, a bason, quart pott, a salt & a pint pott, 2li. 10s.; 3 brass ketle, on Irn ketle & an Irne pott, a brass chaffen dish and a brass candle stick and a bell metle morter & Iron pestl, 5li.; a duzn of napkens, 2 table cloths, 1li. 5s.; six pear of sheetts, 3 pr. of pillowbys, 6li.; a cloth coat & sut of clothes, 3li. 10s.; 7 new blak hatts, 2li.; 2 small tabls, 2 chests, 2 boxes, 1li. 5s.; a form, 3 Join stools, 10 chayers, 1li. 6s.; on pear Andiorns, a pear of toungs, a pear of bellows, a spitt & warning pan, 2 pear of tramells, 2 pear of pott hooks, 1li. 8s.; 8 cushins, a pear of stillierds, a basket & Hatt case, 1li. 8s.; frying pann, a coker, baskett, an hower glass, brush, books, and som smal od things in ye new roome, 1li.; a fowlling peece, muskett & a sword, 2li.; 2 oxen, 2 cows, on 3 year old hayfer & on yearling, 23li. 10s.; 3 yews, 2 lambs, 2 swine, 6 smale pigs, 3li. 15s.; on mare, 2li.; 3 eighths of the catch vnity now abroad at sea, 60li.; in mouny, 1li. 10s.; 2 ackers of corne & 6 bushells in house, 6li.; about 7 Load of hay, 4li.; a Trundle bed, 2 spining wheels, sled, yoke, span shakle & bolt & table in ye old Roome, chamber pott & a barell, 1li.; barells, milk vesells, chees presse,

payles, buketts, Latten pans, trenchers, dishes, spoons, &
other such kind of Lumber in ye old Room, 2li. 10s.; 2 axes,
hatchett & his chest of working toolls, 3li. 10s.; 6 bushells &
a grining stone, 1li. 4s.; total, 328li. 1s.

This is only of wt estat he have in Massachusetts as far as
yet appears, but nothing of his estat at Conectecut except only
the Catch of wch the rest of owners Live at Conecticot all but
Nehemyah Goodal who hath an eighth.

Attested in Salisbury court 14 : 9m : 1676 by the widow
Goodale.

Debts due to ye estat from Richard Smith som post &
Rayles as by agreemt.

More that was omitted when the inventory was taken : a
bridle & sadle, o ; a hors coller, o.

Essex County Probate Files, Docket 11,136.

ESTATE OF MATTHIAS BUTTON OF HAVERHILL.*

Upon motion of the administrators of the estate of Mathias
Button that a division of the estate be made, Court Nov. 14,
1676, ordered that the estate be divided into five equal sums,
a part for each child, and that the share to the two daughters
be delivered to their husbands as soon as possible and the
other shares at age or marriage.

Salisbury Quarterly Court Records, vol. 2, leaf 67.

ESTATE OF THOMAS HAWKSWORTH OF SALISBURY.†

Upon motion of Onezephorus Page, that the remainder of
the estate of Tho. Hawksworth, deceased, now left, said Page
having married the only child of said Hawksworth, be settled
upon him as heir to the estate by virtue of his present wife,
court Nov. 14, 1676, ordered that it be so settled.

Salisbury Quarterly Court Records, vol. 2, leaf 66.

GUARDIANSHIP OF JACOB ROWELL OF ANDOVER.‡

George Norton, guardian of Jacob Rowell, was granted 28 :
9 : 1676, power to take into his hands said Rowell's estate
which was ordered to him on 30 : 7 : 1662, at Ipswich court.

Salem Quarterly Court Records, vol. 5, leaf 100.

Bond, dated Nov. 24, 1676, given by George Norton,
Thomas Hart and Samuell Hart of Ipswich, as security for

*See *ante*, vol. 2, page 299.
†See *ante*, vol. 1, page 140.
‡See *ante*, vol. 2, page 389.

the estate of Jacob Rowell.   Sworn, Nov. 24, 1676, before Daniel Denison.

George Norton's petition: that his apprentice ran away from him about 2 years and a quarter before his time, according to indenture, and having an estate valued at 29li. besides some household stuff due to him next May, and petitioner fearing that there might be some fradulent conveyance of it, he asked possession of the said estate as guardian of Jacob Rowill.

Essex County Quarterly Court Files, vol. 26, leaf 12.

Whereas George Norton of "Southfeild in Hamsheer in the Masachusetts Collony" was appointed guardian to Jacob Rowell of Elizabeth Towne in New Jersey and he approving of the same, acquits the said George Norton of what estate of mine he had in his hands and of all debts and demands, in court held 28 : 4m : 1681, and notice to be given to the next court that further order may be taken for allowance of the entry and discharging of said Norton.

Signed June 6, 1681.   Witness: Francis Dane, Dudley Bradstreet.

Salem Quarterly Court Records, vol. 6, leaf 15.

Petition to the court June 28, 1681 of Jacob Rowell, that whereas my father died intestate in 1662 and administration of his estate was granted to my mother, and the estate disposed of by the court according to an agreement made betwixt my father and mother before marriage which was just, as things were then represented to the court, myself then being hardly out of my infancy and my mother not so much taking notice of my future right and now knowing things were not fairly represented to the court, requests a revision of the premises that as the only child of a deceased father I may have my due of his estate; also that they would recall the administration granted to my mother and to invest me with the same, being now of age and the estate wholly my father's.

This court grants power of administration to Jacob Rowell only son of Thomas Rowell of whatever estate of his father's was omitted to be inventoried by Margerye his mother, she being removed out of this jurisdiction.

Essex County Quarterly Court Files, vol. 35, leaf 130.

The inventory* made June 28, 1681 is in Essex County Quarterly Court Files, vol. 35, leaf 131.

*See *ante*, vol. 1, page 395.

ESTATE OF SAMUEL PUTNAM.

Samuell Putnam dying intestate, Elizabeth, the relict, brought in an inventory of his estate 28 : 9 : 1676, and was appointed administratrix.

Inventory of the estate of Samuell Puttnam, deceased, taken Nov. 17, 1676, by Jacob Barney and Joshua Rea: foure Cowes, 11li.; tow steers, 5li. 10s.; three yearleing, 3li.; one horse, 2li. 10s.; Eighteen sheep, 4li. 8s.; one feather Bed & bedsted And Curtains, valins, one Rug, Tow Blainkets, tow par sheets, one pillow, one thinn Rug, 8li.; warring aprell, 5li. 6s. 6d.; seaverell lining, 2li. 17s. 6d.; waring apprel, 5li. 6s. 6d.; Table Cloathe, napkins, with other Linin, 2li. 17s. 6d.; putter, iron & Brasse, 2li. 17s.; Cuberd, Chests & Booxe, 3li.; 26 pound of yarne, 2li. 9d.; 20 pound woolle, 1li.; one gunne, 1li.; one wheell & Chair, hors takell, 7s. 6d.; iron ware, 9s.; five swinne, 1li. 10s.; one Reaper, 16s.; Cottenn wooll, Cheair tow, Tow earthen dishes, plow, 9s.; one Blankett & sive, 11s.; one Chaine & Bible with other things, 1li. 1s.; one hundred ackers of land, 75li.; one halfe of prices medow Being about tenn ackers, 15li.; one house, 5li.; total, 191li. 7s. 3d.

Attested in Salem court 29 : 9 : 1676 by Elizabeth the relict of the deceased.

Essex County Quarterly Court Files, vol. 26, leaf 22.

Nathaniell Putnam, presenting a writing for settling his daughter Elizabeth's estate which was drawn up by the mutual consent of parties concerned, it was allowed 26 : 4 : 1677, and confirmed.

Salem Quarterly Court Records, vol. 5, leaf 107.

Agreement dated Mar. 22, 1676-7, between Nathanell Putnam and his daughter-in-law, Eleisabeth (her ⌐—⌐mark) Putnam : "The said Nathenniell Puttnam hath giuen vnto his daughter The dwelling house with Twelve ackers of land and tow ackers of medow to Bee layed outt Conueniently to the dwelling house for euer allsoe the said nathenniell puttnam doth giue vnto her the fenced feild with the Broken land and all the improuement of itt soe long as she liues, prouied That his daughter pay or Caues to be paide the full summe of twentie pounds in current pay: to hir daughter Eleisabeth Puttnam if she liue to be eighteene yere of age: Alsoe The saide natheinnel puttnam doth giue to his daughter fouer ackers of medow mor in prices medow for her life time And the saide nathennel puttnam doth Consent that his daughter shall haue all the Rest of the estat And he doth giue her his debts. And that the house and land Be made ouer for the paiment of the aboue said twenntey pounds to her Chilld: And the Rest of the land to be att the Aboue said nathennil Puttnams disposeing. the other lands not mentioned are to returne to nathell putnam."

Signed by Nathanel Putnam, Richard (his R mark) Leech, Eleisabath (her⸻mark) Putnam.

Witness: Thomas Fuller, Joshua Rea.

Allowed by the Salem court 27 : 4 : 1677.

Essex County Quarterly Court Files, vol. 26, leaf 127.

ESTATE OF JOHN FULLER.

Administration upon the estate of John Fuller was granted 28 : 9 : 1676 to Rebecka, the relict, and she was ordered to bring in an inventory to the next Salem court.

Salem Quarterly Court Records, vol. 5, leaf 100.

Inventory of the estate of John Fuller deceased 25 : 6m : 1676, taken 8 : 9ber : 1676 by Nathaniell Ingerson and Joshua Rea: wearing apparell, 5li.; 1 fether bed & blanket, 4li., 9li.; 1 rugg, 7 sheetes, 5li., 14 napkins, 40s., 7li.; 4 pr. pillowbeers, 32s., 2 tablecloaths, 6s., 1li. 18s.; pewter & spoones, 20s., a sadle, 26s., 2li. 6s.; 3 cowes, 1 calfe, 10li., 1 horse, gun & sword, 4li. 15s., 14li. 15s.; 1 pot & ketle, 2 wheeles, 21s., 15li. wool, 20li. flax, 21s., 2li. 2s.; 60 bushells of corn, 7li. 10s., smith's tooles & coale, 9li. 10s., 17li.; 1 frying pan & skillet & chest, 15s.; Houses, 5 acres of land, 60li.; 2 bedsteeds with other lumber, 1li. 5s.; debts due to the estate, 6li. 7s.; total, 122li. 8s.

Attested in Salem court 29 : 4 : 1677 by Rebecka the relict of John Fuller.

The petition of Rebecka Fuller wife of John Fuller, deceased, to the court June 27, 1677, that whereas her husband departed this life and made no will, that the estate may thus be settled: her children Elizabeth and Bethia, to have 20li. apiece when they come to age and if either of them die before that time the survivor to have 30li. and the rest to be to herself, and this with the consent of her fathers, Thomas Fuller and John Putnam.

Copy, Essex County Probate Records, vol. 301, page 104.

John Fuller dying intestate, administration upon his estate was granted to Rebecka, his wife, who made oath to an inventory. Court 29:4:1677, approved of the disposal of the estate according to the mutual consent of the persons concerned as appeared by a writing brought in to court.

Salem Quarterly Court Records, vol. 5, leaf 107.

ESTATE OF EPHRAIM SKERRY OF SALEM.

Administration upon the estate of Ephraim Skerry, was granted 28:9:1676, to the relict, who was to bring in an inventory to the next Salem court.

Salem Quarterly Court Records, vol. 5, leaf 102.

Administration upon the estate of Ephraim Scerry, intestate, was granted to Martha, the relict, who brought in an inventory 26:4:1677. Court ordered that the estate remain in the widow's hands, except 30li. which was to be paid to the children of deceased, being daughters, in equal shares, and whereas there were 10li. due to Henry Skerry, sr., he freely gave that to the three children to be equally divided, and their shares to be paid at age or marriage.

Salem Quarterly Court Records, vol. 5, leaf 107.

Inventory taken 19:8:1676, by Francis Skerry and Henry Skerry, jr.: pleate, 5li.; 25 yds. of Carscey at 3s. pr. yd., 3li. 15s.; 22 yrds. Carcsey at 3s. pr. yd., 3li. 6s.; cash, 4li.; 3 holand sheetes, 2li. 5s.; 3 pr. of sheetes, 2li. 10s.; 5 pr. of pilobers, 1li. 11s.; 3 shurts & 4 pr. drawers, 2li.; 5 blew shurts & pr. blew drawers, 12s.; pr. very fine holand pilebers, 1li.; 8 Towles, 10s.; 20 napkens, 1li. 10s.; 4 small table clothes, 10s.; 8 neckcloths, 16s.; 2 pr. of holand sleeves, 8s.; 7 hankerchefers, 7s.; a bed quilt & eastend carpet, 2li.; a great beed, blankets, Ruge, bolsters, pillows & all to it, 11li.; a trickel beed, bolster, Ruge & blanketts, 3li.; a sea beed, two blankets & Ruge, 15s.; all his woolen waring cloths & cloke, 5li.; all his sea cloths, gloves, stockens, shoes, hatt, bible & other small books, 3li.; tinning things, 1li. 8s.; all the peuter things, 2li.; all the brass things, 2li. 16s.; all the Iron things, 1li. 14s.; a chest of drawers, two trunkes, 3 boxes & a chest, 2li. 14s.; a longe Table & 6 Joyn stolls, 1li. 2s.; two letel tables & 8 chayers, 1li.; all the earthen things, 1li. 10s.; two pr. worsted stockings, 5s.; a looking glass & slekston, 6s.; a litel box, two brushes & pr. stillyards, 5s.; a muskett & Cutlash, 1li. 8s.; 3 Sea chests & a case of glases, 1li. 2s.; all the Lumber, 10s.; all the Sea Instruments, 2li. 13s. 9d.; the house & ground, 103li.; three meale bages, 3s.; total, 177li. 11s. 9d. Debts due to ye estate: by Mr. Huske, 2li. 10s.; by Daniell Lunt, 1li.; by Henry Skerry, jr., 18s.; by Robt. Cannon, 18s.

9d.; total, 5li. 6s. 9d. Debts due from the estate: in England, 30li.; to Mr. Boudeth, 5li.; to Mr. Jno. Higgenson, 6li. 19s. 1d.; to Jno. Crumwell, 5li.; to Henry Skerry, sr., 10li.; total, 56li. 19s. 1d.

Allowed in Salem court 26:4:1677 upon oath of the widow Martha.

Essex County Quarterly Court Files, vol. 23, leaf 21.

ESTATE OF MICHAEL LAMBERT.

Michaell Lambert dying intestate, administration of the estate was granted 29:9:1676, to Ellenor, the relict, who made oath to the inventory brought in and was ordered to pay to the four children of the deceased, Michaell, Abigaile, Moses and Rebecca, to the eldest son, 40s., and to the others 20s., payable to the sons at twenty-one years of age and the daughters at eighteen years or at marriage.

Inventory of the estate of Miell Lambard, taken by Thomas Farar and William Bassett: one cow, 3li.; one hors and on mare, 4li.; 8 sheep and 2 lambs, 3li. 14s.; 2 great swin and 3 shouts, 3li. 10s.; 30 bushells of Ingen corn, 4li. 10s.; 9 bushells of barly, 1li. 16s.; 2 bushells of pees, 8s.; 3 bushells of ots, 6s.; 10 bushells of ell corn, 15s.; 4 pare of shetes, 2li. 10s.; pilobars and napkins and touells, 1s.; 12 yards of linsy wolsy cloth, 1li. 10s.; 20 pound of wool, 1li.; wearing clothes and 3 shorts and 1 hat, 1li. 10s.; in beds and beding, 3li. 2s.; 1 cobard, 1li.; 4 chests and 1 box, 15s.; 1 tabel and 2 whells and cards, 1 kneding trof, 15s.; chars and 1 cradl, 12s.; pots and ketells and Iorn ware, 3li. 15s.; putr, earthen ware and wooden weare, 3li. 5s.; flax, 10s.; 1 hous, 5li. Debts, 17s.

Allowed in Salem court 29:9:1676.

Essex County Quarterly Court Files, vol. 26, leaf 23.

ESTATE OF JOHN HUTCHINSON.

Administration on the estate of John Huchenson, intestate, was granted 29:9:1676, to Sarah, the relict, who brought in an inventory, and was ordered to appear at the next Salem court for the ordering of the estate.

Petition of Sarah Huchinson that the estate of her husband John Hutchinson be divided between herself and child; that she have all the moveable goods and the bringing up of the child; that she have all the land until her child was eighteen years of age and then the child to have one-third

part; that at her death to have one part more of all the land
and the other third part to be at her disposing.

Essex County Probate Files, Docket 14,407.

Inventory of the estate of John Hutchison, who deceased
about Aug. 2, 1676, taken Nov. 8, 1676, by Nathaniell Inger-
soll and Joshua Rea: waring apparrell, 6li. 10s.; foure oxen,
18li.; five Cowes, 15li.; two three years old, 5li.; tow yearling,
3li. 10s.; tenn Sheep, 3li. 10s.; five Horskind, 5li.; one Horse,
4li. 10s.; tow Calfes, 1li. 10s.; five Hogges, 3li.; sevenn
pigges, 1li. 15s.; two hundred ackres of land & medow & or-
charde, one house & Barne, ——; in iron, 12s.; one friing
pann, 1 iron pott, 13s.; tow axes & other tooles; 13s.; three
parre Sheettes, 2li.; one wheell, tow pare pillowberes, 10s. 6d.;
napkins, table cloth, 1li. 2s.; Bassen & putter, 17s.; wooden
ware, Cheste, 9s.; one fether bed, 3li. 10s.; woollen yarne &
woolle, 2li.; Rug, Blanketts new Cloath, 2li. 5s.; tow gunnes,
2li. 15s.; yokes, chaine, sheer, coulter, 1li.; cleves & pinn,
foure pillowes, 1li. 3s.; Engling corn & hay, 6li. 10s.; money,
7s.; 100 ackers of land with halfe the houseing In present possesion & 100 ackers of land, Revertion as appeareth By deed of
giffte, 130li. Debts due to the estate, 7li. 14s.; 250 ackrs of
land, 40li.; debts due from the estate, 15li. 10s.; total, 273li.
5s. 6d.

Allowed in Salem court 29 : 9 : 1676.

Essex County Quarterly Court Files, vol. 26, leaf 23.

Sarah, widow and administratrix of her husband John
Hutchenson's estate, petition to the court, dated Jan. 29,
1676, for a division of the estate between herself and her
child, that is, that the child should have one-halfe of the land
when she becomes of age, as may appear by two deeds given
by her father and father-in-law, and that at said Sarah's decease she should have as much of the other halfe as to give
her two-thirds of the whole; that the rest of the estate be for
Sarah's own use, the child to have a feather-bed when of age.
Her father Putnam and father Hutchinson witnessed and
consented to this agreement.

Witness to their consent: James Bayley, Jonathan
Putnam.

Court Mar. 27, 1677, allowed this distribution, Sarah to
bring up the child until she reached the age of eighteen or
marriage.

Essex County Probate Files, Docket 14,407.

ESTATE OF JAMES BROWN OF SALEM.

"The 29 : 11ᵐᵒ. 1674 I James Browne of Salem, being weake of body yet of pfect memory doe make this my last will & testament Impʳs: I giue & bequeath unto my beloued wife Sarah, my dwelling house & out housing, with the ground adjoyning lying heare in Salem, duering her naturall life, and at her decease to be disposed of as followeth, It my will is, that my eldest son John Browne, whoe haue had his portion giuen him formerly, And doe further will & order, of that estate, left by Henry Bright of water Towne, deceased, which is my proper right & due, in consideration of moneys lent to him or paid for him many years agoe, which said estate I leaue my son to recouer all my right & interest in that estate, or that of right doe belong to me, he the said John Browne shall haue the one half there of to himself his heires & assignes, he paying the one halfe of the charge of what he does recouer, & the other halfe of what estate he shall recouer as aforesaid to be to Sarah my said wife & to her heires & assignes for euer.

"It wheare as there are certaine writings drawne betweene my said wife & my son James Browne, bearing date 10 march 1672 : wherein on my wiues pt, all the houseing & land lying in Newbery, Giuen & bequeathed to my said wife, by her father John Cutting deceased in his last will & testament, are made ouer to my said son James Browne, & to his heires for euer, he on his pt paying, p Annum to his mother soe long as shee liues, soe much as is exprest in sd writing, & at her decease to pay or cause to be paid thirty fiue pounds, to be paid for the use of my other children, according as is heare after exprest, which is my will with the mutuall agreement of my said wife.

"It. I giue to my son Samuell, my dwelling house & out houseing with soe much of the ground belonging therevnto, begining next to Samuell pickworth grounds & from thence, northerly, to take in one pole beyond, on the north side of the barne, & soe right cross the ground from the highways to John Gedney deceased his Ground, to haue & inioy the same, to him his heires, & assignes foreuer, next after his mothers decease, he paying fifteene pounds for the use of my daughters, to be deuided as is heare after exsprest, & my will is that my son Samuell shall liue with his mother to be helpfull to her untill he come to yᵉ age of one & twenty yeares

"Item I giue to my son Abraham, about thirty two pole of

the ground belonging to my dwelling house to begin at one pole beyond the barne as aforesaid & to exstend fower pole in bredth next the highway & soe to run right cross ye same Bredth to the land of John Gedney aforesaid, to haue & to Injoy the same, to him his heires & assignes, next after his mothers decease, but in case the said Abraham dept this life befor he come to the age of twenty one yeares, then the said pcell of ground to fale to my son Samuell & further my will is that my son Abraham shalbe under my wiues care & dispose, the time after he haue serued his apprentice ship untill he come to the age of one & twenty yeares.

"It. I giue vnto my said wife Sarah, the rest of the ground, beyond that thirty two pole of ground giuen to my son Abraham, northward, to the ground of John Cromwell, for her to dispose of for the paiment of my debts or for her necessary use the time of her life, & in case she be not necessitated to sell the said land in her life time, for paiment of debts or for her necessary vse, then at her decease my son Abraham shall inioy it, he paying fower fifthes of the value thereof for the use of his fower youngest sisters: viz: Anna: Mary, Abigaile & Martha: equally to be deuided amongst ym or the longest liuers of ym: If any dy before they come to ye age of eighteene years or married

"It further my will is that the thirty fiue pounds, that my son James is to pay & the fifteen pounds that my son Samuell is to pay at their mothers decease, which is fifty pounds, in all be equally deuided amongst my fiue daughters, viz: Sarah Beasly: Anna: Mary, Abigaile & Martha Browne, that is to say ten pound each of them, to be paid at their mothers decease, at ye age of eighteene yeares or marriage, & my will is that in case any of them dy before they come to age or are maryed, then her or theire pt to fale to those of my daughters y^t doe suruiue, to be equally deuided amongst them

"Lastly I giue to my said wife all the rest of my estate when my debts are paid: & doe appoynt her my sole executrix of this my will, & doe appoynt my Brother Nicholas Noyce And Hilliard Veren, sen. to be ouerseers & heerunto I haue set to my hand & seale this 29: of Janury 1674."

James Browne. (SEAL)

Witness: Hilliard Veren, Senr., Samuell Pickworth.

Proved in Salem court 29: 9: 1676 by Hilliard Veren.

Essex County Quarterly Court Files, vol. 26, leaf 24.

Will of James Browne, glazier, was proved 29 : 9 : 1676, and Sarah, the relict and executrix, was ordered to bring in an inventory to the next Salem court.

Salem Quarterly Court Records, vol. 5, leaf 102.

Inventory of the estate of James Browne, sr., who deceased Nov. 3, 1676, taken Nov. 30, 1676, by Nicholas Noyes and Nathaniell Beadle: a dwelling house and barne and aboute 3-4 acre of land in Salam, 100li.; bead and bead stead and all furniture, 5li.; trundell bead and all belonging to it, 10s.; a bybell and other bookes, 10s.; wareing Cloths, 1li. 10s.; 6 Charies and a desck, 18d. a pease, 10s. 6d.; putter, 17s. 6d.; tene ware, 1s. 6d.; a selfeer cupe and spoone, 10s.; a pare of cards, baskit and brush, 2s.; brase things, 12s.; 2 eyrene pouts & 3 weagis and tongs, spade, 1li. 14s. 6d.; woodin ware, 10s.; a uysce and other glasein toulles, 2li.; earthin ware, 1s. 6d.; a bead in ye Chamber and things to it, 2li. 10s.; 2 Cheasts and seattell, 4s.; 6 bushells of Corne, 12s.; 20li. of Corse yarne, 12d. a li., 1li.; Lining, 15s.; total, 119li. 10s. 6d.

James Browne's debts: to Mr. Edmon Batters, 7li. 17s. 3d.; to Goodwife Bonfeild for caring for Mary's Legg, 8li.; to Doctor Wells, 3li.; to Captaine George Corwin, 4li.; to Mr. William Browne, Junior, 4li. 9s. 4d.; to Mr. Jonathan Corwine, 10li. 6s. 8d.; to funerall charges, 2li. 4s.; to Mr. John Higgison, 2li. 10s.; due for Legacies for fower Children wch. Mr. John Cutting gave to his grandchildren & was James Browne's, due to pay, 6li.; to his sonn James Browne, jr., 43li.; total, 101li. 5s. 3d.

Allowed 26 : 4 : 1677 upon oath of Sara, the relict.

Essex County Quarterly Court Files, vol. 26, leaf 25.

Administration granted to James Browne, jr., son of Mr. James Browne, only male heir of his grandfather, Mr. James Browne late of Salem, deceased, on a legacy given to Samuell Browne, son of said deceased, who also deceased without making any disposal of same, and whereas Sarah Browne executrix to the will of said deceased dyed before.

Bond of James Browne, jr. of Newbury, with John Browne of Rowley and Collen Frazer as sureties, for 100li., to administer on a legacy given by his grandfather James Browne late of Salem, deceased, and upon any other part of the estate not bequeathed in his will. Dated Dec. 1, 1707. Witness: John Stangly, Daniel Rogers.

Essex County Probate Files, Docket 3,592.

ESTATE OF CHRISTOPHER WALLER OF SALEM.

"The last Wil and testament of Christopher Waller made the seauenth day of october 1676 I Christopher Waller of Salem although weak in body yet of perfect memory doe thus dispose of my estate and make this as my last Wil and testament: Imprimis I giue vnto Margaret my wife my dwellinge house, my outhouses, and my orchard with al my land therevnto belonginge to be hers and at her disposinge. Item I giue vnto the sayd Margaret my wife my Catle with al my moueable goods that she may be the better enabled to pay my debts. Item I giue vnto Joseph Woodrow ten pounds to [be] payd unto him out of my estate at the age of twenty one yeares he Continuinge to liue with my wife as formerly vnto that age. Item I doe appoynt my wife Margaret to be executrix and my brother in law Nathaniel Felton ouerseer, to this my Last wil and testament."

Christopher (his ⊕ mark) Waller.

Witness: Nathaniel Felton, Edward Berry.

Proved in Salem court 30 : 9 : 1676 by the witnesses and Margeritt, the relict, was ordered to bring in an inventory to the next Salem court.

Essex County Quarterly Court Files, vol. 26, leaf 19.

ESTATE OF JOHN PORTER, SR. OF SALEM.

"In the name of God Amen. I John Porter of Salim Senr. in the Count. of Essex in New England yeom^n. do declare & make my last Will and testam^t. in manner & forme following. Imp^r. my imortall soul I do desire humbly & beleiveingly to comitt unto ye everlasting mercyes of God father, Sonne, & holy Ghost. my body I comitt to ye earth to be decently buried at the discretion of my Xian freinds. And my outward estate I do dispose thereof in manner following. Imp^r. I do constitute & ordeine my loveing wife Mary Porter sole Executrix of this my Will. unto whome I do give the one halfe of all my goods, debts, chattells, & cattell &c. and also dureing her life I do give her one third pt of the yearly vallew of all my houses & lands, or the thirds thereof as the law directeth. To my Sonne Jo Porter who by his Rebellious & wicked practises hath been a great greife to his Parents, & hath greatly wasted my estate, on condiccons hereafter expressed I do give unto him one hundred & fifty pounds in currant pay of ye country at three paym^ts annually i e. fifty pounds p anno. Provided alwayes before the paym^t of any

p^t thereof he ye said Jno. Porter shall make signe & seale
unto my Sonnes ‖Joseph‖ Benjamin & Israell, their heyres
& assignes, or to some one of them ‖in behalfe of ye rest of
my children‖ an absolute & full release of any further clayme
to any pt of my houses & lands whereof I am now possessed,
& in speciall to any pt of y^t necke of land y^t was sometime
m^r Skeltons, & in ye meanetime shall not directly or indi-
rectly make or signe any alienation thereof to any other and
in case ye s^d Jno. Porter shall faile in pformance of this con-
dicion for more then one yeare after my decease, then the
above named legacy of one hundred & fifty pounds shall be
utterly voyd, and in lew yr of I do give him five pounds to be
payd in Country pay within three yeares after my decease at
the discreccon of my Excecutrix. Item, I do give & bequeath
to my Sonne Benjamin Porter these following parcells of
land, namely all that parcell of land comonly called Bishops
farm also two hundred acc^{r}s of land more or less lying in
blind hole, given me by the Towne, also one hundred acres of
land purchased of m^r Broadstreet also five acres of fresh
meadow purchased of Jaffery Massey, also eight acres of
meadow & upland more or less purchased of Wm Necholls &
formerly was a pt of Bishops farme, also ten acc^{r}s of upland
bought of John Hawthorne of Linn. & was formrly appteyneing to Wm Baily also one hundred pounds to be pd in
Country pay at two equall paym^{ts} annually within two yeare
next aftor my decease
"To my daughter Mary the wife of Thomas Gardiner to
whom I haue already done according to my ability, I do give
to her three children forty shillings a peece, and also I do
give to my daughter Mary & to my daughter Sarah to be
equally divided between them, the farme called Smiths farme
conteyneing Eighty acres more or less, & one hundred &
twenty five acres lying between the farme y^t was sometime
Kenistones, & Lawrance Leaches, also ten acres purchased of
M^r. Gotte, and is lying next to Putmans ag^t m^r Downeings
farme, also the above named Kenistones farme, conteyneing
two hundred acc^{r}s more or less, with twenty acres of meadow
appteyneing thereunto. Item. I give & bequeath unto my
Sonne Joseph Porter five pounds to be payd within two
yeares after my decease and forty shillings a peece to each
of his children to be pd at ye same time. To John Porter
Sonne of my sonne Samuel Porter I do give ten pounds to be
payd him at 21 yeares of age It. I do give & bequeath to my
Sonne Israel Porter, my now mansion Place, with all ye hous-

ing thereupon, Orchard & lands adjoyneing vizt. So much as was by mee purchased of m^r Sharp, with all ye appurtenances to ye same belonging, also I do give him sixty acc^{r}s of Skeltons neck. i e. that pt wch I purchased of m^r Skeltons daughters. It. I do give & bequeath to Joseph, Benjamin, & Israel Porter the remainder of Skeltons neck of land, conteyneing 150 acres more or less, and I do order them to make paymt of the one hundred & fifty pounds by mee bequeathed unto my Sonne John Porter. To my sonne Benjamen I do give a parcell of land wch I purchased of m^r Gott. conteyneing eighty acc^{r}s, more or less, and thirty acres purchased of Jacob Barney Junr, and forty acc^{rs} purchased of Jafery Massey, and forty acc^{r}s purchased of Gm. Watson & forty acc^{r}s purchased of Jno. Peckard and my will is that he shall pay to my two daughters Mary & Sarah fifty pounds a peece, vizt. in five years time ten pounds p anno. to each of them. It. I do give to my sonne Israel Porter my interest in the saw mill neer Skeltons neck. It. I give & bequeath to the Reverend m^r John Higgison forty shillings, and to the Poor of Salim five pounds, to be distributed by my overseers, as they shall in their discreccon judge meet. To my wife over & beside w^t is before given her, I do give her my best featherbed, with all appurtenances necessary to compleat ye same, and also five pounds in money and it is my will y^t w^t shee shall spare of y^t p^t of my estate y^t I haue above bequeathed to her, that shee do in speciall wise consider my two daughters. and be helpfull to them in confidenc whereof I haue disposed to her, and to my sonnes my estate as is aboue exp^{r}ssed. To Cornelius Baker, & Jno Glover. I do give forty shillings a peece. to be payd within twelve m^{os}. after my decease in country pay.* finally. I do nominate, & intreate my loveing friends, m^r Edmund Batter & m^r Hilyard Veren, to be the overseers of this my will To whome I do give full power & authourity to determine any doubt or difference y^t may arise conc^{r}neing the true meaning of this my will. & in case any legatee shall refuse to submit thereunto hee or they shall loose all y^r interest therein. and as a toaken of my love & respect to my overseers. I do give them forty shillings a p^c to be p^d in money. In witnes hereof I do hereunto put my hand & seale this 28th day of Aprill. 1673."

John Porter Senr. (SEAL)

Witness: Samuel Danforth, Peter Olliver, Thomas Brattle, Juni^r.

*"And the residue of my goods & chattels not [already] disposed of, I do give & bequeath to my Sonnes Joseph, Ben-

jamen & Israel, & my two daughters Mary & Sarah to be equally divided between them."

These last lines were pt. of the will of Jn°. Porter deced. as appeares in the *fowle* draught & should have been inserted as attest Tho. Danforth, 26 : 7 : 76.

Proved in Ipswich court Sept. 26, 1676 by Peeter Oliver and Thomas Brattell, jr.

Essex County Probate Files, Docket 22,468.

Inventory of the estate of John Porter of Salem, taken Sept. 22, 1676; his dwelling house with the barn, outhouses, orchard and all the land thereunto belonging called Sharp's farme, 600li.; land commonly called Skelton's Neck being 200 acres or thereabouts, 400li.; land called Bishop's farme with the land belonging to it called blinde hole beinge about 500 acres whereof 45 acres meadow, 500li.; land called Smith's farme being about 90 acres 10 acres of it meadow, 90li.; land called Cromwell's farme being about 200 acres, 20 acres of it meadow, 200li.; 130 acres adjoining to Cromwell's farme, 100li.; 10 acres of meddow called Got's meadow, 20li.; 180 acres called Gott's corner, 300li.; 70 acres bought of John Robinson, 40li.; 1 1-2 acre of land neare bass poynt, 5li.; 3 poole of land in the towne, 1li. 10s.; 12 acres bought of John Hathorne, 8li.; 12 acres of barly, 27li.; 2 acres of Pease, 3li.; 1 acre of wheate, 1li. 12s.; 12 acres of Indian corne, 24li.; 33 load of hay, 33li.; 46 ewe sheepe and wethers, fourteen lambes, 25li.; eight oxen, 35li.; fifteen Cowes, 52li. 10s.; nine two yeare old catle, 22li. 10s.; 8 yearleings, 12li.; 2 three yeare qld steirs, 7li.; 10 Calves, 7li. 10s.; 1 bull, 3li.; 14 swine, 21li.; 11 younge shots, 5li. 10s.; 6 mares, 9li. 10s.; 5 horses, 15li.; 2 Colts, 1li. 10s.; 1 younge Calfe, 10s.; a feather bed, bolster, 1 pillow, a payre of sheets, a Rug and blanket, 6li.; a feather bed, 3 bolsters, a coverlet, payre of blankets, 2 pillows, a bedstead, with Curtains and vallens, 8li.; a feather bed and 2 bolsters, 1 Rug, a payre of blankets & pillow, 5li. 10s.; a bed & bolster, 1 Rug, a blanket and payre of sheets, 4li.; 1 bed & bolster & Rug and blanket, 2li.; 1 bed and bolster, 2 Rugs, & 2 blanketts, 3li. 10s.; a bedstead an old Rug and coverlet, a bolster and pillows, 1li. 10s.; 2 Rugs, 3li.; 2 payre of holland sheets, 4li.; 8 payre of sheetes, 8li.; 8 yards of linnen cloth, 1li.; a fine table cloth, 11 Napkins, 6 course napkins, a table cloth, 2 pillow beares, 3li.; 1 old trunke, 1 case botls, a litle truncke, a box and chest, 1li. 10s.; 1 flaggon, 12 platters, 2 potts, 2 old platters, 2 old cups, 2 candlesticks, a salt, an old pestle & morter, 3li.; silver

spoones, a porringer and two spoones, 1li.; 3 brasse pans,
1li.; 2 brasse pots, 2 skillets, 1li.; an iron pot and ketle, 1li.
10s.; 6 keilers, 6 payles, 16s.; 4 hakes, a fire shovel and tongs,
2 spits and a drippinge pan, 1li. 8s.; 6 Cushions, 12s.; 40li.
wollen yerne, 3li.; 60li. sheep's wool, 2li.; 1 Table, 6 joynd
stooles, 1li. 10s.; 1 Carpet, 10s.; 1 old Table and forme, 5s.;
1 Trundle bedstead & Chest, 10s.; 3 Andirons, 1li.; a Chafe-
inge dish & warminge pan, 5s.; a fowlinge peice, 2 muskets,
a Rapier and two swords, 4li.; Chayres, 10s.; 2 broad axes, 6
old axes, a hatchet, 12s.; 5 wedges & betle Rings,
10s.; an iron pot and brasse pan, 1li.; an old
trough and old barrels, 1li.; a thwart saw, 5s.;
2 Carts with yookes and chaynes, 6li. 10s.; 6 plowes,
2li.; 5 forks & a muck forke, 5s.; a harrow, 10s.;
3 Augers, a handsaw, a tenant saw and Ads & iron
Crow, 1li.; 2 sythes, 5s.; old barels & tubs, 1li.; Bookes, 3li.;
2 negro servants, 40li.; 3 Inglish servants, 30li.; his wearinge
apparell, 20li.; total, 2,753li. 5s.

Allowed 30 : 9 : 1676 upon oath of Mary, the relict.

Essex County Quarterly Court Files, vol. 26, leaf 26.

Whereas Benjamin Porter's father Mr. John Porter late of
Salem, in his will gave unto me and my brothers Joseph and
Israel a parcel of land lying in ye township of Salem in a
place known as Skeltons Neck which we improved together,
and my part of said land I disposed of unto my brother Israel
and unto Joseph and Nathanael sons of my brother
Joseph, but no division being perfected and for as much as
my brother Israel in his will hath given me the improvement
of that part given to him during my life and my brother
Joseph's son Joseph being deceased & leaving minors by reason whereof I being disadvantaged on the account of the
land not being divided, these are to petition the court to appoint a committee to divide my part into two equal parts according as disposed of by me to prevent further trouble.

Witnessed by Jonathan Rayment, Joseph Herrick.

John Appleton, Esq., Judge of Probate of Wills, &c. commissioned Capt. Jno. Gardner, Mr. Jona. Rayment, Mr. Jo.
Herrick, jr., Mr. Thorndick Procter & Mr. Thos. Fuller, all
freeholders in the County of Essex, to divide & set out all the
lands belonging unto Mr. Jno. Porter, sr. and to his two sons
Mr. Joseph and Mr. Israel Porter all of Salem, deceased, viz.
The land called Skeltons Neck into so many parts and divisions as are bequeathed in the three respective wills of ye

deceased aforesaid, and to make return to the court. Dated
Mar. 28, 1716. Danl Rogers, Reg^r.

In accordance with the petition of Mr. Benjamin Porter to
have his share of said Neck which he derived from his brother
Israell Porter's will to be divided according to said will the
above committee are impowered to annex this division to
their former commission. Dated April 2, 1716.

The return of the committee appointed, signed by John
Gardner, Jonathan Rayment, Joseph Herrick and Thorndik
Procter and dated July 9, 1716. The division of a neck of land
known as Skeltons Neck to ye Porters hearafter named having respect to the three wills expressed in our commission:
"in observance to ye will of Mr. John Porter Senr. we have set
out Sixty Acres at ye uppermost or northwesterly end of said
neck to Israel Porter ye son of ye abovesaid Jno. Porter And
ye Rest of ye Land in S^d neck we have equally Devided Between the three sons of ye sd. Jno Porter to wit Joseph Benjn
and Israel Porter: Israel to have his Part at ye upper end
Anext his sixty acres first layd out: Benjamin to have ye mid-
dle Part and Joseph ye lowermost or most southeasterly end
of sd Neck.

"In observance to ye will of Mr. Israel Porter we have set
out to Benj^m. Porter Junr Son of Israel Porter ye sixty Acres
and one third Part of ye Remainder of ye neck: which was
Given to Mr. Israel Porter By his father Mr. Jno. Porter as
abouesd. And have set out to Mr. Benj^m. Porter, Sr. one
Sixt Part which was half his third which ye sd Benj^m. gave
to his Brother Israel and Israel in his will Returned to him
again during his life as by Deed and will may apear.

"In observance to ye will of Mr. Joseph Porter we have
laid out together ye remainder of S^d neck of Land which is
one Third and half third into four equal shears for quantity
& quality unto ye Four sons of Mr. Joseph Porter: and then
drew Lots for ye same which came out as followeth: to
Joseph Porter Junrs. Heirs ye uppermost Lot in that Part
ye next was Nathanel The third was Samuels and ye southeast most and last was Williams."

Also have declared and shown "to Capt. Putnum who is
Atorny to ye Gardean of ye children of Joseph Porter junr.
and to ye other three their Parts or Sheares; and thay have
accepted of ye same," and by "consent of all parties concerned we have allowed liberty to pas and repas through
each part for every one of them and their heyers for ever to
come to his sheare or Lot. It is to be understood that ye

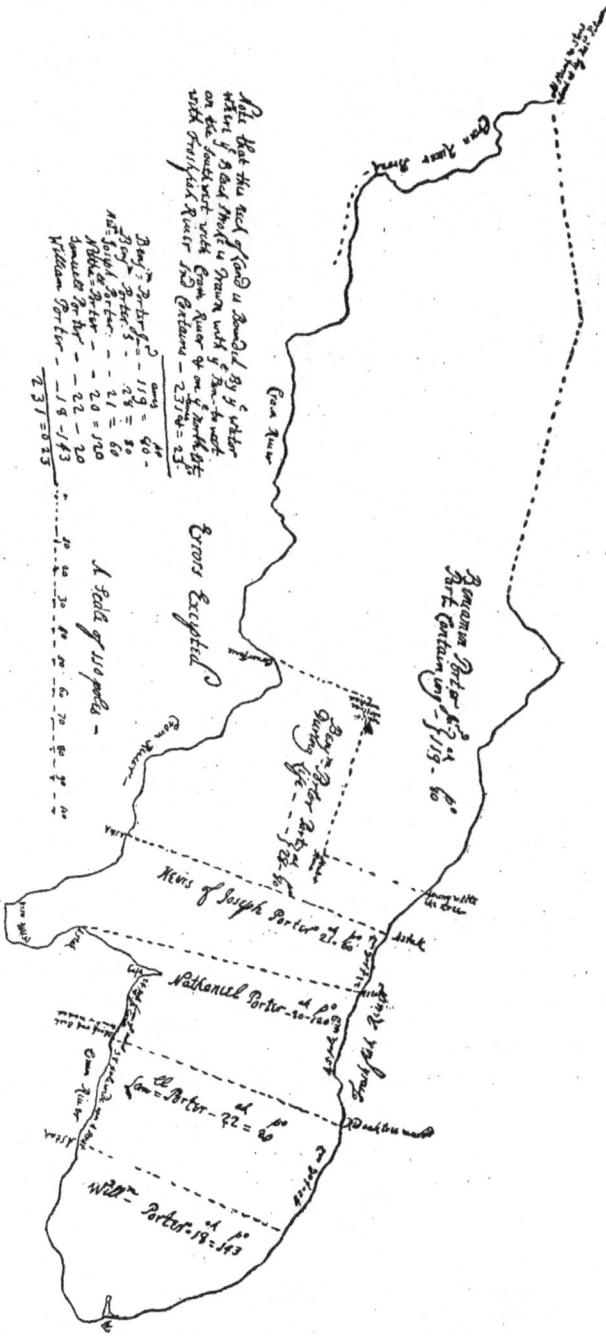

DIVISION OF SKELTON'S NECK.

way or liberty to pass over Benj^m. Porters Junr. Part is to go in at a gate or way By Crain River Bridg."

Account of ye committys work in dividing Skeltons Neck: John Gardner wth ye sarvice in Laying out every Devision as by a Plann given in, 2li. 4s. 8d.; Jonerthon Rayment, 1li. 2s.; Thorndick Prockter, 16s.; Joseph Herick, 16s.; total, 4li. 18s. 8d. Ipswich July 9, 1716. Cost of *Prob.*, 10s., making total, 5li. 8s. 8d.

Joseph heirs to comittee &c., 1li. 3d.; other charges, 17s.; total, 1li. 17s. 3d.

To obtain committee, 1li.; to give County no^ts, 6s.; expenses of comity and all persons attending, 2li. 10s.; expence for ye comity at Ipswich, 12s.; total, 4li. 8s.

The whole charge of ye committee with disbursements come to 9li. 16s. 8d.; an order upon Widow Porter her part of ye charge, 1li. 17s. 3d.

Essex County Probate Files, Docket 22,468.

Estate of Ezekiel Sawyer of Rowley.

Administration upon the estate of Ezkiell Sawyer, intestate, who was slain in the war, was granted on Jan. 11, 1676 to Mary Sawyer, his mother, who was to bring in an inventory to the next Ipswich court.

Ipswich Quarterly Court Records, vol. 5, page 284.

Estate of William Pritchett of Topsfield.

Administration upon the estate of William Pritchett, intestate, was granted Feb. 13, 1676-7, to John Pritchet, his eldest son, who was to bring in an inventory to the next Ipswich court.

Ipswich Quarterly Court Records, vol. 5, page 284.

Inventory of the estate of William Prechard taken 27 : 1 : 1677 by Thomas Chaniler and Thomas Baker: a house and 20 ackers of upland and three ackers and a halfe of medow Lying in topsfield and six ackers of medow in Ipswich in the west medow, 70li.; 4 cows on three yere old and 3 yearlins, 19li.; 2 phather Beeds and 4 rugs, bolsters, 9li.. 5s.; 4 payer of sheets and on ode on and tow pillowbers, 2li. 13s.; jack, wheele, mele trofe, saddle and musket, 2li. 13s.; payer of showse, old putter, tramell and pothoks, 15s.; cotton wheele, iorn pot, a chase, a bocks, a friing pan, 15s. 6d.; old barell, chane, plow tackling, 12s. 9d.; debt deu to the estate, 4li. 15s.; total, 109li. 9s. 3d.

The Land at Broukfild that was my fathers and my Brothers and the quarter part of the mill thire that was my fathers is not put into this envoys. The debts due from the estate: to Majer Pinching, 9li. 5s.; Mr. John Pinching in mony, 11li. 12s.; Samuell Ela in mony, 2li. 11s.; dacken Goodhugh, 4li. 12s.; dacken Knolten, 3li. 11s.; William Howard, 2li. 7s.; Samuell Hart, 6s.; my silfe for charg and exspenc to harford, 3li. 8s.; clothing for my mother, 5li. 15s. 9d.; wintering tow cowse, 1li. 10s.; prisers and records, 7s. 6d.; a debt due to my father denison, 1li. 10s. 10d.; debt due to the marshall, 10s.; total, 47li. 6s. 1d.

Attested in Ipswich court Mar. 27, 1677 by John Pritchet administrator of the estate of his father, Wm. Prichet.

Division of the estate of William Prichard deceased: to the woman, 10li.; to John Prechard, 13li.; to William, Joseph, Elizibeth and Sarih, 6li. 10s. each; to Mary, 2li. 5s.; Hanah, 2li.; Esther, 2li. 3s. The land at Brokefild and mill John to have one half and William and Joseph the other half.

Allowed by the Ipswich court Mar. 27, 1677.

Essex County Probate Files, Docket 22,818.

ESTATE OF THOMAS SKILLIN OF SALEM.

Inventory of the estate of Thomas Skillin, who deceased Dec. 30, 1676, at Salem, appraised by Francis Neale and Hen. Williams: 4 old Blanketts on Bed & Boulster & a pr of Curtaines & on sheet, 4li. 8s.; 6 smal pewter Dishes & 3 pewter plates, 13s.; 1 pewter botle & pewter Cup, 2s.; earthen vessels, 3s.; 2 smootheing Irons, 3s.; 1 Iron pot & an Iron skillet & p of an Irons, 1li. 10s.; wearing Cloaths & 2 p stockins & shoes, and a hat, 3 skives & a smale box, 2li. 4s.; 1 spit, 1 old sword, 1 p of Tongues & a Lampe, 12s.; 4 old Cheares & wooden ware, 5s.; 1 gread Iron, 1 dung forke & a p snow shose, 5s.; 4 Iron weidges, 2 Rings, 2 Iron Tramers, 14s.; old Iron & 6 old bags, 1 bushell of Indyan, 1li.; 6li. of sheeps woole & 15¹¹ & ½ of yearne, 1li. 16s.; 1 frying pan & Lataine ware, 5s.; 1 old flocke bed & old Nailes & 2 old bibles, 1li.; beefe, porke, fish, 1 Cannow, 1 brase spun & 2 pecks, 2 old wheles, 1 barrell & a shoot bag & horn, 2li. 3s.; total, 17li. 3s. Goods Leift in Boston, 2 gunns, 2 Indyan swords, 1 frying pan, old Lins, 1 smal Iron pot, 2 or 3li. feathers & about 60li. of shote; 32li. of Lead, 1 grindstone, 1 bar. & 1-2 of Lead. In Piscatequa, 1-2 a barrell of melases, 2 hogshead of salte, one beare skin.

Allowed, Mar. 14, 1676-7, upon oath of Mary, his wife, by the Worshipfull Samll. Symonds, Dep. Gov., and Edward Tinge, who appointed her administratrix.

Essex County Quarterly Court Files, vol. 26, leaf 75.

ESTATE OF ELIZABETH HARDING.

"7th: of: 6: moneth 1654 The Last will and Testament of Elizabeth Harding being weake of Body but of pfect memory blesed be god Imprs I Bequeath to my sone Joseph Harding my now dwelling house and the two acres of Land together with the ten acres of vpland in south feild that which was mr skelltons together with the one halfe of the Catch Called the Guift that the said Joseph is now in prvided that he pay to mr Gafford twenty fower pounds starlinge Item I Giue my sone Joseph the table board and forme in the parlor I giue to my son Joseph Hardinge one Cow. Item I giue unto my daughter Elizabeth Hascall that pt of house and Land I bought of mr Garford to be at her proper disposing without haueing any Relation to her Husbands Leaue in it and one Cow according to the donation of house and land as abouesaid and I giue to my son in law Roger two Cowes Item I giue to my daughter Elizabeth Hascall the standing bedsteed and bed and all furniture belonginge thereunto according to the donation of house and Land as abouesayd together with a fetherbed and two small Ruggs at the house of Roger her son and one great Chest "It. I giue to Joseph Swasy one heafer Calfe. It. to the wife of Joseph Swasy I giue one old ewe sheep. It. I giue to Roger Haskall his chilldren fiue ewe sheep. It. I giue to my son Joseph Harding's Chilldren two ewes. It. I giue my two Ram Lambs to the Chilldren of my son Joseph to be equally diuided It. I giue my weather sheep unto Nathaniell Pickman. It. I giue to John Hascall one Steere It I giue the Remainder of all my Estate within the house and without to my son Joseph & to my daughter Elizabeth & son Roger to be equally diuided only to pay twenty shillings to Mr Samuell Sharpe which I giue him out of my Estate And I appoynt sergent John Porter to be in the Roome and steed of a feoffe for my daughter Elizabeth for the land and Goods giuen to her And I appoint Sergeant Porter and Jeffery Massey to be ouerseers."

Elizabeth (her + mark) Hardinge

Witness: Edmond Batter, Nathaniell Pickman.

Proved in Salem court 1:10m:1654 by the witnesses. Copy, attested by Hilliard Veren.

Essex County Quarterly Court Files, vol. 26, leaf 41.

ESTATE OF THOMAS GREENSLETT.

Administration upon the estate of Thomas Greenslett, intestate, was granted Mar. 27, 1677, to Ann Greenslett, who was to pay the debts as far as the inventory, which was 3li. 16s. 2d., would allow.

Ipswich Quarterly Court Records, vol. 5, page 287.

Inventory of the estate of Thomas Greenslet taken Mar. 21, 1676-7 by Edmund Batter and John Massey: one flocke bed & apertenances, 1li.; 2 old Chests with raggs, 6s.; a lampe, ticke & Hauke, 4s.; table, 2 wheels & Chairs, 10s. 6d.; one Irone pott, 6s. 8d.; wood & old bedsteed, 7s.; potts, 2s.; 2 swine, 1li.; total, 3li. 16s. 2d. The debts many & not knowne.

Attested in Ipswich court Mar. 27, 1677 by An Greenslet administratrix of the estate of her late husband Thomas Greenslet.

Essex County Probate Files, Docket 11,851.

ESTATE OF JOHN COLE OF MARBLEHEAD.

Administration upon the estate of John Cole of Marblehead, intestate, was granted Mar. 27, 1677, to Mr. Thomas Gardner, and there being an inventory brought in contained in two papers, and one child left, court ordered that the one paper containing 25li. 6s. 6d. be for the child wholly. For the rest of the estate, court ordered that said administrator be gathering in and paying debts and account to the next Salem court.

Ipswich Quarterly Court Records, vol. 5, page 287.

Inventory of the estate of John Cole sometime of Pemaquid, deceased at Marblehead, taken Feb. 16, 1676 by Samuell Cheever and Moses Mavericke: 2 3-4 yds. blew cotton, 5s. 6d.; 6 yds. green ditto, 9s.; 12 yds. red ditto, 21s.; 6 yds. red ditto, 13s.; 3 yds. red kersey, 12s.; 1 1-2 yds. ditto, 6s. 9d.; 3 3-4 colld kersey, 11s. 3d.; 3 1-4 yd. black serge, 11s. 4d.; 4 yds. wt. flannell, 6s.; 9 pr. stockins, 13s. 6d.; 1 1-2 yd cotton, 2s. 6d.; 4 1-2 yd. Irish cloth, 3s.; 6 3-4 yd Linnen & 11 yd. ditto, 21s. 3d.; 2 yds. East India *Silt,* 2s.; 5 yds. striped Linnen, 3s. 9d.; 1 1-2 Linnen, 18d.; 1 3-4 yd. calico, 18d.; 14 knives, 3s. 6d.; 1 parcell statute Lace, 2s. 6d.; colld thread & buttons, 5s. 2d.; wampanpeag, 20s.; thread & silke, 1s. 11d.; silver, 3li. 5s.; manchester, 18d.; coat & doublett, 20s.; bands, 8s.; 3 neckcloth, 6s.; 1 jackett, 10s.; 2 coats & 1 jackett, 25s.; 1 coat, wescoat & breeches, 35s.; 1 cloak, 30s.; 2 hatts, 20s.; wearing Linnen, 20s.; Furs, 13s. 6d.; 8 pr. shoes, 30s.; Iorn ware, 5s.; 1 parcell of damnifyed Tobacco, 10s.; 1 feather bed, boldster, 3li.; 6 blanketts, 35s.; 1 Rugge & coverled, 25s.; 1 Bed, Rugg & 2 blanketts, 3li.; 1pr. old steelyards & 4 yds. truckeng cloth, 16s.; 1 trammell, 5s.; 1 old gunn & cutlass, 20s.; 6 yds. cape cloth, 18s.; 1 pr. old boots, 12s.; 4 hhd. salt Tuterdas, 2li.; 1-2 small boat, 8li.; 1 shallop & furniture belonging to her, 50li.; total, 96li. 8s. 5d. Upon examining his book we find the debts contracted at ye Eastward due to the estate amount to 297li. 3s. 5d.; many of which persons are not now to be found. Debts contracted at Marblehead, 28li. 8s. 11d. Debts due from ye estate disbursed on Funerall charges & otherwise, 3li. 5s., which was all the money we found left. Due to Mr. Davie & brought in by him already, 127li. 3s. 4d.; to Mr. Fairweather, 13li. 2s. 11d.; Mr. Higginson, jr., 34li.; Thomas Gardiner, jr., 4li.; dues for bread, 4li. & caske 40s. at Boston, 6li.; Mr. Devereux of Marblehead, 10s. 6d.; Mr. Maverick, 1li. 4s.; Thomas Dixey, 3s. 9d.; total, 189li. 9s. 6d.

Delivered in to Ipswich court Mar. 27, 1677 by Mr. Thomas Gardner with another paper amounting to 25li. 6s. 6d., ordered to the child.

Inventory of goods of John Cole, deceased, found in the trunk which long before his death, at the desire of the grandmother were given freely to his child now living, upon & after the decease of his wife being mostly her Linnen, apprized Feb. 16, 1676, by Samuell Cheever and Moses Mavericke: a womans petticoat & wescoat, 1li. 5s.; Tammey petticoat & black gowne, 2li. 12s.; Nine sheets, 2 tablecloths & nine napkins, 7li.; Two shifts, 12s.; 2 bolster cases, 5s.; 3 pillowbeers, 10s.; Five aprons, 25s.; three whisks, 18s.; 3 neckcloths, 8s.; Five dressings, 10s.; 2 handkerchiefs, 8s.; 2 ditto & 2 hoods, 4s.; Two pr. sleeves, 2s.; 2 pr glovs old, 12d.; Caps, 2s.; 1 green apron, 5s.; Childbed linnen, 10s.; A Scarfe, 12s.; 2 whisks, 1 hood & vail, 12s.; One pr. stockins, 2s.; 1 looking glass, 6s.; Clomen ware, 5s.; Childrens Linnen, 10s.; One wine cup, 4 silver spoons, 3 gold rings, 1 bodkin, 1li. 18s.; Three pr. gloves old, 2s.; 1 womans bible, 5s.; 1 muffe, 2s.; 1 childs blankett, 5s.; 2 coats, 10s.; 11 pewter dishes, 1li. 19s.; 2 basons & 2 small dishes, 4s.; 5 porringers, 4s.; brass candlestick, 12d.; 1 collender, 2 cups, 18d.; 1 warming pan, 5s.; 2 iron potts, 6s.; total, 25li. 6s. 6d.

Delivered in to Ipswich court 27:1:1677 by Mr. Thomas

Gardner who is granted administration, and the above ordered to the child.

Essex County Probate Files, Docket 5,975.

Mr. Tho. Gardner, sr., brought in an inventory 26 : 4 : 1677, of what he found more of John Cole's estate since he carried in the first inventory to Ipswich court.

Salem Quarterly Court Records vol. 5, leaf 107.

The estate of John Colle debtor to several since the delivering into Ipswich court of the account by Thomas Gardner, sr., the administrator, to be added to the inventory: to Alice Peach for house Rent, Hors Hier, Beefe & Cabagges, 2li. 18s. 6d.; to Doctor Knott for Phisick & Tendance as his Bill, 2li. 4s.; to Doctor Wells, 2li. 11s. 3d.; to Richard Reith, 2li. 16s. 4d.; to Richard Norman for diet & drink, 2li. 4s. 11d.; to John Michels wife & daughter for the Childs diet & Tendance, 1li. 1s.; to Joseph Edmonds which he undertook to pay for Richard Hull, 1li. 2s.; to Edward Reed for digging the Grave, 5s., and to the Ferry Man, 4s.; to William Biggford to Ballanc his Account, 3li. 1s.; to 15s. in A Gun for Makeing of Sayles to the saied Biggford, 15s.; to Mr. John Battle of Boston by Agreement with the Administrator, 3li.; to John Dollen upon an Arbitration with the Administrator, 3li. 10s.; to Robert Hobs for Triming the Boat, 8s.; to William Forde for Salt Received by William Biggford, 1li.; to Mr. John Deverike for three Barrills, 9s.; to James Dennis, 2li. 1s. 3d.; total, 30li. 3d. The estate of John Colle, Creditor: to fish Received as his share of the smale Boat he kept out, 11li. 4s. 1d.; fish, 11li. 4s. 1d. at 15s. p. Quint & in hake & Refus Cod, 4li. 11s. 7d.; 45 Quintalles of Merchantable Fish at 16s. p Quintall, 16li. 16s.; to 12 Quintales & 1 qtr. of Merchantable Cod at 16s. p., 10li. 3s. 8d.; to 3 blls. of Mollasses Returned by John Gardner For fish Adventured, 3li. 12s.; By a Quarter an Acer of Ground & left in the hand of Thomas Junior being bought of him to satisfy his debt he Returning the surplus, 6li.; 1 pr. of Smiths Bellowes & An Iron Kettle & small Anvill, 2li.; total, 54li. 7s. 4d.

Payed by the Administrator out of the Estat of John Colle, deceased, since Ipswich court last: to Mr. John Fairweather, 13li. 18s., he being 15s. in debt, 13li. 18s.; to Henery Wolfe of Boston Baker, 4li. 14s.; to Mr. John Higerson of Sallem, 37li. 12s. 4d.; to Alice Peach, 2li. 18s. 6d.; to Doctor Knott, 2li. 4s.; to Richard Reith, 2li. 16s. 4d.; to Richard Norman, 2li. 4s. 11d.; to John Michell, 1li. 1s.; to Joseph Edmonds, 1li. 2s.; to Edward Read & the Fery man, 9s.; to William

Bigford, 3li. 10s.; to him A Gune, 15s.; to Robert Hobs, 8s.; to William Ford, 1li.; to Thomas Gardner, jr., 4li. 16s.; total, 74li. 13s. 1d.

Essex County Quarterly Court Files, vol. 26, leaf 122.

ESTATE OF DANIEL BUTTON OF (HAVERHILL?).

Administration on the estate of Daniell Button, intestate, was granted Mar. 27, 1677, to John Bartlett, sr., of Newbury, who was ordered to bring in an inventory to the next Ipswich court. The estate was to be ordered according to his mind, a cow to James Kingsbury, and the rest of the estate to the rest of his brothers and sisters.

Ipswich Quarterly Court Records, vol. 5, page 288.

Inventory of the estate of Daniell Button as it cost at the marchants taken by Wm. Chandler and John Webster, sr.; 10 yds. of woosted prunella, 3li.; 7 yds. of Collored linen, 17s. 6d.; holland shirt & making, 16s. 8d.; a paire of breeches, 12s.; two shirts, 7s.; 2 bands, 3s.; neck Cloth & a pockett hand-carcher, 3s.; his wages from ye Contrey in the hands of ye Constable, 1li. 17s. 8d.; a cow desposed of by ye Order of ye Court to his Brother Kinsbury, 1li. 1s. 6d.; total, 6li. 15s. 4d.

Daniell Button debtor to Jno. Barttlett, 4li. 14s. 2d.; Daniell Button Crdr., 4li. 6s. 8d., Rest, 7s. 6d.

Attested in Ipswich court 25 : 7 : 1677 by John Bartlett.

To pay to the children of Mathias Button 33s. 6d. a peice.

Essex County Probate Files, Docket 4,379.

GUARDIANSHIP OF BENJAMIN KIMBALL.

Benjamin Kimball chose Walter Fairfield to be his guardian, Mar. 27, 1677.

Ipswich Quarterly Court Records, vol. 5, page 288.

GUARDIANSHIP OF PRISCILLA LAW OF ROWLEY.*

Pricilla Law chose John Bayly to be her guardian and the court Mar. 27, 1677, allowed it, upon the same terms that his father James Bayley was, to whom she was formerly committed by the court.

Ipswich Quarterly Court Records, vol. 5, page 288.

ESTATE OF OSMUND TRASK OF BEVERLY.

Administration upon the estate of Ossmund Traske of Bev-

*See *ante*, vol. 2, page 110.

erly, intestate, was granted Mar. 27, 1677, to Elizabeth Traske, relict and widow of said Ossmund, and an inventory amounting to 84li. 9s. 5d. was brought in. The estate was ordered according to an agreement in writing presented and allowed.

Ipswich Quarterly Court Records, vol. 5, page 288.

Inventory of the estate of Osmond Traske of Beauerly taken Mar. 5, 1676, by John Raimente and Andrew Eliott: one bed and bedstead with other furniture, 8li.; another bed & bedstead with the furniture, 3li. 15s.; another bed & bedstead with the furniture, 4li. 10s.; another bed and furnituer thereto, 2li.; furniture for another bed, 4li. 10s.; his wearinge Apparell, 7li.; his Lininge & other Lininge in the house, 4li. 18s.; two brass kettles, 4li.; two brass skellets, one warming pan, 4li. 6d.; two Iron pots, 1li. 5s.; one Iron kettle & one postnet, 10s.; pewter and Earthen Dishes, 2li.; one hatt & hatt case, 15s.; chests, boxes, chaires & two spinninge wheels, 1li. 15s.; other smalle Utencills, 1li.; three guns & two swords, 3li.; one bedstead, 8s.; Six plowgh Oxen and ten Cowes, 64li. 10s.; three heifers of 3 years old, 8li. 5s.; one bull and one Steer, 5li. 5s.; Six two year old cattle & three Calves, 15li. 15s.; two horses and one colte, 8li. 10s.; forty Sheep and Lambs, 16li.; Eleaven pigs, 3li. 14s.; his Dwellinge house and barne, 100li.; Twenty Acres of Land with the Orchard next adjoining unto the dwellinge house and Smalle housinge with a Sider press, 150li.; Twenty Acres more nere his house, 120li.; one Acre and halfe of Salte marsh, 10li.; three acres and halfe of meadow and three and halfe of upland by John woodberries, 24li.; one Acre and quarter of land by Chubs, 8li.; fourty Acres of land by Edward Bishop with a house upon it, 160li.; 6 Acres of meadow in wenham meadow, 6li.; 20 Acres of upland behinde wenham pond, 40li.; 20 Acres of upland in burch plaine, 40li.; 14 Acres of upland by Cornelius baker, 21li.; another smale parcell nere vnto it, 1li. 10s.; 80 bushells of Indian Corne, 12li.; fourty bushells of barley, 8li.; foure flitches of bacon, 3li.; one cart, sled, two plowghs, hoes, Axes, Chaines & other tacklinge, 5li. 17s.; 2 Saddles and bridles, 2li. 11s.; another old Saddle, 5s.; foure bushells of pease, 16s.; two bushells of Rye, 8s.; total, 888li. 12s. 6d. Debts due unto Ozmund Trask; martin hall miller Debtor, 3li.; John Gyles of Salem, 2li.; Jonas Jonson, 1li. 10s.; Edward Hellard of Salem, 8s.; dew from John Trask his brothers son, 2li.; sum total, 897li. 10s. 6d. The debts being 56li. 1s. 1d., the estate remaining is 841li. 9s. 5d.

Attested in Ipswich court Mar. 27, 1677 by Elizabeth Traske, administratrix of the estate of her husband.

An account of what Ozmund Traske owed at his death: to
Mr. William Browne, Sr. of Salem, 9li. 13s. 5d.; Mr. William
Browne, Jr. of Salem, 4li. 1s. 3d.; John Stone, 4li. 9s. 6d.;
Hugh Woodberrie, 1li. 2s. 11d.; Mr. Hardy, 1li. 16s. 6d.; Mr.
Hardy in money, 1li. 1s.; John Wallice, 16s.; Nathaniell
Wallice, 14s.; Edward February, 1li.; Mr. Bowditch of
Salem, 15s.; Zacharia Herrick, 12s.; Joseph Morgan, 1li.;
David Perkins, 19s.; the Docter, 2li. 10s.; Nehemiah Grover
in money, 1li. 6s.; Daniell Davenson in money, 5s.; other
debts the creditors beinge at Sea that we cannot justly give
an account of about 5li.; Richard Stackers, 1li. 10s. 6d.;
Phebe Wiles, 8s.; Edmund Berry of Salem, 5li. 13s.; Nehemiah Grover, 9s.; Mr. Becket of Salem, 18s.; John Wallice,
11s.; Richard Neuard, 1li. 10s.; total, 48li. 1s. 1d. Beside on.
Aker and quarter of Land that is Dew to John Trask which
is his brothers son lieth ner to Thomas Chubs, 8li.; total, 56li.
1s. 1d.

Administration on the estate of Osmond Trask of Beverly
granted by the Ipswich court Mar. 27, 1677 to Elizabeth the
widow. After the debts are paid the estate is 841li. to be disposed of as follows: to John Trask the eldest son 40 acres of
land and one house upon it near to Edward Bisheps valued
at 160li. and the other eight children namely Sarah, Mary,
Samuell, Benjamine, Joseph, Elizabeth, William and Jonathan and also the child unborn, to receive from Elizabeth
their mother, 50li. each, as they come to age; the remainder
of the estate belongeth to Elizabeth the administratrix and
if any of the children die before they come to age their part to
be divided equally amongst the rest of the children, and the
land to stand bound for the payment of the children's portion
except that land that belongs to John the eldest son. Allowed
by the court Mar. 27, 1677.

Note to Capt. Sewall from John Croade for a citation to be
sent to Mr. Giles and his wife upon that petition and also to
send him in writing the amount of the estate of Ozmond
Trask.

The whole inventory amounts to 888li. 12s. 6d.; debts due
to the estate, 8li. 18s.; total, 897li. 10s. 6d. Debts due from
the estate, 56li. 1s. 1d.; the Real Estate is 677li. 10s. Signed
S. Sewall.

Account of John Giles and Elizabeth Gyles, alias Traske,
administratrix of the estate of Ozmond Trask given in to the
court June 24, 1695: the real estate 677li. 10s., the personal,

220li. 6d., debts due from the estate, 56li. 1s. 1d. according
to the first inventory; paid to Joseph and Samuel Trask, 50li.
each, their portion; to Elizabeth Trask wife of Steven Herrick, William Trask, Benjamin Trask, Mary Friason, Sarah
Holland their portion and their share of one of the children's
portion, deceased, 55li. 11s. each; to John Trask the eldest
son, 160li.; due to Edward Traske under age, 55li. 11s. which
is ready to pay on demand in case he would choose his guardian to receive it; due to Joseph, Samuel and John Traske
5li. 11s. each, which is ready to be paid to them.

Attested July 15, 1695 by John Gyles and Elizabeth Gyles
alias Traske.

Benja. [Brown?] acknowledged June 25, 1695, the receipt from Jno. Giles of 9li. 16s. 2d. which was due unto his
[father] from Hosean [Trask] deceased, at the time of his
death.

Joseph Traske acknowledged June 23, 1691, the receipt
from —— my mother, Mrs. Elizabeth, his wife, of 50li.
as his present part and proportion of the estate.

Witness: Samll. Hardie, Benjamin Traske.

Acknowledged June 29, 1697 before John Higginson.

Essex County Probate Files, Docket 28,058.

ESTATE OF ROBERT HOLMES OF NEWBURY.*

Hester Holmes, relict and administratrix of the estate of
Robert Holmes, having brought in an inventory of 20li. clear
estate and two children left her, court Mar. 27, 1677, ordered
the estate to her for the bringing up of the children.

Ipswich Quarterly Court Records, vol. 5, page 288.

ESTATE OF BENJAMIN HERRICK OF BEVERLY.

Administration upon the estate of Benjamin Herrick, intestate, was granted Mar. 27, 1677, to his brothers Zachry
and Ephraim. The estate was to be divided among all the
brothers and sisters excepting Thomas, viz., Zachariah,
Ephraim, Henry, Joseph, John, and Elizabeth, wife of Philip
Fowler. The mother of said Benjamin was to have the income of the land during her natural life. Zacheriah and
Ephraim were bound.

Ipswich Quarterly Court Records, vol. 5, page 291.

Inventory of the estate of Benjamin Herrick taken by

*See *ante*, vol. 2, page 380.

Richard Hutten and Andrew Eliott: eighteen Acres of Land, 126li.; Six Ewes and Lambs, 3li.; one Cow, 3li. 5s.; total, 132li. 5s.

Attested in Ipswich court Mar. 27, 1677, by Zachariah and Ephraim Herick.

Administration on the estate of Benjamin Herrick, intestate, granted by the Ipswich court Mar. 27, 1677, to his two brothers Zachery and Ephraim. The estate to be equally divided between all the brothers and sisters excepting Thomas, viz., Zachariah, Ephraim, Henry, Joseph, John, and Elizabeth, the sister, wife of Phillip Fowler. The mother of the said Benjamin to have the income of the land during her life.

Zachary and Ephraim acknowledged themselves bound in the sum of six score pounds to fulfil the division of the estate according to the above order.

Essex County Probate Files, Docket 13,111.

Mary Woodberry, Abigaill Stone and Elizabeth Kellem all aged above thirty years testified that Benjamin Herrick son of the widow Herrick was above twenty one years of age the first day of this instant March. Sworn in Ipswich court Mar. 27, 1677.

Ipswich Deeds, vol. 4, page 80.

ESTATE OF WILLIAM FELLOWS OF IPSWICH.

"The last Will of William felows nouember 29 : 76 I hauing my perfit memory I commit my soull to god and my body to yᵉ graue and bequea my earthly goods as followeth my will is yᵗ my wif shall haue one rome in my house to her self and for her uese dewring her life yᵗ is to say yᵉ parler and to haue twelve pounds yearly paid her in good marchantable pay by my three Sons ‖Ephram Samul Joseph‖ and likewis it is my will yᵗ my wif should haue two of my ‖best‖ Cowes and to be kept by my sonns winter and Somer for my wifs uese and my wif shall haue liberty to keep two swine and like wise my sons shall maintain her with conuenient fiering winter and somer as long as she lius a widow and like wise tis my will yᵗ my wife shall haue a conueanant peice of land for a gearding and a quarter of a acker of good land yearly to sow flaxe on and it is my will yᵗ my wif shall haue all yᵉ houshould goods at her dispoasel tis my will yᵗ my sonne Isack shall haue my march lote at hog Iland adid to that which I haue giuing him allredy and my will is yᵗ my other three sonns yᵗ is Ephram Samuel and Joseph shall haue yᵉ other half of my farme and ye rest of my sault march with ye buildings and stock ‖and corn‖ upon ye farme to be posest of it after my deseas only to fullfill to thr mother what is aboue menchoned and to pay all ‖my‖ depts and legisis as foloweth tis my will y^t my daughter mary shall haue ten pounds paid her within two yeare after my deseas and ten pounds after my wifes deseas and it is my will y^t my othr three daughters Elisebeth abegill Sary shall haue tewenty pounds a peice one half paid them two years after my deseas ore one thr day or mariag and ye othr half two years after y^t and after my depts are all paid my will is y^t my daughters should be maid equale with ther three brothers Ephram Samuele Joseph only fifty pounds y^t my Sonne Isack is to pay after my wifs deseas shall be deuided equaly amongst my three daughters Elisebeth abigil Sary and then to be equallised with thr brothrs aboue menshnd."

Willaim Fellowes

Witness: William (his ∮ mark) Story, Senear, Thomas Burnon, senier, Samuel Ingals, Seanir.

This writing produced in Ipswich court Mar. 27, 1677 as the will of Wm. Fellows, but no executor being named, administration was granted to the three sons, Ephraim, Samuell and Joseph and they were to order the division of the estate according to the mind of the father as expressed in this will.

Inventory taken Dec. 27, 1676, by Henry Benet, William Story, Sener and Thomas Burnum, Senior: his wearing Apparrell, 9li. 4s.; paire of Oxen, 12li.; Three Cowes, 10li. 10s.; five Heifers, 14li. 10s.; Two yearelings, 4li.; Three Calves, 3li. 10s.; Horse kind, 12li. 10s.; Sheep, 21li.; Swine, 5li.; Timber Chaine, Draft Chains, Carts, wheeles, hoops, boxes, Spanshackle, Plowe, Plowe Irons, Beetle, wedges, slead & sum other small things, two Axes & Muck forke, 13li. 1s. 10d.; 15 bushells of wheat, 3li. 15s.; Rie, 1li. 18s.; Three scoare & ten bushells of Barly, 14li.; 4 bushells of pease, 16s.; flax, 12s.; Ten bushells of Indian corne, 2 bush. of oates, 1li. 15s.; Sixty bushells of Indian Corne in ye Barne, 9li.; 38 Acres of upland at home and 26 Acres of Marsh, 250li.; all the Howsinge, 100li.; hookes & Ringes, 2s. 6d.; Cart roape, Traisses & Coller, 15s.; oard & other small things with a hamer, 7li. 11s. 6d., bridle & Saddle, 1li.; Sythes with their taceling, 11s.; one piece of old Iron & 2 pr. sheepe sheers, 3s. 4d.; one dore Lock & yoake hookes, 6s. 6d.; fowre Rod of Ground on the meting house hill where ye old house stood. A pair of Stillyards, 1li. 5s.; beefe, pork, Chese, Apples &

butter, 11li. 2s. 6d.; Bedd & bed Cloathes with the boulster & pillow in the Parlor Chamber, 6li. 10s.; three bedds, 12li.; flax teere, 16s.; Sheeps wooll, 5li.; one Chest, 12li. of Cotton wooll, tooe old wheeles, sacks, 1li. 15s.; Sheets & one table Cloath, 9li.; other small Lening, 1li. 11s.; tooe Chests, 1li. 4s.; one Cupbord, 2li.; one bedd in the Parlor, 10li.; Chairs & one basket, 1li.; Table & Forme, 14s.; for Cushens, 4s.; warming pan, glasses & earthen potts, 1li. 3s. 6d.; Tubs, keelers, panns, pewter & tinn, 3li. 9s.; woodden ware, 4li.; Table & a meale trough, 14s.; Iron potts & Kettles, 1li. 18s.; Brass Kettles & Skillets, 6li. 2s. 6d.; Tramells, Spitts, slice & other small things, 2li. 1s. 6d.; Bookes, pillion & Riding cloth, 1li. 7s.; 2 Cowes, 8li.; 2 Swine, 24s.; a Lead, 30s.; hive of bees, 10s.; total, 581li. 17s. 11d. Debts due to the estate, 8li. 5s. 3d. Debts to be deducted out of the estate, 83li. 11s. 7d.; total remaining, 498li. 6s. 4d.

Attested in Ipswich court Mar. 27, 1677 by the administrators.

Bond of Jonathan Fellows, yeoman, with James Brown, yeoman, and Isaac Knowlton, cordwainer, all of Ipswich, as sureties, for the sum of 300li., dated Feb. 13, 1722-23, for administration on estate not already administered upon belonging to his grandfather William Fellows. Witness: Robert Holmes, Daniell Appleton, Reg.

"These ar The undersigned to segnefi we desire Cosen Jonathan Fellows to administer on the intestate estate of our father William Fellows." Signed Abigel (her X mark) Fellows, Sara (her + mark) Fellows.

Essex County Probate Files, Docket 9,367.

Whereas an agreement hath been made Mar. 27, 1702, among Isaac Fellowes, Ephraim Fellowes, Ruth Fellowes widow and administratrix to the estate of her husband Joseph Fellowes, all of Ipswich, and Samuell Ayres of Newbury attorney to Samuell Fellowes of the same town, to settle and divide the real estate of their father William Fellowes formerly of Ipswich, according to his donation in his will, Ephraim, & Ruth Fellowes and Samuell Ayres do by these presents quitclaim to their brother Isaac Fellowes the land as now divided and set out by these bounds following: westerly upon a stake by the river north east side upon Samuell Ayres about sixty nine rods to a stake with stones about it & then westerly fourteen Rods upon Samuell Ayres land to a stake with stones about it which is Ephraim Fellowes corner & then northeasterly by Ephraim's land Till it comes to a stake with stones about it at the common & easterly by the common & southerly by the land that was Quartermaster Kinsman and southwesterly by the common with all the priviledges thereunto belonging.

Signed and sealed Mar. 30, 1702. Witness: William Fellowes, Jarvas Ringe

Acknowledged July 24, 1702 by Ephraim Fellowes, Samuell Ayres, Ruth Fellowes.

Whereas an agreement hath been made Mar. 27, 1702, among Isaac Fellowes, Ephraim Fellowes, Ruth Fellowes, widow, and administratrix to the estate of her husband Joseph Fellowes, all of Ipswich and Samuill Ayres of Newbury attorney to Samuell Fellowes of Newbury to settle and divide the real estate of their father William Fellowes formerly of Ipswich according to his donation in his will, Isaac Fellowes, Samuell Ayres and Ruth Fellowes do by these presents quitclaim to their brother Ephraim Fellowes the land with all the buildings thereupon as now divided and set out by these bounds: southeasterly by Isaac Fellowes land, northwesterly upon Samuell Ayres land to a white oak tree marked by the common which is the bounds between said Fellowes and Ayres, northerly & easterly by the common and also eight acres more bounded northerly upon the common, easterly upon Samuell Ayres land, southerly upon the river, westerly upon Joseph Fellowes land, and also to his divisions of marsh as formerly divided and bounded out unto him with all the priviledges thereunto belonging. The widow Fellowes signed to all except eight acres of land which was conveyed to her husband per Ephraim Fellowes by a deed dated Feb., 1697.

Signed and sealed Mar. 30, 1702. Witness: Thomas Manning, William Fellowes, Jarvas Ringe.

Acknowledged July 24, 1702 by Isaac Fellowes, Samuell Ayres, Ruth Fellowes.

Essex County Probate Records, vol. 308, *pp.* 24-26.

Administration on a common right or rights of William Fellows, late of Ipswich, which have not been already administered upon, was granted Feb. 11, 1722-3, to his grandson William Fellows (son of ——— Fellows, late of Ipswich), ——— having renounced their right of administration, he giving bond to administer according to law.

Essex County Probate Records, vol. 313, *page* 566.

ESTATE OF WYMOND BRADBURY OF SALISBURY.*

Robert Pike of Salisbury, administrator to the estate of Wymond Bradbury of the same town, by act of the Salisbury Court 9 : 2m : 1672 has received of Thomas Bradbury of the same town 16li. sterling due from him to the said estate in lieu of house and land appraised at 60li. and releases him from all claims.

Signed Mar. 20, 1676-7. Witness : Edward Colcord, Rodger (his T mark) Easman.

Acknowledged by Maj. Robert Pike in Salisbury Court Apr. 10, 1677.

Norfolk Deeds, vol. 3, pt. 2, leaf 22.

GUARDIANSHIP OF WYMOND BRADBURY OF SALISBURY.

Capt. Thomas Bradbury was appointed Apr. 10, 1677, guardian of his grandchild Wymond Bradbury.

Salisbury Quarterly Court Records, vol. 2, leaf 71.

ESTATE OF MRS. ANNE WINSLOW OF SALISBURY.

Administration upon the estate of Mrs. Anne Winsly, widow, was granted Apr. 10, 1677, to Ensign Buswell and Ephraim Winsly.

Salisbury Quarterly Court Records, vol. 2, leaf 73.

Inventory of the estate of An Winslow of Salisbery taken by John Ilsly and Samwell Feelowes : a round boxe and what is in it, 40s. ; fether bead and bouldsteres, 40s. ; a Rudg and some other things with it, 40s. ; her wareing Cloth and a Chest and thosse things that are in it, 6li. 5s. ; two pare of showes, 5s. ; a looking glass, 2s. 6d. ; pewter, 3s. ; a leetle boxe and what is in it, 2s. 6d. ; a byble, 4s. ; Courtine, 8s. ; peice of woollen cloth, 5s. ; total, 13li. 15s.

Inventory of the charge at the funerall of Ann Winslow of Salisbery, widow : the coffin, 12s. ; suger 10li., 6s. ; spice, 1s. 6d. ; Butter 8li., 4s. ; the cakes, 16s. ; sixe gallons Cider, 6s. ; due to Ensigne Wm. Boswell for fower yers Diatt & 5 months, 53li.

Attested in Salisbury court Apr. 10, 1677, by Wm. Buswell and Ephraim Winsly.

Essex County Probate Files, Docket 30,179.

*See *ante*, vol. 2, page 170.

ESTATE OF ANTIPAS NEWMAN OF WENHAM.*

Mr. Daniell Epps, attorney to Mrs. Newman, relict and administratrix of the estate of Mr. Antipas Newman, late of Wenham, desiring liberty to make sale of some land for the payment of debts, court Apr. 24, 1677, granted liberty to sell that land on Royall side in Salem.

Ipswich Quarterly Court Records, vol. 5, page 292.

Petition of Mrs. Elizabeth Endecott to the court 30 : 9m. : 1680, desiring that her son John Newman might be joined with her to administer upon the estate of her husband Mr. Antipas Newman. The court grants her petition, and appoints her son John administrator with her, but is not to act anything about the estate but by the advice of Mr. Richard Wharton and Mr. Daniell Epps, sr. or one of them.

Salem Quarterly Court Records, vol. 6, leaf 12.

GUARDIANSHIP OF ISAAC RING OF IPSWICH.

Isaack Ringe chose his brother Daniell Ringe to be his guardian, and the court, Apr. 24, 1677, allowed it.

Ipswich Quarterly Court Records, vol. 5, page 292.

ESTATE OF NICHOLAS RICHARDSON.

Administration upon the estate of Nicolas Richardson, who was slain in the war, was granted Apr. 24, 1677, to Robert Kinsman who was ordered to bring in an inventory to the next Ipswich court.

Ipswich Quarterly Court Records, vol. 5, page 293.

ESTATE OF REV. THOMAS PARKER OF NEWBURY.

"I Thomas Parker pastor of the church of christ in Newbery in New England being Groune into yeares, the Infirmityes of Age dayly increasing upon me Considering the Comand of God & my duty to be dayly preparing for my departure out of this world & sett in order what the Lord hath bestowed on me, being thro the patience & rich mercy of God in Good health & of a disposing minde doe desire to put in practise my duty in disposing thereof and therefore make Ordeyne & declare this present writting to be my last will & testament Imp^r I doe fully & freely resigne up my Soule into the hands of my most gracious God & father that gaue it me & my body to the dust from whence it Came in hope of a

*See ante, vol. 2, page 324.

Glorious resurrection amongst them that are Sanctified in christ Jesus. Item My minde & will is that after my funerall expences be dischardged that my estate of lands goods debts moneys &c be disposed of as heere after is expressed. Item I Giue & bequeath my estate in lands or money in old England next & imediately after my death to my deare Nephew[s]. m[r] John woodbridge & m[r] Benjamin Woodbridge equally part & part like. Itm I Giue & bequeath Unto my Cousin Nicholas Noyes all such debt or debts that he shall owe Vnto me at my decease for Rent for that land of mine which he hath in his possession on the left hand of the Ridge Coming from the old Toune to the new ouer & besides the land & my Interest in it which I formerly made ouer to him by a deede of guift Item. I Giue & bequeath all the rest of my estate in lands vpland & meadow being on y[e] right hand of the Ridge aboue mentioned in Catle Clothes bedding bookes or what els soeuer & haue now in possession or shall dye possest of to my deare Couzin m[rs] Sarah Noyes. the beloued widdow & relict of my deare Cousin the late m[r] James Noyes for hir sole vse during hir naturall life & the Remainder by hir to be disposed of & Giuen to & amongst the children or such of them as shee shall see cause of the late m[r] James Noyes & theire heires for euer.

"Item I further Give & bequeath to my beloued Cousin m[rs] Sarah Noyes as a further testimony of my Endeared loue to hir for hir faithfull love to me & paines she hath taken with me all such estate & debt as the Toune of Newbery shall owe to me for the yearely recompence at the time of my decease w[th]er for a quarter of a yeere or more or lesse together w[th] the Annuall Rent & Arrerages of Rent as shall be due unto me for my land or money in England (now in the hands or order of my deare Cousin m[r] Benjamin Woodbridg) to the time of my decease w[ch] I Request my sajd Couzin Benjamine Woodbridge to take Speciall Care may be sent to my Sajd Couzin Sarah Noyse or hir order or the order of any of my executo[rs] hereafter named for hir best advantage ffinally for the better & more full accomplishment of this my will I doe here by Revoake & make null & voyd all former will or wills & doe Constitute & Appoint my beloued Couzins m[rs] Sarah Nojes m[r] James & m[r] Moses Nojes hir Sonnes my sole execcutrix & execcuto[rs] of this my last will & testament desiring my louing frends Capt w[m] Gerrish Couzin Nicholas Noyes & Richard Knight to be my ouerseers. In testimony

where of I haue hereunto sett my hand & seale this twelfth
day of September 1663."

Thomas Parker (SEAL)

Witness: Edward Rawson, Wm. Gerrish.

Proved May 23, 1677 in Boston before Samuell Symonds
Esq., Dep. Gov. and Wm. Hathorne, Esq. by Mr. Edward Rawson and Capt. Wm. Gerrish, and they also declared that the
said Mr. Parker committed the will to the keeping of the said
Rawson until his death.

Inventory of the estate of Mr. Thomas Parker late pastor
of the Church of Newbury who deceased Apr. 24, 1677 taken
May 30, 1677 by Wm. Gerrish, Nicholas Noyes and Anthony
Somerby: his farme both upland pasture & meadow, 250li.;
his weareing apparrell, 30li.; featherbed, flockbed, bolsters,
curtaines, vallons, pillowes, Rugg, blankets, sheets & pillow
beares, 20li.; 2 Chests & other things, 1li.; his books & Ly-
brary, 40li.; debts due to the deceased, 60li.; debt in England, 10li.; Land in England, 200li.; total, 611li. Four or five
other small books.

Attested in Ipswich court Sept. 25, 1677 by Mrs. Sarah
Noyse.

Essex County Probate Files, Docket 20,564.

ESTATE OF ISAAC CUMMINGS, SR., OF TOPSFIELD.

"The Last will and testament of Isaac Comins Senier. I
being Sencabl of my aproaching desolation being att present
weak in body yet perfect in my vnderstanding: haueing by
the grace of god bene helped to provid for my futur state in
another world. doe now in ordering of what god hath been
pleased to bestow upon me of the blesings of this life take
Care and order that in the first place my debts be duly payd:
nextly I doe by this my last will and testament confirme to
my Son Isaac the ten Acres of division Land on the South
Side of the great riuer be it more or less: nextly I doe give
unto my Son in Law John jewet ten pounds part in Cattel
and part in houshould goods: nextly I doe will and bequeath to my grand Son Isaac: the Son of my Son Isaac on
year old hefer on littel Sow the indian corne which he hath
planted for himself and the flax which he hath Sowne item
I doe giue unto him my chest the 2d in bignes with the lock
and key: item my history book with Such books as are his
owne: i e a bibl and testament item I do giue him ten pounds
to be payd att Seuenteen years of age in Country pay item I

doe giue vnto my Son in Law John pease thirty pounds to be
pay out of the stock of Cattell and houshould goods as much
as may be att present: and the rest in two years: item: I doe
make my Son John my sole executor and doe giue unto him
my house and Lands being fourty Acres more or less consist-
ing of upland and meddow with all the priviledges and Em-
molvments ther of and apurtainances therunto belonging:
provided that this land shall stand bound in part and in
wholl for the payment of these Leagacyes and in case that the
sayd legacyes shal not be payd according to this my will: the
land shall be sould and payment made out of the price therof:
and the remainder shall be the executors:: item my will further is that if any of these my children shall through discontent att what is done for them in this my will: Cause troubl
to arise to the executor then there shall be nothing payd to
him or them but the Legacy or Legacyes willed to them shall
return too and remain in the hands of the executor as his
proper right: dated the 8th of the 3^d mth 1677.

"my desir farther is that Isaac ffoster and Thomas Dorman
would take Care that this my will be duly performed."

Isaac Cumings S^r

Witness: John (his † mark) poore, Sr., Thomas Dorman,
Isaac Foster.

Proved June 14, 1677 by Thomas Dorman and Isack Foster before Samuell Symonds, Esq., Dep. Gov. and Maj. Gen.
Denison, Esq.

Inventory of the estate of Isake Comings, Senior, late of
Topsfield, taken May 22, 1677 by John Whipple and John
How: a Cloth Sute, 2li.; a Grey sute, 1li. 15s.; 6 yds of cloth
with butons silk & thred as they cost at the merchants, 1li.
19s. 3d.; an old Grat Coat, 9s.; wascot, 6s.; payer of Gren
brchis & two payer of drawers, 9s.; 3 payer of shoos, 1s.; 5
payer of stokins, 8s.; 4 shirts, 10s.; 7 caps, 7s.; one slke Cape,
4s.; 10 bandes, 10s.; 7 handcerchrs, 3s. 6d.; 4 hates, 8s.;
cloth hood & startups, 1s. 6d.; fether beed, bolser & pillow,
4li.; nu coverlet, 24s.; an old Civerlit, 5s.; Curtins & valants,
beedsted, Cord & matt, 1li. 10s.; smale beed with a pilow & a
Rugge, 1li. 15s. 6d.; one payer of sheetes, 30s.; & other
payer, 16s.; one payer of sheets, 18s.; one sheet, 7s.; 3 pilowbers, 6s.; 3 napkins, 3s. 6d.; 2 table cloths, 5s. 6d.; 7 towels,
5s. 6d.; thre sacks, one willit, one bage, 10s.; 3 small Remnants of Cloth, 2s. 6d.; flax and tow, 6s.; 6 pownd of cotton
woole, 6s.; a broad howe, 2s.; one broad how, 3s. 6d.; an Iron
foot, 1s. 6d.; 3 haye forks, 4s. 6d.; an Iron spitt, 3s.; ades,

5s.; handsawe, 2s. 6d.; axe, 3s. 6d.; old spad, 3s.; betle & 4 wedgis, 6s.; a mare, 40s.; yearling colt, 15s.; Sadle & panel with bridle, gurts & crooper, 20s.; brase pott, 20s.; one Iron pott, 9s., two payer of pott hooks, 1li. 12s.; an old Ketle, 6s., 3s. 6d., bras candlstik, 4s., potlid, 1s., 14s. 6d.; pewter, 18s.; tine 9d.; one glac, 1s.; 5 spons, 2s.; earthn ware, 6s. 8d.; tramell, tongs, bellis, 12s.; hamer, pinchers, 5s.; fann, 3s.; Chern, 5s.; a nu powdering tub, 3s. 6d.; 4 paiels, 7s. 8d.; 2 Kelers, 4s.; old powdring tub, 1s.; two old barels, 2s.; half bushel, peck, halfe peck, 3s. 6d.; 4 trayes, 4s.; 4 bouls, 4s.; dishes & Ladle, 1s. 8d.; one duz. trenchers, 1s.; two barels, 5s.; 3 sives, 3s.; 3 chayers, 7s.; a litle table & form, 4s.; desk, 6s.; one chest, 11s. 6d.; two old chests, 4s.; 3 books, 10s.; chest, 5s.; two books, 10s.; corn, 10s.; malt, 6s.; baken, 3s.; Kneding trof, 2s.; warming Pann, fring pann, 10s.; eight swine, 5li.; 3 cowes, 12li.; one 2 yer old ster, one yerling, 16li. 2s.; howsing and Lands with all priveledges & apurtenances, upland and meado is about 40 accers, 100li.; depts due to the estat, 4li.; total, 166li. 1s. 6d. Depts due from the estat about 19li. 16s. 5d.

Attested June 14, 1677 by John Comings to be a true inventory of his father's estate.

Essex County Probate Files, Docket 6,705.

ESTATE OF THOMAS TURVILL OF NEWBURY.

Inventory of the estate of Thomas Turvill of Newbury, deceased May 22, 1677 taken June 25, 1677 by Caleb Moodye and Joseph Pike constable of Newbury: his weareing clothes, 1li.; an old pewter pint pot, two sawcers & a poringer & a earthen pitcher, 6s. 8d.; 3 caps, 2 handkedchers, pr. of linnen stockings, 3 bands & a litle box, 10s.; 3 leather purses or pouches with Allum in them, 3s.; pr. of old sturups & old spurs & a snafle & 4 buckles, 2s.; A munteer cap & a calfe skins, 8s. 6d.; An Iron foot to mend shooes & a pr. of old shooes & 1-2 pound of woolen yarne & a tin pint pot, 3s. 6d.; severall bookes, 1li.; In mony, 7s.; A barrel with Iron band & 2 staples & a locke & key, 6s.; flock bed, 3 bolsters, 2 old torne rugs, 2li.; 4 Tanners knives, 5s.; wooll neere 40 lb. or upwards, 2li., Allum, skins, if they be his, 16s.; his booke debt, 2li. 8s.; total, 11li. 15s.

The deceased hath been maintained by the Towne neere about foure yeare sometimes we have paid for his maintenance 3s. 6d. a weeke, sometimes 5s. a weeke and sometimes 4s. a week in all about 35li. and besides we paid to the sur-

geon at one time 5li. and now in his sickness we have not yet
an account of for phisicke: besides for his funerall neere 40s.
as wee suppose. Anthony Somerby, Thomas Noyes, Selectmen.

Essex County Probate Files, Docket 28,349.

Administration upon the estate of Thomas Turvill, intestate, was granted Mar. 26, 1678, to Joseph Pike, and Anthony Somerby and Henry Jaquis were appointed a committee
to examine the debts and make return according to law.

Ipswich Quarterly Court Records, vol. 5, page 303.

The committee appointed to find out about the estate of
Thomas Turvill having made a return, the court Apr. 1,
1679, ordered Joseph Pike, the administrator, to pay the
debts so far as the estate would go, he being paid for his
charge.

Ipswich Quarterly Court Records, vol. 5, page 345.

ESTATE OF JOHN PICKWORTH.

John West and John Elletrap were ordered by the court
26:4:1677, to make inquiry after the estate of John Pickworth, supposed to be dead, and to account to the court, and
in case the widow Pickworth, mother of said John, be in
want, she was to be supplied out of the estate.

Salem Quarterly Court Records, vol. 5, leaf 105.

ESTATE OF BENJAMIN PICKWORTH.

John West and John Elletrap were ordered by the court
26:4:1677, to make inquiry after the estate of Benjamin
Pickworth, supposed to be dead, and to account to the court,
and in case the widow Pickworth, mother of said Benjamin,
be in want, she was to be supplied out of the estate.

Salem Quarterly Court Records, vol. 5, leaf 105.

GUARDIANSHIP OF SAMUEL SOUTHWICK OF SALEM.

Samuell Sothwick, son of John Sothwick, chose Frances
Nursse as his guardian, and John, son of said John, chose
Tho. Fuller as his guardian, which the court 26:4:1677, al-
lowed.

Salem Quarterly Court Records, vol. 5, leaf 105.

ESTATE OF JOHN WHITE.

Administration upon the estate of John White was granted 26:4:1677, to William Swetland who presented an inventory.

Inventory of the estate of John White, tailor, taken Apr. 28, 1677, by Edward Grove, Nicholas Manning and Tho. Bridge: a Coate of Cloth, & a serge paire trowsers, 15s.; 2 Cametto Coates & a pa: breeches Mutch worne, 2s.; an old Coate & 2 pa: old breeches and a Jackett, 8s.; 6 neckcloths & 1 Carvette, 5s.; 3 paire Sleeves & 3 pocket handketchers, 2s.; 3 shirtes wheareof 2 weare new, 12s.; a paier of buckein buskins, 2s. 6d.; paire old shoes, 2s.; 2 paier old worne stockins, 1s.; 2 yards galloons & a bible, 2s.; 4 small rubons, a powder Horne & An old old Rapier, 2s. 6d.; A pressing Iron, a pa. taylers sheeres & a yard, 3s.; and old Snapesake & 2 hatts, 12s.; a demety Wascoate & a pa. Linnen drawers mutch Worne, 2s.; an old redde wasecoate, 1s.; a walking Cane, a small old Chest, a trencher Knif, a pen knife & a bodkin, 4s. 6d.; a nutte megge grater, a needle Case & 5 needles, 6s.; a small bagge & 2 sliper linnen, 1s.; total, 5li. 1s. "Since this inventory was taken I haue found of his A paire of shooes & stockns & 2 old Rasers which in my Judgment may bee worth 5ˢ."

Allowed in Salem court 26:4:1677.

Essex County Quarterly Court Files, vol. 26, leaf 115.

ESTATE OF HENRY DISPAW, SR., OF LYNN.

"I hinere despaw Sʳ being weke in body yet through mercy sound in mind doe make & ordaine thes my last will & testament in maner following first I desyr too committ my sole to God through yᵉ hands of yᵉ Lord Jesus Christ And my bode too bee desently enterred In the earth & I doe despose of the worldly Good things the Lord hath gevin me as folloeth: Afftor my decese my will is that my duttefoll sonn hinnery shall have Alle my part of the bond of five hundred pounds of lafoll monie of Ingland being the forfit for non paing of my waggis: and Allso my will is that my sonn Edward shall have outt of thes bond forty shillines and the half of my Clothes and If any shall aske the Resin whi I Geve hinery so much and nott doo no mor for Edword it is becaes hinery hath bene at a grate dealle of trobell with me in tim of my lamenis and siknis and Alle soe my will is that my lovin atorne John Floyd shall be satisfied for his trobell at Cortee too Recover

my Right of John write John Gifford and Ezekell Fogg; and
for the performance of this my will I doe Anomant: & ordayne my loving sone hinery too be my Exceketer and I doe
chues my lovin frind John Floyd too be my overser of this
my will in witnis where of I have ‖set‖ vnto my hand thes
twintith seventh daye of febewary in the yeare of our lord
one thousind six hundred sivinty and fore."

hinery (his ‖ mark) Despaw, Sʳ.

Witness: John Floyd, Sarah Floyd.

Proved in Salem court 26:4:1677 by John Floyd and
Sarah, his wife.

Inventory of the estate of Henry Dispaw, sr., of Lynn,
taken by Samuel Stocker and John (his 𝔐 mark) Chil-
son: two old Coates & a payre of Breeches, 10s.; his old Hatt
& all he had, 1s. 6d.; his bed which was all declared & no
thing belonging thereto was his & an old flock bed, 1li.; one
shirt, 6s.; a pair of old stockings & shooes, 1s.; Two Linnen
Neckclothes, 2s.; one Black Sattan Capp, 2s.; total,
2li. 2s. 6d.

To his one halfe pt. of 500li. bond due from John Wright,
John Gifford & Ezekiell Fogg, for forfeiture of non-payment
of his wages, 250li.

Attested in Salem court 26:4:1677 by Hen. Dispaw, jr.

Essex County Quarterly Court Files, vol. 26, leaf 128.

ESTATE OF WILLIAM WOODBERRY OF SALEM.

"I William Woodberry the elder being of good understanding & memory doe constitute and ordein this my last will &
testament the 5th day of the 4th mo: 1663. Imprimis I giue
and bequeath vnto my wife Elizabeth my Dwelling house with
the land adioyning vnto it as allso whatsoeuer other Land I
Doe posesse and enioy, saue what I shall except in this I will
to giue vnto my sonne William. It: I giue vnto my said Wife
all my household stuffe and other goods debts Dews Cattle or
whatsoeuer elce aperteines vnto my wife paying these Legacyes here under expressed. It: I giue vnto my eldest sonne
Nicholas twenty shillings It: I giue vnto my sonne William
ten shillings as allso fiue akers of land which lyes nere snake
hill and adioynes vnto ten akers of his owne It I giue vnto my
sonne Andrew & Hugh my sonne Isacke and Daughter Hannah Haskels to each of them ten shillings the piece Consti-
tutetinge & ordeining my said wife Elizabeth sole Executrix
of this my will & testament."

William (his M mark) Woodberry

Witness: John Thorndike, Nicholas (his N mark) Pache, Richard (his R mark) Brackenbury.

Proved 26:4:1677 upon the obligation of Hugh Woodbery as is entered in the inventory.

Inventory of the estate of William Woodbery, aged about eighty-eight years, deceased 29:11:1676, taken by William (his O mark) Dixsy and John Hill: cotes, 1li.; lining cloth, 2li. 16s.; ticking, 12s. 6d.; shets and shirts, 1li. 12s. 8d.; 4 yds. of carsy, 1li. 4s.; yards and 3 quarters cloth, 11s.; bags, 15s.; 4 yards sad colerd cloth, 18s.; 12 yds. penisstone, 1li. 16s.; to yards coten, 6s.; one paire stockings, 2s.; bed and furnituer, 3li.; plators, 5s.; brass pots, 12s.; 3 kitells, 1li. Debts, due from Nicolas Woodbere, 18li.; from Hugh Woodberre, 4li. 9s.; from Hana Bradford, 2li. 2s.; from John Patch, 1li. 10s.; monney, 3li.; total, 45li. 11s. 2d.

The will and inventory of William Woodbery, deceased, was brought in to court 26:4:1677, by Hugh Woodbery, the witnesses being deceased, leaving only one who was not able to appear. Mr. Hugh Woodbery, in behalf of himself and his brother Nicholas, was bound upon condition that his mother, the relict of deceased, should be maintained during her life, and that the will should be fulfilled.

Essex County Quarterly Court Files, vol. 26, leaf 129.

ESTATE OF ELIZABETH SPOONER OF SALEM.

"I Elisabath Sponer of Salem hauing throug Gods Goodnes liued in this world unto owld Age: & now ffinding my strength to decay not knowing how neere my Glas is Run: I doe now leue thes lines behind me for to declar what my mind & last will & Testement is for the disposing of whatt worldly estatt God hath blesed me with: as is heerafter exspresed & I doe apoynt & desier my Sonne in Law John Rucke my solle exsecetor for the seeing of this my will performed It I giue vnto our Reverant pastor Mr John Higenson fiue poundes in money: & to Mr Nicolatt forty Shillings in Goods & I doe giue vnto my Cusen Margitt Rucke at boston ten pounds & to my Cusen Thomas Clark at Cambridg I doe Giue fiue pounds I doe Giue vnto the widow Elisabeth Owin fiue pounds I doe Giue vnto my thre Grand Chilldren daftors: Elisabath osborn & Hanna Rucke & Sarah Rucke: all my linen that I shall leue behind me: to be Equally devided among them & I doe giue vnto my young Granchild John osborn Junyer too siluer spones: & I doe giue vnto my

Grand Chilldren Hana & Sara & John & Thomas Rucke Ech
of them A siluer spone: & the Rest of my plate to be devided
Amongst them fouer: or the valewe thar of & the Rest of my
Estate I doe leue with my sonne Rucke to his disscrestion for
the disposing of it amonght his fiue Children Elisabeth &
hanna & Sara: & John & Thomas wch he had by my dafter
Hanna Sponner: Her son-in-law John Rucke, executor & to
this my will I haue heerunto subskribed my hand: being at
this present time Through Gods marsie to me: of Good &
perfect memory & understanding what heer I haue dun: witnes my hand this twenty second day of July one thousand
six hundred seventy and thre."

Elizebath Spooner.

Witness: Hannah Rucke, John Rucke, Juneare.
Proved in court 26:4:1677, it having been sworn to by
the witnesses, 26:1:1677, before Wm. Hathorne, assistant.

Inventory of the estate of widow Elizabeth Spooner, deceased in 1676, taken Mar. 6, 1676-7, by Hilliard Veren, sr.
and Thomas Rix: In ye Parlour, 1 bed bolster & 2 pillows,
rugge & blanketts & Curtains and all other appertinances, 3li.
10s.; 1 trundle bed with all appertinances, 1li. 5s.; 1 table &
Carpett & 6 joyne stools, 1li.; 11 Chaires & two small stooles,
16s.; 6 Turkie Cushins, 12s.; 1 pr. Andierns & small tongs,
4s. 6d.; halle, 1 warming pan, 2s. 6d.; 2 chests & 1 bord, 8s.;
waringe Clothes with a hat all giuen away, 4li. 10s.; 7 yds.
searge by har grand Children, 1li. 2s.; a parcell of linning
yarn, 1li.; 1 bedstead settle & rodds, 12s.; kitchen, doggs, 2
hakes, 2 spitts & tongs & slise & old brick, 12s.; pewter, 16s.;
brasse, 2 candlesticks, Chafendish and 2 skimers, skillet & 2
kittles, 1li.; Iron pots & Kittle, 2 pr. pothooks, 8s.; tubs, barrells, payls, trays & boales, 1-2 bushell, pck & 1-2 peck, Skales
& weights, 1pr. bellows, with all other wooden ware & wooden
grater, 16s.; ye Childs Chamber, 1 bed, boulster & 2 pillows,
1li. 15s.; barly, 7s. 6d.; 45 bushels Ind. Corn, 4li. 10s.; Chest
with Iron lumber in it, 16s.; Kings Chest and waring Clothes
3li. 10s.; in ye parlor Chamber, 2 bedsteds & bedding, with
ropes, matts with ruggs & blanketts, 2li. 5s.; 1 pillion &
saddle, 12s.; 4 Cowes, 10li.; 1 pr. oxen, 6li. 10s.; 4 swine, 1li.
5s.; ye horse, an ould one, 1li. 15s.; 3 Calves, sucking, 1li.;
body of a cart & tumbrell, 1li.; 6 1-2 bush. pease, 15s. 6d.; 2
Chaines, 10s.; forkes & rakes & iron box & all other trifling
Lumber, 5s.; 1 barrell sider, 12s.; beefe & porke, 2li.; plate,
6li. 7s. 4d.; cash, 12li. 15s.; linen, 3li. 15s.; the dwelling
house, out housing, orchards & in all about 7 acres of land ad-

joining, 110li.; about 4 acres called Cotta's lott, 40li.; 1 acre 3-4 of marsh & about 5 acres of upland in the south feild, 16li.; 3-4 an acre of marsh in ye north feild, 6li.; about 34 acres of upland in the north feild, 40li.; total, 293li. 4s. 4d. Debts due, 9li. 12s. 4d. Debts due from the estate: to legases given as by will, 27li.; to what was laid out & spent at the funerall for mornings & other wayes, 22li. 9s. 6d.; debts & Rattes to pay, 15li. 12s.; to har waring Clothes given away by her Grandchildren to poor folk, 4li. 10s.; total, 69li. 11s. 6d.

Attested in Salem court 26:4:1677 by Mr. Ruck, the executor.

Essex County Quarterly Court Files, vol. 26, leaves 119, 120.

ESTATE OF WILLIAM BARBER OF (LYNN?).

Inventory of the estate of William Barber was brought in 26:4:1677, by Elizabeth, the relict, who was appointed administratrix, and was to have the estate for her livelyhood.

Inventory of the estate of William Barbar, taken by Rich. Knott, Robert Bartlett and John (his H mark) Martayn: one Kow, 2li. 15s.; one Horse, 1li. 10s.; one old Sadell & 2 old Bridles, 6s.; one sord and Belt and powder & bullets, 10s.; To a snapt sack and Bullett molds, 2s.; Beed and Furnetture, 6li.; Wearing Cloaths and Hatt and Shirts, 1li.; 2 Chests, one Table and A small Box, 1li.; 2 potts, one Brass skillett & a frying pan, 1li.; puter platers & potts and porrengers, 1li. 2s.; a standing Cubbard, 8s.; Books and a bible, 5s.; a payle & wooden Dishes and Trenchers, And 2 earthen potts and a Tray, 5s.; one old pillion and an axe and two smoothing Irons and fire shoufell and other old Lumber, 10s.; land lying in the bounds of Dorchester as praysed by a former Inventory, 9li.; total, 25li. 13s. Debts to be paid, 8li. 2s. 6d. Due to be paid to Goody Farnenum, 3li. 8s.; to Richard Knott of Marblehead, 2li.; to Joseph Fiske of Line, 1li.; to Michell Bouden, 1li. 7s. 6d.; to John Leeg, 6s.; total, 8li. 2s. 6d.

Allowed in Salem court 29:4:1677 upon oath of Elizabeth, the widow.

Essex County Quarterly Court Files, vol. 26, leaf 121.

ESTATE OF MRS. [SARAH] CHARLES.

The will and inventory of the estate of widow Charles were proved and allowed in court 26:4:1677.

Salem Quarterly Court Records, vol. 5. leaf 107.

Inventory of the estate of widow Charles, deceased, Dec. 21, 1676, taken by Moses Mavericke and Samll. Ward: 1 petticoat & wascoat & 1 iron small ketle, 1li. 10s.; 1 gowne & 1 cloake, 1li.; 1 old felt, 2s. 6d.; 1 old cloke & apron, 2s. 6d.; 1 mans wt. wascoat & 1 Frying pan, 10s.; 1 women's coat, 2s. 6d.; suit & more old cloths, 1li. 10s.; Her Bed & covering, 5li.; 1 old warming pan, 5s.; 2 brass ketles, 1li. 3s.; 1 tin ketle, 1s.; 1 iron skellett, 4s.; 1 tongs & old fire shovel, 3s.; 1 small old Frying pan, 1s. 6d.; Wooden Lumber, 15s.; 1 old dimicaster, 5s.; 1 small brass ketle, 4s.; 1 ketle of brass, 5s.; 2 iron potts & 3 pot hooks, 1li.; 1 iron trammell, 4s.; 2 old Bibles, 10s.; total, 15li. 7s.

Mary Dennis, aged about thirty-three years, deposed that being with her aunt Charles in her last sickness, she told her on the day she died that she would like to make her will and wished to have deponent look after her burial. That "after her death she did give unto her sister Tryphena Geer, her gowne & cloake, & to Tryphena Fairfeild her daughter her red kersey petticoat and wescoat, & the litle iron ketle and to John Fairfeild her husbands w^t wascoate & ye Frying pan, & to Sarah Fairfeild, a flannel petticoat, and to Goodw: Goldsmith an old cloak & 1 apron and to Goodw: Haggett, her felt hatt, And to Mary Dennis jun^r her warming pan, to James Dennis, jun^r the 2 Bibles, to Agnes Dennis, her Iron trammell, fire-pan & tongs: to Agnes Dennis her Bed and Covering belonging to it, and to Robert Charles his two daughters fifty shillings a peice, to be paid to him when he came over for it" and she desired to settle her accounts and what was left she gave to deponent. James Dennis and his wife Mary were appointed administrators.

Essex County Quarterly Court Files, vol. 26, leaf 123.

ESTATE OF JOHN HATHORN OF LYNN.

"At Lynn y^e. 19th. day of October 1676 In the name of o^r Lord god Euerlasting Amen I John Hathorn of Lynn. being very weak & sick of body. but through the grace & mercy of the Lord. of good & perfect memory & in my cleere & good vnderstanding. & being willing to prepare my selfe for the good pleasure of the Lord to sett my house in the best order the Lord enableth mee, doe therefore make this my last will & testament. Viz I committ my body to the dust from whence It was taken, & to rest Untill the Resurrection vntill the Lord Jesus shall quicken it & cause it to arise agayne. And my Spirritt into the hands of the Lord Jesus. as my faithfull redeemer the Lord hauing at length through his abundant grace, given mee some hope of his euerlasting mercy through Jesus Christ ye son of his loue in whome I trust to be found at that day: And as for that little outward estate of this world wch the Lord hath beene pleased to leaue me to dispose of I giue & bequeath as followth Imp^r. I doe appoynt & desire that there bee a decent & an orderly buriall of my body in conuenient tyme after my decease It I doe will and appoynt that all my Just & honest debts that I doe owe wth the most & principall thereof according to my best memory I haue inserted in a list left for direction therein that they may bee honestly & duly paid: out of my estate, &c. And as for the remaynder of my little estate I bequeath viz It I hauing foure old fetherbeds. I giue & bequeath vnto my foure children, each of them one with ‖ a Couerlett ‖ a blankett. bolster pillow. & what else thereto belongeth: And my daughter Called marah to haue the choice in the first place. And my little daughter Phebe. next And my son Ebenezer Hathorne next & my son Nathaniell Hathorne. in the next place being younger It. I giue vnto my daughter Marah the new Red Rugg. And as for my houshold stuff. viz. My Brasse & pewter. & Iron vessels my will is that it bee equally diuided among them all according to ye discretion of prudent freinds in conuenient time only whilest the prouidence of god shall Continue them together ‖ to use al together ‖ Only that my daughters Marah & Phebe shall haue each of them. one large new platter: beside or before diuision bee made. Item I giue vnto my son Nathaniell a flock bed y^t I haue. least his p^t aforesaid of bedding may not bee soe good. as ye rest, &c. It I giue all my housing and land vnto my two sons. Ebenezer and Nathaniell to be equall betweene them. if it be the good pleasure of god to Continue them & to giue them Issue but if it bee his good pleasure to take either of them out of this world without Issue. then that part. to fall & belong to that son suruiuing & living. But in case it should bee the pleasure of the lord to take away both my sons aforesaid: without any Issue. Then my will is That my housing & lands goe & belong to my two daughters. Marah & Phebe, Equally. I giue vnto my two Sons aforesaid. my two working Bullocks each of them one. together with my utensels for husbandry as also a steere & a heifer one to one, & the other to the other.

"I giue vnto my two daughters, to each of them one Cow: I giue vnto my two daughters, to each of them one standing or

high Cubbard and Marah to haue the choyce of them. I giue to
my daughter Phebe, the finest Hollon sheete I giue to my two
sons each of them a Table cloth of flaxoncloth I giue my two
sons each of them a p^r of sheets & a p^r of pillowbers & halfe a
dozzen of Napkins I giue vnto my two daughters the rest of my
Linnen to be diuided equally betweene them in a conuenient
tyme. I giue vnto my foure children each of them one table. I
giue vnto my foure children each of them one Chest. I giue
vnto my daughter Priscilla Shore out of my estate as a remembrance of my loue the sum of Fourty shillings I giue
vnto my Grandchild Phebe Shore ye sum of Twenty Shillings
I giue vnto my daughter Marah ye bedsted y^t I & my wife ly
on I giue vnto my foure children aforesaid my horses & horse
kind that are abroad to be sold & then their value to be
diuided Equally amongst them all I giue vnto my two Sons
Ebenezer & Nathl my Gray horse I doe appoynt & ordein my
welbeloued & deare wife ‖ Sarah Hathorne ‖ to bee my executrix to this my last will & testament and my Son Ebenezer
Hathorne as Executor with her hereunto : And doe heereby
bequeath & order this & my whole estate to bee to her use &
Comfort for the tyme of her naturall life without Contradiction by any, &c. It. I doe ordeine & desire my louing & respected freinds & neighbors : John Fuller, Thomas Newhall
& Oliuer Purchis to bee my ouerseers of this my last will &
testament earnestly desiring them not only to bee my ouerseers but also to be of assistance & helpfull to my deare &
welbeloued wife aforesaid & my children that they with more
Comfort & cheerfulnes, be holpen forward in their business &
espetially in the way of the Lord to their good & eternall
peace in Christ Jesus : And for the full confirmaton. & testi-
fying this to bee my last will & Testament I haue heereunto
Sett my hand & seal. this Nineteenth day of October in y^e
yeere of o^r Lord one thousand six hundred and Seauenty
Six."

John Hathorn. (SEAL)

Witness : Robert (his R B mark) Burges, Oliver Purchis.
Proved at Linn, 26 : 1 : 1677 by the witnesses before Thomas Danforth, assistant, and in Salem court 27 : 4 : 1677.

Inventory of the estate of Mr. John Hathorne, deceased,
taken Feb. 21, 1676, by Quartermaster Thomas (his T mark)
Stocker and Robert (his R. B. mark) Burges, both of Lynn :
his dwelling house with the outhouses Barne & stals & stable
with the Orchard adjoyning & the land lying to it by estimation 3 acres more or less, 60li. ; Two acres of Marrish in Rum-

ney Marrish in ye lower devidend, 8li.; a pcell of land Commonly Called Bloods lott, 6 Acres, 15li.; 3 Ten acre lots neere Thaddeus Brann, 6li.; 5 acres of vacant land Called Burchams land, 2li.; 7 Cattle, viz. 2 Oxen, 3 Cowes, & 2 younger Cattle, 21li. 10s.; 13 sheep, 3li. 18s.; A Cart, & wheels, a sled, yoke & Copling & other appurt. as chayne & Ladders, &c., 2li.; old Iron & Lumber of Iron, 8s.; 2 pr. Andirons, 2 potracks & a fire shovell & tongs, 1li.; 9 Iron Vessells, pots, Kettles, morters, 1 pestl., 2 pothooks, 2li. 10s.; 1 Great Iron Fornace pan, 2li.; a Jack, & two spits & two smoothing Irons, 1li. 10s.; Brasse Vessels, 1 pot, 2 pans, 1 Skillett, 1 Skimmer, 2li.; pewter vessells, all new & old, 3li.; Tinsey Vessels, 4s.; plate, 2 Cups & spoones, 1li.; 1 Brasse Chaffing dish & 1 old warming pan, 5s.; 1 Fether bed & bolster with ye bedsted & 1 fether pillow with ye Blankets & Coverlett & Curtaynes, 7li.; 1 Trundle bed with a fether bed, 1 fether pillow with a flock bolster, with ye blankets & Coverlett, 3li.; 1 fether bed, 1 fether pillow, a flock bolster, with ye Coverings, Bedsteed Vallens & old Curtaynes, 6li. 10s.; 1 Fether bed, fether bolster, 1 pillow with Coverings & bedsted with vallens & Curtaynes, 9li.; 1 Flockbed, 2 fether pillowes & two Coverings & bedsted & one blankett, 3li. 10s.; 1 Livery Cubbart, Cubbart Cloth, Cushion with a long table & one old Carpett, 4li.; 1 Table, 12s.; 8 yds. wool cloth, 4s. p yd., 3 yds. 3-4 Lynsey woolsey at 3s. p., 2li. 3s. 3d.; To a Red Cradle Rugg, 6s.; Wearing apparrell of woollen & a hatt of his, 8li.; Linnen of his wearing also, 1li.; a pr. of bootes well worn, 10s.; seaven payre of sheets, 7li.; 5 Table clothes & a fine sheet, 6li. 10s.; 14 pillowbers, 3li.; 13 Napkins, 1li. 6s.; 18 Napkins, 2li. 5s.; 2 pr. of old sheets, 1 old pillowber & 3 Towels, 1li. 4s. a bundle of childs Linnen, 3li.; 4 lb. & 1-2 of Combed Wool, 1 old sheet & a pr. old drawers, 10s.; 2 Guns, 2 pistols & a Cutlas & belt, 3li.; 40 bushels of Indian Corn, 6li.; 22 lb. of Linnen yarn, 2s. p. lb., & 9 lb. of woolen, 2s. p., 3li. 2s.; 40 lb. of wool, 2li.; 34 lb. of Tallow Rough & tryed 4d. p lb., 11s. 4d.; an old pillion & pillion cloth, an old saddle, brest plate, a payre of new Bits & a Curb bridle, 1li. 10s.; a Small Hatt, 3s.; 17 lb. of yarne more, linnen & Cotton at 2s. 6d. p., 2li. 2s. 6d.; 2 lb. of Red hose yarn at 3s. 6d. p & 10 lb. Tallow, 8s. 4d.; 3 wheels, 1 p wool & 2 p Linnen & a Sweep, 11s.; 2 Swine shoats, 1li.; 2pr. Cards, 3s. 6d.; 4 Chests, one Trunke, one Small Table, 1li. 10s.; A livery Cubbart & two small Boxes, 1li. 10s.; two old bibles & a parcell of bookes, old, 15s.; one Table, 10s.; a long Table, two Fourms, & a

Carpet to ye table, 3li.; a Livery Cubbart with Cloth & a
lined board, 15s.; a short rope, a horse Collar & Traises, 9s.;
3 dozn. trenchers, 2s.; & 2 hand brushes, 2s.; 3 forkes & a
shovell, 5s.; Flax dressed & undrest, 14s.; two pr. small
Scales, Iron Beam, weights, earthern potts, small stone
Juggs & Glasse bottles, 10s.; a churne, a small Butter
Tubb, 2 Cheese fatts & one wooden Bole & two Trayes, 10s.;
Beefe & porke, 4li. 10s.; Two Barrels of Sydar, 1li.; Cheeses,
5 small ones, 5s.; 2 old chayres & payles & some such Lumber,
10s.; 2 meale sives, 2s.; 5 Barrels, 10s.; 2 Runlets, 3s.; 2
wooden bottles, 2s.; Two wrought Cushion Coverings, 10s.;
horses and horse kind in number eleven yt many of them have
not beene seene together this twelve months, 22li.; total,
263li. 6s. 11d.

Allowed in Salem court 27:4:1677 upon oath of Sarah,
the relict and executrix.

At Lynn, Oct. 19, 1676, a list of accounts, taken from Mr.
John Hathorn's own mouth, by Oliver Purchis, of debts due
from and to him according to his best memory as he did then
express being on his sick bed, when he made his will: from
Mr. Richard Cutts or his executors as by a bill to Lieutenant.
John Gilman, for 2,000 boards not received although demanded, 4li.; from Bonney Cowell three & foure pounds & to
write to Mr. Moodee to take care of both; from Mr. John
Todd of Rowley, 30s.; from Mr. Joseph Jewet's executors,
3li.; from Mr. Seaborn Cotton of Hampton, who is to pay it
to Capt. George Corwin, 15li.; from Mr. John Ruck, sr., if
he pay 10li. 5s. for Thomas Looke, sr.; from Quartermaster
Thomas Stocker, about 4 or 5li.; from Monseiur John Divan
about 6li. which he is hereby assigned to Capt. Marshal; from
Thomas Looke, sr., about 40s., besides Mr. Ruck's account;
from Oliver Purchis who is to be examined about an old bill
to Captayne Savage & a bill of 12li. Debts due: to Capt.
George Corwin, 25li.; to Mr. Batters, 14s.; to Thomas Newhall, sr., 3li. 9s.; as for Mr. William Bartholmew when I
paid him 20li. p Mr. Bennett then we were even; at Mr. Bennett's arbitration, Mr. Bartholmew sent me word that he
would pay me 10li. for Mr. Bennett; I had a Barrell of Rhum
of Mr. Bartholmew for which I paid him 40s., so there remained due to him 7s. 6d.; at one election time I scored with
him, 18s.; I had of him a Barrell of Fyal wine for which I
paid him 2li. 15s. and a bill of Mr. Jno. Bennet's hand of
40s.; to Major Thomas Clarke, 4li.; to Mr. Kellum, what the
sum is I know not but if hee give the full price for the wood

it will not be much; to Major Thomas Savage, 10li.; to Mr. Coalman, 18s.; to Thomas Fitts, shoemaker, 8s.; to Capt. John Corwin, who had Mr. John Blano's bill for 20 cord of wood, which he accepted as I understood for he took the bill and received part of the pay and had of mee a Cow of late time which I judge worth 4li.; to Mr. William Browne, sr., of Salem, I owe a debt.

Essex County Quarterly Court Files, vol. 26, leaves 124-126.

ESTATE OF JEFFERY MASSEY, SR., OF SALEM.

"The Last will and Testament of Jaffery Massey Senr of Salem which is as ffolloweth. Affter my Debts And ffunerall expences Discharged Imprimus I giue vnto Ellin my wiffe All my housing Lands Cattell and goods For her Maintenance during her Naturall Liffe And If Neede require to sell either Land Cattell or goods by the Advice of the oversears to witt Henry Skerry senr: and Francis Skerry. Item I giue Affter the desece of my wiffe what Estate Is Lefft vnto my sone John Massey Duering his Liffe And after the desece of my sonne his wiffe Sarah Massey is to haue one thirde part of the Land and the other two thirds of the Land with the Cattell and goods is to be devided betwixt the children then Living only After her deseace the Next Eaire Is to InJoye her thirds Item I Constitute my sonne John Massey as on exsecetor of this my will and If the Corte please to Appoynt another Item my will is that my overseers shall be sufisiently satffied for what time and expenses they shall be Att In the parformance of my will. In witnes hereof I haue here vnto put my hand the 6: of 9 mo: 1676."

Jeffrye (his ♂ mark) Marssye, Sener. (SEAL)
Witness: Henery Skerry, Sener, Frances Skerry.
Proved in Salem court 29: 4m: 1677 by the witnesses.

Inventory of the estate of Jeffery Massey of Salem, taken, 25: 9: 1676, by Henery Skerry, sr., and Francis Skerry: his dwelling house and an Aker of upland and an orchard In it with halfe a barne & an old house & fence to it, 40li.; 4 akers of salt & English gras meddo belowe the house, 40li.; 4 akers of pasture land fenced in Neere the house, 32li.; one Ten Aker Lot over the River Against ye house, 30li.; one Fether Bed & Boulster, 2 pillowes, A Rug And thre Blancits, 6li.; a bedsted, Curtins, vallants & Bed Cord, 1li. 7s.; An ould small fether Bed with Boulstars & Coverlet & two Blankets, 1li. 10s.; An old Cow, 3li.; his waring Clothes, on Cloke & An old Cote & 2 pare of Breches & a dublit & Apare of Gloves, 4li.; a hat & thre hancarchars, 4 band & 2 Caps, 8s.; A box, Iorne & pot hucks, 3s.; a pare of AndIornes, a spit, tongs, a hake, one pot And Cettell & fier pan, one mortising Ax, & a wedg, 1li. 5s. 6d.; for old putar, a Tabell & forme & small Tabell & Joynt stoole, 1li. 2s.; 2 Chests, one of Joynar worke & one sea chest, 2 chayres & 2 Cushins, 1li. 2s.; Thre old brasse Ceettels, a brasse Candellstick, a scimer & pott Cover, 14s.; A Linin Whele & To[w] Come, 7s.; a parsell of old Lumbar, of severall Things, 14s.; total, 163li. 12s. 6d. Debts, 1li. 15s.; funeral expenses, 2li. 7s. 9d.

Attested in Salem court 26 : 4 : 1677 by John Massy.

Essex County Quarterly Court Files, vol. 26, leaves 116,117.

An account of the estate of Jeffrey Massey: inventory total, 163li. 12s.; Debt received that was due to the estate by 10 cord of wood, 4li., corne, 1li., 5li.; money, 16s.; breaking up of land, 2li. 8s.; the use of the land during my Father's and Mother's life which was about 7 years, 42li.; from John Batchelder in fencing stuff, 12s.; total estate, 214li. 8s.

The estate indebted for the keeping and maintaining of my father and mother with both Food, Physick & Tendance both in sickness & health for the space of four yeares untill ye time of my father's departure, which account was well approved of by ye overseers nominated in my Father's will, namely, Henry Skerrey, sr. and Francis Skerrey amounted to 106li.; funerall expence, 3li. 15s.; Debt to Mr. William Browne, sr., 3li. 12s.; to Capt. George Corwine, sr., 4li.; to Jno. Bachelour in money, 1li.; loss of halfe an aker of land aprised in ye inventory, 5li.; total, 123li. 15s.

Charges layd out upon my mother after my fathers decease for ye space of three yeares & upwards for Food, Phisick & Tendance while she was in a very weak condicon amounted to 30li.; funerall expence as money, 2li. 7s.; Damage to ye Estate in ye time of my mothers weakness, 5li.; total, 37li. 7s.; making total expence, 161li. 2s.

Attested by John Massey, sr. July 2, 1694 before Hon. Bartholmew Gedney.

Essex County Probate Files, Docket 17,991.

Quitclaim of Jeoffry Massy of Wells in County of Yorkshire in New England, taylor, he having received of his father John Massey of Salem, yeoman, two acres of land in Salem bounded "northerly by ye land of Thomas Elkins, Southerly wth y^a land of s^d John Massey, Westerly by ye Country Road or River, Easterly by ye Comon highway to ye Ferry together wth Orchard Fences comonages and all profits and privilidges & Appertenances of w^t nature or kind so ever thereunto belonging" these two acres being the full payment of the 22li. left to him by his grandfather Jeofry Massey, deceased, as by his last will may more fully appear. Signed and sealed Sept. 3, 1700.

Witness: Daniel Eps, John Trask.

Acknowledged by Jeoffry Massey Sept. 4, 1700 before Hon. Jonathan Corwin, Judge of Probate.

Essex County Probate Records, vol. 307, page 44.

Account of what charges John Massey have been at with my Father and Mother in the tyme of there Age & weaknes Begining in March, 1672 and for my Father & Mother continewed togeather for the space of fore years & a half in much weakness before the time of his deceas: there is alowed for there dyat & Tendance, 90li.; alowed for 8 cords of wood by the yeare for 4 years & upwards, 14li. 8s.; wine & Lickars as there needs Required, 1li. 12s.; funerall expences for my father, 2li. 10s.; Debt to Mr. Browne, sr., 3li. 12s.; to Capten Georg Corwin, 4li. 8s.; total, 116li. 10s. Charges about my Mother after my fathers decease by the means of hir long weaknes of Boddy for the space of two yeares & a half or more no waies Able to help hirself but we mostly to help hir In that condition, 30li.; hir Funerall Expences, 1li. 18s.; losses to the estate by waste of Beding & other things, 5li.; the Oversears considdering the extreordenary Troble that was with my Mother have thought good to ad 11li. more Tords my satisfaction; total, 164li. 8s. The whole inventory of my Father's estate, 214li. 8s.

Henry Skerry, sr. and Francis Skerry the overseers to the will of Jeffery Massey, approved of this account of John Massey as executor to his father's estate, July 1, 1680, and there being fifty pounds remaining to be paid to the children according to the will after his and his wife's decease, we have set apart one house and one acre of land with half an orchard thereto belonging and half a barn thereunto belonging valued at forty pounds for their security, as also another acre and quarter of land in the pasture toward the North Ferry at ten pounds.

Essex County Quarterly Court Files, vol. 33, leaf 108.

ESTATE OF EDMUND NEEDHAM OF LYNN.

"The will and Last Testament of Edmund Needham of Lin in Nu England being Blesed be God in his perfect knowl-

edge memory and understanding tho other wies ill in Body
made & writen by min on hand & acording to min on mind
to my Children and Grandchilldren as follows: first I humbly desire my only True God maker ‖& creator‖ of ‖exodus.
20.11. Psalms 95 : 3.4.5. and. 146. 5.6. Jonah 1.9. ‖heauen &
earth the sea & all that is ther in and me his most por & un-
worthy creature amungst yᵉ Rest. &. to reseue my poor and
on worthy soull of his meer pur & only free Grace and Loue
for yᵉ sake of his only & well beloued ‖son‖ Jesus Christs
sake alone excluding ‖all‖ things of min ‖carnall or‖ cor-
rupte natur in or of myself in any mater or means in hol or
in part to my Justification but to Jesus Christ alon my only
& alon mediator aduocat & intersesor at yᵉ thron of Grace &
alon propisiation for all my sinnes. 1ˢᵗ John. 2. 2. next I de-
siar & impower my sun Ezekiell Needham my tru & Lawfull executor to this my Last will & Testament to se my body
desently & Christianly Buried as neer my old wif being his
on mother as may be Next I giue to my sun daniell Needham
be sids all the housing dwelling house he now dwells in Barn
& all yᵉ out housing all yᵉ Land that was laid
out to him planting land upland & sallt marsh
medo condisionally as is in a deed ‖to him‖ ex-
presed towards my maintenance while I liue in this world: &
also yᵉ bedsted yᵗ stands in my last built nu room wᵗh yᵉ bed
I leue him & to blankets & the curtains & valence belonging
to it and to his fiue Chilldren fiue yu sheep yᵗ is to say John
Needham on & Ezekiell Needham on & iudah Needham on
and Mary Needham on and Elizabeth Needham on Next I
giue to my sun Ezekiell Needham all the upland & yᵉ fresh &
salt medo on both sides yᵉ riuar and all the rest of my mouables on the conditions mensioned in a deed to me yᵗ he
should prouide for me & my wife when then she was liuing &
all things nesesary conuenient that we stood in need of for
our comfortabell liuelyhood in heallth & sicknes whill we
liued her in this world euery way sutabell to our old age &
seuerall condisions & all my mouables I giue to him besides
where as he my sun Ezekiell Needham my Lawfull Executor
hath discharged yᵉ to doctars & all other if any du debtes or
demands what so euer yᵗ any can iustly demand of me: allso
my Chilldrens & gran chilldrens legasies in this my will ex-
presed & then to his to Children to yo sheepe all yᵉ rest to be
as hir on proper goods; that is to say my sun Ezekiell Need-
hams on proper goods as proper to him as euer they were
proper to me: Next I giue to my dafter Hanah diuen & hur

to Chilldren Twenty fiue pounds to be paied them halfe in
Catell & y⁰ rest in good & honest suficient pay that is to say
fifteen pounds to hur selfe present if liuing or ellse to hur
husband if he be liuing after hur & fiue pounds to her dafter
Hanah Armitag & fiue pounds to hur last born son John
diuen when they shall come to age but if any on of them shall
dy before they com to age the longest liuer of them to haue
yᵉ holl ten pounds but if they both dy then ther mother to
haue yᵉ holl ten pounds at yᵉ time yᵗ if they had liued should
haue com to age but if yᵉ mother & hur sun & dafter should
all three dy then my sun Ezekiell Need. to haue yᵉ holl ten
pounds only giuing yᵉ on hafe of it that is to say fiue pounds
of it to hur ‖brother‖ my sun daniell Needham.

"Next I giue unto my sun in Laws ‖Samuell Harts‖ Chilldren first to his dafter in Law born of hur first husband
Elizabeth How but now by mariag Elizabeth Chadwell on yo
sheepe, next to his elldest sun Samuell Hart on Cow & on yo
sheepe ye sheep not exeding four yers old next to Joseph Hart
on yo sheepe next to abigall Hart on yo sheep & thirty shillings mor in good & lawfull pay for her great Car of me in
my sicknes be sides the wages yᵗ I shall giue hur for yᵉ time
she staies wᵗʰ me & to hir dafter Rebeck Hart on yo sheep
all the sheep not exseding four yers old. next I giue to my sun
in Law Joseph Mansfield chilldren first his son Joseph Mansfielld on yo sheep & to his next sun John mansfield wᶜʰ I haue
brot up euer since his Childe hood till now he is about fiften
yers old to him this John mansfielld I giue on Cow & on yo
sheep not exceding four yeres old & to his dafter Elizabeth
wheat on yo sheepe & to deborah mansfild on yo sheep. and
further this I ad as a Codasell or breefe inuentory to this my
last will and Testament that my sun Ezekiell Needham my
Lawfull Executor shall not be put to any oath or oaths at any
Court or any man ——n what soeuer then her I haue set according to min one valuation of my holl estate & if this will
not saue him from any oath abou — it he shall safly swer
that ‖ yᵗ is ‖ all my holl estat I hauing firmly giuen him as
his on proper o— as if it had neuer ben min so son as euer
yᵉ breat is out of my body & I quite dead an I rest I well
knowing yᵗ he canot giue any iust oath wᵗʰ out wronging
his Consienc as I only best know how my estate lies & this
min on valuation or inuentory followes

"first all my housing barn & out housing and al my Lands
wᵗʰ all the chargs of ston wall fensing &c. 400li., to holl peses
of baies on red & yᵉ other of yᵉ collar of a Chestnut on or to
& forty yards a pece at yᵉ lest, 12li., one holl peese of red pen-

iston on or to & forte yards long at ye lest, 6li., 3 parselles of
Canuis ner about on hundred yards & other parsells of linen
cloth & Calico, 10li., my silluer wach & siluer box & other
silluar cupes & spoones & other plate, 15li., my Clock y^t
strikes & another watch & larum that dus not strike, 5li., sum
puter sum old & sum new, 2li., sum parselles of Carsies &
sum parselles of serges & my wering Clothes, 26li., sum potes
& ketelles & trunkes & Chestes & bedsteed, 7li., beds & beding, 7li., debts in old England in suffisient Bonds & most in
abell mens hands as the company of ye marchant aduentorers
& a nother loked at as a great rich Citizen fit for an alldar of
London tho they do what they can to deseue us y^t is to say my
brothers & sisters to whom they o us abou three thousand
pounds, 600li., total, 1,090li., & on horse y^t was forgot, 3li.,
& 4 coues & to young bulloks forgot allso, 17li., allso 20
sheepe forgot, 7li., total, 1,117li.

"But as for this debt in old England y^t is sumthing un-
sartain what my to aturnies in England being my to Brothers
may get for me & them sellues wth sumthing mor y^t may be
coming both to them sellues & me I desier to leue it to my
Chilldren in ye best order as I can amungst them Thus first I
institute my sun Ezekiell Needham my Lawfull executor &
lawfull aturny in this *in this* business as in min on steed &
in min on nam as in mine on person to look ye best after it as
posibell he can & what euer shall com ouer of it wth y^e
charges about it discharged them foreuer twenti pounds y^t
shall cum thus safe in to his hands he shall pay vnto his
Brother Daniell Needham if he be liuing six pounds & to his
sister Hanah diuen four pounds if liuing or ells ye four
pounds to hur to Chilldren Hanah armitage & John diuen if
they be liuing & ther mother dead or ellse to *to* ether on of
them if on should be liuing & ye other dead.

"and further if this will not satisfi any Court or Courts
man or men what so euer wth out my sun Ezekiell Needham
my Law full executornies oath to my wholl estate then my
will is that my sun Ezekiell Needham my Lawful Executor
shall safly mak oath y^t this my holl estate I hauing fully &
wholy desposed of all ye rest in my life as if had neuer ben
min for other wise I can not se how he shound make oath wth
out ronging his Conscience my estat lying as it dus wch is
only best known to myselfe."

Edmund Needham. (SEAL)

Witness: Rich. Walker, Ralph King.

Proved in Salem court 29 : 4 : 1677 by the witnesses.

Essex County Quarterly Court Files, vol. 26, leaf 118.

ESTATE OF CHRISTOPHER COWES.

Administration upon the estate of Christopher Cowes, intestate, was granted Aug. 11, 1677, to Gyles Cowes, his brother, who was ordered to bring in an inventory to the next Ipswich court.

Ipswich Quarterly Court Records, vol. 5, page 293.

ESTATE OF MRS. SUSANNA ROGERS OF NEWBURY.

"All men shall knowe by this p^{r}sent writeing that I Susanna Rogers of the towne of Newbery widdow, doe giue & bequeath unto my three sones Robert Thomas & John Rogers all my upland & mash vppon plum iland, that is to say halfe of it to my son Robert & the other halfe to be equally deuided betwene Thomas & John Rogers, & I doe ingage my tow sones Robert & John when they shall com of age to pay ech of them ffiue poundes a peece to my Daughter Ellezabeth, & I giue likewise to my son. Robert a gun wch was his fathers, & I giue to my Daughter Ellezabeth one payre of sheetes & a payre of pillabears at her day of marriage & I giue to my son Thomas at the day of my death his fathers bible, as for the upland & mash at plum iland I my selfe am to make use of it till my sones com of age & to this I haue set my || hand || this 3^d of July 1665."

Susanna Rogers.

Witness: Abraham Toppan, Senior, Peter Toppan.

Proved Sept. 24, 1677 by Peter Toppan before Jo. Woodbridge, Commissioner.

"I William Thomas doe giue consent freely to this present writeing as witnesse my hand Sept: 28th 1677."

W^m: Thomas.

Witness: Anthony Somerby, Joseph Muzzey.

Proved Sept. 28, 1677 by the witnesses.

Essex County Probate Files, Docket 24,069.

Susanah Rogers, deceased, having made a writing as a will which was presented to this court and no executor named, court Sept. 25, 1677, granted administration of her estate to John Rogers, son of Susana Rogers, the estate to be ordered according to the said writing.

Ipswich Quarterly Court Records, vol. 5, page 298.

ESTATE OF JAMES FORD OF IPSWICH.

Administration upon the estate of James Fooard, intestate,

was granted Sept. 25, 1677, to John Wainwright and he was
ordered to bring in an inventory to the March court.

Ipswich Quarterly Court Records, vol. 5, page 296.

Inventory of the estate of James Ford taken Oct. 6, 1677:
2 1-2 yards of serge, 10s.; 5 yards 3-4 galoone silk, 9d.; 2
yard of calico, 8s.; all rcd. of John French; 20, 1 old axe sold
Ephra. Fellows, 5s., 1 coate sold Robert Shelite, 23s. 2d., 1
chest Fr. young, 5s., 1li. 13s. 2d.; Mar. 18, 1 old cutlas without a scabard to Sam. Ingalls, 4s.; his armes alowed by the
country, 1li. 6s.; total, 4li. 11s. 4d.; 23, goods apprized pr.
Nath. Tredwell and Francis Young, Francis Young as followeth: 1 pr. of stockings, 3s.; 1 pr. spaterlashes, 1s. 6d.; 1
pr. shoes, 3s.; 1 glas, 1 pr. woolen gloves, 1s.; 1 old bible, 4s.;
2 pr. of breeches, 1 jacett & wastcoat, 6s. 6d., 10s. 6d.; 2
shirts, 8 neckcloths, 1li.; 4 hancherchifs, 2s.; 1 Hatband, 3d.,
1 ax, 3s., 3s. 3d.; 1 beetle & 4 wedges, 6s.; total, 3li. 14s. 3d.
making total estate, 8li. 5s. 7d. James Ford Dr. to John
Wainwright, 5li. 10s. 1d.

An account of disbursements, Sept. 25, 1677: for administration, 1s.; one day attendance, 1s. 6d.; for recving ye goods
of Jo. French, 1s.; 1 day receiving goods of Ephraim Fellows,
2s.; cartage of a chest, 1s.; apriseing the goods, 1s. 6d.;
total, 8s.

Attested in Ipswich court Mar. 26, 1678 by John Wainwright administrator, and the court ordered him to be paid
his debt of 5li. 18s. 1d. and the remainder to be paid to any
creditor that make claim.

Copy, Ipswich Deeds, vol. 4, page 160.

ESTATE OF THADDEUS BRAND OF LYNN.

Administration upon the estate of Tadeus Brand, intestate, was granted Sept. 25, 1677, to Capt. Thomas Marshall
and he was ordered to bring in an inventory to the next
Salem court.

Ipswich Quarterly Court Records, vol. 5, page 296.

Capt. Thomas Marshall, administrator of the estate of
Thaddeus Brand, who was slain in the wars, brought in an inventory of the estate 27:9:1677, and was bound.

Salem Quarterly Court Records, vol. 5, leaf 112.

Bill of charges about settling the estate of Thadeus Brann:
to Leutenant Purchis and John Fuller for procuring the appraisers, Thomas Newhall and Roberd Potter, 10s.; to Capt.

Marshall, Leut. Purchis and John Fuller, for fetching the goods down to the town out of the woods and making them safe, 7s. 6d.; to Elisha, son of John Fuller, with his cart and oxen to fetch down the goods, 5s.; to Capt. Marshall and John Fuller, as clerk of the writs, 12s.; to Capt. Marshall and John Fuller with two appraisers, Edward Baker and Thomas Stocker, and to looking up the Hogs, two men two days apiece, 8s.

Toodeas (his +∝ mark) Brain certified, Nov. 16, 1676, that he freely gave his child Mary Bran to Zacheus Courties, sr., and if he left any estate, she should have an equal portion with his other child or children. Wit: John (his T mark) Towne and Zacheus Courties.

Inventory of the estate of Teague alias Thaddeus Brann, who was impressed a soldier of Lyn for the country's service and was sent forth from Lyn on June 22, 1677 and slain in the fight at Blackpoynt on June 29, 1677, taken July 4, 1677, by Thomas Newhall and Robert Potter: A dwelling house, a little out house or Hovell, with four acres of land, a small part of it orchard, 30li.; 1 heifer, 2 yeer old & upward & one yearling heifer, 3li. 10s.; 1 mare about 5 or 6 yeers old, 1li.; 6 bo. & 1-2 of Corne in the house, 19s.; 2 Iron pots, 1 small Kettle, 2 pr. pothooks & an old frying pan, 1li. 10s.; a beetle with Rings, 4 wedges & 3 Axes, 12s.; a pitchforke with a parcle of broken Iron, a bullet or mustard bowl, 6s.; 3 Augurs, 2 Lettle chizzles & an old sickle & file, 6s.; 1 Barrell, 1 Bottle of a Gallon, 2 pailes, 3 Trayes, 7s.; 8 wooden Vessels, platters, dishes & six Trenchers, 2s. 6d.; 1 small Brass skillet, with a frame, 2s. & 1 stone bottle, 6d.; 1 glass bottle, 6d.; a little pewter bottle, 6d.; 2 seiles, 18d.; 1 wood Ladle & 3 wooden vessels, 6s.; An old Rapier & 2 pr. of old Bandileirs, 8s.; 3 old Hats, 8s.; & a pcell of old clothes, 10s.; 4 blew neckclothes, 2s.; 1 Lether Apron, 18d.; a Gimlet, 3d.; a Nal, 2d., & Knifes, 4d.; 2 pcells of wool, 18d.; a sithe, one Snead & Tugs or nebs, 3s.; a pcell of Toe, 3s. 4d.; a horne & powder, 1s.; a Box & Lumber, 3s.; 1 sack with about 2 pecks & 1-2 meal & 3 smal bags, 5s. 6d.; 1 Barrell & 1 old Chest, 3s. & a Trough, 6d., & 3 chayrs, 2s. 6d.; 1 old saddle & haire Rope, 2s.; a parcel of meat, 20 lb., 5s.; the bedsted with mat, Ticken & Coverlett, 10s.; thre Hogs and 4 pigs, 3li.

In house with Allester Dugglas; A fether bed & bolster, wa. 40 lb, with a sheet & Coverlett, 4li. 10s.; In a chest there, 2 pewter platters, 2s., 2 porringers, 8d., 1 chamber pott, 3s.;

1 Course sheet, 5s.; 1 halfe sheet finer but old, 5s.; 1 Searg Coat, 24s.; 1 pr. of searge Breeches, 8s.; 3 shirts, 24s.; 1 pr. of drawers, Linnen, 3s.; 2 pr. of stockings, 6s.; 1 pr. white Gloves, 6d.; Certayne peeces of Linnen, neckclothes, Caps & handwipers, 3s.; the chest, 2s.; Tallow at Allesters, about 8 lb., ——; a warming pan at Josiah Rhoades, being lent; a churn & a cheese fate at Jno. Provenders; a sow & 5 pigs, 2 Hogs, abroad now; a parcell of Turmett seed, 1-2 lb., sold by Allester & d. to Mr. Appleton, 1s.

Estate disposed of July 4, 1677: To Macam Downing's wife, ye saddle & rope, as pt. of what is due them from the estate for nursing the young child, 2s.; to Allester Dugglas, 8 lb. of Tallow, 2s.; to Mr. Samuell Appleton, 1 lb. 3-4 Turnett seed, 1s. 4d. Sarra & mary were the two children of deceased. On July 24, 1677: to Macam Downing, ye 8 wooden vessels, & ye platters, dishes & 6 Trenchers, 2s. 6d.; 1-2 ye meat, 2s. 6d.; Corne 16 pecks, in ears, 2 bo., 4s. 6d.; 1 Barrell, 2s.; 1 paile, 1s.; ye sack with meal & 3 other bags, 5s. 6d.; The mans Black Hatt yt. was Teagus, 3s.; the 3 Trayes yt. were adjudged, 1s. 6d.; the old saddle, 2s.; total, 1li. 4s. 6d.; to Allistor Duggles, 1-2 ye meat, 2s. 6d.; corne, 10 pecks in ears, 5 pecks, 2s. 10d.; Oliver Purchis had: a little gallon Bottle or runlet, 1s. 6d.; the sithe, snead & Tugs, 3s.; the old sickle & ye little file.

Attested in Salem court 28:9:1677 by Capt. Tho. Marshall, administrator, who gave bond.

Essex County Quarterly Court Files, vol. 27, leaves 116, 117.

ESTATE OF JOHN BROWNE, JR., OF SALEM.

Administration upon the estate of Mr. John Browne, intestate, was granted Sept. 25, 1677, to Hanah Browne, widow, who was ordered to bring in an inventory to the next Salem court.

Ipswich Quarterly Court Records, vol. 5, page 296.

Inventory of the estate of Mr. John Browne, Jr., of Salem taken Aug. 10, 1677 by Christopher Babbidge and Richard Croade: a peece of Land in Salem neer to ye Land of Mr. James Browne by ye marsh called planters marsh being about 3 acres, 50li.; one eighth part of a Trackt of Land at ye Sowthward in partnership with others ye whole Trackt containing fifteen myles Square, 160li.; a piece of Land lyeing next to ye Land of Robert Glanfield & Thomas Jeggells in Salem, 20li.; Bedding with what belongs to it, 34li. 8s.;

Trunks, chaires, Boxes, stooles & cushens, 10li. 17s.; his Bookes, CuppBoard, Table, Carpett &c., 4li. 4s.; in pewter, 9li. 14s.; Brass ware, 7li. 5s.; howsehold Lyning, 12li. 5s.; Iron ware with some woodden Lumber, 5li. 7s.; debts oweing to ye Estate as at present probable, 20li.; total, 334li. Besides what may be due to him by his owners in London at his decease but it cannot be proved by account as yett appearing; but according to my best information from my husband & what I have heard by others it may be about 100li., a desperate debt; total estate, 434li. Debts oweing to be paid out of ye estate, 334li.

Attested in Ipswich court Mar. 26, 1678 by Hanah Browne relict of John Browne, administratrix of his estate.

Essex County Probate Files, Docket 3,615.

John Browne, Sr. acknowledged the receipt from his daughter in law Hannah, relict and administratrix of the estate of his son John Browne, of a debt of 190li. due to him from his said son. Signed Jan. 16, 1678-79. Witness: William Gill, John Archer.

Attested in the last month 1678 by the witnesses.

Richard Croad, Sr. of Salem acknowledged Oct. 8, 1679, the receipt from Mrs. Hanah Browne of Salem, relict and administratrix of the estate of her husband, Mr. **John Browne** the sum of 49li. 9s. due by bill from the said **Browne.**

Witness: Richard Flinder, James Browne.

Acknowledged 20: 8m: 1679 by Richard Croad.

Richard Flinder of Salem, mariner, acknowledged Oct. 14, 1679, the receipt from Mrs. Hannah Browne of Salem, relict and administratrix of the estate of her husband Mr. John Browne of 50li. due by bill from the said Browne and likewise do deliver up the mortgage on about three acres of land near to planters marsh in Salem which was for security.

Witness: Richard Croad, James Brown.

Acknowledged 20: 8: 1679 by the witnesses.

John Micarter of Salem, cloth worker, acknowledged Apr. 16, 1679, the receipt from Mrs. Hannah Browne, administratrix to the estate of her husband Mr. John Browne, 54li. 11s., due to him by bill and likewise to deliver up the mortgage given for security. Witness: Rebecha Mecarter, Rhoda Meachem.

Acknowledged 7: 5m: 1679.

Ipswich Deeds, vol. 4, pages 290, 291.

ESTATE OF JOHN BROWNE, SR., OF IPSWICH.

Administration upon the estate of John Browne of Ipswich, intestate, was granted Sept. 25, 1677, to John Browne, his eldest son, who produced an inventory amounting to about 450li. The estate was ordered to be divided as follows: besides the 50li. each, paid or designed to be given by the father to his two daughters, Jacob and Thorne, he shall pay within one year to each of them 10li.; to his brother Nathaniell who hath already received upon his marriage 200li., they see no cause to allow more; the rest of the estate, houses, lands, cattle, goods, etc., were ordered to said John Browne, provided the houses and lands were bound to pay to his mother 16li. per annum and a room in the house with necessary furniture during her life, and also pay such legacies as she shall bequeath at her death to her children, not exceeding the value of 21li.

Ipswich Quarterly Court Records, vol. 5, page 298.

Inventory of the estate of John Browne, Sr. deceased Sept. 13, 1677, taken Sept. 20, 1677 by Richard Hubberd and John Whipple: Thirteen acres of Land belonging to the dwelling howse, 65li.; Dwelling house, Barne & Comonage, 65li.; Thirty Acres of Marsh wth some Islands of upland, 120li.; total, 250li. Lands towards Wenham engaged to his younger Son Nathaniell, 150li.; Two small parcells of Marsh one at Plume Island, the other at the Hundreds, 20li.; a dwelling howse, 30li.; total, 200li. Six Loads of Hay in ye barne, Eleven Loads at ye marsh, 8li.; Four Acres of Barly in the Barne, 12li.; One acre of Rye in ye Barne, 2li. 8s.; Foure acres Indian Corne, 7li.; Indian, Ry and malt in ye house, 3li. 16s.; total, 25li. 4s. In Cattle: Two oxen, 10li.; 3 Cowes, 10li. 10s.; Three 3 yeare old Cattle, 7li. 10s.; Foure 2 year old, 8li.; Three year old, 3li.; Two Calves, 1li. 4s.; Twenty three sheep, 8li. 10s.; Fifteen Lambs, 3li. 15s.; Eight Swine, 8li.; Thirteen Shotes, 3li. 5s.; Five horse Kind, 4li.; total, 67li. 14s. Plowghs, Carts, wheeles, slead, yoaks & chaynes, 3li. 5s.; Axes, Sithes, Sawes and other utinsills of Husbandry wth some Armour, 3li. 12s.; total, 6li. 17s. In the dwelling howse: In money, 2li. 6s. 9d.; The Apparrell of the deecased, 7li. 6s.; Woollen & Linnen Cloath, 4li. 12s.; total, 14li. 4s. 9d. In the Hall: A Featherbed wth ye appurtenances, 7li.; In Peuter, 1li. 6s.; Tinne ware, 10s.; Brasse Kettles, skillets, mortar & warming pan, 1li. 19s.; Three Iron Potts, 1li. 5s.; Three pr. of Pothookes, 5s.; Tramell, firepan, Tongs, slice,

Tosting Iron, Flesh fork, &c., 1li. 6s.; total, 13li. 11s. Foure
chayres, 8s.; Table & two chests, 16s.; Payles & other coopers
ware, 14s.; total, 1li. 18s. In the Parlor: Bed wth Furniture,
3li.; Flax and yarne Linnen & Woollen, 4li. 14s.; Wheeles &
Cards, 1li.; total, 8li. 14s. In the chamber: Bed wth ye appurtenances, 2li. 15s.; Hoggesheads and other Lumber, 7s.;
Kneading Trough, Hetchell, 8s.; Wooll, 2li.; Sheets, 2li.
10s.; Table Cloths, 1li.; Napkins, Pillowbeers, 1li. 7s.; Bridle
& Saddle, 10s.; total, 10li. 17s. Sum total, 606li. 19s. 9d.
Debts due from the estate: to his Daughter Martha as part
of her portion, 20li.; Funerall charges, 5li.; to Deacon Goodhue, 5li.; to Rates, 3li.; worke done this summer, 3li.; to the
Malsters, 3li. 4s.; total, 39li. 4s.

Attested in Ipswich court Sept. 25, 1677 by John Browne
to be a true inventory of his father's estate.

Essex County Probate Files, Docket 3,614.

Petition of John Browne to the Ipswich court Apr. 1,
1679, shewing that when the court settled the estate of his
father, they were not rightly informed of his father's mind,
nor in what condition he left his estate which causes the petitioner to inform the court how his father determined his estate
should be disposed of and what he gave in his lifetime to his
brothers and sisters: he settled my brother Nathaniell upon a
better estate than he left to me, he gave 30li. to my sister
Martha Thorne and willed that I should pay to her 20li. more,
and he gave to my sister Sarah Jacobs, 50li. and this was all
my father intended and willed that they should have, but as it
is now settled the least of them will have more then may prove
to be clear from the estate to me; for the estate my brother Nathaniell now possesses I paid 150li. of the purchase and when
my brother married my father desired me to let him have my
interest in the estate which I did whereupon my father promised me the estate he lived upon after his decease. Administration upon the estate was granted to me and the court ordered
that I should allow my mother 16li. per year and I was willing
so to do, but it was not his will that I should pay to my sisters
10li. a peice more and give to my mother 21li. for her disposal,
and the estate is left with debts to be paid and my mother is
now living with my sister Sarah to whom the 16li. must be
paid, and he desires the court to so order the estate that he
will not haue to pay the amounts to his sisters and to lessen
what he will have to pay to his mother.

Deposition of Nathaniell Browne aged about 25 years that
his father said he would "give to your brother John all my

Liueing boath Land & stock afture my desease, onely he shall
mainetaine my wife and pay to my dafture Martha Thorne
twenty pounds for said my Father I haue giuen to you all that
I intend you shall haue and I haue paied my dafture Sarah Jacobs Fivety pounds and that is all that shee shall
haue, and I haue paied to my dafture thorne thirty pounds and
twenty pounds more my sonn John shall pai to her if I should
not Live to paie it."

Mary Lamberd, aged 20 years, testified that she heard her
master Browne often speak the words above written.
Sworn in Ipswich court Apr. 1, 1679.

The deposition of Andrew Burlay aged about 21 years that
when he lived with old goodman Browne he often heard him
speak concerning what he had given to his son Nathaniell
Browne and unto his daughters Martha and Sarah, and that
his son John should have all the estate which he had then in
his possession, etc. Sworn in Ipswich court Apr. 4, 1679.
Essex County Quarterly Court Files, vol. 31, leaves 17, 18.

Upon the complaint of John Browne to this court, it was
ordered Nov. 6, 1678, that he should not pay the two ten
pounds to his sisters until the March court next and then the
court will consider of it.
Ipswich Quarterly Court Records, vol. 5, page 339.

Whereas by order of court held at Ipswich Sept. 25, 1678,
John Browne was ordered to pay unto his two sisters Martha
and Sarah ten pounds a peice and twenty one pounds to his
mother, upon the consideration of the petition of the said John
Browne and the testimony of Andrew Birdley, Nathaniell
Browne and Mary Lamberd the court Apr. 1, 1679, sees cause
to release him from paying the same.
Ipswich Quarterly Court Records, vol. 5, page 345.

· ESTATE OF JAMES BAILEY OF ROWLEY.

"James Bayley of Rowley being weake of body, but pfect in
understanding and memory, do make this my last will and
Testament, in manner & forme as followeth, After my debts
are payd I do give and bequeath, the rest of the estate, God
hath given me as followeth, I doe give, unto my daughters
Lidia Platts and Damaris Leaver each of them, Twenty pound
a peece and to my daughter Platts, seaven pounds more, which
is in the hands of Thomas Remington, she to have that seaven
pounds when it is due the twenty pounds a peece, that I do
giue unto my two daughters, to be payd in four yeares time,

Also I do give unto my Eldest son John all that land and meadow, *and meadow*, that he is now possesed of and halfe of the farme, that I purchased of m^r Rogers and that Land, that Goodman Jackman doth improve, from merimack River downe to the meadow, my meaneing is from the River, untill it doth come, as far as m^r Phillips his meadow, or the peece comonly cald the five acres, and the rest of that land, that goodman Jackman doth hire, that is betweene the sayd five acres, and crane meadow, to be equally devided, betweene my son John and James.

"Also I doe give unto my son John Bayley, four acres of land more or less lyeing at the Plaine comonly cald, the Rye Plaine. Also I do give unto my son James Bayley, all my lands and meadow that I am possessed off in the Towne of Rowley, with all the buildings upon the same together with that two acres of meadow that I purchased of goodman Lyon wch was sometimes Phillip Nellsons of Rowley, the other halfe of the ffarme, that I purchased of m^r Rogers both upland and meadow, I do give unto my sonn James Bayley, also I do give unto my son John Bayley one ox gate, in east end ox pasture of Rowley and thre cow gates, and to my son James two ox gates, in the sd pasture & thre cow gates. Also I doe give unto my wife, one third part of my lands in Rowley that James is to have, for her life tyme, and my son James, for to alow her or pay to her one third part that the halfe farme that I have given him doth yearly produce, also my son John is to pay to her one third pt that the halfe farme I have given him doth yearly pduce, and this both of them to pay dureing her life, my meaneing is, when I say, w^t it doth yearly pduce, is one third part of the rent of it, w^t it is lett for, also I doe give unto my wife two cowes, for her life tyme, and my son James is for to maintaine them winter & sumer. Also I do give to my wife one third part of my houshold goods, within dores & without. I doe give unto my son James Bayley Allso all my apparrell I do give to my son John, And I do make my son James Bayley sole executor of this my last will & testament. Also my will is, that if my daughter Platts or my daughter Lever doe dye before the legasies, that I do give them be payd that then the sayd legasies be payd to their children, and this I do deliver as my last will August the 8 1677."

James Bayley.

Witness: Phillip Nellson, Ezekiell Northend, Edna Northend.

Proved in Ipswich court Sept. 25, 1677 by the witnesses.

Copy, Ipswich Deeds, vol. 4, page 117.

Inventory of the estate of James Baley of Rowley: in his purse, 4li. 17s.; in pewter, 1li. 7s. 6d.; Bras and Iron ware, 3li. 3s. 6d.; Looms and tackling and all belonginge to it, 1li. 10s.; carpenters tooles, sithes and sickells, 1li. 6s.; Lumber, Earthen vessells and wooden vessells, 1li.; wollen yarne and Linnen yarne, 1li. 9s.; cotten wool and sheepe wool, 1li.; bags, 10s.; thre beds, bedsteds and the furniture belonginge to them, 17li. 10s.; corne and mault, 4li. 10s.; a paire of scales, 5s.; chares and Cushings and two tables, 1li. 10s.; in arms, 5li. 15s.; saddell and bridell, 17s.; two locks, 2s.; in Linnen, 2li. 10s.; his apparrell, 3li. 10s.; books, 1li.; A paire of oxen, 12li.; four cowes, 14li.; A stere, 3li. 10s.; 3 two yeare olds, 7li.; 2 yearlings, 3li.; 3 calves, 2li.; horse, mare and a Colt, 6li. 10s.; swine, 4li.; sives and other Lumber, 8s.; Cart, plowe, yoaks and chains, 2li. 5s.; butter and chese, 2li. 10s.; Bacon, 12s.; English Corne in the barne, 5li. 5s.; Indian Corne upon the Ground, 4li.; hay, 8li.; the house and house lot that John Baley is possesed of, 23li. 10s.; four Acres upon the mill hill that he is possesed of, 8li.; thre Acres at the mill feild that he is possesed of, 9li. 6s.; thre Acres of meddow in the oxe pasture that he is possesed of, 15li.; two Acres of sault marsh at cowe bridge that he is possesed of, 10li.; one Acre of rough meddow that he is possesed of, 5li.; four Gates that he is possesed of, 15li.; four Acres at the Rie plaine, 2li.; house and house Lot in the Towne of Rowley, 27li.; plowe lande in the Common feild 8 Acres, 20li.; four Acres at Simons feild, 4li.; five Acres of sault marsh by Shad Creeke, 25li.; two Acres of Rough marsh, 10li.; two Acres of Sault marsh by Newbury Gate, 10li.; one Acre as you goe to hog Iland, 5li.; five Gates, 21li.; a farme at Bradforth of 3 hundred Acres, 200li.; a peece of Land that Goodman Jackson hireth of 70 Acres, 40li.; in Linnen yarne, 1li. 1s. 6d.; a bill in the hands of Thomas Remington, 7li.; more debts from severall persons, 8li.; total, 586li. Debts due from the estate, 6li.

Attested in Ipswich court Sept. 25, 1677 by James Bayley, executor.

Essex County Probate Files, Docket 1,326.

ESTATE OF JOHN LYNDE.

Administration upon the estate of John Line, intestate, was granted Sept. 25, 1677, to John Wainwright and he was ordered to bring in an inventory to the March court.

Ipswich Quarterly Court Records, vol. 5, page 296.

Inventory of the estate of John Lyne taken Oct. 6, 1677 : Joseph Fellows, 1li. 10s.; a debentour assigned per Joseph Aires, 1li. 17s. 6d.; 1 old hatt, 1 old shirt & 2 neckcloaths sould Joseph Fellows for 12s.; his wages from Capt. Hull, Treasu^r., 9s. 2d.; 2 sheepe Qm^r. Perkins recd., 18s.; total, 5li. 6s. 8d. John Lyne Dr. to John Wainwright, 4li. 1s. An account of disburstments Sept. 25, 1677 : for administration, 1s.; 1 day attendance, 1s. 6d.; fetchinge his goods from Jo. Fellows, 1s.; 2 Jorneys to Boston, 10s.; total, 13s. 6d.

Attested in Ipswich court 26 : 1 : 1678, by John Wainwright, administrator, and the court ordered him to have his debt 4li. 15s. 3d. and the remainder to any other creditor that make just claim.

Essex County Probate Files, Docket 17,485.

ESTATE OF JOHN WILD, JR., OF TOPSFIELD.

"This may satisfy whome it may concarne: that I John Wilde Juner haue Resaiued of my ffather that Land which he promised to my brother Johnnathan: and was ingaged to him and to my salfe by our Grandfather Gould or fifty Pounds to be paied and than my father Redemed his land againe and I doe herby declar that my ffather hath satisfied and paied me both what was promised or in gaged to my Brother Johnnathen and to my salfe to my full satisfaction and the intant of this is that my father may com to no trobell by any claime of my onkell Gould: the fifty pounds that was in Gaged to me and my brother Johnnathen is paied to me by my father to my full content in part of that land which was formerly goodman dormans And now I being prest to go to the war being desirous to satell things befor I goo: not knowing how God may daell with me in respact of Returning againe: If I doe not Returne againe: than I doe dispose of ‖ what ‖ God hath Given me as foloweth: I haue fiue Sistors and one Brother Sarah Elisabath: Phabe: Pracelah: martha: and Ephrem and my will is that my land at Hauerell and at topsffeld and my mouabells be Equaly deuided amongst all the aboue named Sistors and brother: and Let the lands be prised and thos that haue ye lands shall paye to the other that which is there proporshon:: and I doe hereby apint my Honered ffather and Louing onkell John Radington to be admenistrators of this Estate: and to paye all my debts out of the Estat be fore it be deuided: and this is my last will and testament in wetnes whereof I have Set too my hand this toó and twentieth day of october one thousan Six hundred Seventy and Six : : yᵉ 22 : of october 1676 :"

John Wild, Juner :

Witness : John How, Marah How.
Proved in Ipswich court Sept. 25, 1677 by the witnesses.

"This is to declare that I John wild of topsfeald do purpos and intend that my formor will writen in october : before my going to the Eastward shall stand good : prouided it be the will of god I retur not again writen the : 22 of June : 77."

John Wild.

Witness : John Herrick, Sarah (her O mark) bishop.

Inventory taken Sept. 27, 1677, by Thomas Perkins and William Auerell : a percell of upland and medow which hee does by writing under his hand acknowledge to have received of his father in lieu of 50li., 50li.; a peece of Indian corn on the ground prised at six bushells, 18s.; four sheep, 1li. 10s.; three ould woollin garments, 14s.; a sarge westcote and som ould linin, 4s.; an Iron pott, 7s.; an ould saddle, 3s.; three saws, 16s.; two ould axes, 5s.; two Iron wedges, 3s.; two chisills, 1s. 6d.; one augre, 1s. 6d.; a pair of beetle Rings, 1s. 6d.; som sheep wooll not apearing how much Rests unprised. Debts due to him, 1li. 1s. 8d. The debts he oweth the credithers not haveing given in their acounts remain uncertain.

Delivered in Ipswich court Sept. 25, 1677 as a true inventory of the estate of John Wildes, Jr.

Essex County Probate Files, Docket 29,826.

Estate of John Roberts of Manchester.

Administration upon the estate of John Roberds, intestate, was granted 27 : 7 : 1677, to John Elithorp.

Inventory taken by the desire of John Elithrope of the goods of John Roberds, deceased July 13, 1677 by murdering himself, who then lived in Manchester with the said Elithrope, taken July 17, 1677 by John Sibly and Thomas West : one hat, 5s. 6d.; one Coat, 20s.; a pare brichise, 12s.; one weascoat, 12s.; a peare brichise, 9s.; one ould Coat and brichise, 3s.; a pear stokins, 4s.; pear Linin drewers and one shert, 6s.; one nekcloth, 2s.; pear gloves, 2s.; on Ancarcher & on nekcloth, 1s. 6d.; butens and thred, 1s.; tow knivs and coame, 1s.; one pear shoos, 2s.; tow axes, 7s.; one cheare, 2s. 6d.; tow yards of Cotten, 6s. & one old axe, 1s. 6d.; total, 4li. 10s. 6d. The depts of

the party deseased: to my selfe upon acounts, 14s. 3d.; to Ambros gale, 2li. 16s. 2d.; Israell niccols; 1li.
Attested in Ipswich court 27 : 7 : 1677 by John Elithorp.
Essex County Probate Files, Docket 23,825.

GUARDIANSHIP OF SARAH BRADBURY OF SALISBURY.

Upon request of Sarah Bradbury, Mr. John Pike, her uncle, was appointed her guardian Oct. 9, 1677, and he was ordered to put in security at the next Salisbury court.
Hampton Quarterly Court Records, vol. 2, leaf 77.

GUARDIANSHIP OF ANNE BRADBURY OF SALISBURY.

Mr. Jno. Stockman was appointed guardian of Anne Bradbury, Oct. 9, 1677, and he was ordered to put in security at the next Salisbury court.
Hampton Quarterly Court Records, vol. 2, leaf 77.

ESTATE OF THOMAS BARNARD, SR., OF AMESBURY.

Administration upon the estate of Tho. Barnard, sr., late of Amsberie, who was killed by the Indians, was granted Oct. 9, 1677, to Elener, the relict, and she with as many of her husband's children as she could get were ordered to come to the next Salisbury court for a division of the estate between the children and the widow.
Hampton Quarterly Court Records, vol. 2, page 76.

Inventory of the estate of Thomas Barnard, Sr. taken 21 : 6m : 1677, by Phill. Challis, Thomas Wells and John Weed : ye Dwelling house, Barne, orchard & homestead, 140li.; a 40 acre lott at ye back River, 25li.; 3 acres of meadow att ye pond meadows, 6li.; twoe acres of meadow att ye new meadows, 2li. 10s.; 4 acres of meadow in ye higglety pigleyes, 20li.; a sweepage lott, 12li.; 10 acres more or less on salisbury side on ye powow River, 20li.; 200 acres att ye great lotts, 40li.; a 40 acre lott in ye Champion land, 20li.; a 50 acre lott att ye childrens land, 25li.; a Bugmore lott, 5li.; a 40 acre River lott, 38li.; a 40 acre Lott on ye division beyond ye pond, 16li.; a 10 acre lott in ye ox pastures & a swamp lott, 10li.; twoe lotts in ye Lyons mouth, 10li.; a payre of oxen, 14li.; 4 Cowes, 16li.; 2 2 yr. old heiffers & advantage & 3 yearlings, 12li.; 3 calves, 2li.; eight sheep young & old, 3li. 5s.; a young horse, 2li.; 10 swine old & younge, 7li.; 8 hives of bees, 2li.; English, Indian corne & Flax, 12li.; Cart wheels, Irons, chaine, plow & Irons,

yokes, 3li.; Betle Rings, wedges, axes, howes, forkes, shave,
10s.; Iron potts, Kettle, tramells, spitt, Frying pan, tongues,
2li. 10s.; Brass & pewter ware, 2li. 16s.; Bedds, Bedding, Bedsteads, curtains, vallants, 25li. 10s.; Table linnen & hand towells, 2li. 10s.; his wearing clothes yt were left, 8li.; His Bible
wth twoe other Bookes, 10s.; woll & wollen & linnen yarne, 3li.
14s.; Cubbard, Table, chaires, wheels, formes, 3li.; old caske,
trayes, Dishes, spones & other necessaries, 3li. 14s.; Baggs,
saddle & grindlestone, 1li. 10s.; a bull: & 7 yds. of cloth, 4li.
10s.; his right in common land drawd for but undivided, 5li.;
in money, 4s.; a bill from Nathaniell Griffin due to ye sd
Barnerd, 15s.; Due from his son att Nantucquett pr. Bill,
80li. where of is payd & received 4 barrells of beefe & 30lbs of
sheeps wool; shingle nailes, 4s.; total, 607li. 12s.

Attested in Hampton court 9 : 8m : 1677 by Ellenor
Barnard, widow of Thomas Barnard, and administratrix of
his estate.

Essex County Probate Files, Docket 1,785.

Elenor Barnard, administratrix of the estate of Tho. Barnard of Amesbury, with four of her sons, asking for a settlement of the estate, court April 9, 1678, ordered to the widow,
200li., comprising the house and home lot, half of the higgle-
dee piggledee lot of salt marsh and the whole sweepage lot at
the beach at the prices entered in the inventory, and such
things as she desires as per the inventory. Court ordered that
unless there be a necessity, as the court should judge, for the
sale of any of the lands for her maintenance, she should not
sell it or give it away except to one or more of her children.
Court also ordered that a due respect being had to what any of
the children have already received as portions, the same
should be divided among the rest of the children, the eldest
son having a double portion.

Capt. Tho. Bradbury, Leift. Phillip Challis and John
Weed, upon request of some of the children of the widow
Barnard, were impowered to divide the estate of their father
Tho. Barnard which was given to them, and to make return to
the next Norfolk court.

Salisbury Quarterly Court Records, vol 2, leaf 87.

Tho. Bradbury, Phillip Challis and John Weed having
been appointed by the court Apr. 9, 1678 to divide the estate
of Thos. Barnard of Amesbury, who died intestate, have accordingly apportioned to the widow Barnard 200li. and to
Tho. Barnard the eldest son 83li. and to the rest of the chil-

dren, eight in number, 41li. 10s. each, and some overplus their mother to have. Dated Apr. 6, 1679, and approved by the court Apr. 8, 1679.

Salisbury Quarterly Court Records, vol. 2, leaf 69.

The disposal of part of the lands of Tho. Barnard, sr. of Salisbury, who died intestate, by a committee appointed by the court: to his relict, the dwelling house, barne & homested, 140li.; halfe ye higledee piglede lot of salt marsh, 10li.; ye whole sweepage lot at ye beach, 12li. To Tho. Barnard ye eldest son, a lot at ye back River, 25li.; halfe ye higle piglee marsh lot, 10li.; ye right in comon land, 5li.; 10 upland & 2 acre lot of meadow, 14li.

Acknowledged and accepted Mar. 24, 1683-4 by Thomas Barnard.

Norfolk County Records, vol. 3, leaf 316.

Acquittance of Nathaniell Barnard, sr. of Nantucket to his brother, John Barnard of Amesbury, administrator to the estates of their mother Elener Little of Amesbury, deceased, who was administratrix to the estate of their father Thomas Barnard of Amesbury, of all portions due unto him from said estates. Dated Aug. 29, 1695. Witness: Tho. Currier, Samll. Weed.

Acknowledged Aug. 29, 1695 by Nathaniell Barnard before Robert Pike, Just. of Peace.

Acquittance of William Hackett and Sarah Hackett his wife, of Salisbury, to their brother John Barnerd of Amesbury, administrator to the estate of their mother Ellenor Little, deceased, they having received full satisfaction out of the estates of their mother Ellenor Little and their father Thomas Barnerd. Signed and sealed Jan. 31, 1695-6. Witness: Thomas Wells, John Hoyt, Samuel Clough.

Acknowledged Feb. 20, 1695 by William Hakat and Sara his wife.

Acquittance of Samuell Bucknum of Newbury, feltmaker, and Martha his wife, to John Barnerd administrator to the estate of their mother Ellenor Little of Amesbury, deceased, they having received a great iron kettle out of the estates of their father Thomas Barnerd and mother Ellenor Little of Amesbury. Signed and sealed June 22, 1697. Witness: Thomas Wells, Jeremiah Easman.

Acknowledged June 22, 1697 by Samuell Buckeman and Martha his wife, and she also yielded up her right of dower.

Acquittance of Hannah Stevens of Salisbury, relict of Benjamin Stevens late of Salisbury, and administratrix to his estate, to John Barnerd of Amesbury administrator to the estate of her mother Ellenor Little of Amesbury, she having received full satisfaction out of the estates of her mother Ellenor Little and father Thomas Barnerd. Signed and sealed Nov. 5, 1695. Witness: Thomas Freame, Joseph Hoyt.

Acknowledged Feb. 20, 1695 by Hanah Steevens, widow.

Acquittance of Samuel Fellows, jr. and Abigail his wife, of Salisbury, to their brother John Barnerd of Amesbury, administrator to the estate of Ellenor Little of Amesbury, they having received full satisfaction out of the estates of their father Thomas Barnerd and mother Ellenor Little. Signed and sealed Jan. 24, 1695-6. Witness: Thomas Wells, Thomas Weed.

Acknowledged Mar. 14, 1695-6 by Samuell Fellows and Abigal his wife and she yielded up her right of dower before Robert Pike, Just. of the Peace.

Acquittance of Phelep Eastman and Mary Eastman to their brother John Barnerd of Amesbury, administrator to the estate of their mother Elenor Little of Amesbury who was administratrix to the estate of their father Thomas Barnerd of Amesbury, they having received full satisfaction out of the estates of their father and mother. Signed and sealed June 25, 1695. Witness: Thomas Wells, Thomas (his X mark) Barnerd, Senr.

Mr. Thomas Wells and Thomas Barnerd, Senr., made oath June 22, 1697, that they saw Elizabeth Estman and Mary sign, seal and deliver this acquittance.

Acquittance of Joseph Peasely of Haveril, husbandman, and Ruth Peasly his wife to John Barnerd of Amesbury, administrator to the estate of their mother Ellenor Little of Amesbury, they having received 8li. in money out of the estates of their mother Ellenor Little and father Thomas Barnerd. Signed and sealed May 24, 1697. Witness: Thomas Wells, Thomas Currier.

Acknowledged Nov. 29, 1697 by Joseph and Ruth Peasely before Nath. Saltonstall, Just. of the Peace.

Essex County Probate Files, Docket 1,785.

ESTATE OF ROBERT QUINBY OF AMESBURY.

Administration on the estate of Robert Quenby was granted 9 : 8m : 1677, to Elizabeth Quenby upon her request.

Inventory of the estate of Roberd Quinbe taken Aug. 27, 1677 by William Barens, Roberd Jons and Thomas Fowler being chosen by Elesebeth Quinbe the wife of Roberd Quinbe: the coren upon the ground, 5li.; the hows and howslot, 35li.; Six akers of land at Whitthoren hill, 10li.; his land at bugmoer, 3li.; his land at burchen medo hill, 20li.; Seven neat Cattell, 22li.; Six swine, 3li. 10s.; tow meares and a fold, 4li.; Six Sheep, 2li.; bedding and howsell stouef, 6li.; tenn yardes of cloth, 2li.; depts due to him, from Frances Deves, 1li. 18s.; total, 114li. 8s.

Attested in Hampton court 9 : 8m : 1677 by Elizabeth Quenby and she to attend to the order of the court about the disposal of the estate.

Bond of Robert Quinbe of Amesbury, with Jarvis Ring of Salisbury and Thomas Currier of Amesbury, husbandmen, as sureties, of 200li., dated Sept. 26, 1694, for the administration of the estate of Robert Quinbee and Elizabeth Quinbe of Amesbury, his father and mother. Witness: John Croade, Joseph Eaton.

Inventory of the estate of Robard Quenby and Elizabeth his wife both late of Amesbury, deceased intestate, taken Nov. 3, 1694 by Jacob Morill, Jarves Ring and Thomas Currier given in by Robard Quenby their son : his house and homsted, 25li.; a Lot at white thorne hill, 8li.; a lot at burchin meadow, 18li.; lot at bugmore, 4li. 10s.; one ox, 5li.; one cow, 3li. 15s.; three sheep, 1li. 10s.; five swine, 3li. 10s.; money, 13s. 8d.; 11 geese, 15s.; 2 pots on at 18s. the other at 8s., 1li. 6s.; tramel, on ax, pot hooks, 8s.; cards, yarne, wool, flax, 1li. 7s.; bed and beding, 2li.; aples, 1li. 5s.; total, 76li. 19s. 8d.

Attested Dec. 25, 1694 by Robert Quinby, administrator.

William Quinby son of William Quinby of Amesbury, deceased, having agreed with his uncle Robard Quinby of Amesbury who was appointed administrator of the estate of his grandfather Robard Quinby of Amesbury, and it appearing by a paper dated Dec. 24, 1694 that two thirds of the homestead and 1li. 3s. in moveables belonged to his father, have divided the land as follows: William to have the eastwardly end bounded with a white oak southeastwardly and from thence to a white oak which is the ancient bounds of sd lot and so to a small pine across the swamp and upon his receiving the said land together with all the abell trees upon it and all priviledges belonging thereunto,

acquits his uncle of all that might be due unto his father
as his portion of his grandfather's estate.
Signed 21 : 2m : 1713.   Witness: Jacob Rowell, Jacob Morrill, Josiah Clarke.

The division of the estate of Robart Quenby of Amesbury
and Elezbeth his wife, deceased intestate, to William Quenby
two thirds of the homestead and 1li. 3s. in moveables; to John
Quenby the Bugmore lot and the ox; Thomas Quenby the
white thorne hill lot and 20s. of the moveables; to Phillip and
Joseph Quenby Burchin meadow lot; Lidea the daughter 9li.
out of the moveables to be paid by the administrator upon demand; Robart the administrator, to have the remainder of
the estate.   This agreement made by the children Dec. 24,
1694.   Witness: Jacob Morrill, Jarves Ring, Thomas Currier.

Phillip Quinby acknowledged the receipt from his brother
Robbart Quinby administrator to the estate of their father
and mother, Robbart and Elizabeth Quinby, of one half of the
Burchin Meadow lot, his share according to agreement.
Dated Jan. 16, 1699.   Witness: Jarves Ring, Thomas Freame.
Acknowledged Jan. 23, 1698 by Philip Quinby before Robt.
Pike, Just. of Peace.

John Quinby acknowledged the receipt from his brother
Robbart Quinby administrator to the estate of their father
and mother, Robbart and Elizabeth Quinby, of the bugmore
lot and one ox, his share of the estate according to agreement.
Dated Amesbury Jan. 16, 1699.   Witness: Jarves Ring,
Thomas Freame.
Acknowledged Jan. 23, 1698 by John Quinby before Robert
Pike, Just. of Peace.

The acquittance of Joseph Quenby of Amesbury to his
brother Robart Quenby of Amesbury, of all portions and demands whatsoever. Dated July 19, 1711.   Witness: Benjamin
Currier, Thomas Currier.

Essex County Probate Files, Docket 23,160.

ESTATE OF NATHANIEL MIGHILL OF SALEM.

Administration upon the estate of Nathanael Miguel, late
of Salem, granted Oct. 23, 1677 to Thomas Miguel and John
Bayly, two of his brethren, they giving security to administer
according to law and to bring in an inventory to the County
court of Essex.

Bond of Thomas Miguel, of Milton, John Baily, of Rowley
and Thomas Swift, of Milton, to the treasurer for the Co. of
Suffolk, in the sum of 200li. to administer the estate of Nathaniel Miguel of Salem, dated Oct. 23, 1677.   Signed
Thomas Miguel, John Bay——, Thomas Swift.

Suffolk County Probate Records, Docket 917.

Inventory of the estate of Nathaniel Mighell, deceased the
13:8:1677, taken, 27:9:1677, by Wm. Browne, jr., and
Benja. Browne, 27:9:1677: New England money in his
mother's hand, 23li. 4s.; Old England money, 2li. 2s.; one
Guinne, 1li.; ten fifty nine pieces of eight and six Rayalls,
16li. 7s. 6d.; in Mr. Nowel's hands in Boston, 13li. 14s.;
mony received of John Endicot of Boston, part of the effects of 3,904 lb. of sugar in partnership with John Apleton,
17li.; the effects of 4,875 orringes and 7 baskets sould at Boston in mony, 14s. 4d.; In stuff, 17 yds. 1-4 at 4s. per yard, 3li.
9s.; eleven pair of french heeld shooes left at Boston and delivered to Ezekiell Mighill, 3li. 14s.; Orringe flower butter as
per invoice, 8s. 10 1-2d.; Money in Mr. Benjamin Browne
hands, being effects of sugars sould by John Appleton, 33li.
10s.; John Appleton debtor, 9li. 8s.; book debts, 30li. 16s.
4d.; a bill under Samuell Browns hands, 6li. 10s. 9d.; several
things appraised at Rowly in apparel, woollen, linen, stockings and shoos, 8li. 18s.; a horse and sadle, 4li.; One inkhorne, 6d.; severall things appraised at Salem by Mr. William and Mr. Benjamin Browne, in Mr. William Jordins hand
in Barbados as appears by letter, 2,000 sugar, 10li.; one chest
and severall things in it, 16s.; one cabin bed, a rug, two pillows and blanket, 2li.; 29 Baskets, at 6d. per, 14s. 6d.; one
chest at Mr. William Brown, sr.'s, 7s.; in that chest, a ham-
mock, 10s., a camlet cloak, 2li.; a stuff coat and breeches,
10s., 2 pair of shooes, 12s.; a parcel of linnen clothes in a new
pillow beer, 2li. 10s.; a bible, 3s.; a new pocket book, 6d.;
parcell of white thread, buttons, 13s. 6d.; seven Ivory combs,
7s.; piece of red ribbon, 16s.; remnant of black ribbon, 4s.
and bone lace, 13s.; fine piecis of cource cambricke,
7li.; course kenting, 8 pieces, 6li.; sugars in Mr.
Bartholmew's warehouse, two hogsheads, one Terce ¹ and
a barrell Judged in partnership with Mr. John Apleton and
the one-half appraised at 10li.; one small case with five bottles, 5s.; one half of a barrell of Indico, 2li. 10s.; one-half of
3-4 of a hundred Ging., 4s. 6d.; 10 baskets at 6d. per, 5s.;
about 700 orringes at Marblehead, 10s.; total, 224li. 7s. 3
1-2d.   Due from Mr. William Brown, jr., on balance 21:9:

1677, 6li. 14s. 10d.; sperma: Cati, half a pound or there-abouts at 8s. p., 4s.; a receipt of Samuell Williams, dated 12 : 10 : 1676, of seven bushels of peas at 3s. 4d., 1li. 3s. 4d.; bill of Thomas Grinslett, 1li. 13s.; total, 9li. 15s. 2d.

Attested in Salem court 28 : 9 : 1677 by Mr. Thomas Michaell and John Baily, the administrators.

Petition of Ezekiel Mighel, John Bayly and Stevin Mighell, dated Nov. 26, 1677, that the estate of their brother by will belongs to them, they being the youngest children, by expressions in their father's will which says that if Thomas die under age, his portion should fall to Samuell and John, and if any of the youngest die under age, their portions to fall to the youngest children. Therefore their brother dying without a will, they considered themselves the beneficiaries, and if not they, then their mother should have it, she having put her own estate into their brother's hands to trade, having no receipt, etc.

Essex County Quarterly Court Files, vol. 27, leaves 98, 99.

There being an inventory of the estate of Nathanll Michaell, who died intestate, presented to this court by Tho. Michell, administrator, amounting to 234li., court 27 :9 : 1677, judged that although the estate may of right belong to the youngest children had by the mother now surviving, yet Mr. Thomas Michell, administrator, should have 34li.; Ezekiell, the eldest brother, 60li.; the daughter, viz., his sister Mary, 40li.; and the mother and other brother Steephen, 50li. each; the debts being paid first out of the whole estate, and the rest of the estate, according to proportion as above expressed.

Salem Quarterly Court Records, vol. 5, leaf 111.

ESTATE OF ABRAHAM WARR.*

Henry Goold was appointed 27 : 9 : 1677, administrator of the estate of Abraham Warr, deceased, with Phillip Fowler as surety, and was ordered to bring in an inventory to the next Ipswich court.

Salem Quarterly Court Records, vol. 5, leaf 111.

Inventory of the estate of Abraham War, deceased: received by Henerey Goold of Mister Baker by judgment of Ipswich court, 10li.; more in land, 14li.; deduction by agreement with Mr. Baker, 2li.; leaving 22li.

Attested 2 : 9 : 1677, by Henry Gould.

Essex County Quarterly Court Files, vol. 27, leaf 98.

*See Records and Files of the **Quarterly Courts of Essex County,** Mass., vol. 6 (1917) p. 350.

GUARDIANSHIP OF MARTHA ROGERS OF IPSWICH.

Martha Rogers, aged about sixteen years, chose her mother Mrs. Margrett Rogers as her guardian, 6 : 9m : 1677, and she was also appointed guardian of the other children of Mr. Ezekiell Rogers who were under age, Nathaniell, Ezekiell, Timothy and Samuell.

Ipswich Quarterly Court Records, vol. 5, page 299.

Mrs. Margrett Rogers having received of Mr. William Hubbard 200li. for land in England belonging to Ezekiell Rogers, she bound her houses and all land she possessed in Ipswich excepting about three quarters of an acre near to Andrew Peter's land as security.

Copy, Ipswich Deeds, vol. 4, page 113.

ESTATE OF THOMAS LOW, SR., OF IPSWICH.

"In the Name of God Amen. the Twentith day of Aprill in the yeare of grace one Thowsand Six hundred Seauenty & Seauen, I Thomas Low Senr. of Ipswich in America in the Shire of Essex, being weake in body; but of good & perfect memory, thanks be vnto God, Doe ordaine & make this my last will & Testament in manner & forme following, first I bequeath my Soule into the hands of the Almighty God my Creator & redeemer, by whom, through whom, & in whom I trust to haue remission of all my Sinnes, & to be an Inheritor of the Kingdome of Heauen, & my body to be buried at the discression of my Executor. Item I giue & bequath vnto Susannah my loueing wife, what goods she brought with hir, And also I give hir the vse of that roome which I Lye in & the free vse of those things that are in it, And also the vse of one Cow which she liketh best, & will is that my sonne John shall mainteine it winter & Sumer & also my will is, that if the Cow Come to any Casualty hee shall find her another Cow & maintaine it likewise as beforesaid, Also I giue vnto my wife one fourth part of her labor that she hath Spunn both Lening & woollen, & Also she shall haue hir beere as shee hath now, & also free vse of the fire: & Also John shall reare hur vp a shoate yearely for Sum meate for hir, & also shee shall haue the free vse of a Garden plott, & also a litle ground to sow half a peck of flax seede yeerely. And also I giue vnto hir Thirty shillings yeerely to be payd by my Executor in Such things as shee shall stand in neede of, during her naturall life: moreouer I giue vnto my loueing wife five pownds to dispose of as shee shall thinke good. And my will is That in

Case my wife shall thinke meete to remoue from my Sonne John, Then my will is, that John Low shall pay or ca[use] to be payd vnto hir forty Shillings yearely & euery yeare during hir natu[ral] life in Such pay as shee needeth. And Also I giue hir the cowe to be hir [own] & John to send hir the pay to Boston or Charls Towne.

"Item I Giue & bequeathe vnto my Sonne John Low all my Howsing & all my lands in Ipswich both meadow & vpland, to him & his heires for euer. Item I Giue & bequeath vnto my Sonne Thomas Low Thirty pownds, to bee payd him by my Executor in tooe yeares after my decease. Item I Giue vnto my Daughter Margaret forty pownds, to be payd by my Executor in tooe yeares after my decease. Item I Giue vnto my daughter Sarah forty pownds to be payd by my Executor within tooe yeare after my Decease. Item I giue vnto my Grandchild Thomas Low five pownds; when hee is Twenty yeares of age, or at his day of marriage. Item I give vnto my Grandaughter Margaret Dauison five pownds, when she shall be Twenty yeare old, or at hir day of marriage. Item I give vnto my Grandaughter Sarah Safford, five pownds, when she shall be Twenty yeare old, or at hir day of marriage. Item I giue vnto my Grandaughter, Sarah Low, five pownds, when she shall be Twenty yeare old, or at hir day of marriage. All the rest of my goods & Chattells vnbequeathed, I Giue unto my Sonne John Low, whom I doe ordaine & make my Sole Executor of this my last will and Testament. In witness whereof I haue herevnto sett my hand & Seale the Thirtith day of Aprill in the yeare of Grace Sixteene hundred Seuenty & Seauen. 1677"

Thomas Low. (SEAL)

Witness: James Chute, Mary (her + mark) Chute.
Proved in Ipswich court Nov. 6, 1677 by Ja. Chute.

Inventory taken at Ipswich Nov. 5, 1677 by Samuel Ingals, Sr. and Nathaniell Wells: half the hous and half barne, 50li.; the mault hous and the things belonging to it, 35li.; Six acers of areable land, 36li.; a devision of marsh in the hundreds, 20li.; fouer acres and a half at Plumb Island, 10li.; Six acres of marsh at Chebacko, 24li.; fouer oxen, 20li.; five Cows, 17li. 10s.; two heifers and a calf, 5li.; one hors, 2li. 10s.; eight Sheepe and Six lambs, 5li. 5s.; Swin, 4li. 3s.; half of the Cart and other tackling, 2li. 10s.; an old Saddle, bridele, pillion and feetters, 1li.; about fifty boushels of unthrest barly, 9li. 3s. 4d.; about fouer and forty boushels of Indan Corne, 5li. 10s.; eight Sacks, 2li.; nine loads of hay, 4li. 10s.;

hemp and flax unbroak, 5s.; brass kittles and a skilet and
Candlestick, 2li. 10s.; pewter, 1li. 2s. 6d.; one old Iron pot
and other iron uttensels, 1li. 5s.; earthen and wooden wair,
1li. 10s.; two spining wheels, chairs and cushens, 1li. 5s.;
table and meall trough and other smal things, 12s.; new
hom spun cloth, 1li. 19s.; his wearing clothes, 9li. 16s.; five
yards and a half of Seearge, Silke and buttons, 1li. 15s.;
Sheeps wooll and cotton wooll, 16s.; a dousen and a half of
napkins, 2li.; Six pillowbears and tabel Cloth, 1li. 6s.; nine
sheets and a table Cloth, 4li. 18s.; four towels, old pillow-
beare, a pound of Hopps, 10s.; in mony, 13s. 2d.; chest and a
box, 15s.; twenty three pound of yarn, 2li. 17s. 6d.; one
Sword, belt, powder, boullets, 1li.; total, 290li. 16s. 6d.
Debts due from the estate, 14li. 16s. 2d.; clear estate
276li. 4d.

Essex County Probate Files, Docket 17,242.

ESTATE OF JOHN PAINE OF (IPSWICH?).

Inventory* of the estate of Mr. John Paine who died at
sea taken Oct. 25, 1677 by John Appleton and John Whipple:
fetherbed with one pillow, 5li.; fetherbed with one bolster,
3li.; thre meane straw beds, 15s.; fetherbed with one pillow,
5li.; 4 pillos & two bolsters, 2li. 16s.; 2 blankits, 1li. 4s.; one
Coverlit, 30s.; one ruge, 10s.; two homspun blankits & a small
flok pillo, 1li.; one flock beed & bolster, 1li. 10s.; one Cotton
Ruge & a pece of Ruge, 1li. 10s.; 6 Rede Chayers, 3li.; 4 Lowe
cuchin stools, 1li. 12s.; 8 fether cushins, 1li. 12s.; 3 elbo
chayers, 3 other chayers, 1li. 6s.; a Cobbinit, a voiding baskit,
1li.; a bermodas baskit, 1s. 6d.; 6 Joyned stools, 17s.; a smale
squar boxe full of mean books, 10s.; a Desk with 3 drawers &
old cardes, 10s.; a Large brase Ketle & a 3 quart brase scilit,
3li.; a quart scilit, a smale pot with a handle, 7s.; a Large
iron driping pane & a pint scillit, 16s.; an old brase Ketle &
small iron Ketle, 10s.; friing pan, 3s.; morter & pestle, 8s.;
gridiron, 4s.; payer of horse fetters, 3s.; firepan & two payer
of tonges, 15s.; payer of Andirons with brase heads, 10s.;
peele & payer of doge Cobirons, 1li. 4s.; payer of Large Andiron rackes, 1li.; fire shovell, an axe, payer of pot hooks, 6s.;
two spits, two Iron pottes, 1li. 7s.; 5 peces of Curtin rods, an
old Jak, betle ringes, 12s.; one broken Cobiron, a fending
iron, 2s.; a brassel Rowling pin & a hat bruch, 2s.; a bermodas
baskit, one old hatt, one Sive, 5s.; 2 bedcords, an old flaskit,
Kneding trofe, 8s.; 2 mean bedsteds & hengings of a bed, old

*Copy, Ipswich Deeds, vol. 4, page 134.

belles, 1li. 2s.; worming pan, 9s.; a hamac, 10s.; tine puding pann & an old Lanthorne, 2s.; one small Chayer, 2s.; 4 Large pewter dishes, 1li. 12s.; 3 smaler pewter dishes, 15s.; nine porengers, 13s. 6d.; 9 old pewter dishes, 1li. 16s.; smal pye plaat, 2s.; 6 small nu plaats, 12s.; two basson a small & a biger, 7s.; Larg flagin & a Leser flagin, 1li. 5s.; 3 pewter Candlstiks, one of brase, one Iron, 1li.; 10 Saussers, 2 pinte potts, 12s.; small Urr, 5 old peces of pewter, 10s.; old brase Chafin dish, bermoodas baskit, 5s.; wood strainer & a fleking dish, 1s.; 5 striped Curtins & Vallants, 15s.; Large Chest, 15s.; Chest with drawers, 6li.; Syd Cubbard, 1li. 10s.; Cubburd with tinn doares, 2li.; smalle table, 5s.; tramell & a barr, 6s.; 4 pint boxes with small things in them, 2s.; thre yrds of osted fringe, 1s.; 20 trenchers, a hatt bruch, 2s. 6d.; small table Cloth, napcin, a pilowbeer, 4s.; litle trunk, 3s.; Sute of red Curtins & vallants, 3li. 10s.; dyall, 10s.; Sute of striped Curtins & vallants, 1li.; two blankits, a small pillo, 1li.; Case of Knives, 2s. 6d.; trunck, 6s.; blankit, 5s.; Red Rug osted, 40s.; old cubert cloth, 5s.; small trunck and Ironing Cloth, 2s.; trunck, 8s.; 4 pillow beers, one small pilowbeer, 2li. 1s.; 4 payer of pilowbeers, 2li.; two dieper towels, 6s.; two dieper table clothes, 1li. 12s.; one holon table cloth, 4s.; one holon towell, 2s.; 2 duz. half of dieper napcins, 1li. 10s.; 7 osenbrig napcans, 4s.; a Chest, 15s.; 4 cours table clothes, 8s.; 3 cours towels, 2s.; 9 hom made sheets, 2li. 10s.; two Cours tablecloth, 4s.; 7 hom made pilowbers, 10s. 6d.; 3 small holon tablcloth, 8s.; one pillowbeer, 1s.; one duz. of hom made napcins, 12s.; eleven napcins, 11s.; 6 hom made towels, 6s.; 4 towels, 3s.; Remnant of Callico, 1s.; a turthshell Coam, 2s.; pownd & a half of wool yern, 3s.; payer of brase Scales & 5 waites, 10s.; in plaate, 10li.; goole Ringe, 1li.; baskit, 3s.; payer of stokins, 3s.; 4 napcins, 4s.; a nu serge sute & coat, 4li.; and old Serg Sute & coat, 1li. 10s.; two stuff Coats Lyned, 3li.; two hates, 12s.; payer of shoos, 7s.; 3 books, one bible, 16s.; one Chamber pott, one porenger, 8s.; 3 old waskoats, payer of drawers, 12s.; 9 handcerchifs & 7 neckcloths old, 12s.; caps, 2s., eight shirts, 3li. 2s.; two payer of stokins [11s. *Copy*]; small trunke, 4s.; sea chest, 4s.; horse, 3li.; total, 138li. 10s. 6d.

[a raper, 20s.; box iron, 2s.; in plate, 16s.; one napkin 1s. *Copy*.]

Attested Nov. 7, 1677 by Mrs. Elisabeth Paine except the debts which she knoweth not but feareth exceeding the estate.

Essex County Probate Files, Docket 20,384.

The court Mar. 26, 1678 allowed Capt. John Appleton, Capt. John Whipple and Deacon Wm. Goodhue until next September court to make an accounting of the estate of Mr. John Paine.

Ipswich Quarterly Court Records, vol. 5, page 302.

ESTATE OF ROBERT WILKES OF SALEM.

"September 24th. 1677 Robert Wilks of Salem in New England though sick in body yet perfect in memory do make this my Last will and Testament as followeth: Imprimis. I give unto my Brother Isaac Woodberry's wife named Mary Woodberry my Sister, my Shop & ground thereunto belonging Lying and being neere m^r Higginsons house in Salem and all my movable goods, and my dwelling house being neere m^r Curwins warehouse neere the water side & all the Land thereunto belonging during the time & term of her naturall Life. Item. I giue unto Robert Woodberry eldest son of my Brother Isaac Woodberry next & imediately after the decease of my s^d Sister Mary Woodberry the s^d Shop & ground thereunto belonging before bequeathed unto her for Life with the s^d goods hee to possess & enjoy the same next & imediately after her decease. Item. I give unto my Brother Isaac Woodberry's daughter Mary, which hee had by my s^d sister Mary his now wife next and imediately after the decease of her my s^d sister, my house being neere m^r Curwins warehouse neere the water side & all the Land thereunto belonging shee to possess and enjoy the same next and imediately after the decease of Mary my s^d sister. And as concerning my Servant John Smith I Leave him to his choise either to Live with my Brother Woodberry or else my Brother Woodberry to binde him over to a Ship Carpenter and if the s^d Smith do serve out his full time with my s^d Brother Woodberry then hee to have ten pounds at the end of his Apprentiship: And I do hereby nominate and appoint my s^d Brother Isaac Woodberry Executor of this my Last will & testament."

[no signature]

Witness: William Clarke and Thomas Knill, on board the vessel sd Wilks being then sick. Sworn by the witnesses, Nov. 27, 1677, before John Leverett, Esq., Gov., and Simon Bradstreet, Esq., Assist., who said that Robert Wilks deceased in his late voyage from Bristoll to New England.

Proved in Suffolk court Nov. 27, 1677, Copy made by Isa. Addington, cler.

Inventory of the estate of Robert Wilkes of Sealem deceased 24 : 7 : 1677, appraised by Bartho. Gedney and Daniel Bacon: twelve Ring bolts & 4 settbolts, 16s.; 5 augers, 6s., ould Ropes, 18d., 7s. 6d.; an old saw, 2s.; 1 Iron pott & a frieing pan, 10s.; 1 bible, 3s.; 1 pr. sleevs, 3s.; 1 paper book, 6d.; 1 gun, 10s.; 1 Cutlash & belt, 12s.; 1 old holbert, 5s.; a sarvant, 3li.; 1 shop & ground neer Mr. Jno. Higginsons, 30li.; horses & mares, 7li.; house and outhouse neer Corwins, 50li.; debts due the estate, by Daniell Bacon, 6li. 16s. 6d. by Bartho. Gidney, 3li.; by Tho. Greesled, 5li., one half belonging to this estate, 2li. 10s.; By Ishack Woodbery, 1li. 4s. 3d.; By Edward Wharton, 3li.; Jno. Stark, 1li. 10s.; per Benjamin Small, 1li. 10s.; By Abram Wellman, 5li.; total, 117li. 19s. 9d.

Inventory taken, 29 : 9 : 1677, by John Hill and William Woodbery: One Cloke part worn, 1li. 5s.; 1 Cote, 1li. 15s.; 1 wastcote & 1 par trosers, 12s.; 1 Jackit & briches, 2li. 5s.; a parcell of worn Cloathes, 3li.; stokins & shues, 15s. 6d.; 5 rugs, 7li.; sea beding, 1li.; wearing Linging, 4li.; 1 sadell & Cloath, 1li. 10s.; 10 yds. 1-2 sarge at 6s., 3li. 3s.; 3 yds. & 1-2 Corce Carsi, 15s. 9d.; 5 yds. 1-4 Lining Cloath at 18d. per, 7s. 10d.; 2 yds. & 1-4 sarge, 9s.; 3 yds & 1-2 brod Cloath at 16s., 2li. 16s.; 5 yds. brod Cloath at 12s. per, 3li.; 5 yds. Carsi at 6s., 1li. 10s.; 8 yds. Corce Carsie, 5s. 6d., per, 2li. 4s.; 12 dozen buttens at 2s., 1li. 4s.; 1 Caster hat, 16s.; 12 dozen gimblits at 3s., 1li. 16s.; 1 dozen falling axis at 4s., 2li. 8s.; 1 brod ax & 1 ads, 10s.; 3 drawing Knives, 5s.; 4 Cupers axis, 13s. 6d.; 10 calking Irons at 1s., 10s.; owld tools, 1li. 5s.; 1 steelbow, 1 two fut rul & 3 knives, 8s.; trifling things, 3s.; rundlits & bottels, 6s.; 1 Chist & 1 trunk, 10s.; trifling things, 4s.; 1 grindstone, 10s.; 1 par of stilyards, 18s.; total, 49li. 13s. 7d.; Indebted to several persons, 5li. 18s., leaving clear estate, 162li. 14s. 4d.

Attested 30 : 9 : 1677 by Isaack Woodbery, executor.
Essex County Quarterly Court Files, vol. 27, leaves 106, 107.

Isaack Woodbery, executor of the will of Robert Wilkes, deceased, brought in a copy taken out of the records of Boston court, and also made oath to an inventory.
Salem Quarterly Court Records, vol. 5, leaf 112.

Estate of John Collins of (Gloucester?).

Administration upon the estate of John Collens, intestate, granted 27 : 9 : 1677, to Mehitabell, his wife, who brought in an inventory. Court ordered that Ezekiell, the eldest son, should have 6li., and the other five children 3li. each, at age or marriage, and the rest of the estate was to be for the use of said Mehitabell, the house and ground in Salem to stand bound for the payment of the children's portions.

Salem Quarterly Court Records, vol. 5, leaf 112.

Inventory of the estate of John Collins, jr., which he had in Gloucester, taken Sept. 18, 1677, by William (his mark) Vinson and William Ellery: a House & the Land with the orchyard & Commonage, the Land about the House being an Acker together with the sayd House, 30li.; Two Acres of upland & two of meadow at Fishermans Feild, so called, 14li.; Six Acres of Land at the eastern Poynt, 6li.; a cow & calf, 3li. 8s.; Table & forme, 12s.; Case of Glasses, 3s.; total, 54li. 3s.

Inventory of what was in Salem, taken, 20:9:1677, by Hilliard Veren, sr., and Walter Whitford: dwelling house with a quarter of an acre of ground belonging, 25li.; one cow, 50s.; pork, 15s.; swine, 6s.; fether bed, bolster, blanket and sheets, rugg, and all appurtenances with the bed steed & old curtains with 2 pillows, 4li. 10s.; fether bed, bolster, trundle bedsted & covering, 2li. 10s.; his arms that were left, 20s.; 2 coats, 25s.; some linen, 1 pr. stockens & 1 pr. gloves & drawers, 10s.; some lumber in the chamber, 4s.; som carpenters tooles & a wedg & betle rings, 10s.; som wooll & cotten yarne, 7s.; warming pan, 5s.; sheets & pillowbers & 1-2 dozen napkins & smale table cloath & 2 or 3 old towels, 1li. 10s.; 2 old pine chests & 4 old boxes, 16s.; a hanging cubord & old case broken, 5s.; 5 or 6 old chayrs, 6s.; Iron potts & Kettle, hake & pothooke & scillett, 10s.; pewter, 22s.; tubs, pailes, earthware & lumber in the lentoo, 10s.; white earth ware, 2s.; bellowes, gridiron & som other lumber, 5s.; wooll wheele & cards, 4s.; frying pan, 2s.; a fork, old hoe & axe & such lumber, 4s.; mallasses, 12s.; a stoole table, 2s.; cash, 11s.; estate credit, 10s.; total, 47li. 3s.; a hat, 5s.; estate debtor about 15li.; total inventory, 101li. 11s. There were six children, Ezekiell, Ebbenezer, Daniell, Amos, Benjamin and Mary.

Allowed in Salem court 28:9:1677.

Essex County Quarterly Court Files, vol. 27, leaf 109.

ESTATE OF NICHOLAS FOX OF MARBLEHEAD.

Administration upon the estate of Nicholas Fox, intestate, was granted 27:9:1677, to Elizabeth, his wife, and she

brought in an inventory of the estate amounting to 16li. 3s.
10d., which she was ordered to keep for the bringing up of the
children, paying to Nicholas, the eldest, 10s., and to the
daughter Elizabeth and William, 5s. each, at age.

Salem Quarterly Court Records, vol. 5, leaf 112.

Inventory of the estate of Nicholas Fox, taken Nov. 16,
1677, by Samll. Ward and John Legg: 1 hous and Land,
36li.; 1 bed, 2 pillows, 3 shetts, bedsted, Curtins and vallance,
6li. 10s.; 2 Coats, 1 wastcoat, 1 paier of briches, 1li.; 1 Chest,
5s.; 1 table, 4s.; 4 pewter platters, 12s.; 1 old Chest, 2s. 6d.; 2
potts and Croks, 10s.; 1 frieng pan and grediron, 2s.; 1
Chaier, 1s.; 4 earthen dishes, 1s.; total, 45li. 7s. 6d.; due from
the estate: to Mr. Bowdish, 4li. 10s.; John Elethrop, 3li. 18s.;
Mr. Will. Browne, jr., ——; John Furbush, 2li. 10s. 6d.; Mr.
Legg, 2li. 11s. 6d.; Mr. Gale, 2li. 6s. 8d.; Samll. Morgan,
1li.; George Harvey, 1li. 1s.; Vincent Stilson, jr., 19s. 2d.;
Mr. Batters, 1li.; Mr. William Browne, sr., 10s. 6d.; Thomas
Dixey, 13s. 4d.; Mr. Weld, 13s.; Mr. Rodes of Lynn, 10s.; Mr.
Heath of Boston, 1li.; Thomas Hawkins, 1li. 1s.; widdow
Stasey, 10s.; total, 29li. 3s. 8d.

Attested in Salem court 28:9:1677 by Elizabeth, the
relict.

Essex County Quarterly Court Files, vol. 27, leaf 118.

ESTATE OF JOHN CLAY OF MARBLEHEAD.

Administration upon the estate of John Claye, who was
slain in the war against the Indians was granted 27:9:1677,
to William Woods who with John Legg was bound to bring in
an inventory to the next Salem court and to administer according to law.

Inventory of the estate of John Clay, being then a fisher-
man, killed by the Indians, appraised on Nov. 8, 1677, at William Woods' in Marblehead, by Richard Knott and John (his
? mark) Farsbush: a muskett, otherwise a Fier Lock, 16s.;
a Hangger and Belt, 16s.; a Linen Sute, 12s.; a Wastcoate,
10s.; too shirts, 3s.; too payre of old Linnen drawers, 3s.; to
a Neckcloath & handkerchife, 1s. 6d.; a bible,——; total, 3li.
4s. Debts due: to William Woods, 1li. 10s.; to Richard Reath,
17s.; to John Darby, 3li.; total, 5li. 7s.

Essex County Quarterly Court Files, vol. 27, leaf 119.

ESTATE OF RICHARD CRANIVER OF SALEM.

Administration upon the estate of Richard Cranaver, intestate, was granted 27:9:1677, to his wife, who swore to an

inventory. Hilliard Veren and Henry Skerry were commissioned to examine the debits and credits, said Cranaver being indebted more than the estate is worth and make return to the next Salem court, posting notice so that all creditors will come in to demand their debts.

Salem Quarterly Court Records, vol. 5, leaf 112.

Inventory of the estate of Richard Craniver, taken by Edmond Bridges and Peter (his P mark) Cloys: two beds and furniture to them, 5li.; tow chessts and 3 boxis, 1li. 8s.; one pott, one Iron kettle, skilit, 15s.; 2 hakes, tongs, fryin pan, gridiron, fiarshuvil, 15s.; six ould chairs, 6s.; peutir, earthin ware and wooden ware, 1li.; ould lumbar, 1li. 10s.; 2 bushils of Ry, 7s.; 2 ould bibels, 6s.; warin cloethes, 2li. 16s.; lining, 2li.; total, 16li. 3s.

Richard Craniver (also, Cranifurt, Cranifud), Dr. Nov. 29, 1677, to William Andrew, 23li. 16s., balance of account due to the latter's grandfather, Capt. George Corwin; to Jno. Price, 66li.; to Phillip Cromwel, by John Cromwell, 6li. 10s. 6 3-4d.; to Tho. Gardner, 1li. 8s. 7d.; to Jno. Higginson, jr., 3li. 9s.

Essex County Quarterly Court Files, vol. 27, leaves 120, 121.

ESTATE OF RICHARD WATERS OF SALEM.

"I Richard Waters being ancient and allso weak of body yet of good & pfect memory blessed be God do make this my last Will & Testament the 16 Day of July 1676 Imp[r] after all my real Debts be truly paid out of my estate with what charge doth arise about my Funerall, I do will & bequeath my whole Estate that God hath giuen me in this world to say house & Lands chattells, goods, Debts or what ever Estate I haue or of right belongs to mee, movable and unmovable, To Joyce my beloued Wife for her to haue and to hold after my decease the time of her naturall Life for her necessary use & Comfort, and for that end whilst she remaine a widow to haue Liberty for her necessity to sell any p[t] of the s[d] Estate first of the movable and afterward of y[e] house & Land if need require (provided it be with the aduise and assistance of my ouerseers hereafter named,) but in case she be married then to haue no power to sell allinate or dispose of any of y[e] s[d] estat but to keep the housing in tenantable repair and the movables from damage to be disposed of as followeth.

"It   I giue what remaines of my estate at my wives decease to my Son William to be Secured in the hands of my Sonne

Ezekiel for to maintain his Brother William During his naturall life, in case my son Ezekiell be not willing to keep him
if my Son John undertake it then he shall haue Williams estate during his naturall life and at williams Death to be disposed of as followeth.   It. I giue to my son James ten shillings.   And to my son John ten shillings & to my son Ezekiell
ten shillings and to my Daughter Martha ten shillings provided there be left forty pound clear estate at my son Williams Decease Allso my will is that the rest of my children
viz Abigail punchard Mary English Susana Pulsiver and
Hanah Striker who neither of them haue had any pt. or portion of my estate already as my fore mentioned Children have
had, shall haue the rest of my estate that shall be left at my
son Williams Decease, the Legacies *The Legacies* to my other
Children being paid or deducted out as aforesd to be equally
devided between them be the Estate more or less it being
likely that what is left then will be most in the house &
Ground Therefore my will is that my son Ezekiel shall haue
the first refusall of the sd house & Ground, & next any one of
my children If neither of them will not or cannot, then it may
be sold to any other psons, to be devided as aforesd further I
do declare and it is my will that the piece of ground for a
housplott which I formerly gaue my Daughter Susana by
word of mouth shee shall hold & injoy forthwith & forever
hereafter.   It. I entreat my Louing friends Mʳ Edm. Batter,
mʳ Hilliard Verine, Senʳ & Christopher Babbidge & ‖ John
Swinerton ‖ to be my overseers, to take care that this my will
be truly & faithfully pformed.   It I appoynt Joyce my sd beloued Wife to be my sole Executrix."

Richard Waters (SEAL)

Witness: Hilliard Veren, sr., John Swinnerton.
Proved in Salem court 28 : 9 : 1677 by the witnesses.

Inventory of the estate of Richard Waters, taken 25 : 7 :
1677, by John Swinnerton and Hilliard Veren, sr.: the west-
ern end of the dwelling House with the brew house and about
halfe an Acre of Land, 70li.; 4 Barrills of Molasses, 5li., and
36 Bush. of malt, 10li. 8s.; 8 Dozen of quart stone Juggs, 2li.;
A Copper with worme and Appurtenance, Tubs, barrells with
all the lumber in the brew house & wood, 6li.; Cash, 3li. 19s.;
a standing bedstead with bed, bolster, 3 pillows, Rugg, blankets, sheets, vallence & Curtains withall appurtinances, 7li.;
A Truckle bed and beding, 2li. 10s.; warming pan, 5s.; scales
and waights, 10s.; Books and Lumber in the parlor, 17s.;
wearing Apparril, woolin and linin, 5li.; 3 old Chests, wheel &

Cards, 10s.; in the hall, earthen & wooden platters & pewter potts, 8s.; 4 old Chayers, Table, stooles, payles & lumber, 10s.; 7 yds. of blew linin, 7s.; swyne, 4li.; Ropes & Tacles, 4li. 12s.; Iron, viz., 2 pots, Kettle, tongs, fire shovel and hawks, 1li.; in the hal Chamber, a straw bed, 10s.; 4 Bushels of wheat & a barril of meale, 1li. 16s.; linin, 4 p of sheets, bags and lumber, 2li. 13s.; Creditor by severall psons, 28li. 7s. 4d.; total, 148li. 10s. 4d.; Debtor to several persons, 16li. 1s. 10 1-2d. Remainder of estate is 132li. 8s. 5d.

Essex County Quarterly Court Files, vol. 27, leaves 114, 115.

ESTATE OF THOMAS PICKTON OF SALEM.

"In the name of god amen: I Thomas pickton being in perfit memorie doe make this my Last will and Testement this ninteenth day of october In the yeare of our Lord one Thousand six hundred seaventy seaven. my will is: first I commit my soule into the armes of my saviour Jesus Christ desireing to rest with hime for ever and my body to be buried at the discression of my executor heerafter mentioned. Item I doe make my Loueing wife Anne pickton my whole and sole executrix and doe giue unto her all my goods and Estate that god hath giuen me in this world within doores and without to dispose of it for her Liuelyhood and Comfort in this world And I doe appointe John Galley and Henry Bayley to be overseerers to the true intent and meaning of this my will for the maintainance and Comfort of my wife: And in witness I haue heareunto sett my hand the day & yeare first aboue written." Thomas Pickton.

Witness: John (his J mark) Galley, Henry (his H mark) Bayley.

Proved in Salem court 28:9:1677 by the witnesses and the overseers to take care the estate be not wasted whereby the widow may come to suffer want.

Inventory of the estate of Thomas Pickton: Debts, to Mr. William Browne, sr., 17s. 8d.; Francis Collings, 6d.; John Stone, 5d.; Edmund Gale, a bushell of Indian corne, 3s.

Inventory taken by Joseph Dodge and Joseph Eaten: bill due to him, half money and half cloath, Lineing and wooling and shooes, 30li.; by Thomas Blashfeild, 8s.; by Richard Hutten, nineteen bushels Indian corne to be paid the last of Febuarie or Mar. 1 & 20 more that time next year following; Guilbard Tapley, 3li.; in his house in money, 23li.

Another inventory: due upon bill by Joseph Dodge & Joseph Eaten, 30li.; due upon bill by David Perkins, 18li.; by Gilberd Tapley in sterling money, 3li.; In his house in money, 23li.; Beding, 11li. 16s.; his wearing Cloathes, 8li. 6s.; Armes to traine with, 1li. 16s.; Pewter & Brass, 3li. 14s.; Tooles and Iron, 2li. 7s.; Chests, Boxes & Coubberd, 2li. 8s.; English Corne, 2li. 16s.; Indian Corne, 9li.; all his housing, 23li.; Nate Cattle, 12li. 10s.; 2 Horses, a mare & colt, 8li. 15s.; A horse Cart, 1li. 5s.; swine, 5li.; sheep, 1li.; In Land 20 Acres, 104li.; Due by Richard Hutten 39 bushalls Indian corne, 5li. 17s.; by Thomas Blashfield, 8s.; total, 277li. 18s. Small debts to be paid, 3li. 8s. 9d.

Attested in court 28 : 9 : 1677 by the overseers.

Essex County Quarterly Court Files, vol. 27, leaves 112, 113.

ESTATE OF OBADIAH BRIDGES OF IPSWICH.

Administration upon the estate of Obadiah Bridges, intestate, was granted 6 : 9m : 1677, to Elizabeth, the widow, who was ordered to bring in an inventory to the next Salem court.

Ipswich Quarterly Court Records, vol. 5, page 298.

Elizabeth, widow of Obadiah Bridges, brought in an inventory of his estate amounting to about 76li. and there being three children left, court Apr. 30, 1678, ordered that she pay 6li. to the eldest son and 5li. each to the other two when they come to age, the house and land to stand bound for the payment of the children's portions.

Ipswich Quarterly Court Records, vol. 5, page 335.

Inventory of the estate of Obadiah Bridges taken Nov. 2, 1677 : houseing and land, 60li.; one Anvell & backe Iron, 2li. 10s.; one pr. of Bellowse, 2li. 10s.; severall small tooles, 1li. 10s.; skalls & waights & hammer & naile rod, 14s.; hay in the barne, 15s.; one feather bed & furniture belonging, 11li. 9s.; one Trundell bed & what belonging to it, 1li. 16s.; pewter, Brass and one Iron pott, 11li. 17s.; 2 tramells, tongs, fire slice and andirons, 1li. 14s.; 1 gunn, raper, belt and powder horne, 2li. 14s.; wooden wares, 16s. 3d.; Earthen wares, tining ware and chairs, 19s. 2d.; 2 bibles, baskets & other small things as cradell, table wheele, friing pan, 1li. 17s.; severall tubbs & other things in the seller, 1li. 10s.; 2 holand pillebers & 2 paire of sheets & 2 table cloths, napkins, towells and shorts, 3li. 11s. 8d.; his owne weareing cloaths & other linings, 6li. 13s. 6d.; one pillion cloathe, 2 chests & 2 boxes, 2li. 12s.; Indian corne & wooden wares, 3li. 4s.; one howe, 3li. 5s.; one

horse, 4li.; one coult of four yers ould, 2li.; seven shepe, 2li.
10s.; seven swine, 3li. 6s.; total, 133li. 14s. 1d. Debts due
from the estate, 56li. 7s. 10 1-2d.; total estate remaining, 76li.
10s. 3 1-2d.
Attested in Ipswich court Apr. 30, 1678 by the administratrix.

An account of the debts due from the estate of Obadiah
Bridges: due to Mr. William Goodhue marchant, as apers by
Mr. Goodhews Book, 12li. 4s.; to Mr. Frances Wainwrite as
apers by book, 9li. 6s. 5 1-2d.; to Andrew Peters as apers by
his Afermation on his book and bill, 11li. 19s.; Mr. Jno.
Wainewrite, 2li. 1s.; Mr. Jno. Backer, 1li. 6s.; Joseph Safford, 1li. 1s. 6d.; Thomas Newman, 15s. 6d.; Jno. Bridges,
1li. 10s.; Edmond Bridges, sr., 8li. 1s.; Jams Foller, 4li. 12s.;
ould goodman Fellows, 13s.; Nathaniell Rust, 15s. 5d.; Samuell Bushop, 1li. 10s.; Simond Stase, 7s.; Cristifor Bouls,
13s.; Georg Hadlay, 5s.; Richerd Sachwell, 1li. 10s.; Roger
Darby, 13s.; Samuell Yonglove, jr., 17s.; Eleihew Wardwell,
14s.; Frances Yonge, 1li. 5s.; Isack Foster, 13s.; John Chapman, 7s. 6d.; Walter Roper & his son Nathaniell, 13s.;
Samll. Hart, 6s.; Jno. Haris, 9s.; Jno. Spark, 14s.; Jno. Tod,
14s. 4d.; Thomas Knoulton, 3s. 6d.; Robert Pearce, 1li.; to
the constable for Rates, 2li.; Samll. Eires, 1li.; Thomas
Eires, 14s.; to ye widdowe Kimball of Boston, 3li.; Samll.
Noyses, 3s.; Mr. George Person of Boston, 16s.; total, 56li.
7s. 10 1-2d.

Essex County Probate Files, Docket 3,308.

Whereas the house and land of Obadiah Bridges stand
bound for the payment of the children's portions which is
16li., the court Mar. 29, 1681 releases the said house to Nathaniell Rust, he giving security with his own bond of 30li.

Ipswich Quarterly Court Records, vol. 5, page 366.

ESTATE OF NICHOLAS BATT OF NEWBURY.

"In the Name of God Amen I Nicolass Batt of Newbury,
in N : England being Aged and weak of body; though in full
and perfect Memory; Doe make and ordaine my last will and
Testament, for the disposing of my esteat in maner and forme
as followeth. Imp^r: I give my body to ye dust to be buried,
and my Soul unto god that gave it, And as for my worldly
goods I doe will and dispose of as followeth. first I give to
my daughter, mary Elithorp or har haiers a fether-bed, bolster, and pillow, w^t a p^r of Sheets, and a p^r of blankets. 2 to

Sarah mihill, I doe give a cow, and a p^r. of Sheets, w^t the six yew's and lambs thay have alredy 3 to my two grand-Children Nicolas Webster, and Nicolas mihill, I give ech of them yew and a lamb. 4 to my: 3 grand-daughters, Sarah Webster, mary Elithorp, and Sarah Mihill, I give to ech of them a pewter plater. 5 All the Rest of my esteat, both Lands, housing, orchard, and Chattells or moveable estat I give to my Wife dureing har lifetime provided y^t She Continew a widdow; exept a lott of meadow wch I gave to John Webster att his mariege: also I make my wife Sole Executrix of my estate 6 And after my Wife is deceased I doe order and appoint y^t all ye estat that is remaining, Shall be equally devided into five equall parts, and y^t my daughter Anne Webster, Shall have two parts: and ye other three parts, Shall be equally devided, betwen my two daughters, mary and Sarah, or thaier haiers, allwaies provided y^t John Webster, or his haiers being my daughter ann's Children, Shall have liberty to buy the land of both my other Children, that is, thaier parts, if he or his haiers will give full as much for it, as any other man will give, 7 Also I doe desier, and appoint my Lov: freinds, Richard Dole, and Benjamin Rolfe over-seers to see that this my will and Testament be performed according to the full intent thereof in evry perticuler; and for to declare y^t this is my last will and testamet I have hereunto Sett my hand and Seall this eighteenth day of June Anno Dom: one thousand, Six hundred, Seaventy fouer."

Nichlas   Batt (SEAL)

Witness: Richard Dole, Jno. Dole.
Proved in Ipswich court Mar 26, 1678 by the witnesses.

Inventory taken Dec. 12, 1677, by Samuell Ploumer and Benjamin Rolef: houesing and orchard with the land the trees stand on, 40li.; aboute to akers & halef of land called coulmans lot, 20li.; a lott of meadow called silvers lot about 5 akers, 25li.; another lot of medow about 5 Akers below Ileslyes, 30li.; a lott & halef of meadow att plom iland, 18li.; a free hould, 20li.; halef an Aker medow at pine Iland bredg, 2li.; a hoores, 2li.; to cowes, 7li.; 18 sheepe, 8li. to pigs, 14s.; feather bed, bouster, pelow, pr. blanchetes, pr. sheates, rugg & bedsted, 10li.; another fether bed, bouster, pelow, cooverled, pr. blancketes, a small bedsted, 8li.; seven pr. of sheetes, 5li.; 6 napkens, 3 towels, tabell cloth, 1li.; to chests & 3 boxes, 1li.; pewter, 1li. 10s.; to ketteles, to skilletes, to poots, 2li. 10s.; tabell, chahers & couchons, 1li.; gunn, swoord, 1li. 5s.; warming pann & frying pann, 15s.; fire tramell, pott houkes & other things, 1li.; loome & tackling, 5li.; part of a bar. poarke, 1li. 10s.; sadell — peilling, 1li.; wooll & yearne, 1li. 10s.; lumber, 1li.; deptes if gotten, 20li.; to yd. 1-2 cloth, 7s. 6d.; wareing Clothes & boocks, 12li. 10s.; 3 barreles seider, 1li. 10s.; total, 239li. 1s. 6d.; about 6 load of hay, 3li.; to pellow ceases, 10s.

Attested in Ipswich court Mar. 26, 1678 by Lusie Batt relict of Nicolas Batt.

Mr. Nois, 14s.; Capten geris, 6s.; Jhon bartlet, 3s. 2d.; Richard knit, 1li. 2s.; Amos stickni, 5s.; Josep plumer, 2li. 3s. 4d.; gorg litel, 1li. 5s.; Tomas hale, sen., 6s.; Franses thuril, 1li. 2s.; Daniel cheny, 1li. 3s.; Danel thostin, 1li. 8s.; Danel meril, 19s.; Richard thoril, 1li. 2s.; nat. merel, 1li. 6s. 6d.; Capt. gerish, 13s. 6d.; Jonathan more, 11s.; Edman more, sen., 3s. 10d.; Jhon halle, 13s. 6d.; Edman more, Junr., 12s.; Jhon wilkot, 4li. 2s.

Essex County Probate Files, Docket 2,134.

Will of Nicolas Batt was proved Mar. 26, 1678, and objection was made by John Webster.

Ipswich Quarterly Court Records, vol. 5, page 303.

Whereas Nicholas Batt of Newbury is lately deceased and the law gives liberty to prove a will before two magistrates, the clerk John Webster, who married the eldest daughter of said Batt, came to the Worshipfull Major Generall Denison, Esq., 6:9m:1677, and desired that no such will might be proved in private without his or his wife's knowledge, as they had something to say. They were so advised by the Honored Major Generall to have this caution entered.

Ipswich Quarterly Court Records, vol. 5, page 299.

Deposition of John Emery, Sr. and Mary his wife, that in 1653 John Webster married Ann Batt, daughter of Nicolas Batt and in consideration of their marriage Nicolas Batt promised to give to the said John Webster with his daughter Ann his house he then lived in and all his lands that he had with all the priviledges belonging unto them after his and his wife's decease, and did immediately give to the said Ann possession of part of it in lieu of the whole and John Webster hath enjoyed it as his own proper estate to this day without molestation; furthermore Nicolas Batt promised to weave all the cloth that she made for nothing. Sworn in Ipswich court Mar. 26, 1678.

Deposition of John Emery, Jr., aged about fifty years, that in 1653 on the day that John Webster was contracted to Ann

Batt eldest daughter of Nicolas Batt of Newbury he being at
his father Emryes house heard Goodman Batt say that while
he lived he would weave her cloth and after his decease and
his wife's she as his heir should have all his houseing and
lands for as his eldest daughter she should have a double portion and he accounted the houseing and land would amount to
such a value; further Batt said that he would give his other
children their portions as he could in his life time as he was
able and in case he should die the other two daughters should
have their portions out of his other estate.

John Emery, Jr. confirmed this testimony Feb. 28, 1677
before Jo. Woodbridg, com.

Sworn in Ipswich court, Mar. 26, 1678.

Deposition of John Webster, Jr., aged 22 years that about
four or five months before the death of his grandfather Batt
he heard his father and grandfather discoursing about building a room to his grandfather Batt's house and if he did, of
his grandfather giving him security from damage and his
grandfather said he need not fear coming to loss for he had
made a will and all his land was given to him after his death
and his mother's; further, that ever since he took notice of
things his father had enjoyed the orchard behind the house
as his own and he had heard both his grandfather and grandmother say that the orchard was his father's and that after
their death he was to have all the rest of the lands.

John Webster, Jr. confirmed this testimony Feb. 27, 1677
and John Webster, Sr., before Jo. Woodbridge, com. Sworn in
Ipswich court, Mar. 26, 1678.

Ipswich Deeds, vol. 4, page 150.

Petition to the Ipswich court Apr. 30, 1678, of John Webster of Newbury, showing that Nicolas Batt late of Newbury
did before the marrage of the petitioner to his daughter Ann,
freely promise his house and lands with the priviledges
thereto belonging, after his own and his wife's decease as a
portion to his said daughter, yet notwithstanding, the said
Nicolas Batt made his will and disposed of his land as his
other estate, (which your petitioner conceives was not be-
queathable being before disposed of to him on the marriage of
his daughter) and the petitioner is debarred from the possession of the said land till after the death of the relict of the
said Nicolas, who being made executrix of the will offereth
the land to sell, whereby the petitioner is endangered to be de-
feated of his just right, and he asks that the land may be se-

cured and not alienated, or at least to accept this address into the public records of the court as a testimony of the petitioners continued claim.

The Court Apr. 30, 1678 ordered that it may be recorded.

Ipswich Deeds, vol. 4, page 155.

ESTATE OF WILLIAM HOLLINGWORTH OF SALEM.

Ellinor Hollingworth informed the court of several uncertain reports of the death of her husband Wm. Hollingworth and having wasted some time and not being able to get any certain information from all the vessels that have arrived, court 27 : 9 : 1677, ordered that the estate be placed in her hands and that she should act in the improvement of it as if her husband were yet alive until more information be received or the court order otherwise. Said Elenor was given power of attorney.

Salem Quarterly Court Records, vol. 5, leaf 110.

Administration upon the estate of William Holingworth, intestate, granted 26 : 9 : 1678 to Elenor the relict of the deceased, who brought in an inventory of the estate and gave oath to the truth of it. The estate being debter much more then the inventory amounts to it is ordered that all creditors make their claim to Mr. Edmond Batter and Mr. Wm. Bowditch of Salem who are to make return thereof to the next November court that the estate may then be proportioned as far as it will go to pay the debts.

Salem Quarterly Court Records, vol. 5, leaf 123.

Account of what debts of her husband William Hollingwood, Elinor Hollingwood have paid since his departure, out of my owne labor not diminishing his estate, but making use of other mens estate which I was trusted for and am in debt for most of it still : to Mr. Thomas Kellon paid him in part & am Engaged to pay him the remainder, the whole being 19li. 18s. ; to Mathew Nickson paid him for a hogsd. of tobacco my husband had of him & for his wages to Virginea being arrested, 12li. ; to Hugh Woodberry paid him for his wages to Virginea with my husband I being threatned to be arrested for it, 3li. 3s. ; to Mr. Edmond Batter paid him for a debt of my husbands, 20li. 18s. ; to Mr. Heman of Charlestowne paid him for a debt of my husbands being arrested, 9li. 13s. ; to John Becket paid him for ship carpentry worke due to him from my husband, 1li. 16s. ; total, 67li. 8s.

Inventory of the estate of Mr. William Hollingwood, deceased, taken by Joseph Grafton and Thomas Gardner, sr. and given in Aug. 29, 1677 by his wife, Mrs. Elinor Hollingwood: the Howse and land being mortgaged to Mr. Phillip Crummell; one Bedd, one Blankett, one Coverled, one Bolster & Bedsteed & curtains, 5li.; one cubbard & 2 Tables, 2li. 10s.; Five leather chaires, 1li. 5s.; Six old chaires, 10s.; one chest, 18s.; Seven Framed pictures & 2 Boxes, 9s.; one paire of Andirons & one warming pan. 5s., total, 10li. 17s. These things being in the best roome. In the Kitchen: 2 Kettles & 3 skilletts, 2li. 10s.; 2 potts, 5s.; 2 paire of scales, one skimmer, a Basting Ladle forke and Leaden weights, 10s.; 6 pewter platters, 1li. 4s.; 2 plates, one candlestick, 3 qrt potts, 2 cupps, 2 Basons & salt, 10s.; one Jack & 2 spitts, 1li.; 2 paire of tongs, one paire of Andirons & firepan, 8s.; one Fryeing pan, 2 hakes & a griddiron, 10s.; one morter & pestell & 1 doz. of Trenchers, 5s.; one paire of Bellowes & a smoothing Iron, 3s.; one Table & Forme, 5s.; total, 7li. 10s. In the chamber above: one feather Bed, one paire of Blanketts, 3li.; one Flocke Bed & Bolster, one Blankett & one old Rugg, 1li. 5s.; 2 Bedsteeds, A table & one chest & settle, 1li. 5s.; total, 5li. 10s. In the other chamber: one Feather Bedd, Bolster & pillow, one Blankett, Bedsteed & curtaines, 6li.; one coverled & one cubbard, 2li. 10s.; one Table & 3 green chaires, 15s.; 3 trunks & a chest, 1li. 10s.; Looking glass & Trundle Bedsteed, 1li.; 4 paire of sheetes & one sheete, 5li.; 4 paire of old sheetes, 1li. 5s.; 4 paire of pillowbeers, 1li.; 3 Table cloathes, 2 cubbard cloathes, eleven Napkins, 1li. 15s.; 13 Napkins, 10 Towells, 1li.; one paire of pistolls & holsters, 2 Rapiers & 2 Belts, 16li.; one saddle, 1li. 5s.; 3 carpetts & one little one, 1li. 4s.; A Blacke Suite & cloake, 5li.; one paire of drawers, one Wastcoat & Boote hose Topps, 18s.; total, 46li. 2s. In the Brew Howse: the Copper & Brewing Tubbs, 20li.; a Fowleing peece & Sword, 1li. 10s.; A port mantle, 2 chamber potts & a dripping pan, 1li.; total estate, 92li. 9s. Also severall debts that are supposed to be due exceeding the estate.

Elen the relict of the deceased was granted power of administration upon her husband's estate who attested to this inventory in the Salem court 26: 9m: 1678.

Essex County Quarterly Court Files, vol. 30, leaves 19, 20.

The debts of William Hollingwood brought in Nov. 25, 1679 by Edmund Batter and Wm. Bowditch: to Mr. Hayman of Charlestown, 23li.; Mr. Edward Groves, 5li. 11s.; Mr. Edward Norrice, 30s.; total, 30li. 1s.

The court at Salem ordered Ed. Batter and Mr. Bowditch
to pay the creditors as far as the estate would go.

According to an order of the court 26 : 9 : 1679 Edmund
Batter and Wm. Bowditch proportioned the estate as follows:
to Mr. Grove, 5li. 4s. 6d.; Mr. Haman, 21li. 12s.; Mr. Norrice, 1li. 8s. 6d.; to expences & paying the ————.

Essex County Quarterly Court Files, vol. 32, leaf 22.

ESTATE OF JOHN JONES OF NEWBURY.

Administration upon the estate of John Joanes was granted
27 : 9 : 1677, to Mr. Tho. Woodbridg, with Capt. Nicholas
Page as surety, and he was ordered to bring in an inventory to
the next Ipswich court.

Salem Quarterly Court Records, vol. 5, leaf 111.

"In ye name of god amen: I John Jones of Newbery in y^c
County of Essex in New England shipcarpenter: being at
present of a sound minde & memory and in competent health
of body yet considering that I am now taking a uoyage to sea,
& knowing the danger thereof, and ye uncertainty of my life.
haue thought it meet, & doe accordingly make this my last
will and testament: Impr: I bequeath & resigne my soul into
ye hands of god that gaue it And as for my worldly goods and
outward estate, whether reall, personall, or mixt, of what kind
or natuere soeuer they be (my just debts being first payd) I
giue and bequeath wholly and absolutely and euery
part, and pcell thereof, unto my Dear and Louing mother
Anne White to be ordered and disposed of by her, as shee in
her wisdome shall judge meet whoe alsoe I doe hereby make
my sole Executrix of this my last will and testament. By all
my estate, I mean my third part of a plantation at St Thomas
his parish in Barbadoes which was left me by my father
Thomas Jones his will, and alsoe whatsoeuer else of his estate
there which in right belongethe to me & alsoe all my debts
there or in New England together wth my tooles or w^{t}euer is
mine, and I doe hereby make voyd all former wills or ingagements of this kinde either by word or writing whatsoever.

In wittness whereof I haue hereunto sett my hand and seal,
this seuenteenth day of July in ye year of o^r: Lord one thousand six hundred seuenty and six 1676:"

John Jones.

Witness: Hilliard Veren, Junr., Hilliard Veren, Senr.
Proved in Salem court 30 : 9 : 1677 by the witnesses.

Essex County Quarterly Court Files, vol. 27, leaf 108.

Mrs. An White presenting a written will of John Joanes, proved by the oath of two witnesses, was ordered to bring in an inventory to the next Ipswich court.

Salem Quarterly Court Records, vol. 5, leaf 112.

Whereas John Jones of Newbury died intestate and under age, and there had been produced in this court an authentic copy under the hand of the secretary of Barbadoes of the will of Thomas Jones, father of said John, in which it was provided that if John Jones should die under age, his estate should revert to the only daughter, now wife of Thomas Woodbridge of Newbury, to whom administration had been granted, said Woodbridge brought in an inventory Mar. 26, 1678, and it was allowed.

Ipswich Quarterly Court Records, vol. 5, page 302.

Inventory of the estate of John Joanes who died in 1676, taken Mar. 25, 1678 and brought in by Thomas Woodbridge: his third part of his plantation in the Barbados, 100li.; the Rent of it one yeare 2000li. suger, 10li.; mony due from Mr. Car, 1li. 18s.; one mare & colt, 2li.; 2 small sheepe, 14s.; 1 cloake, 2li.; total, 116li. 12s. The estate is Dr. to Mr. Marsh, 11s.; Thomas Woodbridge, 4s.; Mr. Dole, 3s.

Allowed by the Ipswich court Mar. 26, 1678.

Copy, Ipswich Deeds, vol. 4, page 153.

ESTATE OF NICHOLAS POTTER OF SALEM.

"I nicholas Potter of Salem, being weak in body, but of good & perfect memory & vnderstanding blessed be God, doe make this my last will & testament this 10: 8mo: 1677, first, after my debts & funerall charges be paid, the rest of my estate I dispose of as followeth, viz: whereas I lately made a deed to my sonn Robert Potter of my house & land at linn, dated 26 of May 1675, which conveyance I doe by this my last will & testament confirme, upon the condition therein exspressed, to be observevd, 2 for the land in the north feild in Salem, which I had in a former will giuen to my daughter Elizabeth Newall, but made it voyde in the aboue said conveyance, which said land I doe now giue & bequeath the said land be it more or less, to my two sons had by my last wife viz: Samuell & Benjamin, to be to them & theire heires for euer in equall part. 3 Alsoe I giue & bequeath to my said two sonns, Samuell & Benjamin all that my house & ground at Bostone, to them & theire heires, an equall part, to injoy it at the age of twenty one years & if either of them dy before, the whole

to be to the surviver, only my will is that out of the said house
& ground, there shall be pd to my two daughters viz: Sarah
& Mary each of them the value of ten pounds to be paid them
within one yeare after my sons come of age to injoy the sd
house & ground. 4. I giue & bequeath that which will be due
to me from Isaack Williams at or after my decease, as by his
mortgage to me doe appeere, which is eighty pounds: viz: to
my Daughter Bethiah fiue pounds, & the reast I giue to all my
six children, borne by my last wife viz: Samuell,
Benjamin, Sarah, Mary, Hannah & the said Bethiah, to be
equaly devided betweene them. 5. Alsoe I give & bequeath, to my said six children, viz. Samuell, Benjamin, Sarah, Mary, Hanna, & Bethiah, my house &
ground adjoyning in Salem, to haue each of them an equall
part or the value of it, alsoe about four acres of ground caled
Pigden's lot to be equally deuided. 6 I giue & bequeath to
my fouer daughters, viz: Sara, Mary, Hanah & Bethiah, all
my moueables & houshold stuff &c: to be equally deuided betweene them. 7 And my will is that what I haue giuen aboue
said to all or either of my children, they shall haue & injoy
it to them selues & theire heires foreuer, when they come to
the age the sons at twenty one years & the daughters at eighteene yeares or marriage & in the meane time the rents &
profits of the whole estate viz: houses & land & efects of whateuer is elce, to be for the breeding up of my sd children, soe
far as it will goe, at ye ordering & discression of my executor
& over seers (here after exsprest)

"8 My will is that if God should see good to take by death
any of my said children before they come to age or are
marryed, as aforesaid, that then there p^t to be equally deuided amongst the suruiuers: that is to say respectiuely where
they are all concerned, there all to share in ye deceased's pt:
& the sons Joyntly, the suruier to haue ye whole of the deceased sons, but if both die before they com of age then the
daughters to haue theire estate deuided amongst them, &
where Sarah & Mary are concerned together in the twenty
pound out of the house at Boston: the suruier to Injoy the
whole, or if both dy before they come of age, then the whole
to be equally deuided amongst the rest of the suruiuing children, & if Bethiah dy before she be of age or married her fiue
pound to be deuided amongst the suruiuing children Lastly
I doe desire & apoynt my Hon^d father John Gedney to be sole
executor of this my last will & testament, & my son Robert
Potter & my brothers, Bartholmew Gidney & Elezaer Gidney

to be ouerseers. In witnes heare of I haue put to my hand &
seale the day & yeare aboue written."
                    Nicholas (his P mark) Potter (SEAL)
Witness: Hilliard Veren, Senr., Nathaniell Beadle.
Proved 29 : 9 : 1677 by the witnesses.

Inventory of the estate of Nicholas Potter, taken Oct. 25,
1677, by Hilliard Veren, sr.: his dwelling house in Salem
with about halfe an acre of Ground adjoyning, being most pt
an oarchard, 70li.; about 4 acres of ground called Pigdens
Poynt, 20li.; about 5 acres of land in the north feild, 10li.; an
old feather bed, bolster, 3 pillowes pt of a bolster, an old blankett & Rugg, 3li.; a smale old feather bead, 2 blanketts, old
Rugg & old flock pillows, 2li. 5s.; severall smale lumber in a
chest, 5s.; wearing apparrell, 5li.; 1 ell cloath rash, an old
child's blanket & old child's coat, 16s.; an old cattaile bed, old
curtaines & 2 or 3 old pillowes with an old blankett & covering,
1li. 6s.; pewter, 18s.; brass pan & warming pan, 8s.; an Iron
kettle, 2 potts, hake & fire pan, 1li. 2s.; a chest with a small
pr. Doggs, 2 old swords, with some Iron lumber, 12s.; earth
ware, 2s.; a wooll & linen wheels, 8s.; 3 or four old hats &
pr. shooes, 10s.; 7 old chaires at 7s., a Joyne stoole & som
old barrells, 2s.; linnen, 46s.; bookes, 10s.; swine, 16s.; a
cow, 40s.; a cubbord & 3 bedsteeds, 30s., 4li. 6s.; a chest, 6s.;
13 B. aples, 10s.; wood, 7s.; a flock bed with feathers, with 2
Jarrs, 20s.; curtain rods & spitt, 5s.; due from Isaack Williams to be pd in 4 yeare, 80li.; one house & Land att boston
apprised by Mathew Barnard & Edw. Grant, besids the house
& land at linn formerly giuen to his son Robert Potter, 90li.;
total, 206li. 11s. Estate debtor to severall, 15li.; several
charges, 4li.
Attested in Salem court 29 : 9 : 1677 by the executor.

Nicholas Potter, Dr., to Capt. George Corwin, a boat, 1li.
8s.; John Milk, 2li. 12s.; Goodwife Bamfeld, 10s.; Tho. Rix,
9s.; Mr. Batter, 5s.; Mr. Wm. Brown, sr., 6li. 7s. 6d.; Mr.
Neale, 7s.; Philip Crumwell, 2li. 19s.; Walter Skinner, 2s. 6d.
Essex County Quarterly Court Files, vol. 27, leaves 110, 111.

Agreement made between William Roch and Hannah his
wife daughter of Nicholas Potter late of Salem, deceased, and
Mary (her † mark) Elson and Bethia (her † mark) Witt the
other daughters of said Potter as a final settlement and distribution of said estate: that Mary Ellson and Bethia Witt
shall have for their part the house, land and appurtinances
that was their father's being in Boston situate in the back

Street in the north end of the Towne near the dwelling house of the Rev. Increas Mather, in equal parts; that William Roch and Hanah his wife shall have for their part the dwelling house, Land and appurtinances that was the said Potter's situated in Salem bounded on the south with the street or highway, on the east with the land of Wiliam Bath and land that was formerly the widow Eastwick's, on the north with the land of Joseph Miles, deceased, and on the west with the land of Nathaniel Gedney & also a peice of land on the Neck in Salem called Picdens point being about four acres. Signed and sealed Aug. 14, 1697. Witness: Bethiah Gedney, Debora Gedney.

Acknowledged Aug. 14, 1697 before the Hon. Bartho. Gedney, Judge of probate, which is allowed and confirmed by him.

Essex County Probate Files, Docket 22,582.

ESTATE OF JOHN LANGDON.

Administration upon the estate of John Langdon, intestate, was granted 30: 9: 1677 to Steephen Haskett, who brought in an inventory amounting to 17li. 6s., and whatever more estate came to his knowledge he was to make return.

Michaell Comes and Peter Joy, aged about forty years, deposed that they heard John Langdon say that he gave to Elizabeth Haskitt, daughter of Mr. Stepheen Heskitt, 10li., and what else there was left was to be divided among said Heskitt's children. This was said Langdon's desire when he went away with Mr. Eliezer Devenportt out of the country in December, 1676. Sworn, 22: 8: 1677, before Wm. Hathorne, assistant.

Inventory of the estate of John Langdon: tene quintals of merchantable Cod fish, 7li. 10s.; bill of William Smaldridg, 3li.; by Lilford's bill, 3li. 2s.; by his wages and clos to portaingall, 6li. 18s.; total, 20li. 10s. Debts to Edward Bus, 3li.; to Gelbard Taply, 1li. 4s.

Attested in Salem court 30: 9: 1677 by Mr. Steephen Haskett.

Essex County Quarterly Court Files, vol. 27, leaf 105.

ESTATE OF OBADIAH RICH OF SALEM.

Administration upon the estate of Obadiah Rich, intestate, was granted 30: 11: 1677, to Bethia, the widow, who made oath to an inventory brought in.

Inventory of the estate of Obadiah Rich, taken 28:11: 1677, by Hilliard Veren, sr. and Henry West: bed, halfe filled with feathers, the old rug & old blanketts & certaines with an old broaken bedsteed & aprtenances & 2 feather pillowes, 2li. 10s.; an old trunk & in it an old hamaker & 3 old sheets & two old pr. pillow beeres, 4 or 5 old towells & naptkins, 16s.; a little looking glass, 1s. 6d.; a little old pewter & 4 porringers, 6s.; a lattin candlestick & funell & glass bottle & 2 or 3 old peeces of tin ware, 2s.; a spitt, cottrells, a pott & litle Iron kettle, fier shovell & tonges, 10s.; a cushion & beaker & old cloath & old chest, 5s.; 3 old chaires & old little tabel made of a peece of pine board, broaken stoole & som lumber, 5s.; 2 piggs, 16s.; an old paile & som lumber, 2s.; due for nursing a child, 3li. 10s.; for som old codlines, 15s.; total, 9li. 18s. 6d. Estate Dr. to several men: to Mr. Batter, 5li.; to Capt. Price, 20li.; to Capt. Corwin, 10li.; Thos. Ives, ——; to Samuell Williames, 12s. 6d.; to som other men not yet known.

Attested in Salem court 30 : 11 : 1677 by Bethiah, the relict.

Essex County Quarterly Court Files, vol. 27, leaf 124.

ESTATE OF MRS. EDITH DODGE OF BEVERLY.

"Know all persons whom it may concerne that I Edeth Dodge of Beauerle neere Salem in the county of Essex ‖widdow‖ being weake of bodie but of good and perfect memory blessed be god doe make this my last will and Testament in manner as followeth Impr I giue vnto my two daughters ‖Mary herric and Sara Woodberre‖ for there children, equally to be deuided between them for there childrens vse all my wearing apparrell with my bed bedstead and furniture therevnto Belonging my Cubbard Chest warming pan and all other goods belonging to mee in the roome where I now [live] Also I giue vnto my daughters for there children my two Cowes and sheepe Item I giue vnto my son Edward Dodge my horse and what els may be comming to mee from him for his daughter Also I giue vnto the rest of my sons all that *that* remaines due vnto mee which I was to haue had by my husbands will for there children and my will is that my Cubbard Bedstead and chest if my son Edward please to retaine it in the roome where it is that he may buy it uppon reasonable tearmes."

Edith Dodge dying intestate, administration was granted Feb. 14, 1677, by Samuell Symonds, Esq., Dep. Gov., and Maj. Gen. Denison, Esq., to John Dodge and Zachiah Herrick, and the estate to be divided according to the above writing.

Inventory taken Jan. 28, 1677 by John Rayment and Isaac
Hull : bed, Bolster and two pillars, 4li. 10s. ; Seaven Blanketts
and one rugg, 2li. ; Curtaines and vallens, 10s. ; One bed and
boolster, 1li. 5s. ; bedsteed, 10s. ; bed cord, 2s. 6d. ; new Wooll-
en cloth, 1li. 10s. ; new linnen cloth, 2li. 2s. ; sheetes, 1li. 10s. ;
Pillowbees, 1li. 2s. ; Napkins, 10s. ; other Linnen, 3s. ; In silk,
10s. ; hat and hat case, 10s. ; her woollen clothing, 13li. ; Iron
and brasse, 1li. 16s. ; In puter, 1li. 8s. ; Earthen vessells, 6s. ;
One Cubbard, two chests, 2li. 18s. ; Two Cowes, three sheepe,
8li. ; A Box, 2s. ; In money, 6li. 6s. ; total, 50li. 10s. 6d.

Attested in Ipswich court Mar. 26, 1678 by the administrators.

Also to this inventory of the Widdow Dodg, due from her
son John Dodg, 9li. ; from her son Richard Dodg, 7li. ; son
Edward Dodg, 6li. ; son Samuell Dodg, 12li. ; son Josepth
Dodg, 8li. ; total, 42li.

The estate was divided according to the directions given by
their mother and all were well satisfied as witness Mar. 26,
1678, John Dodge, Zacharia herrick, Richard (his ⊙ mark)
Dodg, Edwarde (his X mark) Dodge, Sammule Dodge, Peter
Woodbery, Josepth Dodge.

Attested in Ipswich court Mar. 26, 1678 by Zachery Herick
and John Dodge.

Essex County Probate Files, Docket 7,824.

ESTATE OF JOHN KNIGHT OF NEWBURY.

Administration upon the estate of John Knight of Newbury, intestate, was granted Mar. 26, 1678, to Bathshebah his
widow, who was ordered to bring in an inventory to the next
September court, and she was bound.

Ipswich Quarterly Court Records, vol. 5, page 303.

Inventory* of the estate of Jo. [John *dup.*] Knight taken
Mar. 15, 1677-78 : his [hous] and barn, 100li., 75 akers of
land 5li. pr. acker, 475li. ; 9 Cowes, 36li., 4 oxen, 22li., 4
steares and hefers thre year owlds, 58li. ; 4 steares and hefers
tow year owld. 8li. ; tow yearlings, 2li. ; tow stears, 8li. ; hors
and cowlet, 4li. ; 38 shep, 15li. ; 8 swin, 7li. ; his waring
aparill, 8li. ; 9 pare of shetes, 7li. ; 36 napkins, 2li. ; bostar
Casis and pillo Casis, 2li. ; 5 fether bedes, 4 boasters, 3 pillose,
18li. ; cortins, 1li. ; 3 Roudges, 2 Coverlites, 9 blinckites, 9li. ;
5 beade stedes and a cubard, 4li. ; tow tabels, 1li. 10s. ; 3
Cheste and a trownck, 1li. ; 4 Chares, 10s. ; 3 Cushins, 6s. ; tow

*Duplicate Inventory, Docket 15,982.

warmin pans, 15s.; puter, 3li.; bras Cetels and scillites, 3li.;
potes and pot huckes, tramills, spite, fring pans, anddears,
3li.; barills, Cillars, treaies, dishis, trenshars, 1li., bookes, 1li.,
botels, lantron, 2li. 12s.; 3 guns, 3li., Cotelish, 10s., wightes
and scales, 10s., sadell and pillion, 5li. 5s.; 3 sewefes, 4s.; 40
bou. of Indean Coren, 5li.; barill of porck, 3li.; a whell and
2 pare of Cardes and a Rell, 10s.; Carte and dung pot, wheles,
youckes and chaines, 3li.; shovell, spade, 2 howes, 3 axis, 3
widgis, 16s., a plow and eiern, 5s.; betell Riengs and owld
tubes, 5s.; 2 dripin pans and erthen potes, 6s.; [tow lampes,
2s. dup.]; pare of townges and pele and gredieron, 5s.; tow
sawes, augars, Chissels, hamar and pinseares, 1li.; mortar
and pesell, 6s.; 3 prownges, 4s.; a negar man, 25li.; severall
biles if all due and nothing Reseved, 127li. 14s.; eight part of
a vesill and parte of a Cargoo gon to barbados, 40li.; 20 bou.
of barly due from Jo. [Joseph, dup.] downar, 45li.; for a
Cowe, dwe for a hors, 4li.; of Josep Knight, 45li.; dept of
Rich. dole, 55li.; book depts due to the Estat, 50li. 5s. 7d.;
total, 1011li. 18s. 7d. Debts to be paid out of the Estat: to
John Bartlets wife, 40li.; Josep downers chidren, 30li.; Capt.
Gerish in money, 9li.; Josep toppan in money, 7li.; Mr.
Clarke, 3li.; Mr: byfeeld, 4li.; Mr. Moss, 1li. 10s.; Peeter
topan, 4li.; Tristam Coffin, 7li. 10s.; total 106li. abated out of
the Estate leaves 904li. 13s. 7d.

Attested in Ipswich court Sept. 24, 1678 by Bathsheba
Knight wife of John Knight.

Essex County Probate Files, Docket 15,983.

The administratrix and overseers of the estate of John
Knight of Newbury, deceased, petition the court to settle the
estate as follows: the three sons of John Knight, Richard,
Benjamin and Isaack to have the house and barn valued at
100li. and seventy five acres of land valued at 375li., divided
equally among them; and the three daughters eighty pounds
a piece and the rest of the estate to the widow Bathsheba
Knight who is to pay the debts out of her part. Allowed by
the court Sept. 24, 1678.

Ipswich Quarterly Court Records, vol. 5, page 337.

ESTATE OF JOHN HAMONS OF GLOUCESTER.

Administration upon the estate of John Hamons, intestate,
was granted Mar. 26, 1678, to Mary, the widow, who was to
have the estate for the bringing up of the children.

Ipswich Quarterly Court Records, vol. 5, page 303.

Inventory of the estate of John Hamons taken at Gloucester Mar. 20, 1677 by James Steevens, Timothy Comes and
Thomas Riggs: one dwelling house, 8li., upland ground, 10li.,
18li.; bedding & household stuf, 30s., one chest & 2 wheeles,
8s., 1li. 18s.; one bible, 3s., one small swine, 5s., 8s.; one old
canoe, 5s., one old axe & other iron tooles, 5s., 10s.; total, 20li.
16s.

Attested in Ipswich court Mar. 26, 1678 by Mary, administratrix of the estate of John Hamons.

Copy, Ipswich Deeds, vol. 4, page 143.

ESTATE OF EDWARD WHARTON OF SALEM.

Administration upon the estate of Edward Wharton, intestate, was granted Mar. 26, 1678, to Samuell Shattock, sr., and
Samuell Shattock, jr., who were ordered to bring in an inventory to the next Salem court, and were bound.

Ipswich Quarterly Court Records, vol. 5, page 303.

Samll. Shatock, sr., and Samll. Shattock, jr., administrators of the estate of Edward Wharton, brought in an inventory 25 : 4m : 1678, to which they made oath, and they were
ordered to carry out the will of deceased as appeared by a writing given in upon oath expressed a little while before he
died.

Salem Quarterly Court Records, vol. 5, leaf 117.

Samuell Shattock, sr., aged about fifty-eight years, deposed
that he was often with Edward Wharton in the time of his
sickness, the latter having desired him to look after his estate as per a writing under his hand, and was of good understanding when he spoke as follows : "he said he would giue
fiue pounds towards a burrying place, and he said he did giue
to Mary Trask the wife of Henry Trask fiue pounds: alsoe he
did giue to Hannah Sibly widdow fiue pounds: alsoe he did
giue to Sarah mills & her children ten pounds, all which he
often exspressed in the time of his sicknes, & as he drew neere
to his end: he exspressed the same before other witnesses: and
I asked him what should become or how he disposed of the remainder of his estate, after all things were cleered, as debts &
legacies he said it should goe to his Brothers. Samll. Shattocke, James Mills." Martha Robinson affirmed as in the
presence of God and this court 27 : 4 : 1678, before Hilliard
Veren, cleric. "he alsoe told me that his vice should be returned to England amongst his kinred, for he said it was his
fathers before him & it should be returned into the Genera-

tion & that his eldest brothers son bore his fathers name &
he should haue it."

"And further he said as for his trackt of land lying at
Shrewsbery at New Jarsy: which he purchased with other
purchasers, of the Indians, he told me he had sold one half
of it, when he was in England to one John Harwood marchant
in London & had taken pay for it & further said he had ordered one John Starke to settle upon it & soe to keep it in
possession for him & his freind the other partner, & told me
he would giue him twenty acres of land in his will.   Samll.
Shattocke and James Mills. Samuell Shattock, sr., affirmed
as in the presence of God and this court, before Hilliard
Veren, cleric.

"And further the said Edward wharton did exspress himselfe and say that John winditt a youth which he brought
with him out of England: viz: his sisters sonn (whome he
tooke as his owne & did intend he should share in part of his
estate, as he haue exspresed to some) the said Edward wharton, being asked when he was like to dye, if the said youth
should be sent to England to his mother he answered yea (&
I doubt not but he intended the boys mother should haue a
part of his estate as alsoe the youth) but being after six
weekes Illnes (not app^rhended dangerous) he was taken in
very great exstremety & after that liteness of head, that he
was unable of making an orderly will, & though I was with
him often in order there unto, but he would put it of untill
another time, hoeping he might gett up a day or two to looke
after som writing, & to understand his estate the better before disposall (as I did Judge) by which meanes things were
deferred, but not app^rhending his condition soe dangerous, as it
after proued, I was not soe urgent upon him about his will as
other wise I should haue beene he was taken uery sudent about
three dayes before his death only one smale respitt he had, in
which before seuerall witnesses he confirmed the four legacies
& the remainder to his brothers as is before exsprest."

Samll. Shattock certified that "Divers other smale legacies
he gaue to severall that came to see him in his sicknes neere
his end ; & forty pounds to the youth but in these things he
was ‖ not ‖ soe distinct in his understanding as when he exsprest the last aboue written, it being in the time of the two
or three last days he liued ‖ before his end ‖ & I canot giue
Testimoney to it as his will, he not being of a disposing
mind."

"Edward wharton haue two brothers in England by father

& mothers side: & one brother & sister by the mothers side: & this brother is in verginea. he dyed ye 3^d of ye 1st month 1677-8."

Inventory of the estate of Edward Wharton, deceased, and what goods were in his possession, consigned to him by several, taken 12:1:1677-8, by Hilliard Veren, sr., John Hathorne and John Higginson, jr.: Valued in England as by Invoyce, 1 plaine cloath cloake, 1li. 8s.; 1 boyes worsted cloake, 1li. 5s.; 1 heare camlett cloake, 2li. 18s.; 5 cloath cloakes, 28s. p., 7li.; 1 cloath cloake, 1li. 8s.; 1 fine cloath cloake, 1li. 15s.; 1 cloath cloake, 1li. 12s.; 6 cloath cloake, 28s. p., 8li. 8s.; 3 childs stuff coates at 9s., 1li. 7s.; 1 yeolow Tamy, 10s.; 1 ditto, 13s.; 1 boyes coate, 13s.; 1 doz home made wooll hose, 1li. 14s.; 1 doz. ditto, 1li. 10s.; 8 pr. of youths ditto, 14s.; 10 pr. of woemens home made wooll stockens, 1li. 2s.; 7 pr. of sale wooll hoase, 10s. 6d.; 17 pr. of weomens & youths stockens, 14s. 10d.; 7 pr. of home made woemens 4 thrid, 3s. 2d. p., 4 pr. ditto sale 4 thrid, 3s. 4d. p., 1li.10s.10d.;4pr. youthes 4 thrid ditto, 3s. 4d. p., 3 pr. youthes ditto, 3s., 1li. 2s. 4d.; 4 pr. of wooll home made hose, 14s.; 1 pr. mens worsted home made stockens, 5s.; 8 pr. of home made worsted: 4 thrid, 1li. 14s.; 6 pr. sale ditto, 18s.; 2 pr. of fine home made, 10s.; 1 childs coate, 7s.; 1 greene say frock, 5s.; 9 childs wascoates, 5d. p., 3s. 9d.; 6 Ditto, 7d. p., 3s. 6d.; 5 Ditto, 9d. p., 3s. 9d.; 4 Ditto, 10d. p., 3s. 4d.; 2 Keasy ditto, 2s. 6d., 5s.; 1 ditto, 2s. 8d.; 2 ditto, 3s. p., 6s.; 6 childrens, 12d. p., 6s.; 4 woemens yeolow wascoate, 22d. p., 7s. 4d.; 1 Cloake of lite collrd. haire camlett, 3li. 7s.; 4 coates of the same camlett, 36s., p., 7li. 4s.; 1 cloath collrd. haire camlett cloake, 35s.; 2 worsted camlett cloakes, 34s., 3li. 8s.; 1 fine haire camlet cloake, 5li.; 2 trunks, 16s.; 3 ditto, 1li. 1s.; 1 ditto, 6s.; 2 dittoes, 5s. p., 10s.; 2 boxes or little red trunkes, 3s. 2d. p, 6s. 4d.; 1 ditto, 2s. 8d.; 3 silk say under pettecoates lite collrd, at 12s. 6d. p., 1li. 17s. 6d.; 2 Ditto, 1li. 8s.; cloath woemans wascoats, 8s., 7 ditto, worth each 8s., 10s., 8s., 10s., 6s., 13s., 15s.; 1 cheny sad: collrd. uper woemans coate, 7s.; 1 sad collrd. woemans searge coate, 17s. 6d.; 1 black fine searge upper pettecoate, 19s.; 1 stuff cloake for woeman, 10s.; 1 ditto for a girle, 7s.; 1 large worsted Rugg lite collrd, 1li. 14s., 1 large sad collrd. ditto, worsted, 18s.; 1 ditto worsted sad collrd, 1li.; 6 greene & blew plaine Rugge, 8s. p., 2li. 8s.; 1 sad callrd thrum Rugg, 11s. 6d.; 1 cabbin Rugg, 4s. 8d.; 1 Cource 8-4 Rugg, 10s.; 3 coverleds, ordinary, 6s., p., 18s.; 2 ditto at 5s., 10s.; 2 coverleds, large at 7s. 6d., p, 15s.; 1 smale one, 6s. 6d.; 1 red plaine

rugg, 8s.; 1 peece wt. cotton, 19s.; 1 darnex carpett, 5s. 6d.;
1 ditto greene, 6s. 6d.; 4 pr. wt. drawers, 10s.; 6 peeces of
searge at 40s., 12li.; 7 peeces narrow searge at 25s., 8li. 15s.;
1 peece padaway searge, 2li. 15s.; 13 yds. clarett collrd Tamy
at 19d. p, 1li. 1s. 1d.; 1 large draft lite collrd, 14s.; 1 2d sort,
12s.; 1 small ditto, 10s.; 1 doble 10 qrtr. coverled, 1li. 4s.; 1
ditto, 9 qrts, 1li.; 2 dittos, 8 qrts., 15s. 6d. p, 1li. 11s.; 8
yrds 3-4 striped Tamarene at 18d. p, 13s. 1 1-2d.; 12 yrds.
3-4 Turky mohaire 2s. 10d. p., 1li. 16s. 1 1-2d.; 6 yrds. 1-4 of
striped stuffe at 22d. p, 11s. 5 1-2d.; 9 yrds. striped camlett,
2s. 4d. p, 1li. 1s.; 1 peece oringe collrd worsted draft, 2li. 5s.;
4 yrds. Haire camlett, 3s. p, 2li. 2s.; 10 yrds. of ash collrd,
silk moheare, 4s. p, 2li.; 6 yrds 1-2 of ash collrd silk farren-
dine, 4s. 6d. p, 1li. 9s. 3d.; 12 yrds ash collrd. haire camlett at
3s. p, 1li. 16s.; 1 peece sad collrd. stuff, mixt with Gold collrd,
2li. 10s.; 24 yrds. flowered silk draft, 2s. p, 2li. 8s.; 13 yrds.
striped vest at 22d. p, 1li. 3s. 10d.; 18 yrds. Scotch Tabby at
16d. p, 1li. 4s.; 16 yds., Scotch Tabby at 16d. p, 1li. 1s. 4d.;
10 yrds. Tiking at 15d. p, 12s. 6d.; 8 yrds. padaway at 2s.
6d. p, 1li.; 7 yrds. of Linsy at 12d 1-2p, 7s. 6d.; 2 pr. boyes
cotten drawers, at 2s. p., 4s.; 3 cotten wascoate at 2s. 10d. p,
8s. 6d.; 2 pr. blew drawers, 2s. 5d., p., 4s. 10d.; 1 boyes haire
sad coll. camlett cloake, 2li. 15s.; 1 large flanders tike & bolster, 1li. 9s. 6d.; 30 yrds. of upper Tiking, at 18d. p, 2li. 5s.;
42 yrds. diaper at 15d. p, 2li. 12s. 6d.; 12 yrds. of Tabling,
2s. 6d. p, 1li. 10s.; 21 yrds. of diaper for napkins, 18d. p, 1li.
11s. 6d.; 2 pillow Tikins, at 2s. 2d., 4s. 4d.; 1 light coll. boyes
cloake, 1li. 12s.; 2 yrds. 1-4 of plush at 8s. p., 6s. 9d.; 20 tobaco boxes at 1d 1-2 p, 2s. 6d.; 3 ditto at 20d. p doz., 3 3-4d.;
4 brass roles for chalk lines, 5s. 6d. p doz., 1s. 10d.; 8 ditto
large at 6s. 6d., p doz., 4s. 4d.; 8 chalk lines at 18d. p doz.,
1s.; tinware, 4 Cullenders, 5s. 4d.; 6 ditto, 5s. 6d.; 2 doz.
wood savealls, 3d. 1-2 p, 7d.; 1 large ketle, 2s. 3d.; 1 next size,
2s.; 8 6 qrt. Ketles, 14d. p., 9s. 4d.; 3 gallon Kettles, 12d. p,
3s.; 5 3 qrt. Kettles, 9d. p., 3s. 9d.; 2 3 pt. Kittles, 7d. p. 1s.
9d.; 5 best savealls, 2s. 4d. p doz., 11 1-2d.; 11 second sord at
8d. p doz., 7 1-4d.; 3 exstinguishers, 8d. per doz., 2 3-4d.; 3
doble plate pans, 18d., p., 4s. 6d.; a doble puden pan, 9d.; 2
midle sised lanthornes, 18d. p., 3s.; 4 band candlesticks, 5d
1-2 p, 1s. 10d.; 5 tinder boxes & steele, 7d. p., 2s. 11d.; 4 writing candlestickes, 2d 1-2 p, 10d.; 2 pt. sace pans, 3s. 8d. p
doz., 7d.; 3 bread or flower boxes, 3d. 1-2 p., 10 1-2d.; 4
Casters, 2d p., 8d.; 1 peper box, 2d., 1 fish plate, 8d., 10d.; 6
smale bread graters, 8d. p doz., 4d.; 2 pts. at 3d. 3-4 p., 1

funell, 4d., 2 covers, 8d. p., 2s. 3 1-2d.; 3 brass savealls, 7d.
p., 3 larger graters, 3d. 1-2 p., 2s. 7d.; 2 egg slices, 2d. 1-2 p.,
5d.; 3 whip sawes & tillers, 5s. 6d. p., 16s. 6d.; 2 marking
Irons, 2s., 1 cloase stoole & pan, 8s. 9d., 10s. 9d.; 2 steele
handsawes with screws, 3s. p., 6s.; 1 large steele hand saw,
2s. 2d.; 8 hand sawes at 14d. p., 9s. 4d.; 1 handsaw, 10d.; 2
faling Axes, 1s. 5d., 2s. 10d.; 8 bright smale Hamers, 6d. p.
4s.; 9 Rivited hamars at 10d. p., 7s. 6d.; 2 hamers, 4d. p, 8d.;
5 hamers, steele heads, 10s. p. doz., 4s. 2d.; 4 choppers at 15s.
p. doz., 3s. 8d.; 2 mincing knives, 12d. p., 2s.; 7 small ditto,
13s. p doz., 7s. 7d.; 9 hatchetts, 12d. p., 9s.; 7 smale mincing
knives, 9s. p doz., 5s. 9d.; 3 steele sawes & screwes, 3s. p., 9s.;
5 doz. 8 gimletts at 12d. p doz., 5s. 8d.; 27 pensills at 8d. p
doz., 1s. 6d.; 10 percer bitts at 2d. p. 1s. 8d.; 1 large pincers
to shooe horses, 1s.; 3 curry combs, 10d.; 2 large ditto, 6d. p,
1s.; 1 pr. spincers for shoomakers, 1s.; 5 pr. nippers, 4d. p,
1s. 8d.; 2 bundles of files, 20d. p bundles, 3s. 4d.; 12 doz. of
straite all blades 5d. p doz., 5s.; 7 doz crooked blades at 5d. p
doz., 2s. 11d.; 14 doz. of fire steeles at 6s. p grosse, 7s.; 21 pr.
of spurrs at 7s. p doz., 12s. 3d.; 8 pr. dove tailes at 2 1-2d. p,
1s. 8d.; 22 pr. sid hinges, 3d. p., 5s. 6d.; 6 pr. Esses at 8d. p,
4s.; 1 smooth Iron, 1s. 4d.; 3 doble spring lockes at 20d. p,
5s.; 1 single ditto, 9d.; 2 doz. trunk lockes at 6s. p doz., 12s.;
1 doz. of single ditto, 3s. p, 3s.; 1-2 doz. large ditto, 4s.; 2 ship
scrapers, 2s.; 6 pr. Coll. yarne mens hose, 12s.; 6 pr. worsted
ditto at 3s. 4d., 1li.; 12 pr. stockens, 7d. p, 7s.; 7 pr. ditto, 9d.
p, 5s. 3d.; 6 pr. ditto 8d. p., 4s.; 6 pr. ditto at 5d. p, 2s. 6d.;
10 pr. ditto at 6d. p, 5s.; 6 pr. ditto at 13d. p., 6s. 6d., 5 pr.
ditto at 18d. p, 7s. 6d.; 1 pr. fine woemens red worsted, 3s.;
2 pr. mens worsted, 3s.; 2 pr. mens worsted black & colld, &
1 pr. white, 7s. 6d.

Valued heare as money in N. England: 2 linsy woolsey
pettecoates, 6s. p, 12s.; 1 little boyes coate of camlett worsted,
6s.; 2 linsey woolsey & 1 pr. of fustian draws, 9s.; 1 pr. linen
drawers, more, 3s.; 1 boyes coat, 4s.; 2 red childs blanketts
bound wth feret, 4s. p, 8s.; 1 smale childs camlet pettecoat,
3s.; 9 sashes at 12d., 9s.; 50 yrds. of Irish searge at 2s. 2d. p,
5li. 8s. 4d.; 10 yrds 1-2 broad worsteed camlett duble, 2s. 6d.
p, 1li. 6s. 3d.; 16 1-4 yrds. narrow camlett, 1li. 12s. 6d.; 20
1-4 yrds mixt stuff, very bad, 12d. p, 1li. 3d.; 14 yrds. new
Coll. Stuff at 2s. p, 1li. 8s.; 1 ell of farrindine, 2s. 4d. p yd.,
2s. 11d.; 6 yrds. coll. fustian, 14d. p, 7s.; 3 yrds. red p
petuana at 2s. 6d. p, 7s. 6d.; 6 yrds. 1-4 greene say at 5s. p,
1li. 11s. 3d.; 42 mens & woemens shifts, 4s. 9d. p, 9li. 19s.

6d.; 12 youth & girls ditto, 3s. 6d. p. 2li. 2s.; 8 finer mens, woemens ditto, 6s. 6d. p, 2li. 12s.; 5 white dimity wascoates, 3s. 6d. p, 17s. 6d.; 1 yrd. 1-2 cambrick, 4s. 6d. p, 6s. 9d.; 2 ends of fine wt. callico, 20s. p, 2li.; 2 peeces broade white calico, 40s. p, 4li.; 2 peeces cource holland, cont. 69 yrds. 30d. p, 8li. 12s. 6d.; 5 1-4 yrds. fine dowlas at 2s. 6d. p, 13s. 1 1-2d.; 7 yrds. cource dowlas at 20d. p, 12s. 6d.; 1 ell cource holland at 2s. 6d. p, 3s. 1 1-2d.; 9 yds. scimity, 6s., 2 peeces of dimity, 6s. p. 18s.; 1 callico table cloath, 7s. 6d.; 2 callico shirts, 6s. p, 12s.; 2 callico painted table cloathes, 8s. p, 16s.; 1 large ditto, 14s.; in English money, 2li. 7s.; New England money, 99li. 4s.; Spanish money, 1li. 16s.; 1 peece of goold, 20s., 3 rings, about 25s., 2li. 5s.; a dram cupp, 6s.; 3 yds. fine greene say at 6s. p., 18s.; 3 cloath coates at 20s. p, 3li.; 1 cource gray youth coats, 10s.; 7 yrds. 1-2 of striped linen 16d. p, yrd., 10s.; 1 silk thrum Rugg, 2li.; 28 pr. plaine shooes, 4li. 4s.; 15 pr. fale shoos & 2 pr. woemens, 3s. 6d. p, 2li. 19s. 6d.; 9 straw hats, 2s. p, 18s.; 2 pr. fishing bootes at 14s. p., 1li. 8s.; 6li. of combed worsted at 2s. 6d. p, 15s.; knives, 5s., 2 spoones, 6d.; 6 1-4li. wt. suger at 8d. p, 4s. 4d.; 6 brushes, 18d., 1 pr. smale stilliards, 4s., 5s. 6d.; 8 1-2 oz. pins, 10d. p, 7s. 1d.; 2 peeces 1-2 ferrett, black Ribbond, 12d. p, 1li. 10s.; 5 gross & 1-2 thrid, buttens, 15d p, 6s. 10 1-2d.; about 2 gross thrid laces at 9s. p, 18s.; 1 gross great buttens upon cards, 3s.; 2 doz. 1-2 tweezers, 3s. 6d. p doz., 8s. 9d.; 3 childs swathes, 8d. p., 2s.; tape & filliting, 2s.; 10 oz. fine thred, 12d p., 10s.; a little pcell of thrid of severall coll., 1s. 6d.; 13 pr. scissers, 4s., 1 gross thrid, wt. buttens, 18d., 5s. 6d.; 19 yrds. red Ferrett, 4d. p. yrd., 6s. 4d.; blew tape, 4d., green cotten ribbon, 4d., silk, 18d., 1s. 8d.; 1 pr. bodies, 3s. 6d., 1 woemens worsted cap, 12d.; 6 pr. childs yarne gloves, 3s.; 11 yrds. green ferrett, 4d. p., 3s. 8d.; 6 doz. pack needles, 5s.; soweing needles, 6d.; 4 oz. peper, 6d., 3 pr. spectacles, & 5 cases, 22d.; 16 yrds. yellow taffaty Ribbond, 3d. p, 4s.; 6 boxes of Lockeers pills & papers, 24 yrds. 1-2 silk galoone, 2s. p. doz., 4s.; 16 contry Ruggs & 2 cradle ditto waying 223li. at 14d. p. li., 13li.; 8 Bushells of pease at 3s. p, 1li. 4s.; 1 old sheete of cource canvas, 2s.; 1 old table, 6s., 1 brasse yoare, 20s.; 1 perpetuance under pettecoate, 9s.; 1 woemans Shamare lined, 16s.; a womans Jerkin, 6s.; 1 pr. wooll cards, 1s.; 8 hand basketts, 12d. p, 8s.; 60li. of sheeps woll., 6d. p bagg, 2s., 1li. 12s.; 2 sadles & stirrops, 1li. 4s.; 4 Iron plates or fenders, 3s. p., 12s.; 125li. of sheeps wooll at 6d. p, 3li. 2s. 6d.; 4 baggs, 2s. p, 8s.; hops & a bagg, 2s.; 3 smale skins, 8d. p, 2s.; 79 narrow

brimd. hats, 2s. p, 7li. 18s.; 1 new, 10s.; 4 bands, 4s.; 1 boyes
w^t caster, 3s.; a large chest, 7s.; 2 tray makers adses, 3s.; 1
square & a broaken one, 1s. 6d.; 2 coop. axes, 30d. p, 5s.; 1
bill, 12d., 3 hollow shaves, 12d., p, 4s.; 2 cooper adzes, 2s. p,
1 pr. sheers, 12d.; 3 doz. 9 curtaine rings, 1s.; 4 large, 6
smale shaves, 6s.; 7 shooe punches, 6d. p., 3s. 6d.; 9 pr. Hinges,
5d. p, 3s. 9d.; 2 gouges, 2 chessell, 4d. p, 1s. 4d.; 1 tinder
box & pump nailes, 1s. 6d.; 1 coopers knife, 10d.; 5 staples,
12d.; 4 bolts, 2s.; 1 auger, 12d.; a rasp & smale auger, 1s.; 5
pr. sissers, 12d.; a pewter salt, 12d.; 3 pr. snuffers, 18d.; a
standish, 2s. 6d.; 6 cod hoockes, 12d.; 1 bed quilt, 10s.; 1
thousand & 1-2 of pins, 1s. 1 1-2d.; 21 doz. of w^t thrid buttens, 18d. p grosse, 2s. 7d.; pewter Bottle, 9d.; pcell of beaver
stones, 2li. 10s.; 2 pr. small scalls & some waites, 6s.; a
glasiers vice & moulds, 4li.; a pcell of glass, drawne lead, sod-
ering to mak up about 200 or 300 foot of glass, 4li.; 29li.
cheese at 3 1-2d. p li., 8s. 5d.; 1 B. 1-2 wheat, 3s. 6d., p. 3
bagges, 3s., 8s. 3d.; 6 old shirts, 7s., 5 very old sheetes, 15s.,
1li. 2s.; 2 old drawers, 2s.; 3 wascoates, 8s.; 4 pillow beeres,
6s.; 1 table cloath & 4 naptkins, 6s.; 1 chest, 5s.; 1 sash, 12d.;
1 carpett, 18d.; 1 bed pan, 5s.; 1 brass chafindish, 3s.; a fether
bed & bolster, 2 blanketts, 7 pillowes, a rugg & bedsteed, 7li.;
a pcell of pack cloath, 7s., a hamer, 18d., 8s. 6d.; his woolen
wearing apparell, 5li.; 1 chest, a smale table & 2 old cushions,
12s.; 2 old seives, 10d.; 1 bed, bolster, 1 pillow, 2 Ruggs, bedsteed & blankett, 4li. 10s.; 1 old trunk marked E. W., 3s.;
some odd trifling lumber, 2s.; 2 tables, 4 Joyn stools, 18s.,
tinn ware, 14s., 1li. 12s.; brasse ware, 1li.; pewter, 35s., 2
spitts, 2 fire pans, 8s., 2li. 3s.; 2 Iron potts & a skillett, 12s.;
4 rasors, 1 pr. sissers & a hoand, 9s.; some Indian dishes &
other lumber, 8s.

Furrs: 49 Racoone skins, 12d. p, 2li. 9s.; 38 fox skins,
2s. 6d. p, 4li. 15s.; 2 woolves skins, 12d. p, 2s.; a cub beare
skin, 1s.; 31 Otter skins, 6s. p., 9li. 6s.; 4 wood chuck skins,
21d. p, 7s.; 21 martins & sables at 15d., 1li. 8s. 3d.; 7 musk-
quash, 6d. p, 3s. 6d.; about 50li. beaver, 6s. p., 15li. 13 B.
mault, 3s. p, 1li. 19s.; 150li. oacum, 25s., 3 pecks wt. salt,
1li. 6s. 9d.; 36 gall. Rume, 2s. p, 3li. 12s.; 2 new chests with
ticks, 6s. p, 12s.; 4 new barrells, 8s.; 2 shovells, 18d., 301li.
sheeps woole, 15s., 16s. 6d.; 1 bagg, 18d., 200 foot of board,
8s., 9s. 6d.; 2 B. wheate, 3s. 6d. p., 3 b. Ry, 3s. p B., 9s. 3d.; 6
B. pease, 3s. p., 1-2 B. Beanes, 19s. 6d.; 11 hides, 5s. p., about
600 foot bord, 3li. 19s.; 16 B. Indian corne, 2s. p, 1 barrell,
2s., 1li. 14s.; 6 chests, 6s. p, about 13 C. spanish Iron, 2s. p.,

C, 14li. 16s.; 2 barrells of porke, 50s., 5li.; almost 2 barrells
of tarr, 7s. 6d. p, 15s.; 100li. tobbacco at 3d p, 1li. 5s.; 11
moose skins, 5li. 8d.; 2 Racoones, 12d. p, 2 sealls at 12d. p,
4s.; 1 hhd. 1-2 passader wine much decaid, 4li.; pt. of 5 barrell very much decaid & pricked madera, ——; 2 hhd. mallasses nott full, 5li. 10s.; an old small catch exceeding out of
repaire almost worne out, both Hull & all apprtenances, valued
by Mr. Bar. Gedney & John Norman, ship carpenters, 15li.;
a dwelling house & land neere the meeting house & apprtenances, 80li.; a smale peece of land part of a frame for a
warehouse & wharf, not finished & stones upon the ground,
14li. 10s.; a small pcell of timber & old board, 10s.; an old
smale cannoe, 10s.; a horse runing in the woods if alive, ——;
a remant of stuff, 2s.; a pcell of land at New Jerzey but doe
not know the quantity yett & some goods at som other places
not yett knowne what they are, ——; total, 630li. 6s. 5 3-4d.
Samll. Shattock's account of the debts: To several in England above, 300li.; to several in New England which cannot
yet be known how much, nor Justly what yt is in England,
but as himselfe said when he was sick & I ptly finde it by
Invoys of Goods.

Appraised since the foregoing, goods brought home from
the eastward as cost per invoice: 2 coates, 19s. p coate, 1li.
18s.; 2 coats, 16s. p, 1li. 12s.; 3 white childs coates, 1 at 11s.
& 2 at 14s., 1li. 19s.; 2 coates, 19s. p, 6 or 7 yeare old, 1li.
18s.; 1 Coat tamet, 16s.; 1 boyes coate, 13s.; a flanders Tick
& bolster, 1li. 9s. 6d.; a draft, 8 qrts., 14s. Valued as cost
here in New England: 2 silke barateene under coates, 1li.
6s.; 1 large silk Rugg, 3li.; 1 calico India carpett, 4s.; 7 bushell & 1-2 malt, 1li. 2s. 6d.; 3 B. & 1-2 of Indian, 7s.; 1 B.
wheate, 3s. 6d.; a speckled pillow beere, 1s.; to sugar sold at
5s. 3d.; a gold ring, 7s. 6d.; an Iron Casement, 5s.; 460 foot
of board, 3s. p, 13s. 8d.; 8 narrow brimed hats, 2s. p, 16s.; 3
old rusty curry combs, 1s.; 2 old sawes, 2s. 6d.; 4 pr. sissers,
1 twissers, 1 gimlet, punch, som ales & steeles, 4s. 6d.; 3
firkins of old butter, 3li.; decayed wine, 1li. 15s.; an old pr.
of hand screws, 1li. 10s.; debt of 12s.; suposed 3 acres of land
at merimake, to a silver seale, 2s.; bookes, 12s.; mincing
knife, 6d., 2 curry combes, 2s.; Glass redy made & som lead,
1li. 10s.; 2 chests & 1 trunke, 15s.; 8 & 2 yd. of narrow
serge, at 2s. p, 17s.; Debts, 40li.; total 69li. 6s. 11d.

Allowed in Salem court 27:4:1678, Samuell Shattock, sr.,
being a Friend affirming, and Samuell Shattock, jr. making
oath to the truth of the inventory.

Essex County Quarterly Court Files, vol. 29, leaves 33, 34.

Whereas at the court held at Ipswich Mar. 26, 1678 there was granted administration upon the estate of Edward Wharton of Salem, glasier, to Samuell Shattock, sr. and Samuell Shattock, jr. and they giving bond and now at this court they having presented an administration granted to George Wharton living in London and brother of the said Edward Wharton, under the seal of the prerogative court of Canterbury, which this court judge legal, and they having also received a letter of attorney and orders about the estate, the court 26 : 9 : 1678, ordered them to send the estate that is in their hands to the said George Wharton administrator, to England or his order; accordingly they paying all debts and charges due from the estate here in New England & renounce their power of administration and are released of their bond.

Salem Quarterly Court Records, vol. 5, leaf 124.

ESTATE OF HENRY HAGGET OF WENHAM.

"The last Will and Testement of Henry Haget Aged 80 three years or there abouts made in yᵉ year of our Lord one thousand six hundred Seuenty & six one 7ᵗʰ of ‖th‖ 12ᵗʰ Moneth he being Very sick & weak of body but of good Understanding and memorie Imp: I Bequeth my Bodye to yᵉ Dust, & my Spirit to god yᵗ gaue itt Itᵐ I Bequeth vnto my Son Henrey all my Estate, namely, my house, Lands, Medow, with all Chatle goods namely all my whol Estate, with all my Rights, Titles, & priuiledges, & singuler its Appirtainances therevnto belonging To haue and To hold to him and his heirs for Ever it is allso my Will, that, my aforesaid Son Henrey, he, Being my heir, & Excutor shall Alow his Mother her Reasonable Maintaince, Dureing yᵉ Terme of her Naturall Life, and, allso, pay vnto my fore Chilldren, Namely, to Moses, to Mary, to Deliuerance, & to Hannah, I say pay to them yᵉ Dowry of Tenn shilling vnto each one of Them, in Marchantable pay att Currant price within yᵉ space of twelue Moneths After my Decease for the Confirmation whereof yᵉ aforesaid Henry Haget seniʳ: hath herevnto set his hand & seale."

Henry (his ✔ mark)ˉ Haget (SEAL)

Witness: Charles Gott, Joh[n] ffiske.

Proved in Ipswich court Mar. 26, 1678 by the witnesses.

Inventory of the estate of Henery Hagget of Wenham taken Mar. 13, 1678 by Thomas Fiske and Charles Gott: howseing & Land, 100li.; Neate Catle, 22li.; two Jades, 5li.; sheep,

12li. 10s.; swine, 3li. 10s.; Corne, 8li.; plowe tackling & other
Utensels, 1li. 15s.; howshold stuf, 2li.; porke, 1li. 10s.; Bed-
ing & wearing Cloathes, 6li.; total, 162li. 5s. Debts Due to
Severall persons, 15li.

Attested in Ipswich court Mar. 26, 1678 by Henry Haggett,
executor, and the land to stand bound for the performance
of the will.

Henry Haggett the 11 of Aprill added to this inventory, 6li.
        Essex County Probate Files, Docket 12,054.

ESTATE OF DANIEL PEIRCE, SR., OF NEWBURY.*

"Bee it knowne unto all [men by these *copy*] p^rsents that I
Daniell Peirce Senr of newbury beeing sencible of my [owne
copy] weakenes and mortality beeing of perfect memory doe
hereby make my last will and testament Comending my Soule
into the hands of my blessed Redeemer the Lord Jesus Christ
and my body to the dust in an assured hope of a blessed Resurrection. And for my worldly goods which god of his mercy
hath lent vnto me I dispose of as followeth Nouember 12st
1677 Imp^rs I giue and bequeath my houseing lands goods &
Chattells vnto my Son Daniell Peirce that is to say all my
houseing & lands that are vndisposed of & appoint him my
true & lawfull heire of all & also my sole Executor of this my
last will & testament Desireing him to Doe for his brother
Joshua Peirces children as he shall see in his discretion meet
to be done for them. And whereas vpon my marriag agreement with Anne my wife she was to haue twenty pounds a
yeare dureing her naturall life I appoint my said executor
that in all conditions shee shalbe in, that he prouide all such
necessaryes for her that shee shall stand in need of and that
she shall inioy her former libertyes in the house dureing her
life And for my wiues son in law Thomas Thorpe prouided he
wilbee content & neuer trouble nor molest my son after my
decease I giue him a farme at new Jarsy scituate vpon Row
Riuer Joyneing to John Bishops lande but if he shall trouble
or molest my executor for any cause he shall forfeit the said
gift And wheras I haue giuen my houseing & lands as abousaid vnto my said Son that is the farme I now Dwell vpon I
giue it vnto my heire & his heirs so that it shall neuer be sold
nor any part deuided from the lawfull heire, Male Upon
forfeiture of all the said premises vnto the next heire male of
the same name & kindred but if it should fall out hereafter
that my son Daniels Male posterity faile that it should come

*Copy, Ipswich Deeds, vol. 4, page 158.

to Joshuas posterity then the said heire male of his posterity shall pay eight hundred pounds to the daughters of my son Daniels posterity. My funeral being discharged."

Daniel Perce Sener (SEAL)

Witness: Anthony Somerby, Jno. Dole.

Proved in Ipswich court Mar. 26, 1678 by the witnesses.

Inventory of the estate of Daniell Peirce, Senr. of Newbury, deceased Nov. 27, 1677 taken by Anthony Somerby and Robert Long: A farme of about two hundred & thirty acres of upland & meadow with the houseing, Barnes & orchard 1200li.; A Mault house with about twenty acres of upland and three & thirty acres of meadow & furniture to ye malthouse, 255li.; his weareing Apparrell, books & Armes, 40li.; horse & mare & yearling colt, 7li.; about forty head of neat cattle, oxen, cowes & young Cattle, 94li.; about an hundred & sixty sheep yong & old, 40li.; eighteen small swyne, 5li. 16s.; foure feather beds with other bedings, Rugs, sheets, blankets, pillows, bedsteads & 2 paire of curtaines, 30li.; Anvill, vice, shop tooles with Iron potts, kettles, Brass, pewter, 2 old furnaces, 2 pr. of cottrils, spits, fire shovel & tonges, 20li.; 2 truncks, chests, 2 tables, carpet, table linnen, chayres, cushions &c., 8li.; Barrels, tubs, keylers, bowles, & trayes with other lumber, 2li. 10s.; Carts, wheels, dunpot, ploughs, chaynes and all other utensils for husbandry, 5li. [10s. *copy*]; corne & grayne of all sorts in the house and in the Barne, 60li.; Negros, 60li.; Debts about 10li.; total, 1837li. 10s. [more a farme & stock at new Jarsye, 60li. *copy*.]

Attested in Ipswich court Mar. 26, 1678 by Daniell Pearce to be a true inventory of the estate of his father Daniell Peirce.

Essex County Probate Files, Docket 21,151.

ESTATE OF JOHN CHAPMAN OF IPSWICH.

Inventory of the estate of John Chapman of Ipswich, deceased Nov. 19, 1677, taken Mar. 1, 1677-78 by John Denison and Simon Stace: one dwelling house, ten Rods of ground, 30li.; two acers of tillage land, 10li.; two acers of marsh land, 6li.; two acers of marsh land, 6li. 13s. 4d.; two Cowes & one yearlinge, 8li.; twelve sheepe, 4li.; bed and bedinge, 6li.; two chests, two boxes, 16s.; wearing clothes, 4li.; peuter, Earthen ware, tine, trenchers, trayes, 1li.; two whealles, 4 chayers, one table, Cushen, 1li.; one Iron pote, on scillit, 12s.; musquet, sword, beallt, 1li. 4s.; total, 79li. 5s. 4d. Debts due to the estat, 8li. Debts due from the estate, 9li. 3s. 4d.

Attested in Ipswich court Mar. 26, 1678 by Rebeacha Chapman, relict of John Chapman.

For the settlement of the estate of John Chapman the court held at Ipswich 27 : 7 : 1681, ordered that the administratrix (his widow) shall have the estate in her hands for her own and her child's maintenance and that when the child shall come of age or to choose its guardian, the child shall have the dwelling house and two acres of tillage land and two acres of marsh as mentioned in the three first articles of the inventory, for his portion, he paying to the administratrix or her heirs twenty pounds out of that sum which is 46li.

Essex County Probate Files, Docket 5,037.

ESTATE OF JOSEPH PRINCE OF SALEM.

"The Last will & Teastiment of Joseph P[r]ince Aged thirtie And one yeare: Nouember 14th 1677 Inpmis I giue vnto my brother Richard Prince my now dwelling house & my shop & barne with all the ground belonging there vnto, because he is to puid for my mother the time of her Life, Moreouer I giue my brother Richard all my moueables: only he is to paie vnto his brother Jonathan ten pounds And unto my sister mari Daniell: twentie pounds out of those things that are in hare house of mine: in Lue of that twentie pounds that my father Apointed at his death; And the rest of my goods at my sisters Danyells house I giue to be Equally parted betwin her two Chilldren. Itam I giue to my brother Samuell Prince one meare with a bald face: Itam I giue unto my brother Jonathan Prince halfe the ground in the south feild: allsoe one meare that was Richard Croods & my fowling peece: Itam I giue to An Daniell one meare I bought of george Darling moreouer I giue my brother Richard one Cow: & one Meare with bridell & sadell: the meare is blacke marked R. P. Itam I giue the other hallfe of my ground in the south feild to my brother Stephen Danyells two Chilldren."

[no signature]

Witness: John (his † † mark) Ingersell, Joseph Grafton.
Proved by the witnesses.

Joseph Prince dying intestate, the Ipswich court Mar. 26, 1678, granted power of administration to Richard Prince of the estate of his brother and ordered the estate according to the mind of the deceased expressed in the above writing.

Inventory taken 11 : 1m : 1677-78 by Joseph Grafton and Samuell Gardner, Jr.: A dwelling house, shop, Cowhouse &

about sixty poale of land, 150li.; 3 1-2 Acors of land in ye
South field, 20li.; psell of household Stuf in ye hands of Mary
Daniell, 20li.; 4 mares at 1li. 10s. per. & 1 Cow & 1 hogg,
4li. 10s., 10li. 10s.; 4 Chests, 3 tables & 2 trunks, 1li. 17s.; 7
Chaires, 3 Joint Stools & old lumber, 19s.; psell of Iron ware
& earthen ware, 19s.; psell of brasse ware, 2li. 1s.; 2 beds &
1 boulster, 4li.; 6 pr. sheets & other linin, 3li.; psell of peuter,
3li.; bridle & Saddle, 10s.; his wearing Clothes, 3li.; debts
owing to ye Esstate, 9li. 5s. 3d.; total, 229li. 1s. 3d. Debts
owing out of ye Estate, 69li. 10s. 4d.

Attested in Ipswich court Mar. 26, 1678 by Richard Prince,
administrator.

Essex County Probate Files, Docket 22,783.

ESTATE OF THOMAS HARDY, SR., OF MERRIMAC.

"The last Will and Testiment of Thomas Hardee, Sen[r].
liuing at merimack towne, near Hauerill, I Thomas Hardee,
being in bodyly health, and of perfect memory, through the
goodness of god, yet not knowing how short a time I haue to
liue in this world; do make my last will and testiment; **and in**
the first place, I Comitt my Soul vnto god who gaue it, and
my body to the earth, (from whence it was taken) to a decent
& Comely buriall: and for that little portion of outward
things which the lord hath lent mee in this life; I do thus.
dispose of them, first I do will that all Just debts be discharged, I do giue to Thomas Hardee, my eldest Sonn, that
two hundred acres of land which was lately laid out to him,
be it more or less, acording to the bounds of it. I do giue
vnto my Sonns John Hardee to Joseph Hardee, & to Jacob
Hardee, to each of them one hundred acres of land a piece,
be it more or lesse, as it was laid out & bounded to them, also
I do will that Thomas, John, & Joseph shall enjoy that
meadow, which at y[e] same time was laid out to them, and that
Jacob shall haue an equall proportion of meadow, with his
brethren, John & Joseph, to be taken out of that meadow
which is not yet diuided, Also I do giue unto my Sonn in
law william Hutchins, one hundred acres of land, to take it
right crosse the farme at y[e] further end, not intrenching
upon y[e] land already laid out to his brethren, also what
meadow is within y[e] sd hundred acres, and in case y[e] meadow
wants of an equall share, it shalbe made vp out of long
meadow. Also I do giue vnto my daughter mary & to her
children, tenn pound sterling, the which ten pound, in case
I pay it not my self while I liue, (that is besides what shee

grand children twenty shillings apeece. to be paid by my executor after my decease, as I shall hereafter order. also I do giue to my beloued wife two acres of land lying by ye Riuer on ye east end of ye house to be at her owne dispose at her death; Also I do will that forty acres of land be set out, immediately after my decease, which forty acres shalbee Security for my wife touching her maintenance, in case of need, & I do will that in case Joseph & Jacob hardee shall contribute to my wife for her maintenance they shall each of them be repaid out of this forty acres, accounting it at twenty shillings pr acre. Also I do will that twenty acres of land more be added to the former forty acres, to ly on ye north side of it, & all to joyne to Joseph Hardee his sixty acres: to be laid cross ye farme, from bayleys line to Jacobs lot. this last twenty acres shall ly for security, for ye payment of twenty pounds to my grand children, the which in case my executor shall not pay ye said twenty pounds to ye children aforesaid within ten year next after my decease, then ye land may be sould to some other of the brethren that will pay those legicys, & in case any of ye present grand children should dy in the interim, Then the said twenty pounds to be equally diuided amongst those that shall Suruiue, or shalbe borne of those four familys, i. e. Thomas, & John Hardee, & my two daughters, mary and Sary. further I do giue to my sonne John Hardee, ten acres of land to be laid out adjoyning to ye south end of the three ten acres of land lately brooken up for plow land, by John Joseph & Jacob Hardee. Also I do will, that Jacobs lot of one hundred acres granted before, shall not extent further northward then my feild, and what is taken off at y^n north end shalbee made up next adjoyning & to ly betwen my plowfeild and ye ten acre lots aforesd. Also I do will that my Son Thomas shall not haue power to alienate his land from his children, without ye approbation of such psons whom I shall here after nominate, for ouer-seers of this my will. also I do giue unto my son Jacob that two acres of meadow which was mine, and was laid out by it self to mee in long meadow. Also I do ordaine my son willm Hardee to bee my Sole executor of this my will, And further do Nominate and impower my loueing & respected frinds the reund. m^r Zachary Simes, m^r Shuball Walker and Jonathan Danforth, sen^r. of billerica, to be the ouer-seers of this my will and do impower them to giue the true sence and meaning of this my will, in all things that may be doubtfull, and in all matters of difference that may arise among any of my children, in reference to any ‖thing‖ contained in this my will, it shall be always issued and determined by their judgment in case any two of the psons nominated agreing concerning ye same. & giuen under their hands: that hereby all suets of law may be prevented, & further I do exort all my children, to liue in ye fear of god, & in the exarcise of loue & charity each to other, releiuing each others nescissity acording to their ability as ye case may require. finally I do declare this to be my last will and testiment, hereby rattifying and confirmeing what I had formerly done acording as is expressed in this scadell vnder my hand & seal; so far as it is not contradicted by this addition, but this latter to stand in full force & efficacy, the former not withstanding, & ye former to stand in full force and effica. so far, as it is not contradicted by this latter addition, and both are comprized in three sids of this sheet of paper, witness my hand and seal, this 12. 10^m. 1677."

Thomas (his ♄ mark) Hardee, sen^r

(SEAL)

Witness: John Newmarch, Senr., Samuell Wosester, Jonathan Danforth, Senr.

Proved in Ipswich court Mar. 26, 1678 by the last three witnesses.

Inventory of the estate of Thomas Hardee, Senr., deceased Jan. 4, 1677, taken at Bradford Mar. 7, 1677-78 by Jonathan Danforth, senr., Shubaell Walker and Samuell Wosester: his waring apparrell, 4li.; money in his pocket, 3s. 3d.; one feather bed, & one flock bed with their furniture, 7li. 10s.; wooll and yarne, 2li.; 2 spining wheeles, 5s.; wooden ware & old lumber in ye house, 3li. 5s. 6d.; Iron chaines, wedges, saws & such utensells of ye feild, in iron ware, a how, spade, shovells, old fan, 2 measures, yoak, heckle, tumbrill & such like, 3li. 6s.; four neat cattell, 9li.; ten sheep, 2li. 10s.; one horse, one mare & colt, 3li. 10s.; corne & provisions in ye house, 8li. 10s.; house & barne, orchard, fences & 800 acres land more or less joyning to ye house, 800li.; swine, 20s.; Iron pots, brass & pewter & Iron ware in ye house, 3li. 11s.; total, 848li. 10s. 9d. Debts due to ye estat from John marable, 1li.; a spanshackle for a cart & pin, 2s. Due from ye estate: to Rich. Dole, 5li. 9s. 4d.; Richard woullery, 18s.; Francis willit, 16s.; Jno. Bartlet, senr., 1li. 8s.; Ensigne Greenleife, 1li. 2s. 11d.; Jno. Knight, 2li. 13s. 6d.; more John marobl, 2li.; John addekornes, 1li. 19s. 2d.; marchnt wainwright, 2li. 19s. 6d.; total, 19li. 6s. 5d.

Attested in Ipswich court Mar. 26, 1678 by William Hardy, executor.

Essex County Probate Files, Docket 12,405.

ESTATE OF ANTHONY MORSE, JR., OF NEWBURY.

"Bee it known vnto all men by these psents that I Anthony Morse——of Newbury being sick & weake of body but of perfect memory desir here to make my last will and Testament Comending my soule into the hands of my blessed Redemer, and my body to the dust from whence it was taken in an assured hope of a blessed resurrection, & do here dispose of my worldly goods as followeth Imp^{rs} I giue and bequeath unto Mary my wife my goods & cattle & appoint her to be the sole Executrix of this my last will & testament and to haue the house and all my land in her possession untill my son Anthony shall be of the age of one & twenty years, and he my said son Anthony shall liue with her vntill he be eighteen yeares of age, & then I would haue him put to learne a trade, And if my wife shall chang her condition then my said son when he is of the age of one and twenty years shall haue my house Barne Orchard & all my land & freholde for himselfe & heirs foreuer, paying to his three brothers viz. Joseph John & Peter; ten pounds a peice, & to his sister mary ten pounds when they shall be of the age of one & twenty years but if my said wife mary shall not marry againe she shall haue the said house & land in her possession vntill my said son Anthony shall marry, and then the said house and land to be diuided between them dureing my wiues life & after to be wholy to the use of my son. Anthony, And then when the house & land shall come wholy into his hands then within four years after he shall pay the abousaid forty pounds to his three brothers & sister abouesaid, and also pay to his sister Elizabeth forty shillings at the day of her marriag: And I also giue to my daughter Elizabeth aforsaid her owne mothers apparrell. and I desire that my son Joseph may be put to learne a trade that is I desire he may be a Tailor; and for my debts & funeral to be discharged by my Executrix this is my last will & Testament reuokeing all other wills In witness wherof I haue set to my hand & seale february 23 1677."

Anthony mors jun. (SEAL)

Witness: Anthony Somerby, henrey Jaques.
Proved in Ipswich court Mar. 26, 1678 by the witnesses.

Inventory of the estate of Anthony Morse, Junr. of Newbury, deceased Feb. 25, 1677, taken by Peter Cheny, Henrey
Jaques and Anthony Somerby: house and barne, orchard and
about seaven acres of Arable and pasture land, 110li.; foure
oxen, 20li.; foure cowes, 12li.; an old mare, 1li. 10s.; About
thirty eight sheep, 9li. 10s.; two swyne, six shootes & two
piggs, 4li.; bedstead with featherbed, bolster, Rug, thre blankets, sheets, Curtaines & vallons, 2 pillows and Matt, 8li.;
trucklebed & bolster, two coverlets & a pr. of sheets, 3li.; another bedsted, 2 coverlets, mat, pillow & 3 sheets, 3li.; his
wearing apparrell, 10li.; about Eighteen bushells of Barly,
3li. 10s.; about three bushels of Rye & wheat, 14s.; twenty
bushels or thereabouts of Indian corne, 3li.; about Fifty
pounds of woollen yarne, 6li. 5s.; about thirty pounds of wooll
& about ten pounds flax, 2li.; one cheste, two boxes, 2 dry
hogsheds & smaller dry casks & lumber, cart rope, seith, snede
& about four pound of hops, 3li.; two Brasse kettles, two Iron
potts, bras skellet & belmettle skillet, 3li.; seaven pewter
dishes, four porringers, small bason, quart pot, tin candlesticke & a chamber pott, 2li. 5s.; sadle, pillion, bridle & warmeing pan, 1li. 12s.; two barrells, 2 halfe barrells, churne, halfe
a dozen trayes & dishes, trenchers, earthen vessells, table, two
wheels, foure chayres & other lumber, 2li. 5s.; cart & wheels,
chaynes, yoake, plough, dung pot, boxes, linch pins, round
pins, horsharnes, 2 hooes, 2 axes, prongs, & other utinsills,
6li.; about 6 pound of cotton wool & 2 pr. of Cards, 10s.; frying pan, tongs, cottrills, 2 flitches of bacon, gridiron & bible,
3li. 10s.; total, 219li. 11s. Due to the deceased from Amos
Stickney, 3li. 10s. Debts of the deceased: to the constable,
1li. 15s. 9d.; James Kent, 1li.; goody Bat, 1li.; Capt. White,
1li. 4s. 9d.; goodman Grenleafe, 16s. 9d.; Davied Bennet,
12s.; Peter Tappin, 4li. 3s. 9d.; total, 10li. 3s.
    Attested in Ipswich court 26 : 1 : 1678 by the executrix.
                Essex County Probate Files, Docket 18,902.

ESTATE OF EDMUND BROWNE OF NEWBURY.

Administration upon the estate of Edmond Browne, intestate, was granted by the Ipswich court Mar. 26, 1678 to Elizabeth Browne his mother, she to administer according to an
agreement dated Mar. 4, 1677-78, and owned in court by Elizabeth Browne, John Badger, Richard Browne, Sarah Browne
and Mary Browne.

Inventory of the estate of Edmon Browne of Newbury
taken Mar. 1, 1677-78: a cloake and wescoat, 3li. 10s.; thirtie

yards of stuf, 3li.; chest and Lether stokins, 8s.; gun & 2
belts, 1li. 10s.; coopers tooles, 12s.; grindeing stone, 7s.; two
horses, 6li. 10s.; cow, 3li.; half a mare, 1li.; a debt from
Richard Browne to ye estate, 3li.; staves and heding, 8s.;
Peter tappan oweth, 1li.; oweing from the estate in munney
while Edmond Brown lay sik at mevis, 5li.; to Benjamin
Mors, 3s.; to Daniell Lunt, 4s. 6d.; Six akkers and three
quarters of plow land and twentie akers of meadow and pastor which is in Revertion, the plowd ground, 33li. 15s.; the
meadow and pastor, 60li.

> *Essex County Probate Files, Docket* 3,511.

Articles of agreement between John Bager, Richard
Browne, Sarah Browne and Mary Browne all of Newbury
with the consent of Elizabeth Browne their mother: forasmuch as Edmond Browne late of Newbury second son to Richard Browne, deceased, and Elizabeth his wife, died intestate
leaving a considerable estate in movables and also a reversion
of land, after the decease of his mother Elizabeth Browne,
which land was bequeathed to the said Elizabeth by the will
of Gyles Badger (the father of John Badger) her former husband, and the said John Badger being willing to recover to
himself the said reversion of land bequeathed by his father
to the said Elizabeth, which by the will of Richard Browne
(second husband of the said Elizabeth) was bequeathed to the
said Edmond Browne, and to avoid all contest the following
agreement is made: John Badger agreeth that Richard Browne
shall have a parcel of marsh of about five or six acres in
Plumb Island and to give him a legal bill of sale thereof within six months after the date hereof.

The said Richard Browne receiving the said marsh and 13li.
of the estate of his brother Edmond Browne releases all claim
to the estate of Edmond Browne unto the said John Badger.

The said John Badger having right to some money and
goods left with his father Gyles Badger by Nath. Badger
(brother to the said Gyles) which on the marriage with Elizabeth his mother came into the hands of her husband Richard
Browne, on consideration of this agreement acquits his mother
Elizabeth, and Richard Browne from the payment of anything
on this account. John Bager agrees to pay to Sarah Browne
and Mary Browne, the two daughters of his mother Elizabeth,
30li. each, in any payment that the parties shall agree before
the decease of his mother and if any part remain unpaid at
her decease to pay to them their portions in barley, Indian
corn and neat cattle, and upon the payment thereof they re-

linquish all claim to John Badger, from any part of the estate formerly belonging to their brother Edmond Browne; if either of the sisters should die before the payment of the 30li., John Badger to pay the remainder to the survivor. John Badger also agreed to pay the 5li. due for charges for Edmond Browne while he lay sick at Mevis. Signed Mar. 4, 1677-78.

Witness: Tristram Coffin, Robert Long, Richard Kent.

Ipswich Deeds, vol. 4, page 161.

ESTATE OF JOHN SOOLART OF WENHAM.

"The Last will & Testament of John Solart made this 26: 7:1672: I Being well & In bodily Health through Gods Goodness yett by his providenc being bound to sea & for old England; And therfore for my settling of what it hath pleased God to Give mee for my Inheritanc in this present world: I doe as here after will & despose of it I say all that my portion which was left to me as my part & portion by Ipswitch Court which is exprest in the Courts setlement of it; to be as the sum there is Eighty four pounds which is my right in the estate of my father deceased Also a Bill of four pounds which is due to mee from M^r. Richard Oliver of Monhegon: This mentioned before I doe dispose & will as ffolloweth. To my Beloved wife Sarah Solart now In England I say the whole sum to her If It shall please God that I shall nott be heard of more or shall by his providenc be taken out of this world; If she have never a Child by mee I leave it wholy to herself but If it please God that she have a child by mee then two thirds to the child: when it Comes of Age: & one third to be her owne It a Colt in the hands of my *bro*ther to be disposed of wth the rest in that maner I further Appoynt my Loveing freind Walter ffairfeild of wenham my soal exceqhiter to this estate & will & to se that it be disposed of for the end above mentioned whether it be for their use here or in England If they send for it I further appoynt & desire my Loveing friends Nehemiah Jewett & Roger Darby to be overseers of this my last will & Testament; & doe will And Appoynt that these my freinds walter ffairfeild Roger Darby & Nehemiah Jewett be fully sattisfied for what cost & paynes they shall be att in acting about the sajd estate & for good of the parties mentioned: or If shee die & have noe child then I will the whole estate to my Broth^r Joseph Solart: & vnto this I sett too my hand & seale this day & yea^r aboue written."

John Solart (SEAL)

Witness: Robert Lord, Junier, Philip Fowler.

Proved in Ipswich court Mar. 28, 1678 by Robert Lord, Jr. and Philip Fouler, Jr.

The estate of John Soolart, Jr. is 84 pounds as doth apper by the Records of Ipswich court which together with a cowlt of about two yers old is all the estat that he Left in this country that we doe know of which cowlt is aprised at 40s. by Richard Hutten and John Killam, making total, 86li.

Also he received from his mother 5li. in silver and 49s. in goods as appeareth by his receipt and also 22s. more in silver all which amounteth to 10li. 11s. 6d. according to the custom of the country.

Dated Mar. 23, 1676-77.

Attested in Ipswich court Mar. 27, 1677 by Walter Fairefield, executor.

Essex County Probate Files, Docket 25,862.

ESTATE OF JOHN KINGSBURY OF ROWLEY.*

In the settlement of the estate of John Kinsbery who left two children, upon the widow's marriage to Peter Green, court having ordered that the land that was Kinsberry's should be security for the childrens' portions, and now the woman who was John Kinsberies wife and administratrix being also dead, Henry Kinsbery, father of said John and grandfather of the two children, having agreed with Peter Green to take the two children and their portions of forty acres of land into his hands, court Apr. 9, 1678, approved and said Green, who was a second husband, was discharged from any further care of the children.

Salisbury Quarterly Court Records, vol. 2, leaf 84.

GUARDIANSHIP OF NICHOLAS CHAVERLY.

Nicolas Chaveley chose Arter Abbot as his guardian, Apr. 30, 1678.

Ipswich Quarterly Court Records, vol. 5, page 335.

ESTATE OF EDWARD CHAPMAN OF IPSWICH.†

"[In the name of God *copy*] Amen I Edward Chapman of Ipswich in the [county of Essex *copy*] being weake of Body but through the mercy of God [Inioying my *copy*] understanding and memory do make and ordaine this [my

*See *ante*, vol. 2, page 224.
†Copy, Ipswich Deeds, vol. 4, page 169.

last *copy*] will and Testament Inprimis I comitt my Soule
into the hands of Jesus Christ my blessed Savior and Redeemer in hope of a joyfull resurection unto life at the last day,
and my Body to decent Buriall. and for my outward Estate
that God hath Graciously lent vnto me I do dispose of as ffolloweth viz / my beloved wife there being a covenant and contract betweene us upon mariage my will is that it be faithfully
fullfilled, Twenty pounds of that conteined in the covnant to
be in such household goods as she shall desire, also my will is
that my beloved wife Dorithye Chapman ‖ shall have ‖ the use
of the parlour; end of the house both upper and lower roomes
with the little celler that hath lock and key to it, with free
liberty of the use of the oven, and well of watter, with ten
good bearing fruit trees neare that end of the house which
‖ she ‖ is to make use of, to have the fruit of them, also the
garden plot fenct in below the orchard and one quarter of the
barne at the further end from the house also to have the goeing of one cow in the pasture And all dureing the time she
doth remaine my widdo Item my Son Symon haveing allredy
done for him beyond my other children my will is that he shall
have thirty pounds payd him by my executor as followeth
viz. / to be payd five pound a yeare to begin the first five
pound three yeares after my decease and five every yeare next
after and this to be his full portion And for four pound that
is comeing vnto him of his Grand. father Symonds gift, which
is yet behind my will is that it shall be payd vnto him out of
that Six acre lott lyeing at wattells neck which was his Grandfathers' as it shall be prised by indiferent men

"Item I give and bequeath vnto my Son Nathaniell Chapman thirty pounds to be payd unto him by my executor by five
pound a yeare, the first five pounds to be payd three yeares
after my decease and the rest by five pounds a yeare the next
following yeares & that to be his full portion. Item I give and
bequeath vnto my daughter mary the wife of John Barry the
sum of thirtye pounds to be payd vnto her by five pounds a
yeare, the first five pounds to be payd three years, after my decease, and soe every yeare after five pouds a yeare vntill it be
all payd All the aforsayd Legasies to be payd in current country pay vnto the sd children Also I will and give vnto my sayd
daughter mary one coverlet that is black & yellow Item I
apoynt my Sonn Samuell to be my sole executor of this my
last will and testament and do give vnto him all my house
and lands and chattells, he paying and pformeing all my will
vnto my wife and Brothers and Sister as is above exprest and

also all my debts and funerall charges I say I give vnto him
my sayd Sonn Samuell Chapman all the rest of my estate both
reall and psonall, my will further is that all my children shall
rest satticefied with what I have done for them, and if any of
them shall through discontent make trouble about this my
will, that then they shall forfit and loose what I have heerin
bequeathed vnto them vnto him or them that shall so be mo-
lested by them, In wittnes that this is my last will & testament
I have heere unto put my hand and Seale this 9th of Aprill
1678."

Edward (his] mark) Chapman.

Witness: Moses Pengry, Senr., Robert Lord, Senr.
Proved in Ipswich court Apr. 30, 1678 by the witnesses.

Inventory taken Apr. 27, 1678, by John Whipple and
Simon Stace: his dweling hows & homstead with out housing,
150li.; six accers of planting lande, 30li.; two accers of Land
in the Comon feild, 8li.; sixe accers of upland in watls his
necke, 18li.; 12 accers of marche in the hunderds, 36li.; two
accers of march in the hunderds, 6li. 13s. 4d.; fowr oxen
small, 18li.; fower Cows and thre Calves, 12li.; one haifer &
one steer of 3 years old, 5li.; one horse, two mares, one
yearling Colt, 6li.; fivetene sheepe, five Lames with one
yearling Calf, 7li.; 40 bush. of Indian Corne, 6li.; berly 14
bush, Rye two bush., wheat 3 bush 1-2, 4li. [6d. copy] his
waring Clothes Linon & woolin wth hats, shoos, 7li.; [1s.
copy] fetherbeed & bolster with thre pillows, 4li. [5s. copy];
a strawbeed, a red & blue Coverlit & 3 blankits, 2li. [7s. copy]
an old Rugg, 10s.; fowr payer of old sheets, 40s.; Sixe pilowbeers, 12s. & sixe small napcins & a table cloth, [18s. copy];
chest, 5s.; sixe pecis of pewter, 14s.; 4 poringers, 4s.; small
pewter, 5s.; tinn driping pan, 3s. 6d., quarte pot & chamber
pot, [8s. copy] old warming pane, 4s.; two Iron potts, 10s.;
two scillits, 5s.; two Keetles, 20s.; old grat bible,
9s.; old Looking glase & ouer Glase, 2s.; old slice,
2s. 6d., a two quart Glase, 4s. 6d.; a box Iron, 3s.; hatt
bruch, 9d.; 5li. Cotton woole & two pound of Cotton yern,
9s.; thre Cuchins, 13s.; small Chest, 4s.; old Chest, 5s.; beedsted & trund. beed, 10s; old Curtins, vallans, 4s.; old chest,
3s., 10 chayers, 19s.; Linon yearne, 16s. 6d.; table, 5s.; Lanthorne, 2s.; small pillo, 3s.; five books, 8s.; old pewter, 12s.
6d.; old payer of sheet & other old Linon, 8s.; old Rugg &
blanket, 10s.; old beedsteed with som beeding on it, 1li. 10s.;
two Curtins, Valanc, 10s.; an old Coslit, pike & sword, 1li.;
49 yds. of homemade Cloth, 4li. 18s.; two spining wheeles,

5s.; old bedsted, 3s.; 3 sikls, 2s.; 4 old hogsheads, 4s.; three saks, 6s.; Earthen ware, 4s., Iron pott wth pott hook, 9s.; gridiron, 3s.; two old Kettls, 10s.; tramell, payer of tonges, 4s. 6d.; paiels, dishes & trenchers, 5s. 6d.; old spade, hammer, 3s.; beetle, 4 wedges, thre old Axes, 12s.; Syth, taklin, old forke tynes, 5s.; an old sadle & bridle, 3s.; som old things, 5s.; barels & tubes in the seller with a Cherne, 16s.; tobako, 5s.; half a barrell of poorke, 30s.; small table & a stoole, 3s.; persel of undresed flaxe, 7s.; Cart & old wheels, sleed & tumbrell, 2li. 10s.; set of wheele hoops, 3 yoaks & two chaines, 1li. 2s.; plow & plow Irons, 15s.; three howes, haye hooke, pease meage, spanshakil, 8s.; sixe swine, 3li.; small depts due to the estat, 11li. 16s.; boards at the Saw mill, 3li.; by John warner, 8s.; a dunge fork, roape & duz. trenchers, 8s.; total, 373li. 8s. 7d. Severall depts due from the estat, 171li. 12s. 8d.; due to Doctr. Rogers, ——; to Mr. Juit, 5s.; Samuell Graves, 14s.; total, 172li. Du to Nathll. Rust, 1li. 5s.; Due in thre Leagisis to be at severall payments according to will, 90li.

Attested in Ipswich court 30: 2: 1678 by Samuell Chapman, executor, the house and land to stand bound for the performance of the will.

More debts due from the estate: to Docter Rogers his name put in but no sum, now knowne to be, 10li.; Docter David Bennett, 2li.; Samuell Ingalls, 1li.; John Denison, ——; Goodwife Homes, 4s.; John Kimball, 1li.; John Gaines about 12s.; total, 14li. 16s. To brother Simon, 15li.; brother Nathaniell, 15li.; Decon Jewet, 10li. A croscut saw to be added to the estate, 8s.

Essex County Probate Files, Docket 5,018.

Andrew Peeters entered a caution Apr. 30, 1678, that Goodman Chapman's will be not proved until said Peeters had liberty to speak.

Ipswich Quarterly Court Records, vol. 5, page 304.

ESTATE OF RICHARD SWAN OF ROWLEY.

"The Last will & Testament of Richard Swan of Rowley In the County of Essex in New England I Richard Swan, being weak of body, but of perfect Memory & understanding doe make & appoynt this my Last wil as followeth: Imp^{rs}. my Soul I Comitt Into the hands of the Almighty God my Maker in & through the Lord Jesus Christ whome I trust hath redeemed it, & my body to decent Burial in hope of a comfortable Resurection, through the death & Resurection

of the Lord Jesus Christ. As to my outward Estate
that God of his goodness hath graciously Lent, &
bestowed upon mee, I leaue Give & bestow it as Followeth:
Imp^rs. To my dearly Beloved wife Ann Swan I Give, and
freely Bestow upon her dureing her Natural Life: what I Contracted wth her to have upon our agreement before mariage
vizt. my now dwelling house, orchard, Barne, & out houses &
yards wth the pviledges thereof upon the Comon: & plow
ground behind the Barne; and the English pasture Ground
Joyneing upon the house Lott, and the pasture Ground lying
betweene the English Grass pasture, & pollipod Lotts: &
Three Acers of Salt Marsh, Joyneing upon the Ox pasture at
the East end of the Towne: Further not exprest in our contract before mariage, I bestow upon her dureing her naturall
Life, prouided she live in the house: The Rest of my Meadow
joyneing to that which is before exprest: & the pviledg of
keeping two cows yearly in the East end Ox pasture. Further
I acknowledg the Twenty five pounds to be her due according to our Contract before mariage, & hereby confirme it to
her, to be paid in *in* houshold stuff, & in what she shal desire
of my other estate except Lands. Further I Give my wife Ten
Bushl of Indian, & English corne that may be for her use, till
she Can provide Corne for her self after my decease & a Third
part of what other provission I Leave, vizt, pork, Beef, &
Bacon, &c.
    "Item. I give to my Son Robert Swan as Fol-
loweth: Imp^rs. I hereby Confirme to him my Village Lands
which is about Two hundred Acers: and my Right in an Acer
& half Lott that was Thomas Lilfords Joyneing upon my
owne Land in Rowley, & the pviledges that belonged to my
Right in that Lott: also I give him my now dwelling house
Barne Orchard, yards, & house Lott, & pasture ground Joyneing thereto all but Two Acers: which I have added after in
my will to what I have given Joseph Boynton my Son in Law
already from of y^t pasture Land: This with all the pviledges
thereto belonging I give him the sd Robert, to be at his dispose, & for his vse after the decease of Ann my wife, provided
he pay or cause to be payed, vnto the Three children of my
Son in Law & daughter Stickney namely. Elizabeth. Samuell, & Sarah Each five pounds, when they shal come to be of
the age of Twenty one years: and Fifteene pounds to my
Grandchild Richard Sutton at the Age of Twenty one yeares:
Item. I Give vnto my Grandchild Son of Robert swan. Richard Swan. Three Acers of meadow after my wives decease, and

the pviledg of Two Cow Gates in the East end ox pasture after
her decease which she hath given for the Tearme of her Life
If she dwell her life time in the House: also I give to my sd
Grand child, a sorrel mare colt one year old: & If my son Robert swan doe bestow upon the sd Richard my Granchild (as
sometime he told me he would) what Estate I give to him my
son Robert in Rowley Towne which will fall to him after my
wives decease then the Legacies before given of Thirty pounds
to my four Grand children. Samuell. Elizabeth, Sarah &
Richard, & to be by him paid out of what I Gave him is thereby, & hereby remitted, which then shall be paid by my Execu-
to^r. If they live to ye age aforesaid: & then I Give Richard
More Two Acers; & half of Land that lies (of my Land) next
the ox pasture Land. at Gate. Item. I Give vnto my Four
daughters. vizt. Jane Wilson. Franciss Quilter. Dorothy
Chapman & Mercy Warner Each Ten pounds. Item. I Give
unto my Son in Law Joseph Boynton & Sarah his wife with
what children of theirs that shall live to the Age of Twenty
One years. Two Acers of from that part of pasture Land
given to my wife for her life; which shall be layd out Joyneing to his owne I formerly gave him, & pollipod Lotts, &
David Ben[net] also I give him & them my Land in the Feild
Caled Symons feild: & the Remaynder of that my Land not
given to Richard swan in the Littlefeild by the ox pasture Gate
in the East End of Rowley: also. my salt marsh in the marsh
farme Joyneing upon the pond & Casway: also my Lands in
the Ry plaine (soe cald) ten acers more or Less. also my
meadow Comonly Caled Crane Meadow. also a Comonage in
Towne of Rowley that belongs not to my House I live in but
fell to mee by Gates wth what devission or devissions may hereafter bee upon Rowley Comon that belongs to Gate Land &
Rate Land:
"Item. I Give vnto Joseph Boynton all the Rest of my
Lands & moveables, & estate what ever not mentioned before
to the parties. And give the Lands mentioned to them &
theirs: to him & his wife dureing their naturall life, wthout
they or either of them, that survive the other before their
death dispose of it to them before. Item. I apoynt & Constitute my Son in Law Joseph Boynton my Executo^r to this my
Last will: who I appoynt hereby to pay all my debts, &
legacies & disburstments whatever may be for my Burial:
which debts Legacies, & disburstments I apoynt be paid out of
what moveable Estate, I have left him, or I shall leave, which
s^d estate If it reach not to ye value to pay debts &c: I hereby

Give him leave to sell any part of what is before given him, & his wife, & children, for to pay withall and hee is hereby Empowred to Give deed or deeds of Conveyanc of the same. Further my will is that If any person or persons that I have given Legacie or Legacies vnto, (upon the Sight of my will:) will not promiss my Executo^r (or whome he shall after his decease appoynt in his stead) upon their demaund of what I have given them, to Give him &c. before sufficient wittnesses a full dischardg from any further demaund or any further claime to any part more of my estate, then what I have in this my will given them, then my Executo^r or any he shall leave in his Roome after decease, shal be at liberty whether he or they will pay any such Legacy or Legacies as I have given in my will to any: My desire is & I Intreat my Respected Teacher m^r Samuell Philleps, and my Loveing freind Nehemiah Jewet to be Overseers of this my Last Will For full confirmation of the premises, I have hereunto set my hand & Seal this Twenty Fifth of Aprill Anno. Dom. one Thousand Six hundred & Seaventy & eight: the peice of cloth I leave for cloathes for my wife, & Richard & mary."

Richard Swan. (SEAL)

Witness: Abell langlay, Nehemiah Jewett.

Proved in Ipswich court May 23, 1678 by the witnesses, before Samuell Symonds, Esq., dep. Gov., and Maj. Gen. Denison, Esq.

Inventory taken May 22, 1678, by John Johnson, John Pearson, Sr. and Nehemiah Jewett: cloathes for himself & Linnen, 11li. 2s.; Mony & Books, 2li. 3s.; Corne, Wheat, Ry & Indian, 6li. 5s.; Armes & Coslet, 3li.; Barrels in ye Cellar & meat & Tubs in ye chamber & a chest wth corne in it, 1li. 7s.; Meat, hops, oyle, Runlet, measurs & 1 Ridle, 19s.; 3 old Baggs, a Peck pease, 2 wheels & 1 Runlet, 10s.; 1 pr. sheep sheers, 4 sithes, peuter & Tin ware, Tramil, &c., 1li.; Bedding, 9li. 10s.; peuter, Brass & Tubs, 1li. 5s. 6d.; warmeing pan, Forme, Tramil, Andirons, Tongs, 16s.; pott & hooks, ketle, skillet, frying pan & Brass ketle, 1li.; kneading Trow, 2 sives & 3 cheirs, 8s. 6d.; wood and Earthen ware & 1 Glass, 12s. 3d.; 1 spitt, morter of Brass & pestle, 1 glass & Earthen ware, 6s.; 5 chairs, 2 Tables, an old Cubboard, old Cushins, 18s. 6d.; Hemp, unpilld & pill'd & Calf skin, 2s.; 3 Axes, 4 wedges, betle, frow, 2 Hoes, plow & plow sled, 1li. 5s.; 2 Augers, drawing knife, saw & old Iron, 6s.; Hoops & Boxes, pins, bolt & shackls, 1li. 10s.; yoaks with Irons & Bows, 8s.; 1 sled & some 5 Holed posts, 9s.; 1 draught cheine & hors Tacklin,

10s.; Spade, shovels, forks, Hay Hooks & drag, 6s.; an old
Sadle & Bridle, 10s.; yarne, Basket, old bedstead, old box &
Lumber, 10s.; Houshold stuff, total, 46li. 19s. 9d. 3 pr. oxen,
6 cows, Three 3 yr. olds, 1 2 yr old, 2 year olds, 1 Calf, 64li.
10s.; 2 Horses, 2 mares, 1 Colt, 17 sheep, 10 Lambs, 18li.;
swine, 5li. 10s.; Cattle, total, 88li. House & pviledges on
Comon belonging to it, yards, Orchard, Lands, pasture & plow
ground Joyneing to ye Homestead, 120li.; Village land 200
Acers, 40li.; his right in Acer & half Lott that was Lilfords
wth pviledges that belonged to it, 50li.; Six acers Meadow in
Ox pasture & 7 Acer upland by ye ox pasture gate, 61li.; 3
ox gates in East End Ox pasture, 2 acer meadow at Crane
meadow, 24li.; 8 Acer upland at Symonds feild & 8 acer at Ry
plaine, 20li.; 3 Acers marsh at Casway, 4 Cow Gates, 27li.;
A Frehold belonging to Gates & pviledges on Comon to Rates
& Gates, 10li.; Lands, total, 352li. Total estate, 486li. 19s. 9d.
Attested May 23, 1678 by Joseph Boynton, executor.

Debts and legacies due from the estate to persons following:
to his widdow, 25li. & Corne & provision, 2li. 6s.; Land to his
son Robert Swan, 210li.; to his grandchild Richard, son of
Robert, 25li. 6s. 8d.; his grandchild Richard a conditional
Legacie, 40li.; his four daughters, 40li.; merchant Wainewright, 10li.; Doctor Bennett, 2li. 2s.; Mr. Dole, Doctor,——;
Mr. Jno. Rogers per phisick,——; Nehemiah Jewett, 5s.;
Jno. Pearson, Senr., 8s.; Ed. Herd, shoemaker,——; Richard Leighton, 14s. 8d.; Sugar & wine at Funeral, 1li.; Joseph
Kilburne & Caleb Hopkinson, 5s.; the Hatter for Richard's
hat, 7s.

Essex County Probate Files, Docket, 26,893.

Acquittance of Robert Swan of Haverhill only son of Richard Swan of Rowley, to his brother in law Joseph Boynton,
executor of the estate of his father Swan, he having received
full satisfaction by a deed of lands, to all his right in the estate of the said Richard Swan, except what is expressed in the
agreement. Signed and sealed May 20, 1678. Witness: Daniell Wicom, John Pickard, Sr. Acknowledged June 20, 1678
by Robert Swan.

Robert Swan, sr., of Haverhill, acknowledged the receipt of
what was given him by his father, Richard Swan of Rowley,
in his last will, namely, his dwelling house, barn, orchard,
pasture lands and priviledges thereunto belonging, and releases Joseph Boynton of Rowley, executor to the will, of all

further demands upon the estate. Signed July 31, 1678. Witness: Samuell Phillips, Isaac Coulby.

Acknowledged in Ipswich court Apr. 1, 1679 by Isaac Coulby and 31: 1m: 1681 by Mr. Samuell Phillips, before Nath. Saltonstall and Barthol. Gedney.

Ipswich Deeds, vol. 4, pp. 176,383.

ESTATE OF ROBERT DORTON.

Whereas Robert Dorton left by will 25li. to several persons, John Ring, Edward Deare, Phillip Welch and William Danford, and said Dorton having been out of the country these four years and a half and not heard from, court 25:4m: 1678, ordered that Edward Deere have 10li. and the other three, 5li. each, Deere to pay the charge of settling the estate. Each was to give security in case said Dorton should return.

Salem Quarterly Court Records, vol. 5, leaf 116.

Petition of Edmund Dear, William Danford and Phillip Wealch: that the court would take cognizance of a "verbal will, or Guift madde by Robert Dorton which will be proved now at court; the manner is as followeth, Robert Dorton hauing some estate to the value of twenty five pounds in good specias, which he left in the hands of John Ring, and ordered it so, that if he came not here within the space of three years, then he willed the said summes with the use thereof to four of his countrymen, Namely Edward Dear, William Danford, Phillip Wealch, and John Ring, and that perty of the four that was in most need at the three years end, he was to haue ye bigest share; Now it is allmost six years sinse. the said Dorton went out of thes Cuntry."

Edward Neiland, aged thirty-eight years, and Elizabeth Dear, aged upward of fifteen years, deposed that they asked Dorton a year after he made this will if he still wished the same carried out and he said he did. Also that the bill which Dorton had of John Ring for the money, he had committed to William Danford. Sworn, June 20, 1678, before Daniel Denison.

Edward Allin and Killicrist Ross testified that they being in Goodman Sparks' orchard where John Ring was, heard the latter say he had the money in his hands, etc. Sworn, June 20, 1678, before Daniel Denison.

Essex County Quarterly Court Files, vol. 28, leaf 144.

ESTATE OF THOMAS PURCHASE, SR., OF LYNN.

"In the name of God & in his feare I Thomas Purchase
Senio^r being mindefull of my owne mortallitie & certainetie
of death & the vncertainetie of the time, being now in good
health & perfect memory doe make appoint & ordaine this to
be my Last Will & Testament renounceing all other will or
wills formerly made by me, first I giue & bequeath my soule
into the hands of my blessed Redeemer, the Lord Jesus who
dyed, & his blood cleanseth from all Sine, & through his right-
eousnes I doe only Looke for justification & salvation, & doe
comitt my mortall body after this life is ended, vnto the dust
from whence it was taken there to be preserved by the power
of the faithfullnes of my Redeemer Jesus Christ vntill the
resurrection of the just & then to be raised vp by the same
power to Imortallitie & life where I shall see him as he is,
& shall ever be with him, & in this faith & hope I desire
through his grace & assistance to liue & dye in & at last to be
found of him in peace, nextly my will is that my debts shall
be truely & justly payd vnto euery one to whome I shall be indebted, as for all the Estate, which the Lord hath beene
pleased to bestow vpon me, (Excepting all my siluer plate)
which I intend to dispose of my selfe, I giue & bequeath All
my goods, Chattels, houses & Lands (If any standing) one
third part unto my welbeloved wife Elizabeth Purchase, And
two third parts of my said estate vizt Goods, Chattels, houses,
& Lands, I giue unto my fiue children equally to be devided
amongst them, And as for the third part which I haue giuen
to my wife my will is that it shall Returne againe unto my fiue
children ‖ after hir decease ‖ equally to be devided amongst
them, And as for the supervisors of my will I doe desire my
welbeloved friends Mr Henry Jocelin my cousine Mr Olliver
Purchase of Hamersmith, & my cousine Mr Edward Alline of
Boston, And as for theire Labour & paines herein I doe giue
unto each of my said overseers, twentie shillings a peece to be
payd vnto them in Currant New England siluer by my sonne
Thomas Purchase, whome I doe appointe & ordaine to be
executor of this my last will & Testament. In witnes whereof
I haue set to my hand & seale this second day of May Sixteen
hundred Seventie & Seven."

Thomas purchas senior (SEAL)

Witness: George Robinson, John Ferniside.

Essex County Quarterly Court Files, vol. 28, leaf 146.

Thomas Purchase dying intestate, and a writing having
been given in as his will, in which his son Thomas was named

as executor, court 25:4m:1678, granted administration to
Elizabeth, the relict, and son Thomas, who were to bring in
an inventory to the next Salem court.

Salem Quarterly Court Records, vol. 5, leaf 117.

Inventory of the estate of Mr. Thomas Purchas, sr., who
deceased in Linn, May 11, 1678, aged 101 years, allowed,
25:5:1678, in Salem court, upon oath of Elizabeth, the relict: to a parcell of land at Pechepscot containing about 1000
acres more or less, ——; a mare & mare Colt, 1li. 10s.; one
Cow & 2 Calves, 3li. 15s.; a Sylver tancker, 3li.; a Sylver
Cupp, att 1lb. 10s. given to his sonn Thomas before his decease, 1li. 10s.; a Sylver dram Cupp, 1s. 6d. & a broaken
Sylver spoone att 3s., 4s. 6d.; 2 shirts & 2 p. of drawers, 12s.;
on bolster tick & a feather bed, 1li. 16s.; 2 fether beds & 2
bolsters, 4li. 10s.; 4 pr. of pillowbeeres, 1li. 15s.; one pr. of
wrought pillow berers and Cubbott cloath, 12s.; a diapar table
Cloath & towell, 7s.; 5 sheets, 1li. 10s.; 5 table Cloathes, 3li.;
20 napkins, 1li. 5s.; 2 old Coates & 2 pr. of Bretches, one dub-
lett, one pr. of drawers, 12s.; 3 baggs, 3s.; 7 old sheetes, 1li.
10s.; 3 white Blancketts, 15s.; 5 pillowes, 3s.; 4 Ruggs, 2li.
10s.; one Coverlede & 5 old Blanketts, 1li. 5s.; one great byble
& 3 other bookes, 16s.; 4 Brasse Kittles, 1li. 10s.; 2 sives att
2s., one iron pott, 4s.; 3 wooden dishes, 3s.; 4 pewter Dishes,
14s.; 6 old pewter vessells, 12s.; 2 old sckilletts, a ladle &
sckimer, 6s.; one Brasse Chaffin dish, 4s.; one warming pan,
5s. 6d.; one old Chest, 3s.; one Spitt, 4s.; one old Blanckett,
5s.; old trunck, 5s.; one Chare, 1s.; total, 35li. 1s.

Account presented by Samuell Pike of the charges and
disbursements concerning Mr. Thomas Purchas, deceased,
and his four children: For Mr. Thomas Purchas's diet seven
months, 5li. 13s. 4d.; two children's diet a year and a half,
24li.; one child's diet a year, 8li.; one child's diet a year and
a quarter, 10li.; wintering a mare & colt, 1li.; charges for his
funerall, 1li. 16s. 8d.; total, 50li. 10s. 8d. Received of Mr.
Thomas Purchas: att one time 20 bushell of Indian corn att
5s. 6d. a Bushell, 2li. 10s., att another time tenn bushells of
Indian corn, 1li. 5s., In Linen & wollen cloth, 1li., 4li. 15s.;
total, due, 45li. 15s.

Petition of Elizebeth Purchas, widow of Thomas Purchase: "your petitioners husband being an hundred & one
yeares of age, Deceased aboutt fiue or six weekes since att
Lynn, who left behind him besides your petitioner fiue Children to bee prouided for, And butt Little or noe estate haue-

ing lost most of what he had by yᵉ Indians to the East-ward, Butt itt pleased him to make a Will wch. wee here withall present unto yʳ Honours, in which will he made his Eldest sonn Thomas Purchas his executtor, who by reason he knowes nott how much his father was indebted, butt knowes his father left little or noe estate behind him besides a parcell of land to yᵉ Eastward, and being a young Man is fearefull to accept of yᵉ executtorship for feare of involveing himself into many troubles, And your petitioner understanding that yᵉ law requiers either some executtor or Administrator to bee approued of by yᵉ next court in yᵉ countie where yᵉ partie Deceased, Humblie supplicates this Honord Court that by reason that he that was appointed executtor refuseth to Accept thereof, humbly requesteth that this Honord Court would be pleased to grant letters of Administration to her and her sonn Thomas or otherwise to order & settl yᵗ little estate that is, as in yʳ wisdome you shall think meet." Elizebeth Purchas, Thomas Purchase.

Essex County Quarterly Court Files, vol 28, leaves 147-148.

Inventory of the estate of Thomas Purchase taken June 27, 1685, by John Blany and Henry Skerry, jr.: one fetherbed and all the furniture belonging to it, 7li. 18s. 6d.; 3 pr. pillow cases, 12 napkins, 3 tablecloths, 6 towels, 1li. 8s.; 1 wastcot, 10s., a neckcloth, 5s., 1 pr. sleeves, 3s., 18s.; plate, 6li. 10s.; 1pr. andirons, fire shovel & tonges, 13s.; 1 Iron pot, brase skillet & Iron hake, 14s. 6d.; 3 peuter platters, 3 basons, 3 porengers, 2 sasers, 13s. 6d.; earthen ware, 3s.; 1 small table, 1 joynt stool and 6 chayrs, 15s.; 2 chests, 1 trunk and 2 boxes, 1li.; 1 gun, 1 sword & belt, 2li.; 1 warmeing pan smale one, 7s.; 1 mare, mare colt, 3 sheep and a lamb, 3li.; money and goods of Mr. Wharton, 18li. 8s.; total, 44li. 8s. 6d. 100 acres of vacant land at eastward,—; Debts due out of the estate, 2li. 13s. 6d. Debts due to the estate, 2li. 5s.

Attested in Salem court June 30, 1685 by Elizabeth Purchase widow and administratrix.

Essex County Probate Records, vol. 302, page 138.

ESTATE OF RICHARD RICHARDS.

The relict of Richard Richards, deceased, brought in an inventory of her husband's estate, and was sworn 25 : 4 m : 1678.

Salem Quarterly Court Records, vol. 5, leaf 117.

Inventory of the estate of Richard Richards, deceased, taken June 25, 1678, by Edward Flint and Richard Croade:

in ye lower room, a Feather bed & Bolster with yᵉ Bedsteed, a Rug and ye Furniture being old, 3li.; a Table & Forme, a chest & 2 Boxes, 1li.; 4 old chaires, 5s.; An old Iron pott, 3s., an Iron kettle, 8s.; 2 Iron hakes, 6s., a paire of Tongs & fire shovell, 4s.; A Fryeing pan & Brass skillett, 4s.; A grid Iron, 2s., an old smoothing Iron, & 2 heaters, 2s.; 4 old pewter platters, 8s.; 2 Jarrs, 2s., 5 Cheese Fatts, 18d.; 4 Woodden Boles & 3 Trayes, 5s.; An old Broken woollen wheele, 6d., an old Lynnen wheele, 2s.; 6 old Trenchers & 3 old earthen potts, 1s.; an old ax, 1s.; an old paire of cards, 6d.; in the chamber, An old bed, an old Bedsteed & Furniture to yᵉ Bed, 1li.; A horse coller, a paire of hames & a cart saddle, 3s. 6d.; an old rideing saddle without stirrops or girts, 4s.; A peece of Tarrd roape & some old Iron, 5s.; 3 old Tubbs, 2 old Trayes & old Troff, 3s.; An old hoe, 18d., an old paire of wheeles & cart with yᵉ Appertenances, 16s., 17s. 6d.; total, 9li. 8s. 6d.

Allowed 28 : 4 : 1678 upon oath of the widow.

Essex County Quarterly Court Files, vol. 29, leaf 2.

ESTATE OF MOSES MORGAN OF SALEM.

Administration upon the estate of Moses Morgaine, who was slain at Black Poynt, was granted 25 : 4m : 1678, to Samuell Morgaine, who was ordered to bring in an inventory to the next Salem court.

Salem Quarterly Court Records, vol. 5, leaf 117.

ESTATE OF SAMUEL CONDIE OF MARBLEHEAD.

"The Laste Will and Testamente of Samuell Condy Being in his perfecte Memory the 9 of ffebrewary 1677 ⅞ Impʳ That I doe giue my whole Estate To my wife Anne During The Terme of her Life after my Depts are paide and after the Death : of my sd : wife I giue It all To my Daughter Ane and her Children, only I doe giue to my granddaughter mary Hester greenes daughter The Cubberd that Nowe Is In This House and to Hester greenes soone Charles I giue thurty shilings when he Is of aboute fouer yeares of age If he Liue and To Hester greene I giue one of the pewter dishes That was Her mother Rebecah Condys and one pewter Dish To my Daughter Ane That was Her mothers and I doe make my wife Ane Condy and my Daughter Ane Salter my full and whole Excexetrixes for paying all my Depets and Receiuing all

Deptes and paying all Legaties, as wittness my Hand this 9th february 1678⅞."

Samuell (his Sam mark) Condy.

Witness: John (his J B mark) Brimblecom, Richard Reed, John Pedricke, Thomas Trefry, Samuell (his SR mark) Reede.

Sworn by John Brimblecom, June 25, 1678, before Moses Mavericke, and by Richard Reade 29:4:1678, in Salem court.

Inventory of the estate of Samuell Condie, taken Apr. 30, 1678, by Moses Mavericke, Samll. Ward and Richd. Oliver: two dwelling houses, two thirds of an orchard, a small barn, 65li.; 1 Cow and one yearling, 4li.; four young swien at 8s., 1li. 12s.; 1 hatt, 2s. 6d.; 2 paier yarn stokins, 4s.; 3 red wast-kots, 15s.; 2 paier of Cloth briches, 10s.; 1 Cloth Coat, 12s.; 1 Cap Cloth Coat, 7s.; 1 paier of woolen drawers, 4s.; 2 shirts, 1 paier of drawers, 10s.; 1 paier of sheets, 10s.; 2 pillow Cases, 3s.; 1 silk gras bed and boulster, three fether pillows, Curtins, bedsted, 2 old rugs, 2 blankitts, 1 sheet, 6li.; 1 paier of boots, 10s.; 1 table and a form, 14s.; 1 muskitt, 15s.; 1 Cutlas, 8s.; 1 pistoll, 5s.; 1 Chest and a box, 1li.; 2 Iron pots and 1 Iron ketl, 1li. 10s.; 1 paier of Indirons, 12s.; 1 paier of tongs and a pot Crock, 4s.; 1 spitt, 2s.; six pewter platters, 18s.; 2 plats, 5 poringers, 5s. 6d.; 1 beker, 1 Candlstik, a pint pot and a Cup, 2s. 6d.; 1 warming pan, 6s., 1 Lattin pan, 7s.; 1 Lanthorn, 2s.; a parcill of Earthen ware, 1s.; 1 pewter Cup, 1s.; old Chaires and other lumber, 5s.; 1 bras skillett, 2s. 6d.; 1-2 a maer and Colt, 15s.; total, 89li. 9s. Debts: to Richard Knott, docktor, 9s.; Vinson Stillson, jr., 1li. 1s.; John Walldron, 11s.; Thomas Dixsy, jr., 12s.; Thomas Hawkings, 13s.; Edward Homan, Copper, 14s.; Mr. Sam. Gardner, 1li. 15s.; Cristopher Lattemore, 16s.; Mr. Danell Welles, docktor, 1li. 10s. 6d.; Richard Hood of Linn, 1li. 10s.; Richard Rowland, sr., 1li. 15s.; Phillip Brimellcome, 1li.; Edmund Batter, 27li. 10s. Allowed 29:4:1678 upon oath of An, the widow.

Essex County Quarterly Court Files, vol. 29, leaves 28, 29.

ESTATE OF PHILIP ROUNDY OF SALEM.

Administration upon the estate of Phillip Roundy, intestate, was granted 25:4m:1678, unto Ann, the relict. She brought in an inventory and the estate was ordered to remain in her hands for her necessary use.

Salem Quarterly Court Records, vol. 5, leaf 117.

Inventory of the estate of Phillip Roundy, deceased, appraised, June 24, 1678, by Richard Croade and William Hollis: a small feather Bed & small Bolster with Two little pillowes, a paire of pillow beers & a paire of Linnen sheetes & a paire of Blankets & a Rugg, all being well worne, also ye bedsteed & old curtains & old canopy, 4li.; an old brase Kettle, 6s.; an old fire shovell & a paire of Tongs & a spitt, all little more in vallue then old Iron, 3s. 6d.; an old small Iron pott & poott hookes, 3s. 6d.; A Trammell & an old Fryeing pann, 4s.; 3 pewter platters, 8s.; 3 pewter porringers, an old pewter drinking cup & pewter Bole, 3s. 6d.; 6 old chaires whereof 2 or 3 Broken, 3s. 6d.; 1 Table with an oake leafe about six foote Long, 10s.; 1 Little old Table & a chest, 5s.; 3 Latten dripping panns, 2s.; one very small Trundle beadd being but Few Feathers in it, with ye Bedsteed and that Little Furniture belonging to it, 1li. 10s.; a Letten candlesticke, 6d.; total, 7li. 19s. 6d. Possibly some debts that may be oweing to this estate but what ye widdow cannot tell, neither doth shee know how much ye abovesaid estate of her deceased husband's may be indebted, "Thereforeyepoore‖widdow‖humblyrequests this honored Court to direct her in a way what to doe in this her desolate case that shee may be cleare & also that shee may haue some consideration out of ye estate towards ye maintenance of her poore orphant since her Fathers decease to this tyme." Allowed 27 : 4 : 1678 upon oath of Ann, the widow.
Essex County Quarterly Court Files, vol. 29, leaf 3.

ESTATE OF GEORGE BECKFORD OF MARBLEHEAD.

Christian Bigford was appointed 25 : 4 : 1678, administratrix of the estate of her husband George Bigford, and brought in an inventory. The estate was ordered to remain in her hands for the bringing up of her children.

Inventory of the estate of the husband of Christian Beckford, taken at Marblehead, June 26, 1678, by Willam Woods and Robert Bartlett: to old Rooges, 17s.; three old bed blancketes, 12s.; one old hameck, 5s.; three old feather pelares, 12s.; one Canvas Cattail bolster, 2s.; one old feather bead, 2li. 10s.; one old pare of Cortenes, and fanenes, 1li. 5s.; one pare of shetes, 10s.; one bedstead, 4s.; to Eiaren potes and Cetell, 1 1li.; to pare of pot Crockes, 3s.; one frian pan, 2s. 6d.; one Croock for to hang the pot in and one par of tongs, 5s.; tools, spardes and one hoo and one billhoock, 6s.; to seefes and one

pare of beles, 3s.; six puter dishes, one quart, one to quart
bason, one salt selar, 1li. 12s. 6d.; three porengeres and on
bole, 2s. 6d.; som earthen potes and deshes, 6s.; fouer old bar-
eles and to spening wheeles, 12s.; one bras skelat and one box
and heateres and one Lamp, 7s.; one wascot and one par of
breches, 1li.; one bibell and to small boockes, 5s.; one Chest
and to boxes, 8s.; total, 13li. 9s. 6d.

Essex County Quarterly Court Files, vol. 29, leaf 4.

ESTATE OF MRS. ELIZABETH KING OF LYNN.

Administration upon the estate of Mrs. Eliza. King was
granted 25 : 4m : 1678, to Mr. Ralph King, who presented an
inventory of the estate.

Salem Quarterly Court Records, vol. 5, leaf 117.

Inventory of the estate of Mrs. Elizabeth King, taken May
26, 1678, by William Bassett and Thomas (his F mark) Far-
rar: one long table and Joyn Stools and a chist, 1li. 17s.; two
great chayers, 3 cushins and a carpit, 1li. 7s.; one small table,
one bedsted, one prest and cabbin bed and trundle bed, 1li.
18s.; one trunk, one chist, pewter, brass and skellet and Iron
ware, 2li. 13s. 6d.; a payer of Stilliards, head pece and corslit,
10s.; courtins and vallanc, a Rudg and 2 blankets, being very
old, a *back ford*, 14s.; baskets, beds and bedcloths belonging
thereto, 4li. 14s.; linning, 5 sheep and lambs, 2 silver spoons,
a crank for a grindstone, 5li. 12s.; an ould horse, 10s.; a bed
and bolster, 1li.; a small old tramell and old bellows, 4s.;
total, 21li. 19s. 6d. "my mother in here liue time disposed of
her waring aparrell by her perteculer desire to her grand dautor
hannah blanay, alsoe my mother in her liue time gaue to her
dautor sarah nedom one bed and boulster at her decease which
is not Inuentered And alsoe to my self one greate bibill and
a small siluer dram Cup and to my wife a siluer wine Cup
which is not In the Inuenteree."

Allowed in Salem court 29 : 4 : 1678.

Debts due from the estate of Mrs. Elizabeth King, executrix
of the will of Mr. Danill King: to Ralph King, attorney to
Elizabeth King in behalf of the children of Hanah Blayner at
two courts at Salem petitioning, 3li. 3s.; in the action against
Blainer as we sued in her Right and what he the said blayner
Recouerd against us and that which we expended on that account, 14li. 15s. 4d.; to Docter Knott, 12s.; to Docter Weels,
—; to my mothers funerall Charges, 5li. 10s. Sworn by Ralph
King, June 29, 1678, in Salem court.

Essex County Quarterly Court Files, vol. 29, leaf 32.

ESTATE OF EDMOND TOWNE OF TOPSFIELD.

"The Intent and purpose of Edmond Towne presented by
mary his wife Conscernin his estate presented to this Hounored
Court now sitting Imprimis The minde of the deceased was as
is mine allsoe; and is consented too by all partys conscernd
that the four sonns shall haue all the Lands Equally devyded
amongst them, And the rest of the estate to be Equally
devyded amongst the 5: garles only Sarah the secong Daughter is already marryed and Hath rescievd to the vallue of
twelve pounds already. Soe Leaveing my Cause to god, and
to your Honnors searious Consideration I subscrybe myselfe
mary Towne. Only provided that the widow's thirds of the
whole be taken out fust. Jacob Towne deposed that Thomas
Towne, eldest son of Edmund Towne, deceased, declared himself to be satisfied with an equal share with the rest of his
brethren." Sworn in court, 27 : 4 : 1678.

Proved by the widow, 27 : 4 : 1678, with the consent of all
the surviving persons concerned.

Essex County Quarterly Court Files, vol. 29, leaf 30.

Administration upon the estate of Edmond Towne was
granted' 27 : 4 : 1678, to Mary, the relict, who was to dispose
of the estate according to the mind of the deceased, as by mutual agreement of all surviving persons concerned, which writing was allowed. An inventory was also presented and sworn
to.   *Salem Quarterly Court Records, vol. 5, leaf 117.*

Inventory of the estate of Sergeant Edman Towne, taken
at Topsfield, May 3, 1678, by Frances Pabody and Thomas
Baker: Books, 1li.; wearing clothes, 7li. 14s.; linning sheetes
and neckpins, 11li. 6s.; house and landes on the north of the
Riuer, 220li.; upland and mado on the south side River, 72li.;
five oxen and seven coues, 52li.; young Cattel, 19li. 17s.;
shepe and lambes, 6li.; two horses, 7li.; swine, 8li.; iron
tooles, 3li.; kittels and potes and other iron ware, 4li. 4s.;
peuter and earthing ware and glas, 2li. 15s.; swordes and
gones, 4li. 6s.; wheles and other lumbur, 6li. 3s.; a cubbard
and cheastes, 2li. 10s.; bedsted and beddin, 16li. 10s.; pillin
and saddel, 2li.; wooll and flax, 17s.; five barrels of sider, 2li.
10s.; wollin and linnin yarne, 2li. 10s.; home spon cloath, 7li.
10s.; corne and porke, 4li.; for halfe the farme which was
given to Sargent Toune in Revertion by Thomas Browning;
total, 453li. 12s. Depts owing, 26li. 3s. 3d.; by the death of one
cow, 3li. 10s. Allowed in Salem court 27 : 4 : 1678.

Essex County Quarterly Court Files, vol. 29, leaf 31.

Acknowledgment of John How, dated Mar. 5, 1679-80, of the receipt from his mother Towne, executrix to the estate of his father Towne, of his wife's portion.

Acknowledgment of Abigaile Peabody, dated Mar. 21, 1694-5, of the receipt from her mother Towne of her portion.

Acknowledgment of Rebecca Knitte, dated June 2, 1698, of the receipt from mother Towne of her .portion.

Acknowledgment of John Prichett and his wife, dated July 27, 1698, of the receipt of her portion.

The widow Mary Towne of Topsfield testified in Ipswich court, Sept. 6, 1714, that as administratrix of her husband's estate, she had paid to Thomas Wilkins who married one of her daughters, her portion of the estate.

Essex County Probate Records, vol. 311, page 181.

An agreement made between Thomas Towne, William (his W mark) Towne, Joseph Town and Samuel Town, all of Topsfield, that whereas the court settled the lands of our father, Edmond Town of Topsfeild upon us, and also our mother Mrs. Mary Town hath given to us her share of land which belonged to our grandfather Thomas Browning, and we have divided all the said lands amongst ourselves as is hereafter expressed (excepting only two acres and a half of medow of said Browning's which our mother hath given by her will to our sisters) : "Thomas Town hath two twenty acre lotts in the first Division where he now dwels and about six acres of medow joyning to his Land and to the Rever also about foure acres of medow Lyeing betwen Beverly medows and Wenham medows which he had of our father for Twenti and Two pounds willed to him by our grandfather Browning."

William Town's share of upland "is all that which was our fathers on the north side of the Rever where he now dwells as also a peace of medow of about three acres joyning eastward on Jacob Easte and westward upon Joseph Town and also six acres of medow on the south side of the Rever over against his dore."

Joseph Town's share is "all our fathers second devision where he now dwells it being about fifty acres also Three acres of Rever medow joyning to Jacob Este on the west and William Town on the east, also foure acres of medow on the south side of the Rever joyning upon Joseph Town on the east and on John Curtice on the west."

Samuell Town's share is "all the upland and medow that was our grandfather Brownings on the north side of the Rever In which is included William Towns share of land and medow which he and Samuell Town bought of our Unkle James Symonds, also about an acre and halfe of Revir medow joyning to Joseph Town to the west and Jacob Town to the east."

Signed Feb. 1, 1709-10. Witness: William Porter, Jonathan Putnam.

Acknowledged Dec. 16, 1717, by Thomas Town, William Towne, Benja. and Daniell Town sons of Joseph Towne and executors to their father's will.

Essex County Probate Files, Docket 27,886.

ESTATE OF JOHN WOODHAM OF IPSWICH.

Inventory of the estate of John Woodum of Ipswich, taken July 1, 1678, by John Whipple, Sr. and Thomas Dennis: his dweling hows with out housing & homsted, 70li.; abought fiv acers of march, 27li.; five accers of Lande in the comon feild, 20li.; one horse, 2li. 10s.; one cow, 3li. 10s.; two steers 2 yers old, 4li.; two swine, 1li. 5s.; his wareing clothes Linon and woollin with shoos, 4li. 10s.; two small fetherbeds with what belongeth to them, 7li. 10s.; two chests, 16s.; a smal table & fower chayers, 8s.; one old sword, 4s.; worming pan, 8s.; friing pan, 4s.; Gridiron, payer of tonges, firepan, 8s.; an old axe, 3s.; pewter, 6s.; one sikle, 1s.; two trowels, one hamer, 5s.; one betle, one Iron wedg, one haye fork, 4s.; two old shovels, two howes, 6s.; two Iron pottes, a brase scilet, 1li. 6s., one beare barill, 2s.; one paill, 1s.; two old spining wheels, old fanes & a cow bele, 8s.; a small Cart roape, payer of trayce, a horse sleed, 7s.; one bibel, one other booke, 13s.; kneading trofe & two large trofes, 16s.; a hemp braake & a hechell, 7s.; old Cherne, sadle & panell with bridle, 18s.; tramell, earthen wear, 6s.; severall small inconsiderable things, 5s.; due from Hanna Robiohn which is now wiffe to Isake Howe for one yeares boarde, 7li. 10s.; tammy for a Coate, 1li. 14s.; pd. for hure to Sergt. bruer for making a wascoat, 7s.; due from Thomas fowler in pipe staves, 1li. 10s.; total, 160li. 7s. The estate is deptor to sevrall men, 64li. 4s. 7d.

Attested in court by Mary Wooddam, relict of John Wooddam.

Essex County Probate Files, Docket 30,565.

There being a will of John Wooddam produced in court without proof, the court Apr. 1, 1679, granted administration unto the widow, Mary Wooddam, she to have the estate while

she lives and what she leaves at her death to be to her daughter
Mary Eyr the only child of John Wooddam.
Ipswich Quarterly Court Records, vol. 5, page 344.

ESTATE OF WILLIAM PEARCE.

Ambross Gale of Marblehead was appointed 24: 5m: 1678,
administrator of the estate of William Pearce, who, with
Denis Bartlett and Robert Pike, was drowned in the winter
of 1677, and he brought in an inventory of his estate, which
was to be settled at the next court.
Salem Quarterly Court Records, vol. 5, leaf 120.

Inventory of the estate of William Pears, deceased, taken
Apr. 29, 1678; 105 lb. of pork at 3d. p., 1li. 6s, 3d.; 1 gun,
1li.; 1 felt hatt, 4s.; 2 paier of shoos, 7s.; 1 Corsie Coat, 1li.;
1 Jackett and Briches, 1li. 3s.; 1 Coat, 12s.; 1 paier
wosted stokins, 5s.; 1 paier striped briches and a paier of old
drawers, 5s.; 1 whiet shirt, 1 blew ditto, 1 paier drawers and
on neckcloth, 12s.; 1 lien and half, 4s.; 1 bedsak, 6s.; 3 lb. of
shott, 14 hooks, a ball of twien, 2s. 6d.; 1 Chest, 8s.; 1-8 of
hundred bred, 2s.; 7 bbs. of mackrell sent to barbados by Robert Coks, 5li. 5s.; total, 13li. 1s. 9d. Debts: to Ambrose gall,
2li. 9s. 7d.; James Stilson, 1li. 4s.; John Chine, 14s. 8d.;
John Furbush, 1s. 4d.; 3 cord of wood and 100 C bread to
Sam Morgan, 1li. 17s. 6d.; Robert Cox, 3li.; Christopher Lat-
tamore, 16s. 6d.; Robt. Cox, 1li. 10s.; more, about 15s.; total,
12li. 3s. 11d. William Peerse, debtor to Cr. Lattomor,
16s. 6d.
Allowed in Salem court 25: 5: 1678.
Essex County Quarterly Court Files, vol. 29, leaf 53.

ESTATE OF DENNIS BARTLETT.

Ambross Gale of Marblehead was appointed 24: 5m: 1678,
administrator of the estate of Dennis Bartlett, who, with William Pearce and Robert Pike, was drowned in the winter of
1677, and he brought in an inventory of his estate, which was
to be settled at the next court.
Salem Quarterly Court Records, vol. 5, leaf 120.

Inventory of the estate of Denis Bartlott, deceased, taken
Apr. 29, 1678: 1 suett of Cloth Cloas, 1li. 2s.; 2 paier of
striped briches, 1li. 2s.; 1 Cloth Coat, 15s.; 1 Red wastkott
with silver lases, 15s.; 1 Red wastkot, 7s.; 1 shirt and a paier
of old drawers, 8s.; 2 long neckcloth and hankercher, 8s.; 2

French liens, 7s.; 5 dozen 1-2 of Codhooks, 13s. 9d.; 2 paier french fall shoes, 11s.; parsill of worstid and a paier of worsted stokins, 8s.; 1 Cabin Rug and old bedsack, 9s.; 1 old Coat and Briches, 5s.; 1-8 of a hundred of bred, 2s.; total, 7li. 12s. 9d. Debts: to Ambros Gall, 5li.; John Furbush, 3li. 4s. 6d.; Richd. Read, 15s.; John Chinne, 8s. 6d.; Grigory Codner, 2li. 15s. 9d.; Robert Cox, 1li. 10s.; Samuell Morgan, 5s.; Christopher Lattamor, 1li. 7s. 7d.; total, 15li. 15s. 4d. Denes Bartlot, debtor to Cr. Lattomor, 1li. 7s. 7d.

Allowed in Salem court 25:5:1678.

Essex County Quarterly Court Files, vol. 29, leaf 53.

ESTATE OF ROBERT PIKE.

Ambross Gale of Marblehead was appointed 24:5:1678, administrator of the estate of Robert Pike, who, with William Pearce and Denis Bartlett, was drowned in the winter of 1677, and he brought in an inventory of his estate, which was to be settled at the next court.

Salem Quarterly Court Records, vol. 5, leaf 120.

Inventory of the estate of Robert Pek, deceased, taken Apr. 29, 1678: hooks, Leins and leads, 10s.; 1 old Cloth Coat and stuff briches, 12s.; Cloth Coat, 1li.; 1 hatt, 2s. 6d.; parsell of old hooks and 1 led, 5s.; 1 old shirt, 1 paier drawers, 2 old neckloths, 4s.; 1 old pillow and bed sak, 5s.; 1 old Chest, 4s.; one gun, 10s.; total, 3li. 2s. 6d. Debts: to Ambrose Gall, 4li. 10s. 11d. Allowed in Salem court 25:5:1678.

Essex County Quarterly Court Files, vol. 29, leaf 53.

ESTATE OF AMOS STICKNEY OF NEWBURY.

"August 27th 1678 Bee it knowne vnto all men by these presents that I Amos Stickney of Newbury in the Countie of Essex N E: Massac: being sicke & weake of body but of perfect memory do here make my last will and Testament Comending & Comitting my soule into the hands of my blessed Redeemer Jesus Christ, & my body vnto the dust from whence it was taken, in hope & full assurance of a blessed Resurrection. And for my worldly goods I dispose as followeth Imprs I giue and bequeath unto Sarah my wife all my houshold goods withall my stocke that is to say my cattle horses sheep & swyne & also to haue the house & land in her hands vntill my Son John shalbe of the Age of one & twenty years, And dureing her widdowhood to haue a Roome in the house as long as she

liues a widdow. And I appoint her to be the sole executrix of
this my last will and testament & to discharge my debts &
funerall. 2dly I giue to my son my houseing & ‖all my‖ land‖
meadow ‖ & frehold ‖ and preuiledges ‖ to my son John when
he shalbe of the Age of one & twenty years as aforsaid, And
my said son John shall pay out of the said land to euery one
of his brothers & sisters ten pounds within three years after
each of them shall attaine to the said age of one & twenty
years in corne & cattell as indifferent men shall Judge. And
if my said son John shall decease this life before he shalbe of
the aforsaid age then I appoint my Son Amos to haue the
said ‖ houseing & ‖ land when he shall attaine to the said age
And to pay out of it to his brothers & sisters according as it is
aboue mentioned, as his brother John should haue done, And
my said son John dureing his nonage I appoint that hee shall
dwel with his mother to help her & all the rest of my children
to be at their mothers dispose & my two daughters to haue
their portion paid them when they shalbe of the age of twenty
years and if any of them shall dy before they come of the said
age then *then* their said portions shalbe equally diuided
amongst the rest of those that suruiue And I desire my loueing Brothers John stickney & Andrew stickney & Samuell
stickny to be the ouerseers of this my last will & testament."

                              Amos Stikney. (SEAL)
    Witness: Anthony Somerby, Anthony Morse, Sea., Samuel
Stickny.
    "The names of the children are John Andrew Amos Joseph
Beniamin Moses Hannah & Sarah."
    Proved in Ipswich court Sept. 24, 1678 by Anthony Som-
erby and Samuell Stickny.

    Inventory of the estate of Amos Stickney of Newbury, de-
ceased Aug. 29, 1678, taken by Anthony Somerby, Peter
Cheney and Samuel Stickney: house, barne with fifteene
acres of land upland & meadow, 150li.; Corne in the barne &
Indian corne upon the land, 20li.; two mares, 5li.; two steeres,
7li.; seaven Cowes, 21li.; one two year old, 2li.; three yearlings, 3li.; foure calves, 2li.; about forty sheep, 10li.; twelve
swyne smal & great, 6li.; his wearing apparrell, 7li.; bedstead,
fetherbed, bolster, 2 blankets, Coverlet, Curtaines & vallons,
8li.; other beds & beding, 5li.; three paire of sheets & pillowbeares, 3li.; wooll in the house, 3li.; a Loame with all tackling
for weaveing, 10li.; parcel of new homemade cloth, 3li. 10s.;
parcell of cheese, 2li. 10s.; two Iron potts, 2 Iron kettles & 3
bras skillets, 2li. 10s.; 5 pewter platers, Chamber pot, smal

flagon, pint pot, glass bottles, stone bottles & a warmeing
pan, 2li.; thre chests, 2 litle tables, 2 boxes, settle, 3 chayers
& other small things, 1li. 10s.; hogshead, bear barel, churne,
milk trayes, buckets, firkin & other lumber, 1li. 10s.; fire
shovel, tongues, 2 tramells & pot hooks, 10s.; musket, sword
& pike with Ammunition, 2li.; sadle, bridle & pillion, 1li.;
Cart & wheels, sled, plow, Irons, three chaynes, 3 wedges,
three hooes, an Axe, prongs & other utinsills for husbandry,
5li. 10s.; total, 284li. 10s. The deceased indebted to Henry
Jaques, 2li.; to the executrix of Anthony Morse deceased, 3li.;
Mr. Davison, 1li. 10s.; Mr. White, 1li. 8s.; Francis willet, 1li.
3s. 4d.; Penuel Titcomb, 3li.; marcht. Dole, 10s.; Dr. Dole,
16s.; Anthony Somerby, 11s. 6d.; Peter Cheny, 10s.; total,
14li. 8s. 10d.

Attested in Ipswich court Sept. 24, 1678 by Sarah Stickny,
executrix.

Essex County Probate Files, Docket 26,463.

ESTATE OF FRANCIS JORDAN OF IPSWICH.

"In the name of God Amen: I ffrancis Jordan am now
weake in body yet in perfect strenth of memory do Comit my
spirit to god who gaue it, and my body to bee desently buried
in full hopes: of a blessed & glorious resurrection at the great
day: Item: My will is that my deare and Louing wife Jane
shall Injoy my dwelling house: wth all my: outhouses: as also
al my lands: that I now stand possessed wth all in one place
and another: wth all the appurtenances priuileges thereunto:
belonging as also al my Chattell's: let them bee more or less:
and all my goods both wth in & wth out doores: what soeuer:
in mouable or vnmoueable I do giue to my wife during her
natural life: shee to dispose of to any of my Children or
Gran children: that shal carry and behaue themselus: best towards her: my: will is that my: wife shall not giue any part
or parsell of my Estate of one kind or another: to none, but
either to my Children or Granchildren and that not for them
to receaue or posses or improue, before my wife by the will
of god shall bee called out of this world my wil is that my
deare wife: shall haue power to sell what soeuer part of my
Estate shee shall haue occation of for her Comfortable subsistance & maintainance in her ould age and what then shall bee
left at my wiues death: my Will is that After my wiues decease my Grandchild Mary: Simson shall haue twenty:
pounds if so much left, Undisposed of by ‖ my ‖ wife: for
her Comfortable liuelyhood: & my will is that after that

twenty pounds: is payd: to: my Grandchild Mary: that then
my deare wife shall: haue full power & liberty to giue it as
aboue sayd to them who: do behaue themselus best towards:
her: I say to: my children: or Gran children: & to no other
whatsoeuer: my will is that *is that* my wife Jane shall bee my
sole Excetrix: of this my last will and testament, dated April
23 : 1678 : "

ffrancis (his + mark) Jordan.

Witness: Thomas Knoulton, Sen., ffrancis Wainwright.

Proved in Ipswich court Sept. 24, 1678 by the witnesses.

Inventory of the estate of Frances Jordan of Ipswich,
taken June 8, 1678, by Thomas Knoulton, Sr. and John
Staniford: house, Barne & home lott, 100li.; a pasture in ye
feild of 2 Acres, 10li.; 4 Acres & 1-2 planting land in manings
neck, 22li. 10s.; 4 Acres marsh at ye neck, 16li.; a lott at hogg
Island of 3 Acres more or less, 9li.; 2 oxen, 3 Cows, 2 yerelings, 20li.; 6 sheepe, 6 swine, 7li. 10s.; Cart, slead & plough,
1li. 10s.; pr. of traise, spanshakle, Coller & a yoake, 6s. In ye
Parlor: fether bed & bolster, rugg, blanket, Curtaines & valents, 1 pillow, bed Case, matt, bedsted, trundlebed & 2 Cords,
9li.; his aparrell & woollen ware & shooes, hats & stockens,
10li. 5s.; his waring lenneng, Caps & gloves, 4li.; 5 pr. sheets,
5li. 5s.; 8 pillowbeers, 40s.; napkins & towells, 32s.; remnants,
18s.; bible & psalme boke, 7s.; chest, 12s.; warming pan,
10s.; musket, sword & tackling, 1li. 5s.; rugg, 2 old pillows, a
blanket, 2li.; 6 Chaires & a box, 25s.; lanthorn, 2s.; 2 Cushens, linnen whele & 2 baskets, 10s. In ye halle: A pr. tongs, 2
potts, a pr. Andirons, potthookes & spitt, 2li. 7s.; 1 skillet,
kettle, frying pan, candlestick, 1li. 7s. 6d.; pewter & alcumy
spoones, 3li. 6s.; tin ware & a box Iron, 10s.; earthin ware,
5s.; wooden ware, 25s.; 5 Chaires, table, forme, 8s.; 3 bookes,
6s.; musket, sword & tacklin, 25s. In the old parlor: bedsted,
bed, boulster, rugg, pillow, blanket, 3li.; a whele, 3s.; Cubberd
& sum trifles in it, 15s.; table, forme, Chest & a Chaire, 1li.
7s.; 2 sickles, 2 mesures, tray, pr. sheres, 6s. 6d.; hows, forks,
shovell & implements, 1li.; 30li. woollen yarne, 3li. In the
parlor Chamber: Corslet & pike, 1li. 5s.; Fan, 7s.; 20li. of
wooll, 20s.; wheate, 10s.; 3 sythes, 6s. In ye hall Chamber:
8li. woollen yarne, 16s.; 7li. Cotten yarne, 17s. 6d.; 3li. fine
Cotton yarne, 10s. 6d.; 3li. fine flax yarne, 9s.; 5li. tow yarne,
5s.; 3li. Cotton wooll, 3s.; beame & scales, 5s.; a pr. bootes,
5s.; 3 tubs, 5s.; 2 barrell & fethers, 4s.; flax, 30s.; keeler, 4s.;
2 half bushells, a knapsack, 5s.; 2 sacks & 2 sives, 7s.; hopps
& tow, 5s. In the Cellar: 8 barrells, 3 half barels & other

tubs, 1li. 10s.; 5 keelers, 16s.; Churn, 3s.; hogshead & trifles, 4s.; beere stall & a forme, a piggen, 7s.; sider press & apertinances, 1li. 3s.; flax, hemp & 2 ladders, 14s.; 3 Axes, 1 hatchet, 2 wedges, a betle, 13s.; a well bucket, 4s.; hetchell & betle, 5s. 6d.; total, 262li. 6s. The debtes that are owing, 10li. 6s.; remainder, 252li.

Attested Sept. 24, 1678 by the executrix.

Essex County Probate Files, Docket 15,242.

ESTATE OF JAMES BARKER OF ROWLEY.

"The Last will & Testament of James Barker of Rowley in New England In the County of Essex: Borne at stragewell in Low Suffolk in Old England. Being at present of Competent Understanding though weak of Body, & not knowing how Soone or Suddenly the Lord may call me hence by death I Make & Ordeine this my Last will & Testament: being little altered from what I made a year Since & Left in keeping in the hands of Nehemiah Jewett though not Signed & sealed then: I Comit my Soul Into the hands of God my Maker & my body to decent Buriall in hopes of a Blessed Ressurection through the death & ressurrection of the Lord Jesus Christ my Redeemer. And for my outward Estate which God hath Giuen mee I dispose of it in maner following: Imp^{rs}. to my Beloued Wife Mary I Giue the things she Brought wth her when I maried her, & the vse of the Roome wee liue in, wth firewood Ready Cutt for the fire from time to time: her Rent at Ipswitch & Twenty shillings yearly for her life: to be payed by my Son Burzilai in work or as she shall se need to Call for it. not monie: & If any agreement appear of our Contract at Mariage that it be fullfild equally by my Executo^{r}s: It. I Giue to my Son Burzillai my Eldest child one half of my pasture Land below the orchard: to lie next to B^{ro}. Georg Kilburnes Land: & the Remayneing part of the Six Acers of Land at the farme made ouer to him before & all the Rest of my Upland in the farme Comonly caled Mr Dumers farme: & Three acers of Meadow in meadow (Cald Seetchwell meadow) bought of Daniel Harris being part upland: & Two Acers of meadow at Cow Bridg one of it salt & the other Ruff marsh: & one ox Gate in the ox pasture. (only Grace my daughter to haue the vse of it while she Remaines unmaried) Also a percell of meadow about Two Acers Lying at the place wee call Newberry hole. & one acer of Salt Marsh that was Layd out to mee Towards Mr Nelsons Isleand: and a Quarter part of my Right in the Three Thousand acers aboue the

Cow Commons: & a Third part of my Land at Merimack & Bradford of the great Lott that is six score acers wth this prouiso that the other Two Lotts haue a way throw it to the Riuer on one side or other most Conuenient. My will is that he pay or Cause to be payd the one half of my Engagement to my wife & Twenty shillings as is exprest in her Legacy: & Twenty shillings in Corne yearly to my daughter Grace till she be Maried.

"It. I Giue to my Son James Barker Fifteen Acers of Land in the Addition to my Merimack Land: & also my Gate Marsh deuided to mee at Hog Isleand in Rowley: It. I Giue vnto my son Nathaniel Barker half my Homestead to lye next to the Highway to Br°. Kilburnes house wth the Building upon it: & half the pasture below the orchard which I haue not Giuen to my Son Burzilai next to Jn°. Sticknays Land. More I Giue him the Lott Cald Wilds Lott in Bradford street Lotts: & Three Acers of Land at Long hill: Also my Land at New plaine: & my meadow at Great Meadow: also Fiue acers of Ruff Marsh at Newberry Gate & the Third part of my Land at Bradford that is to say of the Six Score Acers soe cald: to lie next the Village: & more I giue him a Quarter part of my priuiledg in the Three Thousand Acers aboue the Towne Cow Comons: My will is that he pay or Cause to be payd the other half of my Engagement to my wife dureing her natural life: also that he sumer & winter & be at al chardg of the keeping of a Cow for his Sister Grace, while she is unmaried If she desire it: Also my will is that Nathaniell shall haue his dwelling in the part of the house that he now liues in: soe that he suffer not the other parts of the Houseing to want Repairing from time to time to time & doe not disturb his sister liueing in the other part of the House while she is vnmaried If she see good to liue there: which said Houseing & the rest of the Homestead he shall haue after the decease of his said sister or mariage: but he not performeing what I haue specified then upon her Just Complaint to my Ouerseers it shall be in their power to disposes him of that part giuen him: Then I giue & bequeath that wch Grace is to Enjoy wth the rest after her decease & my wiues to Ebenezer Barker my Grandchild If he liue to age of Twenty one y^rs or els to his Father: also I Giue Nathl. two Acers of salt marsh y^t was Leu^t. Remmingtons. It. I will & Giue vnto my daughter Unice Watson my Fifty Acers of Land be it more or Less at Bradford: being my part of the Right of Nehemiah Abbots Lott I giue it to her & her Eldest son after his fathers & mothers decease prouided he liue to

Heir it: And If that child die I giue it to the Rest of their
children as she shal see good to dispose of it at her death:
Also I will & giue vnto her the Best Cours Blanket: & Two
Twild Cotton Blankets: & one flockbed & bolster belonging to
it & a pillow: And one Quarter of the Comon Land that belongs to mee in the Three Thousand Acers aboue the Cow
Commons in this Towne when it shall be deuided: or the vse
and Emprouement til it bee.

"It. I will & Giue vnto my daughter Grace Barker that part
of the house I now dwell in not giuen my wife & that also
after her decease wth half the Homestead & half that part of
the pasture ungiuen to Burzilay & a Third part of the great
Lott at Bradford which Burzillai & Nathl. hath their Thirds
of: & a Quarter part of the Comon Land that belongs to mee
in the Three Thousand acers aboue the Townes Cow-Com-
mon: Also I Giue her forty pounds out of my houshold stuff
& Catle as she shall chuse: And In Case my daughter Grace
die w^thout Issue and not in a Mariage Estate then Burzillai
shal haue the Lands at Merimack or what els I haue Giuen her
in Land: for Ebenezer his Son to Enjoy If he liue to Heir it,
or upon his decease as Burzilai shall dispose in his life or at
his death: And the Moueable Goods that Grace shall leaue If
she die unmaried I Giue to Unice or her children. Further my
Will is that the Rest of my Estate that shal be left when my
debts is payd & all chardges for funeral defrayd be Equally
deuided betwext my Son Burzillai & my daughter Grace. Also
my Vtensels for husbandry I Giue to my Son Nathl. Barker.
Also my wearing Apparrell I will that it be deuided by my
Ouerseers half to Burzillai: & the other half between my
son Nathaniel & my son in Law John Watson: My will is
whateuer deuission or deuissions may or shall be Laid out as
belonging to Gates or Rates upon the Cow Commons be
equally deuided betwext Burzilai & Nathaniel: Also I giue
Nathaniel my Freehold belonging to Gates. Also my will is
Nathaniell Prouide wood for Grace while she is a maid. My
will is Further & I hereby apoynt my Sons Burzillai & Nathaniel to be my Executo^rs to this my Last will, & Testament
and I desire my Loueing friends John Trumble & Nehemiah
Jewet to be Ouerseers: & desire them to Apprize my Estate:
& Giue them full power to Issue any differences that may arise
about my Estate amongst my children that soe sutes at law
may bee preuented: ffor full confirmation of the premises &
euery part thereof I haue Sett to my hand & Seal this Third

day of the Seauenth moneth anno: domin: one thousand six
hundred & Seauenty Eight."

James Barker (SEAL)
Witness: Hannah Brocklebank, Nehemiah Jewett.
Proved in Ipswich court Sept. 24, 1678 by the witnesses.

Inventory taken 12:7br:1678, by Ezekiell Northend,
John Trumble and Nehemiah Jewett: Books, 1li. 3s.; Wearing Apparell, 24li. 17s.; Beding & other houshould stuff his
late wife brought, 11li. 2s. 6d.; Beding, viz., Beds, Rugs,
Blankets, Coverlets, bedsteads, one chest & Linnen in it, 29li.
5s. 6d.; Cotton Cloth & Cotton & Linnen & woolen Cloth, 12li.
17s. 10d.; Brass, Iron & peuter vessels, 7li. 9s. 6d.; Indian
Corne, Mault, Ry, in & wth the 2 Tubs & butter & chese, 5li.
8s. 6d.; 1 Costlet, pike, musquet, Rapier, Bullets, powder,
Match, &c., 2li. 12s.; Utensels for a Tailors Trade & knife,
Inckhorne, sizars, Cane, belt &c., 17s. 6d.; 1 chest, Cuboard,
box, flax, nailes, Hamer, &c., 2li. 8s. 6d.; Sadles, Bridle &
Bags, 1li. 11s.; Bedstead, Chairs, cushings, Tables & Formes,
3li. 10s.; Andirons, Tramill, Gridiron, Tongs, firepan, frying
pan, 1li. 11s.; Earthen & wooden vessels & Tin, spit, Glasses,
skailes & weights, 3li. 5s. 3d.; Brushes, Basket, Trenchers,
Sive, Cards, Leather & Trow., 15s.; utensels for Husbandry,
two Trundle beds & 1 pine board, 3li. 1s.; Stock in Catle, 25li.
1s.; total, 136li. 16s. 1d. Dwelling house, orchard, Barne and
pasture, 40li.; 3 Acers of Land, 9li.; 1 Acer, 3li.; 3-4 Acer,
1li. 15s.; 1-2 Acer, 1li.; 3 Acers of meadow in Setchwell
meadow, 12li.; 2 Acers at Cow bridg, 10li.; One ox Gate, 4li.;
Two Acers at a place wee call Newberry hole, 10li.; one Acer
towards Mr. Nelson Isleand, 5li.; six score Acer at Bradford,
60li.; The Addition, 7li. 10s.; Gate marsh, 5li.; Bradford
street Lott, 18li.; 3 Acers at Long hill, 1li. 10s.; Land at New
plaine, 1li. 10s.; Meadow at Great Meadow, 2li.; 5 Acers of
Ruff meadow at Newberry Gate, 20li.; 2 Acers of salt marsh,
10li.; 50 Acers at Bradford, 30li.; a Freehold Belonging to
Gates, 3li.; Marsh allowed for waies, 10s.; Debts Due to the
Estate, 20li. 3d.; total, 411li. 11s. 4d. Debts due from the Estate, 4li. 6d.; Overchardged in the pticulers above, 1li.
Attested in Ipswich court Sept. 24, 1678 by the executors.

Deposition of Elizabeth Sticknee, aged about seventy, and of
Samuell Sticknee, aged about forty five, that "James Barker
Senior promised upon condition of marriage betwen his son
James Barker and mary the daughter off William Sticknee
deceased that hee the said James Barker Senior would give

his son James a portion equall with any off his other chilldren his elldest son onely excepted and neyther before nor in
his last will hath performed the same." Sworn in Ipswich
court Sept. 24, 1678.

Essex County Probate Files, Docket 1,668.

The court Sept. 28, 1680, ordered that Nehemiah Jewett and
Mr. Willson, overseers to the will of the deceased husband of
widow Barker of Rowley, call the executors of James Barker
to account about what provision hath been made for the
widow, and to see that her dues are laid out for her comfortable subsistance and provide what shall be her dues for the
future.

Ipswich Quarterly Court Records, vol. 5, page 360.

Estate of Thomas Howlet of Ipswich.

"In the name of god Amen I Thomas Howlit of Ipswich in
Newingland being at this present time of perfit understanding
& memory Though weak in body. Comitinge my Soule into
the handes of almyty god & my body to deasent buriall in hope
of reserection to eternall life by the power & merit of Jesus
Christ my most mersyful father & redemer doe thus dispos of
the Temporall estat that god hath graciosly giuen me Imprimis I Giue to Rebeka my wiff: one Cow and two heyfers
that ar Caled hurs also my litle Grey mare: Also I giue to my
wiff an anvety of fiue pownds a yeare: to be pd yearly: fiuty
shilings in Corne And fiuety shilings in Catle: the Corne part
to be pd half in wheat & malt and the other half in indian
Corn: this to be pd at Ipswich wher my wife shal appoint:
also that my wifes goods be returned to her she brought It I
Giue to my Son Samull Howlit fiuety accers of land by
mecher of that which I formerly intended for my Son John
Howlet & also two twenty Accer lots in the thick woods in
topsfeild & also foure Accers of medo. [It I giue to my dafter
Sarah Comings fower accers of the hasakey medo lying at the
moth It I Giue to my son Samull howlet the rest
of the hasekey medow at the bridg. *written in margin*]
Also my wil is that my Son Samull Howlet shall paye fiuety
shiling yearly of the anvety of fiue powndes that I haue
Giuen to my wife in specea according to my will It I giue to
my wife a Ketle in stead of a bed teck I promesed It I Giue to
my dafter Sarah Comings 4 pownds to ‖ be ‖ pd with in fowr
yeares after my desseas if she be liuing elc to her heyers: Also
20ˢ to allis Comins at her mariag or at 18 yers of age It for

my dafter mary perly I haue Giuen her twenty thre pownds
which my wil is shud be made up fiuty powndes the one half
of it within a year after my Desseas the other half within thre
years after my desseas

"It I Giue to mary Howlit my Son John Howlits dafter
forty fiue pownds to be pd to her at the age of eighteen years
or at her daye of maryag, if she liue not to receiu it then my
wil is that ther shal be ten pownds pd to my Son John Howlits wiff Lastly I ordain my Son william Howlit my Sole
executor of this my last wil and testyment to whom I giue my
depts being pd all the rest of my estat housing Lands Goods &
catle Utensils of all sorts and depts from whome soeuer due
unto him & his heyers foreuer. I doe appoint my Louing
freinds Capt. John Applton: major Samull Applton and John
whippl senior the ouerseers of this my last will and Testement: & I doe herby Giue them power to determin any differ-
anc that maye arise betwen my executor and any of the
Legetes aforsaid a bought the payments aforesaid It my will
is that my Son Thomas Howlits wife shall injoy that hundred
accers of land I possesed him of til his eldest dafter be at the
age of eighteen years or at her daye of mariag & then she shal
Injoy one quarter of it: also when my Son Thomas howlits
yongest dafter is of the age of eighteen years or at her daye of
mariag she shal injoy on quarter of the hundred accers giuen
to her s^d father: & after ther mothers desseas they shal injoy
the other fiuty accers equally deuided betwen them my wil
is that if one of ‖ my ‖ Sonn Thomas Howlits dafters dy
befor she is possesed of her portion it shal goe to her sister my
wil is that if my Son Thomas howlits two dafter dy befor
they are eighteen years of age or ar maried that then my dafter in lawe my Son Thomas Howlits wiff shal injoy all the
hunderd accers of land her lif and at her desseas shall paye
out of it, to my children then living one hundred pownds
which shal be equally devided among them in confermation
wherof I hau set to my hand and seal this forth of nouember
1677."

Thomas (his T mark) Howlit (SEAL)
Witness: John Appleton, Samuell Appleton, John Whipple.
Proved in Ipswich court Sept. 24, 1678 by Capt. John Ap-
pleton, Maj. Samuell Appleton, Capt. John Whipple.

Inventory of the estate of Deckon Thomas Howlett taken
10 : 7m : 1678, by John Gould and Abraham Redington : 5
oxen, 20li.; 2 steres, 6li.; 2 yearelings, 1li. 10s.; 5 Coues, 12li.
10s.; 2 heferes & bull, 2li. 10s.; 1 horse, 1 Coult, 3li.; 3 Coues,

7li. 10s.; 1 mare, 2li.; ye farme with housing, barne, orchard, upland and medo with one parcle of march at Ipswich, 200li.; some other percicles of land, 100li.; 16 sheepe & Lams, 18 hoges & piges, 7li.; Clothing woolon & Linnon, 1 saddel, saddel cloth, bridell, pilion and pilion cloth, 13li. 9s.; 1 fouling pece, bookes, 1 brosh, 2li. 16s. 4d.; 1 fether bed, 1 bolster, 2 piloes, 1 ruge, 8li.; 4 chainges, 3 plowes, shares, colters, 20 haroe teeth, 1li. 5s.; 3 yoakes, 1 cart & wheels, cart rope, 4 forkes, 2 siges, 1li. 10s. 6d.; wheges, betell rings, axses, howes, 1 spade, 14s. 6d.; 1 hadess, froe & ringer, 12s.; toules, chisel, plaines, ageres & swass, 1li. 2s.; one heckel teeth, smoething Iron, could chisels, punchies & Lantrone, 4s.; and Iron, spite, tramiell, slise, hath Iron, gridiron, friing pan, tonges, 1li. 4s.; old Iron & the blad of a whipswae, 8s.; 1 bed, 1 blankat, 1 ruge, 2 bolsters, 1li. 10s.; 1 coverlide, 2 blankat, 1 bolster, 2li. 12s.; 2 brass citteles, 1 brass Kandelstik, 1 brass Ladell, 4li.; 1 waring pan, 3 Iron potes, 2 pothookes, 1 Iron morter, 1li. 10s.; 5 poringers, 2 dram Cups, 1 wine Cupe, 1 pint pote, 8s. 9d.; 5 puter platters, 1 tin cittell, 1 tin pot, 2 tin pans & tunel, 1li. 7s. 8d.; earthen ware, 6 brase spones, 7s. 6d.; small woodden ware, 1li. 9s. 11d.; 4 barieles, 1-2 bariel, 6 tubes, 2 coueles, 2 salt boxes, 1li. 3s. 6d.; 1 Bakin troofe, 3 wheeles, 2 melee troves, 1 chease press, 1li.; 1 stand, 1 Cubbord, 2 tabeles, 1 chest, 1 tronke, 1 boxe, 2li. 2s. 2d.; 2 drie caske, 1 fane, 5 chares, 2 chasing, 1 peec Lether, 19s.; 28 yards of nue woolon Cloth, 5li. 12s.; 5 pare of sheets, 2 tabele cloths, 9 napkins, 3 pillobeers, 6li. 19s. 6d.; 1 pare of Curttins, sarge golome & silke buttons, 1li. 17s.; Chase and yarne, 2li. 1s.; 15 pound of sheep woole, 12 pound of fethers, 2li. 6d.; 4 spones, 1 poringer, 1 sirige, 1 yard of genting, 9s. 6d.; 1 pound 1-2 starch, 1li.; plomes, thred, silke & bone Lase, 5s. 9d.; 1 parcell of Linon Cloth, suger, spice & butter, 1li. 10s. 6d.; foueles of all sorts, 1li. 10s.; Indon Corne apon ye ground, 8li.; Ingliss Corne, 9li. 6s. 8d.; 2 sifes, 1s. 4d.; 1 grindstone, 1 plow, 15s.; total, 452li. 11s. 4d. The dets of Deckon Howlet: To Deckon Goodhue, 6li. 10s. 8 1-2d.; Edmon Hard, 9s.; Capt. Whippell, 14s. in malt & 7s. in money; Isaac Cummings, Jr., 40s.; Mar. Francis Wainewright, 29s. 5d.; Mr. John Wainwright, 8li. 15s. 9d.; Goodman Rust, 4s. 4d.; Mr. Darby, 1s. 3d.; Elisha Perkins, 25s.; more detes as doe apeire, 12li. 11s. 5d.; total, 34li. 7s. 10 1-2d.

Attested in Ipswich court Sept. 24, 1678 by William Howlet, executor of his father's estate.

Essex County Probate Files, Docket 14,093.

ESTATE OF MRS. ANN SWAN OF ROWLEY.

"The Last Will & Testament of Ann Swan of Rowley Relict of Richard Swan of Rowley deceased. Imp^rs. I Comitt my soule Into the hands of God my Maker In & throw the Lord Jesus Christ & my body to decent Buriall In hopes of Blesed ressurection: And as for my outward Estate My will is that it be Giuen as followeth: & I doe hereby Giue & bequeath the same: Imp^rs: I Giue to my daughter Abigaill Baily: that Bed that was mine before Mariage to my husband swan: wth the new Bolster & Gray blanket, & a Couerlet & pillow: & a platter & a pair of sheets. & one pillow bear: & one chamber pott. & one porringer one Iron skillet. & one peuter candlestick. & one Beaker Cup. I Giue to my daughter Mary Killburne my other Feather Bedd & Bolster & pillow. & white Blanket & 1 Greene Rugg & the Rest of the sheets & pillow Bears. & one Brass Ketle & .1. Iron pott: & Trammils & Tongs, & pothooks & frying pan: & Bedstead that Mary Lyeth on: and Further all the Wooden Ware & vessells I Giue betwext Abigaill & Mary: Equally to be devided & all my Apparell both woolen & Linnen I Giue to be Equally devided betwext Abigail & Mary: Further I Giue my daughter Mary A peuter platter & Brass Candlestick: & to Abigail My Curteines & vallance: & one chair & to Mary one chair. & peuter pint pot I Giue My Son Caleb Hopkinson the Old Bed in the Chamber & Bolster & Cotton Rug & Blankett: & a chest that his Father Gott made: I Giue my Son John Hopkinson one Iron ketle A pair of Andirons & one Great cheir. My Will is that my Sons Jonathan Hopkinson & John Hopkinson bee Executo^rs to this my Last will: to whome when they haue paid my debts & funerall Chardges I Giue all the Rest of my Estate: only one Book of Mr Boltons works to my Son John Trumble: & for full Confirmation of ye premises & every part thereof I haue Sett to my hand & seal this fourth day of July Anno. Dom: one thousand Six hundred & Seauenty Eight."

Ann (her & mark) Swan. (SEAL)

Witness: Hanah Hazzen, Nehemiah Jewett.

Proved in Ipswich court Sept. 24, 1678 by the witnesses.

Inventory of the estate of Ann Swan, widdow, taken 22 : 6 : 1678, by Nehemiah Jewett and Joseph Boynton: Two Beds, Boulsters, pillow, sheets, 2 blankets & Coverlet, 8li.; the bedding in the chamber, 1li. 10s.; cloathes Linnen & woolen, books, cloth, 2 pr. Cards, 8li. 14s.; 1 Little Barrel, meat Tub, 1 Barrell, 5s. 6d.; peuter & 1 brass Candlestick, 1li.; Wooden

Ware & Earthen & 1 Glass, 12s. 3d.; Table, warmeing pan & kneading Trow, 6s.; 1 Brass ketle, Iron pott, pot hooks, Iron ketle, skillet, frying pan, 1li.; Tramil, Andiron, Tongs, 12s.; 3 cheirs, Two sives, 6s. 6d.; Runlet, oyle, yarne & Baskets, 9s.; 1 pr. sheets, 4 Napkins, 2 pillowbears, 1li.; 2 wheels, 5s.; 2 pigs, 12s.; 1 Hog, 15s.; 2 Cows, 7li.; 1 bag, 1s.; Ry & wheat one Acer upon Ground, 1li. 10s.; Indian one Acer upon Ground, 2li. 10s.; Corne in the house, 1li. 2s.; Hemp upon the Ground, 12s.; 1 Acer of Indian Corne at home, 2li. 10s.; 4 Load of Grass, 12s.; total, 41li. 4s. 3d. Debts due from the Estate: to Mr. Rogers, Mr. Wiglsworth & mercht. Wainewright, 4li.; Mr. March of Newberry, 2s.; Capt. White, 2s.; Edward Hazzen, 2s.; Richard Leighton, 1s. 6d.; Joseph Boynton, 1li. 5s. 6d.

Attested in Ipswich court 24 : 7 : 1678 by John Hopkinson, executor of the estate of his mother Ann Swan.

Essex County Probate Files, Docket 26,876.

ESTATE OF JOHN BREED OF LYNN.

Administration upon the estate of John Bread, intestate, granted Sept. 24, 1678, to his brother Allen Bread, who gave bond and the land also to stand bound.

Ipswich Quarterly Court Records, vol. 5, page 337.

Inventory* of the estate of John Bread taken by Thomas Fuller and John Maskall [Nuhall. *copy*] : load of hay and other things, 1li. 5s.; on hors, 2li. 10s.; to Oxen, 7li.; 4 cowes, 10li. 10s.; in younge Cattell, 5li. 5s.; swine, 3li. 10s.; shepe, 3li. 14s.; the ferry peece of land, 45li.; the hous and to parcel of land, 35li.; 16 acker of land in Rumly marsh, 74li.; to ackers in hoows necke in Rumlle marsh, 10li.; 12 ackers bought of John Haucks, 6li.; a part in a boatt, 13li. 10s.; in Englesh corn, 2li.; Inden corn, 2li.; wearing Cloths, 6li. 12s.; Lining, 7li.; beeding,—; to hatts,—; arms and bostts, 1li.; to silver spoons, —; pewter, 1li. 12s.; Cettells and pott and skellett, 1li. 5s.; Loomber, 6s.; a poot hanger, spit and Chamber pot, 15s.; in other things, 1li. 15s.; coverleds, blanketts and beed, 7li. 13s.; lining, 5li. 2s.; Iron things, 2li.; pewter, 1li.; other things 7s.; Cloth, 16s.; a pillin Cloth, 5s.; presing Iron, 2s.; to Chaiers, 7s. Debts due from the Estate, 20li. 14s. 10d.

Attested in Ipswich court Sept. 24, 1678, by Allen Bread brother of John Bread.

Debts in money: to the nurse, 2li. 15s.; the Dockter, 1li.

1s.; John Dawes, 17s.; John Fewkes, 6s.; Goodman Mechham, 2s. 4d.; Mr. Nowell of Boston, 9s.; Thomas Ivory, 6li.; Samuell Johnson, 2li. 10s.; Clement Colldon, 8s.; Allin Bread, 11s.; mor to Allin Bread, 5li. 3s. 6d.; Timothy Bread, 9s.; Samuell Hartt, 3s.; total, 20li. 14s. 10d.

Agreement between Allin Bread, jr. and Sarah Bread, widow, that said Sarah Bread give up all her right and title that she might claim from the estate of her husband John Bread by law, upon consideration that Allin Bread, jr., administrator to the estate, shall pay her forty pounds, to be paid in cattle, Indian corn, and twenty pound of sheeps wool and twenty pounds in silver in four years, five pound a year and likewise what goods she brought to her husband and six loads of hay. Signed and sealed Sept. 24, 1678. Witness: John Fuller, Nathaniell Ballord, Joseph Bread.

Allowed in Ipswich court 24:7:1678.

For the distribution of the estate the court ordered to the eldest son seventy two pounds, and the others thirty six pounds each, and they to be brought up with the produce of the estate and if that fall short, to be deducted proportionably out of their portions, and the three sons to have their portions out of the lands.

The children of John Bread and Sarah his wife that are living, "John ther Eldest Sonn was born the 15 of November 1664, Sarah ther Daughter was born the 28 of December 1667, Ephram ther Sonn was born the 16 of December 1672, Ebenezur ther Sonn was born the 15 of April 1676." A true copy taken out of the records of Lynn by John Fuller, clerk.

Essex County Probate Files, Docket 3,218.

Addition to the inventory taken by Joseph Armitage, John (his a mark) Neuhall: 15 bushel of Indian corn, 1li. 10s.; 3 bushel of Ri, 10s.; 10 cord of wood, 1li.; more debts that John Bred owes: to Ambros Gal, 1li. 5s.; Nathanel Kirtlan, 5s.; Wiliam Craft, 5s.

Attested in Salem court 29:9:1678 by Allen Bread.

Essex County Quarterly Court Files, vol. 30, leaf 11.

Allen Bread, administrator of the estate of John Bread, brought in an additional inventory, and court held 26:9: 1678, being informed that there are three children of the said John Bread, ordered that he appear at the next court held at Ipswich for the distribution of the estate.

Salem Quarterly Court Records, vol. 5, leaf 123.

ESTATE OF RICHARD ALLEN OF HAVERHILL.

"Martha Hubbard y[e] wife of Rich[d]: Hubbard of Salisbury testifieth that being present w[th]: her Brother Rich[d]: Allin imediately before his death in y[e] sumer 78; she then ‖y[e] s[d] Richard being‖ weake in body yet well composed in mind & of perfect understanding, did heare her Brother Richard as his will w[th]: relation to his estate declare, that hee did will and bequeath unto his Sister Mary Hewes the bigger or better part of his whole estate. And that what was left or the other part of his whole estate he did in like manner bequeath to his brethren ‖Joseph & Jeremiah‖ to be equally diuided between them; A chest w[th]: what was in it which then stood at my Bro[th]: Peter Ayers his house in Haverhill he then excepting which at y[e] same time he declared to be his will & did bequeath to Samuel Ayers y[e] Son of his Bro: Peter Ayers at Haverhill: And then I understood that w[t]: he ment of his gift to his Sister Hewes was the better half of his whole estate.

"Mary Hewes & Jeremiah Allin being present wth Martha Hubbard at y[e] same time as above written doe testifie to y[e] truth of all y[t] y[e] s[d]: Martha testifieth unto, & doe both of them testifie that Richard Allin did at that time declare his mind to be that his Sister Hewes should have the better half of his estate after his death." Sworn Oct. 8, 1678, before Nath. Saltonstall, Comis.

Inventory of the estate of Richard Allen, deceased July 8, 1678: Sargant Stevenes and John Esman prised the wering cloues of richard Allen at Salisbury, 7li. 13s.; robart Clemance and daniel Lad junr. prysed forti acares of land being more or les at haverill, 90li.; to acares and halfe of medo more or les, 7li.; three comman rites, 10li. 10s.; daniel Clemence and Abram Clemence prised a ches with somm goodes in it at haverill, 2li.; total, 117li. 3s.

Attested in Hampton court Oct. 8, 1678 by Josepth Allin.

Essex County Probate Files, Docket 493.

Administration upon the estate of Richard Allin was granted Oct. 8, 1678, unto his brother Joseph Allin.

Bond of Joseph and Jerimie Allin for 200li., upon condition that Joseph shall administer according to law upon the estate of his brother Richard, and abide by the order of the court from time to time.

The court ordered the administrator to the estate of Richard Allin, his debts being paid, to make a division of the estate according as is declared in the evidences of Martha Hubbard, Mary Hews and Jerime Allin to be the will of the deceased.

Hampton Quarterly Court Records, vol. 2, leaf 64.

ESTATE OF HUGH SHERRATT OF HAVERHILL.

Concerning the inventory of the estate of Hugh Sheratt, late of Haverhill, deceased, being presented to this court, the court Oct. 8, 1678, ordered that the matter in difference concerning a bed be referred to Salisbury court next, and that the selectmen of Haverhill or their attorney do then appear with all persons concerned, that the estate may be settled according to law.

Hampton Quarterly Court Records, vol. 2, leaf 65.

ESTATE OF SAMUEL GILES OF (HAVERHILL?).

Administration upon the estate of Samuel Giles was granted Oct. 8, 1678, unto Samuell Watts and he to bring in an inventory to the next court.

Hampton Quarterly Court Records, vol. 2, leaf 65.

ESTATE OF ROBERT ROBERTS OF IPSWICH.*

Nicolas Wallis and Simon Stace gave bond Nov. 6, 1678, of 20li., jointly, to pay unto Ephraim Roberds ten pounds at the age of twenty one years, and the security of marsh and bond that Thomas Perrin gave for the payment of the portions of Robert Robberd's children is released.

Ipswich Quarterly Court Records, vol. 5, page 340.

ESTATE OF JOHN SPOFFORD, SR., OF ROWLEY.

"The last will and testament of John spofard senior I Comit my soull into the hands of god that gaue it and my body to the earth to be decently buryed and as for that estate the lord hath giuen I dispose of as followeth after my debts are payd Imprimus as for my dear and louing wife I giue to her the lease of the house and land of Mrs Prudence Cottons also I giue to her all the houshold stuff to be at her dispose excepting the arms and amunition also I giue her two cowes and one calfe also foure shep I giue to her and my son francis to be equally diuidded betwext them and I giue to my wife

* See *ante*, vol. 1, page 422; vol. 2, page 352.

one young horse also to haue *to haue* the use of four acres of land at ye farm during her life furthermore I will that my son francis his portion be at my wifes dispose till he come to the age of twenty one years if she liue so long: for that end that he may be helpfull to her to cary on her husbundry worke Item that which I giue to my son francis is the two young oxen one mare and the cart and all the furniture belonging to husbandry also one yearling calfe these to be at my wifes dispose till he be at the age abouesaid and then these things or the worth of them to be faithfully payd to him also I giue to him the small gun and the Rapier also four acres of land towards great meadow and what may befall by vertue of *of* any towne grantes

"Item I giue to my son John two stears coming thre year old and the long fowling peice and one halfe of the lease of the farm together with twenty pound stocke I formerly gaue him Item I giue to my son Thomas my vilage land and the gray horse and two shep and one spring hog and one two year old heifer and the great musquet Item I giue to my son samuell the other halfe of the lease of the farm and two young stears one that comes 3 year old and one that comes two year old one spring hog with about ten pound stock I haue already giuen him Item I giue to my daughter elizabeth one two year old heifer and two shep Item I giue to hannah one cow one thre year old heifer and two shep Item I giue to my daghter mary one cow and one calfe and two sheep Item I giue to my daughter sarah one cow and one calfe and two sheep also I apoynt my louing wife and my son Thomas to be joynt exequoters of this my last will and my childrens portions to be payd at their mariage or at twenty one years of age and if any dy before, their portions to be diuided amongst the Rest in witnes heirof I set to my hand and seall october 7 1678."

John (his ⬜ mark) spofard(SEAL)

Witness: John Johnson, Philip Nellson.

Written in margin:

"Wheiras here is two cows and calfe and foure shep mentiond the foure shep onely is to be divided betwen her and francis

"This tweenty and ten pound that is giuen to John and Samuell they haue owned that they haue formerly receaved."

Proved in Ipswich court 6 : 9mo : 1678 by the witnesses.

Inventory* of the estate of John Spofforth, Senior, of Rowley, taken Oct. 23, 1678, by John Johnson and Thomas

* Ipswich Deeds, vol. 4, page 222.

Patch: twenty pounds in John Spofforth, Junior, hands and
10li. in Samuell hands, 30li.; money, 10s.; wearinge cloaths,
8li. 12s.; one bed and furniture belonginge to it, 5li.; another
bed, 3li. 5s.; linnen, 2li.; a peece of home made cloath, 4li.;
one fowlinge peece, 2li.; one muskett, 1li. 5s.; in brass, 2li.
12s.; two Iron pots, one skillet, two friinge pans, two saws, 2li.
10s.; other small things, 1li.; tubs, chairs and other woodden
things, 2li. 6s.; A trap, coslet and other things, 1li. 9s.; Books
and other small things, 2li. 10s.; Butter and cheese, 2li.;
seaven Barrills of syder, 4li. 4s.; thre Barrills of small syder,
1li. 4s.; two oxen given in the will to Francis, 11li.; a mare
given him, 2li. 10s.; to him in cart and wheels, 2li. 15s.; to
him in a tumbrell and wheels, 1li.; to him in chains, yoakes,
spanshakkells and one old share and boult, 1li. 6s.; to him a
new plowe, 15s.; to him in axes, hows and other things belonging to husbandry, 1li. 5s.; more in husbandry things to
him in two saws and other tools, 1li.; to him two sheepe, 10s.;
to him four Acres of Lands and thre siths, 4li. 11s.; to him
a small gun and a rapier, 2li. 5s.; wedges given to him and
old Iron, 5s.; two horses, 9li.; four two yeare old cattell and
vantage, 10li.; thre yearlings and vantage and four Calves,
8li. 10s.; fourtene shepe, four swine and five pigs, 11li. 4s.;
the village Land, 30li.; one musquet and Rapier, 10li. 10s.;
cotten wooll, sheepe wooll and other things, 5li. 16s.; Indian
corne and English corne, 15li.; Eightene loade of hay, 13li.
10s.; five cows, 17li. 10s.; total, 228li. 9s. Debts oweing from
the Estate: the rent for the land this yeare, 7li.; to marchant
Wainright, 5li. 14s. 7d.; Sammuell Graves the hatter, 13s.;
John Wainright, 8s. 5d.; Deacon Goodhew, 2s. 8d.; Caleb
Bointon the Smith, 10s.; Edward Hazon, 5s. [6d. *copy*];
George Killborne, [9s. 4d. *copy*]; Doctor Bennit, [32s.;
copy]; Mr. Darby [10s.; total, 16li. 4s. *copy*.]

Attested by Elizabeth Spaford executrix of her husband's
estate.

Essex County Probate Files, Docket 25,994.

ESTATE OF MARK QUILTER OF IPSWICH.*

"Marke Qwillter being sicke and weake of bodye the forth
day of november 1678 made this onkitive will as followith did
giue his Soule into the hands of the Lord Jesus his body he
desired to be desently Buried Item I giue to frances Qwillter
my wiffe my house and Lands and movable goods withinge
the house to her during her naturall Life and also half the

* See also Records and Files of the Quarterly Courts of Essex
County, Mass., vol. 7.

Cattell and halfe the Corne I had groeing this last yeare item
I giue to myhill Cresy ten pounds to willyam Cresy
fiue pounds to mary Cresy fiue pounds; to Richard
Sutten ten pounds and alle the Rest: I giue to my
brother Joseph desiring him to: be my Executor to my last
will and did desire his brother Joseph and Edward Lumis &
Simon Stace: to dispose of what I leue to my wife during
her naturall life after her desese amongst my oine Relashons
as to them ‖that are‖ In most nead as thay thinke meet: and
desired Edward Lumis Senior & Simon Stace to be overseers
of this his will."

[no signature]
Attest Edward (his E mark) Lumis, Simon Stace.
Proved in Ipswich court Nov. 6, 1678, by the witnesses.

Inventory taken Nov. 6, 1678, by Edward (his E mark)
Lumis and Thomas Lovell: his howse and whomestead, 80li.;
a Six acre lott, 20li.; aboute five bushels of Barly, 1li.; aboute
3 score and five Bushels of Endian Corne, 3li. 15s.; the hay at
whome and a Braude, 5li. 10s.; 2 oxen, 10li.; 3 Cowes, 10li.; 1
steere, 4li.; 1 Bull, 2li.; 1 hayfor, 2li. 10s.; 24 sheepe Ewes
and lambs together, 8li.; 5 Swine, 3li.; 1 horse, 2li.; 1 Cart,
plow, Sled, yoke and Chayne, Spanshackles and harrow, 3li.
10s.; Sithes and tackling belonging to them, 10s.; Saddle and
Saddle Cloath, 1li.; muskett, Rest, powder, bulletts, pouch,
Sword, Belt and Pike, 2li. 4s.; Beetle, 4 wedges, 8s.; 4 ould
axes, 6s.; 2 Auger, 2s. 6d.; horse tackling, 6s.; lathing hamer
and other hamer, 4s.; one acre of marsh at the hundereds,
3li.; one acre and halfe of meadoe by Muddy River, 8li.;
Brass and ockamy Spoones, 1li. 17s.; Pueter, 1li. 12s. 6d.;
warming pann, 10s.; lanthorne, 2 tin panes, 1 drinking Cupp,
7s.; Smoothing Iron and heators, 3s. 6d.; Iron pot, 2 Iron
kettles, pot hooks, hanger, fier Slice, 1li. 4s.; Bed, Boulster,
pilloes, pillobeere, sheetes, Ruges, blanketts, Bedsted and Cur-
tines, 7li. 10s.; Chests, box, Small Baskets, 14s.; 3 Coats, 1
pr. ould Briches, shooes, Boots, 2li. 3s.; earthen ware, 2s. 8d;
Chayres, 7s.; one Cart rope, 4s.; one looking glass, 2s.; Bellowes, table, tub, boules, trays, piggin, wheele and Sives, 18s.;
woollen wheele, Cards and Spindle, 6s.; Table Board and
Bookes, 4s.; Blank t, Cloath, woollen yarne, lining yarne,
sheeps woole, Cotten woole, Sackes, mortissing ax, 4li. 18s.;
hoe, shovle and a peece of an Exeltree pin, 3s.; 2 Barrels of
Sider, 1li. 8s.; barreles, tubs, Bottle, Crockes, hopes, tunnel,
1li. 12s.; one Chest with the Clouse in it given to Joseph

Quilter, 10li. 16s. 6d.; Small waring lining, 16s.; debts in Bills due to Mark Quilter, 178li. 12s. 1d.; total, 387li. 15s. 9d. Marke Quilter Indebted about his Buriall and other things aboute 17li.

Attested in Ipswich court 6 : 9m : 1678 by Joseph Quilter, administrator of the estate of his brother, Mark Quilter.

The Court being informed that the widow of Mark Quilter is in a probable way to waste the estate left by him and in obedience to and prosecution of an order of the General Court, May 28, 1679, that one half of the estate after the widow's decease be to the relations of her deceased husband, and that the true intent of the order may not be frustrated, the County Court Mar. 30, 1680, ordered that said Mark's house, land and meadow with commonages belonging thereto which amount to 111li. be security. The widow who hath the use of the whole estate shall give bond for the securing of 82li. 10s., which is the remaining part of what is ordered to the relations, and that she shall not make any strip or waste upon the said lands without due restitution.

Essex County Probate Files, Docket 23,154.

Administration upon the estate of Mark Quilter, intestate, granted Nov. 6, 1678, to his brother Joseph Quilter, he to dispose of the estate according to the mind of his brother, declared in a paper testified unto by Edward Lomas and Simon Stace.

Ipswich Quarterly Court Records, vol. 5, page 339.

Petition of Frances Quilter, widow, and of Robert, *son* of Marke Quilter, late of Ipswich, to the court at Boston, May 28, 1679, that whereas the husband of the petitioner died possessed of an estate valued at 600li., considerable part of which was money, and was chiefly the product of what your petitioner brought to her husband as a portion given her by her father Richard Swan, and also of their hard labour for about twenty three years that they lived together and her husband having died without making a will, and in attempting to when his reason and understanding had failed, was prevented by death, from finishing, and yet, the writing was presented to court, and administration was granted to Joseph Quilter, and he taking the greater part of the estate, the petitioner asks for consideration of her condition that she may have enough for her support.

The reasons of the widow Twilters address to the General Court: 1st. Concerning the will by which Joseph Twilter as administrator did proceed, it was neither the will nor the mind of the deceased, because he was not in a disposing capacity. Witness: Ann Pegey, Dorothy Woodman, Dr. Bennett, Joseph Bennett. 2d. He was prevented by death, before he had said what he would. Witness: Simon Stacy, Ed. Lummax, Tho. Willson, Dorothy Woodman. 3d. In contradiction, he said his wife should have what was in the house and yet said that Joseph should have the chest, etc. Witness: Simon Stacee, Edw. Lummex, Robert Swan, Mary Kimble, 4th. Some things named by him were not put into the will, one of which was, the widow to have her portion to dispose of at her death. Witness: Simon Stacy, Edw. Lommax, Mary Kimble, Robt. Swan. 5th. That one of the witnesses was deaf and could not hear what he said, and the other witness could not well understand. Witness: Lommax, Stacy, Tho. Wilson, An Peggey, Dorothy Woodman, Robt. Swan. The land and homestead was bought with the widow's portion that she had of her father. Witness: Decon Pingrise, Rich. Shatchwell, Mary Shefeld. The money taken out of the thatch was not given to Joseph Twilter, but only to fetch it. Witness: Ann Peggey, Edward Lummax, Simon Stacy, Dorothy Woodman.

Petition of Francis Quilter, widow of Mark Quilter, to the Ipswich court, that they would order the settlement of her husband's estate, and presenting reasons why that which is presented as his will should not be so accepted; and also that the administrator hath not given in a true inventory of the estate, there being 200li. not inventoried, and the whole estate amounting to 600li., your petitioner having but 145li. 16s. 6d. for her use. Robert Swan and James Barnet testified that this petition was presented to the Ipswich court.

A note of some estate of Marke Quilter's that was not in the inventory: Six Akers of marsh, 30li.; Larance Clenton Debter by bill, 7li.; Joseph Quillter sewes for a debt in book a bill of 6li. 10s. of John Wits; Joseph hath a booke of severall Debts that I Doe not know what they are Debts that I knew of that hee had no bill for; Thomas Hart hath payd 20s. but what more I do not know; Thomas Lule, 2li. 4s.; John Brooer, 1li. 2s.; Thomas Gidins, 1li. 10s.; Epheram Felows and Many more that are in debt that my husband did not acquaint me with the sum, besides the money yt Joseph Quilter carried away and which Goodman Lomas told him ought to bee put in the inventory, and also several papers that Joseph Quilter put in his pocket and did not have them inventoried.—Witness, Dority Woodman, Mary Kimball, Frances Quilter.

John Newmarch, Richard Shatswell, aged about fifty two years, Moses Pengry, Sr. of Ipswich, aged sixty seven years, John Edwards, aged about forty years, John Shatswell, aged about twenty six years, Marsy Warner, aged about thirty eight years, David Bennet and Joseph Boynton, aged about thirty years, testified in court June 2, 1679, concerning the settlement of the estate of Mark Quilter.

In the case of Francis Quilter, widow of Marke Quilter of Ipswich, concerning a settlement of the estate of the deceased, the deputies find that said Quilter died intestate and that the pretended will presented to this court ought to be accounted null and void, and that the widow have the use of the whole estate during her life, and at her death one half to be disposed of as she sees good, and the other half to the relations of her husband, to be ordered as the County Court at Ipswich shall see meet. Consented to by the court, June 11, 1679.

Mass. Archives, vol. 16, papers 104-124.

Agreement dated Nov. 11, 1678, between Joseph Quilter, administrator of the estate of Mark Quilter, and Frances Quilter widow of Marke Quilter, both of Ipswich, that Edward Lumis and Simon Stace should arbitrate and end the differences between them, and gave bond of 20li. to stand to what they may agree upon. Witness: Thomas Lovell, Simon Stace. Sworn Sept. 1, 1679.

Joseph Quilter acknowledged the receipt of his part of the goods that were in the house of Marke Quilter, and Frances Quilter owned that she had her part. Signed Nov. 12, 1678. Witness: Edward (his E mark) Lumis, Tho. Lovell. Sworn Sept. 1, 1679, by Thomas Lovel, and Sept. 30, 1679, by Edward Lomase.

Essex County Quarterly Court Files, vol. 31, leaves 116-118.

ESTATE OF SAMUEL SYMONDS OF IPSWICH.*

"I Samuel Symonds of Ipswich in New England gent. being desireous by setting these things in order, now in tyme of my health that I may be the more free (if God please) when death approcheth to leave this world, & to attende the matters of my soule, & the blessed hopes for life to come, doe make, & ordayne this my last will, & testament, in manner, & forme following, viz: First I comend my soule into the

* See also Records and Files of the Quarterly Courts of Essex County, Mass., vol. 7.

handes of Jesus Christ, my ever blessed Saviour, in hope of a
joyfull resurreccon & meeting of my body at the last day,
wch I leave to be decently buried (without any vayne pompe)
and my fun^rall expences, & debts, to be paide & discharged.
Item my will is that all the estate of my deare wife Rebeckah
Symonds, be returned to her in kinde, to her owne pp use,
to have & to hold the same to her, her heires & assignes for
ever: viz: the lande at Salisbury, being six acres of meadow,
now in the tenure of Henry Browne Senr and the seaventy
acres of upland at Salisbury newtowne, now called Amesbury:
Alsoe sixty two pounds twelve shillings of new England mony,
which I received of Mr Clerke Ironmonger of Boston, whereof
there is now in Mr Russells hande, as Treasurer of this country
fifty pounds, and twelve pounds twelve shillings in my owne
handes. Alsoe the cattell, for numb. & kinde, with all other
particulars of estate & howshowld stuff, & goods as they ‖are‖
exprest in a note of particulars* Bearing date the last day of
Novemb. Anno Dom. 1669 under my hande & seale; alsoe what
is impaired, or lost of the very things in the said
note of particulars, are to be made goode, according to her
owne word & Judgment. Item I give to my wife a good breeding mare, or one of ‖my‖ riding horses which she shall chuse.
Item I give to my wife two milch yonge cowes, Beside the
three expressed in the saide note of particulars. Alsoe I give,
or leave to my wife (in steade of Dower) twelve pounds per
anno. to be paid to her, or her assignes, out of my farme called
Argilla, during her naturall life, in two severall payments
viz: Six pounds on the 25th day of March, & the other six
pounds on the last day of Septemb yearly: this payment to be
made in wheat 40^s, mault foure pounds at the price current
amongsts the merchants of Ipswich, and the other six pounds
to be paid in porke, & indian corne, accordingly and to be
paid where she appoynt in Ipswich. Alsoe my will & meaning is that my wife shall have the sole use of part of my dwelling howse at Argilla, viz: The east end of it with free liberty
of ingresse, egresse, & regresse into the said part of my howse,
as alsoe the use in comon of the kitchin or hall, seller, dayry,
backhowse, brewehowse, or other places to the said howse belonging during her naturall life. Alsoe my will is, that wife
shall keepe or have liberty soe to doe, upon my farme during
her naturall life six neate cattell, 10 sheep, & one horse, to be
pvided for, all of the cattell both sumer & winter at the care,

* See Ipswich Deeds, vol. 4, page 259; also Mass. Archives, vol.
16, paper 280.

& charge of my executor : alsoe my wife shall comande attendance of the servants of my executor for her selfe & creatures, & she may as she please require horse meate, & attendants for her frends, that come to vizitt her, from tyme, to tyme, at the charge of my executor. Alsoe my mind is that all the wood she please to spende shall be brought out of my farme to her dore, ready cutt out for her fire at the charge of my executor from yeare to yeare. Alsoe she shall have liberty to make use of my Towne howse in comon with my children, as formerly. Alsoe my wife shall have liberty to keep what foules she please at my farme of Argilla. Alsoe my wife shall have liberty to take what apples, peares, & plumes for her use, & to take what ground she please, for her garden. All which liberties, & priviledges she shall have during her naturall life, with free liberty of water at the well, & elsewhere upon my farme. Provided allwayse, & it is intended that upon my wife her acceptance of these things before menconed, she shall relinquish the agreement made betweene me & her, before marriage, & stande onely to this my last will & testament: moreover my will is, that whatsoever rent debts, & estate is due to me at the tyme of my death by reason of marriag wth my wife Rebeckah, being due by her right in England, shalbe hers, & at her owne disposing. Provided alwayse that if my wife shall chuse rather to leave Argilla, & live elsewhere signifying her desire soe to doe under her hande in writing, during her absence from off Argilla, then she shall have her 12[ll] allowed in stead of Dower made twenty pounds pr anno. to be paid in mann[r] & quality as in her foresaide Dower: for which eight pounds being added to her Dower she shall abate all these pticulars following viz: The keeping of six neat cattell, ten sheep, horse attendance of the servants, requiering of horsemeat for frends, bringing of wood to the dore, useing of ground for gardening, and the use of the howses, except one roome which she shall chuse for for her owne use during her naturall life, with free ingresse, egresse, & regresse. Provided alwayse that when she thinkes meete to returne, & live at Argilla againe, she shall have liberty soe to doe. expressing her minde in writing Things shalbe as aforesaide for her more comfortable being there, and the eight pounds added to her Dower aforesaid is to be abated againe. Moreover I binde my farme called Argilla for the due payment of what is in this my will exprest.

"Item I give to my sonne Harlakinden Symonds all my part of my farme at Lamprele River with the sawing mill there upon erected, with all the utenses, & app[r]tenances there-

unto belonging, with all my part of the howses thereunto ap-
ptayning. And alsoe ‖one halfe of‖ my part of the meadow
& upland lately laid out to me, which the honrd gen^rall Court
latly granted to me, lying beyond the Bounds of Dover: &
mostly out of the Bounds Exiter. And alsoe all my liberty
in the lands of Dover, which I latly purchassed of Robert
Wadley, wth all its singular priviledges & app^rtenances To
have & to hold the p^rmisses to him, ye said Harlakinden during his naturall life, and to the heires of his body [lawfully
begotten, male or female] and for want of such heires, to remayne to the said Harlakinden & his heires forever Item I
give to my sonn Harlakinden my great silver saltseller, and
my best suit of apparrel [both] linen, & woollen. Item I
give to my grandaughter Sarah Symonds all that pcell of
lande lying in Coxall which remaynes of that I had of her
father it being three hundred acres be it more, or lesse. Item
I give to my sonne & daughter Epps one hundred pounds
pmised before marriage to be paid within one yeare, or two,
after *after* my decease, and if she still desire to have the sute
of damask which was the Lady Cheynies, her grandmother,
let her have it upon apprizment. Item whereas I pmised to
give my daughter Martha one hundred pounds, as a porcon
upon marriage with her husband Mr John Denison, it being
desired by the Major & herself soe to doe, according to the
bonde I entered into I do by this my last will confirme the
same. Item I give to my sonne & daughter Emerson four
score pounds, haveing given them 20^{li} at the least soone after
her marriage, to be paid within one yeare, or two, after my decease. Item I give to my daughter Baker, having paid my
sonne Baker Thirty pounds already Three score & ten pounds
to be paid within one or two yeare after my decease. Item
I give to my daughter Dunkin Twenty shillings. Item I give
to my daughter Hale Twenty shillings Item I give to my sonne
Chewte Twenty shillings. Item I give to the Reverend M^r
Cobbett our Pastor Forty shillings. Item I give to my wives
grandaughter one Cow viz: Rebeckah Stacy, because of her
diligent attendance on me. Item I give to my deare wife my
fetherbed & boulster which we usually lye upon. My mind, &
meaning is that the legacies here given to my children shalbe
paid not in mony nor according to mony, but in such pay as
they usually passe, from man to man, which is called the Currant price. And I doe make, & ordayne my sonne William
Symonds, to be my executor of this my last will & testament.
And considering there are many payments to be made, & dis-

charged by my executor, I doe give, & bequeath to him my said sonne ‖William‖ Symonds all my howses & lands in Ipswich, with all my comonages, & priviledges thereunto belonging. Item I give to my sonne William Symonds (having ingaged to him. before the writing of this my will soe much) half of my meadow, & uplands ground, which lieth beyonde my farme at Lamprele River, beyond the Bounds of Dover, & mostly out of the boundes of Exiter, together with all the priviledges, & app᷒tenances thereunto belonging. Also my will, & desire is that my loving frends, Captaine John Appleton, & Levetenant Samuel Appleton, & my sonne John Hale, to be overseers of this my last will, & Testament. My request is that the advice, & counsell of my saide Overseers, be indeavoured ‖to‖ be taken about my executors arduous concernments, that soe love & concorde may continew, & be increased amongst those I leave behinde me. In witnesse that this is my last will & Testament, I have hereunto sett my hande, & Seale the sixteenth day of February Anno Dom 1673."

Samuel Symonds. (SEAL)

Witness: Henry Archer, John Greaves, Edward (his £ mark) Bragg.

Proved in Ipswich court Nov. 6, 1678, by John Graves and Edward Bragg.

"A codicil testementary to the last will & testament of Samuel Symonds gent which will beareth date the sixteenth day of February Anno Dom. 1673: Whereas in that my will I bequeathed to my sonne Harlakinden Symonds all my part of my farme at Lamperele River with the Sawinge Mill thereupon erected with all the utenses & app᷒tenances thereunto belonging, with all my part of the howses thereunto belonging and alsoe one halfe of all my part of the meadow & upland lately laid out to me which the hon᷏ᵈ Gen᷏ᵃll Court lastly granted to me lyinge beyound the Bounds of Dover & mostly beyound the Bounds of Exiter, and alsoe all my liberty in the lands of Dover, which I lately purchassed of Robert Wodley with all its singular priviledges & appurtinances To have & to hold the p᷒misses to him the said Harlakinden during his naturall life and to the heires of his body lawfully begotten, male or female and for want of such heires to remayne to the said Harlakinden & his heires forever: Now therefore I doe hereby disanull & revoke all this my gift to my sonne Harlakinden as for Terme of his naturall life and doe give him all the p᷒misses to have & to hold the same together

with all & singular its appurtenances to him the said Harlakinden Symonds & his heires & assignes forever. Alsoe
whereas I bequeathed in my Will to my sonne Harlakinden
Symonds my fourth part of the sawing mill on Lamprele
River with all its priviledges & appurtenances the pvidence of
God hath soe ordered it that the mill it self hath bene fired
& wholly ruined by the enymy and soe made unprofittable for
the pʳsent : and considering that my sonne William Symonds
who is my executor is in my debt for rent for my said mill
more then the building & finishing the fourth part of the said
mill will cost, my will is that when the rest of the owners doe
rebuild & finish the saide mill that then this my fourth part
soe bequeathed be alsoe carried on to the finishing of the
same at the onely cost & charges of my sonne William
Symonds for the onely use of my sonne Harlakinden
Symonds. Alsoe considering what lands I formerly have
given to my sonne Harlakinden, and that I highly esteeme this
at Lampreele River. My advice & desire now is that he doth
not sell, or putt it away or any part of it unlesse extreame
necessity compell and that he doth what he doth in reference
to the mill &c with very good advice and though I have gained
very little by it, yet if he can waite, & pcure honest dealing
workmen he will finde sufficient recompence for his waiting,
for there is store of timber with that which is added to it
from Dover, & the meadow & the Court gave me up into the
country. In witnesse whereof I have hereunto sett my hande
& seale the thirteenth day of January 1676."

Samuel Symonds (SEAL)

Witness : William Goodhue, sr., William (his vv mark)
Smyth, jr.

Proved in Ipswich court 6 : 9m : 1678 by the witnesses.

"A codicile testementary which is added to the codicile
bearing date the 13ᵗʰ day of February 1676, which refereth to
my last will & Testament dated 16ᵗʰ of February 1673. I
Samuel Symonds being in good health of body & of good
understanding (blessed be God) thought good to add by this
codicile annexed to the former bearing date as above. I say
some consideracons moving me thereunto I give to my sonne
Harlakinden five pounds (in comon pay) per and during his
naturall life, to be paide by my executor : Provided that if in
the life tyme of my sonne Harlakinden my loving brother mʳ
Richard Fitts Symonds decease in the interim and be bounti-
full to my sonne Harlakinden (which I believe he will) and

bequeath to him more then the value of five pounds per anno.; Then my will & minde is, That this five pounds shall cease and that my executor thenceforth be wholly free from the payment thereof. In wittnesse whereof I have hereunto sett my hande & seale. Dated November the eighth day 1677."

Samuel Symonds (SEAL)

Witness: John Wood, John Woodin, Martha Graves.

Proved in Ipswich court 6:9m:1678 by John Wood and John Woodin.

"This third codicill testementary I Samuell Symonds doe now add to the former, which refereth to my will dated 16 day of February 1673. The occasion & reason of my soe doeing is because I mistooke in my date of my last codicill viz. I dated it 13th day of February 1676, which should have bene January 1676. Alsoe whereas I have mentioned in my will 100li to my daughter Martha Its onely named I doe not thereby give it, for I have given my bond for it for that mention is voide. The reason why I make these codicills is to spare writings being longe Dated January 8th 1677."

Samuel Symonds (SEAL)

Witness: Edward (his V mark) Brag, Timothy Brag.

Proved in Ipswich court 6:9m:1678 by the witnesses.

Inventory of the estate of Samuel Symonds, Esq., of Ipswich, who deceased Oct. 13, 1678, besides 236li. set apart by the agreament of Mris. Rebecka Symonds, relict of Samuell Symonds, and Mr. William Symonds, executor, which was her owne proper estate before marriage & by there mutuall agreament to be disposed of by her, and to be returned againe in kind according as the will provides & is to be delivered to her by the executor when the will is proved, taken by Edward Bragg and Robert Kinsman: his wearing apparrell, 49li. 15s. 6d.; A Downe bed & boulster in ye pler Chamber, 5li.; a paire of holland sheets, 2li.; Curtaines & vallents, 4li., 6li.; a plaine Cupbord & Cloth, 10s., mony, 4li., 4li. 10s.; A suite of Damask being very old, 5li.; Couch Chaire, leather Chaire & a stoole, 1li. 10s.; Clock, 5li., a bedsted, 12s., 5li. 12s.; fetherbed, rug, Coverlet, blankets, sheets & bedsted, 7li. 6s.; bed, Covering & blanket, 2li. 6s.; Chest, 3s., a marble morter, 20s., a Cabinet, 25s., 2li. 8s.; household table linnen, 40s., a Chest, 15s., a Coslet, 40s., 4li. 15s.; gridiron, 8s., hopps & Cask, 20s., 1li. 8s.; fetherbed, bolster, rug, sheets, blankets & bedsted, 5li. 10s.; A paire stockins, 4s., birding peice, 15s., 19s.; Cheses of the better sort, 5li. 5s.;

sheepe wooll 125lb., 9li., bookes, 5li., Cotton wooll, 24s., 15li.
4s.; 2 sives, 2s. 6d., flockbed, bolster, beding & bedsted, 4li.,
4li. 2s. 6d.; other beding, 12s., sword & belt, 15s., 1li. 7s.; 4
leather Chaires & a Turky work stoole, 1li. 8s.; paire of andirons & other irons, 1li. 5s.; an inlayd bedsted, 25s., sheeres
& other Iron, 10s., 1li. 15s.; 60li. of Pewter, old & new, 4li.;
a Copper Cann, 14s., skillet, 10s., 1li. 4s.; an Iron Candlestick
& a dredging pott, 1s.; frying pan, 8s., morter & pestle, 10s.,
18s.; beame & scales, 10s., paire of stillyards, 20s., 1li. 10s.;
paire brass scales & weights, 7s.; paire of racks, a tramell,
firepan & tongs, 1li. 8s.; spitt, 5s., Cupbord, 15s., kettle, 5s.,
driping pan, 3s., 1li. 8s.; an Iron pott, 8s., A Copper, 8li., 8li.
8s.; an old malt mill, 10s., cheese press, 10s., 1li.; 3 potts &
greace, 3s., 3 Tubs, 10s., a table frame, 3s., 16s.; handsawe, a
bushell, a winch, 9s., Cowle, 5s., 14s.; in Silver plate, 14li.;
3 tubs of butter with 2 of the tubs, 3li. 19s.; Cheese tub, 2
sives & earthen Panns, 12s.; Tubs, old Iron & Sythes, 6s.;
Churne, 2 tubs, keeler & 3 barrells, 18s.; Tubs, trays, 8s.,
table, forme, Chaire & 2 pailes, 12s., 1li.; musket, 28s., saddle,
bridle & furniture, 30s., 2li. 18s.; horse fetters, 6s., 17
Cheeses, 23s., 1li. 9s.; Apples & Syder, 2li. 8s., 2 sythes, 12s.,
nayles & lumber, 8s., 3li. 8s.; Cheese hoope & bord, 2s., look-
inglas, 5s., an old rug, 8s., 15s.; 1 bush. of oate meale, 9s.,
10 oxen, 55li., 55li. 9s.; 3 steeres 3 yeres old, 9li., 15 Cowes,
60li., 2 bulls, 5li., 74li.; 4 heyfers 3 yeres old, 13li., 5 two
yeare olds, 10li., 23li.; 8 yearelings, 8li., 9 Calves, 6li. 10s.,
14li. 10s.; 47 sheepe, 23li., 20 lambs, 6li. 15s., 2 horses, 8li.,
30li. 3s.; one mare & a yereling Colt, 2li. 10s.; 8 swine 1 yere
& halfe old, 8li., 12 spring shoats, 6li. 10s., 14li. 10s.; 2 Acres
& a halfe of wheate, 4li. 5s.; 11 loads of barly, 36li., 18 tum-
brells of Indian, 30li., 66li.; 50 loads of haye, 37li. 10s., an
axe, 3s., Cart & wheles, 3li. 3s., 40li. 16s.; an old Tumbrell
& wheeles, 20s., 2 plow Irons & a harro, 36s., 2li. 16s.; 4 yoakes
& Irons, 9s., 3 Chaines, 24s., 2 spanshackles, 4s., 1li. 17s.; 2
shovels, 3 howes, forks & rakes, 1li. 3s.; 13 bush. Indian
Corne, 1li. 19s., 9 bush. of oates, 18s., malt, 8s., 3li. 5s.; about
12 Acres of marsh & a little upland nere Wells land, 50li.;
6 acres more of marsh there to the use of Mrs. Martin for her
life, 12li.; Argilla Farme conteining 300 Acres meadow &
upland, 1500li.; howses & barnes & out houses upon the farme,
200li.; 40li. of yarne, 4li., Lamprele river 200 acres upland &
marsh, 130li., 134li.; a part of 1000 Acres at Coxwell beyond
Wells, 6li.; the house & about 2 Acres of land at Towne, 50li.;
Debts due to the estate, 65li.; total, 2534li. 9s. Funerall ex-

pences yet unpaid in mony, 51li.; other debts due from the
estate, 85li.; to make up Mrs. Symonds 236li. out of the estate there is yet unpayd, 37li. 15s.

Attested in Ipswich court Nov. 6, 1678, by Mr. Wm.
Symond, executor of his father's estate.

Essex County Probate Files, Docket 27,134.

Agreement made Apr. 10, 1694, between Harlackinden
Symonds of Ipswich, John Emerson and his wife, Ruth Emerson of Gloucester, Thomas Baker and his wife, Priscilla
Baker of Topsfield, Daniel Epes of Salem, Simond Epes of
Ipswich, and Joseph Jacob and his wife, Susannah Jacob,
Dorothy Symonds, Col. Wade as guardian to Mary and Elizabeth Symonds, all of Ipswich, that Rebekah Symonds of
Ipswich, widow of Samuell Symonds, shall have all things
performed according to the will of said Samuel, and that all
the land sold in Argilla, viz., thirty five acres of upland and
eight acres of meadow sold to Bragg, and eight acres sold to
John Emerson, and four acres to Thomas Baker, towards paying legacies by Richard Martin, Daniel Epes and Harlackinden Symonds, as administrators, shall stand good, and
also marsh of about fourteen or fifteen acres, bounded by
marsh of Simonds Epes, the Rings and Wells, and all the
stock which was upon the farm, together with all utensils;
also what estate William Simonds, deceased, hath disposed of
to his own use which once belonged to the estate of Samuell
Simonds, Esq. and that which was his interest in Lampereele
River shall be accounted valid; that the whole remaining part
of the farm called Argilla shall be equally divided into two
shares, one half to Harlackinden Simonds, John Emerson and
Ruth his wife, Thomas Baker and Priscilla his wife, Daniel
and Simond Epes, Richard Martin's children which he had
by his second wife Martha, and her other children, that is to
say to be divided into six shares whereof Harlackinden Simonds to have two shares during his life; the other half
of the farm equally to Joseph Jacob and his wife Susanna,
Dorothy, Mary and Elizabeth Simonds and their heirs
forever.

Witness: Samuel Appleton, jr., John Newman, Thomas
Low. Acknowledged by Harlackinden Simonds, John Emer-
son, Ruth Emerson, Thomas Baker, Daniel and Symonds
Epes, June 12, 1694, before Barth. Gedney, Judge of the
Probate.

Mr. Nathaniel Martin son of Richard and Martha Martin, chose Mr. John Emerson, sr. of Gloster, to be his guardian, who gave bond, and it was allowed and confirmed, June 13, 1694.

Essex County Probate Records, vol. 303, pp. 233-235.

An agreement same as the above, signed Apr. 10, 1694, by Joseph Jacob, Susanna Jacob, Dorothy Symonds, Thomas Wade as guardian to Mary and Elizabeth Symonds, and acknowledged by them June 12, 1694, before Barth. Gedney, Judge of the Probate.

Essex County Probate Records, vol. 312, pp. 326-328.

Petition of Daniell Epps to the court June 27, 1679, that there may be an inventory taken of the estate of our father Samuell Symonds, as it now is, it being near eight months since his decease, and our brother William Symonds dying intestate about one month since, and little being performed by him, as executor, of the considerations in the will enjoined.

The petition was granted, and Mr. Daniell Epps, sr., ordered to take an inventory of the estate as it now is, and to give in an account to the next court at Ipswich that further order may be taken.

Salem Quarterly Court Records, vol. 5, leaf 129.

An account of particulars was delivered unto Daniel Epps and Harlakenden Symonds by order of Richard Martyn, by the marshall Robert Lord, jr., and read to our sister Symonds, Robert Kinsman and Samuel Ingalls being present in all the aprizements and deliveries, as witnesses, Nov. 12, 1679.

Upon the petition of Mr. Daniell Epps, sr., administration upon the estate of Samuell Symonds, Esq., was granted 25: 9m: 1679, unto Mr. Daniell Epps, Mr. Harlackenden Symonds, and Mrs. Rebecka Symonds relict of said Samuell, and Daniell Epps gave bond of 1000li.

Mr. William Symonds late executor to the will of Mr. Samuell Symonds, Dep. Gov., dying intestate, and making no provision that the legacies of the will might be fulfilled, administration upon the estate was granted June 18, 1680, to Mrs. Rebecka Symonds widow of Samuel, Mr. Harlackinden Symonds, his eldest son, and Mr. Daniell Epps, husband to Elizabeth, his eldest daughter living. They gave bond of 1000li. to administer according to law, the farm Argilla to stand engaged for the payment of the legacies.

Mr. Daniell Epps, sr., administrator, presented an inventory of the estate of Samuell Symonds, Esq., and attested to the truth thereof in Salem court 30 : 9 : 1680. After all debts and legacies are paid, he is to attend the order of the court in the distribution of said estate.

Salem Quarterly Court Records, vol. 6, leaves 6, 13.

Rebecha Symonds, widow of Samuel Symonds, testified Oct. 22, 1679, that before the death of Samuel Symonds, jr., her husband spoke to her about settling his lands upon his son William Symonds, and declared that he desired so to settle them as that the wife of said William, might not claim her thirds in the lands, and purposed to that end to consult Mr. Bellingham, the then Governor, about it.

Petition of Rebecha Symonds, relict of Samuel Symonds, late Dep. Gov., to the court Oct. 23, 1679, that an administrator may be appointed upon the estate of her husband, and that they would choose some of her late husband's own children or son-in-law, if the court see not meet to admit them as heirs, and not leave her and her concerns to the care of strangers.

Petition of Jonathan Wade, May 14, 1681, in behalf of himself and Mary Simonds his daughter, joint administrators to the estate of the late William Simons of Ipswich, showing that by the will of Samuel Simonds, Esq., there was devised unto said William Simonds a farm called Argilla with other estate to enable him to pay certain debts and legacies as expressed in said will, and that he sold much of his own estate in order to pay the legacies, to save said farm Argilla entire. William dying intestate, administration was granted unto his widow Mary Symonds, and your petitioner in her behalf, and they were in possession of that estate as belonging to said William, and according to an order of the General Court in Oct. 1679, said estate was taken from them and put into the hands of other children of Samuel Symonds, and upon another hearing in May, 1680, the order was reversed, and the estate left as before, which however, has never been performed, and they desire the court's consideration of the case and a final issue thereof, that no more uncertainty may remain.

In answer to the motion May 26, 1681, of Jonathan Wade in behalf of Mary Symons his daughter, the court for a final issue of the matter ordered that the estate of the late Samuel Symonds, Esq., and the farm Argilla, be committed into the hands of the administrators to be in behalf of the children and heirs of said Wm. Symonds, they to give bond of 1000li. and the farm Argilla liable to the payment of the legacies and bequests in the will of Samuel Symonds, and to repay unto Harlakenden Symonds and Mr. Epps late administrators to said estate, what they paid of said legacies during their administration.

Petition to the court Oct. 14, 1681, of Harlakinden Symonds, the only surviving son and heir of Samuel Symonds, that there may be a speedy determination and ordering of the estate of his father by the court.

In answer to a petition of Mrs. Rebeca Symonds the court Oct. 25, 1681, ordered that the farm Argilla be put into her hands and of Mr. Harlakanden Symonds and Mr. Eps, who are to improve said farm and receive all profits, that the surplus may be returned to those to whom it doth of right belong.

Mass. Archives, vol. 16, *papers* 170-172, 213, 218, 219, 261, 272.

An account respecting the payments of the debts and legacies in our father's will presented Nov. 29, 1681: The Estate Dr., to our fathers funerall expences, 3li. 9s., in money pd. at Boston, 3li. 9s.; pd. to severall creditors at Ipswich in small debts & small Legacies, 7li. 12s. 9d.; what remained due to our Mother, 20li.; a horse lent my brother Samuell Symonds pr. my fathers order to ride to Boston wch horse dyed at Winnesymmet in yt. Journey 16 or 17 yrs. agoe, 22li.; wt is due to Mr. Martyn pr. legacie & Debt, 105li.; Daniell Epes, sr., 108li.; Mr. Jno. Emerson, 88li.; Mr. Thomas Baker, 58li.; ye farm Argilla being destitute of all kind of grain I Daniell Epes, sr. supplied the same wth pvisions, seed & corn ye first year & 3 loads of hay, 20li. 6s. 9d.; John Woodins service being an apprentice his clothing according to covent. & also 4 months & 2 weeks work, 23li. 10s.; necessary expences for carrying on affairs in provisions & small Legacies to Rebek. Stacy & Debt to our mother out of that wch was the common stock amongst us as per writing may appear, 32li. 2s. 10 1-2d.; to workmen yt I sd. Danll. Epes, sr. procured & payd for at Argilla ye last year, 3li. 7s.; 2 loads of hay pr. sd. Eppes to Argilla this year, 1li. 10s.; Mr. Duncans Legacie, 1li. due to him pr. will of Samll. Symonds, jr. & part of his 8li., 5li. 9s.; Caution money at Genll. Court in 79 & other charges, 15li. 12s. 6d.; Robert Lord for extending ye first execution, 2li.; Marshall Genll. John Green for extending last execution, 2li.; time wch sd Epes spent about ordering affayres in Argilla & paying workmans wages these 2 last years, 10li.; pvisions that sd Epes supplied this year at

Argilla, 2li. 4s. 10d.; fencing, plowing, planting, howing, mowing, hay making & other work, 11li. 1s. 11d.; Interest of the stock, Tackling & for plows, carts & household goods for one year, 12li.; charges expended in money upon the prosecution of the case referring to Argilla occasioned by Mr. Wade since October 1679 as may appear particularly pr. sd. Epes his book of accts., 33li. 4s. 10d.; more charges last Court at Boston, 2li. 19s.; 117 days for myself and horse, 11li. 14s.; my mother Symonds for her mans work she finding all things needfull for him, 16li. and 5 bush. of wheat, 1li. 5s., Oats for her use, 20s., 18li. 5s.; Harlakindin Sym: for him & wife working upon the farm one year in 1679-80 in order to ye performance of our fathers will, 16li.; Mris. Symonds for her mans meat drink clothing & work for this year, 17li.; Harlak. Symonds & wife for this year, 16li.; total, 668li. 10s. 3 1-2d.

Per Contra Cred.: By cattell & goods according to apprizment taken amongst ye four Legatees Nov. 12, 1679, all wch were left upon the farm to supply all necessary occasions in order to ye fulfilling our fathers will & performing duties therein, 132li. 19s. 6d.; Jan. 30, 1679 took into possession 35 acres of land by us Harlak. Symonds & Danll. Epes pr. consent or order from Richard Martyn administrators at 5li. pr. Acre upon comon acct. wch wee sould to Edward Bragg wch land was esteemed the most unprofitable upon the whole farm, wch according to apprizement came to 175li.; sould unto Mr. Jno. Emerson Eight acres of land next adjoyning to sd Braggs at 5li. pr. acre upon comon acct. 40li. as part of his Legacie; sould to Mr. Thomas Baker 4 Acres as aforesd as part of his legacie, 20li.; 8 acres of meadow sould to Edward Bragg wch we sd. administrators took at 5li. pr. acre wth ye rest at comon acct. all things being prised much above their value, 40li.; payd to Mr. Duncan, 3li. 11s.; Cattell, 22li. 10s. according to apprizement to Danll. Epes, sr. as I charged myself Debtr. in ye Inventory but there was 10s. more then they were valued at as apprd. wn I came to speak wth those yt prized them, 22li. 10s.; Swine, 9li. 10s.; severall particulars of ould goods charged to particular accts. of sd. Legatees, 25li. 18s. 3d.; the whole crop in ye year 1680, 48li.; total, 517li. 8s. 9d. Ballance of accts. of the estate is indebted, 151li. 1s. 6 1-2d.

Mr. Harlakinden Symonds recd. of the estate of our father Samuell Symonds, since the judgment of the General Court at Boston Nov. 13, 1679, in severall particulars to the value of 27li. 19s. 2d. which he apprehends may be set off for the trouble and charges he hath been put to about his father's estate since the death of his brother William Symonds.

Attested Dec. 3, 1681, by Daniell Epps, sr., and Har. Symonds.

An account made Nov. 24, 1680, of what Daniell Epps, sr. and Harlakinden Symonds, administrators to the estate of our father Samuel Symonds, find wanting of the said estate as may be seen by comparing the inventory taken by our brother Mr. William Symonds, executor unto ye abovesd estate, about the begining of Nov., 1678, and the inventory taken by us Nov. 10, 1679, together with what Mr. Wade and our sister Mrs. Mary Symonds relict of William Symonds, hath had and disposed of from ye Farm Argilla: in corne of all sorts of the groath of the yeare 1678 about 70li.; payed unto Brother William by Killigreest Ross, 6li.; old corne of all sorts about 3li. 5s.; Land sould of our Fathers at Towne by William to a saddler, 9li.; Land sould unto Mr. Wade of ye same Lott for halfe money & halfe wheat & mault as we understood by our Brother William, 40li.; silver plate, 10li. 10s.; cheeses of ye better sort, 5li. 5s.; Sheeps wooll 75li., 5li. 2s.; Cotten wooll about 10s.; 3 tubs of Butter, with two of ye tubbs, 3li. 19s.; Syder & apples, 2li.; 50 Loades of hay, 37li.; 40li. of yarne, 4li.; cattle wanting about 18li.; Sheep & Lambs about 38, 16li.; a Steere sould to Isaack Fellowes at about 3li. 10s. wch our brother William had ye pay for in corne as wee understood, 3li. 10s.; the Cropp in the yeare 1679 which Mr. Wade & our Sister Symonds had all away and left ye Farme whollie destitute which was upwards of 80li.; total, 314li. 1s. Now besides this acct. our Sister Mary Symonds had all the benifitt of the Increase of all the Cattle & sheep and of the Dayrie, the keepeing what cattle and sheep shee had viz. 16 or 17 Lambs, 5 calves sumer and winter, 3 or 4 cowes the winter, 5 or 6 swine, two horses, the Drawing the wood she made use of with the oxen, wee had of our estate for the payment of our Legaceys which oxen cowes and other creatures & goods wee left upon ye Farme in order to the fulfilling of our Fathers will as to all concerns, the charge & damage of which unto us we judge is upwards of 20li.; This last winter our Sister Mary Symonds kept 4 cowes, 5 yearlings & vantage, two calves, about 13 swine, one mare, about 12 or 13 sheep, all the cattle, mare and two oxen shee kept upon ye Farme this last Sumer aboutt 6 shoats raysed 4 this sumer and most of her wood carried by our team all wch at 25li. Attested by Daniell Epps, sr. and Har. Symonds.

Essex County Quarterly Court Files, vol. 36, leaves 134-136.

ESTATE OF EDWARD VINTON.

Administration upon the estate of Edward Vinton, intestate, was granted 26 : 9 : 1678, to Elias Henly, who brought in an inventory and gave oath to the truth of it.

Salem Quarterly Court Records, vol. 5, leaf 123.

Inventory of the estate of Edward Vinton taken Oct. 17, 1678, by Samuell Ward and John Chin: 1 old shirt and an old paier of whitt drawers, 5s.; 1 paier of whitt drawers, 1 paier of blue ditto, 1 whiett wastkoat, 9s.; 1 Cloth Coat and a sarg paier of briches, 1li. 4s.; 1 paier blue drawers, 18d., 1 sarg wastkoat, 5s., 6s. 6d.; 1 sack, 9d.; 5 neckcloths, 6s.; 1 paier of old boots, 5s., 2 paier of shooes, 5s., 10s.; 1 paier of old stokins, 1s., 1 old Coat, wastkoat and briches, 6s., 7s.; 1 paier of wosted, 1 paier of yarn stokins, 2s.; 1 old rugg, pillow and an old Capcloth Coat, 6s.; 2 parsells of old Liens, 1s. 6d.; 1 bibl and 3 other books, 6s.; hatt, 10s., 1 old hatt and Cap, 3s., 13s.; 1 old Chest, 3s.; mony, 9s., 12s.; total, 5li. 8s. 1-2 kentel refuse fish, 5s. There is due to him from Elias Henlie for boats hier this Last Sumer, 4li. 17s.; the half of a shallop bought of him to pay the next spring, 11li.; for mackrell in John meritts hand, 1li. 8s.

Attested in Salem court 29 : 9 : 1678 by Elias Henly, administrator.

List of debts due by Edward Vincent given in Nov. 25, 1678: to John Forbuish by bill, 4li. 10s. Money and 1li. 6s. money per Accompt; to Richard Knott 15s. money per Accompt; to John Buckley, 2s. 6d., money per Accompt; Christopher Latimor per Accompt, 2li.; Elias Henly, 4li. 14s. 4d. per Accompt; total, 13li. 8s.; more by Geo. Michell, 4s.; Mathew Salter, 2s.

Essex County Quarterly Court Files, vol. 30, leaf 10.

ESTATE OF EDWARD CARLETON OF ROWLEY.

Administration upon the estate of Mr. Edward Carleton, formerly of Rowley, was granted 26 : 9 : 1678, to Jeremiah Jewett and Nehemiah Jewett, and they were ordered to bring in an inventory to the next court held at Salem.

Salem Quarterly Court Records, vol. 5, leaf 123.

The court Apr. 1, 1679, granted liberty to the administrators of the estate of Ed. Carlton to bring in the inventory at the September court next, in respect to his estate in New England.

Essex County Quarterly Court Files, vol. 31, leaf 19.

Petition of Christopher Babbage and Hannah his wife, dated Nov. 27, 1678, that whereas Mr. Edward Carlton sometime of Rowley, left an estate in New England when he went out of the country part of which he sent his son John Carlton, by virtue of a letter of attorney did receive in his behalf, and we conceiveing that there being some of his estate unreceived by his said son, desire that this court would appoint some of our relations, Jeremiah Jewett or Nehemiah Jewet, or both, to be administrators to the estate, that if anything may be preserved it may be forth coming to the children of the said Hanna relict of the said John Carlton, the only heirs to any such estate.

Administration upon the estate of Mr. Edw. Carlton formerly of Rowley, was granted by the Salem court 29 : 9 : 1678, to Jerimiah Juett and Nehemiah Juet, and they were ordered to bring in an inventory to the next Ipswich court.

Essex County Quarterly Court Files, vol. 30, leaf 19.

ESTATE OF JOSEPH PARKER OF ANDOVER.

"In the name of god Amen I Joseph Parker of Andov^r: in the County of Essex in New England Tanner, being at present, of a sound minde, & memory, but considering my great age, and the many infirmities accompaning the same, and not knowing how soon my change may be, have thought it meet and doe accordingly make this my last will and testament, in manner and forme following. Iprimis. I bequeath and resigne my soul into the hands of god that gaue it, and my body to be decently interred in the earth from whence it was taken, in hope & firme assurance of the pardon of all my sins & of a blessed and happy resurrection, through the alone meritt and mediation of my Lord and Sauiour Jesus Christ. And as for my worldly goods and outward estate, whether reall, psonall, or mixt of what kind or nature soeuer they be, my just debts and funerall expences being discharged, I giue and bequeat in manner following. Itm. I giue unto my dear and louing wife Mary Parker my dwelling house and houselott, with all my household stuf, and that parcell of meadow lying upon the mill Riuer, and two of my best Cowes allsoe that land I haue in Shawshin feild, expecting she should out of the same prouide for my son Thomas, my second son, whoe by gods prouidence is disinabled for prouiding for himself, or managing an estate if Committed to him, by reason of his distemper of mind att certaine seasons, I doe allsoe will and require my s^d: son Thomas to be obedient to his mother and any of her sons she shall imploy about her business, in ye managing her husbandrie affaires and this abouesd given to my wife is during her naturall life, and afterwards to returne the one half to my son Stephen, my meaning is the one half of the upland viz ye notherly part of the s^d Lott leauing my household stuf to be disposed of by my wife att her diseas among her children as god shall direct her the easterly part of ye s^d lott, and that land in Shawshin feild, to goe to my son Thomas, and to be improued for his liuelihood either by himself, or those he shall make choise of for his Guardian but not to be alienated by him, but after his decease prouided he dies without issue, then to returne to my Son Samuell, my dwelling house hortyard barne and ground about ye mill, I giue to my son Josep after his mothers decease, and allsoe ye abouesd meadow upon ye mill riuer.

"It. I giue unto my son Joseph, my grist mill with all ye priuiledges belonging to it, allsoe fourty acres of upland lying on ye south easterly end of ye great pond, with ten acres of swamp land adjoyning to it, alsoe, all my interest in a meadow called shoe meadow, and another parcell of meadow, called ye bounds meadow, allsoe threescore acres of upland which I haue yett to take up. It. I giue to my Son Stephen my last diuison of upland and meadowe, ye upland containing eight score acres, threscore ‖ acres ‖ of ye sd diuision of upland, is that aboue mentioned, giuen to my son Joseph this sd diuision of meadow being ten acres, allsoe two acres of upland lying by Hauerill High way being part of my swamp diuision. It. I giue to my son Samuell all my interest in a meadow commonly Called millers meadow and allsoe ten pounds to be payd by my son Joseph fiue pounds, and by my son Stephen fiue pounds within a, twelue month after my decease, only I doe reserue two acres of ye abouesd millers meadow for my son Joseph to be taken on which side he likes best. It. I giue to my three daughters Sarah Mary and Ruth ten pounds apeice to be payd by my Executo^rs within four years after my decease It I giue to my dear wife all my estate in old England, that at Rumsey, and alsoe any legacies that is left me by any freind there, to be disposed of after her decease among her children, as god shall direct her. It. I doe appoint my son Joseph to be my sole Executor and to pay ye legacies aboue exprest, and any of my estate which I may happily haue forgott either debts or otherwise, I giue to my sd Executor. It. I doe alsoe appoint for my ouerseers my louing Brother Nathan Parker, and my louing freind Left: John Osgood alsoe my louing freinds

Henery Ingalls and Ensigne Thomas Chandler. Hereby makeing uoid all former wills or writings of this nature, and In
wittness that this is my last will and testament I sett to my
hand and seal this fourth day of Nouemb^r: sixteen hundred
seuenty and eight."

Joseph (his ♀ mark) Parker (SEAL)
Witness: Dudley Bradstreet, Thomas Chandler.
Proved 26 : 9 : 1678 by the witnesses.

Inventory of the estate of Joseph Parker taken Nov. 18,
1678, by John Osgood, Henry Ingalls and Nathan Parker:
the beds & the apurtainances belonging to them, 12li.; the
househould vesells, keetels, pootts peuter & woode, 3li.; books,
1li. 10s.; spining wheeles, tow com & chairs, 15s.; provision
in the house, 1li. 18s.; corne in the house & barne, 20li.; fouer
catell, 1 cow, 2 thre yeare oldes, on yearlinge, 12li.; swine,
6li.; the corne mill, 20li.; dwelling house & barne, orchard &
home lott, 68li.; 12 aker of unimproved land about home,
12li.; 6 aker of land in Shasheen Feilde, 12li.; 50 akers of
land by the ponde, 60li.; 140 aker of land by the seder
swampe, 70li.; 60 akers to bee taken up off the towne, 30li.;
6 aker of medow on the mill River, 24li.; 8 akers of medow in
the miller medow, 32li.; 9 akers of medow att the Ceder
swampe, 27li.; 6 akers at show medow, 24li.; cartes, plows,
plow Irons, chains, yocks & other taklings, 4li.; carpenders
tools, axes, wedges, betell Ringe, sith, how, six alls, 3li.;
armes, gons, swords, 2li. 10s.; a Cow hide, 12s. 6d.; an estat
in Inglande, 100li.; total, 546li. 5s. 6d.
Attested in Salem court 26 : 9m : 1678, by Joseph Parker.
Essex County Quarterly Court Files, vol. 30, leaves 24, 25.

Administration was granted Dec. 6, 1708, to Joseph Parker
of Andover, on a certain parcel of land given by his grandfather Joseph Parker, late of Andover, deceased, in his last will
to his son Samuell, after the death of his son Thomas, Samuell dying before Thomas and leaving no issue it returned to
the donor and became an intestate part of the estate. The
said Joseph Parker gave bond to administer according to
law.
Essex County Probate Records, vol. 310, page 55.

Ruth Giul of Haverhill, having some right to some part of
the estate of her brother Thomas Parker, deceased, which
land lyeth in Andover, in which town the said Thomas Parker
lived, for the consideration of 3li. paid to her by Joseph
Parker, jr., joiner, of Andover, quitclaims all right she might
have in the lands of her brother, namely the land called the

mill lot and the land in Shawshin field or any other of his estate.

Signed and sealed Nov. 17, 1708. Witness: Matthew Herriman, James Ford.

Inventory of undisposed legacies of Joseph Parker, deceased, taken Dec. 3, 1708, by John Osgood, Jeames Bridges and Samuel Huchinson: a parsel of Land Laying in the hom Lot of about three acres and three quarters, 14li.; a parsel of land laying in Shawshin field of about six acres, 12li.; which is to be understood at fiften peny wait. Sworn by committee appointed, represent ye estate not capable.

March 22, 1708, for a leter of gardenshipp, 8s.; a jorney of myself and two men; November 13, 1708, for funierl charges, 1li. 8s.; to the docktor, 18s.; November 20, 1708, for myself and bondsman our jorny for a leter of administration, 7s. 6d.; for a apriesers three men one day.

Joseph Parker's account of administration on the estate of Joseph Parker, grandfather, of Andover, deceased, brought in Dec. 6, 1708: the said estate Cred. per real estate, 26li.; the said estate Dr. to S^r. Saml. Osgood, 1li. 10s.; to guardianshipp, 6s.; travel with bondsman, 9s.; letter of administration, 7s. 6d.; travell to obtain power, 5s.; & expences, 18s.; appriseing ye estate, comission to prise sd. estate, 3s.; recd, inventory & oath, 2s. 6d.; recording ye account, 3s.; allowing ye account, 5s.; swering ye committee, 1s.; conveyance of said estate & record therof, 4s.; 3 bonds, 6s.; a Quietus, 4s.; funerall charges, 1li. 8s.; allowed ye administrator, 10s.; expences on ye committee, 8s.; Divideing said estate, 5s.; total, 8li. 9s.

To Steph. Parker, Mary Parker alias Fry, Sarah Parker alias Sabens, Joseph Parker and Ruth Parker alias Gile, 3li. 13s. 9d. each.

Agreement Dec. 6, 1708, between Joseph Parker and Timothy Johnson, that "ye fence as it now stands from Haverhill highway to ye Mill River shall be the divisionall line strait from ye begining of ye fence straite pointing to ye Mill River ye Johnson paying twenty shillings to said Parker."

Witness: John Ames, Jeames Bridges.

Essex County Probate Files, Docket 20,520.

ESTATE OF MRS. ANN CONDY OF MARBLEHEAD.

"This being the last will and testemeant of Ann Condy deseing being in her right sencis hath giuen to her sister willmet

Red on great Iron pot more giuen to Christian Hooper on
puter platter and on ‖ puter ‖ plater to her daughter Elisebeth Hooper more giuen to Elisebeth Tainner twenty shillings
in mony more twenty shillings in mony to her daughter Elisebeth tainner more three puter platers and all her waring close
more ten shillings to Elias tainner more ten shillings to Jo-
sias Tainner more ten shillings in mony to ann tainner more
ten shillings in mony to Joanna tainner more ten shillings
in mony to thomas tainer to be payd when Christopher hox-
abel pays his last payment concering the house hee bought
more giuen to John Hooper ten shillings in mony more to his
son John hooper a puter cup to Elisebeth tainer a brase scellet
and a candel stick and a puter cup and a becer to John hooper
children a puter poringer a pice more two poringer to Sarah
pick and mathew salter is to fulfill these things and pay the
depts and to Receue what is du I giue him full power and
take all what is left as witness my hand this 9th 9th of october:
78."

                        Ann (her ♀ mark) Condy.
Witness: Elisebeth (her E mark) Briors, Sarah (her ♇
mark) Pick.
Proved in Salem court 29:9:1678 by John Hooper and
Elizabeth Briers.

Account of Samuell Condes depts: to Mr. Jon. Swett at
Boston, 1li. 12s. 9d.; Docktar Wells at Salem, 1li. 10s.; Rich-
ard Knott of Marbld, 15s.; John gathell of marblehd, 10s.;
John Furbush of Marblehd, 10s.; Mr. Roods of Lin, 6s.; John
Waldron of Marblehd, 4s.; wt was layd out in buriing good.
Conde, 2li. 3s. 4d.; total, 7li. 11s. 1d. To Peter bouker of
Epsh., 15s.

Inventory of the estate of Ann Condy, widow, taken by
John Legg and Thaddeus Riddan: a dwelling house and two
thirds of a garden with the priviledge belonging thereto, 25li.;
one small outhouse, 12li.; A Barne with some hay & 2 old
barels in it, 5li.; One cowe, 3li., 3 bus. Indian & 1-2 bus. Rye,
7s., 3li. 7s.; a silkegrass bed & 2 small old Ruggs, 16s.; one
pr. blanketts, 7s., 2 pr. old sheets, 6s., 13s.; one bolster & case
with 3 silkgrass pillowes, 12s.; three curtains & one vallant
old, 4s.; two old bedsteads, 7s., 1 table & forme, 7s. 6d., 14s.
6d.; two iron potts & one iron ketle, 1li.; one trammell, 2 pr.
pothooks, one spit & 2 old Lamps, 7s. 6d.; one old boxe & one
old chest, 5s.; one chest & a warming pan, 12s.; one old coat
& 1 pr. breeches, 7s.; Three peuter dishes & 5 porringers, 10s.;

dripping pan, one quart pot. one pt. pot & 1 cup all old, 5s.; six earthen dishes & 2 milke pans, 2s. 6d.; brass skillett, one pitcher, 2 earthen pots, 4s. 6d.; small old table and old chaire, 4s.; A sowe in the woods, 9s.; 4 gall. molasses, 4s. 6d., 1 axe & 2 old pails, 4s., 8s. 6d.; 1 cord wood, 7s., 1 parcell cabbage sold for 5s., 12s.; A barrell & 1 old leather cushion, 3s. 6d., 3s. 6d.; fire shovell and tongs & beetle, 2s. 6d., 1 pr. bellows & fleshfork, 2s. 6d., 5s.; two old pewter dishes, 2s., 1 old spinning wheel, 2s. 6d., 4s. 6d.; one wescoat sold to Sarah Trevy, 8s.; total, 54li. 14s. 6d.

Attested in Salem court 29 : 9 : 1678 by Mathew Salter.
Essex County Quarterly Court Files, vol. 30, leaves 32, 33.

Mathew Salter having renounced his executorship of the estate left by Ann Condy, the court 26 : 9 : 1678, granted administration to the said Mathew Salter, Samuell Read, Thomas Tainer and John Hooper, upon the said estate according to the inventory, together with the will, being proved and allowed.
Salem Quarterly Court Records, vol. 5, leaf 124.

GUARDIANSHIP OF JOSEPH KIMBALL.

Joseph Kimball came into court 26 : 9m : 1678, and chose Walter Feirefeild to be his guardian, and it was allowed.
Salem Quarterly Court Records, vol. 5, leaf 124.

ESTATE OF JOHN BRIMBLECOM OF MARBLEHEAD.

"The Last Will and Testament of John Brimbellcom Being in his perfecte memory the 11th maye 1678 Imp^rmis That first I Bequeue my Body to the Dust and my spiritte To god that gaue it as for my Estat firist I order That after the Charge of my fennerall (is paide) that all my Deptes Bee fully satisfied By my Excetors : secondly my will is that what Estate is Lefte After my Deptes is paide that Tabitha my wife shall fully and wholly Inioye it for the Terme of Her Naturall Life Thirdly my will is That after The death of my sd : wife That my soon Phillipe Brimbelcom and his Children after Him shall Inioye the full and whole Estat that shee shall Leaue to saye my wife what is Leafte of what I Leaue her fourthly my will is That my Exccecetors out of what Estat I Leaue shall pave to my too Daughters Richard Holman and mary Tucker as a Legaci Twenty shilings a peece. fiftly my will is that my wife Tabitha and my soonn Philipe bee jointe Excecetrex and Exceceter of my whole Estate In Being By

them To bee managed and Emproued as aboue further my
will is That my Trusty frinds John Codner and John Leg
Bee my ouerseeres of my Excetors for the Emprouement of
The Estate according to this my will and Testament my will
ffurther is that if my s^d : sunn Die without Isshue that what
is Lefte of my Estate after the death of my sd : wife and
sonne and his Child or what Childrin he maye haue that it
shall bee Equally diuided Betwext my too Daughters Richard
and mary."

John (his I B mark) Brimbellcom.

Witness : John (his T C mark) Codner, John Legg.
Proved in Salem court 29 : 9 : 1678 by the witnesses.

Inventory of the estate taken Nov. 12, 1678, by William
Nick and Thaddeus Riddan: one halfe of a shallop & connue
& what else belongs to ye half & boat, 15li.; one dweling
house, out house and land with ye priviledge belonging to it,
40li.; one halfe of a servants time, 5li.; one bed filled with
silke grasse with Rugg, Blankets, bedsteed & 2 pr. ould
sheetes, 4li.; 3 Chests ould ones & ould barrells, 8s.; one muskett, one houldbert, one Cutles, one swoard & Belt, 2li.; 4
potts & a small Kittle, 1li. 10s.; two pair pott hangers, two
pair pott hooks, one fire shoovell & tonges, gridiron, &c., 10s.;
pewter dishes, cupes & warming pann, 15s.; Table & forme &
a spitt, 10s.; one frying pan & two ould Axes, 5s.; three ould
Chaires, two pailes, washing tubs, wooden Trays & a dresser,
6s.; wearing apparrell in all, 3li.; one spining wheele, 2s.;
several lean swine, halfe a cow & Calfe, 3s.; total, 76li. 6s.
Signed by Thaddeus Riddan and Christopher Necke.

Attested in Salem court 29 : 9 : 1678 by Tabitha Brimbelcom, one of the executors.

Essex County Quarterly Court Files, vol. 30, leaves 26, 27.

ESTATE OF EDWARD BODIE OF MARBLEHEAD.

Administration upon the estate of Edward Bodie was
granted 29 : 9 : 1678, to Erasmuss James who brought in an
inventory. The creditors to be paid by proportion as far as
the estate will go, and Hilliard Veren, cler. is to proportion
the same accordingly.

Inventory of the estate of Edward Bodie, lately deceased,
taken Nov. 28, 1678, by John (his R mark) Roads, sr., John
Roades and Erasomus James: 1 carsy cotte & Brishes, 15s.;
1 capt cotte & Brishes, 12s.; 1 hatte, 2s. 6d.; 2 ould pare of
drayers and one wascotte, 5s.; 4 kintalls of refus code, 2li.;

1 barill of mackrell, 16s.; total, 4li. 10s. 6d. The dettes of the deceased: to William gover for his buriall & chargdes opon him in his sicknes, 3li. 9s. 8d.; William gover for seaverall months dyett he hade, 5li.; William govers wife for washin of him fiften monts, 15s.; William gover for 4 codlines and two code leads, 1li.; for mony the said gover lent him, 3s.; Richard Knott, dockter, 13s.; total, 11li. 8d.

Attested in Salem court 29:9:1678 by Erasmuss James.

Essex County Quarterly Court Files, vol. 30, leaf 28.

ESTATE OF ALEXANDER BRAVENDER OF WENHAM.

Administration upon the estate of Alexander Bravender was granted 29:9:1678 unto Charles Gott.

Inventory of the estate of Alexander Bravender of Wenham, deceased Oct. 22, 1678, taken Nov. 19, 1678, by Thos. Fiske and John Batcheler: Beding, 1li. 3s. 6d.; two old skilits & working tools, 8s.; wearing cloathes, 3li. 9s.; three old barles, 2s. 6d.; total, 5li. 3s. The estate debtor to Charles Gott: to ten weeks howse room & nursing in his sicknes before he dyed, 3li. 10s.; his funerall, 1li. 10s.; total, 5li. Out of his estate above mentioned he gave to our pastor, 5s.; to some others of his friends several things viz. one dubblet to John Fiske; to Robert Mackclafflin an old stuff Cloake; to Alexander Tomson a paire of stockings; to Jno. Ross a shirt; to Alexander Maxey a Jacket & a paire of Britches, being all prized at 19s.

Attested in Salem court 29:9:1678 by Charles Gott.

Essex County Quarterly Court Files, vol. 30, leaf 29.

ESTATE OF WILLIAM ROBINSON OF SALEM.

"The Last Will & Testament of me William Robbinson of Salem in New England made the nineth day of ffebruary in y⁹ yeare of oʳ Lord one Thousand Six hundred & Seventy Six: 77 being then in good health & of sound & perfect memory blessed be God, but knoweing yᵉ uncertainty of mans life here upon yⁿ earth doe now for ye Settlement & disposeall of what estate ye Lord in mercy hath betrusted me withall declare this to be my mind & will after my decease in manner as ffolloweth vzt Imprimis I giue and Bequeath unto my Son Joseph Robbinson who is now in the Barbados and whom as I heare, the Lord hath blessed with a liberall competency for his owtward Subsistance, & hath no child & his Brothers here haue each of them a greate charge, and want more help then he

doth, upon wch consideration, although he be my Eldest Son,
yet I giue & bequeath unto him but Twelue pounds in Currant
pay of ye Country; & that not to be paid him unless he comes
in his owne person to demand it of ye Executors to my Estate Item I giue & bequeath unto my daughter Sarah newbury
ffiue pounds in Courrant pay of the Country to be paid to her
owne Self and to noe other, and for her owne peculiar use and
benefitt & disposeall.

"Item I giue to my Grand Child Tymothy Robbinson ye
sum of fforty Shillings in Currant pay of ye Country to be
paid him at ye one & Twentieth year: of his Age if it please
god that he liues so long And ffor Excutors to my Estate wch I
may Leaue at my decease, I doe now nominate & appoint, my
Two Sonns Samuel & John Robbinson; Willing them to see
this my Last will performed, & also to defray the charge of my
ffunerall, and pay all just debts wch I may owe; and then for
all the Remainder of my Estate Left, both ffor howseing,
Lands in ye Towneship of Salem, goods, chattles moveables
& unmoveables, and all dues unto me belonging upon my just
accompt whatsoever I giue and bequeath unto them my Said
Two Sonns in equall shares to be devided between them & ffor
there onely & propper use for ever, and for theire disposeall
as they may see good for ye benefitt of themselves & theire
children after them. In witness whereof I hereunto Sett my
hand & Seale ye day & yeare abouesaid."

      William (his R mark) Robbinson (SEAL)
  Witness: Stephen Daniell, Richard Croad.

Proved in Salem court 29:9:1678 by Richard Croad before
Maj. Gen. Daniell Denison and Mr. John Woodbridge.

Inventory of the estate of William Robbinson of Salem,
lately deceased, as it was shown to us by his sonns, Samuell
and John Robbinson, and taken Nov. 22, 1678, by Samuel
Gardner, sr. and John Massey: an old Dwelling house and
Barne with about Six Acars of Land and orchating uppon
which the house stands, 40li.; another small Dwelling house
with a barne and one quatar of an Acar of Land uppon which
it stand and about Thre Acars of Land Nere adjoyning to it,
30li.; one Ten Acar Lott in the North ffeld, 35li.; about a
quatar of an Acar of Moing ground, 5li.

  Attested 29:9:1678 by Samuell and John Robinson.
Essex County Quarterly Court Files, vol. 30, leaves 30, 31.

ESTATE OF WILLIAM SNELLING OF SALEM.

Administration upon the estate of Wm. Snelling, intestate,
granted 1:12m:1678, by Maj. Daniell Googin and Maj. Wil-

liam Hathorne, Esq., to Sarah, the relict of Wm. Snelling, now the wife of Samuell Clark, and ordered that she with Mr. Edmond Batter bring in an inventory to the next court at Salem, that so the estate may be settled according to law.

Essex County Quarterly Court Files, vol. 30, leaf 32.

ESTATE OF CAPT. WILLIAM HATHORNE OF SALEM.

Administration upon the estate of Capt. William Hathorne granted Feb. 4, 1678, in Salem, by Daniell Gookin, sr., and Maj. Wm. Hathorne, to Sarah Hawthorne relict of Capt. William Hathorne in behalf of herself and creditors.

Essex County Quarterly Court Files, vol. 30, leaf 32.

Inventory of the estate of Capt. William Harthorne, taken by Thomas Stace and Resolved White: A Bead and Beading belonging to itt, 6li. 6s.; Curtings, 1li. 10s., and Cushings, 15s., 2li. 5s.; Tabell, Stulls, carpit and Chayers, 1li. 18s.; 2 Chests, 2 littell Trunks & 3 Boxes, 2li. 4s.; plate, 3li. 10s., A parsell of puter & Brasse, 4li., 7li. 10s.; A parsell of Arthing waer, 1li. 10s.; A parsell of Iron waer, 5li. 10s.; Books and Lining and some other things, 19li.; Cash, 4li. 6s., 204 gall. of Rume 20d. per gall., 21li. 6s.; molossus, 4li., a pece of salt mash, 7li., 11li.; A Cowe, 2li. 5s., A maer, 20s., 3li. 5s.; A Case of Bottils, morter & pesell, 14s.; Beadstead and some small Caske, 12s.; Shuger, 12s., parsell of woden waer with 2 whells, 1li. 17s.; Debts due to ye Estate 12li. 9s. 11d.; allsoe due from the Country in mony 5li.; total, 102li. 8s. 11d. Allsoe halfe of a farme lyeing about Groaton not yet pryzed. Debts due from the Estate, 59li. 8s. 5d.

Attested in Salem court 27:4:1679 by Sarah Harthorne, the relict and administratrix.

Essex County Quarterly Court Files, vol. 31, leaf 93.

Sarah the relict and administratrix of Capt. Wm. Hathorn, presented an inventory of her husband's estate, and the whole estate when the debts are .paid, shall be to the sole use of the said Sarah.

Salem Quarterly Court Records, vol. 5, leaf 131.

ESTATE OF JOHN BARTLETT, SR., OF NEWBURY.

"Theise p^rsents wittnesseth y^t I John Bearttlett, senior of Newbury in New England being verry weake in body but in perfct sence memory and understanding: doe make this my last will & testam^t: Inprimis I comit and comend my soule into ye hands of my faithfull Creator, y^t gaue it, and my body after death to bee decently Layd in ye graue. Item I giue unto my well beloued sonne John Barttlett all my house, housinge and lands, now lijng and being in the bounds of ye towne of Newbury aforesd. both uppland and meadoe to him and his heires for euer, and if my sd sonne Jn^n: die wthout heire or heires lawfully begotten of his owne body then my will is that after the decease of my sonne, John my lands both uppland and Meadoe bee disposed of as followeth : Vidz : two Acrees of upland lijng and being in ye feild going downe Ordwaies Lane I giue unto my Kinsman Benaiah Tittcom : and ye two Acrees I now liue uppon I giue unto my Kinsman Christopher Barttlett : And my foure Acrees at my barne Lott I giue unto Thomas Barttlett and John Bartlett my Brother Richards two sonnes to bee equally deuided betwixt them, as Conscerning my meadoe ground my will is y^t my six Acree Lott bounded by Little pine Iland Creeke I giue and bequeath after ye decease of my sonne forenamed dijng as aforesd unto ye ministry ‖ of Newbury ‖ to be continued to ye ministry for euer, and as Conscerning ye rest of my meadoe, my plumb bush Lott I giue to my sonne Jno : to be soly at his dispose to doe with it as hee seeth good, the remainder of my meadoe in Newbury to bee equally deuided betweene my foure Kinsmen before mentioned. As Conscerning my other estate goods and Chattells which I am now posessed with all, to geather wth all my Just debts due to me ye sd John Barttlett by booke bills or bonds my Legall and honnest debts being payd out of ye sd estate ye remainder I will and bequeath unto my beloued sonne paijng unto my Kins woomen my two Brothers dafters and my Sisters dafters twenty Shillings a peice to bee pd in one yeare after my decease. ffurthermore I make my sonne John ye sole Executor to this my Last will and testaint, In wittnes where of I haue hereunto sett my hand ye 31th day of January 1678 :"

John Bartlett.

Witness : Thomas (his A mark) Tittcom, William Chandler.

Thomas Titcomb witnessed on oath Mar. 24, 1678-79, that he saw John Bartlett subscribe the within written paper as his last will, and saw him deliver it to Wm. Chandler desiring him to keep it for him.

Proved in Ipswich court Apr. 1, 1679, by Wm. Chandler.

Inventory of the estate of John Barttlett of Newbury, deceased Feb. 5, 1678, taken Mar. 5, 1678-79, by Stephen Grenlefe, Sr. and William Chandler : eight Acrees of errable land togeather wth ye Orchard, house, shopp and barne, 150li. ;

twenty Acrees of Marsh meadoe ground, 80li.; Neate Cattle, sheepe, horse kind and swine, 50li. 5s.; wearing apparrell, 15li. 17s.; Bedds, bedding, brass and peuter and Iron potts, 57li. 1s.; 2 gunns & sword, 2li. 10s.; Cotten yarne and hemp, 1li.; Sadle and pillion, Linen and Cotten whele & hopps, 3li. 8s.; Cart & wheeles and necessaries for husbandry worke, 5li. 16s.; Indego and pouder, tobacco and lumber about ye house, 3li. 16s.; Porke, beefe, bacon, butter, Lard & Sider, 16li. 5s.; wheate, Barley, rie, Indean and Oates, 5li. 12s.; Leather, Raw hides and working geare, 102li. 10s.; part in two vessells, booke debts, bills and bonds, 101li.; total, 595li.

Attested in Ipswich court Apr. 1, 1679, by John Barlet executor of the estate of his father.

Bond of John Bartlett of Newbury, tanner, and Benjamin Cooker of Newbury, in behalf of his brother Hathorn Cooker of the same town, of 50li., dated May 18, 1709. Whereas John Barlett, Sr. late of Newbury, in his will gave unto his two nephews Thomas and John Barlett a legacy in land, to be divided equally between them, and the said Thomas being dead leaving only a female issue and John claiming the whole as survivor, and the daughter of said Thomas claiming as representative of her father the one half of said legacy, we haue mutually made choice of Col. Jno. Appleton, Maj. Stephen Sewall and Daniell Rogers or any two of them to giue their interpretation of that paragraph in ·the will and whatsoever they shall delare as their opinion in the matter shall be as a final issue thereof and we will abide by the said declaration and the party that doth not comply to pay the 50li. to the other. Witness: John Harris, John March, Junr.

Copy of record attested May 11, 1709, by Richard Brown Town clerk of Newbury: "Thomas Bartlet y[e] Son of Richard Bartlet was born Sept: 7th Anno 1650.

"Tirza y[e] daughter of Thomas Barlet and Tirza his wife born March 29th Anno 1689.

"Hawthorn Coker & Tirza Bartlet were married Decemb[r] 17th 1708."

Essex County Probate Files, Docket 1,887.

ESTATE OF MRS. MARY ROGERS OF ROWLEY.

"The Last will and Testament of m[rs] Mary Rogers of Rowley widdow of m[r] Ezekiell Rogers Pastour sometimes of the Church of christ of Rowley. I m[rs] Mary Rogers of Rowley beinge weake of body but perfect in understandinge and mem-

ory, not knowinge how soone this earthly tabernackle of mine
may be dissolued doe make this my last will and testament in
manner and forme as followeth, Inprimis I doe giue my soule
into the hands of god who gaue me it, with a full hope of soule
and body to meete againe at the resurrection from the dead.
allso my will is that all my honest and dew debts be payed,
and the rest of my estate I dispose of as followeth, my thre
cows I doe giue to Ann Nellson of Rowley my Cousin allso
all my sheepe and allso all my bees, (allso my bed and all the
furniture belonginge to it,) allso all my cloaths linnen and
wollen allso my trunke ,and my cubbord. and all my pewter,
allso my siluer tanker, and siluer spoone. allso a littell bell
mettell pot. Allso one littell brass pan, and a lookinge glas,
and my warminge pan. Allso four books and two bibells allso
as a small token of my loue I doe giue ‖ ten ‖ Shillings to
mr Thomas Cobbet pastor of the Church of christ of Ipswitch.
allso I doe giue unto my Cousen Ann Nellson my two chairs
and one buffet stoole. and fiue cushens. allso my heckell, allso
what is dewe to me upon accounts of Rents from Thom [as]
Lambert about ten pounds as may apeare by Accounts my will
is that it [be] payed to my Cousen Thomas Nellson, moreouer
my will is that as [con]cerninge the fiftene pounds that is
dewe to me for my husband mr Ezekiell Rogers his wages as
may apeare by the Bill of the ministry rate entred in the
Church booke the whole rate within a small matter beinge
laide but neuer as yet payed to me fiue pounds of this fiftene
I perceiued was deliuered to mr Phillips and he stands
charged with it in the church booke, and I haue longe Since
made my complaint to him about it and his answer to me was
that he would not a had it, but as yet I haue not receiued it
nor any part else of the fiftene pounds and therfore I would
earnestly desire mr Sammuell Phillips and Deacon Jewet that
they would not ronge me in this particular least it be a greefe
to them at the apearinge of Jesus christ, and that this fiftene
pounds care be taken that Thomas Lambert may haue the
same. and I doe make Phillip Nellson of Rowley Exequitor of
this my last will and testament desiringe him that my will in
all these particulars may be performed and to take care that
euery one according to my will may haue there legacies payed
in witnes whereof I haue hereunto set my hand and Seale the
22 day of July 1678."

                    Mary (her I I mark) Rogers (SEAL)
Witness: Jeremiah Shepard, Elizabeth Nellson.
Proved in Ipswich court Apr. 1, 1679, by the witnesses, and

Mr. Phillip Nellson renouncing his executorship, the court appointed Mr. Thomas Nellson administrator.

Inventory of the estate of Mrs. Mary Rogers, deceased Feb. 11, 1678, taken Feb. 14, 1678, by Sammuell Plats, Sr., and Edward Hassen, Sr.: silver Tanker, 3li.; silver spoone, 6s.; one Gowne, 1li. 10s.; one sarge petticoate, 16s.; one Tamme petticoate, 12s.; one cloth petticoate, 12s.; one sarrge Gowne, 14s.; one sarge petticoate, 6s.; another petticoate, 4s.; one sarge cloake, 8s.; olde cloaths and a paire of bodyes, 14s.; one oalde hat, 4s.; one green say apron, 4s.; in linen, 3li. 9s. 4d.; one muffe and a paire of old gloves, 3s. 6d.; In silke, 1li.; one paire of old shoes and 2 paire of old stockings, 5s.; two coverlids, 2li. 10s.; four blankets, 1li. 16s.; one feather bed, one bolster and thre pillows, 3li. 5s.; one straw bed and a mat, 8s.; a paire of curtens, curten rods and a paire of vallance, 1li. 10s.; a bedstead, 1li.; thre chairs and a stowle, 10s.; five cushens, 8s.; one old trunke, 5s.; one small cubbert, 3s.; paire of spectackells, 6d.; two baskets, 1s.; one bibell and a peece of a bibell, 7s. 6d.; an olde booke called the Seauen treatisses, 5s.; moses his choise, 4s.; Doctor Sibs his works upon the Cantickels, 4s.; Mr. Rhenaalls works upon the Sacrament, 5s.; old linse woolse, 3s.; one littell bell mettell pot, 5s.; one warminge pan and a littell bras pan, 5s.; five pewter platters and two pottingers, 1li. 2s.; one lookinge glas, 2s.; one heckell, 3s.; two hives of bees, 1li. 10s.; six sheepe, 2li. 5s.; four pound of sheepe wooll, 6s.; a fringe cloath and two olde bags, 6s.; thre cowes, 9li. 15s.; one halfe barrell, 1s. 6d.; total, 35li. 13s. 8d. Rents dewe to her, 10li. 3s. Debts dewe from the estate: to Thomas Leaver, Sr., 4s.; for funerall charges, 2li. 10s.; to Mr. Wainwright, 10s.; to Samuell Plats, Sr., 4s.; total, 3li. 8s.

Attested in Ipswich court Apr. 1, 1679, by Thomas Nellson, administrator.

Essex County Probate Files, Docket 24,029.

ESTATE OF ROBERT PEIRCE, SR.

"The Laste Will and Testamente of Robert Peirce Sener Made ye 8th of March 1678-9 In the Name of God Amen I Robert Peirce senior beeing in full and perfect Memory by the grace of god doe make this my last will and Testament in Maner and forme following vizt. I Commite my soull into the hands of Allmighty god my body to the dust to be buried in descent Maner, And after my desceasse my lands goods &

Chattells I giue and bequeath as followeth Imprimis I giue
and bequeath Unto my dear and well beloued wife Abigall
Peirce all my lands goodes Chattells at present in my poses-
sion or that is or may bee due to mee or my order by booke
bond or bill or obligation whatsoeuer my sd wife paying these
after mentioned Legacyes in time & forme as follows Item I
giue and bequeath Unto my Eldest sonne samuell that peice of
land that now lyes fenced out from ye orchard next the street
syd that was formerlly the land of Thomas Lords and alsoe
fourty pounds to be payd to him in Convenient time at ye discretion of my wife Item I giue and bequeath Unto my daughter Abigall Lyndall the sum of tenne poundes to be payd her
in Conuenient time at ye discretion of my wife Item I giue
and bequeath Unto my sonne John the sum of twenty fiue
poundes to be payd him in Conuenient time at ye discretion
of my wife Item I giue and bequeath Unto my daugh [t]er
Johanna the sum of twenty fiue pounds to be payd her in conuenient time at ye discretion of my wife Item I giue and bequeath Unto my sonne Robert the sum of twenty fiue poundes
to be payd him in Conueniente time at ye discretion of my
wife Item I giue and bequeath Unto my sonne Moses the sum
of twenty fiue poundes to be payd him in Conuenient time at
ye discretion of my wife Item I giue and bequeath Unto my
daughter Mary the sum of twenty fiue poundes to be payd her
in Conuenient time at ye discretion of my wife whom I doe
ordaine and Constitute my sole Executrix of this my last will
and testament and further I doe ordaine and Constitute my
Louing ffreinds Deacon Knowlton Jacob ffoster John stainford to bee overseers of this my last will & testament in witness wherof I haue heer unto sete my Markes ye day & year
Aboue writen."

Robert (his R P mark) Peirce, senior
Witness: Thomas Knowlton, Sr., John Stainford, Jacob
Foster.

Proved in Ipswich court Apr. 1, 1679, by the witnesses.

Inventory of the estate of Robert Pearce, deceased Mar. 21,
taken Apr. 1, 1679, by Thomas Knowlton, sr., Jacob Foster
and John Stainford: the housing, barne & land one both sydes
of ye way, 160li.; 4 Acres of Marche, 20li.; 2 Acres by ye
necke, 7li.; 15 Acres of Marche at plum island, 45li.; 1 farme
at Rowly Villidge, 100li.; 4 Cowes, 15li.; 25 sheepe, 12li.
10s.; 1 Mare, 3li.; 1 Hoge, 15s.; 2 Canous, 4li.; His waring
Clothes, 11li.; 21 Bookes, 4li. 10s.; 2 Remnants woollen Cloth,
16s.; 3 remnants of Linen, 2li. 2s.; 3 remnants of blue ditto,

8s. 8d.; 6 yards serge, 1li. 3s.; 2 fether beds, 6li.; 4 Boulsters, 2li. 6s.; 8 paire blanketts, 9li.; 7 Rugs, 1 Coverlide, 5li.; 5 pillows, 1li.; 3 flocke beds, 2li. 10s.; 12 paire sheets, 12li.; 6 pr. pillowbeers, 1li. 1s.; 7 tabel clothes, 2li. 9s.; 16 napkins, 16s.; 11 towells, 11s.; 1 remnante silke, 12s.; 1 remnante stufe, 7s. 6d.; 5 Bedsteds, 3li. 14s.; 1 Cubbord, 2li. 10s.; 1 Chest, 16s.; 1 Chest & boxes, 13s.; 2 Casses & glasses, 4s.; 1 Case & knifes, 5s.; 1 boxe & 2 bruches, 5s. 6d.; 2 boxe Irons & heters, 7s. 6d.; 1 hatte Case & warming pane, 9s.; 1 round table, 1li.; 14 Kushins, 1li. 5s.; small blanketts, 18s.; glasses, 8s.; 1 trunke, 16s.; 1 Chaire, 10s.; 6 Joined stoolles, 18s.; 8 Chaires, 17s.; 4 wheelles, 12s.; 5 pr. Cards, 5s.; 2 pr. Cobirons, 12s.; 2 pr. tonges, 6s.; 1 slice, 1 fire shovell, 3s.; 3 tramells, 1 fire forke, 16s.; 1 spite & Crowe, 7s.; 1 gridiron, 1 Chafin dish, 4s.; 1 beetle, wedges & 2 Axes, 10s.; 2 forkes, a sith, 1 axe, 1 bill, 10s.; 1 Morter & pestell, 1 hamer & Ads, 8s.; 4 pr. skalles & weightes, 1li. 16s.; 1 saw & 2 shovells, 10s.; 2 howes, 1 ditto, 4s. 6d.; 6 Iron potts, 2li.; 2 Iron Kettells, 2 skillets, 18s.; 4 brass Kettells, 2 pans, 4li. 4s.; 3 skillets, 3 pr. pothookes, 10s.; Curtaines & rodes, 10s.; 11 peuter dishes, 3li. 17s.; 9 porringers, 17s. 3d.; 2 peuter Candlestickes, 6s.; 7 peuter potes, 1li. 1s.; 3 Bassons, 1 sauscer, 6s. Earthen ware, 8 porringers, 3s.; 12 dishes, 9s.; 12 sauscers & potts, 5s.; 11 potts & panes, 6s. 6d.; 3 tine pans, 3 tunells, 4s. 6d. Wooden ware, 5 Cheese fates, 5s.; 9 trayes & trayes, 10s.; pailles & tubbs, 1li. 3s.; 2 tablles, 1 Cubbard, 1li. 10s.; 4 sives, 1 settle, table, 1 kneadin trough, 1li. 2s.; severall baskets & bee skipes, 11s.; 2 Chests, 10s.; 4 bush. 1-2 rye, 18s.; 3 bush. 1-2 wheate, 17s. 6d.; 12 bush. Indian, 1li. 16s.; 10li. sheeps woolle, 12s. 6d.; 8li. woollen yarne, 16s.; 1 saddle & pillion, 18s.; 7 hatts, 17s. 6d.; severall Caske old & thite, 1li. 1s.; 1-2 barill porke, 1li. 10s.; Mollasses, 2li. 10s.; 2 Muskettes, 1 Carbine with furniture, 1 sword, 3li. 11s.; 3 silver spoons, 2 tasters, 1 whistle, 2li. 4s.; In Cash, 4li. 11s. 10d.; Rigging, 1 topssaill & Iron worke, 6li. 10s.; Debts due to ye Estate, 90li. 17s. 5d.; total, 574li. 5s. 8d.

Attested in Ipswich court Apr. 1, 1679, by Abigaill Peirce, executrix of the estate of her husband.

Essex County Probate Files, Docket 21,216.

ESTATE OF JAMES STANDISH.

Administration upon the estate of James Standish, intestate, granted Apr. 1, 1679, to Richard Hutcheson, and he to pay the debts so far as the estate will go.

Ipswich Quarterly Court Records, vol. 5, page 343.

Inventory of the estate of James Standish taken by Joshua Rea and Joseph Hutchinson: Bead and beding, 4li. 1s.; five yard carsey, 1li.; 1 chest, 5s.; old lumber, 6s.; putter, 13s.; poott, 6s. 6d.; Brasse, 8s. 6d.; tonges, smoothing iron, skilett, 6s.; land at Manchester in the four Hundred Akors, 7li. 2s.; also 19 ackres in Manchester, 8li.; total, 22li. 18s. Debts to be paid out of this estate to Cap. Gorg Corwin, 4li. 13s. 11d. to Philip Cromull, 2li. 10s. 8d.; Thomas Eires, 2li. 12s. 9d.; John Maston, jr., 17s. 11d.

Allowed in Salem court 27 : 9 : 1679 upon the oath of Sara, relict and administratrix of the deceased.

Essex County Quarterly Court Files, vol. 32, leaf 23.

ESTATE OF JOSEPH SOOLART OF WENHAM.

Joseph Soolart dying under age and leaving some estate, the court Apr. 1, 1679, granted administration unto Joseph Levet and Walter Fairefield, they were bound to bring in an inventory at the next Salem court that there may be a distribution of the estate.

Ipswich Quarterly Court Records, vol. 5, page 343.

Inventory of the estate of Joseph Soolart taken Mar. 3, 1679 by Charles Gott and Thomas Patch: that which was ordered to him of his fathers estate by Ipswich court Sept. 24, 1672, 42li.; one cow in Thomas Killams hands & one yearling, 4li. 10s.; one yearling in the hands of Ezekiell Woodward, 1li.; one cittle at Joseph Levetts, 15s.; total, 48li. 5s. Due from Joseph Soolarts estate to his brother John Soolarts estate for one colt that was the sayd John Soolarts, 2li.

Ipswich Deeds, vol. 4, page 265.

ESTATE OF HENRY BATCHELDER OF IPSWICH.

Administration upon the estate of Henry Bachelour, intestate, granted Apr. 1, 1679, to Nath. Tredwell and John Warner, they to bring in an inventory to the next court at Ipswich, providing for the widow and keep an account, that then the court may order the estate.

Ipswich Quarterly Court Records, vol. 5, page 343.

An account of Debts due from the estate of Henery Batchelder, deceased: to Mistris Tredwell,—; to Mistris Mary Tredwell, 6li. 10s.; to Mistris Tredwell, 1li. 19s. 3d.; to mistris Tredwell, 9li. 7s.; to Thomas Tredwell, 1li.; to John Batcheder, 3li. 3s.; to Abraham Foster, 1li. 6s.; to Medcalfe,

6s.; to Cristofer boules, 4s.; Marthy Perey, 2s.; Samuell
Perly, 1s. 6d.; Samuell houlet, 2s. 3d.; George hadly, 3s.; Edward *Werling*, 6s.; John Warner, 12s. 3d.; Nathaniell Tredwell, 5li. 17s.; Marchant Waindright, 12s.; William Smith,
7s.; Mister Willsonn, 3s.; total, 42li. 2s. 3d. Signed Nathaniell Tredwell, John Warner, John Batcheler.

To be deducted out of the estate inventoryed: ten sheep that
died and was cilled with the woulefes, 2li. 10s.; swine lost,
prised, 15s.; lost out of the corn 4 bushels, 12s.; lost by meat,
12s.; total, 4li. 9s.

An account of what John Warner has done for Henery
Batchler: for fouer jagges of hay in the year 73, 2li., of wch
I receaved of him in part of Pay for it, 8s.; for carying bricks
& clay for an oven, 4s.; for carying him a load of bords from
Maning Neck and helping of him to halfe an hundred, 9s.;
on Bushell of Indian corne in 75, 3s.; carying two Jagges of
hay in 77 & 78, 6s.; for tending of him in his time of his sicknes from the 23 of Jenuary to the 5 of feburary in wch I made
it a great part of my imployment boath night & day to tend
him & get such things for him as hee desired, for what I did
tack up in cloathing & other thing at decon goodhew, 3li. 1s.
3d.; for blew Linen, 2s.; for on handekercher, thread &
macking hir cloath, 7s.; ten pound of suger & too pound of
Buter, 6s.; halfe a pound of hony & on quart of wine, 1s. 9d.;
three gallons of beere & halfe a bushell of wheat, 4s. 6d.; halfe
a bushell of ry, 2s.; total, 4li. 5s. 2d.

What John Bachelour did for Heneri Batcheler and for the
securing the estate: too dais while he was seke, 4s.; one dai in
preparin for his beurial, 2s. 6d.; one dai spent about the pris-
ing the estat, 2s.; makin her waskoat, 2s. 6d.; one dai bringin
the shep to John Warners, 2s.; one dai in bringing the corn
to John Warner with mi hors, 3s.; one dai myself and son in
bringing the shep, 4s. 9d.; from John Warners to mi hous
half a dai in caring things to her at Mr. Tredwels, 1s.
3d.; 3 dais and a half miself and mi son, 7s.; to bring the
catel, 10s. 9d.; too pounds of Hopts, 1s. 6d.; too pound of
buter, 1s.; thre pound of seuger, 1s. 3d.; one groat left, 4d.;
for keping ten shep, 8 weks, 1li.; for keping a kow 3
weks, 3s.
Essex County Quarterly Court Files, vol. 31, leaves 145, 146.

Whereas administration was formerly granted unto Nath.
Tredwell and Jo. Warner upon the estate of Henry Bachelour,

the court, Sept. 30, 1679, added John Bachelour of Wenham
to administer with them.

Ipswich Quarterly Court Records, vol. 5, page 348.

Inventory of the estate of Henery Batcheler, taken Feb. 6,
1678, by Abraham Foster and Thomas Metcalfe: the Liveing
Howse, Barne & orchard wth all the rest of the land both upland and meadow wth all the privileges therunto belonging,
180li.; three cowes, 9li.; to hefers, 4li.; on horse, 5s.; twenty
sheepe, 5li.; five Hogs, 35s., Aplls, 8s., 2li. 3s.; wooden weare,
12s.; one fouling Peace, 1li.; a tramell and a croscut saw,
10s.; grinstone, 5s.; Tackling for Husbandry, 1li. 14s.; in
other iron things, 18s. 6d.; a sid and a half of Porck, 1li.
5s.; a quarter of Beefe, 10s.; Barly foure Bushell, 16s.; Indian corne, ten Bushells, 1li. 10s.; total, 209li. 8s. 6d. Debts
from the estate & los of cattle as appeares in a note, 46li.
11s. 3d.

Attested in Ipswich court Sept. 30, 1679, by Nath. Tredwell, John Warner and John Bacheler.

Account of the administration of Nathaniel Treadwell,
John Warner and John Batcheldour on the estate of Henry
Batcheldor, late of Ipswich: The estate is Cr. as by inventory,
the real estate, 180li., the personal, 29li. 8s. 6d. Ye rentt of
ye farm from ye widows Death being 9 yr. 1-2, 19li.; total,
228li. 8s. 6d. The following charges and payments have been
made: charges on ye widow being distempered, to Nathaniel
Tredwell, 35li. 11s.; John Warner for his disbursements on
her, 27li. 6s.; Mrs. Tredwell for ditto, 7li. 17s. 8d.; to Joseph
Knowlton & Thomas Wilson, 14li.; Joseph Knowlton, 21li.;
funerall expences, 1li. 5s.; severall Debts, 28li. 13s. 9d.; total,
135li. 13s. 5d. Debts not yet paid: to ye executors of merchant Jewets, Decd., 2li. 18s.; Mr. Francis Wainwright, 16s.
10d.; John Kimballs wife, 1li.; ye administrators for their
trouble & care about ye distempered woman being grt & very
troublesome, 14li.; allowing ye accot., 5s.; settling & Deviding ye estatt, 5s.; writing & making ye account & time in taking it, 4s.; Admrs. attendance this day 2s. each, 6s.; total,
19li. 14s. 10d. The estate above is 228li. 8s. 6d.; Dr. 155li.
8s. 3d.; clear estate, 73li. 3d. Since to ye Sup. Court, 12s.,
Quits, 4s., Recordin settlements, 2s., com. to Comitte & yr return, 2s., 1li.

The deceased left no children but ye nearest of kin are his
brother's children viz.: ye children of Joseph Bacheldor who
deceased before ye intestate, John, Elizebeth and Hanah

Bacheldor, and the children of John Bacheldor that out lived their uncle, John, Joseph and Hanah Bacheldor. Of Joseph's children that are dead since their uncle died, Hanah Bacheldor alias Warner, who left children. Of John Batcheldor's children dead since ye death of their uncle, John and Joseph, who left children.

The appointment by the court at Salem May 25, 1696, of Lt. Simon Stacy, Deacon Nathaniel Knowlton, Sargt. Thomas Hart, Mr. Nathanil Tredwell and Mr. John Warner, all freeholders in Ipswich or any three of them to make a division of the lands of Henry Bachilder late of Ipswich, deceased, first to the administrators Nathaniel Tredwell and John Warner to the value of forty shillings being what remains due to them, the remainder to John, Elizabeth and Hanah Bachilder children of Joseph Bachilder, deceased, and brother of Henry Bachilder, deceased, and to John, Joseph and Hannah Bachilder children of John Bachilder, deceased, and brother of Henry Bachilder aforesaid, eleven pounds, thirteen shillings 4 pence apeice, which is one sixth part to each of them together with the one moiety of the rights of commonage to the children of John Bachilder, equally. .
Lt. Stacy, Mr. Nathaniel Tredwell, Dea. Nathaniel Knowlton and John Warner were sworn June 23, 1696, to faithfully perform the above order.

Essex County Probate Files, Docket 2,070.

According to the commission bearing date May 25, 1696, Simon Stacey, Nathaniell Knowlton and John Warner made the following division of the farm of Henry Bachilder, Aug. 11, 1696: first we laid out so much land as was worth forty shillings to the administrator: "then made a division of that part which is for the children of John Bachilder & bounded their parts by stakes and trees which parts & divisions Run cross the farme & are equally for quantity being thirteen rod & twelve foot on the northwest side of the farm & eight rods & ten foot on the southeast side & the half moiety or Right of comonage we do appoint to the children of John Bachilder & as to that part which we laid out for the children of Joseph Bachilder we made no division it being sold by those children to Joseph Knolton." Signed and sealed Oct. 1, 1696.

Essex County Probate Records, vol. 305, page 209.

GUARDIANSHIP OF ABIGAIL SOOLART OF WENHAM.

Abigaill Soolart in court, Apr. 1, 1679, chose Walter Fairefield to be her guardian, and he gave bond of 40li.
Ipswich Quarterly Court Records, vol. 5, page 343.

Whereas the land of John Soolart* stands bound for the
payment of John Soolart's children's portions, and being in
Ezekiell Woodward's possession, it was ordered Apr. 1, 1679,
that the produce of what their portion come to be paid by him
yearly.
Ipswich Quarterly Court Records, vol. 5, page 344.

GUARDIANSHIP OF BETHIAH SOOLART OF WENHAM.

Bethia Soolart in court, Apr. 1, 1679, chose Charles Gott to
be her guardian, and he gave bond of 40li.
Ipswich Quarterly Court Records, vol. 5, page 344.

ESTATE OF JOHN LUNT OF NEWBURY.

Administration upon the estate of John Lunt, intestate,
granted Apr. 1, 1679, unto Mary Lunt, the relict of John.
Ipswich Quarterly Court Records, vol. 5, page 344.

ESTATE OF JOSEPH MORSE OF NEWBURY.

Administration upon the estate of Joseph Morse, intestate,
was granted Apr. 1, 1679, unto Mary, relict of Joseph Morse,
and she to bring in an inventory to the next court.
Ipswich Quarterly Court Records, vol. 5, page 344.

Inventory of the estate of Joseph Mose deceased in January
1678, taken by Samuell Plumer and Stephen Grenlefe, Sr.:
on cowe, 4li.; on bede & beding, 7li.; on pesse stufe, 2li. 15s.;
on pese rede stufe, 1li. 2s.; on chest & boxe, 1li. 10s.; a cuberd,
1li. 10s.; five chairs, joneien stoles and a tabell, 1li. 10s.; on
small tabell, 5s.; toe tubes & a paile, 4s.; peuter & earthen
deshes, 3li.; andirens & tramel, pots, stelerds & other smal
things, 4li.; a sedell & pelen, 1li. 10s.; half a mare & 6 p.
yarne, 1li. 10s.; on bed & beding in the chamber, 6li.; a jake,
1li. 10s.; toe pair shets, on dusens napkens, table clothes, other
lenen, 8li.; a chest, box, kneding trough, 1li.; on smal bede,
boulster, ruge, 3li.; coten wole & sheps wol, cards, 10s.;
trondel bedsted & cradall with smal lumber, 1li.; smeth
toles, 9li.; a smeth shope, 3li.; total, 62li. 16s. The estate at

*See *ante*, vol. 2, page 283.

Piscataqua, 50li. 9s.; sum total, 113li. 5s. Debts due from the estate, 54li. when deducted there remains, 59li. 14s.

Attested in Ipswich court Sept. 30, 1679 by Mary, relict of Joseph Morse. and administratrix of his estate.

Inventory of the estate of Joseph Morss at the Gtt. Island Picattuque taken Aug. 20, 1679, by Richard (his R A mark) Abbott and Thomas Parker both inhabitants on the said Island: the dwelling house, 2 small shops & ye land adjacent, 40li.; one acre of land beyond ye bridge by old Dormonds, 10li.; 4 Joynt Stools, 6s.; 3 Chaires, 12d. per chair; total, 50li. 9s.

Essex County Probate Files, Docket 18,941.

GUARDIANSHIP OF NATHANIEL ROGERS.

Nathaniell Rogers and Martha Rogers came into court Apr. 1, 1679, and chose their uncle Mr. Wm. Hubbard for their guardian.

Ipswich Quarterly Court Records, vol. 5, page 344.

ESTATE OF WILLIAM BRADBURY OF SALISBURY.

Administration upon the estate of Mr. Willi. Bradbury of Salisbury, deceased, was granted Apr. 8, 1679, unto Mr. Thos. Bradbury and Caleb Moudy upon their request, who gave bond of 200li. and to bring in an inventory to the next court.

The court, Nov. 11, 1679, granted the administrators until the next Salisbury court to bring in an inventory of the estate.

Salisbury Quarterly Court Records, vol. 2, leaves 68, 74.

Inventory of the estate of Mr. William Bradbury of Salisbury who died intestate Dec. 4, 1678, taken Apr. 4, 1679, by Henry Brown and Samuell Felloes: in cash, 5li. 17s.; his wareing apparrell, 14li. 11s.; his armes & amunition, 3li. 10s.; feather bed, beding & furniture, 14li.; a great brass kettle, warming pan, skillet, morter, 4 poringers, quart pot, bellowes & 1-2 a hundered of Bare shot, 4li.; other brass, 1li. 15s.; 2 payer of Andirons, a pott, kettle & other iron things belonging to ve chymny, 3li. 5s.; in peuter & other small things in a boxe, 1li. 7s.; 4 basketts & other small things, 1li. 10s.; her wareing clothes with other lining in a trunke, 13li. 10s.; linin in another trunk, 6li. 4s. 6d.; 2 hatts, 12s.; some toyes & other things, 10s.; a little trunk with childs linen, 1li. 2s.; a box wth childbed linnen, 3li.; cradle & an old case, 5s.; cotton wooll about 55li., 2li. 15s.; chayers, stooles, livery cubbard & bedstead in ye parlor chamber, 4li.; for tables, 2li. 10s.; 9 chayers, old & nue flag bottoms, 1li. 4s.; barrills, hogshead, keelers & other old tubbs, hors sled and cheese press, 2li. 10s.

Iron worke appraised Apr. 5, 1679 by Richard Hubbard: Augors, 14s.; small tooles & a payer of fetters, 1li. 12s. 10d.; a ring, hookes & a few small spikes, 3s. 8d.; 2 whipsawes, 16s.; old Iron, 7s. 6d.; Iron for ship worke, 1li. 11s. 10d.

Cattle appraised Apr. 5, 1679 by Joseph Fletcher and Henry True: 2 4 yeare old steers & a fower year old heiffer, 2 two year old steers, 22li. 5s.; a 2 year old heifer, 5 small yearlins, a gelding & a young sowe, 4li. 1s.; 2 sacks & 3 pound of cotten yarne, 13s. 6d.

Goods appraised by Richard Hubbard: 4 barrills of molassis, 6li.; 8 tirkie leather chayers, 4li.; 2 barrills of salt & ye barrills, 1li. 4s.; a tymber cheyne, 4 boxes, 4 Iron cart hoops, 1 broad Axe, 1 small maule, a little bottle, lethern pouch, earthen pott, an Ads, 2li. 7s.

Debts appraised by Tho. Bradbury and Caleb Moody: due to the estate, received & in Mr. Checky's hand, 23li.; Phillip Grele for Moses Gillman 4 thousand foot of board, 8li.; from Jno. Garland by bill, 2li. 2s.; from Jacob Brown of Hampton pr. bill, 1li. 10s.; from Georg Carr, jr., 16s. 6d.; by Richd. Smith in staves, 2li.; from Mr. Anthony Stanian 5 C. foot of board, 1li.; from Jon. Stanian about 2li.; from Mr. Anthony Checkly in money, 30li.; from Jno. Davis, 3s.; from Job ye Indian, 8s. Debts due from the estate: to Mr. John Stockman, 30li.; Mr. Davison of Nubery, 10li.; Jno. Severans, sr., 3li.; Joseph Norton for work about 2 vessels, 5li. 12s.; Joseph Eaton for work about ye Pinke, 16s. 3d.; Jno. Easman in mony, 14s.; Joseph Fletcher in money, 9s.; Jno. Bradbury 49 dayes work about ye Pink, 7li. 18s.; claymd by Mr. Rich. Dole in money & other pay, 6li. 13s.; Jno. Dickison, jr., 2li. 7s.; Samll. Felloes, jr., 1li. 2s. 6d.; Samll. Felloes, sr., 10s.; Moses Gill for work about ye Pinke, 1li. 3s.; Mr. Carr, sr., 1li.; Henry True, 3li. 16s.; claymd by Phillip Grele, ——; claymd by Robert Downer, ——; Tho. Bradbury, 2li. 10s.; James Chase about 2li.; Tho. Fowler for his daughters service, 2li. 10s.; Major Pike, 8s.; Mr. Tho. Woodbridg, 1li.; Ensigne Greenleafe, 6s. 6d.; claymd by Edmond Marshall, 19s.; Ms. Hewes for nursing ye youngest child 15 months & attending ye mother when sick, 10li. 11s.

Attested in Ipswich court Mar. 30, 1680, by Caleb Moody and Apr. 24, 1680, by Mr. Thomas Bradbury.

Copy of deed of Thomas Bradbury of Salisbury, planter, who in consideration of my affection to my son William Bradbury of the same town have given unto him "all that my dwelling house lately erected wthall other houseing therunto belonging now standing & being upon that houselott which I formerly bought of John Gill of ye same town Planter wth ye Oarchyards & all ye other upland adjoyning therunto bounded wth north east upon ye street & wth ye south west upon marsh & upland of Isaac Buswell in part & in part upon land which I bought of Isaac Colby as far as the heithermost side being ye northeast of ye range of ye meadow wch I bought of ye said Colby & allowing liberty to bring ye hay out of ye sd Colbies meadow to ye Ferrrie high way & wch way is ye bounds of ye aforesd land upon ye northwest & ye southeast, bounded wth ye marsh of Isaac Buswell Jno. Bayly, Richard Bartlett, Phillip Challis, & yt called Mr. Hodges meadow, As also I do give unto him all ye sd Hodges meadow adjoyning in part, to ye sayd upland & in part, upon ye land of John Severans to Hodges ditch so called: As also all my halfe part of fresh & salt marsh wch I wth John Stevens Senr Bought of Henry Ambross, As also all ye salt marsh lotts wch I bought of George Martyn, as also lying neare a place cald Brushie Iland, As also ye marsh lott wch I bought of Onesiphorus Page, lying in ye range of Mr. Hooks farme so called; As also fower cowes comons, wthall ye marsh & upland therunto belonging . . . , As also my sixscore acre lott att ye beach hill joyning to ye land of Joseph Fletcher upon one side, & all ye rest of ye sd lott incumpassed wth a fresh river or brooke; As also all my division of swamp land towards ye Ferrie Adjoyning to ye land of Samll. Felloes & Rodger Easman wth one end & wth ye other end upon Swamp land of John Severans lying between ye land of Isaac Buswell, & ye lotts or lands of Richard Goodales, & Richard Hubbard As also two thirds of all my pasture land towards the Ferrie," all these to my son and to Ms. Rebecka Maverick after her marriage with him during her life, and to his heirs lawfully begotten forever, provided that during mine and my wife's lives, we have the use of certain parcels of the land. Signed and sealed March 11, 1671-2. Witness: Jane True, Mary (her M W mark) Weed.

The 4 : 3m : 1680, John Severans and Phillip Grelee appraised the houseing and lands contained in this deed of gift to be worth 300li.

The Ipswich court May 4, 1680, ordered that the lands in this deed of gift given by Mr. Thos. Bradbury, be to William the eldest son of William, deceased, he paying unto his other two brothers Thomas and Jacob, 50li. each, when they come to age. The names of Wm. Bradbury's children, Wm. the eldest, Sam. and Jacob.

The court Sept. 27, 1681, upon further consideration of the estate of Wm. Bradbury, deceased, ordered that the estate given by his father as by deed of Mar. 11, 1671-2, be settled upon Wm. the eldest son of ye said Wm., he paying to ye other two brothers Thomas and Jacob, 50li. each, and that the rest of the estate be equally divided between the said younger brothers, Thomas and Jacob.

Essex County Probate Files, Docket 3,013.

Mar. 9, 1695-6, memorandum, that the copy of the inventory and bondsmen of the estate of Will. Bradbury deceased, Caleb Moodey and Thos. Bradbury administrators at the court at Salisbury, Apr. 8, 1679, no record here.

Essex County Probate Records, vol. 305, page 179.

ESTATE OF ISAAC BUSWELL, JR., OF SALISBURY.

Administration upon the estate of Isaac Buswell of Salisbury, was granted Apr. 8, 1679, unto Susanna Buswell relict of Isaac Buswell, jr., who is ordered to bring in an inventory to the next court, and to take the best care of the estate for the maintenance of the children and payment of just debts.

Salisbury Quarterly Court Records, vol. 2, leaf 70.

ESTATE OF WILLIAM SYMONDS OF IPSWICH.

Administration upon the estate of Mr. William Symonds, intestate, was granted June 17, 1679, by the Hon. Gov. Symon Bradstreet and Maj. Hathorne, unto Mrs. Mary Symonds relict of William, and Mr. Jonathan Wade, and they to bring in an inventory of the estate to the next court. Mr. Jonathan Wade gave bond of 1000li.

Ipswich Quarterly Court Records, vol. 5, page 346.

Inventory of the estate of Mr. William Symonds, who died in Ipswich May 26, taken July 8, 1679, the most part, and as it could be found more added, by Edward (his Z mark) Bragg and Robert Kinsam: his wearing apparrell woollen & linen, 11li.; Argilla farme containeing thre hundred acres thereabout more or lesse, 1500li.; houses & barnes & outhouses upon the farme, 200li.; twentie two acres of English & Indian corne grene, 30li.; about twelve acres of marsh & a little

upland about wellses, 50li.; 6 acres more of marsh there to the
use of Mrs. Martin during her life, 12li.; the house & about
twentie rod of ground at towne, 10li.; 1 sow & shoats in the
woods, 5li.; 10 cowes, 36li., 7 oxen, 35li., 8 2 year olds, 16li.,
87li.; 3 horses & a colt, 8li.; 1 stear 3 years old, 50s., 2 heifers,
6li., 8li. 10s.; 1 bull, 55s., 6 yearlings, 8li. 1 heifer 4yr. old,
3li. 10s., 14li. 5s.; 3 yoaks, 3 chayns, 1 cart & tackling, a paire
of wheels halfe worn, 1 spanshackle & 1 new tumbrill, 3li.
6s.; 42 sheep & 21 lambs, 22li.; 4 old axes, an old adds, 1 paire
fetters, 1li.; 2 old sithes & tackling & 3 rakes, 9s. 6d.; 3 forks,
3s., one dung forke, 3s., 6s.; handsaw, a bushel, an iron winch
& a cowle, 12s.; paire of harrows, 20s., an Iron wedg, 1s., 1li.
1s.; good peuter 78li. at 1s. 4d. pr. li., 28li. old puter at 12d.,
6li. 6s.; flaggon, 6s., beetle & wedges, 6s., 12s.; old hoops
& boxes for wheels, 10s.; 2 hooes & a spade, 12s.; 2 parcels of
old iron, 40s., 2 frying pans, 13s., 2li. 13s.; a servant boy for 2
years, 5li.; a cosslet & hed peice old, 1li.; 126li. of timber
chaine, hooks & ring, 4li.; 5 strakes for a cart tire 48li. old
& rusty, 1li.; a heckle, 4s., 4 chests & 3 boxes, 1li. 15s., 1li.
19s.; more old iron & an old churne, 5s.; hollen earthen ware
& other small things, 7s.; cushins & peices for cushins & remnants, a bible, 2li. 3s.; flax tear, 3s., 2 wicker baskets, 3s., 6s.;
small table linnen & other old linnen, 7s.; bed linen & table
linen, 6li. 9s.; carpet, 20s., blancket, 10s., 1li. 10s.; a bed rug
& blankets, 4li. 5s.; an old pistol, 3s., paire curtains & vallence, 22s., 1li. 5s.; rugs, bed bolster & sheet, 6li. 16s.; other
bedding, 1li. 10s., 3 paire keards, 7s., a bottle & oyle, 3s., 2li.;
old rug & blancket, 1li. 2s., 2 old chests, 8s., 1li. 10s.; 3 old barrills, 4 bush. 1-2 of malt, 5li. of hops, 1li. 6s.; 12li. cott.
wooll, 16s., trundlebedstead & rope, 5s., 1li. 1s.; a great kettle
& an old little kettle, 2li. 15s.; 2 skillets, 10s., 2 iron potts,
17s., 1li. 7s.; paire of cobirons, spitt & a drippin pan, 1li. 4s.;
an old chest, 2s., 5 trayes, 5s., 3 chayers, 8s., 15s.; hoe, 3s. 6d.,
tramills, 9s., 2 payles, 5s., 17s. 6d.; dishes, cheese motes, 4s.,
tub, 5s., 2 grind stons, 16s., 1li. 5s.; bridle, saddle &^ pillion,
20s., barrills & earthen ware, 20s., 2li.; 3 spinning wheels,
12s.; 4 acres of salt marsh neere Mr. Epps Island, 12li.; 20
acres or thereabouts more or lesse at the Pequid lotts of upland, 50li.; 18 acres of meddow at or about ye west medows,
36li.; 3 cowes from Nickles Wallis, 9li. 15s.; a cow from Matt
Perry, 4li.; a smoothing box iron & 3 heaters, 4s. 6d.; trenchers & spoons, 5s., earthen ware, 3s., 8s.; 3 red curtains & vallence, 1li. 5s.; a clock, 5li., Andirons, 20s., 6li.; green curtains & vallance, 3li.; a plaine cubbord & cubberd cloth & 3

old stools, 10s.; a Sute of damaske very old, 4li.; a copper
cann, 11s., a cosslett, 40s., 2li. 11s.; 12li. more of cott. wooll,
a marble morter, 15s., 1lj. 11s.; a bell mettle morter & pestle,
10s.; paire of brasse scalles & waits, 7s., a beam & scales, 10s.,
17s.; paire of stillyards, 1li.; a great copper, 8li., an iron pott,
8s., 8li. 8s.; cheese prisse, 10s., malt mill, 10s., 1li.; 3 turkie
work cushins, 12s., 4 lether chayers, 20s., 1li. 12s.; musket,
28s., sword & belt, 15s., 2li. 3s.; coutch chayer, 15s., a great
chest, 15s., 1li. 10s.; a great chayer, 3s., a cabbinett & an old
hatt, 25s., 1li. 8s.; fether bed, boulster, rug & bedsted, 4li.;
cloth dublet & hoas & old cloth cloak, 2li. 5s.; a haire camblett
cloke, 5li.; black cloth cloke, 40s., a wosted cote, 40s., 4li.; a
black tunick, 50s., a bayes gown & old briches, 20s., 3li. 10s.;
2 payer of boot hoas tops & a paire silke sleves, 10s.; fetherbed, old rug, & blancket & coverlid, 5li.; flockbed, blanckit,
rug, bedsted & old sheet, 2li. 6s.; in plate 1li. 3-4 haverdepose
waite that is in troy waite 25 ounces 1-8 1-32 at 6s. per oz.
7li. 11s.; in money, 18li. 9s.; paire of racks, 14s., 1 paire
tonges & firepan, 3s., 17s.; books, 5li., gridiron, 5s., riddle sive,
1s., 5li. 6s.; spitt & tramill, 10s., a cubbard, table & froe,
18s., 1li. 8s.; woollen yarne at the wevers 38li., 5li. 14s.;
sheeps wooll 168li. part pelt wooll the rest fleece wooll, 12li.
7s.; a tin lamp, 1s., brass skellett, 8s., wooden ware, 15s., 1li.
4s.; earthen ware, 2s. 6d., a brasse kettle & pott hooks, 10s.,
12s. 6d.; tub & tray, 3s., old iron dogs, 1s., 2 earthen pots, 6d.,
4s. 6d.; snuffers, 6d., chafin dish, 9d., riddle, 1s., 2s. 3d.; Indian corne about 8 bush., 1li. 4s.; a phisick book, 6s.; due
from Nickles Wallice, 55li. & 55li. & 20li. of which there is
10s. paid so remains 129li. 10s.; due from George Stimson,
1li. 15s.; a farme at Wells about 300 acres, 600li.; 5 acres 1-2
of meddow bought of Wadly, 16li. 10s.; 1-4 pt. of a place for
a saw mill with land & meddow & other necessarys, 200li.;
other land not yet knowne & therefore not yet valued; horse
kind runing in the woods nere Wells, 3li.; cattle at Wells, 6
cowes, 21li.; 1 bull, 1 stear, 3 yeare old, 6li.; 2 bulls 2 year
old, 4li., 1 heifer 2 year old, 2li., 6li.; 6 steres 2 year old, 12li.,
2 calves, 1li. 10s., 13li. 10s.; 6 cowes, 21li., 1 bull, 1 stear 3
yere old, 6li., 27li.; 2 young oxen, 8li., 9 yearlings, 13li. 10s.,
21li. 10s.; 6 calves, 6li.; Iron ware at Wells, 3li.; debts due to
the said estate as appears by writings from Francis Backhous
4100C. mrch. boards payable at Boston at 4s. per, 8li. 4s.;
from Henry Hobs in money, 9li. 15s.; from Abraham Collens
in money, 2li. 5s. 6d.; Abraham Collens in beife, 5li.; Abraham Collens in porke, 5li. 4s.; from William Soyer, 2li. 10s.;

Thomas Avory by bill, 11li. 10s.; most of these Debts above mentioned are desperate debts; total, 3359li. 9s. 3d.   There are also severall other both debts & Credit whose accounts are not yet cleared.   The estate is debtor to funerall expences of Samuel Symonds, Esq., late deputy governor, 37li. 18s. 4d.; also debtor to funerall exspences of Mr. William Symonds late of Ipswich, son of Samuel Symonds, Esq. & executor to his estate, 18li. 18s. 4d.; also Dr. to Mr. Harrison or his assigns a sum; Dr. to Mr. Elikim Hutchinson, 211:00M mrch. pine boards payable at Boston; to Mr. Thomas Andrews in money, 8li. 9s.; and to severall others not yet certainly knowne.   This estate is also debtor to Mrs. Rebecka Symonds, relict of Samuel Symonds, Esq., deceased, and also to Mrs. Epps and to Mrs. Martin and Mrs. Emerson and to severall others, as it is exspressed in the Will of the said Samuel Symonds, Esq., only what they or any of them have received to be deducted.

Delivered to the Salem court 30:9m:1680, by Mr. Jonathan Wade.

Essex County Quarterly Court Files, vol. 34, leaf 80.

Danill Epps and Jon. Emerson pastor of the church of Gloucester "having waited in exspectation of an oppertunity of conferring with such as possible might concerne them selves about our beloved sister Symonds widdow & relict of our brother, Mr. Wm. Symonds, deceased, but there being nothing at all intimated or proposed, Doe therefore in ye behalfe of ourselves & the rest of our relations concerned, lay claime & before these witnesses, doe take possession of the houses & lands, chattells & goods, that were the proper estate of Samll. Simonds Esq. late deputy Governor of the Massachusetts in New England, deceased, And doe heareby declare that there is noe intention, heareby to deprive, our honrd mother of what is bequeathed in the will to her in any measure nor our sister Simonds of her just proportion."

Signed, June 16, 1679.   Witness: James Chute, Richard (his ∧ mark) Brier.

The above demand consented to June 21, 1679 by Richard Martin.   Har. Simonds being more principally concerned in his father's estate, consents to the above written, June 24, 1679.

Mr. Daniell Epps and Mr. Jon. Emerson in behalf of themselves and the rest of the children of Samuell Simonds, Esq., late deputy Gov., who are interested in their father's estate desire this court 24 : 4 : 1679, that the estate may not be settled until they have an opportunity to inform and make appear their right they have in the said estate, which desire is granted by this court.

Salem Quarterly Court Records, vol. 5, leaf 129.

ESTATE OF SAMUEL MANSFIELD OF LYNN.

Administration upon the estate of Samuell Mansfeild, was granted 24 : 4 : 1679, to Sarah, the relict, and she to administer according to that writing presented to the court, which is an agreement made by her consent with the parties subscribed, and she also presented an inventory.

Salem Quarterly Court Records, vol. 5, leaf 131.

Inventory of the estate of Samuell Mansfeild of Lynn who departed this life Apr. 10, 1679, taken by John Newhall and Robt. (his P mark) Rand: his dwelling house, orchard & land ajoyning to the house & 4 acres of marsh, 94li.; 2 cowes, 6li. 10s., 2 two year ould heifers, 4li., 1 year ould heifer, 1li. 6s., 11li. 16s.; 1 Horse, 4li., 6 ewe sheepe & 3 lambes, 2li. 14s., 6li. 14s.; 5 yong swine, 2li., two Hives of Bees, 10s., pistills & houlsters, 1li. 15s., 4li. 5s.; Back sword & belt, 9s., cutt lash & Belt, 18s., a gun, scurer, &c., 1li. 5s., 2li. 12s.; A sadle & croop, 15s., bridle, 4s., pillion & pillion cloath, 1li. 19s.; wearing Apparrill, two hatts & stockings, 3li.; 11 yds. of woollen cloath, 1li. 18s. 6d., 3 coverlids & 3 blanckitts, 3li., 4li. 18s. 6d.; 3 pare of sheets, 1li. 10s., a bed boulster & 3 pillows, 2li., bedstead, curtains & vallens, 1li. 16s., 5li. 6s.; A pare of Boots, 16s., A loome & weavors tackling belonging to it, 3li. 19s. 6d., 4li. 15s. 6d.; 2 chests & a box, 7s., a table & cradle rug, 8s. 6d., sheers & stooles, 5s., 1li. 10s. 6d.; An Iron pott, 2 puter dishes, a chafin dish, tinn ware, earthen ware, glass, 1li. 12s. 6d.; A table cloath, 2 shurts, napkins, towells & a Lether Apron, 18s.; A frying pan, a pare of tongs, an axe, an hoe, 10s., raisier Hone, siser, 6s. 6d., 16s. 6d.; 2 sithes & tackling, 10s., wool, 10s., Lyning yarne, 1li. 10s., a reele & wheele, 10s., 3li.; A Loome, Lathe & blocks, tridles, stretchers & irons belonging to it, 2li. 5s.; 2 pare of temples, 2s., a pare of Blocks & wheels, 1s. 6d., 2 pare of shafts, 2s., 5s. 6d.; 2 sydar barrills & an Hamer, 7s. 6d., sum Lumber, 6s., a pare of scales, 1s., 14s. 6d.; woolen yarne, 9s., 10 dozen buttons, 5s., 2 Lamps, 2s., halfe a coverlid, slea & Harnis, 19s.

6d.; A sheep rack, 5s., a rave, 3s., a shitle, 2s., an ould slea, 3s., 13s.; a forke & rake, 2s. 6d., 2 ell sleas & harniss belonging to them, 1li. 10s., 1li. 12s. 6d.; 1 yard slea for carsye & harnis belonging to it, 8s., 2 sleas & harnis for them for Lyning, 10s., 18s.; total, 154li. 8s. 6d.

Attested in Salem court 25: 4m: 1679, by Sarah, the relict. *Essex County Quarterly Court Files, vol. 31, leaves 89, 90.*

Whereas Samuell Mansfeild of Lynn died of the smallpox leaving a wife and three children, the eldest of them being a son, the nearest relations on both sides, the father of Samuel Mansfeild, and the father of the wife, with the consent of the wife, chose and impowered Mr. Thomas Laughton, sr., Andrew Mansfeild and Nathaniell Bersham to divide the estate which is as follows: "the estate being inventoried amounted to 154li. 8s. 6d., debts 17li. 4s. 7d. being provided for, leaving 137li. 3s. 11d.; to the widow, a third part of the estate as her proper estate, 45li. 14s. 8d.; to the son Andrew Mansfeild, 4 acres of upland ajoyning westerly along his granfather Mansfeild's house lott & three acres of salt marsh in Rumnye marsh ajoyneing northelye uppon his grandfather's marsh & 7li. 14s. 8d. to be paid by the estate in the widow's hand, 45li. 14s. 8d.; the two daughters, 22li. 17s. 4d. per peice out of the estate in the widdow's hand, 45li. 14s. 8d." The widow to have the whole estate until the children respectively come to age, but if the widow die before then, they are to have their portions. The remaining part of the land and dwelling house to be as security, the widow to keep the house and all fences in good repair. This being also to be understood that Samuell Mansfeild, deceased, as his last words on his death bed, gave unto his father Andrew Mansfeild, his son Andrew above mentioned, until he come to twenty one years of age, and his said father accepted of him. Dated Lynn, 20: 4m: 1679. This agreement allowed by the Salem court 20: 4m: 1679.

Essex County Quarterly Court Files, vol. 31, leaf 89.

ESTATE OF BENJAMIN CHADWELL OF LYNN.

Administration upon the estate of Benjamin Chadwell, intestate, granted 24: 4m: 1679, to Elizabeth, the relict of Benjamin, who brought in an inventory of the estate and gave oath to the truth of it. The whole estate when the debts are paid to remain in her hands for the bringing up of the children of the deceased until they come of age, and what estate shall then remain shall be one half to the children and the other half to the widow.

Salem Quarterly Court Records, vol. 5, leaf 130.

Inventory of the estate of Benjamin Chadwell lately deceased, taken June 17, 1679, by John Newhall and Saml. Cobbett: the Dwelling howse and Barn and 4 Acres of Land adjoyning thereunto, 65li.; five Acres more of upland, and nine Acres of meadow, 70li.; A Bedstead and bedding belonging thereunto, 3li. 10s.; in Linnen, 5s.; two small potts and pot hooks and a Tramell, 14s.; an old warming pan and frying pan, 2s.; In Peuter and a smoothing Iron, 5s.; cradle, a small Barrell and other wooden ware, 7s.; foure pound of toe yarne, 5s.; A sow, 12s.; Linnen wheel and a wollen wheel, 6s.; total, 141li. 6s. Just Debts: for an Acre of meadow (taken into the inventory) morgaged for 4li. 11s. in mony; an Acre and a quarter of upland or thereabout taken into the inventory, that was made over for ye widows present supply, received in mony, 5li.; two Acres and a half of meadow morgaged to John Newhall for 7li. in money which 7li. was received by Benjamin Chadwel; to John Newhall, 2li. 5s. 6d. in mony; Thomas Newhall, 1li. 3s. 9d. in mony: John Tarbox, 15s. in mony; Eliezer Lynsee for the Country Rates, 1li. 4s. 11d.; James Walls, 9s.; Elisabeth Engolls, 10s. in money; Thomas Laighton, 3s.; Joseph Armitage, 5s.; Samuel Hart for setting up new fence, 1li. 10s.; Mrs. Hawthorn, 16s.; total, 25li. 13s. 2d.

Attested in Salem court 24:4:1679, by Elizabeth Chadwell, the relict.

Essex County Quarterly Court Files, vol. 31, leaf 86.

Petition of Nehemiah Jewet, attorney to Samuell Chadwell, late of Lynn, now of Rowley, that whereas Benjamin Chadwell late of Lynn, died intestate, administration was granted to his widow Elizabeth Chadwell, 24:4m:1679, and the estate when debts were paid to remain to the widow for the bringing up of the children until they come of age, and what estate should then remain, the one half to the children and the other half to the widow, and the said widow being married again unto John Jewet of Ipswich, yet never having rendered an account of administration, so that Samuel is kept out of that estate he ought to have received when he came of age, desiring the court Sept 1, 1698, that the administratrix may be called upon to give an account of her administration so that Samuel may receive his equal part.

Account of the administration of Elizabeth Chadwell alias Jewett, upon the estate of Benjamin Chadwell late of Lynn, brought in Sept. 5, 1698: sundry debts paid that were given in with the inventory, 25li. 13s. 2d.; to Wm. Craft, 1li. 10s., Moses Chadwill, 12s., 2li. 2s.; Samuell Hart, 5s. 10d., 5 days about ye boys, 10s., 15s. 10d.; expence at that time, 10s.; Thomas Thurley, 24s., Mr. Croad, 33s., 2li. 17s.; 3 days time expended about sd. Debt & Cost, 12s.; Nathll. Rust, 10s. 10d., Henry Stacey for repayr ye House, 8li., 8li. 10s. 10d.; Mr. Gidney, 30s., Mr. Batter, 30s., 3li.; allowing the acct. 5s., setling & Dividing ye same, 5s., 10s.; Reg. ye settlement, 1s., a Quietus, 4s., 5s.; stating & Registring this acct., 4s.; allowed ye adminr. more then ye Income of ye estate towards ye bringing up ye children, 6s. 2d.; total, 45li. 6s. The estate per inventory, 141li. 6s.; a stear omitted, 4li.; total, 145li. 6s. Signed, Elizabeth (her † mark) Jewitt, John Jewitt.

Acknowledged Sept. 5, 1698, by Elizabeth Jewit and also by John Jewett, her now husband.

The estate free of all charge being 100li., the court 24:4: 1679, ordered to the widow one half, 50li.; to Samll. Chadwill only son, a double portion, 33li. 6s. 8d.; to Mary Chadwill only daughter, 16li. 13s. 4d.

Essex County Probate Records, Docket 4,836.

Estate of Robert Starr of Salem.

Administration upon the estate of Robert Starr, intestate, was granted 24:4m:1679, to Mary the widow of Robert, who presented an inventory of the estate and she is to have the whole estate in her hands towards the maintenance of the children until the court take further order.

Salem Quarterly Court Records, vol. 5, *leaf* 132.

Inventory of the estate of Mr. Robert Starr who was murdered by the hands of ye Barberious heathens, taken June 25, 1679, by Joseph Phippen and Edward Wollon: A House and Orchard & Ground, 130li.; on Bed Ruge & 2 blankets, 3li.; on Bed Ruge wth 2 blankets & Curteine, 6li. 10s.; five paire of sheets & 18 table napcins, 7li.; on Cubbard Cloath, 5s.; three paires of pileberes, 12s.; two Chestes, 14s.; on Chest & Cubbard wth a table, 1li. 5s.; on bedstead, table & forme, 1li.; on Iron Citle and two Iron pots, 1li. 2s.; on Litle brase pot & a brase skillet, 5s.; on paire of Dog Irons, 1 hack, two pothooks, on friing pan & spit, 11s.; seaven platers, 4 porrengers, 1 warming pan, on salte seller & a Candle stick, 1li. 10s.; foure cheares, 1 Loockin Glase, 2 boxes, 9s.; on Linen wheel and one woolen wheele, 5s. 6d.; total, 154li. 8s. 6d.

Mary Nick late relict of Robart Star, having been left a widow with four children very young and not able to help themselves, having put out two of them, the other two to be maintained by herself, petitioned the court to grant her, her third part of this estate for the bringing up of her four children.

Essex County Quarterly Court Files, vol. 31, leaves 104, 105.

The court 30 : 9m : 1680, ordered that Richard and Susanna Starr, children of Robert Starr, have present possession of the house and ground their father made over to them by a deed of gift, divided equally between them.

Salem Quarterly Court Records, vol. 6, leaf 12.

Samuell Williams and Isack Foott being desired by Timo. Lindall to appraise a house and land formerly belonging to Robert Star, sr., deceased, have measured the land and find it to be near about an acer, and a very old hous upon it and a few trees or small orchard att one end of it, all wch we value at four score pounds.

Attested in Salem court 29 : 9 : 1681, by Samuell Williams and Isaack Foote.

Upon the return of the above apprisement of house and land which is an estate joynt, as not yet divided, between said Robert Starr, deceased, and his brother Richard and sister Susana, this court impowered Leift. John Higenson and Mr. John Hathorne to make a division of this estate into three parts and deliver or lay out the said Robert's part to Timothy Lindall, as administrator, who is to administer thereupon as the estate of Robert Starr, jr., deceased, according to law.

Essex County Quarterly Court Files, vol. 36, leaf 141.

ESTATE OF JOHN WHITTIER OF NEWBURY.

Administration upon the estate of John Whitteere was granted 24 : 4 : 1679, to John Kelly, who is to bring in an inventory to the next court held at Ipswich, and then the estate to be ordered according to law.

Salem Quarterly Court Records, vol. 5, leaf 128.

Inventory of the estate of John Whityer who died the 20 day of febuary, 1678, taken May 14, 1679, by Nicholas Noic

and John Badger: 4 Cows and 2 Calves, the two old Cows at
7li. and the other 2 Cows and their Calves at 8li., 15li.; 4
young Cattell, 11li.; sadl and a koat, 1li. 10s.; 2 gunes,
Cuttlis, knapsac, horn and pouch, 2li. 10s.; pistol, an axe and
two old shirts, 14s.; 5 sheep, 2li.; bedsack, som old Cloths,
necclothes and a horslok 1li.; blanket, an old koat, 2 glass bottles and other old garments, 1li. 7s.; total, 35li. 1s. A young
horse, 2li.; mare, 3li. Debts due to Rich. Dole he says 9li.
3s. 7d.; to the docter for phisick, 1li. 15s.; to Ensign Grenlef,
4s. 6d., to John Webster, 6d., 5s.; du to John Keley which
he payd to severall men whil he was in the warrs for winter
meat for his Cattell, 1li.; lent him a horse to boston two
Jorneys, 10s.; Lent him a horse to haverill two times, 4s.;
for somering a Calfe and wintering of him, 6s.; feching of
his mad bull Calfe from Plom Iland promised me, 5s.; feching
of his Cattell from Plom Iland in January, 5s.; feching whom
a horse he bought of Toppan, 2 days, 7s.; wintring of a horse
2 months and a load of wood of ours Carid to John Glover,
6s. 6d.; 4 yards of Cloth for a koat both spining, weaving and
milling cost, 5s. 3d.; stoking of 2 pr. of stockings, 2s.; care of
his horse and bulls, 4s.; wintering of a Colt, 5s.; wintering
3 sheep, 10s.; feching of his Cattell and horses from Plom
Iland in May 2 days, 5s.; I went with him to looke a horse
for him & he went with on of ours, 5s.; I went with him to
Plom Iland to fech a hors for him & with him 2 horses of ours,
5s.; lent him a horse to havrill again, 2s.; driving of his Cattell to Plom Iland I and my 2 bois, 3s.; for a 3 yere old wether
sheep, 12s.; to Josep Knight for heye and wintring of 5
Cattell, 3li.; for hey and wintring of 2 Cows & a 3 yere old
steer, 3li.; for 5 weeks dyat, 1li. 2s. 6d.; for a per of knit
stockins when the ship went away, 6s.; for his atendance when
he was sick and Entertainment 20 weeks while his Imploy-
mer was in the ship in the tim of the pox was being in the
oners house and in provision for the last voig in the ship, 5li.;
the Cost and Charg for tim and Expenc & for Evidences about
the Estate and at Salem Court, 3li.; total, 30li. 13s. 10d. Du
unto John Whityer from the owners of the ship for five
months waiges at thirty shilings a month from the first of
october 78 unto the twenty of february 78, 7li. 10s., so that
when this 7li. 10s. is paid ther will Remain of the Estat, 11li.
17s. 2d.

Attested in Ipswich court Sept. 30, 1679, by John Kelley,
administrator.

The testimony of Patrick Ewing aged about 30 years that "John Whitear about 5 or 6 houres before his death finding himselfe very ill, The Master of the Shipp, Benj. Dole & my selfe being there, (being as farre as we discerned of good understanding) did utter himselfe before us, that we might take notice of it, & spake to this purpose. I haue a young horse at Plumm Iland, that I giue to you speaking to Benj. Dole; & haue a Pyeballd mare, wch I giue to Abiel Kelly, for I had her of the old folkes, And all the rest of my goods, I give to the people of the house, (wch I did suppose he meant of John Kellyes house having mencioned his sonne just before) for I haue allwayes found them kind to me: & about 5 or 6 houres after he dyed." Sworn May 16, 1679 before Jo. Woodbridge, Commis.

The testimony of Sam Lowle aged about 33 years that "I belonging to the same vessell wherein John Whitear dyed whereof Benj. Dole was master. I heard the sayd Benj. Dole (who afterwards dyed in the same Shipp) severall times speake the substance of what is aboue written & testifyed by Patrick Ewing: & that John Kelly was to haue his estate as is aboue expressed, & I watched with him when he dyed, & that he spak wel & sensibly & was of good understanding about halfe an houre before he dyed as farre as I apprehended." Sworn May 16, 1679 before Jo. Woodbridge, Commis.

Essex County Probate Files, Docket 29,713.

ESTATE OF JOHN GILLOW OF LYNN.

Administration upon the estate of John Gillow of Lynn, granted 24 : 4 : 1679, to Mr. George Keaser, and he is also appointed guardian of Robert and Sarah, children of John Gillow. *Salem Quarterly Court Records, vol. 5, leaf* 130.

ESTATE OF HENRY BALL OF SALEM.*

Administration upon the estate of Henry Ball, intestate, granted 24 : 4m : 1679, to Samuell Eborne, sr., and he to bring in an inventory to the next court held at Salem.

Salem Quarterly Court Records, vol. 5, leaf 130.

Henery Ball who deceased May 15, 1678, was indebted to Samuell Aburne as followeth: lent him 40s. in mony to pay his passage from Newfoundland, 2li.; payd for him to the Docter, 3li.; the charges of his dyet and tendance in the tyme

*Henry Baily in Probate, Docket, 1,320.

of his sicknes which was 7 months, and for damage done to
cloathinge and beddinge, 10li.; total, 15li. There being some
cloathinge sent to the said Hen. Ball by Mr. Rosse master of
the Apsum, ketch, and 5li. in mony by the way of the Barbados, it is requested by the said Samuell Aburne that the
court would grant him power to recover his debt if there be
so much of the estate in the country.

Essex County Quarterly Court Files, vol. 31, leaf 85.

ESTATE OF CHRISTOPHER CODNER OF (MARBLEHEAD?).*

Whereas there was ordered at a former court in Salem, out
of the estate of Christopher Codner to his two children, Christopher and Joane, 60li. to be paid when they come of age, the
house and ground being bound for security, the daughter
being of age sometime since received her part which is 20li.
and now the son being of age and none appearing that will
pay his part which his 40li., the court 24: 4m: 1679, impowered Mr. John Devorix and Mr. Richard Knott as feeofees in
trust, and upon the request of the mother and son, to sell or
otherwise dispose of the house and ground that the 40li. may
be paid.

Ann Devorix and Mary Downing gave oath in court 24: 4:
1679, that Christopher, the son of Christopher Codner, deceased, was twenty one years of age the latter end of September last past.

Salem Quarterly Court Records, vol. 5, leaf 130.

ESTATE OF PHILIP HARDING OF MARBLEHEAD.

"In the name of god Amen I Phillip herding Being Sick &
weake In Body But In perfect memory Doe make my Last
will & testament: Imp^r I Bequeaue my Soul to the Lord: from
whence it Came hopeing Through the meritts of Jesus Crist
That after this Sinfull Life is Ended I may Injoy Life
Eternally and for my outward Estate I giue as ffolloweth I
giue unto my Loueing wife Elisabeth herding all the Lower
Roomes of my house with the appurtinances thereunto Belonging Item I giue to my Daughter Jane herding all the upper
Roomes with the appurtinances thereunto Belonging to Be
Equally Shared Between my wife & my Daughter: of the
Chamber and if my Daughter will not Repaire that Share of
my house giuen her then my will is that she shall not Liue In
it: till her mothers Discease: and then I doe giue it to my

*See ante, vol. 1, page 325.

daughter and her heires for Euer Item I make m^r Ambrosse
gale my whole Executo^r to Se this my Last will and testament
perfomed: In wittness whereof I haue Sett to my hand and
fixed my Seal this 5th day of nouember 1678."

Phillip harding (SEAL)

Witness: John Eyres, George ffreshwatr.

Inventory of the estate of Philip Harding late of Marblehead, taken June 23, 1679, by Richard Norman and James
Dennes: a house and garden plot adjoyning, 40li.; Bedstead,
bed and furniture belonging, 6li.; Two iron pots, one iron
kettle & one brass kettle, 1li. 6s.; one cupboard, one table &
five joint stools, six chairs, 1li. 11s.; peuter platters and
basons and a peuter pott, 2li. 10s.; three chests, 15s.; old suit
of cloths, two hats and six cushions & pr. andirons, 1li. 10s.;
three sheets and six napkins, 15s.; a desperate debt of 34li.
5s. due from Laurence Barnes.

Attested in Salem court 27:4:1679, by Susana, relict of
Phillip Hardin, and she was granted administration upon his
estate, the imperfect will not being allowed.

Essex County Quarterly Court Files, vol. 31, leaf 91.

Administration upon the estate of Phillip Harden, was
granted 24:4:1679, to Susan, the relict of Phillip, who presented an inventory of the estate. The whole estate to remain
in her hands, only at her decease, 20li. to be paid to Jane, the
only child of the said Phillip and Susan.

Salem Quarterly Court Records, vol. 5, leaf 131.

ESTATE OF THOMAS COLE OF SALEM.

"The fiue & twentieth day of December Ann° Dom. 1678:
The last will & testament of Thomas Cole, made the daye &
yeare abouesd, although sick & weake in respect of bodyly
health, yet in sence & of sound & pfect memorye blessed be
God for it, but well knowing the uncertainty of mans life
heare upon earth, doe now therefore for the setlement and
disposall of what temporall estate ye Lord hath Blessed me
with all, make as aforesaid this my last will & testament: viz:
I giue & bequeath vnto Ann my wife, all my whole estate, both
in lands howseing, goods & chattells, moueables & unmoveables whatsoeuer, to and apptaineth: making my said wife
my only executrix upon all my estate, for her subsistence duering the terme of her naturall life, & at her decease, for what
part of my estate, shee may haue then remayning, my will &
desire to her is, that shee dispose of it to my children as shee

may see cause, In witnes whereof, I haue heareunto sett my hand & seale, the day & yeare abouesaid."

Thomas (his † mark) Cole. (SEAL)

Witness: Richard Croade, Pricilla Hunn.

Proved in Salem court 27 : 4m : 1679, by the witnesses.

Essex County Probate Records, vol. 301, page 136.

Inventory of the estate of Thomas Cole, taken Apr. 20, 1679, by Hilliard Veren, jr. and Richard Croade: a dwelling hows wth about an acker of Land adjoineing pt. of wch being ye Land Abra. Cole built 2 howses, & out howseinge, 50li.; a tenn acker Lott lying in ye Northfeild, 30li.; fower Cows, 10li.; two swine, 1li.; old cask, a chest & other Lumber in ye chamber, 10s.; 1 fether bed wth ye furnitture, 4li.; 1 old trundle flockbed, 10s.; 1 cubbard, 10s.; 1 Chest, 5s.; 2 brass kettles, 1li.; 2 Iron potts, 10s.; 3 puter dishes & smal parcel of Erthen dishes, &c., 10s.; 1 old table, chairs, formes & belos, 5s.; Pott hangers, 1 pr. old Andirons & tongs, 5s.; 1 old bras pott & skillit & spitt, 3s.; 2 bushels of Indian corne, 4s.; 1 old scith, 2s.; some other old Lumber not valeuable; total, 99li. 14s. The estate in Debt to sundry persons about 12li.

Attested in Salem court 27 : 4 : 1679, by the two appraisers, Ann, executrix, being sick.

Essex County Quarterly Court Files, vol. 31, leaf 92.

ESTATE OF NATHANIEL HUNN.

Administration upon the estate of Nathaniell Hunn, intestate, was granted 24 : 4 : 1679, to the relict of Nathaniel, who brought in an inventory, and the estate is to remain in her hands for her and the children.

Salem Quarterly Court Records, vol. 5, leaf 131.

Inventory* of the estate of Nathaniel Hunn taken by Richard Croade and Robert Kitchen: one feather Bed & furniture, 7li.; One Chest of drawers, 2li.; One Chest & box, 15s.; One small Chest & [2 tables: *copy*], 18s.; Fower Chaiers, 8s., 2 [Iron potts, 2 Haukes: *copy*] 1li. 8s.; One frying pann, [brass Ketle: *copy*], 1li. 2s.; One Skillitt, One [lamp, 1 gridiron: *copy*] & fire shovell, 5s.; One pr. andirons [1 pr. tongs. *copy*], 10s.; One Spitt & 2 hamers & one smoothing iron, 8s.; 2 Candlesticks, three [pitchers & glasses: *copy*], 5s.; One Trundlebed, &c., 2li. 10s.; five baskitts, 2 Pailes, 9s.; peuter platters, &c., 1li. 15s.; One spining wheele, 3s.; in Linen as sheets, napkins, &c., 5li.; Barrells & wooden ware, 6s.; Debts oweing to his Estate, 6li. 18s.; Debts due from his Estate,

* *Copy*, Essex County Probate Records, vol. 301, page 142.

6li. 5s., leaving 13s.; his wereing Cloathes, 2li.; Two bibles, 10s.; total, [27li. *copy*] 12s.

Attested in Salem court 27 : 4 : 1679, by relict of Nathaniel Hunn.

Essex County Quarterly Court Files, vol. 31, leaf 94.

ESTATE OF NATHANIEL PARKER OF NEWBURY.

Administration upon the estate of Nathan Parker, intestate, was granted 24 : 4m : 1679, unto Mary his wife. The whole estate to remain in her hands for the education and bringing up of Mary, the daughter of the deceased, until she come of age, and then the daughter to have half the estate, being equally divided, the house and land to stand bound for security.

Salem Quarterly Court Records, vol. 5, leaf 131.

Inventory of the estate of Nathan Parker, who deceased Apr. 6, 1679, taken by Wm. Chandler and Stephen Grenlefe, sr. : a house & halfe an Acree of land, 70li.; about five Acrees of marsh meadoe ground, 19li.; a mare, a cow, 4 sheepe and 3 lambs, 10li. 10s.; three swine, 30s., wearing apparell & sum Linen, 7li. 10s., 9li.; beding, bedsteads and sheetes, 11li. 6s.; Iron Cettles, pott and tramell & small skellett, 2li. 5s.; bridle, sadle and pillion, 1li.; peuter, glass bottles and bookes, 1li.; working tooles, 3li.; a gunn, snappsack, bandelers, pouder hornes, pouder, 1li. 15s.; Chestes, table and boxes, chaires and lumber, 3li.; bedstead, sledd and reele, 1li.; tennant saw & a long percer bitt, 10s.; due to him uppon severrall Accounts, 28li.; total, 161li. 6s. Debts 13li., making total, 148li. 6s.

Attested in Salem court 26 : 4 : 1679.

Essex County Quarterly Court Files, vol. 31, leaf 95.

An account of the debts which were due out of the estate, and since paid by Mary the relict: to John Guile, 7li.; Mr. Hugh March, sr., 2li. 10s.; Mr. Tristram Coffin, 5li. 10s.; Mrs. White, 6li.; John Webster, 1li. 10s.; James Smith, 15s.; Joshua Mors, 1li. 10s.; William Worm, 10s.; Robbert Long, 2li.; Benjamin Mors, 3s.; Hugh March, jr., 6s.; Mr. Davison, 1li.; old Mr. Anthony Somersby, 14s.; Israel Webster, 7s.; Moses Pilsbury, 1li. 19s.; widdow Knight, 11s.; Mr. William Noice, 1li. 8s.; John Bartlett, 13s.; left out of it by providence a cow & 2 swine imediately after the settlement of the estate, 5li.; John Sawyer, 2s.; Docter Dole, 9s.; Mrs. Woodbridge, 11s. 9d.; Mr. Thomas Noice, 6s.; total, 40li. 14s. 9d. Out of the above said account was allowed formerly but

13li., more debts paid since, making total, 27li. 14s.
9d. This addition or after entry of debts more than
was in the first inventory, allowed by the Salem
court 27 : 4 : 1682. *Probate Papers in the Quarterly Court
Records copied by Joshua Coffin, and now in the Probate Reg-
istry, vol. 2, page 628.*

Account of Mary Parker, alias Eliot, administratrix of the
estate of Nathan Parker, late of Newbury, of her administration, brought in Apr. 27, 1696: the estate Cr. per real estate,
89li., personal estate, 72li. 6s., received for rent, 6li., total,
167li. 6s.; debts paid to several persons, 40li. 4s. 9d.; debts
which were due to ye estate wch I could never gett, part of it
being Illegally given to be pd. yearly if sd. Nathan lived or
else to Revert to his Uncle, 28li.; Funeral charges, 16s., cow
that was lost, 5li., 5li. 16s.; 4 sheep & 3 Lambs killed by
wolves, 2li. 18s.; Repairing ye house, 9li., 3 shotes Dyed
strangely, 30s., 10li. 10s.; Doctr. Bradstreets Bill for Physick
& Tendance when Mary Parker was wounded by the Indians
in Mony, 12li. 6s. 8d., 18li. 10s.; Nurse for Nursing her 13
weeks & for Diet & Lodging in mony,—li. which is in pay,
12li.; Coffin & Digging her grave & pd. the apprisers in pay,
1li. 4s.; for making 2 Deeds of sale & 3 dayes time of myself
& father in getting deeds written & signed, 7s. 6d., acknowl-
edging & recording said deeds, 1li. 2s. 6d.; my husbands journey to Newbury to procure ye finishing sd. deeds, 18s.;
Bathsheba Knights for a debt due to her, 9s.; shingles & nailes
for repairing ye house, 8s. 4 1-2d.; shingling ye house & other
work att ye time & filling ye chamb. in part, 2li.
4s.; pd. for glass to ye house, Repaireing ye Cellar, Makeing ye stairs & so on & nailes to do it withall & worke & a
crotch pole for ye well, 2li. 17s. 6d.; making severall Tennants
& Leases from time to time, 1li.; Repairation of ye house severall times more, 6li.; more ground pinning & making a drain
to ye cellar, 2li. 13s.; 1 weeks tendance of myself on Mary
Parker when wounded by the Indians, 10s.; Journeys of my
husband & self to look after her 5 times, 5li.; pd. Mr. Dole,
11s., Docr. Packers's Bill, 2li. 9s. 10d., 3li. 10d.; stating this
acct., Allowing of it & recording & a Quietus, 1li. 8s. 6d.;
Setling & Dividing it & allow ye admrx. for her trouble, 4li.
7s. 6d.; total, 110li. 15s. 8d.

Remains due to Bal. 56li. 10s. 4d. one half of which is to
Mary Parker, 28li. 5s. 2d. Mary Parker Dr. to Dr. Bradstreet,
the nurse, her coffin, &c, 30li. 18s.; a weeks attendance when

wounded & journey of myself to Newbury to look after her
5 times, 5li. 10s.; pd. Mr. Dole, 11s., Docr. Packers bill, 2li.
9s. 10d., 3li. 10d.; total, 39li. 18s. 10d. Attested May 4, 1696,
John Croade, Reg.

Mary Parker, alias Elliot, administratrix of the estate of
Nathaniel Parker of Newbury, carpenter, having made and
rendered an account of her administration on said estate, a
quietus is granted and given to the said administratrix.

Essex County Probate Records, vol. 305, pp. 179, 249.

ESTATE OF VINSON GALLISON.

Administration upon the estate of Vinson Galishon, intestate, granted 24:4m:1679, to Richard Reefe, who is to administer as far as the estate will go.

Salem Quarterly Court Records, vol. 5, leaf 131.

Inventory of the estate of Vinson Gallison taken Dec. 6,
1678, by Moses Mavericke and Samuell Morgan: 1 paier of
boots, 8s.; 1 cap cloth coat, 10s.; 2 parsells of Lien, 5s.; 1
whiett wastkoat, 4s.; 1 old shirt and drawers, 3s.; 2 whiett
neckcloths, 3s.; 1 blue shirt, 1 whiett ditto, 7s.; 1 red wastkoat
and drawers, 12s.; 1 cloth coatt and Sarg briches, 12s.; 1 old
hatt, 4s.; total, 3li. 8s. Due from Richard Reaf for a months
servis, 1li. The sd. Vincent Gallison Dr. to Mr. Rich. Reefe
reckoned with him while he was alive, 2li. 17s. 6d.

Since he dyed pd. to James Stilson for mending of shooes,
3s.; to John Curtis, 2s. 9d.; to Edw. Reede for digging ye
grave, 4s.; James Dennis for a coffin, 10s.; ye jurie & other
charge of his buriall, 9s. 6d.; for mackrell & other things
unreckoned, 2s. 4d.; for his towne rate, 5s.; total, 4li.

Administration upon the estate granted by the Salem court
26:4:1679, to Richard Reefe, and he is to administer so far
as the estate will go.

Essex County Quarterly Court Files, vol. 31, leaf 97.

ESTATE OF JOHN MILLETT OF GLOUCESTER.

Administration upon the estate of John Millett, intestate,
was granted 24:4m:1679, to Sara, the relict, who brought in
an inventory. The house and land to stand bound for security
for paying the several children's parts out of the estate according as the court shall order afterwards.

Salem Quarterly Court Records, vol. 5, leaf 131.

Inventory of the estate of John Millitt taken by James

Stevens and William Sargant: howse & baren and Land, 24li.; neate catell & a mare, 23li.; bedes & beding, 8li.; home-mad cloth, 4li.; his waring clothes, 5li.; in howsall stuffe, 3li.; woole, 2li. 5s.; armes, 1li. 10s.; tooles, 12s.; lumber, 2li.; broadcloth, 10s.; sarge & Tabell Lining, 1li.; sheepe, 11li. 4s.; total, 86li. 1s. Deptes due from the estat, 13li.; the deptes paid the Estate aperes to be 73li. 1s.

Attested in Salem court 24 : 4m : 1679, by Sarah, the relict.
Essex County Quarterly Court Files, vol. 31, leaf 98.

ESTATE OF THOMAS OLIVER OF SALEM.

Administration upon the estate of Thomas Oliver, intestate, was granted 24 : 4m : 1679, to Bridget, his wife, and she is to bring in an inventory to the next court at Salem.
Salem Quarterly Court Records, vol. 5, leaf 131.

Inventory of the estate of Thomas Oliver, taken 21 : 4m : 1679, by Edmund Batter and Hilliard Veren, sr : house & ground adjoyning of about 1-2 an acre, 45li.; about 10 acres of land in the north feild, 25li.; a smale old bed, bedsteed, flock bolster & pillowes with all appurtenances, 2li. 10s.; his wear-ing apparrell, 1li. 5s.; a litle table & 3 old chests, 15s.; 2 Iron pots & old iron Ketle, a hanger & tonges, 10s.; a brass scillitt & som few earth dishes, 5s.; 3 or 4 old chaires, 3s., 2 piggs. 10s., 13s.; 2 pailes & old tubs & som od lumber, 5s.; an old rusty sword & old bandeleers, 5s.; total, 76li. 8s. The estate is Dr. in England, as he said in his sickness, about 30li.; to severall other men heare as he said above, 15s.; due to the Towne when sick & at his buriall, 2li. 19s. 6d.; due to Dr. Swinerton about 2li. 3s.; several other debts owing not yet knowne.

Attested by Bridgett, relict of Tho. Oliver, and allowed, 28 : 9 : 1679.

Administration upon the estate was granted 28 : 9 : 1679, to Bridget, relict of the deceased, and the estate to be for the use of the widow, she paying the two sons of her husband, 20s. each, and her daughter Cristian 20s. and also the debts; and to have liberty to sell the ten acre lot by advice of the select-men of Salem, towards paying the debts and her present supply, and as need shall be, any other part of the estate.
Essex County Quarterly Court Files, vol. 32, leaf 23.

ESTATE OF ALLESTER MACKMALLEN OF SALEM.

Administration upon the estate of 'Allester Mackmallen,

was granted 24 : 4m : 1679, to Elizabeth, the relict, and she is
to bring in an inventory to the next court at Salem.

Salem Quarterly Court Records, vol. 5, leaf 131.

"The last will & testament of Allester Mackmallen, made
this 3ᵈ of June 1679 : being then very sick, but in right & pfect
mind and memory is as followeth, my will is that after my
decease, that litle I haue, in this world both house & ground,
with all my household goods & what ever elce I haue, my
deere wife, Elizabeth, shall haue & injoy all to her owne proper
use & behoofe the time of her naturall life, or marriage &
after her decease, or marriage to any other man then the house
& ground to goe to my son John & to his heires, except the
smale peece of ground behind the house to goodman Baxsters
wards which I giue to my sonn——after his mothers decease
or marriage, or elce five pounds to be pd by his Brother John
out of the house & ground at his the sd——choyce, & then
John to hold all the house & ground & further my will is that
John shall pay out of the house & ground twenty shillings
apeece to the rest of my children, viz.——and also to pay what
debts my deere wife may leaue unpaid if required, that I
shall owe at my decease, and I doe make & appoynt, my sd
wife sole executrix of this my last will & testament In wittnes
whereof I haue sett to my hand & seale."

"The sd Alester haveing not an opertunity to signe & seale,
it being presented to the court the widow consents to this
above written and the court at Salem 28 : 9 : 1679, allowed it."

Essex County Probate Records, vol. 301, page 150.

Allester Makmallen having deceased before his will was perfected, it being drawne up what his mind was, and presented
to this court, and Elizabeth his relict consenting thereto, it
was allowed 25 : 9 : 1679, and this paper together with the
inventory was filed in this court's records.

Salem Quarterly Court Records, vol. 6, leaf 4.

Inventory of the estate of Alester Mackmallen, deceased 20 :
4m : 1679, taken by Richard (his ℬ mark) Adams and Hilliard Verin, sr. : the house and ground, 40li. ; an old smale
featherbead, steed & furniture, 3li. ; his wearing apparrell, 1li. ;
an old brass mettle pot & Ketle, 1li. ; a side cubord & old
warmin pan, 1li. ; hanger & pothookes & gridirons, 10s. ; in
pewter & lanthorne, 10s. ; earthware & botle glasses, 2s. ; an
old chaire or two, an old chest, 3 old axes, 2 old spades & som
other lumber, 10s. ; an old bedstead & a litle old flock bed,

10s.; total, 48li. 2s. The estate is Dr. to Mr. Wm. Browne, sr.; to Mr. Cromwell, 2li. 10s. 9 3-4d.; Mr. Wells; John Cromwell, 1li. 7s. 8d.; Mr. Browne & Willowby, 1li. 4s.

Attested in Salem court, 28:9:1679, by Elizabeth Mackmallon, relict of the deceased, and she was granted power of administration.

Essex County Quarterly Court Files, vol. 32, leaf 23.

ESTATE OF JOHN PEARSON, SR.

"The Laste will & Testement of John Persson ‖senior‖ though weak in Bodey yet perfitt in Mind and Memorey firste I giue My soule to god that gaue it And My Bodey to bee Buried By My Christian friendes in hope of a Joyfull Resurection at the Laste daye secondly My will is That My Deare & Louinge wife Maudlin shall haue the hole Improuemente of ‖all‖ the Land & Catell that I haue in My hands, and of the orcherds & Meddows and all houshold stuf within dores and all Impelments of husbandery with out dores 3 I giue unto My Sonn John Persson all the farme that I now Liue uppon with all the Medowes Belonging Thearunto Excepting Twenty Ackers of the upland, which Twenty ackers of upland I giue unto My Daughter Sarah and to her Cheldren And if euer My Daughter Sarah hath a mind to sell this Twenty Ackers of Land They shale sell it to none But to My Sonn John or to his Children, they giuing for it soe mutch as Tow Indiferent Men shale Judge it to be worth which Twenty Ackers shale Leye as followeth: beging at the heighways and soe alonge By the Line that Runnes bettwen goodman Poles Lande and Mine 4 I giue Unto My Daughter Sarah and to her Cheldren Tenn Ackers of Meddow Leying in the great Meddow, tow Ackers of this Meddow is now in the handes of Edward Tayler and I giue it to you at his deaseas further More I giue Unto My Daughter Sarah and to her Cheldren A parssell of Land Bee it More or Less that Leyeth Beyond Ipswidg River at the head of Redding Boundes that was somtimes Richard Horadels and a parssell of swampy land Leying in the great swampe fiue Ackers or thear aboutes.

"I giue unto My Daughter Marey Burnap and ‖to‖ her Cheldren Thirty Ackers of upland Leying Betwen the Landes of Jonathan Poole and Robarte Burnap be it More or Less further More I giue Unto My Daughter Marey Burnap A parssell of Land forty Ackers or ther abouts Leying near to the Land of Mas. John hauke or Adjoyning to it and to her

Cheldren further More I giue Unto My Daughter Marey
Burnap and to her Cheldren Tenn Ackers of Meddow tow
Ackers of it Leyinge in the wigwam Meddow and eight Ackers
leving in the great Meddow 6 I giue Unto My Daughter
Bethia Carter and to her Cheldren A parssel of Land Leying
in Redding Boundes eighty Ackers or thear abouts with the
Medow Belonging thear Unto and Eight Ackers of Meddow
Leyinge in the greate Meddow further More I giue unto My
Daughter Bethia Carter Three pound A year yearly to Be
payd to her during her naturall life Twenty shillinges a yeare
in Monies of it to be payd to her By My Sonn John Persson
or By his heires excecutors or Administrator or Assignes prouided That the Land and Meddow That I haue giuen to her
and the Three pound a yeare doath not Amount to Aboue one
hundered pounds 7 further more I giue unto My Sonn John
Persson a peese of Cedor swamp that was the widdow Dustins
that Leyeth in the Cedor Swamp in the Boundes of Reddinge
further More I giue Unto My Sonn John Persson An Acker
mor or Less an Acker of salte Marshe that Leyeth in the Towne
Marshe att Linn, with the Remaynder of the Thirty Ackers
of Meddow that Leyeth in the great Meddow to him and to
his Children And all the Landes & Meddowes that I haue
giuen to him shale be to him and to his Children and to his
Childrens Children foreuer And further More all the Landes
& Meddowes That I haue giuen to all the Reste of My Children shalbe to them and to ther Children & to ther Childrens
Children for euer But in Case My Children or Childrens Children shale see cause out of som nessesarytey of concienc shale
see Cause to Remove Ther habitasion that this will of Mine
shale not tey them But that they Maye Sell ther Landes 8 My
will is that My Daughter Sarah Tounsend shale haue the use
of halfe the Barne while they are Capabell of getting one for
them selues further More I giue Unto My Daughter Sarah
Townsend the use of the Tow peeses of Meddow That Leyeth
within the farme for fiften year after the Date hearof and My
will is that the Landes And Meddow that I haue giuen to her
And the Rente of theas tow peeses of Meddow shale bee Made
up one hundred pounds

"9 My will is that My Daughter Marey Burnap that the
Lands and Meddow that I haue giuen to her and her Chel-
dren shale bee made up one hundren pound 10 I giue unto
My Deare wife Maudlin The Time that I haue in My
Seruants that is yet Remayning to serue further More 11 My

will is That My Sonn John Persson shale Improue all the
Land and Meddow for My wife Maudlin his Mother for her
use hee hauing one halfe of the Increase for his paynes And
Care, John Persson is to haue John Lilly at Comand for to
help him for the Improuement of the Land 12 further More
My will is That the three score Ackers of Land That Leyeth
Beyond Ma⁸ Dillingams Meddow shalbe sould for the use of
the famely as My wife Maudlin shale see Cause 13 further
More My will is That the Thirty Ackers of Meddow in The
greate Meddow that I haue giuen to My Children shale equally
Bee deuided amongste ‖them‖ according to each mans proportion 14 Lastly My will is That none of all the Landes and
Meddowes That I haue hear in this My will giuen to my Cheldren shale not Bee Theirs untill After the death of My Deare
wife Maudlin Persson Datted This 19ᵗʰ of Aprill 1679."

John (his O mark) Persson

Witness: William Cowdry, Jeremiah Sweyen.   Proved in
Salem court 25:4:1679, by the witnesses, and the court
granted administration unto Maudline, relict of the deceased, and to his son John Pearson, jointly.

Inventory of the estate of John Persson taken May 14,
1679, by William Cowdrey, Thomas Bancrofte and Hananiah
Parker: the housing and homstead Land and Meddow, 500li.;
Thirty Ackers of upland called Newels Lott, 36li.; forty
Ackers of upland By John haukes, 30li.; one Acker of salte
marshe, 5li.; Thre score Ackers of uplands in the woodes,
16li.; Thirty Ackers of Meddow in the great medow, 120li.;
Tenn Ackers of Land beyond Ipswidg River, 5li.; eighty
Ackers of upland beyond Ipswidg River, 25li.; a parssel of
Meddow in the hundred Ackers, 18li.; five Ackers of wett
swampe, 3li.; tow Ackers of Meddow in the wigwam Meddow, 5li.; A parssel of Cedar swamp, 5li.; Three horses, 4li.;
fower oxen, 20li.; fower Cowes, 15li.; youge Cattell, 9li.; 14
sheep and nine Lambes, 6li.; fower swine, 2li. 10s.; fether
bead, Rugg, boulsters & pillowes, 5li.; coverled & a bead & 2
flock pillowes, 2li. 3s.; another Bead & boulster & blancket,
1li. 5s.; sheets and Tabel Linnen, 6li.; puter one & other,
2li.; Brasse, 1li. 10s.; In Iron, Thre pots and a friing pan, 1li.
15s.; Milke vessels, Trayes, dishes & spones, 1li. 15s.;
Andianers, 2 spits, driping pan and Iron back, 2li. 10s.;
Tramels, fire pan, Tonges and smothing Irons, 15s.; Tabels,
Chayers, a setell, cushins & a fourme, 2li. 10s.; Armes, 2li.
10s.; Chests and Boxes, 1li. 8s.; woolen yarne & Linnan, cotten

yarne, 4li.; Cider Caske, 3li.; chees Toub, poudering toub & meash tub, 15s.; wheels and cards, 1li. 5s.; glasses and erthen ware, 6s.; Books, 2li.; cartes, plowes, chaynes & howes, 4li. 12s.; Beetel Ringes, wedges, Iron morter, 1li. 5s.; Iron Crowes, a spade and shovell, 1li. 8s.; a fann, winow sheete and Mesures, 17s.; scales, wayts and sives, 15s.; Axes, forkes, sawes & sikels, 10s.; carte Rope, sadel and pillyon, 1li. 15s.; sithes, sheep sheeres & a hamer, 15s.; Creditt, 7li.; Three yards of Carsey, 1li. 10s.; his waring Aparell, 10li. 10s.; Total, 897li. 19s. Debts owing, 7li.

Attested in Salem court 25 : 4 : 1679, by the administrators. *Essex County Quarterly Court Files, vol. 31, leaves 87, 88.*

ESTATE OF WILLIAM ALLEN, SR., OF MANCHESTER.

"The Last will of Willallam Allen Sen of Manchester made y* 7 of June 1678 Imprimes I doe make my wife Elezebeth Allen my full & Sole execcuter of all my lands & goods duereing her life & after y*e* deth of my wife to be dissposed in maner & forem as folleth y*t* is to say I give to my Sone Samuell y* remayner of y*e* five & twenty acer lott which he all redy poseseth y*t* is to Say y*e* uplands & y*e* sheare of y*e* fresh medow belonging thereunto I give to my too Sonns onesephoras & Willam Allen my wholle fifty acer lott w*th* all y*e* devissons & apurtenances belongin to it w*th* y*e* propriety of all commons devidded & undevided belongin to it & an acer of Sallt marsh at y*e* lower end of my orchard y*t* I purchesed this I give to my too Sonns onesephoras & Willam Allen to be equally devided betwene them booth after y*e* deth of me & my wife & it is farther to be understood y*t* as my Sone onesephoras hath hallf an acer in present poseson joyning to his hows y*t* lyes in my orchard Soe my Sonn willam Allen to have hallfe an acer joyning to his hows in y*e* Same maner In wittnes where of I y*e* Said Willam Allen have put to my hand."

Willam (his M mark) Allen.

Witness: Thomas (his T mark) Jonnes, Samuell Friend.
Proved in Salem court 26 : 4 : 1679, by the witnesses.

"The Widow Allen Testifieth That her husband William Allen deceaced gaue his Sonne Samuell more then he gaue his other Sonnes thes things following & that therefore he gaue him not A double Portion first at his first mariadg or before helpt to buld him An house Secondly he gaue him Thre

Cattell one After Another Thirdly he hath bin helpfull unto
him Cince as he Could."

Inventory of the estate of William Allen, deceased Jan. 30,
1678, taken Manchester, Feb. 17, 1678, by Thomas West and
John Siblle : hows & land wth all ye medow belongin to it,
140li.; fivetene acers of upland lying in yᵉ bounds of Beverly
joining too ye great pon called wenam pon, 20li.; Two oxen,
a cow, two hyfers, too shepe & a horse, 18li. 10s.; Bed wth
beding & other howsholld stufe, 8li.; total, 180li. 6s. 10d. 6li.
to be abated for the loss of horse & cow.

Attested in Salem court 26 : 4 : 1679, by Eliza., the relict.

William Allin, sr., Dr. unto Phillipp Cromwell, 2li. 16s.
4d.; to Jon. Cromwell, 12s. 5d. Dated June 25, 1679.

William Allen, deceased, his estate stands debtor unto my
Master Capt. Georg Corwin, 8li. 1s. 9 1-2d. Witness: Jno.
Whyting. Dated June 23, 1679.

William Allin of Manchester debtor to Henry Bartholmew,
6s. 6d.; to William Browne, sr., 7li. 16s. 3d.

Essex County Quarterly Court Files, vol. 31, leaf 96.

ESTATE OF EDWARD WALDEN OF WENHAM.

"Known all men by these presents this 22 of March 1678-9
thatt I Edward Walden of Wenham in the County of Essex,
being sick of body butt of good & perfect memory caling to
mind the uncertainty of this mortall life. Doe make constitute & ordeine this my last will & testament in form & manner as followeth. Impʳ: I Committ my soul to God thatt
gave itt, & my body to the earth, & to decent Buriall. Item: I
Give to my Son Nathaniell Walden: all my Land on the
Neck: In account ten acres be there more or less. Item the
rest of my estate, I will thatt itt ‖be‖ equally divided betweene the rest of my children which I here name. John
Walden. Hannah Walden. Ruth Walden. Naomi Walden, &
Elizabeth Walden. If any of these my children dy before
they come of Age to possess their portions. It shall be equally
divided among the Survivinge If they all dy itt shall fall to
the nearest of Kin And I make my Son Nathaniel Walden
sole Excecutor of this my will & I desire my Loving friends
Capᵗ: Thomas Fiske, & Charles Gott to oversee this my will.
In witness whereof I have sett to my hand ‖and Seale‖ the
day & yeare above written."

Edward (his IX mark) Walden (SEAL)

Witness: Joseph Gerrish, Sarah (her S mark) Moulton.
Proved in Salem court 25 : 4 : 1679, by the witnesses.

Joseph Gerrish and John (his J mark) Abby, sr., testified Apr. 29, 1679, that Edward Walden ordered the blotting out of the words that are blotted out in the will.

Joseph Gerrish aged about 29 years, testified that he heard Edward Walden say he had done enough for his two daughters, Mary and Thomasin already, and therefore saw meet to leave them out of his will. Sworn in court at Salem, 26 : 4 : 1679.

Inventory of the estate of Edward Waldern, taken 20 : 4m : 1679, by Thos. Fiske and Charles Gott: ten acres of land, 25li.; twenty pownd Remainding upon a Bill to be paid in fowre yers following, 20li.; another Bill to be paid in 9 yers following, 17li.; one Cowe, 3li. 16s.; one gun, 1li.; Cloathing, 2li. 4s.; Tramell & pothooks, 6s. 6d.; one old kettle & one old ax, 3s.; due from Samll. Fiske, 6s.; in Beding, 1li. 16s.; Bedstead, 5s.; total, 71li. 16s. 6d. Debts due from the estate; to the Docter, 2li. 8s.; to John Fiske, 2li. 2s.; Goodwife White, 10s.; Goodman Woodward, 5s.; Goodman Pearce, 5s.; John Walderne, 10s.; Hannah Walderne in mony, 13s.; mony to Mr. Gerrish, 5s.; Mr. Gerrish by Rate, 6s. 5d.; Joseph Fowler, 2s.; total, 7li. 6s. 5d.

Attested in Salem court 26 : 4 : 1679, by Nathaniell Walden, the executor, and he is to pay to his sister Tamson 5— out of the estate the debts to be paid first out of the whole estate.

Essex County Quarterly Court Files, vol. 31, leaves 99, 100.

ESTATE OF GEORGE GARDNER OF SALEM.

"I Georg Gardner, lying very sick & weak: doe comend my soule into the hands of God through Jesus Christ, to whome I fly alone, as my all sufficient refuge, in this & all conditions, I may be in, yea death itselfe Secondly my body to Christian buriall first I bequeath unto my beloued wife Elizabeth Gardner, the incum of my part in the mills of Salem, duering her life, & I doe give unto my wife abouesaid the rent of that land I bought, of Mr. Joseph ffitch, or the use of the money if he pay for it, according to contract, the terme of her life, againe I giue her the rent of that land I bought of John Terry, during her life, & the two cowes, & two calves: & three swine, at home, for euer, as likewise the use of what household stuff in my house is mine for the terme of her life, 2ly I giue unto my sonn Samuell Gardner, my house & land in

which he now dwelleth, at Salem, with all my upland &
meddow, in the south feild & my part of the mills after his
mothers decease, And the farme & meddow, Thomas Gold
lives upon after his mothers decease & the houseing & all ap-
p^rtenances thereto belonging 3^{ly} I give unto my sonn Ebenezer,
all my houses & land, with all the app^rtenances thereto belonging: at hartford: & windsor & simsbury after his mothers
decease: likewise I give unto him p^rsently after my decease,
that land lyeth by Mr. Babadg, & that acre of saltmarsh I
had of my father foreuer 4^{ly} to my daughter Buttolph I giue
three hundred pounds, of my debts owing me at conetticott,
when they are gott in: & to my son Buttolph I give thirty
pound he was Indebted to me at our last reckoning I mean
the ballance of that acco^t: was made in the Springe, 5^{ly} To
my daughter Turner I doe give the house & land, they now
live in, to him & her, theire naturall liues, & then to whome
of her children he shall give it after him, prouided he give it
to one or more of her children, & three hundred pounds, of
my debts at coneticott, as it can be got in, 6^{ly} To my daughter
Hathorne, I give three hundred pounds, of my debts at conetticott, as they can be gott in. But in case my sonne Ebenezer
dy before he be marryed then the estate given him to be deuided equally amongst the rest of my children And I likewise give to my sonn Ebenezer, the rent of that farme Thomas
Gold liueth on, duering his mothers life and doe giue unto
my Brother Thomas Gardner, twenty pounds in prouissions,
And I giue unto my two Cozens, mirriam Hascall & Susana
Hill, fiue pounds to each of them, money to be layed out by
my sister Grafton, fiue pounds now in household stuff, to
mirriam, & fiue pounds to Susana Hill at her marriage.

"And I doe apoynt Samuell Gardner & Ebenezer my sonns
to be my executors, & what remaineth after my debts be paid
& legacies two parts to my sonn Samuell & one part Ebenezers
and to my seruant Arrah I doe giue fiue pounds when he
hath serued my sonn Samuell fiue yeares: & then his time to
be out. And I doe intreat my loueing friend Capt: John
Allen, to ouersee the pformance of this my will, whoe liueth at
Hartford, to whom I giue fiue pounds: in token of my loue.
And likewise I doe intreat my freind caleb Stanley to ouersee the pformance of this my will, whoe liueth at conetticott, to whose two daughters I giue fifty shillings apeece And
I desire my two loueing brothers, Thomas & Samuell Gardner,
to oversee the pformance of my will at Salem . . . That the
aboue written is now my act & deed being in pfect memorye,

I sett my hand this twenty one of July, one thousand six hundred seauenty nine."

George Gardner

Witness: Thomas Gardner, Samuell Gardner, sr., Joseph Williams.

Proved in Salem court Sept. 1, 1679, by two of the witnesses.

Inventory of the estate of Lt. George Gardner, taken Oct. 17, 1679, by John Browne and John Higgenson, jr., and presented by Samuell and Ebenezer Gardner: the dwelling house, bake house & out housing & the land they stand on & the land belonging & adjoyning to them now in possession of Samll. Gardner, 270li.; a farm of about 400 acres of upland & meddow with the dwelling house & outhouseing upon it now in possession of Thomas Goold & in the towneship of Salem & 12 acres of meddow lying in Redding bounds in possession of said Goold, 320li.; 13 acres upland & 2 acres of marsh or there abouts lying in the south feild, 60li.; 1-8 part of the corne mill, 100li.; 1 acre of land neere the pen, 20li.; a houselot next to Mr. Babadges, 14li.; 1 house & the land belonging to it now in the possession of Habbacuck Turner, 90li.; Dts. due to the estate from Mr. Samll. Shrimpton, Mr. Arther Mason & Mr. John Waite, about 157li.; due to the estate in the hands of Samuell Gardner, Jun., about 588li.; severall small debts in Salem about 20li.; 5 years service in a negro named Arow, 10li.; an Indian servant, 10li.; pcell of household stuff in the possession of Samuell Gardner Jun. & wearing cloathes, 22li. 14s. 2d.; 1 cow in the possession of Thomas Goold, 2li. 10s.; 7 barrells of pork in the hand of Jon. Hathorne, 17li. 10s.; an acre of salt marsh by Strong water brooks, 20li.; total, 1621li. 14s. 2d. Pcell of burnt sithes sold for about 3li.

Attested in Salem court 30 : 4m : 1680, by Mr. Samuell Gardner and Ebenezer Gardner to be a true inventory of their father's estate here in this colony, except what is entered in the inventory and given in and allowed of at the court in Hartford.

Essex County Probate Records, vol. 301, pp. 143-145.

ESTATE OF PHILIP FOWLER, SR., OF IPSWICH.

Administration upon the estate of Philip Fowler, intestate, was granted Sept. 30, 1679, unto his grandchild, Philip Fowler.

Ipswich Quarterly Court Records, vol. 5, page 347.

Inventory of the estate of Phillip Fowler, Sr., taken July 21, 1679, by Phillip Fowler, Jr., Simon Stace and Nicolas Wallis: 4 ould Cotts & an ould cloke, 1li. 15s.; A parsell of ould clothes, 1li.; some ould stockens, 2 Caps, payer of gartars, 5s.; A payer of ould gloves and an ould hate, 2s.; two payer of drawers, two old shirts, 15s.; two caps, two bands & three ould hankercher and also two ould neckclothes, 4s.; total, 3li. 1s. Debt due to the estate, 17s. 6d.

Attested in Ipswich court Sept. 30, 1679, by Phillip Fowler, administrator of the estate of Phillip Fowler, Sr.

Essex County Probate Files, Docket 10,073.

ESTATE OF PAUL WHITE OF NEWBURY.

"In the name of god amen: I Paul White of Newbery in y⁰ County of Essex in New England Marrinor being att psent of a sound minde and memory and in competent helth of body: yet Considering my great age, and the many infirmities accompaning yᵉ same, and not knowing how soon my change may bee, haue thought it meet, and doe accordingly make this my last will and testament, in manner and forme following: Imprs: I bequeath and resigne my soule into the hands of god that gaue it and my body to be decently interred in yᵉ earth from whence it was taken, in hope & firme assurance of ye pdon of all my sins & of a blessed and happy resurrection through yᵉ alone merritt & mediation, of my Lord and sauiouʳ Jesus Christ. And as for my worldly goods and outward estate, whether real Psonall or mixt of what kind or nature soe euer they be (my just debts & funerall expences being discharged) I giue and bequeath wholy and absolutely and euery part and parcell thereof, unto my dear and louing wife Anne: White to be ordered & disposed of by her, as she in her wisdome & discretion shall think meet Whoe alsoe I doe hereby make my sole Executrix of this my last will and testament. I should haue giuen some Legacies to yᵉ children of my sᵈ dear wife and in pticular to my daughter Mary yᵉ wife of Mʳ Thomas Woodbridge but that I haue formerly largely testified my loue towards him in full satisfaction (as I intended & declared) of what he might expect from me, upon any account or consideration whatsoeuer & for yᵉ rest of my dear wiues children, I leaue it freely to her, to doe for them as she shall judge meet hereby making voyde all former wills, writings or ingagements of this kinde: In wittness whereof I haue hereunto sett my hand and seal this fourteenth day of August, in yᵉ year of oʳ Lord one thousand six hundred and seuenty four."

Paul (his △ mark) White. (SEAL)
Witness: Dudley Bradstreet, Richard Lowle.
Attested Aug. 27, 1679, by Richard Lowle (he being not able to travel), before Jo. Woodbridge, Com., and in Ipswich court, Sept. 30, 1679, by Mr. Dudley Bradstreet.

Inventory of the estate of Capt. Paull White, taken Sept. 1, 1679, by Tho. Woodbridge and Wm. Chandler: In the Parlor, Bed, Bedsteed, Bolster, pillowes, Curtains & vallance, 10li.; A good trundle Bed with all Furniture, 6li.; A close stoole with a pewter pan, 15s.; 1 Iron Bound Case of Bottles, 5s.; 1 Larg pair Cast Andirons, 1li. 8s.; 1 Great table & six Joyn stools, 1li. 12s.; 1 small table & Four great chairs, 17s.; 5 Cushins, 1 Rushy carpett, Fire pan & tongs, 1li. 8s.; 1 chest and Box, &c., 15s.; 1 screan, 2 window Curtains & Cubbard cloth, 6s.; his wearing clothes, 20li.; His House and Land & all outhouses, 300li.; 96 Acres Land att haverill, 75li.; 5 Acress more, 12li.; 108 Acress more Land att Emsbury, 60li.; 1 Negrow, 30li.; All the goods in the shop, 53li. Goods in the ware house celler; 8 pd. Butter & 4 empty Butts, 1li.; wines and Salting troff & 3 old Cask, 13li. 3s. In the Haull or great kittchin: 1 great table, 2 Joyn stooles, 4 chairs, 1 cushin, 15s.; 13 pewter Dishes, 3 Bassons, 16 plates, 4li. 1s. 6d.; 9 porringer, 1 Flaggon, 3 pewter tankards, 1li. 11s.; 1 pr. Candlestick, 2 ale quarts, 13s.; wine qt., 2 wine pints, 1-2 pints, gill, &c., 15s.; 5 Sawcers, 2s. 6d.; 1 Still & 3 chamber potts, 2li. 2s. 6d.; 5 larg Brass kettles, 3 Brass skillitts, 4li. 18s.; 1 warming pan, Bras scumer, Bell mettle skillitt, 16s.; 1 Brass morter & pestle & basting Ladle, 4s.; 1 pair Iron Andirons, 3 Iron potts, &c., 2li.; Tramell, spits & one Fender, 16s.; 1 drippin pan, Frying pan & choping kniffe, 12s.; 3 smothing irons, 2 pair tongs, Firepan & Bellowes, 10s.; 1 Iorn morter, 1 Lamp, fleshook, 2 pails & 1 pipkin, 14s.; 7 earthen potts, 2 pans, 1 great bason, 2 dishes & 2 potts, 9s.; 2 pans, 1 pipkin & 1 salt celler, 1s.; 6 larg puddin pans, larg drippin pan, 14s.; 1 Collinder, 1 Lanthorn, 1 Breadgrate, 6s.; Flesh plate, Aple Roster, candle box, Funell & candlesticks, 6s. 6d.; tin ware, trenchers, diat pan, sauce panne, Basting ladles and divers others, 12s. In the millhouse: The mault mill, 1 percell off Briks, 4 cask & 4 sives, 3li. 10s.; to the third part off the sawmill att Emsbury, 23li.; in the parlor Chest, Five Fine pillobees, 1li.; 4 pair Fine sheets, 2 Fine towles, 4li. 14s.;

money, plate & silver Buttons in a small trunk, 9li. 8s. 6d. In
the trunk in the Parlor Chamber: one Doss. new diaper Napkins, 20 cotten & Linen Napkins, 2 doss. 4 more, 23 more
Cors, 6 Fine towles & 4 pillobers, 9 Linen sheets, 3 large
diaper tablecloth and Fine holland in the chest, 17li. 16s.
In the chest in the hall Chamber: 11 pair Cors sheets, nine
table clothes, 10 towles, 6 pair pilobees, 17 cors Napkins, 8li.
15s. In the warehouse: 4000 sugar, 1 Barrill beeff, 2 hhd.
salt, 1-2 Tun. mellossoss, 188 Gall. Rum at 2s., 1 pair Larg
stilliards, 6 Cask, 12 Iron hoops, 1 Adds, &c., 34li. 8s.   In
the parlor Chamber: 1 hie Bedsteed, curtains, vallences, two
Cups, 5 silver spoons, Andirons, dogg, 1 trunk & chest, 15li.
14s. In the kitchin chamber: 1 Feather bed, curtain & vallans, Rugs, Blanketts & four chests, 8li. 16s. In the Garrett
over the kittchin: 1 bed and Furniture, meal trough, 4 Bush.
meale, Feathers, salt, 3 bags, 3 old Cask, 1 Rug, baskett, over
the porch, 1 Flock Bed, Bolster, Rugs & over the parlor chamber 30 pd. cotten, 2 Bags, 1 hanswa, 3 guns, 1 hamer, 1 Reell,
Bandeleers, 1 kneeding tub & boyle in all, 11li. 6s. 6d. In the
Cellar under the house, 3 Barrills of beer, 5 old tubs with
sope & grease, whaleboan & provisions, 6li. 10s.   In the still
house: 1 still worm & tub, 1 Brass Coper, 4 old Butts, 1
wheele, 2 Firkins, 1 tub in the old house, one but, 1 hhd., bedsack, 1 chair, an old sadle, hops, in the yard, 4 cord of wood,
1 beetle, 3 wedges, 3 axes, 1 spade, shovell and how, 25li. 10s.
In the old shop: 84 Gall. Rum, 4 hhd., 2 Barrills, 1 old still
with part of a worm, 1 chest, ammunition and other small
things, 16li. 2s.; 2 great bibles & the Rest of his Printed
Books in number 24, 2li. 12s.; 1 percell of yarn, gimblets,
cards, tapborers, glass bottles, stone jugs, wheat, Indeon and
Rye, 9li. 13s.; total, 8080li. 5s. 1d.; Book debts, 1050li.;
total, 1935li. 5s. 1d.; To the estate in Barbadoss, 100li. Due
in money to be paid out of the estate, 120li.

Attested in Ipswich court Sept. 30, 1679, by Mrs. Ann
White, executrix of the estate of her husband.

"[torn] John   wheed   of   Amesbury——pay   or   cause
to be payd to John Weed three pound sixteen shillings
either in ye —— pine board att ye new Mill at Almsbury w^{th}
in fower —— ye date hereof or so much indian corne good
condicond —— to be prized by indifferent men att ye sd
Weeds now dwelling house in Almsbury aforesd, & shall also
deliver unto ye sd Weed that corne ——Capt. White
tooke from him by virtue of an execucon upon
—— against him by ye County Court held att Salisbury in

Aprill 1667 —— yt ye —— in before any sute was comenct ag^t ye —— abouesd p^{r}mises being according to this agre —— part pformed to bee a finall end & issue —— different —— between them concerning all accounts."

> Paul (his △ mark) White.

Witness: Edward Woodman, Tho. Bradbury, Wm. Chandler.

Essex County Probate Files, Docket 29,616.

ESTATE OF JOHN WRIGHT OF NEWBURY.*

Whereas John Wright late of Newbury died at sea, intestate, and administration being granted unto Edward Bragg of the estate, and he bringing in an inventory of 40li., and 20li. being the remainder after the expenses were paid, and there now appearing John Wright, the son of the aforesaid John, demanding of the estate, the court at Ipswich Sept. 30, 1679, ordered said Bragg to pay him the 20li. and revolves the administration upon said Wright, and Edward Bragg is discharged.

Ipswich Quarterly Court Records, vol. 5, page 348.

ESTATE OF PATRICK EWING OF (ROWLEY?).

John Kent of Newbury being lately a voyage at sea in Mr. Richard Dole's ship, whereof Patrick Ewing was master, and said Kent mate, upon their returning home said Patrick Ewing fell overboard and was drowned, and ye said Kent being then master, with ye first opportunity applied to this court desiring letters of administration, which were granted Nov. 11, 1679, and he bound himself in ye sum of forty pounds to administer according to law.

Salisbury Quarterly Court Records, vol. 2, leaf 74.

Inventory of the estate of Patrick Ewing, who died at sea in the ship Hopwell, taken Nov. 19, 1679, by George Hewes and Stephen Greenlef: one payer of Rough Sleves, 1s. 6d.; 1 1-2 yd. of dowlas, 3s.; 6 neckcloths, 6s.; 2 payer of drawers, 5s.; 4 shirts, 14s.; 3 ould silke Neck cloaths, 4s.; 1 whit Jackit, 2s.; 2 blew shirts, one payer of drawers, 6s.; 1 Carpit, 6s.; 1 Coate and briches, 10s.; one Cloath Sute, 1li. 10s.; 4 payer of stockins, 7s.; 1 payer of ould silke drawers, 3s.; 1 ould See Gowne, 14s.; 1 ould silk wascoat, 2s.; 6 ould Hancarchefs, 3s.; 1 Spoon silver and payer of buttons, 7s.; fore stalfe and gunter scale, compases, 11s.; one Calebash tipt with silver, 2li.; To

*See *ante*, vol. 1, page 275; vol. 2, page 317.

sea books, 5s.; one Hatt, 4s.; 18 glas bottles, 6s.; one bl. of
Rum ct. 30 gl., 3li.; one bl. of Suger, 2li. 10s.; one sea Chest,
8s.; total, 16li. 7s. 6d.

Attested at Rowley, Nov. 20, 1679, by John Kent, administrator of the estate of Patrick Ewing, before Daniel Denison
and Nath. Saltonstall.

Essex County Probate Files, Docket 9,177.

ESTATE OF CLEMENT JARMIN OF SALISBURY.

The court held at Salisbury, Nov. 11, 1679, authorized Mrs.
Abbigail Wheeler to take up the debts due unto Clement Jar-
min of Salisbury, deceased, and pay the charges of his burial
and if there be anything left she is to present it to the Salisbury court next, but if the debts due will not amount to the
discharging of his burial, then the town of Salisbury is to
make it up.

Salisbury Quarterly Court Records, vol. 2, leaf 74.

ESTATE OF EPHRAIM DAVIS OF HAVERHILL.

Administration upon the estate of Ephraim Davis, late of
Haverhill, was granted Nov. 11, 1679, unto Mary Davis, the
widow, and Thomas Johnson her brother, upon their request,
who gave bond of 4li. and they to bring in an inventory to the
next court.

Salisbury Quarterly Court Records, vol. 2, leaf 73.

Inventory of the estate of Ephrim Davis, taken Mar. 26,
1680, by Henry Palmer and Danyell Kendrick; an old house
and a new frame of a house, 10li.; household stufe and beding,
3li.; his weareing clothes, 2li.; hemp and flax unbrakt, 10s.;
12 pound of cotten woole, 12s.; sheeps wool and yearne, 1li.;
two gunes, 2li.; three cowes, 12li.; one old horse, 2li. 10s.;
one colt, 2li.; one sow and two pigs, 1li. 10s.; 14 sheepe and
4 lambs given by will, 7li.; one oxe, 5li.; two heifers, 4li.;
two calves, 2li.; the priveledges of two ox commons and three
cow commans given him by his father, 20li.; 35 akers of land
lying above his house, 100li.; about 5 or 6 akers of land given
to him by his father upon his will which joined to Ephrims
other land in ye Plaine, 18li.; a parcel of meadow in the east
meadow given to Ephrim upon his fathers will, 10li.; one
cow more given to him by his father upon his will, 4li.; total,
197li. 2s.

Attested in Ipswich court Mar. 30, 1680, by Thomas John-

son and Mary Davis, administrators to the estate of Ephraim
Davis.

The depts which are chalinged from the estate of Ephram
Davis: Mr. Davison, 3li. 18s.; Docktor Doell, 2li.; John Ad-
kasin, 1li. 10s.; Joseph Knight, 1li. 15s.; Mistres White, 2li.
5s.; Peeter Ayers, 1li. 10s.; John Grifin, 1li.; Danel Hendreks
40s, as he sayes, he says he has a bil for it which is of 24 years
standing and never demanded til now, 2li.; William Sargent,
1li. 10s.; Deken Goodhue, 6li.; Thomas Johnson, 4li. 10s.;
John Callam, 12s.; Andrew Grely, 1li.; total, 29li. 10s. Dept
payd from the estat, 26li. 5s. Signed, Thomas Johnson, Mary
Davis.   *Essex County Probate Files, Docket 7,239.*

Mary Davis, relict and administratrix to the estate of
Ephraim Daves, moving to the court for a settlement of his
estate, and a determination of her claim of six or seven acres
of land which James Davis claims, this court, Sept. 28, 1680,
leaves the widow to her liberty until the next court to move
for a settlement of the estate, and that then the administrators to the estate may, if they please, make use of the law to
sue for that land which she claims.

Ipswich Quarterly Court Records, vol. 5, page 360.

For the settlement of the estate of Ephraim Davis of Haverhill, the court at Ipswich, 27:7:1681, ordered that the
eldest son Stephen shall have 14li. for his double portion,
and the rest of the children, Ephraim, Thomas, Jonathan,
Mary, Susanna and Hannah, 7li. each, when they come to
age, or shall by law choose guardians, and the rest of the estate to be to the widow and administrators for payment of
debts and her part, the land to stand bound for security.

Essex County Probate Files, Docket 7,239.

In answer to the petition of Thomas Johnson and Mary
Davis of Haverhill, administrators to the estate of Ephraim
Davis of Haverhill, court July 8, 1685, granted them power
to sell so much land belonging to the estate as shall be necessary for the ends proposed.

Mass. Bay Colony Records, vol. 5, page 490.

Hannah (her ₰ mark) Davise acknowledged Mar. 24,
1695-6, the receipt from her brother Stephen Davice, both of
Haverhill, of seven pounds in money and goods, being her
portion of the estate of her father, Ephraim Davis of Haverhill. Witness: Josiah Gage, Christopher Hallett.

Thomas (his † mark) Davis of Norwich, Ct., acknowledged
May 25, 1717, the receipt from his brother Stephen Davis of

Haverhill, of seven pounds, being his part of the estate of his father, Ephraim Davis of Haverhill. Witness: Samuell Luthry, Jonathan Davis.

Ephraim Davis of Canterbury, Ct., acknowledged May 27, 1717, the receipt from his brother Stephen Davis of Haverhill, of seven pounds, being his portion of the estate of Ephraim Davis of Haverhill. Witness: Elisha Paine, John Dyar.

The subscribers upon request made to them by their mother Mary Davis, on the account of their not buying any lands of her, being already to them tendered, give her free liberty to sell to any person. Signed Jan. 18, 1719-20, Jeremiah (X) Rideout. Witness: Joseph (his∫ mark) Peasle, Amos Singelterry.

The request as above, signed and sealed April 13, 1720, by John Kezar, Judith Kezar. Witness: Enoch Sawyer, Judith Hook.

The request as above, signed April 15, 1720, by Patince (her A mark) Daves, wife of Ep. Davis. Witness: Samuel (his K mark) Kinne, Jaini (her X mark) Mor.

Essex County Probate Files, Docket 7,239.

ESTATE OF ROGER CONANT OF SALEM.

"The Last will & testament of Roger Conant dated the first day of the first month 1677 I Roger Conant aged about eightie fiue yeares being of perfit understanding though weake & feeble in body doe heerby declare my will and minde wherein in the first place I doe bequeath my soule unto God that gaue it & my body to the graue in hope of a blessed Resurrection: & for my outward estate & goods I giue unto my Sonne Exercise one hundred & fortie acres of Land lyeing neere adjoyning unto the new towne of Dunstable as part of two hundred acres granted me by the Generall Court also I giue & bequeath unto him ten acres of Land next adjoyning unto his present homelot and land Lying by the side of william Dodgeses his land & butts one the land of Thomas Herrick: also I giue him two acres of marsh at the south End of the great pond by whenham or if my daughter Elizabeth Conant will Exchang to haue so much at the great marsh neere wenham: also I giue him my swamp at the head of the railes which is it undevided betwixt me and Benjamin Balch adjoyning unto william Dodgeses' swamp: also I giue him my portion of land Lying by Henry Haggats on wenham side:

now out of this forementioned Land he is to paye seauen
pound toward the discharge of such Legassis as I haue giuen
& bequeathed according as is heere after set down More I
giue unto my grand child John Conant sonne of Roger Conant ten acres of Land adjoyning to his twenty acres by the
great ponds side he paying twenty pounds for the same towards the payment of legassis as after mentioned more I
giue unto my grand child Joshua Conant seaventeen acres of
Land Lying by the south side of the great marsh neer wenham
and bounding unto the land of Peter woodbery : and the rest
to returne to my Executor.

"Also I giue unto my daughter Sarah two acres of Land
lying between the head of the railes & Isack Hull his ground
as part of six acres twixt me and Benjamine Balch this to her
and ||her|| children also sixtie acres of Land out of my farm
granted me by the generall Court neere the new town of Dunstable I giue and bequeath into the hands of Captain Roger
Clap of the castle neer Dorchester for the use of a daughter
of one M^ris Pits deseased whose daughter now Liueth in Culli-
ton a town in Devon in old England & is in lue for certaine
goods sold for the said M^ris Pits in London and was there to
be paid many yeares since but it is alleged was neuer paid and
the foresaid Captaine Clap to giue a discharge as there at-
turny according as he is impowered and intrusted in theire
behalfe further more as legassis I doe giue unto my sonne
Lot his ten children twenty pounds to be equally devided to
my daughter sarahs children to John fiue pound to the foure
daughters fiue pound between them To my daughter Mary
Dodge her self fiue pound and fiue pound to her fiue children
equally devided To Exercise his children foure pound
betwixt them To adonirum Veren three pound and
to his sister Hannah twenty shillings and her two children each ten shillings. To my Cosen Mary Veren wife to
Hellier Veren three pound as also three pound unto the
daughters of my Cosen Jane Mason deceased to be devided
amongst them including Loue Steeuens her children a share
my wearing apparrill I giue and houshold impelments not
otherwise disposed of and my gray horse and cattle to my
sonne Exercise one sheep I giue to Rebacka Connant my
grand child and one sheep to Mary Leech.

"And whereas there remains in my hands a certaine portion
of cattle belonging unto on m^r Dudeny in England and by him
assigned unto his nephew Richard Conant valued at twenty
fiue pounds and now left in the hands of my sonne Exercise

Conant that there be a rendering up of such cattle or theire valuation mentioned unto the said Richard Conant upon seasonable demaund he giueing a full discharge for the same And further my will is that my sonne Exercise be my Executor to this my will and Testament and for further help in seeing these things performed I desire my sonne William Dodge and my grandchild John Conant senior to be overseears of the same. In witness whereof I haue heerunto sett my hand the day and yeare aboue written."

Roger (his R C mark) Conant (SEAL)

Witness: John Bennet, Benjamin Balch.

Proved in Salem court 25: 9m: 1679, by the witnesses.

Inventory of the estate of Roger Conant, taken Nov. 24, 1679, by John Rayment and William Rayment: 200 Acors of land, 60li.; Liing at Dunstable not improved mor land sould to Elizabeth Conant & not payd for, 40li.; mor land 10 acors, 20li.; land 10 Acors, 20li.; land 23 Acors, 59li.; 2 Acors of medow, 10li.; 2 Acors of land, 5li.; swampy land, 1li.; more land, 1li.; 2 cows and a hors, 10li.; more cattell, 15li.; 4 sheep, 1li. 10s.; a bed & furnytur, 5li.; wareing closse and linin, 9li.; a Chest, trunck and box, 1li.; other things, 1li.; total, 258li. 10s.

Attested in Salem court 28: 9m: 1679, by Exercise Conant, the executor.

Essex County Quarterly Court Files, vol. 32, leaves 25, 26.

ESTATE OF ISAAC GOODALE OF SALEM.

Administration upon the estate of Isaac Goodell, intestate, was granted 25: 9m: 1679, unto Patience, the relict, and John Pease, sr. An inventory being brought in and sworn to by said Patience it was allowed, and the land to stand bound for security, that they administer according to law.

Salem Quarterly Court Records, vol. 6, leaf 4.

Inventory of the estate of Isacke Goodale, taken Oct. 23, 1679, by Nathaniel Felton and Job Swinerton: his dwellinge house and orchard and the land thereunto belonginge, 130li.; five acres and a halfe of fresh meadow, 11li.; 4 Cowes, 12li.; 2 yearelings and vantage, 3li.; 1 horse, 10s.; 6 swine 1 yeare old & 6 piggs, 7li. 10s.; 50 busheles Indian Corne, 7li. 10s.; 2 busheles of Rye, 8s.; 1 musket, 1 Rapier, powder and bullets, 1li. 10s.; on bed and bolster, 2 payre of sheets, an old Rug & blanket, some wollen and linnen yarne, 5li.; 2 Iron pots, a warminge pan, a fryinge pan, & a payre of pot hooks, 1li. 15s.; 2 Chests, 1li.; his wearinge Apparel, 5li.; 3 old axes, 3 wedges, a Reape hooke, 2 sythes, 2 augers, 2 chissels, a gouge and drawinge knife, a hand saw, 1li.; a payre of Cardes & smoothinge Iron and a hammer, 4s.; two trayes and a Churne, 2 payles, two seives, a linnen and wollen wheele, some wood-den platters, tubs and old Lumber, 2li.; 4 load of hay & other fodder, 3li.; total, 192li. 7s. Isack Goodale Dr. to Job Swin-erton, 1li. 6s. 4d.; Jon. Cromwell, 1li. 13s. 1 1-3d.; Nich. Dur-rall, 1li. 12s.; Jon. Pease, sr., 8s.; Jon. Pease, jr., 5s.; ———— Golthrite, 3s. 6d.; Capt. George Corwin, 10s. 6d.; Joseph Huch, 1li. 5s.; John Pease, sr., 1li.; Zack Godle, 4s. 6d.; Wilem benat, 6s.; total, 8li. 13s. 11d.

Attested in Salem court 27 : 9 : 1679, by the administrators.
Essex County Quarterly Court Files, vol. 32, leaf 27.

Patience, relict of Isaack Goodell, and administratrix of his estate, desiring a settlement of the estate, and the court understanding there are five children, ordered 30 : 9m : 1680, that when the debts are paid the whole estate to remain in the widow's hand for the bringing up of the children, and to pay to the eldest son 12li. and the rest of the children 6li. each, when they come to age or marriage, the rest of the estate to be to the sole use of the widow, the land to stand bound for security.   *Salem Quarterly Court Records, vol. 6, leaf 12.*

Citation dated June 12, 1693, to Patience Stimpson, alias Goodale, administratrix on the estate of Isaac Goodale, to give an account of her administration on which it appears that she hath not completed the same, and whereas John Pease who was joined with her in the administration is dead, adminis-tration is granted to Isaac Goodale, eldest son of the deceased.
Essex County Probate Records, vol. 303, page 183.

Bond of Patience (her Ȣ mark) Stimpson and Isaac (his O mark) Goodale, both of Salem, with John How and Samuel (his ∧ mark) Abbey, of Salem and Topsfield, as sureties, in the sum of 200li., for administration on the es-tate of Isaac Goodale of Salem. Signed and sealed, June 12, 1693. Witness: Stephen Sewall, Reg., Thomas Flint.
Essex County Probate Files, Docket 11,115.

Acquittance of Abigaile Goodale unto her brother Isaac Goodale, of all debts and legacies due to her from her father's estate, Dated Salem Village, Nov. 6, 1696. Witness: John Walcott, Samll. Abbey.

Zachariah Goodale, acknowledged Jan. 23, 1698-9, the receipt from Patience Stimson and Isaac Goodale, administrators on the estate of Isaac Goodale late of Salem, of about ten acres of land, being his portion of his father's estate. Witness: Zachary White, Steph. Sewall.

John Goodale, acknowledged Oct. 22, 1705, the receipt from Patience Stimson and Isaac Goodale, administrators on the estate of Isaac Goodale, deceased, of six pounds in money, being his portion of his father's estate. Witness: Zachary Goodale, John Wollcott.

Acknowledged in Salem court Feb. 11, 1708-9, by Zachary Goodale, John Walcott and Zachariah White.

Essex County Probate Records, vol. 313, page 4.

GUARDIANSHIP OF JOHN WHITTIER.

John Whitteere came into court, 25: 9m: 1679, and chose Thomas West to be his guardian, which was allowed.

Salem Quarterly Court Records, vol. 6, leaf 2.

ESTATE OF MRS. ARABELLA NORMAN.

Administration upon the estate of Arrabella Norman, was granted 25: 9m: 1679, to her son John Norman, and he was bound in 100li. to bring in an inventory to the next court.

Salem Quarterly Court Records, vol. 6, leaf 2.

John Norman, administrator to the estate of his mother Arabella Norman, presented an inventory 29: 4m: 1680.

Salem Quarterly Court Records, vol. 6, leaf 9.

Inventory of the estate that Arabella Norman died possessed of Nov. 23, 1679, as administratrix to the estate of her husband John Norman, taken by Jeremiah Neale and Thomas West: 1 fether bed & bolster, 3li. 10s., 2 pr. sheets, 30s., 1 rugg, 23s., 6li. 3s.; 2 pr. pillowbeers & pillowes, 12s., wearing apparell, 4li., 4li. 12s.; 2 pr. pillowbeers & table linen, 15s., 2 Iron potts & Iron scillett, 18s., 1li. 13s.; warming pan & some pewter dishes, 16s.; brass skillett, 2s., 1 pr. doggs Irons, spitt & 1 pr. tongs, 15s., 17s.; house & barne, oarchard & all ye land adjoyning to it, 30li.; ten acres of upland upon ye neck & 2 acres of salt marsh, 40li.; 1 acre of salt marsh at Ketle Cove, 7li.; the remaining part of 400 acres of land granted by the towne of Salem to 8 men his pt., 50li.; 2 cowes & a steere, 9li., 1 swine, 15s., 9li. 15s.; total, 150li. 16s.

The above estate is indebted for this six years, 46li.
Presented and attested in Salem court July 1, 1680, by
John Norman, administrator of the estate.
Essex County Probate Records, vol. 301, page 165.

GUARDIANSHIP OF JOHN BREED OF LYNN.

John Bread, son of John Breade, chose Thomas Newall
and John Putnam to be his guardians, which was allowed
25 : 9m : 1679.
Salem Quarterly Court Records, vol. 6, leaf 2.

ESTATE OF WILLIAM LAKE OF SALEM.

Administration upon the estate of William Lake, intestate,
was granted 25 : 9m : 1679, unto Ann, the relict of William,
who was to bring in an inventory to the next court held at
Salem. The house she dwells in with all the land adjoining
to stand bound for security.
Salem Quarterly Court Records, vol. 6, leaf 3.

Inventory of the estate of Mr. William Lake, taken June
26, 1680, by Edward Mowle and Francis Neale, sr. : the housing and Land, 110li.; Bedding, Boulster, sheet, Ruggs, &
blanketts in ye Little Roome, 6li. 4s.; Beding, Boulsters,
sheetes, Ruggs and Blanketts in ye chamber, 5li. 12s.; Bed,
Boulster, blanketts, sheets, pillow, Rugg, old Curtaines & a
Bedstead in ye Great Roome, 6li. 13s.; halfe a Douzen of
Joynt stooles, 11s.; a Round Table, 12s.; a paire of Andirons,
1li.; Bedstead & Trundlebed in ye chamber, 1li. 15s.; 13 old
chaires, 16s. 3d.; one Chist in the chamber, 3s. 6d.; one chist
more, 12s.; 8 Boxes, 7s.; one Trunk, 10s.; one small old Chist,
4s.; two Cuppboards, 3s.; one paire of old Andirons & a
small paire of Dogges, 10s.; Fier Tongs & a fyer shovell, 8s.;
two Gridirons & a chaffing Dish all old, 5s.; two Haikes, 7s.;
a Jack & a spitt, 12s.; 3 Iron potts, one Iron kettle & a frying
pan, 1li. 10s.; 3 pair of pott hookes, a flesh hook, one Douzen
of Iron skewers, 6s.; 2 small Brass skilletts & a kettle, 12s.;
scales and a paire of stilliards, 9s.; a Callico cuppboard cloth,
2 old cushings and a few Glasses, 3s.; pewter, 8li.; Tinn ware,
10s.; Earthen ware, 10s.; a Carpett, 10s.; 3 old Tables small,
10s.; Nine pair of sheetes, 5li. 5s.; 4 Tableclothes & 4 Cupb-
bord clothes, 1li. 6s.; 68 Napkins, 4li. 6s.; pillowbeers, 14s.;
Tooles, 1li.; wheele and a small Looking Glass, 7s.; a furnace,
2li.; a Mashing Tubb, Tubbs, old barrels and Bucketts, 2li.;

a Grindstone, 6s.; a Sow and piggs, 1li. 10s.; timber to work Upp, 15s.; total, 171li. 12s. 9d.   Debts due from the estate: to Deacon Goodhew, 60li.; Mr. William Brown, jr., 10li.; Captaine John Corwin, 7li.; Mr. John Cromwell, 5li. 8s. 1d.; Mr. Thomas Ives, 11li. 13s. 5d.; Mr. Hurst, 10li.; Mr. Knights of Newberie, 3li.; total, 107li. 1s. 6d.

Attested in Salem court July 1, 1680, by Ann the relict and administratrix.   When the debts are paid the estate to remain in the widow's hands for the bringing up of the two children, Abigaile and Mary, who are to be paid 10li. each, at age or marriage.   The house and land to stand bound for the payment of the children's portions.

Essex County Quarterly Court Files, vol. 33, leaf 105.

GUARDIANSHIP OF JOHN BROWN OF SALEM.

John Browne son of John Browne, deceased, came into court 25: 9m: 1679, and chose John Browne his grandfather, to be his guardian, which was allowed.

Salem Quarterly Court Records, vol. 6, leaf 3.

Steephen Haskett and John Williames testified that Mr. John Browne of Salem took possession of the remainder of that land which was formerly the land of John Browne, jr., deceased, after the execution was satisfied for Hannah Browne relict of James Browne, and likewise a piece of land of said John Browne's which he bought of Job Hilliard, and lyeth near adjoyning to the house which said John Browne, deceased, formerly lived in; these two peices taken possession of by John Browne, sr., in behalf of John Browne son of John Browne, deceased, as his guardian.   Signed Dec. 29, 1679. Acknowledged in Salem court 30: 4m: 1680.

Salem Quarterly Court Records, vol. 6, leaf 9.

ESTATE OF JACOB PRESTON OF SALEM.

Jacob Presson being cast away at sea, the court 25: 9m: 1679, granted administration upon his estate to John Preston, who gave bond of 20li., and to bring in an inventory to the next court at Salem.

Salem Quarterly Court Records, vol. 6, leaf 3.

Inventory of the estate of Jacob Preston, who in all probabilitie hath been departed this life for these severall months haveing bin wanting about nine or tenn months, gon forth in a small Ketch upon a Fishing designe to ye eastward & never

yet returned nor certainly heard of, his goods presented by
Thomas Preston and appraised in Salem, June 30, 1680, by
Richard Croade and John King: a chest with a Lock & Key,
6s.; one Hatt, 4s.; an old paire of Breeches, 6s.; A new red
cloath wastcoate, 15s.; A paire of dowlas drawers, 4s.; a paire
of cotton & Lynnen drawers little worne, 3s.; one yard &
half of holland, 7s. 6d.; A genting neck cloath, 1s.; due to
the estate per Levy Preston, 2li. 5s.; Samuel Preston, 1li. 5s.;
total, 5li. 16s. 6d. The estate is debtor; to Mr. Nehemiah
Willowby, 13s. 1 1-2d.; Nathaniel Ingerson, 7s.; Sarah
Traske, 1li.; Symon Horne, 12s.; Benjamin Horne, 12s.;
Thomas Preston, 2li. 4s.; total, 5li. 8s. 1 1-2d. Unresolved
how ye accot. stands between Mr. Willim Bowditch & ye
abovesaid Jacob Preston, Thomas Preston haveing don his
best endeavor to have had a settlement but cannot as yet attaine it.

Attested in Salem court July 1, 1680, by John Preston, administrator.

Essex County Quarterly Court Files, vol. 33, leaf 106.

ESTATE OF JOHN NEAL OF SALEM.

Administration upon the estate of John Neale, was granted
25 : 9m : 1679, unto Ann his relict, who is to bring in an inventory, and said Ann and Andrew Mansfeild and Jeremiah
Neale stand bound in 20li. that she shall administer according to law.

Salem Quarterly Court Records, vol. 6, leaf 3.

An Neale, relict and administratrix of John Neale, presented an inventory to the court, June 29, 1680, who see
cause to respite the ordering of the estate until the next court
held at Salem, she to appear and fully perfect the inventory.

Salem Quarterly Court Records, vol. 6, leaf 7.

Inventory of the estate of John Neale of Salem, who departed this life Nov. 11, 1679, taken Nov. 24, 1679, by John
Pickering and John Norman: one Fether Bed, Boulster, Bedstead & Curtains, 5li. 5s.; two Rugs, two Blanckets, 1li. 14s.;
one Trundle Bedstead, two Blanckets, one Rugg, 1li. 12s.;
Flock Bed, Boulster, 2 Blanckitts & one Rug, 2li. 10s.; 3
pare of sheets, one single sheet, 35s., 2 pr. of trundlebed
sheets, 12s., 2 Blanckitts, 12s., 9 Napkins, 2 table Cloaths, 2
pillowbears, 10s., 3li. 9s.; one ould pine chest & two Boxes,
5s.; wearing Apparrill, 50s., one Box, 3s., 2li. 13s.; one
Smoothing Iron & heats, 2s., Bookes, 5s., puter & earthen

ware, 6s., 13s.; a pare of compasses, a Rule, a Gimblet, 1s.
6d.; Rapier, 10s., Brass kettle & 3 Iron pots, 30s., 2li.; frying
pan, chaffin dish, skellet, Churne, pails & Lumber, 15s.;
Cradle, cheares, table, fire shovell & a pare of toungs, 16s.;
dripping pan, candlestick, spoones & tynn wares, 3s.; Looking
Glass, shooe Lether & shooe nailes, 10s.; Beife in the powdering tub, 20s., corne, 40s., 3li.; 2 mares, 3li. 10s., 2 oxen 6li.
10s., 2 Cowes, 4li., 14li.; A parcell of Land caled Tucks feild
in estimation 4 acres or neare uppon which is his at his
mothers death, 70li.; ten acres called Harburds lott, 30li.;
His pte of the swamp caled Adams swampe, 5li.; An ould
Cart & wheels & a sett of hoops & boxes for cart wheels, a
pare of Boxes for one wheele & a slead, 2li.; An Axe, Ads,
Mall, two Augurs, 16s.; 6 Ring boults, 5 set Boults, a cauck-
ing iron or two, 12s.; Haye in the Barne, 9li., Tallo, 5s., 9li.
5s.; 15 swine & a wheele, 8li. 8s.; one eight part of the sloope
John & Marye, as monye, 34li. 15s. 10d.; one Kron Kettle,
4s.; pare of fetters & locks, 5s., ould Iron, 9s., 18s.; due to
him as a Legacye to bee paid him by his Brother Johnathan
Neale by his Grandfather Francis Laws will within foure
years after his mother's death as appears by sd. will, 20li.;
total, 221li. 10d. The estate is Debtor 52li. 10s., 18li. of it
being to be pd. as monye.; more debts, 5li. 4s.; the estate is
Debtor in monyes, 11li.; total, 67li. 14s. Due to the estate as
monye, 27li. 1s. 3d.; making total estate, 248li. 3s. 1d., with
debts 67li. 14s., which leaves a free estate of 180li. 8s. 8d.

Attested in Salem court 30:9m:1680, by Ann, relict of
the deceased and administratrix.

Ann Neale relict of John Neale, having power of administration by this court, Nov., 1680, to administer on his estate,
has endeavored to reduce said estate into an inventory, which
amounts to 180li. 8s. 10d., in lands 105li., whereof there is of
it in present possession 35li. and the rest of it not to be possessed until the death of the mother of said John Neale, and
20li. more is in a legacy given by the grandfather of the deceased, not payable until four years after the death of the
mother of the deceased, and the rest of the estate is in moveables.

Essex County Quarterly Court Files, vol. 34, leaves 74, 75.

Ann Neale administratrix of the estate of John Neale ye
younger, her late husband, presented an inventory amounting to 180li. 8s., and the court 30:9:1680, ordered that the
whole estate remain in the widow's hands for the bringing
up of the children, which are four, John the eldest son to

have paid him 40li. and Thomas, Joseph and Rebecka, 20li. each, at age or marriage, the remainder to be the widow's. The land to stand bound for security and the two bondsmen, Jeremiah Neale and Andrew Mansfeild are hereby released.

Salem Quarterly Court Records, vol. 6, leaf 12.

Petition of Ann Neale, relict of John Neale, jr., to the Salem court, June 28, 1681, that whereas she was left with young children, and a fourth not born, and the inventory of the estate being taken soon after her husband died, but not brought into court until a while after, and the estate he left not being clear in part and the other part not in possession nor like to be for many years, desires that the court would consider her estate and order it acordingly.

Essex County Quarterly Court Files, vol. 36, leaf 12.

In answer to the petition of An Neale, relict and adminis-tratrix of John Neale, jr., the court finding they had not a due information of the condition of the estate, and the great loss by the burning of the sloop, this court June 28, 1681, ordered that the children of the deceased shall have paid them out of the estate, to John the eldest 20li., to Thomas, Joseph and Rebecka 10li. each, at age or marriage, and this to be a full settlement of the estate, notwithstanding what may be the last court entered. The rest of the estate to Ann the widow, and the land called Tuckes lot in the inventory to be for security.

Salem Quarterly Court Records, vol. 6, leaf 19.

ESTATE OF ANTHONY DIKE OF SALEM.

Administration upon the estate of Anthony Dike, intestate, was granted 25 : 9m : 1679, unto Margery, his wife, who brought in an inventory and attested to the truth thereof, the house and ground to stand bound for security.

Salem Quarterly Court Records, vol. 6, leaf 4.

Inventory of the estate of Anthony Dike taken by Samuell Wackfield, Nathaniel Pickman, jr. and Nathaniell Pickman, sr.: on howse and ground belongin to the howse, 50li.; nine poyter platers and six plates and six peses of other poyter, 2li. 8s.; olde poyter, 6s.; on silver cup and on silver spone, 12s.; erthen platters and glases, 3s.; on bras pestell & morter and to lattin pans, 7s.; Iron pots and on friin pann, 12s.; on Iron kittell, on pair of Andirens, on spitt, on grid-iron, on hake, 1li.; Iron Rake and on flesh forke, 15s.; bras kettell and on warmin pann, 1li. 15s.;

tongs and fier pann, 2s.; on fether beed and bedsted and
furniture to the beed, 8li.; to small flok beds &
furniture to them, 3li.; on peas of curtin stuf and freng
for the curtins, 2li.; to yards of sarg and on half yarde, 10s.;
fife yards of hollon, 1li.; on paire of briches, to sherts, thre
paire of stokins, 17s.; on lookin glas, 10s.; thre tables. 1li.,
to chests and on box, 15s., 1li. 15s.; thre whells, 15s., thre
erthen platters, 2s. 6d., 17s. 6d.; on Rapier, 4s. and thre
pounds of wollen yarnn, 9s.; six pound of Cotten and sheps
woll, 3s.; on bushell of whitt salt, 3s.; on small trunk and
on small box, 8s.; six olde chayers, 3s., to dusen of olde
trenchers, 1s., 4s.; to olde payels, 1s., on Cow, 2li. 5s., 2li.
6s.; on small swin, 6s.; total, 80li. 8s. 6d. The estat indetted
to severall men, 20li. 10s. 9 1-2d.

Attested in Salem court 28 : 9 : 1679, by Margery, relict
of the deceased.

Essex County Quarterly Court Files, vol. 32, leaf 24.

ESTATE OF REV. JOHN WHEELWRIGHT OF SALISBURY.

"The last will & Testam[t], of y[e] Reverend M[r] John Wheell-
wright, who: died y[e] 15th of Novem[br]: 1679. In y[e] name of
god Amen May y[e] 25 : 1679 I John Wheelright Pasto[r] of y[e]
church of Christ att Salisbury in y[e] county of Norfolk in New
england although aged in yeares & weake in body yet pfect in
& of a disposed minde: Doe make & declare this to bee my last
will & Testament in writing: Revokeing all my former wills &
testaments whatsoever heretofore by mee made & declared:
ffirst I doe comend my soule into y[e] hands of all mighty god,
confidently belieuing in him to bee saved through y[e] riches of
his grace by faith in Jesus Christ my Savio[r] & redeemer. And
my body I comitt to y[e] Earth in an assuered hope of a blessed
resurrection of y[e] same at y[e] last day to enjoy that happie
fruition of y[t] kingdome p[r]pared in heaven for all his elect.
As concerning my estate lands, & worldly goods: I will & do
dispose of them as followeth 1 I doe giue unto my grand child
Edward Lyde that part of my Messuage being & scituate in
Mumby in Lincolnsheire in ould England w[ch] part consists of
Ten acres of pasture lying & beeing in Langhum, bee it more
or less, & all y[t] land of mine w[c] lieth in Minge with the lands
of M[r] Newcomin being in Mumby for w[ch] my pasture in
Minge y[e] sd Newcomin payeth mee three pounds per anum as
appeareth by a lease w[c] hee hath of it, & it is my will that
my aforesd Grand childe Edward Lyde shall haue y[e] aforesd

part wth all ye privilidges & appurtenances therunto beelong-
ing to him & his heires forever, pvided that ye sd Lyde do pay
or cause to bee payd unto his mother Mary Attkinson or her
order the anuall rent or pduce of ye say'd lands duering y^e
terme of her naturall life, but in case that Edward Lyde
should die before he cometh to ye age of twenty one Yeares,
then I doe giue ye lands afore mentioned unto my Sone Samuell Wheelwright unto himselfe & his heires forever hee paying or causing to bee payd ye rent & produce of the said lands
unto my daughter Attkinson duering ye continuance of her
naturall life. 2 I doe giue & bequeath unto my grand daughter Mary Mavericke all ye rest of my land being part of y^e
aforesaid Messuage lying and scituate in Mumby aforesd my
house wth all ye pasture arrable meadow & comones with all
privilidges & appurtenances thereunto belonging to that part
of my Messuage being lately in ye occupation of Ea^{w}st and
his widdow, unto ye sd Mary Mavericke & unto her & her
heires forever, who of her body shalbe Lawfully begotten 3 I
doe giue & bequeath unto my sone in law Edw. Rishworth
fifty acres of upland & twenty acres of marsh land : & my will
is after his decease I doe giue ye sd land & meadow wth all
ye privilidges & appurtenances thereto belonging unto Mary
White my grand Childe daughter of ye said Rishworth to her
& her heires forever, & for want of & for want of such heires
I giue it unto my Sone Sam^{ll} : Wheelwright & his heires forever wch upland & meadow is thus to bee divided lying in y^e
township of Wells, ye bounds on ye South west is Ogunquet
River & soe to runne ye breadth of my farme in that part of
it vntill ye fifty acres of upland bee compleated, & twenty
acres of marsh to runne ye full breadth lying upon ye westerly
end of my farme next adjoyning to or neare ye Estermost part
of ye sd land
"4 I doe giue & bequeath unto my grand children Thomas
& Jacob Bradbury forty pounds Sterlg : a peece to each of
them in Currant money of New england, by my Executo^r
when they doe come unto ye age of ^{x}one & twenty^x years,
either of them dying before they doe come to that age then
ye pson Surviveing shall haue ye whole fower score pounds 5 I
do giue & bequeath unto my Sone Sam^{ll} : Wheelwright of
Wells all my land lying in ye towne of Crafft in ye County of
Lyncolne in ould England neare Waneflitt in ye same County
wth all ye privilidges & appurtenances thereunto belonging to
him & his heires for ever and I doe further giue unto him my
aforesd Sone Samuell all my houses lands Marsh meadows

scituate & being in ye township of Wells in ye County of
York in New england with all ye privilidges & appurtenances
therunto belonging [excepting before excepted] that land &
marsh wch by mee was giuen as aboue specified unto my Sone
in law Edward Rishworth To my aforesd Sone Sam^ll: Wheelwright to his heires & assignes for ever: And I do further
giue unto my Sone Samuel Wheelwright my clock & all my
library & bookes & all my Apparrell & all ye rest of my estate
& goods not disposed of in this will excepting the rents I
haue owing to me in ould england halfe whereof I do giue unto
my Executo^r & ye other halfe to bee divided equally between
my three grand childeren William Thomas & Jacob Bradbury
In case my Executo^r do recover it & if it so happen that one
or more of those three childeren shall die before they come to
age then hee or those y^t doe surviue shall haue ye part of him
or those that are deceased 6 And further I do giue unto my
latter wyfes Childeren all my plate to bee equally divided
amongst them by two indifferent psons chosen by themselues
to make that division: Lastly I doe make ordeine & constitute
my Sone Sam^ll. Wheelewright of Wells aforesd to bee ye sole
Executo^r of this my last will & Testament by whom care is
to bee taken for payment of my just debts & discharging of
ye legasies & funerall expences In wittness wherunto I haue
hereunto affixed my hand & seale at ye day & date hereof."

                              John Wheelwright (SEAL)
Witness: Jno. Flood, John Price, Henry Ambross.
Sworn in court in Boston Nov. 26, 1679, by Jno. Flood
aged 27 years, before Hum. Davie, Assist.
Sworn in the Norfolk court Dec. 4, 1679, by Henry Am-
bros, before Nath. Salstonstall, Esq. and Capt. John Gillman.
Allowed upon the above evidence, Dec. 4, 1679.
                         Norfolk Records, vol. 3, leaf 235.

ESTATE OF MRS. DEBORAH BLAKE.

Administration upon the estate of Deborah Blake, granted
to her sons, Timothie and John Blake, who gave bond of 200li.
to administer according to law, and to attend to the ordering
of the estate and to take care of her two youngest children in
the meantime.

Inventory of the estate of Deborah Blake, widow, deceased
Dec. 20, 1678, taken by Samuell Dalton and Abraham Drake:
two oxen, 10li.; two cowes, 6li.; 1 two yer old steere, 2li.; 1
Heffer & 1 steere, 2li. 10s.; Six sheep & 3 lambs, 2li. 10s.; 5

swine, 2li. 10s.; one sarg petticoat, 1li.; one peniston wescott, 8s.; one fetherbed, bedstead, Rug & 2 blankits, 5li. 10s.; one joyned box, 3s., 1 table, 5s., 1 Chayer, 5s., 13s.; one Iron pott, 12s., an Iron skillitt, 4s., 16s.; one Brasse Kittle, one Hake & pothooke, 16s.; 4 peuter platters, 1 Bason, 1 Beaker & 1 wine cup, 1li. 2s.; one old chamber pott & a Candlestick, 4s.; one warming pan & one brass skillitt, 10s.; Dishes, Trayes and Lumber, 1li.; 4 acres of fresh medow, 16li.; 46 acres of upland, 46li.; 80 acres of outt land, 4li.; 25 acres of outt land of north Division, 1li. 5s.; one cops & pin, 3s., 3 wedges, 2s. 6d., Ring & staple, 2s., 7s. 6d.; total, 105li. 1s. 6d.

Essex County Probate Files, Docket 2,584.

ESTATE OF ISRAEL BLAKE.

Administration upon the estate of Isarell Blake, granted to Timothy and John Blake, who gave bond of 60li. to administer according to law.

Inventory of the estate of Isarell Blake taken by Abraham Drake and Samuell Dalton: his forth partt of the Boat prised as monie, 8li. 10s.; one sarge coate, 1li.; one Black hatt, 7s.; one sword, 5s., a Barrill of a Gun, 5s., 10s.; a pike well Headed, 5s.

Essex County Probate Files, Docket 2,584.

ESTATE OF JOHN HERRICK OF BEVERLY.

"In the name of God Amen; I John Herrick of ye Town of Beverly in ye County of Essex in Newengland. Yeoman; being in perfect mind & memory & ye use of my reason & understanding remaining wth me; though weak & distempered in body; Doe make & ordain this my last will & testament in maner & form as followeth; Imprs. I Give & bequeath my Soull to God who gave it hoping through ye death resurection & Intersession of our Lord Jesus to inherit life everlasting; And my body to ye earth to be decently buried at ye discretion of my executors herafter named Item I will yt my debts, & funerall charges be paid & discharged Item I Give & bequeath unto my Loving wife Mary ye use & emprovment of all my whole Estate untill my children come unto age & ye use of ye one halfe therof during her naturall life & doe apoint her full & sole executrix of this my will & testament Item I Give & bequeath unto my Son John Herick; ye one halfe of all my estate to his own proper use & behoofe when he *when*

he shall come to yᵉ age of one & twenty years Item I Give &
bequeath unto my daughter Mary Herick yᵉ sum of twenty
pounds at yᵉ age of eighteen years or her day of Mariage to
be paid yᵉ one halfe out of my wives, yᵉ other halfe out of yᵉ
boyes halfe of my estate formentioned & yᵉ sum of twenty
pounds more to be paid to her seaven years after; one halfe
out of my wives yᵉ other out of yᵉ boyes halfe of my estate formentioned; & in case yᵉ Child Mary die before she receive
her Legacie then my will is yt her part return equally to both
my wife & John;

"Item I give more unto my son John; yᵗ halfe of my Estate
wᶜʰ I before bequeathed to my wife during her life; to his
own proper use & behoofe after her decease; & in case he
diethe before he come to Age then his part of yᵉ Estate to
return to his sister Mary; & I doe herby disanull & revoke
all former wills by me hertofore made & ratifie & confirm this
present will desiring my Loving freind Exercise Conant &
my brother Zackariah Herick to be my overseers of this my
will & see yᵗ all things be ordered acording to yᵉ true intent
& meaning of this my *my* will; as witness my hand & seall
this fifth of february Ano Domini 1680.

"Item at my wives desece yt yᵉ sd John Herick shall pay
to his sister Mary twenty pounds more."

John Herrick (SEAL)
Witness: Samuell Hardie, John Richards.
Proved in Ipswich court Mar. 29, 1680, by Samuell Hardy
and Zachriah Herrick.

Inventory of the estate of John Herrick who deceased Feb.
14, 1680, taken Mar. 11, 1680-81, by John Rayment and Exercise Conant: a dwelling house & barnes & orchard with sixteen
acres of tillidg land ajoyning, 100li.; 24 acres of pastor land
within fenc, 50li.; 38 acres of land not improved, 66li.; 2
acres of marsh, 10li.; in Cattell, horses, sheep & hay, 48li.;
swine, 6li.; a carte & putt chaine & plow geares, 2li. 10s.;
axes, forks, hoes, fetters, wedges and severall other tools, 2li.
6s.; graine as Indean Corne, barlye, Rie, oats, 8li. 12s.; porke
and Bakon, 2li.; fetherbed & all ye furniture, 6li.; wearing
Aparill, 7li.; Linin, 6li.; more Beding, 6li.; Linin & woolin
Cloath, 6li.; chests & Boxes & Cubbard, 2li. 15s.; Table,
chaires, stools, 1li.; pots & other Iron gear, 2li.; peuter,
Earthen & wooden ware, 1li. 5s.; cushins, 12s.; Gunn & sword,
1li. 5s.; Saddle, Bridle, pillion, panill, 1li. 7s.; Flax, payles,
tubs & many other houshold Implements, 6li.; Bibles & other

Books, 1li. 5s.; total, 343li. 17s. The estate is indebted to
Thomas Herick, 10li. & to others about, 4li., 14li. The Estate is also Crdr. by Debts about 2li.
Attested in Ipswich court Mar. 29, 1681, by Mary Herrick,
widow of John Herrick and executrix of his estate.

Essex County Probate Files, Docket 13,146.

ESTATE OF MRS. MARGARET BOARDMAN OF IPSWICH.

"The Last will and testment of the widdow Borman I Margret Borman bequeue to my Daughter Kindsman one fether
Bed and boulster and a paire of shetes and a Red rug one pillow one pare of cotten piloberes one course shete To my daughter Loe all my peuter and a pare of fine shetese and half a
duson of napkines two cowes that are in thare handes and a
black goune and a Red petticot only one pint pot Resarued
To my Daughter ffellowes all my Corse lining Sauing one shet
and a spit and a chafing dish a Sarge goune and one petti-
cote and a Silk Scarfe and a hud and all the Lining she hath
in hur hands of myne and one bead blancut and allso a pint
pot i Resarue out of my daughter Loes To my Sonn Dannill
a trundle bead ||the bead|| and a Ruge and a blancut and his
wife a cloth petticot and a Sarge petticot and a wastcote and
a great Chest and foure chayres and a cow he hath in his
handes and a debet he owes me I giue it him and half a duson
of shepe he hath in his handes and to his wife a new hat I
giue to my Sonn Thomus thre shepe and the bedstid and
tabell I giue him a payer of cobiarnes and will leaue in his
handes thre cowes one heffer and two oxen and two steres for
seauen yeres and at the seauen yeres end what is left besids
klering my Debtes is to be deuided as foloweth thre parts to
my Daughter Kindsman and the forth part betwen martha
and Johana and to this my last will I leaue my Sonn Thomus
to be my Soule Exseceter the aight day of Agust in the yere
of grace 1679 I giue to Dinah my Sonns mayd two trayes a
milk keler and a payele.

"Half a duson of Arpurns and half a duson of shifts
Equialley to be deuided betwene my Daughters."

Margret (her ⱳ mark) Borman.
Witness: John Dane, Jone Gidins.
Proved in Ipswich court Mar. 30, 1680, by John Dane.

Inventory of the estate of Mrs. Margerit Borman, late of
Ipswich, taken Mar. 19, 1679-80, by John Whipple and Daniell Hovey, Jun.: all her wareing clothes Linon & woollin,

15li.; fetherbeed & boalster, one payer of sheets, a rede rugg, one pillow, one payer of pillowbeers, one sheet, 7li. 6s.; payer of blankits, sute of Curtins with rodes, 2li.; peuter, 3li; a payer of sheets, duz. of napcines, 1li. 15s.; pillion cloth, 12s.; one Iron pott, brase pott, one Irone morter, 1li. 2s.; one Chest, one boxe, 11s.; Linon table cloth, napcins & sheets, 8li.; one spitt, brase chafin dish, 15s.; beed, one rugg, two blankits, 2li. 15s.; large chest, 4 chayers, 18s.; one bedstead, one table, payer of cobirons, 2li. 10s.; paile, trayes & tubes old, 10s.; two oxen, two steers, 17li.; five cows, two of them in Tho. Loo his hands & one in Daniell bormans hands, 16li.; one hayfer, 2li.; nine sheepe, six of them in Daniell bormans hands, 2li. 14s.; total, 84li. 8s.; depts due to the estat, 4li.; depts due from the estat, 19li. 1s.

Attested in Ipswich court Mar. 30, 1680, by Thomas Borman, executor.

Essex County Probate Files, Docket 2,708.

Estate of William Thomas of Newbury.

"Aprill 3ᵈ 1677 I william Thomas being weake of body but of perfect memory considering mine owne mortality and the solitary condition I am in at present doe hereby make my last will and Testament, Comending my Soule into the hands of my blessed Redeemer Jesus Christ, And my body when it shall decease this life I Comitt to the Dust from whence it was taken, In assured hope of a happy Resurrection And for that portion of worldly goods, that the lord hath lent mee In consideration that my Son in law Thomas Rogers, dureing my naturall life find and prouide for mee wholsome & sufficient food & Rayment lodging attendance washing & other necessaryes as shalbe for my comfortable liuelyhood, as well in sicknes & weakenes of old age as in health, reserueing my owne bed to lye upon and two chests ‖& 2 boxes‖ for my owne proper use dureing my naturall life, on these considerations, I giue and bequeath unto the said Thomas Rogers all my house land goods & Chattells to Improue & dispose of for his owne & my comfortable maintenance dureing my naturall life and after my decease to possesse & enioy to him & his heirs for euer, as my sole heire & executor of this my last will & testament my debts & funerall being discharged. But in case the said Thomas shall faile in or neglect his duty in not performeing the conditions abouesaid, then it shalbee lawfull for mee to sell such of the goods for the procurement of such

necessaryes as shalbee needfull for mee. To which agrement well & truely to be performed on both partyes. I the
said william Thomas & Thomas Rogers doe mutually bind &
engage themselues each to other It is also agreed upon that
the said Thomas Rogers shall not sell nor giue away the house
nor land nor any of the goods abouementioned dureing the
naturall life of me the said william Thomas In witness whereof wee haue set to our hands & seales the day & yeare first
aboue written."   Wᵐ. Thomas (SEAL)
                                       Thomas Rogers (SEAL)
    Witness: Anthony Somerby, Daniell Peirc, Jun., Elizabeth
(her E B mark) Bingly.
    Proved in Ipswich court Mar. 30, 1680, by Capt. Daniell
Pearce and Anthony Somerby.

    Inventory of the estate of Mr. William Thomas, who de-
ceased the last day of December, 1679, taken 23 : 11m : 1679,
by Daniell Peirc and Thomas Noyes: a house & two acres and
an halfe of land, 35li.; His weareing Apparrell and bookes,
4li. 10s.; two beds and beding, 2li. 10s.; Chests & Boxes &
cubbards, 2li.; old Casks, 11s.; two Iron pots, one tramel, 2
pr. of tongs & 2 pr. of pothooks, 14s.; one frying pan, 1 spit,
1 peele, a fender & an Iron lamp, 6s.; two wedgs & other old
Iron, 2s.; A little brasse kettle, a warming pan & brass skillet,
10s.; severall peices of pewter, 1li. 3s.; Brasse scales & weights,
8s.; a paire of small scales & weights, 2s.; one bedsted, 4
chayres & 2 Cushions, 6s.; Trayes & wooden platters, 4s.; Latten pan, spoones, cheesfat & dishes, 3s.; three formes, 3s.; foure
knives, one pillion & spining wheel & cards, 13s.; in mony, 7s.
2d.; one Copper & a Trevet, 2li. 10s.; Two tap boriers, 2
chissells and a Hammer, 3s.; Two Rangers, two Oares, four
brushes, 1 comb & two pr. of sissers, 3s.; Earthen ware, 1s.; A
Harpin Iron & Sturgion pooles, 3s.; A Freehold, 5li.; pr. of
woodden scales, a looking glase & Tormenters, a wooden To-
bacca pipe & an Iron ladle & forke, 1s.; total, 57li. 13s. 2d.
    Attested in Ipswich court Mar. 30, 1680, by Thomas Rog-
ers, executor.

                   Essex County Probate Files, Docket 27,476.

             ESTATE OF SAMUEL WHITING, SR. OF LYNN.

    "Lynn: 25ᵗʰ: of ffebruarye one thousand six hundred
seaunty, & eight I Samuell whiteing of Lynn in the Countye
of Essex being of perfect memorye, & right understanding
considering the age god hath lengthened out my dayes unto,

& the dutye incumbent on mee, to set my house in order before I dye doe thinke it now full tyme to attend this worke and therefore after my Committing of my Deare flock, unto the tender care of that great, & good shepheard the Lord Jesus Christ, & bequeathing my immortall soule into the hands of my mercyfull Creator, redeemer, & sanctifier, & my bodye unto a Comlye, & desent buriall: I doe make, & Constitute my Last will, & testament, in manner, & forme following. ffirst I doe Constitute, & appoynt my two sonns (viz) Samuell whiting Liveing at Billericai, & Joseph whiteing Liveing now with mee at Lynn to bee my Lawfull, & onelye Executo^{r}s unto whom joyntlye I Comitt that portion of outward things, or the whole estate that I shall Leaue at my decease to bee disposed of by them, according to my order herein Expressed. My will is that all my Lands I am possessed of bee inherited by my two sonns my Executo^{r}s Samuell, & Joseph, as I shall appoynt it out unto them. My will is that my Eldest sonn Samuell shall haue, & possess for him, & his heires my farme of foure hundred acres of upland, & medow (be it more, or Less) at Dunstable, with all the priviledges appertaineing there unto: As alsoe fourteen acres ‖of marsh‖ Lyeing in Rumnye marsh in the Township of Lynn (be it more or Less) it being in the first devision of Lotts there, bounded according to the Towne records

"Alsoe my will is that my second son John whiteing Liveing in ould England, at Leverton in Lincolneshire, shall by my sonns that are my Executo^{r}s haue thirtye pounds of my estate that I Leave, sett out to him as an addition to what ‖he hath‖ alreddye receiued (viz) ten pounds in monyes, & twentye pounds in common paye according to the ordinarye prises of Corne, catle &c: in the countrye. My will further is that my third sonn Joseph whiteing, shall haue, & possess for him, & his heires after him: my dwelling house with the orchard, & Lott adjoyning, with all the privilidges of Comons, herbage &c: beLonging there unto. Alsoe eight acres of medow, or salt marsh (bee it more or Less): in the medow before the Towne, bounded with the Towne Records. Unto my daughter weld of Roxburye I Leave twentye pounds to bee paid by my executo^{r}s as an Addition to what shee hath received: ten pounds of it in monyes, & plate, & the other ten pounds in Comon paye, as Corne, & Catle &c: pass from man to man. Alsoe to my daughter Hubbard of Topsfeild: I order thirtye poundes to bee paid by my Executo^{r}s as ‖an‖ addition to what shee hath already received: ten pounds of it to bee paid in monyes or plate & twentye in Common paye according to the odinarye prise yᵗ corne or catle &c: passeth from man to man yᵗ is not accounted as monye. I have alsoe promised to Leave to my sonn in Law mʳ. Jeremiah Hubbard a parcell of Bookes set out to him, which I judge to bee well worth ten pounds for his son Samuell, or whom hee shall see meet to Leave them to. And Lastlye my will is that my two sonns my Executoʳs shall haue besydes the Lands beefore mentioned all the remainder of my estate equallye to bee devided betwixt them after they have paide out what I haue ordered to their brethren, & sisters in this my will In wittness here unto I haue sett to my hand, & seale the daye, & year aboue written."

Samuel Whiting, Sen. (SEAL)

Witness: Andrew Mansfeild, Samuel Cobbett, Francis Burrill.

Proved in Ipswich court Mar. 30, 1680, by Andrew Mansfield and Francis Burrell.

Inventory of the estate of Rev. Mr. Samuell Whiteing, late Pastor of the Church of Christ of Lynn, who departed this life Dec. 11, 1679, taken Dec. 18, 1679, by Andrew Mansfeild and Francis Burrill: The dwelling house, orchard Lott marsh & farme at Dunstable, 362li.; monyes & plate, 77li. 2s.; cowes, sheepe & swine, with one Cow hyde, 42li. 9s.; Beding, Bedsteads, Curtaines & vallence, 15li. 19s.; wooden ware, tables, stooles, chairs, Cupboards, chests & caske, 9li. 10s.; Lynnen, 9li. 6s. 6d.; Apparrell, 10li. 11s.; Bookes, 10li. 16s.; Provisions, 4li. 15s.; Brasse, puter, Iron, Earthen ware & other small things, 8li. 15s. 4d.; debts due unto the estate, 15li. 10s.; Linnen & woolen Cloath with some other things before omitted, 4li. 1s. 8d.; total, 570li. 15s. 6d. The estate debter, 4li. 5s. 1d.

Attested in Ipswich court Mar. 30, 1680, by Samuell and Joseph Whiting, executors of their father's will.

Essex County Probate Files, Docket 29,659.

ESTATE OF WILLIAM HOOPER.

Administration upon the estate of Wm. Hooper, intestate was granted Mar. 30, 1680, unto Elizabeth, the widow, and there being three children living, and she being with the fourth, the court ordered 8li. to the eldest son and 4li. a peice to the other three, if any die their portion to be divided among the surviving, the land to stand bound.

Ipswich Quarterly Court Records, vol. 5, page 351.

Inventory of the estate of William Hooper deceased the 8 :
9m: 1679, taken 20: 1m: 1679-80, by Samuell Corning, Sr.,
John Hill and Jeremiah Butman; his owne wearing clothes,
5li. 10s. 6d.; one bed and apurtinances, 5li.; another bed, 3li.;
another bed, 3li.; lining, 2li. 3s.; table lining, 18s.; a new
pece serge, 15s. 9d.; a parsell of fethers, 1li. 5s.; a chest and
boxes, 1li.; brass, 1li.; peuter & portege weare, 15s.; Earthen
weare, 3s.; Iron potes and other Iron weare, 1li. 16s. 6d.;
chairers, & other small woodden lumber, 8s.; three cows & a
tow yer old hefer, 11li.; coultes, 2li.; swine, 12s.; yewes and
lambes, 18s.; hows and land, 50li.; one gune & sword, 1li. 5s.;
Fishing lines, 5s.; severall persells of new cloth, 2li. 18s.;
total, 95li. 12s. 9d. Debts to be paid, 21li. 3s. 2d.; Credit, 1li.
18s. 6d.

Attested in Ipswich court 30: 1: 1680, by Elizabeth Hooper,
the administratrix.

Essex County Probate Files, Docket 13,886.

ESTATE OF JAMES MOULTON, SR. OF WENHAM.

"Know all men by these presents, the twenty Sixth of February in the yeare of our Lord God, one thousand Six hundred & Seventy eight. I James Molton Senr. of wenham in
the County of Essex, well in body & of good & perfect memory,
doe make & ordeine this my last will & Testament in manner
& forme following. Imprimis, I bequeath my body to the
earth; & my soule to God thatt gave itt. Item I leave to my
well beloved wife, my houseing, & land wth all the apurtinances, wth my stock & houshold goods for her use & benefitt
during her life excepting, such as I shall after dispose of
viz: 20 acres of land to my Son Samuell ten acres by cedar
pond & ten acres belonging to Lords farme next the great
pond which I give him & his heires for ever after my decease
Item I give my wife my houshold stuff, to dispose of acording
as she please after her decease. Item, after her decease I give
to my Son Samuell Molton my housings & the twenty acres
of Land belonging to itt more or Less with the ten acres of
Land before mentioned joining to Cedar Swamp, & ten acres
of Lord's farm by the great pond, & Six acres of Meadow
Item I give my Daughter Mary freind & her heires five acres
of Land joining to the backside of his present house & ten acres
of Lords farm next his own Land Item I give to my Eldest
Son James Molton & his heires forever. the residue & remainder of all my Lands and Meadow be itt more or Less. Item I

give him five pounds out of my moveable estate Item I give to
the Colledge five pounds Item 1 give to the church att Wenham five pounds. Item I give to the present Minister Joseph
Gerrish or his heires five pounds which Legacies shall be paid
within a yeare after mine & my wives decease I make &
ordeine, my three children joint executors, of this my Last
will. And I doe entreate my Loving freinds Capt. Thomas
Fiske & William Fiske to oversee the acomplishment of this
my will In wittness where of I have sett to my hand & Seale
the day & date above mentioned."

James Molton (SEAL)

Witness: Joseph Gerrish, Anna Gerrish.

Proved in Ipswich court Mar. 30, 1680, by the witnesses.

Inventory taken 6 : 1m : 1679-80, by Thos. Fiske and William Fiske: the howses & about twenty acres of land of the
homestead, 85li.; twenty Acres of land in the woods mentioned in the will & Given to Samuell Moulton, 30li.; 12 Acres
of medow in the Greate medow neare the Great Illand, 24li.;
3 Acres 1-2 of medow in lords medow, 10li.; 74 Acres of land
which James moulton liveth upon, 180li.; about 6 Acres of
land in lords farme, 12li.; 10 Acres of land more
in lords farme Given (in the will) to James freind,
20li.; 5 Acres of land lying by James freinds howse,
12li.; two fether Beds, 6li.; one Bed Sack, 10s.; one fether
boulster, two pillowes, one Blanket & Rugg with a Sute of
Curtains & valants belonging to the bed wch stand in the
parlor, 4li. 13s.; one flock Bowlster, 5s.; one small bed Sack,
two blankets & two small pillows, 15s.; one Bedstead, 10s.;
one trundle bedstead, bed mat, 3s.; wearing Cloathes, 3li.
14s.; Pewter, 2li. 4s.; Silver spoons, 14s.; Brass & Tinn, 1li.
4s. 6d.; Iron kittle & potts, 1li. 4s. 6d.; two spits, 4s. 6d.; two
Tramels, 12s.; Andirons, fire shovell, Tongs, hamer with some
old Utensils, 14s.; Armes & Ammunition, 1li. 8s.; total, 379li.
15s. 6d.; two holland pillowbeers, 16s. 6d.; thre pillowebeers
more, 6s.; one cubbord Cloath, 10s.; Table Cloath & Napk-
ings, 10s.; one holland Sheet, 1li.; other Course sheets, 2li.;
Books, 12s.; Cattle, 30li.; Cart & wheels, 1li. 10s.; one small
Timber Chaine, 12s.; one Draft Chaine & yoaks & Spanshackle & pine, 12s.; one old share & horse Tackling, 5s.;
beetle & one wedge, 5s.; two axes & howe, 6s.; one Dung
brome, 3s.; Swine, 2li.; cushins, 3s.; wooden Utenciles &
lumber, 3li. 18s.; Earthen ware & Cubbord Cloath, 8s.; one
warmeing pan, 3s.; one meate tubb & one old barell, 3s.; 45

Bushels of Corne, 6li. 15s.; mault 14 Bushels, 2li. 16s.; a
Remmant of Sardg, 1li. 16s.; a Croscut Sawe & fan, 4s. 6d.;
Cotton wooll & flax, 11s.; Bridle & Sadle, 12s. The debts of
James Molton, Sen. are as follows: to Mr. Will. Browne, Sr.,
10li. 11s. 2d.; Mr. Francis Wainright, 5li. 10s. 11d.; Mr.
Lindall, 4li. 19s. 1d.; Deacon Goodhue, 2li. 14s.; Mr. Batters,
2li. 10s.; Capt. John Corwin, 1li. 7s. 7 1-2d.; Thomas Ives,
1li. 2s. 6d.; Capt. George Corwin, 13s. 1 1-2d.; Go. Gaines,
12s.; Deacon Nolton, 10s.; Mr. Farlow, 3s.; Go. Harriman,
7s.; Capt. Gerrish, 5s.; Mr. Gerrish, 2s.; Go. Gage, 2s.; Go.
Stackors, 6s.; Mary Horton, money, 15s.; Mr. Thomas
Gardiner, mony, 15s.; Nathaniell Walden, 12s.; to the Cooper,
6s.; Go. Fiske, 4s.; to the Grave, 2s. 6d.; Thomas Clarke,
2s. 9d.

Attested in Ipswich court 30: 1m: 1680, by Samuell Molton
and James Molton, executors of their father's estate.

Essex County Probate Files, Docket 19,018.

James Molton, sr., often declared his intent in disposing of
his estate at his decease, and desired Mr. Joseph Gerrish to
write the same. He not having had experience in such matters
did not clearly express the wishes of the donor, which may occasion some difference among the legatees, and especially in
that clause of the gift to his son Samuel Molton of "his houseing & 20 acres of Land belonging to it more or less, after his
Mother decease in y^t tis not expressed to him & to his heires
as in other Legacies." I do here offer oath that it was my
default through forgetfulness, and that it was fully expressed
to me by the donor, to be Samuell Molten and his heires. Mary
Molton, widow of James Molton, sr., testified to the truth of
the above. Sworn Mar. 31, 1685.

Ipswich Deeds, vol. 5, page 33.

Guardianship of Nathaniel Walden.

Nathaniell Walderne chose Walter Fairefield to be his
guardian, Mar. 30, 1680.

Ipswich Quarterly Court Records, vol. 5, page 351.

Estate of Mrs. Mary Marchent of Ipswich.

"The Last Will, & Testament of Mary Marchent Widdow,
who, though weake in Body yet of good understandinge, doth
disspose of her Temprall Estate, in maner & forme as ffolloweth, Impri I Give My Daughter, Mary Ossburne her Children my whole estate, Left unto mee by my Disceaced hus-

band William Marchent wch is the one halfe of the whole estate
that hee died Ceaz'd on, as it appears by the Inventory Recorded in the court Rooles of Ipswich, which estate Remaines
yet undevided unto mee, The which, my will is, shall bee, Devided in Equall Proportion, amongst the children aforesd.
Notwithstanding my will is That my daughter Mary aforesd
shall haue the use theroff Dureinge the time off her Naturall
Liffe, & then to be Dissposed off, as abouesd. And allsoe my
will is that in case any of the Children Die Before they haue
Received their Proportion that then that share ‖or shares‖
shall be Equaly Devided Amonge the surviueing. As for any
other Estate of mine as Books wearing Cloathes or the Like,
I Leaue to my Daughter to Disspose as she see cause for her
selfe and the children. This is my Last will as wittness my
hand this 25 June ‖1679‖."

Mary (her M mark) Marchantt.

Witness: Moses Pengry, sr., Aaron Pengry, sr.

Essex County Probate Files, Docket 18,196.

Administration upon the estate of Mary Marchent, widow,
intestate, was granted Mar. 30, 1680, unto Henry Osborne,
he to administer according to a paper declared to be her mind,
the land to stand bound.

Ipswich Quarterly Court Records, vol. 5, *page* 351.

John Osburne of Ipswich, son of Henry Osburne of Ipswich, releases unto his father Henry Osborne, administrator
to the estate of Mary Marchent, widow, and administratrix to
the estate of William Marchent of Ipswich, all claim which
he may have in the estate of Mary Marchent and William
Marchent. Signed and sealed July 29, 1697. Witness: John
Appleton, Elizabeth Appleton.

Acknowledged by John Osborne July 31, 1697, before John
Appleton, J. of Peace, and Aug. 2, 1697, before Barth. Gedney, Judge of Probate.

Henry (his E mark) Osburne of Ipswich, ordained his son
John Osburne, his lawful attorney, and he to appear before
the Court and render an account of his administration on the
estate of Mary Marchant. Signed and sealed July 29, 1697.
Witness: John Appleton, Elizabeth Appleton.

Acknowledged by Henry Osburne, sr., July 31, 1697 before
John Appleton.

William (his ‖W G mark) Goodhue of Ipswich,
who married Mary Goodhue, daughter of Henry Osburne of Ipswich, releases unto his father Henry Osburne, as

administrator to the estate of Mary Marchant, widow, and administratrix to the estate of William Marchant of Ipswich, all claim which they may have in the estate of Mary Marchant and William Marchant. Signed and sealed July 29, 1697. Witness: Wm. Fellows, Martha Brewer.

Acknowledged by William Goodhue, 3d, July 31, 1697, before John Appleton.

Whereas Henry Osborne administrator of the estate of Mary Merchant of Ipswich, being cited to appear and render an account of his administration on said estate, appeared accordingly by his attorney John Osborne, and he producing acquittances for two of the children interested in said estate, and there being but one child more, Elizabeth, who married Anthony Lowden of Portsmouth, and Philip Fowler of Ipswich appearing by his letter of attorney in behalf of sd. Lowden, John Osborne bound himself to pay over to Anthony Lowden or to his attorney, 14li. 13s. 4d., which is the full share of said Elizabeth Lowden, in the estate of Mary Merchant. The land still to stand bound for the payment of the same. Signed and sealed Aug. 2, 1697. Witness: John Croade, Mary Smith.

Philip Fouler, attorney to Anthony and Elisabeth Louden, acknowledged June 23, 1698, the receipt in full, of her share of all willed to her by her grandmother Marchant, and acquitted Henery and John Orsborne from all further claim.

Essex County Probate Files, Docket 18,196.

Estate of John Harris.

Administration upon the estate of John Harris, intestate, was granted Mar. 30, 1680, unto Honor Hall and Lewis bafor and they to bring in an inventory to the next court.

Ipswich Quarterly Court Records, vol. 5, page 351.

Inventory of the estate of John Harris, cooper, taken Mar. 27, 1680, by Richard Walker and Abraham Tilton: a bung boarer and two shaveing Knives, 10s.; A crissiff, 7s.; a Round shave, 6d.; an Ax, 8s.; two Adses, 12s.; A heading Knife and howell, 4s. 6d.; three compasses, 6s.; two Crowsing Irons, 3s.; two breast Wimble Stocks and a head Pullee, 3s.; Chalk, 1s. 4d.; three neckcloths, 14s.; other linnen, 4s.; two shirts and an old neckcloth, 5s.; Woolen Clothes and Stockins and an old pr. of shooes, 8s.; a hatt, 2s.; a chest, 10s.; a Pike Staff, 2s. 6d.; Trusse hoops and other hoopes, 5s.; four yards of Cloath and four dozen of buttons, 1li. 4s.; Woolen Clothes, 10s.;

Stockins, 8s. 6d.; Neckclothes and other Linnen, 5s. 3d.;
Gloves, 9d.; a shirt, 4s. 6d.; shooes, hat & Apron, 9s.; a comb,
Knife and Steel, 1s. 3d.; Ribbin, a purse, 1s. 10d.; in money,
2s.; 1000 of Staves, 1li. 10s.; Debts upon the booke due to the
estate, 7li. 19s. 2d.; total, 18li. 1d. Debts due out of the
estate, 7li. 19s. 3d.

Richard (his R H mark) Hutton and John Knowlton, sr.,
being desired by Hannah Ardway to take account of the pains
and cost she hath expended upon a young man named John
Harris, who lay wholly upon her hands both for meat, drink
washing and lodging for the space of nine weeks, and which
we apprehend she should have 9s. per. week, amounting to
4li.; for expence at the Docter, 4s.; twice goeing to Salem,
4s.; for linnen, 1s.; John Severy providing the coffin & digging the grave, 10s.; total, 5li.

Deposition of John *draire* that "I asked John Haris
whether he and Lewes wife ware a kinn: he told me he
thought she ware but he was not sartaine but he have sent to
his Father: after he told me that he have reseaved a letter
from his father and was informed she was kin."

Deposition of Elizabeth Graves aged thirty nine that "being
at Lewes Befords house, John harise lately deseaced came
into the house and said unto Lewes wife cozen Janne I will
now tell you how you came to be a kinn to me youre fath^r.
and my Fath^rs were owne Broth^rs for I haue now sartaine in-
teligenc by a leter from my fath^r. wch letter the above mentioned Haris then shewed I this deponant further testefy that
I have often observed that John Haris frequently cam to the
house of Lewes sometims the best part of a week to gather."
Essex County Quarterly Court Files, vol. 32, leaves 134, 135.

ESTATE OF MRS. FAITH WARNER OF IPSWICH.

"Whereas there was an estate left by Edward Browne late
of Ipswich deceased and he haveing by will disposed of his
Reall estate unto his two sons Joseph & John Browne, and left
all both Reall & psonall in the hands of his widdow ffaith
Browne for tearme of life (exsept eight acres of Land & a
pcell of meadow) and by his will his sd widdow to dispose of
the rest of the estate to his children, Know all men by these
presents, that I ffaith Warner late wife unto the aforsayd Edward Browne being in good health at present, not knowing
how soone a change may happen wch are all subject unto and

somtimes suddaine, for the settling therfore of that estate left me to dispose off by my aforesayd husband, do make this my last will & testament first for my eldest sonn Joseph Browne, his ffather haveing suficiently provyded for him by his will, to more then a dubble portion, I therfore have only given unto him, the shop tooles, wch amounted unto three pounds six shillings, wch he hath had in full possession ever since his ffather dyed Item I give unto my other son John Browne besyds, the little pcell of land he is to enjoy after my decease, I give unto him a flockbed, & bolster Rugg & blankett and one paire of sheetes, out of the chest & the straw bed all wch are in the house, and left with my sonn Joseph, also I give him a cow wch is also in my sonn Josephs hands, also I give unto him the sd sonn John Browne eleven pounds ten shillings after my decease, wch is due to me by bond from my p^{r}sent husband Daniell Warner, and to my eldest Daughter I have allredy given unto her a feather bed, bolster, downe pillow, and the one halfe of my lenin & other houshold stuf wch I judge to be her full portion, and to my daughter Lidia Browne I give a cow now in the hands of John Browne glasier, and also a featherbed & bolster & pillow after my decease, and the other halfe of the linnen, standing in the house, with the other houshold stuff, and bedstead & tables left in the house, and I do apoint my son John Browne and my daughter Lidia to be my executor & executrix of this my will and desire my present husband Daniell Warner to be overseer to see this my will pformed, In wittnes heerof have sett my hand the 25 of June 1669."

Faith (her mark) Warner.

Witness: Robert Paine, Robert Lord.

Proved in Ipswich court Mar. 30, 1680, by Robert Lord, sr.

Inventory of the estate of Faith Warner, formerly wife of Edward Browne, taken Mar. 31, 1680, by Thomas Knowlton, sr. and Edmond Heard: one featherbed, bolster, Rugg and sheete, 5li.; one pare of sheetes & one pillow-beere, 1li. 3s.; one chest, pewter & bras, wooden ware & earthen in it, 18s. 6d.; one paire of sheetes, thre towells, 3 pillowbeers, one tablecloth & small lining, 1li. 9s. 6d.; two pewter dishes, one quart pott, pr. of bras scales & earthen ware, 8s.; one old trunk, one brass waite, & a peece of bed ticking, 2s.; two old Iron potts, one old brass kettle, one frieing pan & fire fork, one tramell and an old gridiron, 14s. 6d.; one bedstead & bedcord, 3 curtains & vallins, one meale trough, 1li.; one table &

one table frame & one chaire, 4s.; a small flockbed, bolster, one Rugg, one blanket, one pr. of sheetes, 2li. 5s.; debt by bond, 11li. 10s.; total, 24li. 14s. 6d.

Attested in Ipswich court Mar. 30, 1680, by Lidia Chaffen formerly Lidia Browne, executrix to her mother's will.

Ipswich Deeds, vol. 4, page 341.

ESTATE OF HILLIARD VEREN, JR., OF SALEM.

At a County Court held at Boston, Apr. 27, 1680, power of administration upon the estate of Hilliard Veren, jr., late of Salem, (in the Island of Barbadoes), intestate, was granted unto his father Hilliard Veren, Capt. John Price and Hannah the widow of said Hilliard, they giving bond to present an inventory unto the next court at Salem.

Salem Quarterly Court Records, vol. 6, leaf 9.

"Salem Nouember the 10: 1679 I Hilliard Veren Junᵣ of Salem, now being bound to sea & not knowing how it may please God to deale with me make this my last will viz I giue unto my Deare wife Hanna Veren for euer, my now dwelling house, and land adjoyning & furniture: the remainder of my estate which I leaue at home, which I value as money about six hundred pounds I say six hundred pounds: I giue unto my Honʳᵈ father & mother two thirds be it more or lesse, to be kept by them & improued for theire use, the terme of theire lives & at theire decease, if any thing shall remaine, to giue it to the most hopefull & ingenious Grand children & the other third part to my wife. Alsoe the estate I carry with me, if I should miscarry & that pʳserved & com hom my will is that it be equally deuided between my wife & father & mother, & that alsoe improued as aboue mentioned and this I declare to be my absolute mind & will, In testimoney sett my hand, the day aboue mentioned."

Hilliard Veren, Junᵣ.

"I intend by the grand children, my sisters children & Walter Price to haue an equall proportion with them."

H. Veren.

Mr. Benjamin Browne, Mr. John Higgenson and Mr. Thomas Gardner made oath in Salem court, June 29, 1680, that the above was in the hand writing of Hilliard Veren, jr.

Hilliard Veren testified in Salem court June 29, 1680, that "my son Hilliard Veren, that very morning before he went away this last voyage or a morning or two before he came into

my house & brought in his hand & delivered the within
written to me as his last will & read it to me & said pray take
it & seale it up till you heare how God shall deale with me in
my voyage."

Agreement between Hilliard Veren, sr. and Hannah Verin,
widow of Hilliard Veren, that according to the tenour of the
above writing or will the widow aforesaid shall have and hold
the house and furniture, with the land adjoyning, mentioned
in the will aforesaid, to her and her heirs forever; that all the
other real and personal estate already in hand being estimated at six hundred pounds in the will, be divided equally
between Hilliard Veren and the widow, for the uses mentioned
in said will, the debts of the estate to be paid equally by them;
that care shall be taken to draw in what belongs to the estate
in Barbados, England, &c., and upon receipt thereof, to be
divided equally between the above mentioned, and if either
party decease before, then it to be accordingly to the heirs of
the deceased party; that an inventory be taken and presented
to the court, with the request that this mutual agreement be
allowed. Signed and sealed June 29, 1680. Witness: Bartho-
lomew Gedney.

The above allowed and confirmed in conjunction with the
will, by the Salem court, June 29, 1680.

Inventory of the estate of Hilliard Veren, jr. taken June
24, 1680, by John Higgenson, jr. and Thomas Gardner, jr.;
In the shopp, 7 peeces searge at 55s. per, 2 peeces gray collered
searg at 3li. per, 21 yds., 2li. 15s., 28li.; 8 yds. 1-4 cloth searge
at 4s. per., 21 1-2 yds, cource carsey at 2s. per, 3li. 16s.; 15
yds. long old searge at 3s. per, 3 yds. fine carsey at 5s. 6d. per.,
3li. 1s. 6d.; 10 yds. 1-4 Irish carsey at 3s. per, 9 yds. 1-4 sad
gray carsey at 4s. 6d. per., 3li. 12s. 4 1-2d.; 8 yrds. mixt
carsey at 30d. per., 6 yds. 3-4 colerd halfe thick 2 remnants,
2s. 3d., 1li. 15s. 2 1-4d.; 45 yds. Red halfe thick in 2 peeces
2s. 3d. per., 5 yd. collrd cotten, 13d. per., 5li. 6s. 8d.; 4 yrds.
wt. cotten 14d. per., 13 yrds. red cotten at 16d. per., 23 yd.
penestone 2s. 3d. per., 3li. 13s. 9d.; total, 49li. 5s. 5 3-4d. 3
peeces of blew linen cont. 103 yrds. & in remnants 55 yrds.
all is 155 yrds. at 10d. per., 6li. 9s. 2d.; 12 yrds. red flannell,
18d. per., 7 yrds. Irish blanketting at 12d. per., 1 carpett, 4s.,
1li. 9s.; 1-2 peece 2-3 Dowlas, 4li., 4 remnants dowlas cont.
118 yds. at 20d. per., 13li. 16s. 8d.; 3 small remnants qt. 7
yds. 3-4 at 20d. per., 8 yrds. 1-4 broad dowlas at 2s. per., 1li.
9s. 5d.; 33 yrds. 1-2 Irish linen browne at 22d. per., 24 yrds.

1-4 ditto at 19d. per., 4li. 19s. 9 3-4d.; 4 peeces cource Irish
linen, qt. 33 yds. at 12d. per., 10 yrds ditto at 12d. per., 2li.
3s.; 8 yds. 1-2 cource holland at 2s. per., 6 yds. fustin at 10d.
per., 1li. 2s.; 22 yds. 1-2 canvis at 12d. per., 35 yrds. 1-2 ditto
at 11d., 17 yrds. 1-2 ditto at 13d., 3li. 14s.; 19 yrds. canvis at
10d., 62 yds. 3-4 narrow canvis, 9d. per., 3li. 2s. 11 1-4d.; 1
peece & 19 yrds. pole dany at 15d. pr. yd., 12 yds. wt. Duffells
at 2s. 9d., 5li. 1s. 9d.; 10 gross 4 doz. gimp coate buttens, 2s.
3d. per., 7 gro. 11 doz. silck coat buttens, 4s. per., 2li. 14s.
11d.; 13 doz. silk brest ditto 2d. 1-2 per., 5 gro. 1-2 wt. wascoat buttens at 12d. per., 8s. 2 1-2d.; 49 yrd. cotten Ribbon at
1d. 1-4 per., 52 yds. 1-2 galloone 1-2 silk 2d. per., 13s. 10
1-4d.; 33 yrds. of manchester 1d. per., 8 peeces tape 8d. per., 3
Ivery combes, 2s. 8d., 10s. 9d.; 8 yd. wt. flanell 18d. per.,
12s.; total, 97li. 13s. 1-2d.; 3 pr. wt. thrid stockins, 12d. per,
No. 27, 25, 5li. 1-2 wt. browne third at 5s. per., 1li. 10s. 6d.;
1li. 1-2 ditto 5s. 6d. per, no. 20, 22, 23, 2li. 1-4 ditto at 4s.
per. 1-2li. fine thrid, 20s., 1li. 17s.; 5 brushes 8d. per., 4 papers pins 2d. per., 16 pr. mens cource worsted hose 3s. per.,
2li. 12s.; 6 pr. mixt woemens hose, 3s. 6d. per, 2 pr. cource
mens yarne 12d., 1li. 3s.; 4li. silk at 22s. per, 1li. 1-2 collrd
thrid 3s. per., 1 Hatt 2s. 6d., 4li. 15s.; 5 candlestickes 8d.
per, 3 locks 1 pr. dove tailes, 1 gimlett, 3s., 1-2li. bone, 9d.,
7s. 1d.; 21 pewter dishes qt. 127li. 3-4 at 12d. per., 7 large
plates 16d. per., 6li. 17s. 1d.; 23 2d sort of plates 14d. per,
18 smale plates 12d. per., 2li. 4s. 10d.; 6M. 3C. 1-2 20d.
nailes at 9s. per., 7M. 4d. nailes at 2s. 3d. per., 3li. 12s.; 24
pole of land by Pritharches 10li., 1-2 an acre by Abra. Coles,
10li., 20li.; New England money 38li. 10s. peeces of 1-8, 65
&c. 17li. 2s. 6d., 55li. 12s. 6d.; disburst upon mourning wch
layd out in money & alowed on acct. to them yt disburst it for
Mrs. Veren, 16li. 6s. 7d.; total 218li. 11s. 10d. Debts due to
the estate as pticulars good & bad, 435li. 1s. 1d. The dwelling
house & land thereunto belonging, 240li.; furniture of the
house, viz., Parlor, 12 Turkey work chaires at 9s. pr., 5li. 8s.;
2 square tables at 24s., 1 pr. large brass Andirons 20s., 2li. 4s.
Hall, 6 lether chaires, 3s. 6d. pr., 2 tables 8s., 4 straw bottom
chaires, 5s., 2 calico carpetts, 4s., 1li. 18s.; 1 old low lether
chaire, 1s., 1 pr. andirons, 4s., 1 looking glass, 4s., 3 brushes
2 coms, 30d., 11s. 6d.; 1 large Iron candlestick, 14s., 5 small,
1 large booke, 15s., 2 cushions, 18d., 1li. 10s. 6d.; 1 standish
& penknife, 12d., 6 old joyne stooles, 6s., 6 silver spoons &
broken plate & 3 cupps, 5li. 14s., 1 Seale Ring, 1 small & 1
silver Ring, 2li. 3s., 8li. 1s.; 1 Gold Seale, 15s., a vice to open

bottels, 12d., 16s. Halle chamber, 6 searge chaires at 5s. per,
1 chest drawers at 12s., 2 trunkes, 12s., 2li. 14s.; 1 bed, bedsteed, 2 pillowes, 1 bolster, curtains & vallens, 3 blanketts &c.,
7li. 10s.; 9 pr. pillow beers, 30s., 2 doz. diap. napkens, 1 diap.
tablecloath, 24s., 2li. 14s.; 2 doz. dowlas naptkins, 1 small
diap. table cloath, 24s., 16 towells, 12s., 1li. 16s.; 2 table
cloathes, 6s., 1 cubord cloth, 5s., 1 silk cubord cloth, 6s., 17s.;
2 pr. fine sheetes, 24s. per., 1 pr. cource holland ditto 15s., 3li.
3s.; 1 fiue dowlas sheet, 18s., 10 pr. cource sheets, 9s. per, 5li.
8s.; 1pr. new searge curtaines with silck freng, 6li., 1 table
cloath, 5s., 6li. 5s.; 3 pictures & the box; 1 plaine rugg &
flockbed, 25s., 1li. 11s. Shop chamber, 1doz. 10 cource napkins,
1li., 8 tablecloathes worne, 10s., 1li. 10s.; 1 bed, bedsteed,
Rods, 4li., 1 box, 1 old Trunk, 4s., 1 Hamack, 10s., 4li. 14s.;
1 worsted thrum Rugg, 18s., 1 wt. blankitt, 5s., 1 basket &
flaskett, 30d., 1li. 5s. 6d. Lento chamber, 1 sadle, bridle &
furniture, 1 carbine 15s., 1 pr. pistolls, holsters, rapier,
&c., 2li. 16s. Garret lento, meale trof, bagg & lumber, 8s., 50li.
pewter at 9d. per., 13 plates 12d. per., 2li. 18s. 6d.; 1 bason,
5s., 5 sacers 2d. per., 7 porringers 10d. per., flagon, salt, 2
potts, 6s., 17s.; 2 smale brasse candlestickes, 3s., 2 brass scill-
letts, 2 chafin dishes, 7s., 10s.; warming pan, 1 skimer, 8s., 1
brass Ketle, 30s., spit & friing pan, 4s., 2li. 2s.; 1 Iron pot, 1
Kettle, 7s., 1 pr. andirons, 4s., fire shovell, tonges & a forke,
4s., 15s.; gridiron, a clenly, 3s. 6d., 2 tramells, 1 pr. pot-
hoockes, 8s., 11s. 6d.; 1 Jack, 1 pr. bellowes, 17s., 3 chaires &
1 cushion, 4s., 1 case, 7 bottles, 8s., 1li. 9s.; 18 earth plates, 4s.
6d., 6 earth basons, 8s., 2 earth dishes, 2s., 14s. 6d.; chamber
potts & juggs, 4s. 6d., tin ware, 7s., glasses & bottells & other
smale things, 16s., old cask in the seller, 6s., 1 pr. stilliards,
1li. 6s. 6d.; total, 969li. 1d. The estate is due for severall disburstments for mourning & other debts, 57li. 6d.; soe much
layd out by Mrs. Veren for mourning as per inventory, 16li.
6s. 7d.; the estate is Dr. by a mistake upon the casting up of
the silks, 1 gross buttens & browne linen all is 4li. 6s. 6d.;
the estate is Dr. in England, &c.

Attested in Salem court June 29, 1680, by Hilliard Veren,
Capt. John Price and Hanah Veren, relict of Hilliard Veren.

Essex County Court Records, vol. 301, pp. 151-154.

ESTATE OF JOHN SOUTHWICK OF SALEM.*

A proposal being made on the behalf of the youngest child
of John Sothwick, deceased, that her portion of estate might

*See *ante*, vol. 2, page 313.

according to the order of the court at Salem, Nov. 26, 1679, be set out for her, this court May 4, 1680, appointed Capt. John Corwin, Capt. John Price and Mr. Hilliard Verrin or any two of them, to compute the child's proportion and to set it out if it be in land, and make return to the next court for their further consideration and confirmation.

Ipswich Quarterly Court Records, vol. 5, page 354.

ESTATE OF JOHN HUMPHRIES, ESQ.*

Griffen Edwards, husband of Elizabeth, the daughter of Ann the now wife of Mr. John Miles, the only child of John Humphreyes, Esq., deceased, presented to the court June 28, 1681, a letter of attorney under the hand of said Ann, his mother in law, to act in her behalf, relating to any right she might have in the estate of her father, and also produced a certificate under the hand of the Mayor of Clonmell, Ireland, and attested by several, that said Ann is the only surviving reputed child of John Humphryes, and he was granted administration in the behalf of said Ann, of all the estate of John Humphryes here in this Colony of Massachusetts. The court having formerly ordered Mr. Thomas Price and Mrs. Elizabeth Pelham upon their receiving Col. Humphryes farm at Lynn into their hands, to pay 75li. 17s. to Mr. Edmond Batter, which was a debt due from the estate, now order that they may keep the farm in their possession as formerly, until they shall be reimbursed the 75li. 17s. and also be reimbursed the ten pounds which as a legacy of Mr. Joseph Humphreyes they paid to Mr. Samuiell Whiting, pastor of the church of Lynn, and then upon such receipt, that possession to be delivered to Griffen Edwards in right of Mrs. Miles.

Salem Quarterly Court Records, vol. 6, leaf 18.

A letter showing that John Miles of Swanzey, in the colony of New Plimouth, clerk, who married Ann Palmes, widow of William Palmes, late of Ardfinan, Ireland, Gent., and Ann his wife, constituted their son Griffin Edwards of Boston, merchant, their lawful attorney. Signed and sealed Jan. 15, 1680. Witness: Jno. Haynes, Roger Dobelday.

Petition to the court at Salem, June 29, 1681, of Griffin Edwards, attorney to John Miles and Anne his wife, only surviving child of Col. John Humphreys, deceased, that whereas the 26 : 9m : 1672, order was given that Elizabeth Pelham and

*See *ante*, vol. 1, page 345.

Thomas Price should have possession of a farm at Lynn, which at that time was in the possession of Edmund Batter, who was made administrator with Joseph Humphreys to the estate of Col. John Humphreys, here in New England, leaving reservations for any relations of his that might lay claim thereto, now desires the court to consider her claim, that said farm may be settled upon the rightful heir.

Deposition of John Floyd, aged about forty five years, that being at Mr. Mieles house last spring, he heard Mr. John Miells and his wife own that they had both constituted Griffin Edwords to be their lawful attorney. Sworn in Salem court June 28, 1681.

Edward Richards, aged about sixty five years, testified that he knew that John Miles and Anne his wife, constituted their son Griffin Edwards, their lawful attorney, to act in their behalf in all their demands of lands that they laid claim to as their right in New England, that formerly was by grant given to Col. John Humphreys as a patentee; and further Mr. Jonathan Palmes sent for me to Boston, Jan. 17 last, and desired me to be of assistance to the said Griffin Edwards his brother. Sworn in Salem court 28: 4 : 1681.

Essex County Quarterly Court Files, vol. 35, leaves 149, 151.

ESTATE OF JOSEPH ARMITAGE OF LYNN.

Administration upon the estate of Joseph Armitage, was granted June 29, 1680, unto Henry Stacy, who brought in an inventory and attested to the truth thereof.

Salem Quarterly Court Records, vol. 6, leaf 6.

Inventory of the estate of Joseph Armitag of Lin, taken July 1, 1680, by Rich. Haven and John Ballord: on smalle fether bed and two small bolsteres and a pillow, 3li. 5s.; too small ould Ruges, 15s.; parcell of ould clothes, 1li. 10s.; two oulde chestes and beedsted, 10s.; a peare of shears and Iron, 2s. 6d.; total, 6li. 2s. 6d.

Attested in Salem court 29: 4: 1680, by Henry Stacye, the administrator.

The estate of Joseph Armitage Dr.: acount of charges dew to Henry Stacy, ten weeks bord at fouer shiling per week, 2li.; cofin raill and diging the grave, 14s.; my own time tening and my wifes in time of sicknes, 10s.; in wine and sider for his buriall, 2li.; other charges at his buriall, 6s.; total, 5li. 10s.

Essex County Quarterly Court Files, vol. 33, leaf 77.

ESTATE OF JOHN SMITH OF SALEM.

"The last will & testament of John Smith mad ye 20 day of ye 11 month 1678 hauing my understanding & memory doth despos as folloeth first I giue unto my soon Georg Smith the west end of my house wherin I now dwell with half the ground & the use of the ouerns in the tother roome also I giue unto my soon Georg ye tenacker loot and saltmarsh also I giue unto Georg on peutter platter which he will marked G S also I giue unto him ye biggest iron pot & on iron skelet & all my iron tools on new great brass kettel on great chest & great table firpan & tongs old anderens & spit on fetherbed & furnutur belonging to it on heake I giue unto my dafter Exersis on fetherbed & the furnutur belonging to it also I giue unto her on great brass pan & ye midelmost iron pott & on brass skelett on platter marked G S on 3 pint pott on old pottenger the old brass pott to puetter sasers on brass candelstick & Georg the other brass candelstick & to Georg on pint pott: & to exersis the other & to Exersis on pine chest on littel trunk & to Exersis the est end of the house with the other part of the land joyning to it & also on pott heak & pott hookes & to Georg the other pott hookes 3 I giue unto my dafter Tamesen on trundel fetherbed & all ye furnutur belonging on littel iron pott on peutter platter marked G S on half pint *pint* of peuter on old pottenger on coper kittel & 2 sasers on whit earthen basen & the sheets & other lining to be devided eaqally amonst all fouer of my childeren & all this to be don after my deseas if in cause I mak not use of it befor I goe out of this world: all thes pertickelers as houshold it is my will it should be fulfiled acordingly: but as for house & land & cattel or any kind as I haue befor mentioned Georg is to haue a dubl portion & the three dafters to haue eqall shar alike & Georg & Exsersis to ‖pay to‖ Mary & Tamesen: & brother Joshua Bofem & Samuel Shadock iunier to be the childerens ouerseers with the aduic of mother for the performanc of this my will: with full power to order my childeren for ther good as thay see best: and Georg is to dewel with Daniel Suthwick Exsersis to Joshua Bofems Tamesen to her sister mary: & if in caus mother shuld tak Tamesen to her self not to let her be a looser for what she hath don for: her and if in [case] Mary dy her portion to return to her soon Samuel in witnes herof I haue set my hand"

John Smith

Witness: Caleb Buffum, Mary Mills, Damaris Buffum.
Proved in Salem court 29 : 4m : 1680, by the witnesses.

Inventory of the estate of John Smith taken Apr. 16, 1680, by John Pickrin and Samuel Gardner, jr.; ye west end of his dweling house & halfe ye land adjoyning to his house & his barne, 45li.; ye east end of his dweling house & halfe ye land adjoyning to his house, 25li.; his ten Acor lot in ye north feild & an Acor of saltmarsh, 60li.; a stear of 3 year old, 40s., 1 cow, 50s., 1 heifer, 30s., 1 horse, 40s. & a sheep, 6s., 8li. 6s.; a fether bed, bolster, pillow, 3 blanckits, 1 Rug, A winscot bedsted & Curtins and vallians & Iron Rodds, 6li. 10s.; A fether trundlebed & bedstead, 2 pillows & 4 blanckits, 2li. 5s.; A fetherbed & bolster, 2 Rugs, bedstead & 3 blanckits, 3li. 19s.; a bedstead, bedcord & matt, 10s., saddle, saddle cloth & stirrups, 20s., A window Cloth, 2s., 1li. 12s.; 4 pr. large sheets, 3li. 4s., 3 small sheets, 10s., 10 pillowbears, 10s., 10 napkins, 4s., 4li. 8s.; A peuter 3 pint pot, a pint Ale measure, 1 pint pot, halfe pint pot wine measure, 3 old porengers, 2 small old sacers & 1 new sacer, a half pint bottle, a beaker, 3 old platters, 2 small dishes, a new bason, a plate, 2 old chamber potts, 1li. 12s. 6d.; 2 brasse candlesticks, 11s., 5 glasse bottles, 3s., tin ware, 2s., a silver dram cup, 3s., 1li.; A great ston Jug, 3s., 3 small Juggs, a white bason, platter & a pott, 4s., 7s.; 6 small glasses, 6d., 1 doz. trenchers, 9d., a new pair womens shoose, 2s. 6d., 3s. 6d.; 5 earthen potts, 1s., 1 small earthen Jug & saltsellor, 9d., A padd, 18d., 3s. 5d.; 2 linin wheals, 5s., 6 wooden trayes, 4s., A corn baskit, 6d., A old hhd. & 8 old barels, 4s., 13s. 6d.; A great Chest, 10s., a box, 3s. 6d., a meal trough & 3 old meal baggs, 6s. 6d., 1li.; 5 oagers, a speak gimblit, 2 hand playnes, A fore plaine, 2 Cresing playns, 7s. 6d.; severall other working tools, 34s., with old Iron, 1li. 14s.; A small table, 18d., a great table, 5s., 6s. 6d.; 1 fire shovel, 1 pr. tongues, 18d., a frying pan, 1s., an Iron skellet, 4s., 6s. 6d.; 3 Iron potts, & potthooks, 14s., 2 brasse pots, 7s., 1li. 1s.; a spade, pr. fettors, half bushel, peck & 5 wooden dishes & bread Tray, 6s. 6d.; brass morter, 2 presing Irons, 1 box Iron, 2 heators & a pr. sheers, 9s.; an ower glasse, 6d., 3 oald sives, 1s., 6 old chayers, 6s., 8s.; 1 great brasse Kettle, 40s., midling old brasse Kettle, 8s., 1 smal Kettle, Copper, 8s., 2li. 16s.; a great brasse pan, 12s., a little Kettle, a skellet skimer, 3s., a warming pan, 6s., 1li. 1s.; pr. wooden skalls & 4 waits, all 10 1-2li., 3s. 6d., a pine Chest, 4s., 7s. 6d.; Cart & wheals & slead, 22s., 2 hakes 2s. 6d. pr. ps., 1li. 7s.; about 2-3 of a barrel pork, 30s., a swine in ye woods of 3 year old, 15s., 2li. 5s.; total, 174li. 15s. 5d.

There are severall debts demanded of ye estate as alredy

apears to ye value of 13li. od Monys & what more may be we
yet know not, as also about 6li. od Monys due to ye estate, but
what time will farther manefest we know not, for we have
not as yet ye full certinty of things from ye place where he
dyed wch was in Vergenia. Signed, Joshua Buffum, Samll.
Shattock, jr.

Attested in Salem court 29 : 4 : 1680, by Joshua Buffam and
Samuell Nurse, who had power of administration granted to
them upon the estate, they to have respect to the fulfilling of
the will of the deceased, only the court ordered that the administrators pay out of the estate to John Nurse, a grandchild,
20li., payable within six months after George and Exercise
children of the deceased, come of age.

Essex County Quarterly Court Files, vol. 33, leaves 95, 96.

ESTATE OF THOMAS FLINT OF SALEM.*

A return being made by Lt. Thomas Putnam, Lt. John
Pickering and Tho. Flint of a division of some land as by the
will of Thomas Flint, sr., it was allowed June 29, 1680, and
the original filed in this court's records.

Salem Quarterly Court Records, vol. 6, leaf 6.

ESTATE OF ELEAZER HATHORNE.

Mr. Eleazer Hathorn dying intestate, and none appearing
to take administration, the court June 29, 1680, ordered that
the marshall make inquiry what estate may be found and
make return thereof to the next court.

Salem Quarterly Court Records, vol. 6, leaf 8.

ESTATE OF JOHN DAY OF GLOUCESTER.

Administration upon the estate of John Day, intestate, was
granted 29 : 4 : 1680, unto Ann Day, the relict, who brought in
an inventory which was allowed.

Salem Quarterly Court Records, vol. 6, leaf 9.

Inventory of the estate of John Day taken June 26, 1680,
by Edward (his E W mark) Wollond, sr. and Jos. Hardy,
jr.: 2 bedsteads and beding belonging to them, 2li. 10s.; a
hous wich stands apon Mr. Jos. Graftons land, 65li.; 1 chest,
1 box, 2 tables, 7 chairs & 2 stools, 18s.; 1 Iorn pot, 1 Iron
skellet, a pr. bellows and 1 pr. tonges, 1 warming pan, hake,
box and heators, 13s.; 1 muskit and an old cutlis, 11s.; woolen

*See *ante* vol. 2, page 139.

wheel, a pr. cards and Earthen things, 5s.; his old sea cloths, scale, compasses, a forestaf, old callender and 2 sives, 1li.; money, 2li. 4s.; total, 73li. 1s. Debts due from ye estate to Mr. Joseph Grafton about 12li.; Mr. John Grafton about 8li.; Mr. Tho. Ifes about 10li.; Mr. Edm. Batter about 2li.; Capt. George Corwin about 3li. 10s.; Mr. Tho. Skiner in money, 5li.; total, 40li. 10s.

Attested in Salem court 1 : 5m : 1680, by Ann, the relict, and administratrix of the estate, and when the debts are paid the remainder to be to the widow for her own use and bringing up her children.

Essex County Quarterly Court Files, vol. 33, leaf 107.

ESTATE OF WILLIAM SUTTON OF NEWBURY.

Administration upon the estate of William Sutten, intestate, was granted June 29, 1680, unto Sarah, the widow, who brought in an inventory and attested to the truth thereof.

Salem Quarterly Court Records, vol. 6, leaf 6.

Inventory of the estate of William Sutton who deceased May 9, taken Newbury, May 27, 1680, by John Badger and John Kelly: a hors, 4li.; plough and Irons and pin, 15s.; 3 calves, 2li. 14s.; sleed, 7s.; 3 pigs, 1li. 4s.; shovell, 3s. 6d.; whipple tree chayne, 3s.; hors harnes, 8s.; pair of fire tonges, 3s.; wheele for spining, 4s.; 2 chayers, 3s.; pair of buf gloves, 5s.; 3 sheets, 1li. 17s. 6d.; 2 pair of stokens, 8s.; 4 yards of homspun cloth, 14s.; 3 shirts, 19s.; Table lining, 5s.; 2 Bands, neckcloths and handkercheifs, 10s.; pilobeir, 2s., a chest 4s., 6s.; wareing clothes, 2li. 10s.; hat and cap, 4s.; pair of gloves, 2s. 6d.; 2 glas bottles, 1s., awl, Bodkin, hamer, 2 knives, 2s., 3s.; 4 spoones, 1s., wooden ware 1s., tin ware, 5s., 7s.; skillet, grater, poringer, 5s., earthen ware, 1s. 6d., 6s. 6d.; a bible and a pair of bridle bits, 4s.; 2 pair of shooes, 9s.; a saddle, 10s., 19s.; wooll, 12s., mor hors takling, 3s., 15s.; bed and blanket, 5s.; a half barrell, 2s., pair of fetters and lock, 4s., 6s.; 4 sheep, 2li. 8s.; his labor about the Lot, 3li.; five pound of cotton yarne, 15s.; from Thomas Martin for keeping of his Sun, 2li.; a bushell and half of corne, 4s. 6d.; total, 30li. 19s. 6d. Debtor to Richard Kent, 5li.; Georg Maior, 15s.; Joseph Plumer, 7s. 6d.; Joseph Pike, 5s.; John Knight, 5s. 8d.; Joseph Knight, 4s. 9d.; Nicholas Noyes, 4s.; Ms. White, 1li. 10s.; Peetter Uter, 15s.; Richard Dole, sr. 9s.; Doctor Dole, 15s. 9d.; Jabis Musgrove, 4s.; John Emmury pr- a coffin, 7s.; Joshua Morse, 2s.; Steephen Greeneleaf, 15s.

6d.; John Bartlet, sr., 8s.; James Coffin, 7s. 3d.; Georg March, 1s. 6d.; John Hog, 2s. 6d.; Sammuell Plumer, 2s. 6d.; John Kelley per shoos, 6s.; total, 11li. 7s. 11d.

Attested in Salem court 30 : 4 : 1680, by Sarah, the widow.

Essex County Quarterly Court Files, vol. 33, leaf 78.

ESTATE OF JOHN COLLINS OF LYNN.

Administration upon the estate of John Collens, intestate, was granted 29 : 4m : 1680, unto Abigaile Collens, the widow, and there being an inventory brought in and allowed, as also an agreement drawn up by the widow with consent of children and relations of the father and mother for settling the estate, it was allowed.

Salem Quarterly Court Records, vol. 6, leaf 9.

Inventory of the estate of John Collins of Lynn, who departed this life about Dec. 22, 1679, as being cast away at sea, and dyed intestate, taken Mar. 27, 1680, by Andrew Mansfeild and Ralph King and presented by Abigaile the widow of the deceased: weareing apparrill yt was not lost at sea, 3li. 8s.; Beding, Bedsteads, sheets, curtaines, vallenc, 17li. 1s.; cubord, cuboard cloath & a chest, 3li. 5s.; Tables & joyned stools, 1li. 12s.; an ould cuboard, cradle, cheers & wheels, 1li. 5s.; 5 cows, 2 oxen, 2 steers, 33li. 10s.; 19 sheep, 9li. 10s., puter & a Lattin pann, 1li. 15s., 11li. 5s.; Brass, 2li., Iron pott & kettles, frying pan & a morter, 1li. 14s., 3li. 14s.; dog Irons, pot hooks, a pot hanger, 1li. 5s.; Armes, 4li., stiliard, 10s., syths & sickles, 10s., 5li.; smoothing Iron, 3s., wooden ware, 10s., tooles & ould Iron, 1li. 15s., 2li. 8s.; a Hatt, cuboard & a Box, 12s.; plows, carts, yoaks, chaine, 2li. 2s., 2li. 14s.; woolen & Linnen yarne, 1li. 6s., cardes, 3s., Bibles, 8s., 1li. 17s.; pare of tongs & a fire shovell, 3s., Porcke, 1li. 10s., Barrills, 12s., 2li. 5s.; Graine, 3li., A Fann, sadle, ould Boots & Flax, 1li., 4li.; Loome, Harnice & sleas, 2li., an houre glass & a sive, 2s., 2li. 2s.; the Land the houses stand uppon with the houses & orchard, 80li.; thirtye two acres of Land & medow, 160li.; 4 Acres & an halfe of medow in Wigwam medow, 13li. 10s.; pare of scales, weight & Adse, 5s.; Monyes, 5li.; A sixt parte in the saw mill, 5li.; woolen cloath, 2li., more Lynnen Cloath, 10s., 2li. 10s.; an ould chest & a box & an inkhorne, 3s. 6d.; two mares, 1li. 10s.; one Grindlestone, 10s., a warming pan, 2s., 12s.; total, 365li. 1s. 6d.

Attested in Salem court 30 : 4 : 1680, by Abigall Collens, who was appointed administratrix of her husband's estate and an agreement being presented to the court, of the widow and all persons concerned, as also with the approval of the eldest son, it was allowed and confirmed.

John Collins of Lynn who died, intestate, having been cast away at sea, and leaving a wife and twelve children, the widow with her relations, judging it most meet, desired Abigail Collins, Samuel Collins, Joseph Collins, Andrew Mansfield, Henry Collins, sr., and Henri Collins, jr., to divide his estate, which they have done as follows: to the widdow all the moveable estate, both stocke & store within dores and without as her free estate, 111li. 11s. 6d., which being taken out of the sum of the inventorye, the houses, Lands & medow remain to be disposed, which amount to 253li. 10s., of which, one third part to the widow during her life, and the other two thirds to the two eldest sons, Samuell and Joseph Collins, equally, as they come to age. Samuell having a good trade as a gunsmith, maketh up to him his double portion; and this to be understood the widow to have the use of the whole estate until the two said sons come of age, and then to have only her thirds, and at her death the whole estate to the two sons, they to pay to each of their brothers and sisters, namely, Benjamine, Daniell, Nathaniell and John, Elizabeth, Marye, Hannah, Loes and Alice Collins, ten pounds in current pay, as they come to age, their sister Abigaile Townsend having already received her portion. If any of the children should die before they come of age, then their portion equally to the surviving children, also that Samuell and Joseph Collins are not to leave their mother, but to live with her and carry on her business for her upon the consideration of their having the housing and lands as abovesaid, the house and lands to stand bound for the payment of the children's portions.

The eldest son giving his consent to the above agreement in the Salem court 30 : 4 : 1680, it was allowed and confirmed. *Essex County Quarterly Court Files, vol. 33, leaves* 100, 101.

ESTATE OF MRS. ANN COLE OF SALEM.

"Salem In New England ye first day of Novemb^r Anno Dom. 1679 The last Will and Testament of me Anne Cole Relict and Administratrix upon the Estate of my deceased

Husband Thomas Cole and although I am at present trough
gods visitation upon me sick and weake in respect of bodily
health yet blessed be God of sound & perfect memory: & well
knoweing my husbands mind with respect to ye disposeall of
what Estate he left unto me, wch was to be devided Between
his Two children as I see cause I doe therefore in ffaithfull-
ness thereunto: Thus in my last will and Testament made ye
day & yeare abouesaid Bequeath as ffolloweth vzt Inprimis
I give and bequeath unto my Son Abraham Cole upon ye consideration of his being my eldest Son ye sum of Ten pounds
in silver wch is the Tenn pounds he hath alreadie received of
m^r Jonathan Corwin in part of fforty ffive pounds ffor my
Lott in ye North ffield by me sold ye said m^r. Jonathan Corwin Item my Will is that all *all* my debts shall be justly paid
out of my estate wch. I may leaue. after me; wch being don by
the care of my Executo^r & Trustees to see ye due performance
of this my will The remainder I will that it shall upon an
equall valluation be devided. I say equally between my Two
Sonns: Abraham Cole & John Cole: That is to say my son
Abraham shall haue ye Land sowtherly Towards ye Streete
upon wch his Two howses stand and ye ground thereunto now
fenced in, with so much backward in ye said Lott: as in valluation shall be made an equall half of ye said Lott: & ye remainder of my said Lott whereon my old howse stands northerly: I give and bequeath unto my Son John Cole: & this
Land as it shall by my Trustees in equity be devided. I give
to them my said Two Sonns theire heires Executors and Assignes for ever: And also for my moveables Goods & chattells after my debts are paid: I will that it shall be equally
devided between my said Two Sonns Abraham Cole & John
Cole & for my Executo^r. I apoint my Son Abraham; and for
my ffiffees in Trust: whom I would in a christian request
crave ye ffavor of seing this my Will prformed, are m^r. Edmond Batter & m^r. Hilliard Verren Senio^r In witness whereof
I haue hereunto Sett my hand & Seale ye day & yeare
abouesaid"

Anne (her A mark) Cole (SEAL)

Witness: Frances (her F mark) Croade, Dorcas (her D
mark) Rist, Richard Croade.

Proved in Salem court 2:5:1680, by Richard Croad and
Dorcas Rist.

Inventory of the estate of Anne Cole, widow, of Salem; a
dwelling house with out houseing belonging and about one

acre of lands adjoyning, on part of which land Abraham Cole
have built two houses all which was valued and apprised by
2 men after my fathers decease, April 20, 1679, 50li.; due
from Mr. Jonathan Corwin for a 10 acre lott in the north
fields, 35li.; total, 85li. The rest of the goods & chattells
were disposed of by my mother and divided by her before her
decease. , Abraham Cole, Executour.

Attested in court 2 : 5 : 1680, by the executor.

Debts due from the estate of Anne Cole, widow: to Doctor
Welds, 2li.; Doctor Swinerton, 1li. 5s.; the nurse, 3li.; Capt.
Price, 3li. 15s.; Deacon Horne, 1li.; Mr. Rich. Croade, 18s.;
John Leech, jr., 10s.; Benjamin Gerrish, 6s.; goody mansfield of Lyn, 7s.; William Beanes, 2s.; Mr. William Browne,
jr., 1li. 3s.; for writings made, 6s.; the funerall, 3li. 10s.; Mr.
Samll. Gardner, jr., 8s.; to Hilliard Veren, jr., 11s. 8d.; to
the cleark for this & my father's will & inventory, 8s.; total,
19li. 9s. 8d.

Essex County Quarterly Court Files, vol. 33, leaves 102-104.

ESTATE OF JAMES DAVIS, SR., OF HAVERHILL.

"The Last Will & Testament of James Davis Senj[r] of Haverhill, made March y[e] 17th : 1675 : 1676 : I James Davis Senj[r]
of Haverhill in Norfolk in New England being of perfect
memory and through y[e] blesseing of God, though aged, yet
in good health, and knowing assuredly that all men are
mortall & y[t] young men may dy suddenly, & old men must
dy, & how suddaine my owne time may be in these desolate-
ing times; wherein y[e] Enimie seekes y[e] destruction of o[r] New-
England Israel; Being through Grace & y[e] Meritts of my Lord
& Saviour Jesus Christ in good hope of my eternall being in
happynesse; to whome I comitt my Soule; Doe hereby, as followeth, settle my outward estate, w[c]: God in mercy hath hither
unto lent mee; Viz: Inprimis, I hereby revoake & make void
all wills formerly by mee made before the date hereof: 2[dly]:
I give to my Son John Davis all my third division of land
in Haverhill wth all y[e] additions belonging to it, according to
y[e] grant of y[e] Towne of Haverhill. together with my third division of meadow in Haverhill. 3[dly]; I give to James Davis
y[e] Son of my Son John Davis the one half of my fourth division, or y[e] full right to y[e] one half of my fourth division of
Vpland in Haverhill, it not being yet laid out. 4[thly]: I give to
my Son Ephraim Davis all that land being thirty acres more
or lesse w[r] he hath built upon joyneing to y[e] great plaine in

Haverhill: I give him also that half of my East meadow w^c I made use of for my self. I give him also all the sheep & other cattle w^c: he hath of mine in his hands. 5^{thly}: I give to Stephen & Ephraim Davis ye Sons of my Son Ephraim Davis the other half of my fourth division Vpland; to be equally divided between them w^n: it is laid out, my Son John Davis his Son James or his Agent being to have his first choice of his half.

"6^{thly}: I give to my Son Ephraim Davis two Ox Comons, and also five Cow Comons, 7^{thly}: I give to my Son Sam^{ll}: Davis my second division of Vpland, and one ox-Comon and also three Cow Comons, all in Haverhill. 8^{thly}: I give to my Daughter Sarah ye wife of John Page jur the one half of my Pond meadow, and all ye goods of mine w^c: her husband hath in his possession, excepting only my warmeing pan. 9^{thly} I give to James Gild ye Son of Sam^{ll}: Gild the one half of my pond meadow; my Daughter Sarah or one in her behalf being to have ye first choice. 10^{thly}: I hereby leave & give to my Son James Davis all my other estate that I shall leave at my death, and doe hereby constitute and appoint my s^d: Son to be my Sole Executor of this my last will: In wittnesse whereof I ye s^d James Davis, Senj^r doe hereto sett my hand & seale, March ye 17th: 1675: 1676."

James (his ∧ mark) Davis, Sejr. (SEAL)

Witness: Nath. Saltonstall, John (his O mark) Swaddocke.

"Haverhill July ye 22th: 1678. The words [and to John Page ju^r Three Cow Comons] is hereby revoaked & made void, it being at first intended to be but for Two Cow Comons; and, since that, deed by mee given him for ye said Two Cow Comons, I doe hereby also appoint William White & Nath^{ll}: Saltonstall both of Haverhill to be ye Overseers of this my will, & to provide that if I out live the Time & money I thought to spend, justice, according to porportion, in my Will mentioned, may be done to my Eldest Son James Davis; & no disposall of any of my estate to be made till y^t: matter be determined by my said Overseers or their Executors, as to any matter of portion or legacie."

James (his < mark) Davis, Senj^r.

Witness. Nath. Saltonstall, Comiss.

Deposition of John Page, jr., and Sara his wife, that their father James Davis at their house said he had given to his son Samuell Davis the "uper pese of his Este medow", and also that their mother Davis lived with Samuel Davis about one year when she was very weak and not able to help herself and to their knowledge he was very careful of her and did to his ability what he could for her. Sworn Sept. 22, 1680 before Nathll. Saltonstall, Assist.

Deposition of Marthah Tewxbery, that she living sometime near Samuell Daves and going to his house "did often see the great trouble & care y^t he had with his mother that he could hardly spare time to goe abroad about his buesnes." Sworn Sept. 25, 1680 before Nath. Saltonstall, assist.

Deposition of William Barens aged about seventy years and Rachell his wife aged about sixty years, that "James Deues Senier ded promis to giue unto his Son Samuell Deues apon the acount of the maring of my daughter forty ackers of upland and a peas of medo at the est medo wich land hee haue injoyed euer senc wich is about sixteen or seventeen yeares senc and apon the Seam acount I gaue him with my daughter forty aker of upland." Sworn by Rachell Barnes, Sept. 25, 1680, and by Wm. Barnes 29 : 7 : 1680, before N. Saltonstall.

Deposition of Hana Prows, aged about thirty five years, that she was at the house of her brother Samuell Daves about a fortnight when his mother lived there and could see that "hee had a great deall of trobell with her for shee was not any abell to help her self." Sworn Sept. 25, 1680 before Nath. Saltonstall, Assist.

Essex County Probate Files, Docket 7,260.

James Davis, jr., in open court renounced executorship according to his father's will, and the rest of the relations being absent, the court Apr. 8, 1679, appointed him administrator to the estate of his father James Davis, sr., late of Haverhill, he giving bond of 200li. to present an inventory.

It being moved to this court that a settlement may be made of the estate of James Davis, sr. of Haverhill, the court Nov. 11, 1679, judge that the will be attended to by the administrator, and ordered him to act according thereto with relation to legacies therein mentioned after the next court, unless at that court the estate not granted in legacies and the debts due from the estate be computed, at which time he may bring in his challenge if it shall appear that there is need of proportionable abatement to be made out of the legacies which shall then be attended to.

Salisbury Quarterly Court Records, vol. 2, leaves 68, 74.

Inventory of the estate of James Davis given in by James,

John, Ephraim and Samll. Davis to the appraisers, Robert
Swan, sr. and Robert Clement, Jan. 29, 1678: James Davis
gives in to us 4 bills yt Jno. Wells was debter to his deceased
father wch amounts to 78li.; Ephraim Davis in to us one
cow, 4li. 10s., and ten shepe, 5li.; Samll. Davis gives in five
& forty acres of upland, 78li. 15s., and two acres & a halfe of
East meadow, 12li. 10s.; James Davis gives in two acres of
East meadow, 10li.; five acres of ye Pond meadow, 12li.; two
acres & a halfe of meadow at ye Sower meadow, 4li.; eight
comonages, 30li.; two hundred & twenty acres of third division land at Spickett falls, 45li.; five acres of meadow third
division meadow some of it within ye sd land at Spicket
falls & part of it at ye meadow comonly called Pollise, 12li.;
thirty nine acers of upland, 136li. 10s.; the 4th
division of land 300 acers, 30li.; total, 458li. 5s.
Jan. 29, 1678, the wareing clothes both linen & woollen
wth ye bedding appraised by Will. Sargent of Amesbery and
James Pecker of Haverhill at 3li.

Attested in Salisbury court Apr. 8, 1679 by James Davis,
administrator.

Debts due from the estate to Jno. Keisar, 5li.; goodman
Ilsley, 5s.; Jno. Dole, 2li.; Jno. Page, 19s.; James Pecker,
10s.; Jno. Callum, 4s.; Danll. Ela, 5li. 4s. Demanded by
brother Samll. Davis 20li.; 3 cowes in my brother Ephraim
Davis hands due to the estate; received of my father Davis
37li. 13s. Left in Salisbury court Nov. 11, 1679.

Copy, Essex County Quarterly Court Files, vol. 35, leaf 46.

The declaration made to the court at Ipswich, Mar. 30,
1680, by Nath. Saltonstall and William White, in prosecution
of the request of James Davis, sr., of Haverhill in his will,
which was urged to be attended unto, and in obedience to the
desire of the court at Salisbury, that we having considered
their several writings and pleas, now give in our decision
about the estate leaving the whole to this court's determination: that James Davis the appointed executor and now administrator to his father's estate, do according to the clauses
hereafter mentioned attend to the will, we not finding sufficient ground to take off from any legacies to give to him, for
though he is not put in as others with a particular legacie,
yet we find that what hath been in his hands to manage will
be sufficient to satisfy him for his claim; the meadow in Samuel Davis' hand and upland adjoining to the 30 acres given
Ephraim Davis by deed and will, we judge ought to be settled
in law upon the administrator and James Davis,

sr., deceased, having formerly as agent, by letter
from his son John Davis, made sale of his land which
he left at Haverhill upon his removal to Pascataqua about
twenty years since, which John seems now to deny because
the order to his father cannot be found, and threatenings are
made thereupon of the administrator, therefore we judge that
the administrator shall have and keep all that was given by
will to John Davis and his children for restitution of intended
damage, unless said John and his wife give a legal discharge
to James from any molestation about the father's estate; also
that the debts any of the rest of the children of James Davis
may present for his care etc. be cancelled and not recoverable
of the administrator, otherwise their said debts ought to be
deducted out of the legacies given to the other brethren and
sisters or relations. The court ordered this return to be accepted and allowed, unless any appear at the next court to
show cause to alter the same.

Essex County Probate Files, Docket 7,260.

ESTATE OF THOMAS FRENCH, SR., OF IPSWICH.

"In the name of God Amen. I Thomas ffrench senio^r. of
Ipswich being weak of body yet of perfect understanding and
memory doe in case of death make this my last Will and Testament. In the first place I commend my Soul into the hands
of Almighty God who hath redeemed it by the precious blood
of his Son; and I commit my body to the Earth, whence it
was taken, to be buried in a Christian decent manner by my
friends in hope of a blessed resurrection to eternal life. And
as for my outward Estate which God hath graciously given
me in this world I doe thus dispose of it: inprimis, I give and
bequeath to Mary my beloved wife the Bed whereon I use to
ly, with all the appurtenances and furniture belonging
thereto. Moreover I give to my son Thomas ffrench my
cloak and close-coat. Also I give to my son John French
one Cow, which is to make up the full summe of thirty
pounds which I formerly promised him for his Portion. Also
I give to my daughter Mary Smith, one Cow. And to my
son Samuel ffrench I give and bequeath the bed whereon he
usually lieth, together with the Bedding and Bed-stead belonging to the same. ffurther, as concerning my lands at the
Pequod lots, and my division Lot of marsh at plum-Island
my Will is, that my sons Thomas and Samuel French for and
in consideration of twenty pounds by them engaged accord-

ing to my order unto my son Ephraim French as ye remaining part of his portion (which summe of twenty pounds is almost all paid, and the remainer due upon demand), I say my Will is that those my two sonns Thomas and Samuel shall possesse and enjoy the said Pequod lands, and division-lot of marsh to themselves and to their heirs forever, to be equally divided betwixt them.

"ffurthermore, I give and bequeath to my sonn Thomas French my dwelling house and homested with all the appurtenances and priviledges therof and belonging thereto, and also my Lot lying in Labour-in-vain fields containing twelve acres more or less; with all the rest of my cattell, stocke of all sorts and moveable goods (not disposed of by this my Will and testament:) and to my son Samuel I give and bequeath two acres of upland joyning to Joseph Quilter's and two acres of meadow-ground at Reedy marsh; to be possessed by them respectiuely after my decease: Provided always and my Will is, that my son Thomas French doe give full and free libertie to Mary my wife his mother to abide and dwell in the said house and to make use of any room or rooms therof for her convenient accommodation therein; as likewise to make use of all or any such moveables as I doe now leave in the hands of my son Thomas (not disposed of:) as may be necessary and convenient for her use and occasions from time to time; and all these during the term of her natural life: and that after her decease my son Thomas shall deliver to my three children John, Sam^ll. and Mary three of the biggest pewter dishes which shall then be left and remain, that is to say, to each of them, one. Provided also, and my will is, that my two sons Thomas and Samuel doe carefully provide for their mothers comfortable maintenance and livelyhood and what is requisit thereto during her natural life; each of them allowing thereto proportionally to that part of my Estate which shall be by them received by vertue of this my testam^t. And if through any neglect or failure, this way of maintenance should not be to their mother's satisfaction and content, my Will is, y^t those my two sonns Thomas and Samuel shall allow to their mother ten pounds yeerly: nine pounds thereof to be paid by Thomas and twenty shillings by Samuel, in such pay as shall be suitable and necessary for her comfortable maintenance and livelyhood: And further, if it shall please God to exercise her with much prevailing weakness or continuing sickness that the

aforesaid ten pounds should not suffice to defray the charges
of her expences; my Will is, that (over and aboue ye ten
pounds, and according to the like rate of proportion) those
my two sons Thomas and Samuel shall supply her with necessaries suitable as her condition may require, y^t she be not ex-
posed to suffering for want of what ought and might be procured for her. Also my Will is, that my Lot in Labour-in-
vain fields, and the two acres of meadow at Reedy Marsh shall
stand bound respectively to my said wife during her natural
life as securitie for the true pformance of this my Will as
respecting her maintenance by my two Sonns; and after her
decease, the said lands (except what shall bee alienated (if
any so be) by means of the securitie aforesaid) to remain to
each of those my Sonns, and to their heirs for ever as is before
mentioned and declared. And lastly, I doe name, appoint,
and constitute my son Thomas French to be the sole Executo^r.
of this my last will & testament."

August: 3 : 1680.   Thomas ffrench, Sen.
Witness : [no signatures]
Proved in Ipswich court Sept. 28, 1680, by Mary French
and Samuel French.

Inventory of the estate of Ensign Thomas French taken
Aug. 25, 1680, by Jonathan Wade and John Whipple : his
waring apparell Linon & woolin, 4li. 10s.; the grat beed in
the parler with what belongs toe it, 7li. 10s.; a trundle beed
with what belongs toe it, 3li.; thre chests, 20s., 7 cushins, 20s.,
2li.; 4 payer of sheets, 40s., 4 pilowbers, 8s., 2li. 8s.; 22 napcines, 30s., 3 tablecloths, 20s., 2li. 10s.; 11 yds. of hommade
cloth, 1li. 13s.; warming pann, 8s., yd. & halfe of serge, 6s.,
14s.; a cutlach & belt, 6s., 3 small baskits, 2s., 8s.; 2 bruches,
2s., smal looking glas, 1s., 3s.; 6 chayers, 6s., table & foorme,
7s., 13s.; one spitt, fire pan, tonges, gridirone, tramell, 18s.;
9 pewter dishes, 27s.; 2 pint pots & a half pint, two porengers,
one beacer cup, 2 poringer, 1li. 17s.; two bras Ketls, 2li. 15s.;
one Irone pott, 3 scilits, a scimer, 14s.; tine ware, 6s., 9 spones,
18d., 7s. 6d.; barels, payels, trayes, kelers, 14s.; earthen ware,
8s.; old axe & howe, 3s., books, 10s., 13s.; 3 loads of haye,
30s.; a bed given to Samuel French with what belongs toe it,
4li. 15s.; a meane bed with what belongs toe it, 2li.; doz.
halfe of trenchers, 18d., sithes, 2s., 3s. 6d.; 5 sheep & thre
Lames, 2li. 13s.; 4 cowes, 12li.; 8 swine, 3li. 11s.; his dweling
hous & barne & homestead with the privelidg belonging, 70li.;
12 accers of Lande at Laber in vain, 60li.; 2 accers of Land

by Scotes Lane, 10li.; 2 accers of march in the comon feild,
10li.; debts due by booke, 7li. 7s. 6d.; total, 217li. 15s. 6d.
Debts he oweth, 34li. 8s. 5d. making total, 183li. 7s. 1d.

Attested in Ipswich court Sept. 28, 1680, by Thomas
French, executor.

Essex County Probate Files, Docket 10,190.

ESTATE OF HENRY PALMER OF HAVERHILL.

"In the Name and ffeare of God Amen I Henry Palmer of
Hauerill Upon Merimack Riuer in the collony of the Massa-
chusets in New England being sick and weak in body butt
sound and solled in my vnderstanding and of a disposeing
mind Doe make this my last will and Testament as followeth
Haueing comitted my soule to Allmighty God the father of
Spiritts and vnto Jesus Christ my only sauiour & Redemer by
the Helpe of the holy Ghoste my comforter in all my troubles
and Afflictions that haue befalne mee in this world And touching the Disposall of my fraile body I comitt the care of my
Interment to my Exectuers Hereafter mentioned to bee pformed in a Christian and Decentt maner and to bee layd by my
Dear wife in Hauerill Burieing place by Gods pmition And for
whatt Estate God hath Giuen mee in this world my will is
thatt my Just Debts bee Honestly payd and Discharged and
that my land bee Disposed of as is here after mentioned,

"Itt^m I Doe Giue unto my Grand child John Dalton thatt
peece of my East medow thatt lyeth on the East side of the
Riuer y^t Runeth through thatt medow and I Also Giue to
John Dalton all my land in the upper and lower plaine more
or less as itt is Itt I Doe Giue unto John Dalton two cowe
comonages in the Towne of Hauerill Itt I Doe Giue unto
Elizabeth Ayers my Grand Daughter now the wife of John
Clemante fower Acres of planting land lying northward of
the Towne Joyning to the land of Robertt Swan, and one
Acker of Accomadations, Itt I Doe Giue unto my Grand Son
Samuell Ayers the uper peece of my East medow lying on
the west side of the Riuer, to Ad to whatt land he hath Alredy
in possession. Itt I Doe Giue vnto my Grand son Timothie
Ayers the lower peece of my East medows lying on the west
sid of the Riuer with whatt other land hee hath already in
possession Itt I Doe Giue vnto Zacarias whitte formerly my
Seruant Eleauen Acres of land in the ox comon Abuting vpon
the way thatt Goeth to the pond medow, or the vallue thereof
as It shall be Apprized by two Indiferant men Ittem I Doe

Giue Unto my Son Robert Ayers and my Daughter Elizabeth his wife, All my Spickett medows as itt is bounded in the Towne book of Hauerill

"Itt I Doe Giue vnto my sone and Daughter Ayers all my medow in thatt medows comonly called the west medows as itt is bounded in the Towne book and these medows att the Decease of my son Ayers to bee Equally Deuided betwixt my two Grand children Samuell and Timothy Ayers, Itt I Doe Giue vnto my Son Robertt Ayers and my son Samuell Dalton my third and fourth Diuision of land with all other Rights in the Towne of Hauerill nott otherwise Disposed of Itt I Doe Giue vnto my Son Samuell Dalton & to my Daughter Mehetabel his wife my Dwelling house & my House lott and orchyard as itt is bounded in the Towne book of hauerill only my Son Ayers is to haue the one halfe of the frute of the orchyard for fiue years and all the frute this year in consideration of paying of a Debt of fiue pound Due to m^r Russell, and all these pcells of land aboue mentioned I Doe Giue to my children & Grand children as they are mentioned to them and their Ayers for Euer And I Doe Giue unto my Daughter Elizabeth Ayers my Bed thatt I ly vpon with all the furnituer there vnto belonging. Ittem I Doe Giue Unto my Son Samuell Dalton my best cloak & coate & my best sute and all the Rest of the mouables within Dores and withoutt shall be Equally Deuided between my two Daughters Exept one bras pott which I Giue to Mehetabel Ayers And I make & Appoint my two Sons Robert Ayers & Samuell Dalton to bee my Exequtors to this my last will which I Signe & Seale this 10 : July 1680."

henry palmer (SEAL)

Witness: Andru Grele, Sen., Thomas Eatton, Sen.
Proved in Ipswich court Sept. 28, 1680, by the witnesses.

Inventory taken July 17, 1680, by Thomas Whittier, Robert Clement, Robert Swan, sr. and John Griffing: His House, House lott & orchyard containing six Acres, 150li.; nine Comonages, 36li.; his 3 pcells of East medow containing six Acres & Halfe, 30li.; two Ackers of west medow, 20li.; foure Acres in the pond plaine, 4li.; five Acres in the lower plaine, 20li.; five Acres in the upper plaine, 15li.; fower Acres & halfe of Spicket medow, 35li.; aboutt two hundred Acres of 3d Division, 50li.; a peece of medow att Chineris pond, 2li.; his fourth Division of land not yet laid out containing one hundred & 70 Acres, 27li.; a peece of medow bought of Steven Kent, 4li.; 11 Acres of land in the ox Comon, 11li.; two Cowes

& a two yer old Heffer, 10li.; 13 sheep & 4 lambs, 6li.; his bed and other beding, 9li.; wearing cloathes wooling & linin, Hatts, stockins, shoes & Gloves, 18li.; 3 yds. of sarge, 18s.; potts, pothooks, hake, slice, tongs, chafin dish, Grigioron, fire fork & tongs, 2li.; 3 puter dishes, 3 cups, two pots, 1li. 4s.; one table, 4 chaires & stooles, box, chests & trunk, 1li. 10s.; one bible & other Bookes, 1li. 10s.; 2 pitch forks, 2 Rakes, taylors tooles, an ax, wedg, Rings & a shortt Gunn, 1li.; one stock of bees & one yong Swarme, 1li.; old tubes & other lumber, 12s.; total, 456li. 14s.

Attested in Ipswich court Sept. 28, 1680, by Mr. Samuell Dalton and Robt. Ayers, the executors.

Essex County Probate Files, Docket 20,428.

ESTATE OF NATHANIEL ROGERS OF IPSWICH.

Administration upon the estate of Mr. Nathaniell Roger, was granted Sept. 28, 1680, unto Mr. John Rogers, and an inventory brought in. A motion being made by him for the settlement of the estate and producing evidences declaring the mind and will of the deceased, the court doth hereby settle the estate according to the evidences of Walter Roper and Mr. Samuell Belcher, upon Mr. John Roger and his son.

Ipswich Quarterly Court Records, vol. 5, page 359.

Inventory of the estate of Mr. Nathaniel Rogers, deceased June 14, 1680, taken by Deacon Moses Pengrie, sr. and Insigne Thomas Burnum, sr.; the Dwelling house and out housses adjoyning and land belonging, 70li.; Lands at ye Townes end adjoyning to ye lands of Mr. Wade, Deacon Goodhue & Insigne Burnum, errable, swamp & meadow, 112li.; meadow at Haffield Farme or there abouts, 40li.; Plate in five shillings pr ownce, 8li. 5s.; a Debt in Cash part received, 250li.; soe much due to him from mothers estate about 3li.; one chest & wearing Apparrel, 5li. 10s.; Horse, saddle & Armes, 6li.; total, 494li. 15s. Some other Debts there are that at present wee cannot give a perfect accompt of. Debts due from ye estate: to Mr. John Roggers for Liveing about 20 years, 320li.; to him for soe much payed to mother about 60li.; Funerall charges, 19li.; a Debt due to Deacon Goodhue, 40li.; to Mr. Appleton, Mr. Waynwright & Mr. John Hubbard about 10li.; total, 449li. There are some other Debts as wee apprehend yt are not yet come to hand.

Attested in Ipswich court Sept. 28, 1680, by Mr. John Rogers.

Deposition of Walter Roper aged about sixty eight years taken July 15, 1680, before Daniel Denison, that Mr. Nathaniel Rogers lately deceased "being ordered to goe foorth a trooper against the Indians in the yeare 1676, Just before his going from his brother M[r] John Rogers house, where I then was, he would not be satisfyed till he had declared his will to me concerning the disposal of his outward estate, not knowing how it might please God to dispose of him he therefore desired me to remember & signify this as his will as there should be occasion to any court viz I doe bequeath to my kinsman John Rogers Eldest son of my brother John Rogers, all my houses & lands in Ipswich, withall the appertenances & priviledges thereunto belonging and my other estate I haue either heere or in England I doe Leaue or giue to my brother M[r] John Rogers to satisfy & pay himselfe what is or may be due to him from me, which he then sayd he beleeued was as much as it would doe & further sth not." Attested in Ipswich court May 9, 1682 by Mr. John Rogers, sr.

Deposition of Samuel Belcher, aged about forty years taken Sept. 23, 1680, before Daniel Denison, that walking with Mr. Nathaniel Rogers in his pasture ground joining to the land of Deacon Goodhue of Ipswich some years before his death, said Mr. Rogers declared his purpose and resolution, for diverse considerations to bestow and give that place unto his nephew John Rogers, eldest son of Mr. John Rogers of Ipswich, and did also confirm the same to him at another time after, and he had also declared the same to Walter Roper deceased, on his going out against the Indians in the time of the war.

Essex County Probate Files, Docket 24,043.

ESTATE OF MRS. ABIGAIL PEARCE OF IPSWICH.

"In the name of God Amen I Abigaill Pearse of Ipswich in the county of Essex widdow being weake of body, but through the goodnes of God enioying my undestanding and memory doe make & ordaine this my last will & testament, first comiting my soule into the hand of the Lord Jesus Christ my blessed Saviour and redeemer, in hope of a joyfull resurrection unto life Eternall my body to decent buryall, do thus dispose of my outward estate that the Lord hath gratitiously given and lent unto me, that my debts & funerall charges being payd, I give and bequeath unto my Sonn Samuell the house and land on the other syde of the way which I pur-

chased of Thomas Lord the Shop only excepted, and I give &
bequeath unto my Sonn John, the house ‖wherin I now live‖
and Land about it with the previledge therto belonging and the
shop on the other syde of the way also I give unto him my
best flockbed with the furniture belonging unto it, Item I give
and bequeath unto my daughter Joannah my best fetherbed
bolster, new coverlett and best Rugg Also I give unto her
halfe my english mony and my silver ‖wine‖ cup and my Red
Tammy coate and halfe my lennen and weareing clothes, Item
I give and bequeath unto my daughter Mary Perce my other
ffetherbed & bolster and covering and red Rugg, and the
other halfe of my english mony and my silver dram cup, and
my red Stammell coate, and halfe my linnen & weareing
cloathes.

"Item I give unto my two Sonns Robert and Moses Pearse all
my meadow and marsh att plumb Iland, & heere at Towne
behind the Hill Item I give unto my Son in law Josiah
Linden ten shillings and grand children his two sons Twenty
shilling a peece and Abygaill Linden forty shillings, And
further my will is that the rest of my bedding and linnen
both fine and corse with bras & pewter be equally devided betweene my two daghters Joannah and Mary Pearse And my
farme debts & all the rest of my estate, to be valued, and to be
equally devided among all my children only my Eldest Sonn
Samuell to have thirty pounds mor in his share then any of the
rest and my will and mynd further is, that all those pticuler
things before mentioned given in pticular to any ‖&‖ all my
children viz / Samuell John Robert Moses, and Joannah and
Mary, both houses lands & goods be all valued & disposed, soe
as all there parts in value be made equall only as before Sam-
uells to be thirty pounds in his part or share more then any
of the rest and my meaning is that my grandchild ‖en‖ receiue there legasies when they come to age, further I constitute & ordaine my Eldest Sonne Samuell Pears to be my
‖sole‖ Executor of this my last will and testament, In wittnes
heerof that is my last will & testament, I have heerunto put
my hand & seale the 24 day of June In the two & thirtieth
yeare of the raigne of oʳ Soveraigne Lord King Charlse the
Second & Anno Dom 1680 my meaneing is that John shall
have the use of the shop given him in the place where it
stand & not forst to remove it without his consent."

Abigail Perce (SEAL)

Witness: Robert Lord, Sen., Jacob Foster.
Proved in Ipswich court Sept. 28, 1680, by the witnesses.

Inventory of the estate of Abigall Peirce, deceased June
28, 1680, taken by Thomas Knowlton, sr., Jacob Foster and
Jno. Staniford: the Dwelling & land Adjoyning with ye
privellidges, 110li.; ye Land one side of ye way with ye barne
& privelledges there to belonging, 50li.; an old house termed
in ye will a shope, 3li.; 4 Acres of Marsh behind ye hills,
20li.; 2 Acres Ditto at Jeferys Necke Causy, 6li.; 15 Acres
Ditto at Plumb Island, 33li. 15s.; A Farme at Rowlly Village, 100li.; 3 Cowes, 11li. 5s.; 12 sheep & 2 lambes, 5li. 18s.;
1 Mare & 2 swine, 4li. 10s.; Woolling wairing Apparell, 7li.
10s.; Linen wairing Apparell, 4li. 7s.; 6 pr. of pillobeares,
1li. 1s.; 1 Cupboard Cloath & halfe sheete & 6 table clothes,
1li. 8s.; 16 napkins & 14 towelles, 1li. 15s. 9d.; 3 pr. stock-
ines, 1 Mufe, 15s.; 2 tableclothes & 2 shiftes, 19s.; 21 sheettes,
10li.; 1 Cupboarde, 2li. 10s.; 2 Chestes & 1 boxe, 1li. 12s.; 1
Remnante of Kenting, 6s. 6d.; 1 round table, 1li. 12s.; 2
Casses & Glasses, 5s.; 6 Joynte stoolles & 2 boxes, 1li.; 1
hatte & Case & 2 brushes, 15s. 6d.; 2 boxe Irones & heaters,
1 warming pane & basquete, 15s. 6d.; 4 bedsteades, 2 flocke-
bedes & 1 boullstere, 5li. 5s.; 1 Feather bed, 1 boullstere &
2 pillowes, 4li. 15s.; 1 Feather bed, 1 boullstere & 2 pillowes,
5li. 5s.; 1 Flocke bed, 1 boullstere, 1 pillowe, 1 pr. blankettes
& 1 Rugg, 4li. 19s.; 6 pr. blanketts, 5 Ruggs & 2 Coverlides,
14li. 10s.; 22 yds. of linen, 1 trunke, 1 Cheste, 2li. 9s. 4d.; 1
blankette, 1 sackcloth, 1 boullstere, 12s.; 9 Chaires, 13 Cush-
ines & Curtains, 2li. 14s. 10d.; 1 blankett, 1 pr. bodyes, 1pr.
hose, 1 Kersey Coate, 1li. 1s.; 1 sillver whistle, 2 tasters &
Cash, 3li. 16s.; 1 Case wth 4 knives, 2 looking glasses, 9s.
6d.; 4 pr. scalles & weightes, 3li.; 14 peuter Dishes, 3li. 10s.;
9 poringers, 17s. 3d.; 8 pottes, 3 bassenes, 1 scausier, 3
spoones, 1 Candlestike, 2li. 4s.; 4 Kettelles, 2 panes, 3 skilletes, 1 scimer, 1 Mortar & 2 pestilles, 5li. 9s.; severell peices
of tine ware, 8s.; 5 Iron pottes, 2 Kettlles, 2 skilletts, 3li.
3s. 6d.; 2 pr. Andirons & tonges, 3 pr. tramells, 2 panes, 1
slice, 1 forke & hookes, 2li. 12s.; 2 tablles, 1 Cupboard, 1li.
10s.; severall trayes & boulles & keellers about ye dairy, 1li.
14s.; severall caske & pailles & dishes &c., 3li. 3s.; 4 sives, 1
settlletable, 1 kneading trough, 6 baskettes & 8 bee skipes,
1li. 16s.; 34li. fleece woolle, 10li. shorte ditto, 2li. 8d.; 12
bookes, 1li. 17s.; severall peeces of Earthen ware, 1li. 6s. 6d.;
2 Musketts, 1 sword & furniture, 2li. 10s.; 4 wheeles, 3 pr.
Cards & some old Iron, 2li. 7s. 6d.; 2 Canoos, 1 Anchor &
rod, 7li. 9s.; 1 prcell of Iron ware, 1 glass, 3 oores, 1li. 6s.;
Debtes Due to ye estate, 42li. 9s. 4d.; More in Doubtfull

Debtes Due to ye estate, 34li. 16s.; total, 552li. 5s. 8d. Debtes Due from ye estate 35li. 9s. 6d.

Attested in Ipswich court 28 : 7 : 1680, by Samuell Perce, executor of the estate of his mother, Abigaill Pearce.

Essex County Probate Files, Docket 21,138.

ESTATE OF WALTER ROPER OF IPSWICH.

"In the name of god Amen I walter Roper of Ipswich in Neuengland being at this present time of perfit understanding & memory though weake in body comiting my soull into the hands of almity god & my body to deasent buriall in hope of Reserection to eternall life by the pouer & merit of Jesus Christ my most mersyfulle Sauior & redemer : doe thus dispos of the Temperall estat that god hath graciosly giuen me Imprimis I giue to Susan my wiffe the bed she logeth on with all that belongeth toe it : with liberty to dispos of it as she pleaseth amogst my childeren at her death : my will is that my sonn John shall maintaine my wiffe conveniantly comfortably in diet & clothis : & also that my wiffe shall haue halfe the fruit of my orchard : & also the use of the roome she now lodgeth in which is the parler : & also the use of the rest of the roomes of the hous that I leaue to my sonn John for her nesessary ocations :: & if it shall faale out that my wiff doth not like her waye of liuing : then my will is : that my wiffe shall haue the use of my houshould goods : alonge with my sonn John : & allso my sonn John shall maintaine her one cow : & four sheep winter & somer : & if any one of y^m miscary he to put another in the roome of it : also to Kepe her one hogg yearly & also to finde her nessesary firewood : & a horse for her nessesary use : & also paye to her three pounds a yeare : one halfe in wheat & mault : the other half in indian corne : all marchantable : all which she shall injoye so longe as she shall remaine a widdo : also if my wiffe shall marrye my sonn John shall paye to my wiffe fouer pounds a yeare : and be freed from all the pertikelers aboue expressed

"I giue to my sonn Nath^{ll} foure accers of March I bought of Nehemiah Jeuit or twenty pounds in currant paye after my wiffes desseas : also half my carpenters tooles at my desseas : also eight pounds : foure pounds of it to be pd within one year after my wiffs desseas : & foure pounds foure years after my wiffes desseas I giue to my dafter mary fiue pounds to be pd one half within one yeare after my wiffes decceas : & the other halfe foure years after my wiffes decceas I giue to

my dafter Elizabeth fiue pounds to be pd one halfe one yeare
after my wiffes decceas: & the other halfe fouer years after
my wiffes decceas I giue to my dafter Sarah tenn pounds to
be pd one half one yeare after my wiffes decceas: & the other
halfe fouer years after my wiffes deceas I giue to my grandchild Elizabeth Sparks fiue pounds to be pd at the age of
twenty one years I giue to my grandchildren Susan margerit
rose & Sarah Sparks twenty shilings a pecce to be pd at the
age of twenty one years I giue to my grandchild John Sparks
forty shilings to be pd at the age of twenty one years I giue
my grandchild John duch forty shilings to be pd at the age
of twenty one years: & also to my grand children: Elizabeth
& Susan duch twenty shilings apecce to be pd at the age of
twenty one years I doe apoint my louing freinds John Dene-
son ‖seni‖ John bruer ‖sen‖ & John whipple ‖seni‖ of Ipswich the ouerseers of this my last will & testement: & I doe
hereby giue them pouer to determin any differance that maye
arise betwen my executor: & any of the Leagetes aforesaid
abought the payments aforesd I doe ordaine & appoint my
sonn John Roper my sole executor of this my last will &
testement: to whome I giue all the rest of my estate both
houses landes & Cattle goods of al sorts: & depts from whom-
soever due unto ‖him‖ his heyers foreuer: In coufermation
wherof I haue heruntoe sett my hand & sealle this fiuetenth
of Jeuly 1680."

               Walter (his R mark) Roper (SEAL)
  Witness: John Whipple, Sen., John Denison, Sen., John
Brewer, Sen.
  Proved in Ipswich court Sept. 28, 1680, by Capt. John
Whipple and John Denison.

  Inventory taken Aug. 19, 1680, by John Whipple, sr., John
Denison, sr. and John Brewer, sr.: his wareing clothes Linon
& woollin, 3li.; the grat beed in the parler with what belongs
to it, 9li. 10s.; the trudell beed in the parler wth what belongs to it, 4li.; a percell of hommad Linon, 2li.; thre chests
& a small boxe, 1li. 15s.; cushons, 4s., warming pan, 5s., boxe
ioron, 2s., 11s.; sheeps wooll, 8s., Linon yarne, 14s., 6 old
chayers, 6s., 1li. 8s.; a beed in the chamber with what belongs
to it, 4li.; 4 bush indian corne, bush. rye, 6 pecks malt, 1li.
2s.; buter & chees, 16s.; two gunes, 35s., one sword, 6s., 2li.
1s.; an old coslit & pike, 10s.; two iron pots, 10s., two scilits,
5s., friing pane, 2s., 17s.; a bras cettle, 10s., in pewter, 15s.,
1li. 5s.; 3 tine pans, 5s., 5 cheny dishes, 4s., 9s.; dishes,

trayes, keelers & earten ware, 10s.; two glases, lanthorn, shepe
shers, spit, 6s.; two old wheels, 3s., trenchers, 1s., 4s.; slice,
tonges, bellis, tramels, 10s.; a cubburd, 7s., books, 10s., 17s.;
sythes, betle, wedgis, axe, 10s.; cart, tumbrell, sled, two yoaks,
chain, 2li.; a plow, 5s., hors feters, 3s., howes, 5s., 13s.; two
haye forks, old mattuk, 3s.; old barels & tubbes, small table,
5s.; two oxen, one cow, one stear 2 yeares old, 13li. 10s.; one
yeare old, 20s., two calvs, 20s., 2li.; a hors, a mare & a colt,
7li. 10s.; 6 shep, two lames, 2li.; swine, 4li., sadle
& bridle, old pillion, 4li. 10s.; the hous & barne & homstead,
80li.; 10 accers of upland & marsh in the comon feild, 50li.;
in carpendere tooles, 5li.; debts yt are due to the estat, 3li.
9s.; total, 207li. 1s. Debts due from the estate, 16li.; clear
estate 191li. 1s.; a sword, 8s.; total, 191li. 9s.

Attested in Ipswich court Sept. 28, 1680, by John Roper,
executor of his father's estate.

Essex County Probate Files, Docket 24,143.

Estate of Jonathan Platts of Rowley.

"The last will of ionathan Plats I being of parfect memory thof weack in body i comet my soule into the hands of
god wo gaue it and my body onto the dust to be desently
bured and as fore the outward istat which god hath geuin me
first my will is that my tou sons iohn and iohnathan dou
prouid well fore my belouid wife and that they let hire want
nothing that is needfull fore hire self so long as she Remaneth
my wedow and in petickler i giue onto my wife the euse of
the parler which is that end of my hous nexst the barne i geue
to my wife fiue bushels of barly malt and feftene bushils of
indan to be payd yearly so long ashe conteneuith my wedow
by my tou sons iohn and ionathan it is to be payd they are
allso to cepe my wife tou cous both wenter and somer and
allso to find hir with fiear wood what she shall stand in need
of al thees things tou be cept and mantaned fore the euse of
my wife by my tou sons iohn and ionathan so long as she con-
tineuth my wedow theare is ten pound of seluer in the hous
feftey shilins of it i giue to my wif and feftey shilins of it
i giue to my son iohn Plats the other fiue pound is to be
deuided equaly amonst the Rest of my cheldaren

"Allso i giue onto my wife tou yards of brod cloth which is
in the hous allso i giue hir that bed and bedsted in the parlor
which i now ly oupon with all the fornituer that belongeth
tou it allso i giue my wife feftene yeards of stufe and fiue

yards of blew searge which is in the house my will is that the
Rest of my istat be equaly deuided a monst my cheldarin only
my son iohn Plats being my eldest son i giue him ten pound
more then any of the Rest of my childarin and he is to tack it
in land whear he seeith good and as fore my housould stuf
as puter bras and iron and earthen and wodin ware my wif
is to haue the eus of it so long as she contenueth my wedow
and aftear they are to be deuided betwext my tou doughters
as part of thear porshons and if any of my children dy before
they com to ayge theat porshon is to be deuided amonst the
Rest of my children and i mack my wife and my son iohn
Plats my exsecuters to this my will allso i dou apoynt my
cusen Samewell Plats Sener and ezeckell mihill to be my
ouersears to se this my will performed this 24 of iuly 1680."

[no signature]

Witness: Danill wicom, Sarah Plats.
Proved in Ipswich court Sept. 28, 1680, by the witnesses.

Inventory taken Sept. 20, 1680, by Capt. John Jonson,
Daniell Wickam and John Dreser: One house, one barn, 30li.;
5 acker of land about the house at 7li. an acker with the orchard, 35li.; 12 ackers of paster land lying betwixt John
Dreser & Ezekell Jewet, 48li.; 7 acker of land lying at hunsly
hill at one pound ten an acker, 10li. 10s.; 1 acker and a quarter lying at bachler playne, 5li.; 2 acker of salt marsh bought
of Mr. Crosby, 12li.; 2 acker & a halfe bought of wiliam
Hobson, 12li.; a persell of Marsh bought of Leu. Rementen,
15li.; a persell of Marsh caled hyway marsh, 9li.; a persell
of Marsh comonly caled gat marsh, 4li.; 1 payre of Oxen,
11li.; 5 cows, 18li.; 2 stears coming foure years ould and one
cow, 10li. 16s.; 1 hefer 3 years ould, 2li. 10s.; 3 young catell
coming 3 years ould, 7li.; 1 a year ould and 4 calves, 3li.; 1
horse, 4li.; 2 Mares, 3li.; 19 sheep and lambes, 5li. 15s.; 9
swine, 6li.; corn in the house, 3li.; English corn in the barne,
7li.; Indan corn upon the ground, 7li.; Ots in the barne, 14s.;
in mony, 10li.; weayreing clothes as bots, shoose, spurs and
all other clothes lyning and woling with a scarfe for a truper,
11li. 5s.; a child blankit, 15s.; four payr of sheets and 3
pillowbears, 3li. 10s.; one rug and 3 blankits, 3li. 15s.; one
Trunle bed with the furnetur, 4li.; one bedstead and beding
belonging to it, 2li. 10s.; sheepes woole, 1li. 10s.; coton wooll,
3li.; bags, winow cloth, sives, 1li. 10s.; Tubs, kilers and
barels, 1li. 10s.; spining wheells and cards, 15s.; chists, boxes
and chears, 1li.; wooden ware as pals, churn, dishes, treas,

trenchers & botles, 1li. 5s.; Irne potts, pot huck & tramell,
2li.; frying pane, smothing Irne, spit & tongs, 14s.; 3 brass
kettles, 2 skelets & warming pane, 4li.; peuter platers and the
rest of they peuter, 3li.; 2 Muskits one 25s. the other 30s.,
2li. 15s.; one garbine, 1li.; one case of pistls and houlsters,
1li.; on sadle, bridle, brestplat & crupor, 1li. 8s.; one ould
sadle, bridle, brestplat, crupor and a sadle cloth, 1li. 4s.; 1
cutlash & belt, 14s.; powder & al other amonition, 10s.; one
pilion seat, 10s.; one Raper & belt, 10s.; axes, oagers, beetle,
weges, handsaw & other tools, 1li. 10s.; cart, cart rope, plow,
yoacke cheans, horse gears, siths, sickles, hows, spads and
forkes, 6li. 10s.; debts due to the estat, 3li. 12s. 9d.; total,
38li. 11s. 9d. Debts due from the estat, 7li. 10s. Theese was
given to his wife before his death: one bed with all the furnetur belonging to it, 10li.; two yeards of broad cloath, 2li.;
fifteene yeards of stufe, 1li. 10s.; five yeards of blew searg,
1li. 5s.

Attested in Ipswich court Sept. 28, 1680, by John Platts
and his mother, executor and executrix of the estate.

Essex County Probate Files, Docket 22,100.

ESTATE OF JOHN MASHOONE.

Administration upon the estate of John Mashoone, intestate, was granted 30:9m:1680, unto William Shaw and
John Mason.

Salem Quarterly Court Records, vol. 6, leaf 13.

Inventory of the estate of John Mashon taken by Thomas
Flint and John Cooke: one bead, Ruge and two Blankets,
15s.; two shurts, 6s.; Remnant of Cloth, wastcoat and two
neckcloths, 3s.; two necloths, a cape, strip of Cloth and a
pair of draws, 1s.; A looking glass, 3s.; fouer axes, one hatchett, 15s.; fouer wedges and a pair of betell rings, 6s.; one
handsaw, 1s.; a smale case, 2 sisers & Rasior, 4s.; glase bottle
& thre dusen of haire bitons, 1li.; a peise of a fishing Line, a
paire ould stoking & a pair of shears, 2s. 6d.; a hundred of
hobnails, 3d.; hammer, pincher & gimlet, 2s. 6d.; cloves,
mace & peper, 1s.; pair of brase Compasses, 1s.; horse furniture, 8s.; a leather bage and bread, 7s.; cheast and Runlete,
5s.; ould thread bare Cloak, 2s.; total, 4li. 4s. 9d.

Attested in Salem court 3:10m:1680, by Wm. Shaw and
John Mason.

William Shaw's disbursements and charges about the business of John Meechan deceased: to Richard Croade as per his

note, 9s.; 1 qrt. of Rum, 1s.; to Hugh Joanes for his expence
& tyme about sd. Meechans business, 5s.; bringing downe ye
pay to Salem, 1s.; a winding sheete, 10s.; to John Baxter for
6 foote of wood per sd. Meechans order, 6s.; my tyme & paines
about ye sd. occasion, 5s.; total, 1li. 17s.

William Shaw, Dr. to Richard Croad for expence on ye
jury that sate upon John Meechan & other charges at ye
said Croads howse, 9s. Dated 12:7m:1680.

Essex County Quarterly Court Files, vol. 34, leaves 76, 77.

GUARDIANSHIP OF MARY PEARCE OF IPSWICH.

Mary Pearce came into court, 30:9m:1680, and chose
Samuell Peerce her brother to be her guardian, which was
allowed.

Salem Quarterly Court Records, vol. 6, leaf 12.

ESTATE OF ROBERT PEIRCE OF IPSWICH.

Administration upon the estate of Robert Pearce was
granted 30:9m:1680, unto Samuell Pearce, who is to bring
in an inventory to the next court.

Salem Quarterly Court Records, vol. 6, leaf 12.

Inventory* of the estate of Roburt Pearce, deceased
Sept. 28, 168[o. copy], taken by John Dane and Jacob
Foster: one horse, 1li. 10s.; one pr. of sarge Britches
& Jacket, 18s.; two hats, 10s.; two ould coats, 7s.; Drawers,
6s.; one home made sute, 18s.; three home made shurts, 15s.;
two pr. of lining Drawers, 5s.; foure pr. of handkerchifs, 2s.
[4d. copy]; three neckcloths, one pr. of hand sleves, 5s.
[8d. copy]; one pr. of stockings, 3s.; one pr. of showes, 3s.;
In mony, 6s. [2d. copy] one silver spone, 5s. [9d. copy]; sillver Buttens & buckeles, 2s. [6d. copy]; Debts owinge to him,
2li. 17s.; one ould Bibell & one Buck of Mr. Britmans one
thee Revelationes, 5s.; total, 9li. 19s. [5d. copy]; Debts due
from the Estate, 6li. 10s. [5d. copy]; for charges the administrator hath been at, 1li.

The clear estate is 2li. 9s. of which the administrator is to
pay nine shillings a piece to his two brothers and two sisters
and the remainder to himself. Attested by Samuell Pearc,
the administrator.

Essex County Probate Files, Docket 21,217.

*Ipswich Deeds, vol. 4, page 419.

ESTATE OF WILLIAM FLINT OF SALEM.*

The court 30:9m:1680, ordered that some meet persons be appointed to make a division of several parcels of land, or of so much as is needful for the settling and peaceable enjoyment of every one interested in the estate of William Flint, and that it be done according to the tenor of his will.

Salem Quarterly Court Records, vol. 6, leaf 13.

ESTATE OF JOSHUA WARD OF SALEM.

Administration upon the estate of Joshua Ward, intestate, was granted 30:9m:1680, unto Hanna Ward the widow, by William Browne and Bartholmew Gedney, assistants, and she acknowledged herself bound to administer according to law, and to bring in an inventory to the next court.

Administration confirmed by the court 30:9:1680, and the said Hanna is appointed guardian of the children by her late husband Joshua Ward.

Salem Quarterly Court Records, vol. 6, leaf 13.

Inventory† of the estate of Joshua Ward taken Nov. 30, 1680, by Joseph Hardy, sr. and Samuell Gardner, sr.: one Dwelling howse and land, 100li.; one cowe, 2li. 5s.; one fether bed, bolster, bedsteed and furniture thereunto belonging, 8li.; one trundell bed, one pellow, two blancketts thereunto belonging, 5li.; one fether [bed & bolsters: *copy*], 4li.; his wearing clothes, 10li.; 18 yds. of searge, 2li. 9s. 6d.; 2 pr. [blanckets *copy*], 12s. 6d.; 6 pr. of sheets, 3li.; 5 pr. of pellobears, 14s.; board cloth, [6 napkins: *copy*] & towells, &c., 11s.; 6 yds. of Dowlas, 12s.; 2 yds ticken, 5s.; a sea chest and [instruments: *copy*], 1li.; his Armes, 1li.; a waynscot chest and boxe, 1li. 10s.; 5 peces of pewtere, 16s.; brase kettells, stue pane, skellet & warming pan, 2li. 5s.; houshold Iron, 1li. 5s.; coubard & boxe, 2li.; [plate: *copy*] 2li. 15s.; in mony, 4li. 16s.; chests, chayars & such licke, 1li.; earthen, glase and ten weare, 12s.; a Remnant stufe and genting, 1li. 10s.; psell of Cotten wooll, 5li.; Iron Tools, 10s.; total, 163li. 18s. Debets due to ye Estat about 15li. Debets due from the estate about 13li.

Attested in court 30:9m:1680, by Hannah Ward, the relict.

Essex County Quarterly Court Files, vol. 34, leaf 83.

*See *ante*, vol. 2, page 363.
†Essex County Probate Records, vol. 301, page 171.

Hanna the relict, and administratrix of Joshua Ward, presented an inventory to the court 30 : 9m : 1680, and it was ordered that the whole estate remain in the widow's hands for the bringing up of the children, and to pay to Miles the eldest son 32li., the rest of the children 16li. each, at age or marriage, and then the rest of the estate to the widow. The house and land to stand for security.

Salem Quarterly Court Records, vol. 6, leaf 13.

ESTATE OF JOSHUA WARD, JR., OF SALEM.

Inventory of some estate in land of right belonging to Joshuah Ward the younger, late deceased, presented to the court 30 : 9m : 1680, and Hanna his mother was appointed administratrix of the estate. The land valued at 30li., Miles the son of Hanna and brother of Joshua to have one half and the rest of the children of the said Hanna, the other half between them.

Salem Quarterly Court Records, vol. 6, leaf 13.

Inventory of the estate of Joshua Ward son of Joshua Ward, deceased, who died intestate, taken Dec. 2, 1680, by Jeremiah Neale and Samll. Shattocke, jr.; one ten ackre lot lying in the South feild wch said Lot was given him by his grandfather Flinte, 30li.

Essex County Quarterly Court Files, vol. 34, leaf 82.

ESTATE OF EDMOND PATCH OF IPSWICH.

Administration upon the estate of Edmond Patch, intestate, was granted 30 : 9m : 1680, unto Thomas Patch, who presented an inventory and attested to the truth thereof. There being two grandchildren, Edmond and Abraham Patch sons of Abraham, the son of said Edmond Patch, when all debts are paid, they are to have the estate between them when they come of age.

Salem Quarterly Court Records, vol. 6, leaf 14.

Inventory of the estate of Edman Patch who departed this life Nov. 10, 1680, taken Nov. 19, 1680, by John Dodge and Richard Hutten : 3 peses of old putore, 6s.; an old brase Candellsticke, 3s.; & old brase scellete & a smoothing eiron, a' letell pote, 4s.; the great eiron pote & pote hoocks, 12s.; a small speete & a trevet, 5s.; an old winestote chest, 3s.; another winstote Chest, 8s.; a borde Cheste, 1s. 6d.; a Coborde 5s.; tramell, 5s. 6d.; an olde Rouge and a blancete, hate & Cote, 5s.; fether pello, 4s.; a testamente, 1s. 6d.; total, 3li. 3s. 6d. Due to the estate from John Knowlton being the remainder of his purchas, 2li. 10s., Thos. Fiske, Thomas Patch. The estate debtor for diging of the grave & makeing of the Coffin, 9s.; to ye agents Tho. Patch & Tho. Fisk, 1li. 10s.

Attested in Salem court 30: 9m : 1680, by Tho. Patch, administrator,

Wenham, May 15, 1695, to Capt. Sewall, an addition to the inventory made by Thomas Patch, administrator of the estate of his uncle, Edmond Patch, who lived in Ipswich, and died there, Nov. 10, 1680: about half an acre of Bushshe medow ajoyning to Samuell Dodg his land & too Curtain Rods allone aprized at 2s. 4d.; dew from John Knowlton 2li. 10s. and I have received it of him. Dew from the estate; for diging the Grave and coffin, 9s.; to Capt. Fisk & myself by the court order, 1li. 10s.; to me upon former acount for work done, 10s. 9d. and now dew to me for about 15 years administration, 1li. 10s.

"February ye 20th 1673, Know all men by these psents that I Edmund Patch Living in Ipswich doe by these prsents Ingage unto Richard Dodge of Wenham, And unto Samuel Dodge of the Towne of Ipswitch that I will not bargaine sell or diminish ‖or alienate‖ any pt of my Land now in my possesion together with all my moueable good unto any person or psons what euer as acounting my selfe, obliged by this not to medle upon any such an accoumpt without the consent of the forsd pties and being sensible of my owne weekness, Least I should be cheated by any person, for the security therof for my selfe and my daughter in Law and the Children, untill the next court at Ipswitch, that then the Court may take further order concerning it, this obligation only to stand good untill that time."   Edmund (his   mark) Patch

Witness: Richard Walker, Samuell Frayll.

Essex County Quarterly Court Files, vol. 34, leaves 88, 89.

Petition dated May 6, 1695, of Eunice (her   mark) Patch, widow, the daughter in law of Edmond Patch of Ipswich, deceased, and Benjimine Patch his grandchild, showing that in 1674, the said "Edmond Patch was posesed of a dwelling house and about fifty acers of land together with a competent personall estate and sd uniss lived with my sd. father in law Edmond Patch I having two children this my son Benjemin and his brother Abraham now out of this

country I then being left destitute and my father in law being
aged and on a sudden bereaved of his understanding upon
the loss of Abraham Patch his son my then husband and then
the County Court at Ipswich in 74 did sequester the wholl
estate that my sd father in law and myselfe was in the poses-
sion of in the hands and under the care of Capt. Fisk and
Thomas Patch of Wenham and John Powland of Ipswich
that the estat might not be Imbezeled and suddenly after the
sd Fisk and Patch did ridde me from the sd. house and estate
and I and my children have shifted for ourselves ever since
we doe understand that the land is sould to John Knolton and
what they have don with the personall estate we know not
those that were betrusted by the court have not given any
acount of their managment from that time untill now the
sd Edmond Patch our father and grandfather hath bien de-
cesed about fiften or sixten yers and noe settlement hath bien
made," therefore we ask that his estate may be settled on those
that are his next of kin.

Petition of Benjamin Patch for power of administration upon the estate of his grandfather Edmond Patch.

Bond of Benjamin Patch, with John Poland and John
Low, 3d, as sureties, all of Ipswich, dated May 6, 1695, in
the sum of 200li., to administer on the estate of his grandfather Edmond Patch of Ipswich. Witness: Steph. Sewall,
John Croade.

Petition of Benjamin Pattch grandson to Edmond Pach,
deceased, that whereas there is a considerable estate sequest-
ered in the hands of Capt. Thos. Feske, Thos. Pach and Jno.
Poland and the said Thos. Pach being made administrator of
the estate, therefore I request that a citation may be granted
for the abovesaid persons to render an account of the estate. Dated Ipswich May 17, 1695.

In answer to the above petition, Capt. Thomas Fiske and
Thomas Patch of Wenham and John Powland of Ipswich, are
required to give an account of the estate at the house of Mr.
Francis Ellis in Salem. Dated Salem May 17, 1695.

Addition to the inventory of the estate of Edmond Patch,
who died Nov. 10, 1680, made May 25, 1695 by Thomas
Patch: about sixty poles of land lying in Ipswich between Jon. Knoltons land & Samuell Dodges land also about
half of Bushshe medow ajoyning to Samuel his land; also an
old saw, 2s. 6d.; one saucer, 8d.; 3 curtain rods, 3s. 8d.

Account of Thomas Patch, administrator to the estate of

Edmond Patch of Wenham, of his administration upon said
estate, brought in May 27, 1695: the estate valued at 6li. 4d.
and the following charges and payments have been made,
bond and letter of admin., copy &c., 2s. 6d.; diging ye grave
& ye Coffin, 9s.; allowed by ye Court to ye admr. & Tho. Fisk,
1li. 10s.; to the admr. for his trouble, 10s.; allowing the
acct., 5s.; setling & dividing the estate, 5s.; a quietus, 4s.;
total, 3li. 5s. 6d. Remains due to ballance this acct of ye personal estate, 2li. 14s. 10d.

Attested May 27, 1695, by Thomas Patch, admr. The balance of 2li. 14s. 10d. is to be paid vnto Abraham and Benjamin Patch, grandsons of Edmond Patch, equally, and in
case of the decease of either of them to be to the survivor. Ye
above 14s. not yet pd.

Essex County Probate Files, Docket 20,695.

ESTATE OF MRS. BRIDGET GILES OF SALEM.

"The Last Will and testament of Bregett Giles of Salem,
Widow I Being weake of Bodie but well in My understand-
inge Doe Dispose of that Estate the Lord hath Left me in
Maner and forme as ffolloweth Imprimis I giue to my Son
Samuell Very twentie Shillings. It. I giue unto My Son
Thomas Very twentie Shillings It I giue unto Mary Cutler
of Redinge the Wife of Thomas Cutler fortie Shillings It I
Giue unto Briegett Very the Daught^r of My Son Thomas
Very a Cowe to be Due to her when she shall be Eighteene
yeares of age or at the tyme of her Mariage. It I Giue unto
my Son Eliazer Gilles one ten aker Lott which sometime Belonge to Goodman Addams of Nuberie of whom My Hus-
bond bought it & I Giue unto him all My Meadow on both
sides the Brooke to begin at the stump that doth part his Up-
lande and Mine & from that stump to Run over the Brooke to
the Bound tree of the ten aker Lott aboue Menshoned all
my Meadoe be lowe that line I Giue to him p^{r}ouided & my
will is that he pay unto Mary Cutler that fortie shillings I
haue giuen her in this My Will and for the Remainder of
My estate howsing land Meadow ground Cattle householde
stuffe & what euer elce Doth any way belonge or Apertaine
unto me I Doe giue & bequeathe unto My son John Geiles
home I ordaine & apoynt My sole executo^r of this my Last
Will and testament and in Witnes thereof I haue here Unto
set my hande and seale this fourteenth of the 11th Month
1668."

Bredget Gyles (SEAL.)

Witness: John Browne, James Browne.
Proved in Salem court 30:9m:1680, by Mr. Henry
Bartholmew.
Essex County Quarterly Court Files, vol. 34, leaf 84.

ESTATE OF JOHN LOVEJOY OF ANDOVER.

Administration upon the estate of John Lovjoy, intestate, was granted 30:9m:1680, unto Naomie Lovejoy the
widow, who brought in an inventory and attested to the truth
thereof.
Salem Quarterly Court Records, vol. 6, leaf 14.

Inventory of the estate of John Lovjoy, jr., who died July
14, 1680, taken by Richard Barker, sr., and Joseph Ballard:
one house & a crope of corn, 20li.; one hors, 4li.; one steer
4 years old, 4li.; one cow & a year old heifer, 5li. 5s.; swine,
2li.; one carbine, 10s.; wearing apparrill, 2li.; flax, wooll &
yearn, 16s.; one bed & Beding, 5li.; in lumber and tooles, 1li.
6s.; one iron pott, frying pan and one brass skillet, 12s.; one
old saddell and an old Bridle, 6s.; total, 45li. 15s. The
depts that doe allredy apere amounts to 29li. 14s. 7d. The
debts yt doe since appeare due, from the estate is more, 3li.
4s. and heare is 3li. 16s. 9d. of it in mony.
Attested in Salem court 30:9:1680, by Naomi Lovejoy,
relict and administratrix.
Essex County Quarterly Court Files, vol. 34, leaf 85.

ESTATE OF JOHN TURNER OF SALEM.

Administration upon the estate of John Turner, intestate,
was granted Oct. 13, 1680, by Hon. Maj. Gen. Daniell Denison, William Browne and Bartholmew Gedney, Esq., unto
Elizabeth Turner, the widow, who gave bond of 3000li. to
administer according to law, and to bring in an inventory
to the next court. Allowed by the court 30:9m:1680.

Mrs. Elizabeth Turner, administratrix to the estate of Mr.
John Turner, brought in an inventory of the estate amounting to 6788li. 17s. 11d. and the court 30:9m:1680, understanding he left five children, John, Elizabeth, Eunice, Free-
stone and Abiell, have ordered that the estate remain in the
widow's hands for the bringing up of the children until they
come to age or until they be of age to choose guardians if
they see cause, and that she shall have for her portion of the
estate 1500li., provided she pay 100li. to Elizabeth Gedney

which was given her by the deceased, to be paid to her at
age or marriage, and to be educated at the charge of the
administratrix; the rest of the estate to be divided equally
between the children, only the son to have a double portion,
to be paid when they are of age unless by the court's allowance they shall choose guardians who may require their respective portions, and then the administratrix shall be discharged of any further charge for their education. The houses
and lands to stand as security, and if the administratrix
should marry, other security to be given for the payment of
the legacies, otherwise the whole estate except the widow's
portion shall be in the court's hand to take order for the security thereof. Capt. William Brown, Mr. John Hathorne,
Capt. John Price and Mr. Thomas Gardner, jr., are desired to advise the administratrix in the management of the
estate.

Salem Quarterly Court Records, vol. 6, leaf 14.

Inventory of the estate of Mr. John Turner as it is now
found in the hands of Mrs. Elizabeth Turner, widow, taken
by Wm. Browne, jr., John Price, Thomas Gardner, jr. and
John Hathorne: Sundry goods & merchandize amount unto
2843li. 9s. 11d.; househould stuff and in baggs, 1295li. 8s.;
total, 4138li. 17s. 11d. The account of houseing & land: the
dwelling house, land, out houseing, 2 warehouses & wharfe
belonging thereunto, 500li.; a house, househould stuff &
stock at Bakers Isld., 50li.; Land at Castle Hill, 70li.; a
parcell of land bought of Wm. Lake and a pcell bought of
Nathl. Sharp, 40li.; a warehouse at Winter Isld., 12li.;
house and land bought of Mr. Skinner, 140li.; the warehouse
yt is building, boards, &c., 25li.; land by Christopher Babidges,
40li.; total, 877li. The account of Vessells: the Keatch
Blosome, 170li.; Keatch Prosperous, 120li.; Keatch Jno. &
Thomas, 100li.; Keatch Willing Mind, 90li.; total, 480li.;
1-2 of ye Keatch wth Mr. English, 190li.; 1-2 of ye pink
Speedwell, 150li.; 3-8 of the Keatch Society, 150li.; 3-8 of
the Keatch Wm. & Jno., 100li.; 1-4 of the Keatch Freind-
ship, 65li.; 1-8 of the Keatch Fraternyty, 40li.; a shallop at
Marblehead, 50li.; 1-4 of ye sloop with Jon. Hart, 40li.; a
pleasure Boote, 8li.; 1-3 of 3-8 of the Shipp Wm. & John,
500li.; total, 1773li., making total of whole estate 6788li. 17s.
11d. Further, a parcell of Salt at Marblehead; a parcell Refuse
fish at Marblehead. The account of Debts due unto the estate and debts due to be payd out of the estate which cannot
yet be settled or knowne.

Attested in Salem court 30 : 9 : 1680, by Mrs. Elizabeth Turner, relict and administratrix.
Essex County Quarterly Court Files, vol. 34, leaf 86.

ESTATE OF JOHN HILL OF SALEM.

"This may testifye to any whom it may concerne, that I John Hill haueing bene for a long space of time ill & out of order as to the health of my body & not knowing how soone I may be called out of this world, am theirfore willing now while I haue my understanding & memory to dispose of what I haue as followeth imprim I giue to my two sons John & robert my 40 akers of land lying up in the woods by Samuel Cutlers to bee deuided equally betweene them. 2 I giue to John Hill all the land I haue in the pound meddow & that which I haue in coakes medow I giue to robert 3 I giue to my foure daughters Miriam Susan Liddia Elizabeth each of them a cow & fiue pound a peice besides to the two eldest to bee paid in some short time after my decease as soone as conueniently may bee, to the two youngest when they come of age 4 I giue to my wife all the rest of my estate to bee enjoyed by her without any interruption or molestation during the time of her life & at her decease to bee at her sole disposing (as shee may see good) to my children in witnesse whereunto I doe heere set my hand and seal this present 29th of July 1680."

John Hill (SEAL)

"Further my will is that in case my beloued wife shall see caus to sell any part or the whole of that estat giuen her she shall haue full power at the eand of her life to despos of what she shall haue left as aboue said I apoint my wife my executor of this my last will & testiment." I. H.

Witness: Jeremiah Neale, Samuell Nurs.
Proved in Salem court 30 : 9 : 1680, by the witnesses.

Inventory of the estate of John Hill taken Nov. 20, 1680, by William Traske and John Traske: one Dwelling House & Orchard and Barne with other oute Housing, 100li.; 3 akers of upland lying in the Glass house feild, 10li.; Halfe an aker of salt marsh lying at forrest River, 4li.; a parcell of fresh Meddow lying by ye Great Rvr., 10li.; 40 Akers of upland lying neere Samuell Cutlers, 45li.; a five Aker Lott in ye Northfeild, 15li.; 3 quarters of an aker of Marsh lying neare the hill called Gardners Hill, 12li.; 3 Cowes, 9li., on Steare, 3li., 2 young cattle 2 yers and ye vantage, 4li., 16li.;

2 young cattle a yeare & Halfe ould, 2li. 10s.; 3
calves, 2li., 2 mares & 3 colts in the woods if living, 3li., 5li.;
parcell of swine Running in ye woods, 4li.; fetherbed and all
belonging to it, 8li.; fetherbed in ye Little Roome & wt belongs to it, 7li.; one Trundlebed and what Belongs to it, 4li.;
one Bed in ye Chamber and wt Belongs to it, 6li.; one
Cubbard in ye Chamber, 12s., Tooles, 2li., 2li. 12s.; A Cubard
in ye Great Roome, 16s. & one in ye Little Roome, 1li. 10s.,
7 cheares, 14s., one table & 3 stooles, 3li. 10s.; eight paire of
sheets, 6li., 2 Table cloathes, 12 Napkins, 8 Towells, 2li.,
8li.; 4 paire of Pillowbeares, 20s., 2 wenscot chests & 2 Boxes,
26s., one Gun, 20s., peuter, 2li. 10s., 5li. 16s.; 3 skelletts,
10s., 5 Brass Kettles, 3li., 3 Iron potts and one kettle, 25s.,
earthen ware & Glasses, 6li. 5s.; one warming pan & a paire
of Doggs, 15s.; 2 Hakes, 8s., one spitt, 2s. 6d., 2 paire of
pott Hooks, 2s., 12s. 6d.; one fire shovell, Tongues & fire
slice, 7s.; one frying pan, 3s., one little Table, 3s., 6s.; one
Lanthorne, 2s., smoothing Iron, 2s., 4s.; his wareing Cloathes,
8li.; one Looking Glass, 2s., 8li. 2s.; ould chests, cradle and
sum ould Lumber, 12s.; flax & wooll, 2li., home made cloth
wolling & Lining, 4li., Sarge and other Eng. goods, 5li.; one
Grenston, one hors, cart & saddle, 6li. 18s.; Bookes, 10s.;
total, 300li. 6s. 6d.   Due to the estate in Debts, 5li.; The
estate is debter to severall men, 1li. 10s.

Attested in Salem court 30:9m:1680, by Liddea Hill,
widow and executrix.

More added to the inventory 7:10m:1680 by Lidea the
executrix in cash & goods, 9li.

Essex County Quarterly Court Files, vol. 34, leaves 78, 79.

ESTATE OF ISAAC HYDE.

Inventory of the estate of Isac Hyde presented by Susanna
Hyde, taken Nov. 13, 1680, by Joseph Grafton and Samuel
Gardner, jr.: a dwelling house & 24 pole of land, 60li.; fetherbed & furnature as it stands, 4li. 10s.; 4 paire of sheets & 4
pr. pillowbeirs, 2li. 10s.; 8 towels, 8 napkins, 4 tablecloths,
15s.; putor, 25s., brasse, 30s., 2li. 15s.; Iron ware, 20s., earth-
en & tin ware, 10s., 1li. 10s.; 2 small tables & a chest, 1li.; 8
chaires, 12s., 2 truncks, 10s., 1li. 2s.; Carpet & 2 small baskets, window curtin & a pr. bellows, 12s.; old barrels & tubbs,
5s.; total, 74li. 19s. Due to be paid unto Wm. Hill in England, 5li.

Attested in Salem court 30:9:1680, by Susana Hide, and

she was appointed administratrix of the estate of her husband Isaack Hide. The estate when the debts are paid to be equally divided, one half to the widow, and the other half to Richard, child of the deceased, at the age of twenty one years.

Essex County Quarterly Court Files, vol. 34, leaf 90.

ESTATE OF ROBERT COKER OF NEWBURY.

"The last will and Testament of Robert Coker of Newbury made this 20ᵗʰ Sept. 1678 I Robert Coker of Newbury doe ordaine this to be my last will and testament, heerby Revokeing all wills by me formerly made 1 I give to my Eldest son Joseph Coker my house that I now live in with all my out houseing orchard upland and meadow, wᵗʰ the freehold, and all other previledges & apptenances thereunto belonging, (except such parcells of land as are heerafter excepted) to be to him and his heires for ever, together wᵗʰ all the stock and household goods or utensills belonging to the house & all my weareing clothes, by these presents oblidgeing my sd son Joseph to pay all such Legasies as are heerafter mentioned 2 I give unto my younger son Beniamin my land in the Little field being four acres and a halfe more or less together with the frame upon it, as also my meadow at Plumb Iland at the Sandy beach, be it more or less, as it is bounded with the widdow Worths land Northerly and the River westerly, & the beach easterly, and six acres of Land upon the southern part of the highway by my dwelling house, upon that syde of it next to Daniell Lunts, soe many Rod upon the front, as that runing ‖back‖ the whole depth shall amount to six acres, All wᶜʰ parcells of land I give to him the sd Beniamin and to his heires forever, oblidgeing him by these presents, to pay unto my daugĤter Hanah Lunt twelve pounds of that legacie wᶜʰ I doe heer after bequeath unto her 3 unto my Daughter Sarah Smith I give the sum of forty pounds nyne pounds of wᶜʰ sum is allredy payd, and toward the payment of the residue, shee shall have one feather bed with the apptenances therto belonging, and what more I may be capeable of paying while I live, the resedue of the forty pound that shall be left unpayd at my decease shall be payd to her by my son Joseph within four year after my decease 4 unto my daughter Hanna Lunt I give forty pounds part of it to ·be pay in a feather bed and apptenances, and twelve pound of it to be pd by my son Beniamin (as above) and

what remaines that I due not pay in my life time to be payd
by my son Joseph within four years after my decease 5 ffinally
I make my Eldest son Joseph aforesayd ||my|| sole executor,
and request and apoynt my Kinsmen Joshua and Caleb
Moody together with my Son in law James Smith to be overseers to this my last will & testament, heerby giveing full
power to my overseers, abovsaid to decide and determin any
matter of difference that may arise, betweene my children or
any of them as refering to anything heere bequeathed them,
and doe oblidge and require my children to sit downe and
abyd by their determination. In testimony to all and singular
the premisses I have heerunto sett my hand & seale this 20 :
Sept : 1678."

Robert (his mark) Coker. (SEAL)

Witness : Joshua Moodey, Caleb Moodey.

Proved in Ipswich court Mar. 29, 1681, by the witnesses.

Ipswich Deeds, vol. 4, *page* 390.

Inventory of the estate of Robert Coker of Newbury, deceased Nov. 19, 1680, taken 18 of Dec. following, by Stephen
Grenlefe, sr. and William Chandler : ye dwelling house with
ye Barne & out housing together with ye orchard & eight
acrees of land adjoining to ye house, 160li. ; ye hill Lotts on
ye south side of ye house seaventeene Acres & a halfe, 105li. ;
in ye Little feild foure Acrees & halfe of plough land, 36li. ;
thirteene Acrees of Divident Land at ye townes end, 20li. ;
twenty nine Acrees of marsh meadoe ground, 145li. ; a frame
of a house on ye land in ye Little feild, 10li. ; neate Cattle,
16li., 22 sheepe and a hogg, 10li. 6s., 26li. 6s. ; In graine
English and Indean, 16li. ; in hey, 4li. ; thirteene bushells of
old Indean Corne, 1li. 19s. ; Houshold stuff in ye lower roome,
10li. 16s. ; sider & caske in ye seller, 1li. 12s. ; Iron geare,
armes & a copper Kettle, 6li. 10s. ; wearing Apparrell, 8li.
17s. ; Bedding in ye chamber, 21li. 2s., linnen, 3li. 11s., 24li.
13s. ; cloth, sheepes wooll, flax, thread & other necessaries in
ye chamber, 8li. 14s. ; two thirds of a boate, 6li. 10s. ; a sett of
Harroe teeth, 10s. ; In money, 4s. 2d. ; the Freehould to ye
house, 10li. ; some more old Lumber, 6s. ; total, 602li. 17s. 2d.

Attested in Ipswich court Mar. 28, 1681, by Joseph Coker,
executor.

Essex County Probate Files, Docket 5,883.

ESTATE OF THOMAS JONES OF MANCHESTER.

Administration upon the estate of Thomas Joanes of Manchester, intestate, was granted Mar. 29, 1681, unto his sons, Abraham, Tho. and Ephraim Joanes, who brought in an inventory in two papers and attested to the truth thereof.

Ipswich Quarterly Court Records, vol. 5, page 366.

Inventory of the estate of Mr. Thomas Jones of Manchester, taken Mar. 9, 1680-81, by Paul Thorndike and Thomas West: one dwelling hous and outhous & orchard, 45li.; land in the plain by estimation, four Acres, 8li.; three Acres of land upon the neck so called, 7li. 10s.; a parcell of medow by estimation an Acre and half at the sawmill pond, 3li.; neat Cattell and one Colt & two small swine, 17li. 15s.; Beding and wearing Cloaths & one hide, 12li. 18s.; gunn, Iron ware, bras, pewter, wooden ware & bookes, 5li.; in mony due to the Estate from his son Ephraim Jones, 3li.; the land and marsh which belonged to the hous in which the town of Manchester settled said Jones at his first coming to them, 24li.; total, 126li. 3s.

Inventory of the estate of Thomas Joans of Jefferrys Creeck, Lying in the town of Hull taken Mar. 16, 1681, by Zechariah Whitman and Nathaniell Bosworth: one whome lott excepting only thirty Rods of the front of the sd lott made over to Thomas Joans, 18li.; five rod on the front of Samuel Baker lott long since bought by the said Thomas Joans, 4li.; one lott at point Alderton on Acre & half, 9li.; on lott at strabury Hill 1-3 of an Acre, 5li.; one lott at sagamore hill 1-3 of an Acre, 5li.; one lott at Whithead on Acre & halfe, 5li.; one Lots commons, 15li. and two Acres of medow, 20li., 35li.; one lott of 4 Acres at peltoxe island, 20li.; a share in the island appertaining to a single lot, 5li.; in Rent money, 6li.; total, 112li.

Attested in Ipswich court Mar. 29, 1681, by Abraham, Thomas and Ephraim Joans, administrators of the estate of their father.

The widow Elezebeth Jonns, Aberham, Thomas and Epharam Jonns being most concerned in the estate left by Thomas Jonns, have made the following agreement: Elezebeth Jonns, the widow and their mother in law to have sixteen pounds; considering the condition of our brother John Jonns being uncapable for to order and dispose of himself it hath been known that it was the intent of our father Thomas Jonns that all his land at Hull that was not already disposed of was to be made over to his son Thomas Jonns, for the maintaining of his brother John Jonns during his life; the hows and orchard with the land now belonging thereunto being situated in Manchester, to belong to Epharam Jonns for his portion, provided he pay out of the same to his two sisters, Sarah Chaemberlin and Hanneh Goding part of their portions, as indifferent men shall judge meet; the rest of the estate, to be divided equally to Aberham and Thomas Jonns and their two sisters Sarah Chamberlain and Hanah Godin. Dated Manchester, 30 : 1m : 1681. Witness : Sam. Freind, Sarah (her U mark) Allen.

Elizabeth, widow of Thomas Jones, Sr., of Manchester, with Thomas, Abraham and Ephraim Jones his sons, presented this writing in Ipswich court, 29 : 1m : 1680, and declared it to be their mutual agreement for the settlement of the estate, which was allowed, and the administrators ordered to attend to the same.

Essex County Probate Files, Docket 15,230.

ESTATE OF MRS. JANE WILLIAMS.

Administration upon the estate of Jane Williams, was granted Mar. 29, 1681, unto her son Joseph Williams, who brought in an inventory.

Ipswich Quarterly Court Records, vol. 5, page 366.

Inventory of the estate of the widow Jane Williams taken Dec. 1, 1681, by Stephen Dowe and Joseph Page : one iron pote and pote hockes, one *tramel* stick and tramil, 19s. 6d.; two peuter platteres, 10s.; one frieing pan and one warminge pan, 6s.; a payer of cardes and a coten wheele, 6s.; a cotten Ruge and a bead and two sheets, blanckit, 3li. 12s.; boulster and a pilow, 5s.; a sarge goune and a karsy wescoate, 1li. 12s.; two swine, 1li. 10s.; thre cowes, 13li. 10s.; one cowe, two haiefers and a bull, 11li. 15s.; total, 33li. 5s. 6d.

Attested in Ipswich court Mar. 29, 1681, by Joseph Williams, administrator of his mother's estate.

Essex County Probate Files, Docket 30,009.

ESTATE OF SAMUEL WORCESTER OF BRADFORD.

Administration upon the estate of Mr. Samuell Worster, intestate, was granted Mar. 29, 1681, unto Elizabeth Worster the widow.

Ipswich Quarterly Court Records, vol. 5, page 366.

Inventory of the estate of Mr. Samuell Wostor taken Mar. 23,

1680-81, by Shu. Walker, Ezekiel Northend, Thomas Tenny
and John Palmer: wearing aparill wooling and Linin, shoos
and boots, 8li.; armes and ammunition, 3li.; Books, 1li. 10s.;
Beads and beding, 12li.; Beadsteeds, 2li.; peuter, brase, Iron
pots, trammils, fire shovell, tongs, 5li. 10s.; cubbart, chests,
box, chares, tabel, spining wheles, hogsheds, barills and other
Lumber in ye house, 3li.; barill and hogshed staves, 1li. 10s.;
25 bushels Indian corne, 6 bush. rye, 5 bushels wheat,
6li. 4s.; 5 bushels oates, porke and beefe and 1
bushel salt, 1li. 15s.; flax and shepes wool and cotten
wool and yarne, 2li. 6s.; cart, plough, yoake, chaines and
utencils for husbandry, 3li. 10s.; saddell and pillion, 1li.
10s.; 4 oxen, 3 cowes, 2 2 yere old steres, 2 yerlings, 1 bull,
1 calfe, 43li.; 14 shepe, 1 horse, 7 swine, 15li. 10s.; 337
acres Land and meadow, house, barne, and fences, 400li.;
total, 510li. 9s. Debts due to the estate, Thom. Wood, 5s.;
Joseph Palmer, 4s. Debts due from the estate 119li. 13s. 10d.
whereof there is Dew of the aforesaid sum in money 6li.
6s. 6d.

Attested in Ipswich court Mar. 29, 1681, by Elizabeth
Worster, relict and administratrix.

This court ordered the settlement of the estate of Mr.
Samuell Woster who died intestate, which estate amounted
to 384li. 9s. cleare of debts, as follows: to the widow for her
part 54li. for the bringing up of the children, and the rest of
the estate to be divided equally among the eleven children the
eldest son first having a double portion, to be paid as they
come of age. The house, barn and 200 acres of land to
stand bound for security.

Bond of William Worecester and Francis Worcester of
Bradford, with Joseph Bayley and Caleb Hopkinson as sure-
ties, dated Feb. 20, 1692-3, for 600li., to administer according
to law upon the estates of Samuel Worcester and Elizabeth
Worcester late of Bradford, deceased. Witness: Stephen
Sewall, Abigall (her O mark) Mansfield.

Inventory of the estate of Mr. Samuell Woster and Mrs. Elizabeth Woster relict to him and administratrix to his estate
taken May 3, 1694, by John Tennie, Samuell Haseltine and
Richard Kimball: a muskitt and Books, 2li.; Beding and
Bedstead, 4li.; puter, bras, Iron pots, tramills, tongs, 3li.
12s.; an old chest and other lumber, 1li.; a chain and other
utinsalls for husbandry, 1li. 16s.; land formerly inventoryed

wth addition, 350li.; a fram of an old hous remaining, 4li.; total, 366li. 8s.

Attested May 14, 1694, by William and Francis Worcester, the administrators.

Petition of Josiah Wheeler of Salisbury, that whereas he had a legacy due to him by right of his now wife, from the estate of Samuel Worster of Bradford, who deceased in the year 1681, and since by the death of the widow and two of the children of the said deceased, your petitioner hath fallen to him out of the estate some thing more, and having demanded his right of William and Francis Woster who possess the estate, now desireth that the court may grant him redress therein. Accordingly William and Francis Woster are cited to appear at the Ipswich court in May, 1694.

The account of Wm. and Francis Worster, administrators of the estate of Samuell and Elizabeth Worster, late of Bradford, brought in Nov. 22, 1697: Debts paid, 77li. 3s. 5d.; allo. and setling ye estate, 10s.; stating ye acct. &c., 10s.; quietus, 4s.; order for a division & committee & recording ye return, 2li.; loss on ye estate by casualty, 16s.

[Charges paid to Deacon Coffin of Newbry, Tho. Stickny, Ann White, John Tennie, James Coffin, Henry Somersby, Faith Law, Will Osgood, Caleb Boynton. *This entry cancelled.*]

The account of William and Frances Worster, administrators of the estate of Samuel and Elizabeth Worster late of Bradford, brought in Nov. 23, 1697: bond and letter of administration, 7s. 6d.; pd. a debt to Wm. Osgood, 5li.; 2 oxen lost by casualty, 12li.; loss on the buildings for want of timely reparation, as appears by ye estimate of Richard Kemball and Caleb Hopkins, 40li.; 1 swine lost, 30s. 1 horse died, 5li., 6li. 10s.; the widow former administratrix had and spent of the moveable estate more then her part of said estate, 2li. 4s. 6d.; allowing ye acct. setling & deviding ye estate, 10s.; methodifing ye acct. 30s., quietus, 4s., 2li. 4s.; a division & to ye comitte & recording ye return, 2li.; allowed administrators, 15li.; more for extraordinary trouble, 1li. 3s.; total, 100li. Per Contra, 69li. 15s. The widow Elizabeth Worster pd. Caleb Boynton a debt due to him from her 4li. 15s.; 65li. of the moveable estate she kept in her hands more than she paid away in debts and then what was left yt came into the hands of ye new administrators, 69li. 15s.

The names of the children: Wm. the eldest son, Samuell, Moses, deceased, Frances, Joseph, Timothy, Elizabeth, Dorothy, John, Ebenezer, Susanah.

Essex County Probate Files, Docket 30,674.

The court May 16, 1694, granted William and Frances Worcester further time for the settling of their account of administration upon the estate of Samuell and Elizabeth Worcester.

Essex County Probate Records, vol. 303, page 211.

Capt. David Haseltine, Ensigne Joseph Bailey, Corp. John Boynton, Mr. Richard Kimball and Mr. Caleb Hopkinson all freeholders in Bradford, or any three of them, authorized by the court at Salem, Nov. 23, 1697, to make a division of the housing and lands of Samuel Worster late of Bradford, deceased, among his surviving children according to the settlement made, first setting out to the administrators William and Francis Woster, one hundred pounds allowed upon their account, besides their shares. Sworn Dec. 1, 1697.

Division of the houseing and lands of Samuel Worster late of Bradford, deceased, and of Elizabeth Worster his wife, also deceased, made Mar. 10, 1701-2, by David Haseltine, Richard Kimball and Joseph Baily: to William Woster one of the administrators, one half of the hundred pound on the westerly side of the farm laying ye whole length of said farm wch we account at 50li.; to William Worster eldest son, adjoyning to that wch was set out to him in ye first place, at ye rear, it being eight rod wide & so running ye whole length of ye farme to ye uper end there it being Eleven rod wide wth an acre & thirty rod of meadow laying at ye esterly end of a meadow comonly called Worsters meadow all wch we estimate at 41li. 13s. 8d.; to Elizabeth Worster, adjoyning to William Worster, ye one halfe of her share at ye rear, it being two Rod wide & so runing to ye uper end of sd. farme there it being two rod & a halfe wide wth forty seven rod of meadow in meadow called Worsters meadow joyning to Wm. Worsters meadow estimated at 10li. 8s. 5d.; to Susanah Worster, joyning to Elizabeth Worster at ye River, it being four rod wide & so runing ye whole length of said farme at ye uper end being five rod & a halfe wide wth about ninety five rod of meadow in meadow called Worsters meadow laying on ye northwest side of Mr. Symes as it is now bounded, estimated at 20li. 16s. 10d.; to Timothy Worster, next to Susannah Wors-

ter, at ye rear four rod wide & so runing to ye uper end of
said farme being five rod & halfe a rod wide there, wth about
ninety five rod of meadow laying on ye northwest of ye
meadow formerly set out to Susanah Worster, laying ye whole
breadth of it as now staked out, estimated at 20li. 6s. 10d.;
to Ebenezer Worster, next to Timothy Worster, at ye rear
four rod wide & so runing ye whole length of ye farme ye
uper end being five rod & halfe a rod wide, wth ninety five
rod of meadow laying on ye northwest side of meadow formerly set out to Timothy as it is now staked out and bounded,
estimated at 20li. 16s. 10d.; to Dorothy Worster, next to
Ebenezer Worster, at ye rear four rod wide & so running ye
whole length of said farme at ye uper end it being five rod
wide & halfe a rod, wth ninety five rod of meadow laying in
meadow called Worsters meadow on ye northwest side of
meadow formerly set out to Ebenezer Worster as it is now
staked out & bounded, estimated at 20li. 16s. 10d.; to John
Worster, next to Dorothy Worster, at ye river being four rod
wide & so runing ye whole length of said farme at ye uper
end it being five rod & halfe a rod wide, with ninety five rod
of meadow laying on ye northwest side of meadow formerly
set out to Dorothy Worster as it is staked out and bounded estimated at 20li. 16s. 10d.; to Joseph Worster, next to John
Worster, at ye river being four rod wide & so runing ye whole
length of said farme, at ye uper end being five rod & halfe a
rod wide, wth ninety five rod of meadow laying on ye westerly
side of meadow formerly set out to Elizabeth Worster, estimated at 20li. 16s. 10d.; to Elizabeth Worster, the other halfe
of her share next to Joseph Worster, at ye river being two
rod wide & so runing ye whole length of said farme at the
uper end two rod & halfe a rod wide, wth forty eight rod of
meadow laying on ye westerly side of meadow formerly set
out to Joseph Worster, estimated at 10li. 8s. 5d.; to Frances
Worster, the other administrator, next to Elizabeth Worster
her last part set out to Frances, ye remainder part of said
farme and laying on ye easterly side of said farme being his
just part for his 50li. allowed him as administrator for
charges and his share of ye estate ninety five rod of meadow
joyning to meadow last set out to Elizabeth Worster and laying at the northerly end of meadow of Mr. Simes and meadow
formerly set out to Susannah Worster, estimated at 20li. 16s.
10d., also ye surplus wth ye building unto ye administrators.
Essex County Probate Records, vol. 307, pp. 370-372.

ESTATE OF MRS. MARGARET BISHOP OF IPSWICH.

Administration upon the estate of Mrs. Margret Bishop, intestate, was granted Mar. 29, 1681, unto her son Samuell Bishop, and an inventory being brought in amounting to 710li., he gave bond of 500li. to administer according to law, all the lands to stand bound.

Ipswich Quarterly Court Records, vol. 5, page 366.

Inventory of the estate of the widow Bishop of Ipswich, taken Mar. 31, 1681, by Thomas French and Samuel Hunt: A gold ring, 15s., 2 silver spons thimble & clasps, 1li. 19s.; silver cup, silver Ring, 11s. 6d.; pewter, 5li. 16s. 6d.; brass, 1li. 16s.; her woollen Apparill & a silk Apron, 7li.; her Linnen, 1li. 15s.; sheets & other linen, 6li. 10s.; the Bed in ye parlour wth wt belonges to it, 8li.; other bedding, 3li.; table cloths & napkins & Cubbard clothes, 2li.; Iron Kettles & Iron potts, skillet & spoons, 2li. 11s. 6d.; a spitt, Racks and other Irons, 16s. 8d.; an Iron Copper, 2li. 10s.; 2 spinning wheeles, trenchers, sives, scales & querns, meal tub & meal trough, 1li. 16s.; Andirons, tongues, tramill & fire pan, 1li. 10s.; an Iron Jack, 18s.; a clocke, 4li.; box iron wth Heaters, 4s.; 2 buffet stooles, five cushions, 1li. 16s.; a Press, a little table, 1li. 6s.; a great Table, 2 joint forme, 2 stooles, 1li. 10s.; In ye chamber: a great chest, a carved box, 3 chaires, 1li. 1s. 6d.; 2 andirons & candlestick Iron, 5s. 6d.; a cupboard wth cloth & cushions, 3li.; four leather chaires, a chest & box, 1li. 12s.; in ye parlor: a great Table & 2 stooles, 1li. 10s.; 2 payer of stiliards & a voyder, 1li. 6s. 6d.; fowling peice & muskett, 2li.; another cupboard, cloth & cushion, 1li.; a Table, chaires & stooles, 1li.; 2 glasses & foure bookes, 15s.; brass scales & weights, 10s.; 2 oxen, 3 cowes, a 2 year old & calf, 21li.; 8 hoops & a chaine, 17s.; wedges & beetle rings, box, spanshakle, youke & furniture to it & Iron boxes, 13s.; tire for ye wheeles of a cart, 1li. 10s.; 11 acres of land at wattle neck, 25li.; 6 Acres of Meddow at ye west medows, 12li.; House & barne & orchard & Commonage & 14 acres of land on the south side of River adjoining to Doctour Rogers land, 160li.; 6 Acres of marish at plumb Iland, 12li.; total, 304li. 8s. 8d. A payr of gloves, 1li.

There is still due unto the widow Bishop as executrix to Thomas Bishop, by booke, 255li. 8s. 6d.; severall Bills, 323li. 2s. 11d.; by rent, 20li.; ye half of a fishing Ketch, 70li.; 2 years fishing half of her earnings, 50li.; wch belongs to a

Ketch, the half of a great pot, the half of a great payr of
stiliards, 1li. 10s.; total, 720li. 1s. 5d. Due from Widow
Bishop in severall Debts, 315li..9s., leaving the estate, 710li.
1d.

Attested in Ipswich court Mar. 29, 1681, by Samuell
Bishop.

Essex County Probate Files, Docket 2,477.

ESTATE OF MRS. SARAH GAGE OF BRADFORD.

Administration upon the estate of Sarah Gage, widow of
John Gage, intestate, was granted Mar. 29, 1681, unto John
French and William Smith two of her sons in law, and they
are to bring in an inventory to the next court.

Ipswich Quarterly Court Records, vol. 5, page 367.

Inventory* of the estate of Sareth Gage deceased July 7,
1681, taken July 14, 1681, by Stephen Grenlefe and Caleb
Moody: on fether beade, 2 pilos, 3li.; an other beade, 12s.;
an ould gren ruge & blancet, 7s.; on nue boalster, 6s.; a coverled, 7s., a blancet, 7s., 14s.; 2 knete blancets, 1li.; blak petecote, 5s., serge petecote, 3s., 8s.; a red petecote, 10s., another
red petecot, 2s., 12s.; a gray cote, 4s., gray cloth 4 yards &
half, 12s. 6d., 16s. 6d.; pese of white cloth, 6s., a seafe garde,
8s., 14s.; a serge jumpe, 10s., a pair bodes and 2 hodes, 4s.,
14s.; a letel chest, 3s., a knete petecot, 6s., 9s.; a serge wascot,
4s., a brod bage, 4s., 8s.; on pair shetes, 14s., another pair
with a touell, 15s., 1li. 9s.; toe coten pelobers, 2s., 4 spones,
2s., 4s.; toe sheftes & toe scarfes, 12s.; toe napcens & toe
tabel cloth, 8s.; som small lenen clothes in a blue apren, 1li.
14s.; som small lenen in a napcen, 1li.; a cheste & som things
in the tell, 12s.; on dusen trenchers, 1s., 3 peis stokes, 7s.,
8s.; selke hods & hackeches, 1li. 10s.; cortens & valens,
8s.; a bibell, 3s., a wescote, 5s., 8s.; blue lenen, 3s., toe gren
aprens, 7s., 10s.; a stufe petecote, 10s., to cortens & valents,
10s., 1li.; a wescot, 4s.; peuter plates & [lattin: *copy*] ware,
1li. 8s.; a warmen pan & screnie, 11s.; earthen ware & a
brase [ladell: *copy*], 6s. 6d.; wooden ware & ould se [ive],
17s.; 2 potes, scelet, cetel [pothooke: *copy*], 1li. 5s.; frien-
pan, 3s., firpan, tongs, 6s., 9s.; tramel & gredeyren, 6s.; boshal
& halfe rye, 6s.; a coberd & boxe, 1li. 2s.; 2 chaire, 3 coshens,
forme, 2 stoles, 7s.; a bage with 3 small bages [& som malt:
copy], 8s.; som enden bascets, 4s.; a bage with som whete
mele, 5s.; total, 28li. 2s.

*Ipswich Deeds, vol. 4, page 496.

Attested in Ipswich court Sept. 27, 1681, by William Smith
and John French, and the court ordered that the estate be
equally divided to the three daughters, namely, the wives of
Wm. Smith, John French and Samuell Buswell.

Essex County Probate Files, Docket 10,506.

ESTATE OF JOSEPH MUZZEY OF NEWBURY.

"July the 29 1680 Be it knowne to all men, that I Joseph
Muzzey of Newberey in the County of Essex N : E. massachu-
sets being weake of body but of perfect memory considering
my owne Mortality, doe here make my last will and Testament, comending and commiting my soule into the hands of
my Blessed Redemer Jesus Christ and my body when it shall
Decease this life, to be burryed in the buryall place of newbery in hope of a blessed Resurection and for my worldly
goods I Dispose of as followeth. Imprimis I give and bequeath
to my son Joseph all my house and land and meadow exept my
Iland of creeks grasse in plome Iland River when he shall be
of the Age of one and twenty yeares, that is my Eight Ackeres
of meadow at this side of Plome Iland River, and my lote of
meadow on the other side; Also I give to him on yoke of oxon
not exeeding the Age of Seaven yeares with a plough : and
plow chaine and plow-irons compleat, Also two Cowes not
exeeding seaven yeares of Age; Also ten sheepe not exeeding
fower yeares, Also one shovel and spade and Dung-forke and
three pitchforcks and on ffaling axe on morticeing axe one
frow and two broad hoes one betle and Rings, foure Iron
Wedges a flax-combe Also on hamer on Sickle and on Reape-
hooke Also on Iron tramell A fire pan and tonges Also I
give him my fouling peice and sword and pike and a belt my
litle chest and my silver spone my great powder horne and
belt, and my pouch ; and a musterd bowle; also my Iron ketle
and Iron pott and pot-hookes two new peauter platters two
new poringers on quart peauter pott two ocome spoones on two
quart brasse skillet on Iron-lampe; Also my feather-bead and
bed-steade with on Rug on Couerlet on paire of blanketes
and paire of sheets on feather bolster and pillow Also I give
him a new sadle comp[l]eat and a new pilion also I give him
my bible, my booke of the Gouerment of Cattell Lenard
Mascall, my Herball boke Didimes mour mowtione Also my
great chaire and my houre Glass also I Giue him one three
pinte stone Juge and two quart glass Botles Also one Sith
withall furniture belonging Also a spitt also a Raying cive

and on wheate Ruder and on barley Rudder also a paire of
horse trasses collor and whipletree and whiple-tree chaine a
copse and cops-pines Also a cupe-boarde and on paire of bellowes also a Hand-saw and a draght shave a paire of bolet
molds worme and scourer a paire of shott-molds also a smoothing Iron; also a smal coper boxe a trowell a horse fetters Loke
and key Also a yoke staple and Ringle Also a cart-rope.

"2ly I give unto Mary my Daughter two Cowes not exceeding the Age of seaven yeares and eight sheepe not exceeding
foure yeares of Age when she shal be of the Age of Eighteene
yeares or else at the day of marriage if it be before that time
also I giue to her my sayd Daughter my Iland of Creeke-grase
by Plome Iland River Also I giue to her my Brase ketle containeing about a bushell and a half in measure; Also a quart
brass skillet And a peauter pint pott a Basson containeing a
quart; also two poringers two peauter platters and on sucking botle and A warmeing panne and on chamber pot of
peauter; two quart Glasess two Ocome spones and one sauce
Pane on quart Jugg and a drame cup; Also on Bed on paire
of Sheets on Rugg on Coverlet also a new chest and a Cradle
on measheing tub on churne two kellares Also I give unto
my Daughter Mary my Linnen Wheele Also a new chaire
also a Paire of Courtaines Also I give unto her my Horse
also a smotheing iron And a Lattin Tunnell my will is that
my sonn or sonns be put to learne some profitable trade or
trades in due time for theire future goode and benefite

"3dly I apoint Esther my wife to be the sole executrixe of
this my last will and testament and to haue my house and stocke
and land in her handes, for the bringing up of my children
and to have all my Goodes and chattelles undisposed of my
Debts and ffuneralle being Discharged.   And my wife being
now with child, my will is That if the child shall live, that
twenty pounds be payd it as a legacy ten Pounds to be payd
by my Wife when the child shal come to Age, in neat cattell
and merchentable corne and ten pounds to be payd by my
son Joseph in the like pay; and if my wiffe shall marry againe
she shall put in sufficent Securitty, for the payment of my
childeren portiones expressed in this my will and if any of my
children shall Decease this life then it shall be to those that
doe surviue and if all shold faille then the lande Goods and
Chattelles to y⁰ next of my kindred, and I wold Intreate and
Appoint Seargant Coffin and Seargant Clarke & mʳ Tho:
noyse and mʳ Moses Gerish to be ouerseers of this my last will

and testament ‖that it be pformed‖ and herunto I haue set
to my hand and sealle."

Joseph Muzzey (SEAL)

Witness: Stephen Swet, Tristram Coffin.

Esther Muzzy relict of Joseph Muzzy appointed by her husband to be executrix, renounced the same in open court, Mar.
29, 1681.

Inventory of the estate of Joseph Muzzy, 1680: a hous and
barne and 6 akars and a half of land, 60li.; 12 akars of salt
marsh and a Iland of crek thach, 50li.; 3 cowes and 3 steares
and 2 hefares, 22li.; 26 shep and lams, 7li. 5s., 5 swine small
ons, 2li. 10s.; a hors, 2li. 10s., waring aparill, 5li., bookes, 4s.,
7li. 14s.; sadell, pillian, bridel, collar, hos trasis and whipeltre
chain, 1li.; hors feters, chain and plow, a youck and cops and
pin, 14s.; 2 axis, 2 hous, 10s., spad, shovell and 4 wigis, 15s.;
a gun, sword, pike and powder hor[n] and smal things bee-
longing thar untou, 1li. 10s.; a bead, 3 coverlites, 2 Rouges
and 3 par of shets, 9li. 10s.; a boustar, 2 pillos and pillo casis
and cortins, 1li. 10s.; 2 blanckits, 2 owld beadtecks and a
beadstid, 2li. 5s.; tobes, cillars, pails and trais, 1li. 5s.; putar,
bras and Iron, a tramil and pot hucks, 3li. 3s.; 2 chest, a box,
4 chares and 3 seuefs, 19s.; a cart Roap, slid, tow cowmb and
2 whels, 15s.; wool and hemp, 20s., a Rephuck, sickell, a truil,
1li. 2s.; severall small things, 20s., a silvar spun, 5s., 1li. 5s.;
43 bowshils of barly and 9 bowshills of owtes, 9li. 14s. 6d.; a
depte due from Joseph Knight, 14li., timber, 19li.; a parsell
of nails, 15s., a depte due, 4li., 4li. 15s.; total, 201li. 6s. 6d.
Deptes due from the estat: to Tristram Coffin, 3li. 10d., Mr.
Goodhue, 1li. 8s., 4li. 8s. 10d.; Mrs. Whit, 27s., Nathaniel
Clark, 25s., 2li. 12s.; Robard whingooo, 20s., Thomas Noyes,
1li.; Rates to the constabl, 4li. 3s. 1d., to John halle, 7s.,
4li. 10s. 1d.; anthony Sumerby, 23s., John atcison, 7s. 8d.,
1li. 10s. 8d.; abel huss, 7s., Thomas Rogars, 6s., 13s.; John
webstar, 8s., Calib Richardson, 7s., 15s.; Will. bolton, 3s.,
Insin grenlef, 7s. 6d., 10s. 6d.; Jams ordway, 1li. 10s. 8d.,
georg march, 15s., 2li. 5s. 8d.; John Noyes, 2li. 12s., Petar
toppan, 4li. 1s., 6li. 13s.; Jams Jackman, 12li., Georg Littell,
12s., 12li. 12s.; John Dole, 14s., hue march, 2s. 10d., 16s. 10d.;
total, 38li. 7s. 7d. deducted leaves 162li. 18s. 11d.

Attested in Ipswich court Mar. 29, 1681, by Ester Muzzy,
administratrix of her husband's estate.

Hester Muzzy shewing that her husband Joseph Muzzy was
unsatisfied with the will presented to the Ipswich court Mar.

29, 1681, and would have altered it had he been able, petitioned the court "to take such order that she may be inabled to get a livelyhood & bring up her children according as ther necessity doe require being very young. And wheras there is no convenient house to live in and a necessity of building a new one before she can have a comfortable habitation and therefore humbly conceives that it may be judged rationall, that at least that stock of cattell wch is given to my son Joseph may be laid out in building a house, seeing he is likely to possess it and also that she may be repaid or allowed what may be thought fitt for what she shall be necessitated to lay out according to the worth of it when he shall posses the house and land, or any other that shall be heire to it and also that she may have a suffitient settelment in it during her naturall life."

There being presented to this court an inventory of the estate of Joseph Muzy, with a writing said to be his last will, wherein Hester relict of said Muzzy was appointed executrix, and she refusing to accept thereof, the court granted her power of administration, and ordered that the widow have possession and use of the whole estate during her life for her support and bringing up the children and paying the just debts, and after her death, the lands, being valued at 110li. to revert to the children. Joseph Muzey being the eldest son to have a double share, and the rest of the land to be equally divided between Benjamin and Mary Muzey; if the widow shall survive all the children, the next heir to inherit said land, paying unto said Hester or her heirs, the full value of such buildings as shall be built by her for her necessary use.

Essex County Probate Files, Docket 19,130.

ESTATE OF MRS. REBECCA HOWLET OF NEWBURY.

Administration upon the estate of Rebecah Howlet, widow, granted Mar. 29, 1681, to James Smith, who brought in an inventory which was allowed. James Smith and John Smith the children of the widow, having agreed upon a division of the estate to their mutual satisfaction and also equally to pay the debts, the court allows of their agreement to be a full settlement of the estate.

Inventory* of estate of Rebecca Howlett of Newbury, deceased Nov. 1, 1680, taken Nov. 3, 1680, by Anthony Somerby and Abell Huse: her weareing apparrell, foure gownes,

* Ipswich Deeds, vol. 4, page 385.

a hoode and a cloake, foure wastcoats, two paire of bodyes, nine petticoats & 2 sea aprons, 20li.; six yards of sarge, 1li. 16s.; bedstead, featherbed, bolster, coverlet & mat, 4li. 2s.; seaven pewter platters, four smal pewter dishes, 3 porringers, pewter candlesticke, beaker, cup & salt sellar, 2li. 4s.; a smal brasse pot, brass pan, brasse kettle and a posnet, 2li.; eleven sheets, 6li. 10s.; thre tableclothes, dozen of napkins & 3 towells, 1li. 10s.; three Aprons of ordinary [weare 4: *copy*] homemad pillowbears and foure shifts, 2li. 10s.; two blew Aprons [& three quarter of a yard: *copy*] of tammy, 7s.; pillion & pillion cloth [and on old pannell: *copy*], 1li.; two silk [scarfes, 3 hoods, two silke: *copy*] neck handkercher, two whisks, 2li. 4s.; a muff & [2 paire of gloves &: *copy*], callico neck handkircher, 8s.; A yard of holland and [four fine aprons: *copy*], 2li.; eight caps laced & [three dressings: *copy*], 1li. 15s.; seaven neck handkerchers, 1li. 8s.; three pocket handkerchers [4 paire: *copy*] of sleeves, three linnen whisks, thre stock neckclothes, 2 [fillets, 4: *copy*] quoyves, a head band & a paire of knit cotton gloves & a white [hood: *copy*], 1 li. 4s.; silver bodkin, 2s.; two chests and 2 boxes, 1li.; a hatt, 8s.; mare and colt, 3li. 10s.; two cows, 7li.; twelve pounds of cotten yarne, 1li. 10s.; total, 64li. 8s. 6d.

Attested in Ipswich court Mar. 29, 1681, by James Smith, administrator of the estate of his mother, Rebecha Howlet.

Essex County Probate Files, Docket 14,090.

ESTATE OF MRS. ANNIS REDDING OF IPSWICH.

Annis Redding, widow and executrix of Joseph Redding, being deceased, Elizabeth the daughter of Joseph Redding brought her father's will into court, by which it was judged that she is now executrix, who because of some estate of said Joseph spent in the life time of Annis, presented this inventory of what was left at her death, to the Ipswich court, 29: 1m: 1681, who ordered and advised her to attend her father's will as much as may be.

Inventory of the estate of Anice Reding, relict of Joseph Reding, taken Apr. 1, 1681, by Jonathan Wade and John Dane, sr.: the house and housing and homlot &c., 90li.; six acres of areable land at Labor in vaine, 45li.; 4 acres of marsh at Labor in vaine, 30li.; 1 acre and 1-2 marsh and thatch next the necke, 9li.; 6 acres and 3 acres of marsh at Plum Iland, 18li.; one acre and a halfe pasture at hart break hill, 9li.; 6 neat cattle, 28li. 10s.; 6 shepe, 2li. 10s.; a bill from

Thomas bishop, 10li.; brasse and pewter, 5li.; Iron ware, 2li.
10s., 1 fan, 5s., 2li. 15s.; beding, wearing Aparell, boxes,
chayrs, cushons, books, 14li. 10s.; total, 264li. 5s.   Funerall
expences, 2li. 15s.

Essex County Probate Files, Docket 23,395.

ESTATE OF PHILIP WATSON CHALLIS OF AMESBURY.

Inventory of the estate of Lt. Phillip Watson Challis deceased at Amesbury, as it was given in by his widow, and appraised 21 : 8m : 1680, by William Ossgood and Samuell
Foote: the house and Barne orchard and Homestead, 80li.; a
lott of upland in the plaines, 16li.; a Higglety Pigley lot,
10li.; a great swamp lott, 6li.; a lott behind Whitchers hill,
10li.; a Lot in the oxe pasture, 8li.; a bagsmore lott, 6li.; a
lott in the childrens Land, 20li.; a Lott in the Champion
ground, 30li.; a lott in the great devission, 40li.; a lott in
peeke, 5li.; house and Land at Jamaicoe, 100li.; the frogg
pond (comonly so called) 1li. 10s.; a Higglety Pigly Lot
of meadow, 30li.; a beach barr Lott, 5li.; A sweepage Lott,
20li.; a Lott at the black rock creeks mouth, 10li.; lott in the
Tyde meadows, 15li.; lott at the boggy meadows, 15li.; lott
in the new meadows, 4li.; three dayes intrest per anum in a
saw mill, 2li.; company of swine, 10li.; five cowes, 15li.; five
young steers & a yearling & 2 calves, 11li. 10s.; eight sheepe,
2li. 8s.; horse, 3 mares and a yearling colt, 6li.; eight barrells of syder, 2li.; six thousand of hogshead & 1-2 a thousand of pipe staves, 6li.; five thousand of short shingle, 2li.;
Iron tooles & Implements, chaines & plow, 2li. 10s.; Beds,
Bedstead & bedding, 15li.; houshold stuff with two bibles &
other bookes, 20li.; his wearing clothes, 10li.; five geese &
other fowle, 5s.; his armes, 2li. 5s.; corne & hay layd in for
provition for famally & cattle,—; cannoo, 2li.; total, 540li.
8s.   A parcell of Land sold to Isaac Morrell, 45li. Debts due
to the estate from Isaac Morrell for the abovesayd Land, 8li.
2s. 4d.   Debts due from the estate to Anthony Somerby, 1li.
10s.; John Attkinson, 2li., Mrs. White, 9li. 6s., 11li. 6s.;
John Bartlett, sr., 4li. 10s., Edward Woodman, 1li. 10s., 6li.;
Elisha Ilsly, 6s., Thomas Currier, 1li. 10s., 1li. 16s.; John
Hoyt, jr., 3li., Mr. Jno. Dole, 20s., 4li.; John Cluffe, sen. in
mony 10s., John Weed, 2li., 2li. 10s.; total, 27li. 2s.

Attested in Ipswich court Mar. 29, 1681, by Mary Challis,
relict and administratrix.

The settlement of the estate of Phillip Chalice ordered by

the Ipswich court Sept. 27, 1681, as follows: to the widow Mary Challice for her sole use the moveables amounting to about 25li. and of the housing and land to the value of 127li. during her life, the rest of the estate to be divided equally between the eight children, William, Phillip, Thomas, John, Elizabeth, Lidea, Mary and Hannah Challice, to each of them 47li., to be paid as they come of age; and there being an estate in England of 10li. per annum, which will fall to the eldest son, this court ordered that the revertion of what the widow leaves at her death shall be equally divided between the then surviving children, and also if any of the children die before they become possessed of their portions, their parts shall be equally divided between the surviving children, and the whole estate to remain in the possession of the widow for her support and bringing up her children. The lands to remain bound for the performance of this order, only the widow to have power to sell the waste land to the value of 10li. for necessary repairs.

Ipswich Deeds, vol. 4, pp. 392, 416.

ESTATE OF RENOLD FOSTER, SR., OF IPSWICH.

"The last will and testament of Renold ffoster Senr of Ipswich in the County of Essex in New England, mad the last day of Aprill Anno Dom one thousand six hundred & 80, being this day by Gods good providence of perfect understanding, tho, through Infirmatyes of body, dayly mindfull of my mortality Therfore for the setting my house in order I make and apoynt this my *this my* last will and testament as followeth In the name of God Amen my Soule I committ into the hand of Jesus Christ, my blessed Redeemer, In hope of a joyfull resurrection at the last day my body, to a decent comly buriall, And for my outward estate which the Lord hath Graciously given me, I thus dispose of it, in manner following Imp^{rs}. to my beloued wife Sarah, I give the use of the house I now dwell in and the orcyards, and gardens, and five pound yearly dureing her naturall life, and two cowes, which she shall chuse out of my stock, and the keeping of them both summer & winter yearly, also I give her the bedstead with beding in the parler, and the rest of the linnen & woollen yarne, that she hath made and provided into the house, also the use of a bras pot, and chees pres, and kneading trough, with the utensills in the Leantoo, and the great Kettle & two skillets dureing her naturall life, Also I give her three sheepe to be kept winter & summer, also two piggs, and what provisions shall be in the house at my decease, also the table and forme for her naturall life. Further my will is that the household stuff, or things that my wife brought into the house when I marryed her be at her dispose, in life and at death It. I give and bequeath unto my son Abraham Foster my now dwelling house and orchard and ground about it three acres more or less, & halfe the barne and halfe that land in the field lyeing betweene the land of John Denison & Philip Fowlers, and ten acres on this syde the River caled mudy River by major Denisons & John Edwards Land, and six acres of salt marsh, All which I give him after my wives decease, I give him four acres of marsh att Plumb Iland, and the six acres at Hogs Island It. I give and bequeath unto my son Renold Foster all the land which he possesses of myne, at the Falls, that he hath built a house upon, both upland & marsh be it fifty acres more or less, only to pay out of it, within a yeare after my decease to Sarah my daughter Story, the sum that I have given her, except w^t ye sheets & pillobeers amounts to It. I give and bequeath unto my son Isaack Foster my eight acres of Fresh meadow at the west meadows, joineing to meadow of his and four acres of salt marsh at Hog Island Jacob to have the use of the salt till the decease of my wife.

"It. I give and bequeath unto my son William Foster my six acres of land I had of Thomas Smith, & six acres of marsh at Hog Iland, the marsh to Jacob till my wives decease It. I give and bequeath unto my son Jacob Foster the house he lives in & ground about it and my two lotts beyond mudy River ten acres more or lesse, and the remainder of salt marsh att Hog Island, further my will is that my son Jacob have my land at home and barne dureing my wives naturall life, further I give him my pasture on the south syde of the River, by Simon Tompsons, and the pasture by Caleb Kimballs, also I give him a featherbed, only my will is that he pay what I have given my wife & keepe in repaires for her yearly, what I have allowed her, and given her in my will; It. I give and bequeath to my daughter Sarah, William Storyes wife the sum of ten pounds vizt. a payre of sheets and a paire of pillowbeers, and what they amount not to, of the sum, the rest in the hands of my son Renold, which I have willed him to pay as appeares above. It. I give and bequeath unto my daughter Mary the wife of Francis Pabody the summ of ten pound, part of it to be payd in a payre of sheetes and a paire of pillobeers & a fetherbed, the bed after my wives decease. It. I give my Granchild Hanah Story, the sum of six pound vizt. a bed bolster pillow and paire of sheetes & blanketts, which are of my now wives makeing, the rest to be payd by my executors, if she carry it well to my wife while she lives with her as she hath done to us hitherto It. my will is that my son Jacob have the Implements of Husbandry It. my will is wch I desire and apoynt y^t my Two sonns Abraham Foster and Jacob Foster, to be my executors of this my last will and Testament, and request and desire my beloved Freinds Simon Stace & Nehemiah Jewett to be my overseers to this my will fullfild by my executors, and if any difference arise amongst my wife and children, or amongst them, about any perticuler in my will, my will is that my two overseers shall end it, and they rest satticefied as they two shall agree, and if they two difer, then as a third may, who they shall choose joyning with either of them. In wittnes wherof I have sett to my hand & seale Read, Signed, Sealed, and declared to be the last will & testament of me Renold Foster Senr the day and yeare above written 1680."

Renold Foster (SEAL)

Witness: John Starkweather, Nehemiah Jewett.

"Memorandum The things given my wife for her naturall life, be soe exsept she marry againe, and what debts shee shall have due for labor & worke shall be for her proper use & sole benefitt, and that the repaires of the house be out of her estate, and dureing her abode in it, and that my wife shall have liberty to cutt & procure what wood she needeth from of my land at Muddy River. This declared the 5 of March 1680-81 to be his last will."

Renold Foster.

Witness: John Starkweather, Nehemiah Jewitt.

Proved June 9, 1681, by the witnesses.

Inventory of the estate of Renold Foster of Ipswich, deceased, taken May 30, 1681, by John Whipple and Simon Stace: the house and barne with homstead with all previledges, 150li.; the house Jacob Foster liveth in with ye homestead & previledges, 100li.; ten acres of land at Muddy River, 35li.; 4 acres & a halfe in the comon field, 20li.; 29 acres of salt marsh, 84li.; 8 acres of fresh meadow, 16li.; 12 acres of pasture lands, 40li.; 20 acres of land in the common field, 76li.; 50 acres of upland and marsh, 150li.; one ox, 4 cowes, 2 steers 2 years old, 21li.; one calfe, 10 sheepe, three lambes, 5li.; three swine, 1li. 10s.; a bed in the chamber with bed-

ing upon it, 5li.; 20 bushells of Indian corne & Rye, 3li.
5s.; two boxes, severall old tubbs, 1li.; a coslet, 2 pikes, old
rapier, 20s., mony, 20s., 2li.; Featherbed, 2 sheets, 2 pillowbeers, 5li.; paire of sheets & a paire of pillowbeers, 16s.; bedstead in the parlour with beding and curtaines, 2li.; trundlebed with beding, 15s.; flockbed, 1 pillow, 1 bolster, paire of
sheets, 2 blankets, 3li. 6s.; sheets, pillowbeers, table Linnen,
3li.; 3 paire of sheets & one sheet, 1li. 10s.; 2 tablecloths, two
napkins, 16s.; two chests, one old trunk, one box, 12s.; his
wearing apparrell woollen and Linnen, 6li. 10s.; table, forme,
chayer, 10s.; pewter & brass, 2li., tubbes, keeler, pailes, barrells, 1li., 3li.; porke, cheespres and kneading trough, 1li. 8s.;
paire of cobirons, tramell, warming pan, frying pan, tong, spit
& other small things, 1li.; ten pound of yarne, 1li., utencills
of husbandry, 1li. 10s., 2li. 10s.; an old Iron pot & kettle,
10s., a pitt saw & milk vessells and churne, 15s., 1li. 5s.; sixteen pound of sheeps woole, 16s., trowell, halfe bushell, four
Hammers, 1li. 3s.; total, 744li. 16s.

Attested June 9, 1681, by the executors.

Ipswich Deeds, vol. 4, pp. 402-404.

ESTATE OF WILLIAM HATHORNE OF SALEM.

"Know all men by these p{r}sents that I william Hathorne of
Salem doe make this my last will & testament as followeth,
being of sound mind & memore, Blessed be God Inp{r} I Give
my Soule into the hands of Jesus Christ, in whome I hope
to liue for euer, & my body to the earth, in hope of a Glorious
resurection with him when this vild body, shalbe made like
unto his Glorious body. And for the estate God hath giuen
me in this world (my debts being paid) I doe dispose of as
followeth. It I Giue unto the two sonns, of my sonne Eleazer
Hathorne late deceased viz: william & Samuell, forty pounds
apeece, & to his daughter Abigaile, twenty pounds, which one
hundred pounds, I doe order & appoynt my sonne John Hathorne to pay unto them out of what of my estate, I doe giue
him, as is heareafter exsprest, to the sonns, paiable at the
age of one & twenty yeares & the daughter at eighteene yeares
or marriage, and in case either of them depart this life before
they come of age, as aforesaid, then his or theire part to be
to the surviving, an equall part.

"I Giue to my sonne John Hathorne, all my houseing &
land oarchard & app{r}tenances lying in Salem, to him & his
heires for euer. It wheareas I had formerly giuen to my sonne

William (late deceased) in his life time three hundred &
twenty Acres of land lying neere Groaten with two adventures
at Sea, I doe by this my last will & testament confirme the
same, & my will is, that Sarah his wife, my daughter in law,
shall Haue & hold the same to her & to her heires & assignes
for euer It for the other part of my farme at Groaten, Jer-
vice Helwyes my grandchild, I giue it to him & his heires
& assignes for euer prouided he come over out of Urop to
enjoy it, if not, then I giue it to my daughter Sarah Coakers
two eldest sonns, by her husband Coaker, that are now liueing.
It I giue to all the rest of my grand children ten shillings
apeece payable to them, within one yeare after my decease:
It I doe giue unto Ann my deere wife, all my moueable estate both within doare & with out to be at her dispose for
euer, whome I make sole executrix of this my last will & testament and I doe appoint my sonne John Hathorne, & my sonn
in law Israell Porter to be ouerseers of this my will & assist
my wife, and in witness whereof I haue sett to my hand &
seale this seauenteenth day of february: Ann°: Dom:
1679/80."

Wm. Hathorne. (SEAL)
Witness: Hilliard Veren, sr., John Pickering.
Proved in Salem court June 28, 1681, by the witnesses.

Inventory of the estate of Maj. William Hathorne, Esq.,
taken June 10, 1681, by Hilliard Veren and John Pickering:
his dwelling house with the outhouseing, oarchard & land adjoyning & belonging thereto containing of upland & meddow
about 60 acres, 450li.; a smale pcell of land for a warehouse
at the burying poynt, 2li.; 5 cowes, 15li., 2 yearling heifers,
40s., 17li.; 4 swine young, 48s., 31 sheepe, 9li. 6s., 11li. 14s.;
12 lambs, 48s., 2 horses & 1 mare, 6li., 8li. 8s.; 7 mares &
colts wild in the woods, 7li.; severall goods left in the house,
bedsteeds, cubbords, tables, chaires, chests, potts, tooles, cart
tackling, plow geere & other lumber, 7li. 10s.; chest with
severall old bookes, 4li. 10s.; a farme at or neare Groaton containing about 640 ackers, 50li.; plate, 8li.; cash, 110li.; featherbed, bolster, pillowes, curtaines, vallins, & all appurtenances,
8li.; 1 more featherbed, coverings, Rugg & appurtenances,
6li.; 1 more featherbed smaler one, Ruggs, blanketts & appurtenances, 4li. 10s.; flockbed, bolster, & all belonging
thereto, 2li.; a turky carpett & 2 old carpetts, 1li. 15s.; 9
chaires, 8 joyne stooles & 10 cushins, 2li. 10s.; 3 guns, 3 old
pistolls, Rapier & cutles, 3li.; his wearing apparrell wollen &

linen, 15li.; 66 yds. linen & cotten cloath, 8li. 5s.; pewter, 3li.; brase Kettles, pan, pott, scales, skillets, warming pan, &c., 5li.; Iron potts & other housold goods & iron, 1li. 10s.; old axes & other old tooles & lumber, 10s.; 6 yds. home made woollen cloth, 1li. 7s.; a still & appurtenances, 1li. 10s.; 10li. linen yarne & 12li. of cotten & flax, 2li. 4s.; table, bed & housold linen &c., 11li.; horse furniture &c., 1li.; total, 754li. 3s. There is somthing owing from the treasurer, & somthing owing to ye contrye or demanded for powder money not yett knowne. The estate is Dr., for funerall expences, 41li.; oweing to severall men, 1li. 2s.; total, 42li. 2s.

Attested in Salem court 29 : 4m : 1681, by Ann, relict and executrix.

Essex County Quarterly Court Files, vol. 35, *leaves* 140, 141.

ESTATE OF THOMAS WOODBRIDGE OF NEWBURY.

Administration upon the estate of Mr. Thomas Woodbridge, intestate, was granted 28 : 4m : 1681, unto Mary, the relict, who gave in an inventory and gave oath to the truth thereof.

Salem Quarterly Court Records, vol. 6, *leaf* 17.

Inventory of the estate of Mr. Thomas Woodbridge, deceased Mar. 30, 1681, taken June 3, 1681, by Dudley Bradstreet: the dwelling house, warehouse & about 3 qrs. of an acre of land, 150li.; about halfe an acre of land by the water side, 20li.; three feather beds, 1 flockbed with the bedsteads & furniture belonging to them, 20li.; eight pare of housewifes sheets, 3 paire of dowles pillowbyes, 2li. 4s.; foure paire of sheets of a finer sort with 2 paire of pillowbyes, 1li. 10s.; Two paire of holland sheets with two paire of pillowbyes, 2li.; Two holland table cloathes, 23 diaper napkins & two callico cupboard cloathes, 1li. 10s.; Two course tablecloathes & 24 napkins, 12s.; Ten course towells, 5s.; Halfe a dosin of leather chaires, 2 broken, 1li. 4s.; 7 great chaires with armes & 18 small chaires, 1li. 12s.; a chest of drawers, 10s.; Three chests & two trunks, 10s; Three old trunks & two small ditto, 14s.; fifteen pewter dishes, two basins, 1 dosin of plates, 7 pottingers & a mustard pott, 3li.; 2 chamberpotts & a tankard, 5s.; Earthen ware, old pewter & old latin ware, 10s.; five silver spoons & a wine cup, 2li.; 1 brass kettle, 1 warming pan, 2 skillets, skimmer & ladle, 2li. 5s.; 3 paire of Iron andirons, 3 trammels, 1 firepan, 1 paire of tongs, 1 iron forke, 2 iron candle sticks, 1 spitt, 1 chopping knife &

a chafin dish, 1li. 5s.; 2 iron potts, 2 iron kettles, 1 fender, 1
iron drippingpan, 1 gridiron, 2li.; 1 Jack & chaine, 1 old
muskett, 1li.; 3 tables, 1li.; his wearing clothes, 5li.; barrells
& lumber and a sieve, 10s.; 7 cushions, 3s.; 2 bibles & 2
other books, 5s.; 3 boxes, 3s.; cash, 1li. 3s.; 2 load of wood, 5s.
Attested in Salem court 28 : 4m : 1681, by Mrs. Mary Woodbridge, relict and administratrix.

Essex County Quarterly Court Files, vol. 35, leaf 143.

Account of Mary Woodbridge, administratrix of the estate
of Thomas Woodbridge, late of Newbury, presented May 27,
1695. The real estate which is all Intailed, 170li.; the personal estate, 52li.; a pcel of sugar from Bbados, 15li. 10s. 6d.;
another pcel of sugar, 3li.; wheat recd., 12s. 9d., corne of Jno.
Emery, 25s., 1li. 17s. 9d.; so much recd. of ye wid. Hazeltine,
4s.; recd. of Jno. Pearly, 2li. 5s.; 1 bs. corne, 3s., per Tho.
Crosbie, 2li., 2li. 3s.; so much recd. of Hugh March, 5s.; total
of personal estate, 77li. 5s. 3d. This acct. over Ballanced
by ye admx., 1li. 18s. 4d., making total, 79li. 3s. 7d.

The accountant prays allowance for the following payments
made by her since she accepted the trust: pd. Simon Brad-
street, Esq., Gov., 11li.; Robert Bransdon, 8li. 10s.; Mr.
Thadeus Mekarte, 1li. 10s.; John March, 3li. 6s. 4d.; Mr.
Jeremiah Dumer, 10s.; Tristram Coffin, 1li. 9d.; Stephen
Swet, 1li. 5s.; funeral charges, 5li.; Do. Dole, 10s.; Mrs. Ann
White for my own diet & 3 children from March, 81 to
March, 82, 20li.; pd. ditto for diet from March, 82 to March,
83, 20li.; pd. ditto for my own diet from March, 83 to Sep-
tember, 83, 5li.; Mr. Verin for recording ye inventory, 2s. 6d.;
Daniel Ela, 1li.; allowing the acct., 5s.; quietus, 4s.; total,
79li. 3s. 7d.

Attested May 27, 1695, by Mrs. Mary Woodbridge.

Essex County Probate Files, Docket 30,556.

GUARDIANSHIP OF ABIGAIL LAMBERT.

Abigaile Lambert came into court 28 : 4m : 1681, and chose
her uncle Thomas Lambert, to be her guardian.

Salem Quarterly Court Records, vol. 6, leaf 17.

Thomas Lambert, guardian of Abigaill Lambert, gave bond
Sept. 27, 1681, of 200li., for security of what estate he shall
receive into his hands of said Abigaill's.

Ipswich Quarterly Court Records, vol. 5, page 371.

ESTATE OF RICHARD RICHARDSON.

Administration upon the estate of Richard Richardson, intestate, was granted 28 : 4m : 1681, unto Amy, the relict, who brought in an inventory.

Salem Quarterly Court Records, vol. 6, leaf 17.

Inventory of the estate of Richard Richeson, taken June 24, 1681, by Roberd (his ⎰ mark) Rand and William Bassett: on house and land, 40li.; to cowes and on caf, 6li. 10s.; on hors, 5li.; swin, 9li.; on barn, 4li.; beding and bedsted, 2li. 10s.; Iorn ware, 1li. 10s.; wearing cloaths, 2li.; chests, chears, whells, cradle, on setell, on pall and tras, 2li.; putr, 8s.; armes, 1li.; Ingin corne and mault, 1li.; flax, 1li.; met, 6s. 8d.; on pese of serg and linin cloth, 1li. 4s.; total, 77li. 8s. 8d.

Attested in Salem court 28 : 4 : 1681, by Amy, relict of Richard Richeson.

This court disposed of the estate, to the eldest son Richard Richardson, 6li., to John, Francis, Thomas, Ebenezer and Mary, 3li. each, at age or marriage, the widow to have the rest of the estate for her support and bringing up of the children, and the house and land to stand bound.

Petition of Edmond Batter to the court at Salem, 1 : 5m : 1681, for administration upon the estate of Richard Richardson, who died intestate, leaving an estate and a debt of above 20li. to the said Edmond Batter. Court granted administration to Mr. Batter upon the estate of Richard Richardson.

Essex County Quarterly Court Files, vol. 35, leaves 144, 145.

ESTATE OF JOHN TOMPKINS OF SALEM.

Administration upon the estate of John Tomkins, intestate, was granted 28 : 4m : 1681, unto Mary, the relict, and John Tompkins the son of the deceased, who brought in an inventory of the estate. The land to stand for security, and the next court to order the settlement of the estate.

Salem Quarterly Court Records, vol. 6, leaf 17.

Depositions of Josiah White and Remember his wife that they heard "John Tomkins Senr. say sundrey times that it was his will that his son Nathaniel Tomkins being his eldest son shold have his then dwelling house with the barne & ground thereunto belonging; for he had given him little or

nothing & had given his other children something considerable (or their portions)." Sworn Nov. 30, 1681.

Inventory of the estate of John Tomkins taken June 30,
1681, by Edmund Batter and Nathaniel Felton, sr.: dwelling
house, barne, outhouses, orchard with about seaventeene acres
of improved land, 100li.; an acre of fresh meadow, 2li.; bed
and bedstead with all furniture thereunto belonging, 3li. 10s.;
2 payre of sheets, a blanket, 2 shirts, 1li. 10s.; his wearing
apparel, 2li. 10s.; 4 pewtor platters, 1 basen, a drippinge
pan, 9s.; linnen & wollen wheele, 3 chests, 3 seives and other
lumber as tubs, payles, &c., 1li. 10s.; Iron pot, pothookes,
hake, fire shovel, tongs, firepan, gridiron, 12s.; an old brasse
ketle & skillet and a parcel of Linnen Yarne, 10s.; Tow
combe with a brake & toutow, 1li.; flax and hempe, 1li. 5s.;
Indian corne, 2li.; workinge tooles, 10s.; 2 cowes, 3 2 yeare
old, 2 calves, 11li. 10s.; 3 swine, 3li.; musket and sword,
morter, smoothinge iron and some smal bookes, 2li.; corne
upon the ground, 2li.; total, 135li. 16s.
Attested in Salem court 28:4:1681, by Mary, relict, and
Jon, son of John Tompkins.
More to be added to the inventory: an Iron croe, plow
chaine, wheelbarrow, cops & pin with old iron, 1li.; stone
jugg & bill hook, 3s. 6d., sheeps wooll, 4s., 7s. 6d.; load fresh
meddow hay, 10s., 2 B. Ry, 8s., 18s.; By what the estate is
credit by severall men, viz., John Felton, 9s.; Frances Nurss,
8s., John Nurss, 6s., 14s.; John Tompkins, 15s.; Hugh
Joanes, 10s.; more by John Tompkins, 3s. 6d.; the widdow
Tompkins to pay for corne spent, 1li. 4s.; total, 6li. 1s.
John Tomkins debter to Mr. Batter, 1li. 10s.; John Hibbert,
2li. 7s. 6d.; Mr. Roberts, 16s. 6d.; John Foster, sr., 15s. 6d.;
Mr. Geerish, 3li. 2s. 6d.; Capt. Price, 21s., John Cromwell,
11s. 7d., 1li. 12s. 7d.; Mannasses Maston, 5s., Jon. Foster,
24s., 1li. 9s.; Isaack Cook, 9s., Samuell Ebborne, 4s. 6d.,
13s. 6d.; Wm. Osbourne, 14s., Mr. Bowditch, 20s., 1li. 14s.;
Nathaniell Silsby, 14s., John Procter, 3s., 17s.; John Bachelor, 13s., John Pudney, 2s. 6d., 15s. 6d.; a steere dyed,
1li. 15s.; 23 1-2 li. of flax owing Jacob Read, 1li. 3s. 6d.;
spent by the widdow in corne & Ry, 1li. 4s.; Tho. Maule in
money, 10s.; rent for the cows to Mr. Woodbery, and two
cows delivered him, 6li. 12s.; total, 26li. 16s. 1d.
An addition to the inventory of the estate of John Tomkins, which inventory was delivered into Salem court in June
last, 1681, taken by Edmond Batter and Nathanel Felton:

two acres of Indian corne upon the ground, 2li.; thre bushels
of Rye, 12s.; a parcel of Oates, 12s.; five load of hay, 2li. 10s.;
one cow, 2li.; an Iron crow, plow chayne, wheelbarrow, cops
& pin with some old iron, 1li.; stone jugg and bil hooke, 3s.
6d.; sheeps wooll, 4s.; total, 9li. 1s. 6d. The estate of the
Relict before mariage, 35 acres of land with the old house,
120li.; halfe an acre of salt marsh, 5li.; bed and trundle
bedstead, 12s.; total, 125li. 12s.

Nathaniel Tomkins, John Tomkins, Sarah Tomkins, Elizabeth, Mary, Deborah, Priscilla.

2 Load of hay to Goodm. Beanes for Boards to repair my
husband Tomkins his housing, 2li.; halfe a steere to Samll.
Small for building my said husbands Barne, 2li. 1s.; To the
said Small out of my owne estate in money on the same acct.,
1li.; a cow lent my said husband that was my Daughters and
never repaid, 3li.; 23 1-2 li. flax lent him wch was my owne,
1li. 3s.; total, 9li. 5s. 2d. An account of sundry things of
mine mixed with my husband Tomkins his estate contrary
to agreement made: 7 head neat cattle at about 14li.; 7
swine, 3li. 10s.; 50 Bush. corne, 6li. 5s.; 10 load Hay, 10li.;
total, 33li. 15s.

Essex County Quarterly Court Files, vol. 35, leaves 146-148.

Nathaniell Silsby of Salem, joyner, in consideration of
twelve pounds paid by Nathaniell Tompkins of Salem, yeoman, administrator of the estate of his father John Tompkins, who was administrator to the estate of his grandfather
John Tompkins of Salem, deceased, in right of his wife
Deborah Tompkins, daughter of said John Tompkins, sr.,
which is in full and to their satisfaction of all the portion
of the estate due to his said wife from the estate of her
father. Signed and sealed Nov. 27, 1707. Witness: Samuel
Phillips, Daniel Rogers. Acknowledged Nov. 27, 1707, by
Nathaniell Sillsby.

Essex County Probate Files, Docket 27,800.

ESTATE OF RICHARD HUBBARD OF IPSWICH.

Administration upon the estate of Mr. Richard Hubbard,
intestate, was granted June 28, 1681, unto Sarah, the relict,
and an inventory being presented upon oath, the court re-
served the settlement of the estate to the next court held at
Ipswich.

Salem Quarterly Court Records, vol. 6, leaf 17.

Inventory of the estate of Mr. Richard Hubbard late of Ipswich, taken June 14, 1681, by John Appleton and John Whipple: his dweling hous & out housing with orchyard & priveledge of comon and land adjoyning amounting to 220 acres more or less, 1000li.; by the revertion of a hous & lande in the hands of Robert Kolborn, 200li.; his waring clothes Linon & woollin, 10li.; two oxen, one stere, 14li.; 7 cowes, 21li., 3 yeare olds, 2 calves, 4li., 39li.; one horse, one mare & coult, eleven sheep, 4 lambes, 16 swine, 24li.; in the parler, a bedsted with a downe beed with what belongs to it & two trundle beds wth what belongs to them, books, 6li., 28li.; one truncke, one cubbard, one chest, 2 boxes, 6 lether chayers, thre —— a sute of curtins & a cubbard cloth, 9li. 2s.; looking glase, thre baskits, one worming pan, 1li. 12s.; in the poarch chamber, a fetherbeed, bolster, pillows, curtins and what belongeth to it, 12li.; money, 3li., plate, 12li., cubburd with drawers, a trunke, 25s., 16li. 5s.; in the parler chamber, bedsted with a fether beed & sute of curtins with what belongs toe it, 9li.; 3 trunckes, 2 chests, one boxe, 3 chayers, two Rapiers, 5li. 16s.; two payer of Large hollon sheets, 2 payer of flaxen sheetes, 8li.; seven payer of hommade sheets & 5 payer of sheets, 11li.; 4 duz. & a half of napcines, 4li., five diaper table clothes, 7li. 10s.; 6 hollon cubbord clothes, 20s., two paier of holon pillowbeers, 20s., 2li.; eight paiere of flaxen pilowbeers, 40s., 14 table clothes, 40s., 4li.; 12 towels, 12s., payer of pillowbeers, 3s., 10 yds. of coars cloth, 40s., 2li. 15s.; 17li. of yarne, 50s., sheeps wooll, 12s., 4 spining wheels, 2 saddles & bridle, 7li. 2s.; large chest, 10s., 3 sakes wth a remnant of sakin, 2li.; flaskit, 2 tubes, cradle, screne, flockbeed wth what belonges, 3li. 10s.; 125li. of pewter, 12li. 10s., earthen wares & glasses, 20s., 13li. 10s.; flagin, beedpan, 3 candlesticks, 3 chamber pots, 2 quarte pots, two brase candlestickes, 3 Iron candlestikes, 4li.; earth ware & glases, 20s., 2 tables, one cubburd, 8 old chayers, 3li. 10s.; payer of dogg cobirons, 20s., fouling pece, 30s., 2li.; 2 tramels, 2 paier of tonges, slice, 20s., scales & waites, 20s., 2li.; boxe iron, 6 cuchins with some small things, 1li.; 3 brass pots with hooks, a copper, 2 brase ketls, brase pan, 12li.; 2 Irone ketles, 3 brasse scilits, 2 spits, a trevit, a racke, 2li. 14s.; gridiron, 2 driping panes, 40s., 4 kelers, 9 trayes, a churne, 1li. 3s.; tubes, barels, firkins, chespress, paieles, 2li. 2s.; utensils for husbandry, 4li.; a bull, 40s., 6li.; debts due to the estate from sevrall men, 4li. 4s.; total, 1457li.

5s. Debts due from the estate to sevrall men already knowne, 69li. 13s. 3d.

Attested in Salem court 28 : 4 : 1681, by Sara, relict and administratrix.

Essex County Quarterly Court Files, vol. 35, leaf 139.

The court Sept. 27, 1681, ordered for the settlement of the estate of Mr. Richard Hubbard, that the eldest son should have 260li. for his portion, and the rest of the children 130li. each, to be paid in the land, and the rest to the widow for her part of the estate and payment of debts. The land to stand bound for security of the children's portions. If any of the children, namely, Sarah, Richard, Nathaniel, John and Simon, die before they come to age or marriage, their portion shall be divided amongst the surviving children.

Ipswich Deeds, vol. 4, page 414.

ESTATE OF THOMAS ROWELL OF ANDOVER.*

Whereas Margery, relict and administratrix of Thomas Rowell, presented an inventory to the court the 7m : 1672, and it since appearing that part of the estate was not inventoried, and said Margery being removed out of this jurisdiction, this court June 28, 1681, granted administration to Jacob Rowell, only son of Thomas Rowell, of what estate may be found more, who presented an inventory of the remaining part of the estate and attested to the truth thereof.

Capt. Dudly Bradstreete and Ensigne Thomas Chandler made oath that the said Jacob Rowell is the reputed son of Thomas Rowell, deceased.

Salem Quarterly Court Records, vol. 6, leaf 17.

ESTATE OF MOSES VODEN.

Administration upon the estate of Moses Vowden, intestate, was granted 28 : 4m : 1681, unto Mary, the relict, who presented an inventory amounting to about 130li. and she was ordered to pay out of this estate to Mary and Elizabeth, children of the deceased, 10li. each, at age or marriage, and the rest of the estate to be to the widow. The said Mary and John Ormes to stand bound in 40li. for security.

Salem Quarterly Court Records, vol. 6, leaf 18.

Inventory of the estate of Moses Vouden presented by Mary Vouden, and taken June 28, 1681, by John Browne, sr. and Samuell Gardner, jr.: a small Lighter about 15 tun, 36li. ;

*See ante, vol. 1, page 395.

flockbed, 15s., 3 blankits, 15s., 1li. 10s.; 2 cabbin Ruggs &
2 bed Ruggs, 1li. 10s.; muskit, 10s., 46li. in cotten wooll,
2li. 16s.; Iron pott, 7s., small trunck, 3s., 10s.; 3 chests, 20s.,
a chest drawers, 40s., 3li.; 2 truncks, 7s., 8 chaires, 8s., 15s.;
2 small tables, 5s., earten ware, 5s., 10s.; featherbed, bedstead
& furniture, 5li.; pewtor & Brasse, 7li. 10s.; 5 pr. sheets, 2 doz.
napkins, 7li.; 3 table cloths, 6 towels & 6 pr. pillowbeers,
2li. 16s.; 2 cubbard clothes, 10s.; firepan & tongs & glasses,
3s.; debts due to ye estate, 24li. 6d.; about 24 gall. Rom,
1li. 16s.; a barrel molasas, 1li. 5s.; his wearing clothes, 6li.;
cash, 24li. 18s. 6d.; 13 yds. furston, 13s.; 23 yds. blue linin,
1li. 3s.; 6 yds. searge, 18s.; total, 130li. 3s. 6d.

Attested in Salem court 28:4m:1681, by Mary, relict of
Moses Vowden.

Essex County Quarterly Court Files, vol. 36, leaf 5.

ESTATE OF ROBERT WILSON OF SALEM.

Administration upon the estate of Robert Wilson, intestate, was granted 28:4m:1681, unto Ann, the relict, who
brought in an inventory amounting to about 150li., and
whereas there is some legacy or something of an estate of
Tamsen Buffum's which of right is to belong to Robert and
Deborah, children of the deceased, the court ordered that
Ann should pay out of this estate in the inventory, to Robert
the eldest son 14li. and to Deborah aforesaid, children by his
first wife, and to Anna, John, Mary and Elizabeth children
by Ann, 7li. each, at age or marriage, the house and land to
stand bound for security.

Salem Quarterly Court Records, vol. 6, leaf 19.

Inventory of the estate of Robert Willson of Salem, taken
May 8, 1681, by William Traske and Daniell Southwick:
his dwelling howse & outhowsing & ye land wch ye said
howse stands & is belonging to it in ye Towne, 60li.; 30 acres
of Land in ye limitts of Salem neer to Samuel Verries Farme,
38li.; a standing bedsteed in ye lower roome, featherbed &
bolster with ye Furniture upon & about ye said bed, 7li.;
one Trundle bedsteed & flagg bedd, a small bolster, 3 feather
pillows with ye coverings & what elce belongs to ye said bed,
3li. 10s.; 1 Tablecloath & 10 napkins, 15s.; his wearing apparell, 8li.; 1 saddle & bridle & 2 rasors, 15s.; 1 cuppboard,
1li.; 3 chests, 2 boxes, a desk, 1li.; 1 Table & forme, 1li.;
chaires & other woodden Lumber, 1li.; 3 brass kettles, 3 Iron

potts, warming pan, 2 skillets, Ladle, skimmer & dark lanthorne, 2li. 6s.; a spitt, 2 hakes, firepan, gridiron, a pr. bellowes, 16s.; a fowleing peece, musket, sword & belt, 2li.; 12 pewter porringers, 18s., 10 pewter Basons, 25s., 2li. 3s.; 12 pewter platters, 2li., 1 brass candlestick, 2 pewter potts & other small pewter ware, 8s.; glasses, 2s., bell mettle morter & smoothing Iron, 8s.; 2 Bibles, 12s., earthen ware, 1s., 13s.; 16li. Lynnen & woollen yarne, 16s.; his carpenter Tooles & other utensills, 2li. 10s.; his cart & wheels & horse Tacklin, 2li.; ———, 3li., 2 cowes, 6li., a grey horse, 30s., 10li. 10s.; a mare, 1li. 10s.; 3 sheep & a lamb, 20s., part of a canoo & part of a grindstone, 6s., 1li. 6s.; total, 151li. 6s. Debts oweing to ye estate, 15li. 1s. 8d.   The estate is Debtor, 16li.

Attested in Salem court 28 : 4 : 1681, by Ann, relict and administratrix of the deceased.

Essex County Quarterly Court Files, vol. 36, leaf 7.

INDEX

(433)

www.ingramcontent.com/pod-product-compliance
Lightning Source LLC
Chambersburg PA
CBHW050546270326
41926CB00012B/1935